Brief Contents

e **LearningCurve** activities and **Additional Grammar Exercises** are available for the topics in this unit. Visit **macmillanhighered.com/realessays**.

Fifth Edition

Real
Essays
with Readings

Writing for Success in College, Work, and Everyday Life

Susan Anker

with **Nicole Aitken**
Illinois Central College

Bedford/St. Martin's
Boston ◆ New York

For Bedford/St. Martin's

Vice President, Editorial, Macmillan Higher Education Humanities: Edwin Hill
Executive Editor for Developmental English: Vivian Garcia
Developmental Editor: Jill Gallagher
Senior Production Editor: Gregory Erb
Senior Production Supervisor: Dennis Conroy
Senior Marketing Manager: Christina Shea
Copyeditor: Janet Renard
Indexer: Mary White
Photo Researcher: Bruce Carson
Senior Art Director: Anna Palchik
Text Design: Claire Seng-Niemoeller
Cover Design: William Boardman
Cover Art: © Hill Street Studios/Getty Images
Composition: Graphic World, Inc.
Printing and Binding: RR Donnelley and Sons

Manufactured in the United States of America.

9   8   7   6   5   4
f   e   d   c   b   a

For information, write: Bedford/St. Martin's, 75 Arlington Street, Boston, MA 02116
(617-399-4000)

ISBN 978-1-4576-6436-6 (Student Edition)
ISBN 978-1-4576-8875-1 (Loose-leaf Edition)
ISBN 978-1-4576-8878-2 (Instructor's Annotated Edition)

Acknowledgments

A note to students from Susan Anker

For the last twenty years or so, I have traveled the country talking to students about their goals and, more important, about the challenges they face on the way to achieving those goals. Students always tell me that they want good jobs and that they need a college degree to get those jobs. I designed *Real Essays* with those goals in mind—strengthening the writing, reading, and editing skills needed for success in college, at work, and in everyday life.

Here is something else: Good jobs require not only a college degree but also a college education: knowing not only how to read and write but how to think critically and learn effectively. So that is what I stress here, too. It is worth facing the challenges. All my best wishes to you, in this course and in all your future endeavors.

A note to students from Nicole Aitken

I've been working in both the university and community college environments since 2001, and I've had the opportunity to be a student in all different types of situations as well, including a large university, a small private college, and community colleges. I understand how your surroundings affect the way you learn and how important it is to be comfortable in those surroundings. What you bring with you to the classroom is as important to the learning experience as the material you learn in that classroom.

What does that mean? That means that you, as a student, have something to say and something to contribute. Every day you are thinking, reading, and writing in a critical way that is valuable to the college classroom, but you may not be aware of how to access those thoughts or skills in a meaningful way just yet. While this book may introduce you to some new words and concepts, chances are good that many of these concepts or methods are ones you use regularly. Every day you are writing. You are texting, e-mailing, and sending messages, and you are communicating through written or spoken language. When you read or hear someone speak to you, you are analyzing what was said or written and interpreting those words; that is all a part of thinking critically and being a receptive audience.

Come to the classroom ready to share what you already know and understand that a concept we may call by a new and foreign term is actually something that may already be commonplace to you. Let's share our knowledge and ideas. While this book can guide you and help you make the choices you need to be successful in your careers and in college, you are also already an expert: You are the expert in your life, your technologies, and your own experiences. A writing community asks that we all share our experiences to increase the knowledge of the group. Join our writing community and increase our collective knowledge.

Contents

🄴 **LearningCurve** activities and **Additional Grammar Exercises** are available for the topics in this chapter. Visit **macmillanhighered.com/realessays**.

e **LearningCurve** activities and **Additional Grammar Exercises** are available for the topics in this chapter. Visit **macmillanhighered.com/realessays**.

e **LearningCurve** activities and **Additional Grammar Exercises** are available for the topics in this chapter. Visit **macmillanhighered.com/realessays**.

🅴 **LearningCurve** activities and **Additional Grammar Exercises** are available for the topics in this chapter. Visit **macmillanhighered.com/realessays**.

Thematic Contents

Preface

The first aim of *Real Essays with Readings* has always been to communicate to students that good writing skills are both *essential* and *attainable*. When they have this perspective, students can start fresh, reframing the writing course for themselves not as an irrelevant hoop to jump through, but as a central gateway—a potentially life-changing opportunity, worthy of their best efforts. In large and small ways, this book is designed to help students prepare for their futures. It connects the writing class to their other courses, to their real lives, and to the expectations of the larger world.

Real Essays underscores this powerful message in its initial part, "Critical Thinking, Reading, and Writing"; in its practical advice on writing different kinds of essays; and in its step-by-step grammar sections, which build confidence and proficiency by focusing first on the most serious errors. An abundance of readable student and professional selections further encourages students to see the big picture, giving them a context for what they are learning. Profiles of Success provide inspirational portraits of students and former students, now in the workplace, who reflect on the varied, important ways they use writing in their work.

And with **LaunchPad Solo for *Real Essays with Readings,* Fifth Edition,** we bring the book's instruction into an online, interactive space, where students can continue their practice of key concepts such as critical reading, vocabulary, grammar, and mechanics. Please see the inside back cover for more information on packaging LaunchPad Solo with this book.

Real Essays shares this practical, real-world approach with its companion texts—*Real Writing: Paragraphs and Essays for College, Work, and Everyday Life; Real Skills: Sentences and Paragraphs for College, Work, and Everyday Life;* and the new integrated reading and writing text, *Real Reading and Writing.* All four books put writing in a real-world context and link writing skills to students' own goals in and beyond college.

Features

Successful and popular features of earlier editions of *Real Essays* have been carried over to this edition, with revisions based on suggestions from many insightful instructors and students.

A Comprehensive Teaching and Learning Package: *Real Essays* combines carefully curated readings, writing samples, writing assignments, grammar instruction, critical thinking and reading coverage, and online practice in one convenient volume, allowing instructors to focus on their students.

WRITING ASSIGNMENT 2 Writing about images

Look at the chess pieces in the image. What words come to mind as you look at this photo? Is this image about colors? Shapes? Structure? Diversity? Acceptance? Or is it something else? Identify one word that best defines this picture, and then use clear examples to explain that definition to your reader.

Writing Practice: Not only does *Real Essays* feature a number of student model papers, workplace writing, and professional essays, it asks students to write their own essays in multiple assignments throughout the book. These assignments aid students in translating their writing skills to the real world, asking them to practice concepts through the lens of tasks they will need to complete in college and beyond, such as composing an e-mail, building a résumé, and writing a research paper. Each rhetorical mode chapter also features a step-by-step writing guide and checklist that students can refer to when completing their writing assignments.

Profiles of Success: These profiles feature former students who regularly use writing in their careers, highlighting their background and the ways in which they use writing beyond the classroom.

The Four Basics and Four Most Serious Errors: *Real Essays* breaks the writing process down into logical steps, focusing on the four basics of each rhetorical mode as well as the four most serious errors in grammar. This approach lets students digest information at their own pace, helping them really understand each concept before starting a new one.

Profile of Success
Process Analysis in the Real World

Melissa Erb
Counselor at a County Sheriff's Office

Background I was a mediocre student in high school and did not have an interest in applying to colleges. However, my older sister went to community college, so I did, too. I didn't have an exact idea of where I wanted to go or what I wanted to do with my life, so community college was a good option for me. Shortly after starting, I surprised myself by finding the courses I was taking interesting, so I applied myself in each course. Early on, I took a few courses that discussed disparities in the world—topics such as hunger, racism, uneven wealth distribution, and injustice. I identified personally with some of these disparities because I was raised by a single mother. This triggered my interest in helping and empowering people whose circumstances made it difficult for them to help themselves.

After four years, I completed my associate's degree and then transferred to a four-year college, where I majored in psychology and minored in political science. With only a bachelor's degree, I had some trouble finding a satisfying job directly working with people, so I went on to get my master's degree in social work. I had two internships while getting my master's—one in child welfare, working in foster care, and the other in mental health, working in an intensive outpatient program as a therapist. I became a licensed social worker and currently work in my county's jail as a counselor. It's my job to prevent suicide and provide mental health services to inmates.

Writing at work Among other responsibilities, I make regular progress notes containing observations of inmates' mental health status, comments about my counseling sessions with inmates, and recommendations for treatment.

How Melissa uses process analysis My progress notes need to be clear, concise, and accurate so that personnel from other disciplines (attorneys, judges, counselors, and medical staff) can rely on them. This is particularly important because all writings about an inmate's mental health can be used in court, and, during a trial or appeal, counselors can be subpoenaed to answer questions about ambiguous information.

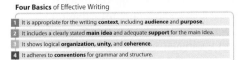

Four Basics of Effective Writing

1. It is appropriate for the writing **context**, including **audience** and **purpose**.
2. It includes a clearly stated **main idea** and adequate **support** for the main idea.
3. It shows logical **organization, unity,** and **coherence**.
4. It adheres to **conventions** for grammar and structure.

2PR The Critical Reading Process: Appearing throughout the book, this process helps students tackle readings using critical thinking skills, asking them to preview, read, pause, review, and respond to each reading.

2PR The Critical Reading Process

Preview the text.

Read the text, looking for the main idea and support.

Pause to question and interpret the text, taking notes as you read.

Review the text and your notes, and **respond** to it.

Research Writing: Two easy-to-follow chapters on writing research essays break down the process into manageable steps. Chapter 19 shows students how to find and evaluate sources in preparation for writing a research essay. Chapter 20 continues with a clear look at writing the essay, avoiding plagiarism, integrating quotations, and citing sources.

New to This Edition

This edition includes carefully developed new features to help students become better readers and writers, in college and beyond.

LaunchPad Solo for *Real Essays*, Fifth Edition: Throughout this textbook you will see icons in the margins indicating when additional online content is available through our LaunchPad Solo platform.

- LearningCurve, innovative adaptive online quizzes, lets students learn at their own pace, with a game-like interface that keeps them engaged. Quizzes are keyed to grammar instruction in the book. Instructors can also check in on each student's activity in an online grade book.

- Additional multiple-choice grammar exercises offer students even more practice with their most challenging grammar concepts. The exercises are auto-gradable and report directly to the instructor's grade book.

Please see the inside back cover for more information on LaunchPad Solo.

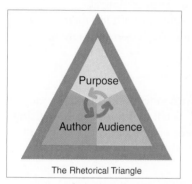

The Rhetorical Triangle

Expanded Rhetorical Situation Coverage: Each writing process chapter now features emphasis on the rhetorical triangle (audience, purpose, and author), helping students think and read more critically, and apply these skills to their writing assignments.

Emphasis on Situational Writing: Real writing samples from the workplace, including a police report, observational notes, a professional and a student résumé, a Web site, and a progress report showcase the various ways in which students will use writing skills beyond the classroom, encouraging them to apply what they learn in their future college courses and in their daily lives.

Updated Readings: This new edition features twenty-six new relevant and relatable readings on themes such as military service, the evolving hiring process, and the effects of media on body image. Also included is a new argument cluster focusing on social media, new Profiles of Success, student papers, workplace samples, and professional readings.

Kimberly Lake

Sample Observation of a Developmentally Impaired Child

Guiding question What is the purpose of recording these specific details?

Vocabulary The following words are *italicized* in the essay: *Caucasian, siblings, co-parenting, phonetic, cognitive, deformities,* and *disposition.* If you do not know their meanings, look them up in a dictionary or online.

Introduction to Subject

Rena is a 4-year-old *Caucasian* female, with curly brown hair and green eyes. Rena is 31 inches tall and weighs 30 pounds.

Rena is experiencing delayed speech. I have known Rena's mother for 15 years and have frequent contact with her and the children.

Individual Functioning Level with the Physical Environment

Rena is not in preschool yet. She does interact normally with her siblings and friends. Rena deals well with her environment and gets along with others easily.

Rena lives with her mother, a 23-year-old female, and 2 female *siblings,* ages 1 and 6. They all live in an apartment on the northwest side of Fresno. The mother is a full-time student. Rena has a close relationship with her father, and the *co-parenting* is very effective between her two parents.

Rena enjoys playing outside. She loves animals and is very happy to interact with adults as well. Rena is very coordinated and enjoys dancing and climbing. She enjoys many physical activities and seems to avoid activities that include sitting, for example, watching television.

Redesigned Interior: A streamlined design allows students to focus on the most important elements of the text, getting rid of the clutter of additional features while remaining visually appealing.

A Slimmer Book: Working from instructor feedback, this edition has been carefully edited to sharpen the instructional content, making the concepts easier for students to absorb and simpler for instructors to teach.

Support for Instructors and Students

Real Essays is accompanied by comprehensive teaching and learning support.

STUDENT RESOURCES

📖 Print   🖥 Online   💿 CD-ROM

Free with a New Print Text

🖥 *LaunchPad Solo for Real Essays with Readings,* **Fifth Edition,** at **macmillanhighered.com/realessays**, provides students with interactive and adaptive grammar exercises. Please see the inside back cover for more information on LaunchPad Solo. **Free** when packaged with the print text. Package ISBN: 978-1-3190-0776-8.

🖥 *Re:Writing 3*. New open online resources with videos and interactive elements engage students in new ways of writing. You'll find tutorials about using common digital writing tools, an interactive peer review game, Extreme Paragraph Makeover, and more—all for free and for fun. Visit **bedfordstmartins .com/rewriting**.

📖 **The** *Bedford/St. Martin's Planner* includes everything that students need to plan and use their time effectively, with advice on preparing schedules and to-do lists plus blank schedules and calendars (monthly and weekly). The planner fits easily into a backpack or purse, so students can take it everywhere. **Free** when packaged with the print text. ISBN: 978-0-312-57447-5.

Premium

📖 **The** *Bedford/St. Martin's Textbook Reader,* **Second Edition,** by Ellen Kuhl Repetto, gives students practice in reading college textbooks across the curriculum. This brief collection of chapters from market-leading introductory college textbooks can be packaged inexpensively with *Real Essays*. Beginning with a chapter on college success, *The Bedford/St. Martin's Textbook Reader* also includes chapters from current texts on composition, mass communication, history, psychology, and environmental science. Comprehension questions and tips for reading success guide students in reading college-level materials efficiently and effectively. Package ISBN: 978-1-319-01165-9.

E-BOOK OPTIONS

Real Essays **e-book.** Available as a value-priced e-book, available either as a CourseSmart e-book or in formats for use with computers, tablets, and e-readers—visit **macmillanhighered.com/realessays/formats** for more information.

FREE INSTRUCTOR RESOURCES

The Instructor's Annotated Edition of *Real Essays* gives practical page-by-page advice on teaching with *Real Essays* and answers to exercises. It includes discussion prompts, strategies for teaching ESL students, ideas for additional classroom activities, suggestions for using other print and media resources, and cross-references useful to teachers at all levels of experience. ISBN: 978-1-4576-8878-2.

Instructor's Manual for Real Essays with Readings, **Fifth Edition,** provides helpful information and advice on teaching integrated reading and writing. It includes sample syllabi, reading levels scores, tips on building students' critical thinking skills, resources for teaching non-native speakers and speakers of nonstandard dialects, ideas for assessing students' writing and progress, and up-to-date suggestions for using technology in the writing classroom and lab. Available for download; see **macmillanhighered.com /catalog/realessays**.

Testing Tool Kit: Writing and Grammar Test Bank **CD-ROM** allows instructors to create secure, customized tests and quizzes from a pool of nearly 2,000 questions covering forty-seven topics. It also includes ten prebuilt diagnostic tests. ISBN: 978-0-312-43032-0.

Teaching Developmental Reading: Historical, Theoretical, and Practical Background Readings, **Second Edition,** is a professional development resource edited by Sonya L. Armstrong, Norman A. Stahl, and Hunter R. Boylan. It offers a wealth of readings from the historical foundations of the developmental reading field to the latest scholarship. ISBN: 978-1-4576-5895-2.

Teaching Developmental Writing: Background Readings, **Fourth Edition,** is a professional resource edited by Susan Naomi Bernstein, former co-chair of the Conference on Basic Writing. It offers essays on topics of interest to basic writing instructors, along with editorial apparatus pointing out practical applications for the classroom. ISBN: 978-0-312-60251-2.

The Bedford Bibliography for Teachers of Basic Writing, **Third Edition** (also available online at **macmillanhighered.com/basicbib**) has been compiled by members of the Conference on Basic Writing under the general editorship of Gregory R. Glau and Chitralekha Duttagupta. This annotated list of books, articles, and periodicals was created specifically to help teachers of basic writing find valuable resources. ISBN: 978-0-312-58154-1.

ORDERING INFORMATION

To order any of these ancillaries for *Real Essays with Readings* contact your local Macmillan Education sales representative; send an e-mail to **sales_support @macmillan.com**; or visit our Web site at **macmillanhighered.com**.

Acknowledgments

Like every edition that preceded it, this book grew out of a collaboration with teachers and students across the country and with the talented staff of Bedford/St. Martin's. I am grateful for everyone's thoughtful contributions.

REVIEWERS

I would like to thank the following instructors for their many good ideas and suggestions for this edition. Their insights were invaluable.

Martha Bowles, Georgia Perimeter College
Jeri Buckner, Lincoln Land Community College
Lynda Dorsey, Harrisburg Area Community College
Tarasa Gardner, Moberly Area Community College
Anita Vail Gilbert, Dean College
Corey Hall, Kennedy-King College
Chrystal Helton, College of the Redwoods
Leota Jones, Prairie State College
Mary Jo Keiter, Harrisburg Area Community College
Andrea Kreft, Gateway Technical College
Melinda Modesitt, Gateway Technical College
Brit Osgood-Treston, Riverside City College
Sherry Rankin, Jackson State University
Brian Reeves, Lone Star College–Tomball
Thomas Stoffer, Ferris State University
Jennifer Thompson, Saint Xavier University
Sandra Valerio, Del Mar College
Shellie Welch, Georgia Perimeter College–Clarkston Campus

STUDENTS

Many current and former students have helped shape this edition of *Real Essays* and I am grateful for all their contributions.

Among the students who provided paragraphs and essays for the book are Deshon Briggs, Jordan Brown, Tam Nguyen, Kimberly Kirwan, Daniel Flanagan, Brittany Philpott, Josef Ameur, Melissa Erb, Anna Puiia, Rui Dai, Laura Huber, Kathryn Arnett, and John Around Him.

CONTRIBUTORS

Art researcher Bruce Carson, working with Martha Friedman, assisted with finding and obtaining permission for the many new, thought-provoking images included in the book.

Kathleen Karcher, working with Kalina Ingham, successfully completed the large and essential task of clearing text permissions.

I am also deeply grateful to designer Claire Seng-Niemoeller, who freshened the look of the book's interior.

BEDFORD/ST. MARTIN'S

I have been extremely fortunate to work with the incredibly talented staff of Bedford/St. Martin's, whose perceptiveness, hard work, and dedication to everything they do are without parallel.

Thanks to Edwin Hill, vice president, Editorial for the Humanities. Editorial assistants Brenna Cleeland, Jonathan Douglas, and Kathleen Wisneski have helped with innumerable tasks, from running review programs to assisting with manuscript preparation. We were very fortunate to have Gregory Erb, senior production editor, shepherding *Real Essays* through production. Overseeing and thoughtfully contributing to all aspects of the design was Anna Palchik, senior art director. Thanks to Billy Boardman for his work on the cover design. I must also extend tremendous gratitude to the sales and marketing team. Christina Shea, senior marketing manager, has been a great advocate for all my books and has helped me to forge greater connections with the developmental market and to stay up to date on its needs. And I continue to be deeply thankful for the hard work and smarts of all the sales managers and representatives.

This book would not have reached its fullest potential without the input and attention it received, from the earliest stages of development, from executives and long-time friends in the Boston office: Joan Feinberg, former president of Bedford/St. Martin's; Denise Wydra, former vice president, Editorial for the Humanities; Karen Henry, editor in chief; Susan Winslow, director of marketing; and Jane Helms, associate director of marketing. I value all of them more than I can say.

Thanks also to my editor, Jill Gallagher, for developing this edition.

As he has in the past, to my great good fortune, my husband Jim Anker provides assurance, confidence, steadiness, and the best companionship throughout the projects and the years. His surname is supremely fitting.

—Susan Anker

In addition to the names already mentioned, I wanted to thank Alexis Walker, former executive editor for Developmental Studies at Bedford/St. Martin's, for asking me to be involved in this project. Although it was a bit of a surprise to be initially contacted to work on this project, it has been a very insightful and rewarding experience. It was a delight to collaborate with Alexis and with Martha Bustin, my initial contacts at Bedford/St. Martin's, and I am grateful for their trust in letting me work with Susan Anker's time-tested materials. I would also like to acknowledge Jill Gallagher, who walked me through the book's development. Jill was certainly one of the most valuable assets to me in the final stages of this process and I owe her a great debt of thanks.

I need to also express my gratitude to colleagues, students, and friends who stepped in and assisted me along the way whenever I asked for help. There were several people in the Department of English, Humanities, and Language Studies at Illinois Central College who were willing to provide any assistance that I needed. In addition, my colleagues who work in developmental studies were always a great help when I asked for materials or feedback. My officemate,

Megan Ames, has seen me at the best and worst of times and walked me through many a draft of a chapter, question, or reading and helped with many revisions. I owe her a significant debt of gratitude that will have to be handsomely repaid. I also need to thank the friends and colleagues who offered up writing samples within a day when asked. I'm blessed to have such a strong group of writers and colleagues ready to step up and offer their work and support.

Finally, I want to thank my family. My husband, Brian Aitken, has been endlessly patient and supportive through this entire process. There have been quite a few times when his encouragement has been my rock, and that was certainly crucial to my success. I also have to thank my precious daughters, Katie and Hope, and ask that they forgive me for not being as available as I could have been during some of the evenings in the fall when they wanted to go to the park. I promise I'll make it up to you this year; I'm sorry that I didn't anticipate the horrible winter we were going to have. Thank you to my entire family for supporting me and believing in me; you are all a blessing to me.

—*Nicole Aitken*

Getting Started

If you are reading this chapter, you probably just started a college writing course, and you might have questions: What will the teacher require? What will class be like? How do I get through it—and all my courses—successfully?

This chapter is designed to answer those questions and set you on the road to success. In the first section, you will learn about common expectations that many college writing instructors have of their students. The second section discusses two important communities: your writing classroom and the larger college community. The third section is designed to help you start to develop your goals for this semester.

Teaching tip This chapter gives students a preview of your course, later writing courses, and other college courses. Setting short-term and long-term goals can help students understand their purpose in this writing community.

> **PRACTICE 1**   **Describing your educational experiences**
>
> Write about your school experiences so far, such as how you would describe yourself as a student, what school activities you have been interested in, and whether you changed schools. Include points that may help your instructor understand what you have done so far and what you hope to learn in this course.

Understanding Instructors' Expectations

You can benefit from thinking carefully about your instructor's expectations right from the start. While every instructor is different, most share the baseline expectations outlined in the following checklist. You should be aware of all of them as you start your course.

Teaching tip Ask students to discuss their preferences after going over the instructor checklist. Which of these tips work for them and why? Which haven't they tried? How might trying those particular tips help them learn?

Instructor expectation checklist

Expectation	Do you do this?
Treat your course as seriously as you would a job. Think of your course work as a job that can lead to bigger and better things if you work hard and perform well.	☐
Come to class on time and stay until your instructor dismisses you. When you arrive late or leave early, you not only disrupt other students, but also might miss vital instructions or information.	☐
Come to class prepared. You have to do your homework or expect to fail. It's as simple as that.	☐
Connect to others in class. Get to know others around you. Class discussion will be easier, and you'll be able to contact a classmate for information if you miss class.	☐
Let your instructor know if you know you are going to miss class, and ask how you should catch up. Instructors can help you make up what you have missed—but only if you have made a connection and communicate in a clear, respectful way.	☐
Read the syllabus carefully and hang on to it the entire semester. Your instructor will expect you to know what the homework is and when assignments are due.	☐
Pay close attention to the instructor's comments on your work. When you get your papers back, do not focus on the grade alone. If you do not carefully read the comments, you will miss a lot of the value in your courses.	☐
Get to know your instructor. If you have questions, ask them either in class or via e-mail, or visit your instructor during office hours.	☐
Ask questions to make sure you understand the instructor's assignments. If something is not clear to you, chances are it is not clear to at least some of your classmates.	☐
Participate in class: Ask questions, answer questions, and make comments. Participation is an important part of how you learn. Plus, many instructors grade on it.	☐

Instructor expectation checklist—cont'd

Expectation	Do you do this?
Listen and take notes. To figure out what you should make a note of, look at the instructor. Important points are often signaled with a hand gesture, a note on the board, or a change in the tone of the instructor's voice.	☐
Don't hide. The farther back in the class you sit, the more tempting it is to let your mind wander.	☐
Pay attention. Instructors do notice, no matter where you sit or how subtle you think you are being, when you are not paying attention.	☐
Keep up. If you can't avoid missing an assignment or class, you should make arrangements to meet with your instructor as soon as possible to catch up.	☐
Take responsibility. When you did not complete an assignment, own up to it and tell the instructor when the work will be completed. Then make sure it is done by the date you have promised.	☐
Schedule your time wisely. Don't wait until the last minute; if you do, chances are you'll do a bad job and get a bad grade.	☐

Teaching tip Go over your own expectations for the course and demonstrate where they can be found in the syllabus.

Making Connections

Your Classroom Writing Community

Part of what makes the classroom writing experience unique is that all of its members—students and instructors alike—learn and grow from one another. Brainstorming a topic or ideas for arguments or evidence benefits everyone involved, as does working with your peers to edit and proofread your papers and theirs.

By sharing your experiences and your writing with others in your class, you are participating in a community, and being an active participant in this community is an important part of the learning process. If you are absent due to illness or fail to contribute, you're missing valuable opportunities to learn.

The assignments in this book are designed to help you learn how to become a better writer and reader in your college classes, but these same skills will also help you in your professional and everyday life. In each of these contexts, writing is

Teaching tip It can be beneficial to put students in groups throughout the semester. Groups allow students to build community within the classroom and give them a comfortable and consistent space for classroom work. Rotating groups also allows students to work with those who have different experiences, backgrounds, and skill levels.

often a communal event. When you are at work and you have to write a memo or a proposal, there may be others working on the project with you who will help you draft that document. When you are sending a text message to your friends, you are participating in their writing community. In joining your classroom writing community, then, you'll be building skills that will help you in the future.

> **PRACTICE 2**   **Learning more about your writing community**
>
> Part of writing as a community is understanding that almost everyone enters a classroom feeling a bit of unease. In most cases you're facing a new semester, new classmates, or a new instructor; in some cases you're facing a new school.
>
> To build trust and establish your writing community, find others in the class near you and speak with them for a few minutes. Find out why they are enrolled in this class and what they want to learn. What are some things they have done in their lives that make them proud? What do they think they are good at? What do they want to work on in this class this semester? Write up the answers in a short paragraph and share it with a small group or the class.

Your College Community

Your college community is not limited to your writing class. It's extremely worthwhile to find out what your school offers beyond the classroom and, perhaps more important, what you might be able to contribute, not least because students who form connections to their college communities tend to succeed more often than those who do not. They know there are people who can help them when they have trouble, and they forge relationships that can help them in the future. Involved students also have opportunities to develop their interests and experiences more deeply.

All colleges offer support services that can help you become a successful student. For example, here is a list of student resources most colleges offer:

- A writing center and writing tutors
- A financial aid office
- An employment office
- An office of student affairs (with many programs)
- A counseling office
- Mini-courses or seminars on a wide variety of topics, such as taking notes, studying for tests, and writing a résumé
- Ride-sharing and babysitting exchange boards
- Academic advising
- Library services, including assistance for specific reference searches of print and online databases

To see what your school offers, visit its home page and click on the "Student Services" or "Current Students" links. Then complete the following activity.

PRACTICE 3   **Finding your resources**

1. Go to your college's Web site and find the page that lists student services. After locating each of the resources listed in column 1, fill in the chart with the information you gather.

Resource	Location	How it can help me (be specific)
Career services		
Academic assistance		
Advising		
Financial aid		
Health services		

2. Choose one of the student services you found on your college's Web site, and make an appointment to interview someone who works there. Pick up handouts or brochures. Then write about the service, describing what you found out in your interview, and how the service helps students.

Many successful students believe that if they had not connected to the college in some way beyond taking classes, they would not have stayed. Consider what one Bergen Community College student wrote for the February 2010 edition of the campus newspaper, *The Torch*.

Islam Elshami

Why Join the Club?

1   Bergen Community College (BCC) offers a variety of clubs and organizations for students to join on a weekly basis. Each club suits each student's desires, whether it is by helping others or learning about and exploring new cultures. Some of these clubs and organizations allow students to promote awareness for something they feel passionate about, such as a culture, a subject, an activity, a sport, a religion, or a tradition.

2   Clubs offer students a wide range of opportunities and benefit members in ways such as meeting new people and gaining experience, whether it is generally for life or by adding it to a résumé or application. Not only do clubs help socially,

but they also <u>help educationally and assist students in subjects that they are tak-</u><u>ing on campus.</u> Everyone should join at least one club in a semester to experience something new and enriching to look forward to every week. You get the <u>oppor-</u><u>tunity to hold a position in a club where you can make a difference in your school.</u>

3   There are clubs about cultures and religions such as the African Student Union, the Christian Club, the Desi Club, the Korean Club, the Muslim Student Association, the Polish Culture Club, the Russian Club, and many more. There are activity clubs such as the Chess Club, the Dance Club, and the Theatre Club. Some of the clubs are also <u>helpful for the community as well as for the college,</u> such as the Environmental Club and the Community Service Club.

4   Professor Rachel Wieland, adviser to the Environmental Club, elaborates on the tasks that this club is most successful in. "When we talk about the green initiative on campus, we are no longer speaking of the environmental club; they are a subset of the green initiatives. In the past, Semester Green has enormously expanded on campus. I advise the Environmental Club, but I also co-run the Green Team, and I am also a co-sustainability officer. If students want to be involved, the best way to jump in is to simply look at what options are available on campus, to join, and go for it. Green is not a side dish anymore at BCC. It is the main event. BCC is positioning itself to be the leading sustainability community college in New Jersey. That leaves a huge amount of room for students to <u>get involved and make a difference,</u>" says Professor Wieland.

5   Students should be encouraged to participate in clubs around their own schools to <u>experience the feel of being able to make a difference</u> in any way pos-sible. Not only does it help within the school, but it also helps the students them-selves by <u>teaching them leadership skills.</u> It is always a good time to <u>brush off the</u> <u>stress</u> that has been building up from exams and assignments and get started on something you can enjoy doing.

| PRACTICE 4 | **Reading to understand** |

Throughout this book (and throughout your college experience) you will practice reading to understand meaning. Although you know how to read, of course, you might still need practice in reading *critically*, a key college skill. As a start, answer the following questions about "Why Join the Club?"

1. What is Elshami's purpose in writing the article for the student newspaper?

   To persuade students to join a club on campus

2. Underline the reasons she gives to persuade her readers.

3. Do you agree with her position? Why or why not?

Answers will vary.

_____

4. If you were responding to Elshami, what would you say? If you do not agree with her points, what would you say to persuade her of your position?

Answers will vary.

_____

PRACTICE 5   **Finding the clubs**

1. Go to your college Web site again, and find "Student Life" or "Student Activities." Click there to find a list of student clubs and organizations. Find out about two clubs or organizations at your college that you might be interested in, and fill in the following chart.

> **Teaching tip** Invite a student from an on-campus club to come talk to the class. Have students prepare questions in advance.

Club name	Description	Location, meeting times, adviser

2. Go to a meeting of the club that interests you most or talk to a student who is involved in it. Ask what the club does and pick up information about upcoming or past events. Write about what you found out.

Setting Goals

You may already know what kind of degree you want to pursue in college and what type of job you want. With these long-term goals in mind, you also have shorter-term goals—steps that help you get where you want to go. For example, to pass this course, you will need to develop your writing skills. Having some specific writing goals in mind will help you become a better writer.

Writing Goals

Think about the writing you have done in previous courses. What kinds of writing did you do? What kinds of grades did you get? When you are given an assignment, how do you begin? What problems do you think you have with writing?

After reflecting on this, complete the following activity. Throughout the course, refer to these goals, changing or updating them as needed.

> **PRACTICE 6** **Looking ahead to writing goals**
>
> List at least four writing goals—skills you want to learn, practice, or improve in this course. Be as specific as possible. For example, "Learn to write better" is too general to help you focus on what you need to do.
>
> 1. _Answers will vary._
> 2. _____
> 3. _____
> 4. _____

Reading Goals

Think about your previous experiences with reading in your courses. How would you characterize your experience with reading? Has it been positive or negative? Do you find reading to be challenging, or is it something you feel relatively comfortable with? After reflecting on this, complete the following activity to sketch out some reading goals. Then, throughout the course, refer to this list of skills and abilities.

> **PRACTICE 7** **Looking ahead to reading goals**
>
> Identify at least four reading skills you want to learn, practice, or improve in this course. Be as specific as possible. Think about what happens when you sit down to read. Do you need to work on limiting distractions when you read? Perhaps you need to take better notes as you read or take the time to look up words or phrases you don't understand. Do you need to learn how to keep yourself focused on what you read?
>
> 1. _Answers will vary._
> 2. _____
> 3. _____
> 4. _____

Degree Goals

Whether or not you have decided what you want to major in, you should still ask yourself some questions now.

- Which majors seem interesting to me?
- Which courses would I need to take for the major(s) I might be interested in?

- What are the required core courses that every student must take to graduate?
- When could I take these courses?

Course requirements for each major are listed in the college bulletin and on the college Web site. It's a good idea, though, to sit down with your academic adviser as soon as possible to plan a sequence of courses. If you are like most students, you are juggling a lot of important priorities, and having a plan to reach your goals will help you achieve them. Write your tentative plans in the spaces provided.

PRACTICE 8 **Looking ahead to degree goals**

I (might) want to major in *Answers will vary.* _____

Courses I will need for that major (If you do not know your major yet, list the courses required for all students.)

_____

_____

Number of courses I can take next term _____

Courses I should take if they fit into my schedule (Remember, certain

courses have other courses as prerequisites.) _____

_____

Career Goals

You may or may not know what your career goals are at this point. Even if you do not have clear goals yet, try the following activity to jump-start your thinking.

PRACTICE 9 **Looking ahead to career goals**

After completing my college coursework, a field I would like to work in

would be *Answers will vary.* _____

_____

Additional degrees or certifications needed (If you need additional course work beyond your current degree or certificate program, list them here.)

_____

_____

In this field, how is writing used? (Reports? Memos? Charts?)

_____

_____

In this field, how is reading used? (Computer records? Articles? Guide-

books?) _____

_____

_____

Part 1

Critical Thinking, Reading, and Writing

"I write multiple drafts of my college essays."

Mary Carmen G., student

PHOTO: PATRICIA LEE

Critical Thinking and Critical Reading

Critical Thinking

Say you see someone waving. How do you know what the message is? Virtually all of us will answer, It depends. Who is waving? Why? At whom? Where and when? What kind of wave is it, exactly? In most cases, we can draw a conclusion about what a particular wave means without thinking too much about it. What we are actually doing, though, is thinking critically. Without necessarily realizing it, we are taking into account a complex set of interactions that can be expressed by something called the *rhetorical triangle*.

The Rhetorical Triangle

What something *means*—whether that something is an action, a message, an idea, an image, or a text—depends on its *context,* which includes the elements you see in the diagram: the *author,* the *audience,* and the *purpose.* Examining all these variables consistently will help you think more critically and read more critically. Similarly, taking all those variables into account as you write will make you a more effective writer at school, at work, and in everyday life.

In everyday life, we reach many conclusions quickly, and often we are not fully conscious of how we reached them. For example, we will decide quickly that that person waving was waving hello when we see him hug someone shortly afterward. We call this kind of thinking common sense. Often, however, you will encounter texts and ideas that are more complex than a wave and that will require more than common sense to truly grasp. In college especially, your instructors are going to expect you to think critically about the topics and concepts that you cover in class and in your reading.

Question Assumptions and Biases

The process of critical thinking is not so different from the process of interpreting a wave. It does, however, require conscious effort and practice. It starts with actively questioning what you see, hear, and read to determine the elements of the rhetorical triangle: author, audience, purpose, and context. As part of this questioning, you should carefully consider two additional factors: *assumptions* and *biases.*

Assumptions are ideas or opinions that we do not question but that we use to form conclusions. Many assumptions have a reasonable basis, but they might not hold true in every case. For example, if we see a woman driving a Mercedes, we might assume that she is rich. In fact, she might be—but she might instead have borrowed the car from a friend, be test-driving it, or be renting it for a special occasion.

Biases are strongly held beliefs or points of view that lead people to certain conclusions but that lack a rational basis. To return to the example of the woman driving a Mercedes: If we assume that the woman is rich, some of us might conclude that she is arrogant. The idea that she is arrogant reflects a bias about rich people; there is no necessary relation between being rich and being arrogant.

Assumptions and biases are not necessarily negative. For example, we can assume the best in people and be disappointed as easily as we can assume the worst in people and be pleasantly surprised. The important point is that we are aware of our biases and assumptions and bring them to light. Being a critical thinker means cultivating self-awareness as well as awareness of others' views. Above all, it means being curious and asking many questions.

It is important to remember that when we think critically about something, we, too, are part of the rhetorical triangle: When we read or listen to someone's ideas or statements, we are the audience. For that reason, to come to reasonable conclusions about an idea or a text, we must examine our own assumptions and biases.

Apply the Critical Thinking Process

When faced with a complex idea or text, take the following steps:

The Critical Thinking Process

1. **Consider the context.** (Who created it? For whom? Why? When and where?)

2. **Identify the main elements.** (What is the main idea? How is it supported? What form does it take?)

3. **Question and interpret.** (What's the meaning, in context? What assumptions underlie it? Is there evidence of bias? What are *your* assumptions/potential biases?)

4. **Review and respond.** (Given all of the above, how would you respond to it?)

The following practice will help you apply the process of critical thinking.

> PRACTICE 1   **Thinking critically about an idea**

ALEXIS WALKER

Work attributed to Banksy, 79th and Broadway, New York City

Banksy, a famous graffiti artist (or vandal, depending on your point of view), took up residence in New York City in October 2013, leaving behind a number of spray-painted images on buildings throughout the city. When asked about Banksy's activities at a press conference on October 16, New York mayor Michael Bloomberg had the following to say:

> "Look, graffiti does ruin people's property and it's a sign of decay and loss of control. Art is art. And nobody's a bigger supporter of the arts than I am. I just think there are some places for art and there are some places [not for] art. And you running up to somebody's property or public property and defacing it is not my definition of art. Or it may be art, but it should not be permitted. And I think that's exactly what the law says."

1. Consider the context of the idea expressed by the quote. (Who spoke it? Why? Where?)

2. Consider the main elements of the idea. (What is the idea? What support is offered for it? How is it delivered?)

3. Question and interpret the idea. (What does it mean, in context? Is there evidence of bias? What assumptions underlie it?)

Discussion Go over the student responses in class.

4. Review and respond. (Do you think graffiti can qualify as art? If so, should it be condoned or even encouraged? Why or why not?)

> **PRACTICE 2**   **Questioning your own assumptions and biases**

Think about how you responded to the idea of graffiti as art in Practice 1. What assumptions underlie your response? Can you detect any biases of your own at work?

Critical Reading

Simply put, critical reading is critical thinking applied to texts, whether those texts are composed of words or images. It requires paying close attention as you read, both to the text and to its context, and asking yourself questions about the author's purpose, main idea, and support of that idea. It also means that you do not just accept everything you read but instead consider why the author arranges the points in a certain way, whether you agree or disagree, and why. Critical reading is reading actively, not just passively looking at the words on the page or screen. It requires that you get involved with what you read to deeply understand it and try to detect the writer's assumptions and biases (and your own).

Apply the Critical Reading Process

In college, critical reading begins with focusing on what you are doing. Whatever kind of text you have in front of you, take a breath and tell yourself, "Focus." Then, take the following steps.

> ## 2PR The Critical Reading Process
>
> **P**review the text.
>
> **R**ead the text, looking for the main idea and support.
>
> **P**ause to question and interpret the text, taking notes as you read.
>
> **R**eview the text and your notes, and **respond** to it.

This four-step process, which we call 2PR—for *preview, read, pause,* and *review*—should be familiar if you have read the first section of this chapter. It is a version of the four-step critical thinking process we discussed earlier (see p. 15) applied specifically to reading.

Step 1: Preview the Text

Before reading any text, skim or preview the whole thing, using the following steps.

READ THE HEADNOTE AND CONSIDER THE FORMAT

Some articles and other documents are introduced by headnotes, which provide information about the selection (Who wrote it? When? Where? Why? Where was it first published?) and sometimes summarize it. At the least, you should see the author's name. What do you know about the author? What can you find out? When there is no headnote, try to derive clues about context from the format of the piece. Does it look like other texts you have read? A newspaper or magazine article? A novel or short story? If you can identify the kind of writing it is, you will probably know something about the intended audience and the general purpose.

READ THE TITLE AND INTRODUCTORY PARAGRAPHS

The purpose of a title is to introduce you to a piece of writing. Good titles usually give the reader a clear idea of the topic of the piece. Once you have considered the title, read the first few paragraphs; writers often introduce their topic and main idea in these paragraphs, so read them and take notes.

READ HEADINGS, KEY WORDS, AND DEFINITIONS

Textbooks and magazine articles often include headings to help readers follow the author's ideas. These headings (such as "Step 1: Preview the Text") tell you what the important subjects may be.

Any terms in **boldface** type are especially important. In textbooks, writers often use boldface for key terms. Read and make note of the definitions of key words as you preview the writing.

LOOK FOR SUMMARIES, CHECKLISTS, AND CHAPTER REVIEWS

Many textbooks (such as this one) include features that summarize or list main ideas. You should always take the time to review summaries, checklists, or chapter reviews to make sure you have understood the main ideas.

ASK A GUIDING QUESTION

Ask yourself a **guiding question**—a question you think the reading might answer. Often, you can turn the title into a guiding question. For example, read the title of this chapter, and write a possible guiding question. As you read, try to answer your guiding question. Having a guiding question gives you a purpose for reading and helps keep you focused.

READ THE CONCLUSION

Writers usually review their main idea in their concluding paragraphs. Read the conclusion, and compare it with the notes you made after you read the introductory paragraphs and thought about what the main idea might be. Comparing your notes not only helps you determine whether or not you understood the material but also keeps you thinking about the writing. When you keep thinking about the material or make connections about the subjects you read about, it will be easier to recall that information later.

> **PRACTICE 3**   **Previewing a text**
>
> Preview one of the readings in the back of this book. Look for all of the features (headnote, title, headings, etc.) listed as part of the previewing process. What information did you discover? What more would you like to know? Record your guiding question here: *Answers will vary.*
>
> _____
>
> _____

Step 2: Read the Text: Find the Main Idea and the Support

After previewing, begin reading the document carefully for meaning, trying especially to identify the writer's main idea and the support for that idea.

DISCOVER THE MAIN IDEA

For more on main ideas, see Chapter 3.

The **main idea** of a reading is the central idea the author wants to communicate. The main idea is related to the writer's **purpose**—which can be to explain, to demonstrate, to persuade, or to entertain—and to the **audience** the writer wishes to reach. Writers often introduce their main idea early, so read the first few paragraphs with special care. After reading the first paragraph (or more, depending on the length of the reading selection), stop and write down—in your own words—what you think the main idea is. If the writer has stated the main idea in a single sentence, <u>double-underline it.</u>

PRACTICE 4   **Finding the main idea**

Teamwork Practice 4 works well as a group activity.

Read each of the following paragraphs. Then, write the main idea in your own words in the spaces provided.

1. Neighbors who are too friendly can be seen just about anywhere. I mean that both ways. <u>They exist in every neighborhood I have ever lived in and seem to appear everywhere I go. For some strange reason these people become extremely attached to my family and stop in as many as eight to ten times a day.</u> No matter how tired I appear to be, nothing short of opening the door and suggesting they leave will make them go home at night. (I once told an unusually friendly neighbor that his house was on fire, in an attempt to make him leave, and he still took ten minutes to say goodbye.) <u>What is truly interesting about these people is their strong desire to cook for us even though they have developed no culinary skill whatsoever.</u> (This has always proved particularly disconcerting since they stay to watch us eat every bite as they continually ask if the food "tastes good.")

   —From Jonathan R. Gould Jr., "The People Next Door"

   Main idea: *Answers will vary. Possible answer: Overly friendly neighbors plague the author.*

2. Personally, I have never been able to take a test in a room with other people. There is nothing that I find quite as distracting as the many idiosyncratic habits that other students bring into the classroom. <u>What I find surprising is that none of my fellow classmates ever appears to have an annoying habit until the day of the test. All of a sudden, all I can hear are distractions.</u> The young man sitting next to me has to blow his nose every three seconds. The girl three seats back can't stop popping her chewing gum. Another student somewhere in the class is rocking back and forth in the chair creating some kind of squeaking noise, while yet another student can't stop tapping a pencil on the desk. <u>How anyone is ever successful taking a test in a "quiet" classroom is a mystery to me.</u>

   Main idea: *Answers will vary. Possible answer: Quiet classrooms may be overly distracting to nervous test takers.*

3. In communities around the United States, people are "time banking," giving their individual skills in return for another's, and building a sense of community in the process. <u>For example, one person might not have a driver's license or a car but needs transportation to a regular appointment. That same person is a good baker, and so offers to make cakes,</u>

pies, or cookies in return for transportation to her appointment. Individuals offer up their skills and get what they need in return, when they need it. Time banking in some large cities is funded by AmeriCorps because the groups are large and need a central administration. People involved in time banking are highly satisfied with the practice because it is local, it saves money, and it connects people who might not otherwise meet, strengthening community ties. It also reminds individuals that they have something to contribute as they offer up their skills to their neighbors.

Main idea: _Answers will vary. Possible answer: Time banking, wherein people swap skills and services, has a number of benefits._

4. Please note that in our class, attendance and participation are not only essential, they are part of your overall grade in the class. Students always ask how many absences are allowed or how many classes they can miss before their grade will be affected. Since being in class and actively participating in our classroom activities is a part of your grade, any absence will have an impact on your grade. Excused absences may be arranged at the discretion of the instructor, but they will require documentation of a family or medical emergency or other noted illness or hardship. If you must miss class for any reason, you will need to meet with me to determine how you will make up the work you have missed. Any student who is actively missing class and not participating will be dropped from the course at midterm.

—From a syllabus for a writing course

Teaching tip Ask students to annotate the main ideas in your course syllabus.

Main idea: _Answers will vary. Possible answer: Students must attend class, do the work assigned, and follow procedures for absences._

CONSIDER THE SUPPORT

For more on support, see Chapter 7.

Support is the collection of details that shows, explains, or proves the main idea. The author might use statistics, facts, definitions, and scientific results for support. Or he or she might use memories, stories, comparisons, quotations from experts, and personal observations. All of it could be good support, but do not assume that: Ask questions about what the writer has used for support. The facts might be incorrect, the memories hazy, the experts questionable, the personal observations biased. When you are reading for college, ask yourself: What information is the author including to help me understand or agree with the main idea? Is the support (evidence) valid and convincing?

Teaching tip Ask students if they can identify the main idea and support in the textbook example on page 40 or in any of the essays in Part 9, Readings for Writers.

PRACTICE 5   **Identifying support**

Go back to Practice 4 (p. 19) and underline the support for the main ideas of each of the passages in the practice.

Step 3: Pause to Question and Interpret the Text

Critical reading requires you to actively think as you read, and asking questions is a part of this process. As you pause to think about what you are reading, use check marks and other symbols and jot notes to yourself so you can understand what you have read (rather than having just looked at the words without thinking about their meaning and purpose). Here are some ways to take notes as you read.

- Note the main idea by highlighting it or writing it in the margin.
- Note the major support points by underlining them.
- Note ideas you do not understand with a question mark (?).
- Note ideas you agree with by placing a check mark next to them (✓).
- Note ideas that you do not agree with or that surprise you with an *X* or an exclamation point (!).
- Mark examples of an author's or expert's bias and note possible sources of the bias.
- Pause to consider your reactions to parts of the reading. Note how a part or sentence relates to the main idea.

PRACTICE 6   **Questioning and interpreting the text**

Practice the note-taking steps in the bulleted list using one of the readings in the back of this book. What ideas did you agree or disagree with? What surprised you? What did you not understand? Did you uncover any hint of bias or questionable assumptions?

Step 4: Review and Respond

After you read a text, pause to *reflect* on the ideas presented in it and on your responses to it. This is important for two main reasons. First, when you take the time to think critically about what you have read, the information will stay with you longer. You will be able to make more connections to other topics and larger issues if you take the time to review and respond to the reading. In addition, when you think critically about what you have read, you will be participating in a conversation with the author.

When you *respond* critically to a reading, you determine how your own positions or ideas relate to what you have just read. When you are not required to respond in writing to a text, you should still take notes for yourself and write a response after reading—writing your ideas down is the best way of remembering and developing them, and preparing to discuss them in class. Often, of course, your instructor will ask you to submit written answers to questions about a reading or to write about it.

Resources For more on teaching critical thinking, see Chapter 6 in the *Instructor's Manual for Real Essays*.

> **PRACTICE 7**   **Reflecting on the 2PR process**
>
> Pick an article out of a newspaper or magazine that you would not normally read and use the 2PR process to help you read and understand it. Write a paragraph about your experience. What parts of this process helped you better understand the material as you were reading? What connections did you make? What did you think of that you would not have thought of otherwise?

> **PRACTICE 8**   **Responding to a text**
>
> Choose an article from the Web site ProCon.org that disagrees with your own personal beliefs. For example, if you defend the practice of using performance-enhancing drugs in professional sports, read an article that argues for banning them. Use the 2PR process as you read. What is your reaction to what you read? Why do you feel that way? What about the article makes you feel that way? What specific points do you agree with or disagree with and why?

Reading Visual Texts Critically

Visual texts like Web sites, photographs, illustrations, graphics, and advertisements play a huge role in our lives today. It is important to "read" visual texts critically, just as you do texts that rely on words.

To approach visual texts insightfully, in a way that uses your critical thinking and reading skills, first pay special attention to the dominant elements of the images. A dominant element is one that draws your eye. Look closely at the image. What draws your eye? Are the figures or people wearing clothes from a certain time period? Are they engaged in a particular activity? Are there colors that the image is featuring or is there a pattern that is capturing your attention? If so, chances are good that the artist, illustrator, or publisher wanted you to focus on those elements for some reason.

Next, study the composition of the image and its arrangement of elements. Keep in mind that people generally read images in the same ways that they read print material: from left to right and from top to bottom, so elements within a visual may be arranged or designed to take advantage of this pattern. Think of a Z pattern, in which a viewer's eye goes first to the top left (the start of the Z) and ends with the bottom right (the end of the Z). Artists, illustrators, and advertisers most often use this pattern of setting up an image, with the most important object in the top left area and the second most important object in the bottom right area.

Finally, to "read" a visual text critically and organize your impressions and observations into a thoughtful response, apply a process similar to the 2PR Critical Reading Process (p. 17):

2PR   The Critical Reading Process for Visuals

Preview the image. (Who created it? Why? For whom? When? Where did you encounter it?)

"Read" the image. (What are its *basic* elements—figures, objects, text? Which are its *dominant* elements?)

Pause to question and interpret the image, taking notes as you go. (What does the image mean? What do you think about it? How does it relate to your experience and/or knowledge? What questions do you have about it?)

Review the image and your notes, and **respond** to it.

PRACTICE 9   **Critically reading an ad**

Study the advertisement on page 24 and answer the following questions.

1. Where does the image come from? *Runner's World magazine*

2. Why? *It seems to be an advertisement for running clothes/shoes.*

3. For whom was it intended? *Readers of the magazine/potential buyers of the company's merchandise*

4. What are its *basic* elements—figures, objects, text? *There's a man running through a curtain of water, which washes him clean of stress and frustration (which are indicated by text). There is a slogan, "sound mind sound body," and the name of the company (Asics), with its Web address and what appears to be a company motto ("Running cleanses the mind and body").*

5. Which are its *dominant* elements? How do they fit together? Is there a message? *The figure of the man and the company name appear to be most dominant. The company wants us to connect the handsome, athletic, newly stress-free man with the company name.*

AMERICA CORPORATION

Print advertisement from *Runner's World* magazine

6. What does the image mean? _The company is betting that we want to be_
   stress-free and good-looking. It wants us to connect those qualities with
   its products, and then to buy them.

7. What do you think about it? How does it relate to your experience
   and/or knowledge? What questions do you have about it? _Answers will_
   vary.

PRACTICE 10   **Critically reading an image**

Browse the Internet, a magazine, or a newspaper, and bring in an image
that interests you. Working with a small group, discuss it, applying the 2PR
Critical Reading Process for Visuals (p. 23). As you discuss the image, take
notes. Then, share your notes with the group before writing a paragraph
about the image. In your paragraph, note what aspects of the image are
particularly important. What are the aspects of the image that give you the
most information? What parts of the image can you read critically? What
information did you learn from them?

3

Effective Writing: An Overview

The Elements of Effective Writing

Effective writing has four basic elements.

Four Basics of Effective Writing

1	It is appropriate for the writing **context**, including **audience** and **purpose**.
2	It includes a clearly stated **main idea** and adequate **support** for the main idea.
3	It shows logical **organization, unity,** and **coherence**.
4	It adheres to **conventions** for grammar and structure.

Effective writing is the result of a multistep process. This chapter will introduce the four basic elements of effective writing and outline the steps of the writing process that will help you produce it. First, however, let us look again at the concept of the rhetorical triangle and how it applies not only to critical thinking and reading but to effective writing as well.

Context

e Log in to
macmillanhighered
.com/realessays
LearningCurve >
Working with Sources

In Chapter 2, we discussed the idea of the rhetorical triangle as it applies to critical thinking and critical reading (pp. 13–25). As you will recall, investigating context—Who created it? For whom? Why? When? Where? How?—is essential when you are trying to understand an idea, text, or communication of any kind.

    Context is equally important in writing. Considering the context for each writing task as you begin to write—especially *to whom* you are writing and *why* you are writing—will help you write effectively not only in your college courses, but also in your everyday and professional life.

AUDIENCE

Your **audience** is the person or people who will read what you write. Whenever you write, always have at least one real person in mind as a reader. Think about what that person already knows and what he or she will need to know to understand your main idea. In most cases, assume that readers will know only what you write about your topic and main idea.

Most of us automatically take audience into account in the writing we do in everyday life, at least to some extent. The more we do so, the more effective our writing is likely to be. Consider the following examples, written by a student named Maggie, and think about who Maggie could be writing to. What clues in each of the writing samples gave you this idea?

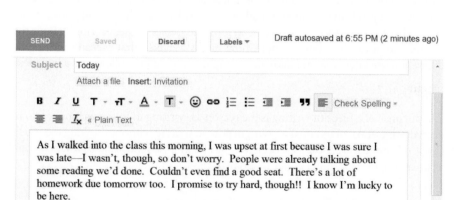

As I walked into the class this morning, I was upset at first because I was sure I was late—I wasn't, though, so don't worry. People were already talking about some reading we'd done. Couldn't even find a good seat. There's a lot of homework due tomorrow too. I promise to try hard, though!! I know I'm lucky to be here.

E-mail

K -- u dunno wat 2day was lik. i was rele nervous n freakin. had 2 sit in front by da teach and h8ed it! cya! :)

Text message

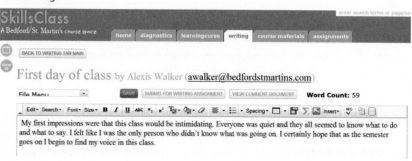

First day of class by Alexis Walker (awalker@bedfordstmartins.com)

My first impressions were that this class would be intimidating. Everyone was quiet and they all seemed to know what to do and what to say. I felt like I was the only person who didn't know what was going on. I certainly hope that as the semester goes on I begin to find my voice in this class.

Web site

PRACTICE 1   **Understanding audience**

1. Identify at least two ways these three accounts are different from one another.

2. How do her different audiences affect what Maggie writes and how she writes it?

3. How do you think the different intended audiences would have reacted if they received the wrong message?

Teaching tip Bring in or have students find a letter to the editor from a newspaper or magazine. As a class, discuss the letter writer's original audience, and then ask how the letter might have to be changed for various other audiences. Choose one of these, and have students form small groups to revise the letter with this audience in mind.

When you write in formal contexts, especially in college, thinking about audience will not necessarily come to you automatically: You will need to consider it explicitly. As you think about your audience, consider what the person knows about you and your topic and what type of writing the person expects. Think about the person's point of view. For example, how might Maggie's first piece of writing be different if she knew that her audience thought that going to college was a bad idea?

PURPOSE

The **purpose** of a piece of writing is the reason for writing it. In the writing we do in everyday life, most of us consider our purpose in writing without thinking too much about it—and the purpose is reflected in our writing. To illustrate this, take a look again at Maggie's accounts of her first day of class, and then complete Practice 2.

PRACTICE 2   **Understanding purpose**

1. What is Maggie's purpose in writing the first account of her first day in class? *Answers will vary but should be similar to those supplied. To report back to someone who cares about her; to reassure them that things are going OK.*

2. What is her purpose in writing the second account? *To check in and share her gut impressions.*

3. What is her purpose in writing the third account? *To write a formal account, probably to/for her teacher, of her first impressions. Secondary purpose: to demonstrate her writing skills to her instructor.*

Understanding your purpose for writing is key to writing successfully, particularly as writing tasks become more complex. In college, your purpose for writing often will be to show something; to summarize, analyze, synthesize, or evaluate something; or to make a convincing argument. Typically, your instructor will want you to demonstrate that you understand the content of the course. To understand the purpose of a particular assignment, be sure to read assignments and exam questions critically, highlighting words that tell you what your instructor wants to see in your writing. If you do not understand, ask your instructor or a classmate for help.

Remember that success in college (and in other areas of life) requires you to keep questioning what you read and write and to use the critical thinking and reading skills covered in Chapter 2 of this book. Now would be a good time to review the Rhetorical Triangle (p. 13), the Critical Thinking Process (p. 15), and the 2PR Critical Reading Process (p. 17).

Teaching tip Using your syllabus, discuss with the class the purpose of some of the assignments.

TONE AND FORMAT

Your audience and purpose for a piece of writing determine what tone you should use and what format you should write in. Most of us pay at least some attention to these factors in everyday writing, as in the examples of Maggie's writing on page 27. As with audience and purpose, however, as your writing tasks become more complex in college, you will have to train yourself to consider tone and format carefully so that they are appropriate for the task at hand. What kind of language is most appropriate? What format will you use? How will you deliver your message? Stop to consider these factors before you write and as you revise.

Formality versus Informality

Tone is the "voice" of our writing, formed by the words we use and the ways in which we use them, and it determines the way our audience perceives us when we write. Because we communicate often today via faceless channels like e-mail and texting, learning to control your tone in writing is more important now than ever.

The degree of formality is one of the most important variables of tone in writing. You probably already know that you should not write to your new instructor, your boss, or your city councilwoman the same way you text to a close friend. Applying that knowledge means thinking about various choices. For example, in formal writing, abbreviations and emoticons are inappropriate, as are ALL CAPS, out-of-control punctuation (!!!!), misspellings, and errors in syntax like fragments and run-ons. When in doubt, opting for a more formal tone is strongly advisable.

> **PRACTICE 3**   **Writing a formal message**
>
> Read the following situation and answer the questions that come after it:
>
> > You have lived in your new apartment for only a few months when you receive a message from the owner of the building telling you that your neighbors have been complaining about the amount of noise coming from your apartment. You were unaware that your neighbors could hear sounds from within your apartment. You have not yet met any of your neighbors, other than an occasional wave hello in the hallway, and you met the owner only once, when you first viewed the apartment.

1. What would be your first response in this situation? Take a few minutes to write it out.

2. Now imagine that you are the owner of the building and you received the message that the renter of the apartment just wrote. What would your perception be of this new renter? Is it positive or negative? Are you willing to speak to the renter and work things out or not?

3. Now imagine that your neighbors are also given the opportunity to read your written reaction to the situation. How would they perceive you as a person or a neighbor? Is this the way you would want to be viewed? Why or why not?

Email, Texting, and Social Media

Format, like tone, is closely linked to audience and purpose. E-mail is still considered by many to be an informal format, and texting much less formal even than e-mail. Additionally, social media platforms that allow people to share text, pictures, videos, and instantly chat with each other also allow them to feel increasingly connected to each other. While this is a wonderful thing for your friends and family, it is important to separate professional contacts and contexts from your personal life. If you are invited to use a format like e-mail to contact someone you do not know or to send information or a request, make sure you do so appropriately so that the person you are contacting will respect your request. Here are some tips for sending an appropriate e-mail:

- Always write a clear subject in the subject line. The subject line should be short, direct, and to the point. For example: *Ride to Class?*
- Always address the person you are writing to. For example: *Dear Mr. White,* or *Hello, Chris.*
- If your message is long, break it up into paragraphs.
- Avoid writing in all capital letters—doing so is equivalent to shouting to the other person.
- Do not overuse color or splashy fonts. The point of e-mail is to convey information, not to create an art installation.
- Do not use texting language; not everyone is familiar with it, and it is generally perceived as extremely informal.
- Use correct punctuation and capitalization.
- Note that many new tablets, phones, and other technologies will either auto-correct words in ways you do not want (for example, *were* automatically becomes *we're*) or does not autocorrect words that it should (for example, *I* is not automatically capitalized).

Avoid texting another person unless you have permission to do so. Even in text messages there are different levels of formality. Save truly informal choices for good friends, and use correct spelling and punctuation when texting others.

When engaging with others on a social media platform such as Facebook, remember that there are different levels of formality. Keep in mind that everything you do online will remain for everyone to see. We tend to think that managing our privacy settings will keep our activity hidden, but that is not always the case. Privacy rules are always changing. Never post something that you would not want everyone to see. Posting a message about a wild party on a friend's wall may seem harmless, but in the future a potential employer could discover it during an online background check. While you may have deleted your account, your friend's account might remain active.

Also, think carefully before you make someone a Facebook friend and post things or chat with them. Some instructors will allow students to be their friends through social media so they can chat or post questions outside of class. It may be nice to have access to your instructor through an app on your phone, but do you want your professor to see all of your posts and photos? What is an appropriate level of formality to maintain on social media sites? If you decide to connect with your professors on social media, be sure to communicate appropriately by using correct spelling, punctuation, and grammar.

> **PRACTICE 4**   **Writing e-mail**
>
> In steps 1–3, write the suggested e-mail exactly as you would in real life. That is, use the same tone and format you would use if you were actually writing to that person.
>
> 1. You have to write a note to your best friend through e-mail explaining that you will not be able to meet up with him or her for dinner tonight.
>
> 2. Now imagine you have to reschedule a meeting with your professor, so you are sending him or her an e-mail.
>
> 3. Now imagine you are writing to a hero or idol of yours asking to meet you for dinner.
>
> 4. When you are done with steps 1–3, answer the following questions:
>
>   - What changes did you notice in the format of your e-mail?
>
>   - What changes did you notice in the language of your e-mail?
>
>   - Why were there differences between the messages? How did context affect the writing and style of the messages?

AVOIDING MISCOMMUNICATION

One of the main potential problems with writing e-mails, text messages, and comments on social media is miscommunication. Why? Electronic communication is as rapid and informal as spoken communication, but it lacks the nonverbal components (facial expressions, tone of voice, gestures) that give layers of meaning to spoken words. Jokes, sarcasm, and other complex statements may not come across as intended in a text, e-mail, or comment. In order to avoid miscommunication in writing, reread before sending or turning in your written work. If you are in doubt as to how your words will be interpreted, revise and edit; then ask a friend or peer to read what you have written and give you frank feedback. Avoid writing in the heat of the moment. If you are feeling emotional about a certain topic, wait a few hours or a day before you decide to hit "send" on your e-mail, text message, or comment.

Main Idea and Support

e Log in to
macmillanhighered
.com /realessays
LearningCurve > Critical
Reading

The **main idea** is the central point you as the writer want to communicate. In an essay, the main idea is expressed as a **thesis. Support** is the collection of details that shows, explains, or proves the main idea. You might use statistics, facts, definitions, and scientific results for support, or you might use memories, stories, comparisons, quotations from experts, and personal observations. The way you express the main idea and the kinds of support you use are determined in large part by your purpose and by the audience you wish to reach.

Developing a main idea and supporting it will be covered in depth in Chapters 4–8, as stages in the writing process.

Organization, Unity, and Coherence

Arranging your ideas in a logical manner is crucial for effective writing. Common kinds of essays, like essays that tell a story (called *narration*), essays that a describe a process (called *process analysis*), or essays that compare and/or contrast two or more things, use conventional organizational patterns. You'll learn more about these in Part 3. All essays need to use some method of organization to help readers follow the thread of the writer's ideas. Three common ways of organizing support for a main idea are **chronological, spatial,** and **order of importance.** You will learn more about organizing your ideas in Chapter 8, in a walk-through of the drafting stage of the writing process.

Two equally important characteristics of effective writing are **unity** and **coherence**. All of what you write in an essay should relate to the main idea (a characteristic called *unity*), and all of it should be connected in a way that is intelligible to the reader (a characteristic called *coherence*). You will learn more about these important principles in Chapter 9, Revising a Draft.

Conventions: Structure and Grammar

Effective writing also depends on the use of clear, appropriate **structure** and **grammar**. Structure, which involves how you connect your main idea and your support and how you organize it, will be covered in Chapters 5–9 in Part 2 of this text. Grammar skills will be covered in depth in Parts 5–8 of this text. As an introduction, the basics of paragraph and essay structure are covered in the following sections.

PARAGRAPH STRUCTURE

A **paragraph** is a group of sentences that work together to make a point. A good paragraph has three necessary parts—the topic sentence, the body, and the concluding sentence. Each part serves a specific purpose.

Paragraph part	Purpose of the paragraph part
1. The **topic sentence**	states the **main idea.** The topic sentence is often either the first or last sentence of a paragraph.
2. The **body**	supports (shows, explains, or proves) the main idea. It usually contains three to six **support sentences,** which present facts and details that develop the main idea.
3. The **concluding sentence**	reminds the audience of the main idea and often makes an observation.

ESSAY STRUCTURE

An **essay** is a group of paragraphs that work together to make a point. Essays vary in length. A short essay may consist of four or five paragraphs, totaling three hundred to six hundred words. A long essay is six paragraphs or more, depending on what the essay needs to accomplish—persuading someone to do something, using research to make a point, explaining a complex concept, or explaining an idea or experience.

An essay has three necessary parts—an introduction, a body, and a conclusion.

Teaching tip Have students interview a second- or third-year student in their major to find out the kind of writing that person does for his or her classes.

Essay part	Purpose of the essay part
1. The **introduction**	states the **main idea,** or **thesis,** generally in a single strong statement. The introduction may be a single paragraph or multiple paragraphs.
2. The **body**	supports (shows, explains, or proves) the main idea. The body of an essay generally has at least three **support paragraphs.** Each support paragraph begins with a **topic sentence** that supports the thesis statement and continues with facts and details that develop the main idea.
3. The **conclusion**	reminds the audience of the main idea. It may summarize and reinforce the support in the body paragraphs, or it may make an observation based on that support. Whether it is a single paragraph or more, the conclusion should relate back to the main idea of the essay.

Relationship between Paragraphs and Essays

For more on the important features of writing, see the Four Basics of Effective Writing on page 26.

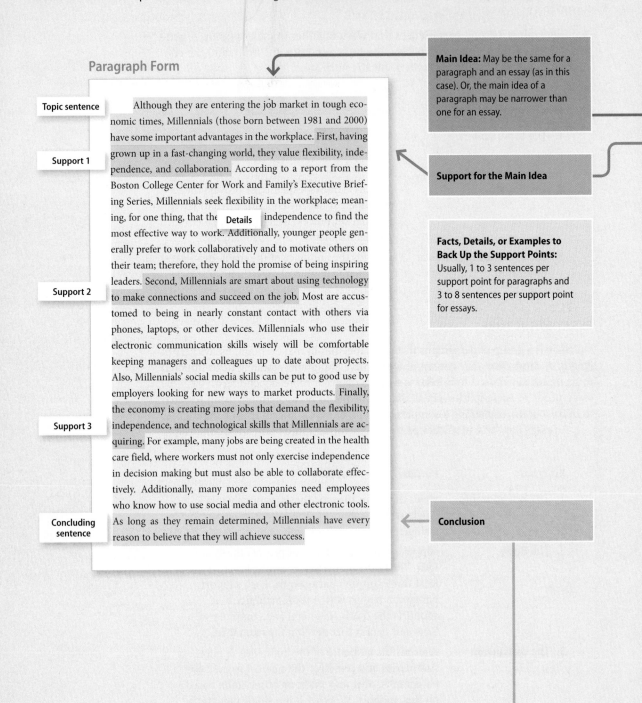

Paragraph Form

Topic sentence

Support 1

Support 2

Support 3

Concluding sentence

Although they are entering the job market in tough economic times, Millennials (those born between 1981 and 2000) have some important advantages in the workplace. First, having grown up in a fast-changing world, they value flexibility, independence, and collaboration. According to a report from the Boston College Center for Work and Family's Executive Briefing Series, Millennials seek flexibility in the workplace; meaning, for one thing, that the **Details** independence to find the most effective way to work. Additionally, younger people generally prefer to work collaboratively and to motivate others on their team; therefore, they hold the promise of being inspiring leaders. Second, Millennials are smart about using technology to make connections and succeed on the job. Most are accustomed to being in nearly constant contact with others via phones, laptops, or other devices. Millennials who use their electronic communication skills wisely will be comfortable keeping managers and colleagues up to date about projects. Also, Millennials' social media skills can be put to good use by employers looking for new ways to market products. Finally, the economy is creating more jobs that demand the flexibility, independence, and technological skills that Millennials are acquiring. For example, many jobs are being created in the health care field, where workers must not only exercise independence in decision making but must also be able to collaborate effectively. Additionally, many more companies need employees who know how to use social media and other electronic tools. As long as they remain determined, Millennials have every reason to believe that they will achieve success.

Main Idea: May be the same for a paragraph and an essay (as in this case). Or, the main idea of a paragraph may be narrower than one for an essay.

Support for the Main Idea

Facts, Details, or Examples to Back Up the Support Points: Usually, 1 to 3 sentences per support point for paragraphs and 3 to 8 sentences per support point for essays.

Conclusion

Essay Form

1

Fairly often, I hear older people saying that Millennials (those born between 1981 and 2000) are spoiled, self-centered individuals who have much less to contribute to the workplace than previous generations did. Based on my own experiences and r— **Thesis statement** I must disagree. Although they are entering the job market in tough economic times, Millennials have some important advantages in the workplace. **Topic sentence 1**

First, having grown up in a fast-changing world, they value flexibility, independence, and collaboration. Unlike their parents and grandparents, Millennials never knew a world without personal computers, and the youngest of them never knew a world without the Internet or ever-changing models of smart phones. They are used to rapid change, and most of them have learned to adapt to it. Consequently, Millennials, for the most part, expect workplaces to adapt to them. According to a report from the Boston College Center for Work and Family's Executive Briefing Series (EBS), Millennials seek flexibility in the workplace—for example, in when and where they work. This attitude

2

does not mean that they are looking out for themselves alone. Instead, they want the independence to find the most effective and productive way to work. Additionally, according to the EBS report, Millennials are more likely than older workers to reject old-fashioned business hierarchies in which managers tell lower-ranking employees what to do, and there is no give-and-take. In general, younger people prefer to work collaboratively and to do what they can to motivate others on their team; therefore, they hold the promise of being inspiring leaders. **Topic sentence 2**

Second, Millennials are smart about using technology to make connections and succeed on the job. Most of them are accustomed to being in nearly constant contact with others via phones, laptops, or other devices. Although some people fear that **Support paragraphs** nectedness can be a distraction in the workplace, these technologies can be used productively and allow effective multitasking. For instance, over the course of a day, Millennials who have learned to use their electronic communication skills wisely will be comfort-

3

able keeping managers and colleagues up to date about projects and responding to questions and requests as they arise. Furthermore, most Millennials are open to continuing such electronic exchanges during evenings and weekends if they feel they are collaborating with colleagues to meet an important goal. Also, many Millennials are skilled in using social media to reach out to and remain connected with others; in fact, some people refer to them as "the Facebook generation." Employers can put these skills to good use as they look for new ways to market their products and find new customers. **Topic sentence 3**

Finally, the economy is creating more jobs that demand the flexibility, independence, and technological skills that Millennials are acquiring. For example, many jobs are being created in the health care field, where workers, such as nurses and physician assistants, must not only exercise independence in decision making but must also be able to collaborate effectively. Additionally, many more companies need employees who know how to use social media and other elec-

4

tronic tools for marketing purposes. Similarly, Millennials with social media skills may have an advantage in finding work in the marketing and advertising industries specifically. There is also always a need for independent-minded people to create new businesses and innovations. Thus, Millennials play a valuable role in helping the economy grow.

As long as they remain determined and confident, Millennials have every reason to believe that they will achieve career success. According to the EBS report and other sources, meaningful, challenging work is more important to this generation than having a high salary. In the long term, workers with those types of values will always be in demand. **Concluding paragraph**

The parts of an essay correspond to the parts of a paragraph. The **thesis** of an essay is like the **topic sentence** of a paragraph. The **support paragraphs** in the body of an essay are like the **support sentences** of a paragraph. And the **conclusion** of an essay is like the **concluding sentence** of a paragraph.

> **PRACTICE 5** **Identifying parts of a paragraph and essay**
>
> Read "Just Walk On By: Black Men and Public Space" by Brent Staples on page 669, and identify the following:
>
> 1. What is the main idea or thesis statement?
>
> 2. How many support paragraphs are there?
>
> 3. Identify the topic sentence of each paragraph.
>
> 4. Where in the conclusion does Staples remind us of the main idea?

An Overview of the Writing Process

The **writing process** consists of four basic stages. The rest of the chapters in Part 1 cover every stage except editing (presented later in the book). In these chapters you will practice every stage, see how another student completed the process, and write your own paragraph or essay. Keep in mind that you may not always go in a straight line through the four stages; instead you might circle back to earlier steps to further improve your writing. This is what it means to call the writing process **recursive.**

Whenever you are first learning to do something—playing a sport, driving a car, riding a bicycle—the steps seem complicated. However, after you practice them, the individual steps seem to blend together and you just do them, often with increasing smoothness and confidence. The same thing will happen as you practice the steps in the writing process.

The flowchart on page 37 shows the four basic stages of the writing process and the steps within each stage. Each stage will be explored fully in a later chapter.

Teaching tip Ask students to describe a process related to their college experiences, such as applying for admission or financial aid, registering for classes, or purchasing textbooks.

The Writing Process	1. **Generating Ideas**
	2. **Planning and drafting**
	3. **Revising**
	4. **Editing and proofreading**

The Writing Process

Generate Ideas

CONSIDER: What is my purpose in writing? Given this purpose, what interests me? What connections can I make among ideas? Who will read what I am writing? What do they need to know?

- Find and explore your topic (Chapter 5).
- Make your point (Chapter 6).
- Support your point (Chapter 7).

Plan and Draft

CONSIDER: How can I organize and present my ideas effectively for my readers?

- Arrange your ideas, and make an outline (Chapter 8).
- Write a draft, including an introduction that will interest your readers, a strong conclusion, and a title (Chapter 8).

Revise

CONSIDER: How can I make my draft clearer or more convincing to my readers?

- Look for ideas that do not fit (Chapter 9).
- Look for ideas that could use more detailed support (Chapter 9).
- Connect ideas with transitional words and sentences (Chapter 9).

Edit and Proofread

CONSIDER: What errors could confuse my readers and weaken my point?

- Find and correct errors in grammar (Chapters 21–32).
- Look for errors in word use (Chapters 33–34) and punctuation and capitalization (Chapters 35–39).
- Before submitting your paper, proofread for typographical and formatting errors.

What do you think the arrows mean?

One of the mistakes many writers make, no matter how long they have been writing, is that they think of writing as something that has an end point or a finish line. Of course, all writing does come to an end. We have to turn in that paper for class or that project for work. However, you can move backward or forward through the steps of the writing process. Sometimes you move back and forth only once or twice. For example, perhaps you have an idea for a paper you want to write, but once you start to draft that paper you get stuck. In that case, you may move back to the "generating ideas" stage of the writing process and start again.

In other cases, you may move through the process several times. It may take you a few times to come up with a good topic. Then, once you have that topic, it may take a while to find the right support and evidence. Once you finally feel like your paper is done, you may turn that paper in to your instructor, and she or he may give you feedback that helps you reorganize your thoughts or add new information. In that case, you would move back to the planning and organization stage again. Good writers know that writing takes time and patience because writing is a journey, not a race to the finish line.

> **PRACTICE 6**   **Reflecting on your writing process**
>
> Think back to the last time you wrote something—not necessarily an essay, but something longer than a text message. Then, answer the following questions:
>
> 1. Did you go through all the steps of the process outlined in the flow-chart on page 37? If not, which steps did you take? Did you follow all the steps in order?
>
> 2. Do you think making any changes to the process you normally use would make your writing more effective?

Responding to Texts

Ways of Responding to Texts

Responding to texts in writing involves entering into a dialogue. At first you may feel a bit uncomfortable because this style of writing asks you to confront an "expert" and you may feel unqualified as a student who is learning about the topic. However, you have your own opinions and thoughts about what you read and write; now you need to learn how to express them in writing in a thoughtful way.

There are five main kinds of writing that you can use to respond to a text: **reader-response, summary, analysis, synthesis**, and **evaluation.**

1. **Reader-Response:** recording your reactions to a text in writing.

2. **Summary**: condensing a longer piece of writing into a briefer version.

3. **Analysis**: breaking down the main parts or pieces of a larger work to see how they work together.

4. **Synthesis**: pulling together information from other sources to make a point.

5. **Evaluation**: judging something thoughtfully based on summary, analysis, and synthesis.

Each of these kinds of response helps you demonstrate your deep understanding of course content. In fact, they are all related; you will often find that in completing a reader-response assignment, you will analyze and summarize the reading as well. By understanding how each of these processes helps you respond to a reading, you will be better equipped to understand which ones are appropriate for your assignments.

Examples are based on the following excerpt from *Discovering Psychology,* an introductory textbook by Don Hockenbury and Sandra Hockenbury.

Daily Hassles
That's Not What I Ordered!

What made you feel "stressed out" in the last week? Chances are it was not a major life event. Instead, it was probably some unexpected but minor annoyance, such as splotching ketchup on your new white T-shirt, misplacing your keys, or discovering that you've been standing in the wrong line.

Stress researcher **Richard Lazarus** and his colleagues suspected that such ordinary irritations in daily life might be an important source of stress. To explore this idea, they developed a scale measuring **daily hassles**—everyday occurrences that annoy and upset people (DeLongis & others, 1982; Kanner & others, 1981). The *Daily Hassles Scale* measures the occurrence of everyday annoyances, such as losing something, getting stuck in traffic, and even being inconvenienced by lousy weather.

Are there gender differences in the frequency of daily hassles? One study measured the daily hassles experienced by married couples (Almeida & Kessler, 1998). The women experienced both more daily hassles and higher levels of psychological stress than their husbands did. For men, the most common sources of daily stress were financial and job-related problems. For women, family demands and interpersonal conflict were the most frequent causes of stress. However, when women *do* experience a stressful day in the workplace, the stress is more likely to spill over into their interactions with their husbands and other family members (Schulz & others, 2004). Men, on the other hand, are more likely to simply withdraw.

How important are daily hassles in producing stress? The frequency of daily hassles is linked to both psychological distress and physical symptoms, such as headaches and backaches (Bottos & Dewey, 2004; DeLongis & others, 1988). In fact, the number of daily hassles people experience is a better predictor of physical illness and symptoms than is the number of major life events experienced (Burks & Martin, 1985).

Why do daily hassles take such a toll? One explanation is that such minor stressors are *cumulative* (Repetti, 1993). Each hassle may be relatively unimportant in itself, but after a day filled with minor hassles, the effects add up. People feel drained, grumpy, and stressed out. Daily hassles also contribute to the stress produced by major life events. Any major life change, whether positive or negative, can create a ripple effect, generating a host of new daily hassles (Maybery & others,

Reader-Response

A **reader-response** assignment asks you to read an article or other document and to respond, in writing, to that particular reading by thinking about what it means to you. When we read something, we always come away with some feelings, thoughts, or ideas, but we often ignore those feelings or find ourselves afraid to express them. A reader-response paper is based first and foremost on your own reactions to what you have read.

PURPOSE AND AUDIENCE IN READER-RESPONSE

Your purpose in reader-response is to clearly articulate your own response to what you read and to explain the reasons for that response. In a college setting, your audience is often classmates who have read the same piece of writing and, of course, your instructor. In an important sense, too, your audience is the author of the piece to which you're responding: You're talking back to the author to share your views on his or her writing.

MAIN IDEA IN READER-RESPONSE

Since reader-response can be based on any reaction you had and since it can come from any aspect of the text, you need to be clear and specific in expressing your main idea. Which part of the article are you reacting to? Have you thought through your response carefully? It's OK to respond quickly and with emotion at first, but then you will want to go through a bit more carefully after you have cooled down and make sure your main idea is more than just a first-blush reaction.

SUPPORT IN READER-RESPONSE

Depending on the assignment, support in reader-response can be either experiential or research-based. Experiential support is support based on your own thoughts and experiences. For example, I may claim that students perform better when they sit in the front of the classroom because all of the students I know who earn good grades sit there. This is support based on experience. Some instructors, however, will want you to express your thoughts and feelings but also find some research and evidence to back them up. In that case, you would have to also find a source that could demonstrate that sitting up front is correlated to higher grades.

You will also need to refer to the original article as you respond. You don't want to write about butterflies if the original article was about heart attacks (unless you have some clear reason for connecting the two). You must stay on the original topic and engage in the same conversation as the original author.

Questions for reader-response

- As a reader, what is your immediate response to the writing? Do you like it? Why or why not?

- Is your response based primarily on the ideas in it or on the way it was written?

- What factors underlie the way you respond—emotions, experience, beliefs, or something else?

- Take a moment to talk with others who have read the piece: Do they agree with you? Why or why not?

- Is research required to support your response? Would it make your response more relevant? If so, what kind of facts do you need to gather?

Here is a sample reader-response to "Daily Hassles."

It's interesting that the authors say that the effect of minor sources of stress adds up to greater overall stress than major events. Every time something stupid happens and I get upset, I tell myself that at least

I'm not seriously sick, and no one's died, and I still have a job. Am I wrong to think I'm better off? Maybe I am. But exactly how many minor sources of stress equals one major one? How is that measured? I'd like to find out, and I think I can, if I can find the study they mention by Richard Lazarus.

> **PRACTICE 1**   **Practicing reader-response**
>
> Respond with your thoughts on one of the following: an article on the front page of your local paper or the *New York Times* online (**nytimes.com**); a blog posting on the *Atlantic*'s photography blog *In Focus* (**theatlantic .com/infocus**); a short story from Project Gutenberg (**gutenberg.org/wiki /Short_Stories_%28Bookshelf%29**); or a poem from the Poetry Foundation (**poetryfoundation.org**).

Summary

A **summary** is a condensed version of something longer. You have used summary when you have told someone what a movie was about. As a written response to a text, a summary briefly presents the main ideas and key support of a text in your own words. (In a **paraphrase,** you also restate something in your own words, but your restatement will not necessarily be briefer. You'll learn more about summary and paraphrase and how they differ in Chapter 20.) The length of a summary depends on the length of the original, as well as on the instructions your instructor gives. Typically, though, a paragraph is sufficient as a summary of an article. With this style of writing, you don't include any of your own thoughts or ideas.

PURPOSE AND AUDIENCE IN SUMMARY

Your **purpose** in summary is to briefly restate the main ideas of a document so that your audience—any interested reader—can understand and process them quickly and easily.

MAIN IDEA IN SUMMARY

In a summary, your main idea is not your own. You simply restate the main idea from the original article.

SUPPORT IN SUMMARY

Teaching tip Have students practice summarizing different types of things together. Try books, movies, lectures, classes, class notes, articles, chapters, and other kinds of writing to give them a variety of practice.

A clear summary presents all the major details in the original document; your job is to clearly determine **major details** from **minor details**. *Major details* are the specific reasons, events, or ideas that the author uses as evidence. *Minor details* are more specific and help describe the major details. A good test to see whether a detail is major or minor is to try to take it out of the paragraph or the paper. If you delete it from the original document and the document still makes sense, then the sentence was probably a minor detail. However, if you delete the detail from the paragraph or paper and then the paper doesn't make sense, it was probably a major detail.

Questions for summary

- What is the context for the piece of writing? (Who wrote it? When? Where was it published?)
- What is the author's main idea? What was the purpose of the piece?
- What information does the author give to support the main idea? What major and minor details does the author provide?

Here is a summary of "Daily Hassles." The main idea is double-underlined; the supporting points are underlined.

> Hockenbury and Hockenbury tell us in *Discovering Psychology* that daily hassles often cause more stress than major problems do. According to studies, men and women report different kinds of daily stress and react to stress differently, though both experience psychological and physical symptoms. Some research shows that daily hassles produce stress because their effects are cumulative—that is, they add up over time to create major stress.

Teaching tip A good writing assignment (or a good discussion topic) is to ask students to discuss their daily hassles and the behaviors or physical symptoms that result from them. They can also discuss the validity of the gender differences identified in the passage.

PRACTICE 2   **Summarizing a text**

Summarize the piece you chose to respond to for Practice 1, or choose a new piece from the following list and summarize it: an article on the front page of your local paper or the *New York Times* online (**nytimes.com**); a blog posting on the *Atlantic*'s photography blog *In Focus* (**theatlantic .com/infocus**); a short story from Project Gutenberg (**gutenberg.org/wiki /Short_Stories_%28Bookshelf%29**); or a poem from the Poetry Foundation (**poetryfoundation.org**).

Analysis

An **analysis** breaks down the points or parts of something and considers how they work together to make an impression or convey a main idea. When you tell someone about a movie, you might describe how the music, lighting, camera angles, and acting worked to create suspense or humor. In an analysis, you can begin with the questions from the Critical Thinking Process (p. 15).

PURPOSE AND AUDIENCE IN ANALYSIS

Your purpose in analysis is to show how something ticks. What parts does it consist of? How do the parts work together? In analyzing a text you might provide an in-depth explanation of the topic or demonstrate your understanding of it. In addition, written analysis will help you better understand how written texts work and allow you to apply what you learn to your own writing.

MAIN IDEA IN ANALYSIS

The main idea in analysis will reflect your insight into the way a text works. What is the main idea in the text? How does it relate to the kinds of support offered? What strategies does the writer use to influence the reader's understanding of the text? What assumptions underlie the writer's claims? An analysis also often includes your own questions about the text.

SUPPORT IN ANALYSIS

The kinds of support you use in an analysis will rely most significantly on the text itself. Where, precisely, do you see the main idea expressed? What kinds of support are offered? Where do you see a particular strategy at work? Where do you see evidence of the writer's assumptions?

Questions for analysis

- How do the text's main elements (main idea, support, structure, etc.) work together?
- What is the intended effect on the reader? How do the elements work to achieve this effect?
- What questions do you have about the text?
- What assumptions has the author made about his or her audience?

Here is an analysis of "Daily Hassles" in which the writer discusses one major point in the excerpt and two other studies included in the piece. She then poses questions that the article raises for her. The writer's main idea is double-underlined, and the support points are underlined.

> We have all read about stress, but Hockenbury and Hockenbury have something new and interesting to say about it: It is not the big life crises but the million petty hassles we face every day that get to us. The authors mention a number of different studies on hassles and their effects on us. Two of these studies explore gender differences, and they conclude that men and women report different kinds of daily hassles and respond to them differently.

These studies seem to involve only married men and women, however, which raises areas for further exploration. Do *all* men and women really experience and respond to hassles differently? For example, would unmarried male and female students be affected in the same ways that married men and women are? In a future paper, I would like to examine the kinds of daily hassles my college friends—both male and female—react to and what symptoms those hassles produce. The subject of hassles and how we react to them seems particularly relevant to students, whose lives are full of stress.

PRACTICE 3   **Analyzing a text**

Analyze the piece you chose to respond to for Practice 1 or 2, or choose a new piece from the following list and analyze it: an article on the front page of your local paper or the *New York Times* online (**nytimes.com**); a blog posting on the *Atlantic*'s photography blog *In Focus* (**theatlantic .com/infocus**); a short story from Project Gutenberg (**gutenberg.org/wiki /Short_Stories_%28Bookshelf%29**); or a poem from the Poetry Foundation (**poetryfoundation.org**).

Synthesis

A **synthesis** pulls together information from other experiences or sources to make a new point. Continuing with the movie example, you might relate the effect a movie had on you to an experience you have had or to something you have read about.

PURPOSE AND AUDIENCE IN SYNTHESIS

Your purpose in synthesis is to draw together ideas from different sources to create something new. Synthesis is required in writing most research papers. The goal is to explore a particular topic through a variety of texts (and, in some cases, interviews, experience, and other sources) and draw conclusions about the topic based on what you learn. Ideas for synthesis can emerge from your in-depth analysis of a particular text. Your audience, in addition to your instructor, would be anyone interested in new ideas about the topic.

MAIN IDEA IN SYNTHESIS

Your main idea in writing a synthesis will be the insight you have forged from your exploration of a topic through multiple sources. This insight is a contribution to the academic conversation on a particular topic.

SUPPORT IN SYNTHESIS

The support you bring to bear in writing your synthesis will come from the sources you have consulted, including (when appropriate) your own experience and the experience of others.

Questions for synthesis

- How does the text relate to other, similar (or different) texts?
- To what aspects of your experience or other readers' experience does it relate?
- What new ideas has reading the piece given you?

Here is a synthesis of "Daily Hassles." The writer wanted to understand the hassles that people experience and the effects that they cause, so she incorporated additional information from published research and her own experience. The various sources the writer pulls together are underlined.

First source

In *Discovering Psychology*, Hockenbury and Hockenbury present evidence that males and females react to different sources of stress and respond differently to them. The studies they use as evidence discuss only married couples, however, and they provide few details about the actual kinds and symptoms of stress. Several other studies, as well as original research done among unmarried college students, provide some additional insights into these questions.

Second source

The Mayo Clinic's Web site, produced by the staff at the Mayo Clinic, suggests that there are two main types of stress: acute stress, which is a response to specific and isolated situations (such as a car accident, a performance, or an exam) and chronic stress, which is longer term and cumulative. Acute, short-term stress can be good for people, prompting them to act. Chronic stress, however, tends to have negative effects, both physical and psychological. Daily hassles can produce either or both types of stress. Physical symptoms include headaches, back pain, stomach upset, and sleep problems. Psychological symptoms include anxiety, anger, depression, and burnout. The site offers numerous articles on stress and stress management, including a stress assessment test.

Third source

The Web site *Diabetes at Work* gives a list titled "Top 10 Daily Hassles." On this list are the illness of a family member, home repairs, loss of work, and crime. It includes the same symptoms of stress that the Mayo Clinic site does, such as shortness of breath, forgetfulness, reduced concentration, trouble making decisions, and irritability. Neither the *Diabetes at Work* Web site nor the Mayo Clinic site distinguishes between male and female stress sources or symptoms. ▸

To these sources, I added interviews with eight friends—four men and four women—who all reported these top five daily hassles: worries about money, transportation problems, waiting in lines, unfair bosses, and automated phone systems that take forever and never get you an answer.

Fourth source

The only significant difference in the kind of hassles reported by the men and women I talked to was that several women (but not men) mentioned worries about physical safety (for example, while traveling home from school at night). When I asked my friends to report how they dealt with their stress, they seemed to confirm the Hockenburys' claim that women's stress spills over into the family and men tend to withdraw. Two men reported no psychological symptoms of stress, whereas the remaining six people (four women and two men) emphasized both psychological and physical symptoms.

These sources suggest that there might be some gender differences in the hassles that people experience and the symptoms that result from these hassles, but they might not be as major as the Hockenburys' passage led me to expect. Most of the stresses mentioned seem to be caused by having to do too much in too little time. Perhaps this is a comment on the quality of modern life, which affects both men and women equally.

New point

Works Cited

Hockenbury, Don H., and Sandra E. Hockenbury. *Discovering Psychology*. 5th ed. New York: Worth, 2010. 543. Print.

Mayo Clinic Staff. "Stress Symptoms: Effects on Your Body, Feelings, and Behavior." *Mayo Clinic*. The Mayo Clinic, 20 Feb. 2009. Web. 13 Oct. 2010.

"Top 10 Daily Hassles." *Diabetes at Work*. United States Dept. of Health and Human Services, 27 May 2007. Web. 10 Oct. 2010.

PRACTICE 4   **Synthesizing**

Use one of the pieces you selected for Practice 1, 2, or 3, or choose something new: an article on the front page of your local paper or the *New York Times* online (**nytimes.com**); a blog posting on the *Atlantic*'s photography blog *In Focus* (**theatlantic.com/infocus**); a short story from Project Gutenberg (**gutenberg.org/wiki/Short_Stories_%28Bookshelf%29**); or a poem from the Poetry Foundation (**poetryfoundation.org**). Now find at least one additional piece of writing on either the same topic or a related one. Finally, in a page or two, explain the different perspectives on the topic that the pieces of writing express.

Evaluation

An **evaluation** is your *thoughtful* judgment about something based on what you have discovered through your summary, analysis, and synthesis. To use the movie example again, if you write about why you liked (or hated) a movie, you are evaluating it. More than a mere opinion, your evaluation is a reasoned demonstration that you've chosen the right criteria for your judgment and applied them correctly.

PURPOSE AND AUDIENCE IN EVALUATION

Your purpose in writing an evaluation of a text (or of anything else) is to persuade your reader that your judgment of it is correct. Your audience is anyone interested in the text itself or in your skill at evaluating it. Evaluation often leads directly from analysis—that is, once you have determined what the parts of the text are and how they work together, you can begin to consider how *effectively* they work together, and whether the intended effect on a likely audience has been achieved.

MAIN IDEA IN EVALUATION

Your main idea in writing an evaluation is your judgment of the text or other object you're evaluating. "It's good" or "It's bad" won't do. A credible main idea in evaluation has to be based on criteria that legitimately apply to whatever you're evaluating and specific about the ways in which the subject of your evaluation does or doesn't measure up.

SUPPORT IN EVALUATION

Your support in writing an evaluation should include examples from the text you're evaluating as well as some demonstration that the criteria you're using for your evaluation are reasonable. Both have to be convincing in order for your readers to accept your evaluation. In evaluation, reference to commonly accepted standards for judging something—the complexity of characterization in a realistic play, for example—is useful. Including the evaluation of other readers and explaining why your evaluation differs (if it does) can also be persuasive.

Questions for evaluation

- Is the work successful? Does it achieve its purpose? Why or why not?
- What is the text's likely effect on a reader? How does this relate to its intended effect?
- Is the main idea logically argued and sufficiently supported?
- Is there evidence of bias or deliberate deception?

Here is an evaluation of "Daily Hassles."

> Hockenbury and Hockenbury present important information and raise some interesting questions about how daily hassles affect our lives. In a few paragraphs, they present a great deal of information on the subject of daily hassles—what they are, who developed the scale of daily hassles, how men and women differ in their reactions to daily hassles, and how the stress of daily hassles negatively affects people. They provide numerous credible references to support their points. Other sources—such as the Mayo Clinic's Web site, the Web site *Diabetes at Work,* and a gender-based poll I conducted—provide more details about some aspects of daily hassles and raise questions about the extent to which women and men are differently affected by them. However, the Hockenburys present a good overview of the subject in a short piece of writing. I think the authors do a great job of pulling together good information for students.

PRACTICE 5   **Evaluating a text**

Evaluate the piece you chose to respond to for Practice 1, 2, 3, or 4, or choose a new piece from the following list and evaluate it: an article on the front page of your local paper or the *New York Times* online (**nytimes.com**); a blog posting on the *Atlantic*'s photography blog *In Focus* (**theatlantic .com/infocus**); a short story from Project Gutenberg (**gutenberg.org/wiki /Short_Stories_%28Bookshelf%29**); or a poem from the Poetry Founda- tion (**poetryfoundation.org**).

Documenting Sources

When you write about readings, particularly when you are writing a synthesis or an evaluation, you may want to refer directly to sources other than the reading itself. For example, in the synthesis on pages 46–47 the writer cites two sources within the text and also in a Works Cited list.

College writers must follow specific rules to document every work they have referred to or quoted from. The writer of the synthesis example uses the documentation style of the Modern Language Association (MLA), which is used in most English courses. Other courses may use other styles, such as that of the American Psychological Association (APA). The MLA style of docu- mentation is presented in Chapter 20. Use that chapter to learn how to quote from another source and how to cite other sources both within and at the end of your paper.

Reviewing What You've Learned

To review summary, analysis, synthesis, and evaluation, read the following text by Deborah Tannen; then complete Practice 6. (The notes in the margins show how one student, Tom, applied the process of critical reading to this text.)

Deborah Tannen

It Begins at the Beginning

Deborah Tannen is a professor of linguistics at Georgetown University in Washington, DC. Linguistics—the study of human language—reveals much about people and their culture. Part of Tannen's research in linguistics has focused on differences in how women and men use language and how those differences affect communication. The following excerpt, adapted from her book *You Just Don't Understand* (1990), describes how girls' and boys' language and communication patterns differ from an early age.

Guiding question How do boys and girls differ in their play and the language they use in their play?

Main idea

She will have to prove this point.

Signals important purpose

What about computers?

Examples (boys' play)

! But don't boys & girls play together—at least sometimes?

More examples (girls' play)

1   Even if they grow up in the same neighborhood, on the same block, or in the same house, girls and boys grow up in different worlds of words. Others talk to them differently and expect and accept different ways of talking from them. Most important, children learn how to talk, how to have conversations, not only from their parents, but from their peers. . . . Although they often play together, boys and girls spend most of their time playing in same-sex groups. And, although some of the activities they play at are similar, their favorite games are different, and their ways of using language in their games are separated by a world of difference.

2   Boys tend to play outside, in large groups that are hierarchically structured. Their groups have a leader who tells others what to do and how to do it, and resists doing what other boys propose. It is by giving orders and making them stick that high status is negotiated. Another way boys achieve status is to take center stage by telling jokes, and by sidetracking or challenging the stories and jokes of others. Boys' games have winners and losers and elaborate systems of rules, and the players frequently boast their skill and argue about who is best at what.

3   Girls, on the other hand, play in small groups or in pairs; the center of a girl's social life is a best friend. . . . In their most frequent games, such as jump rope and hopscotch, everyone gets a turn. Many of their activities (such as playing house) do not have winners or losers. Though some girls are certainly more skilled than others, girls are expected not to boast about it, or show that they think they are

better than the others. <u>Girls don't give orders</u>; they express their preferences as suggestions, and suggestions are likely to be accepted. Anything else is put down as bossy. <u>They don't grab center stage</u>—they don't want it—so they don't challenge each other directly. And much of the time, they simply sit together and talk. Girls are not accustomed to jockeying for status in an obvious way; they are more concerned that they be liked.

Does Tannen think these differences affect how adult men and women work together?

| PRACTICE 6 | **Responding to "It Begins at the Beginning"** |

1. Reader Response: How did you find yourself reacting to Tannen's article? What parts of it surprised/confused/intrigued/irritated you? Why?
   Answers will vary.

2. Summarize: What is the article's main idea? What support does Tannen offer for her argument?

3. Analyze: How do the various parts of the article work together? What effect did Tannen intend to have on her readers? What strategies did she use to achieve this effect?

4. Synthesize: How can you connect the information in this article to your own knowledge or experience? Can you connect it to other texts you've read?

5. Evaluate: Where in the article did the author do a particularly good job supporting her points? What parts were confusing or could have used more explanation? Do you think the author achieved her purpose? What is your response to the article and why do you feel that way?

Writing as a Process

"I write a blog."

Alex V. R., student

Finding and Exploring a Topic

How to Find and Explore a Topic

A **topic** is who or what you are writing about. A good topic for an essay is one that interests you and that fulfills the terms of your assignment. To learn more about finding and exploring a good topic, read on.

Decode the Assignment

Just the thought of a writing assignment can be overwhelming at first. To relieve some of the stress, make sure you always know exactly what the instructor expects from you. Important variables include, but are not limited to, the following:

- How long should the assignment be? Does this instructor expect a certain number of pages or words?

- How formal is the assignment? Is this a quick response to something you read or discussed, or is this a formal paper?

- How much of your grade is this assignment worth? Is it a general homework assignment or a major paper grade?

- How much assistance will you have with this assignment? Will you have the opportunity to generate topics, work on paragraphs, and revise papers in class, or will you be expected to write the paper on your own?

- What freedom do you have in choosing a topic? Is there a particular topic that you are required to write on, or are you free to choose your own topic? In addition, is there a list of banned topics?

- Does the assignment specify a particular type of paper such as a narrative, argument, or cause and effect?

There may be other requirements specific to your own assignment.

| PRACTICE 1 | Decoding an assignment |

Circle the key terms in the following writing assignment, and then answer the questions.

For your first assignment this semester, you are going to write a short biography of the student sitting three seats to your left. Introduce yourself to that person and interview him or her outside of class. This interview needs to take place in person and not through an electronic format or by phone. You should post your biography to the Discussion Board on our Blackboard classroom site, and it should be a minimum of 150 words. In this paragraph, you need to include not only the other student's name but also some unique information about him or her. In other words, you need to find out something that makes this person different from the other people in the class and write about it. This paragraph needs to be grammatically correct with no spelling or punctuation errors and needs to be posted no later than the start of our next class meeting. Any posts later than 9:01 a.m. (our class starts at 9:00 a.m.) will be counted late.

1. What type of assignment is this—a short homework assignment, a major paper assignment, something else? _Short homework assignment_

2. What do you need to do in order to earn a passing grade on this assignment? _Post paragraph on Blackboard no later than 9:00 a.m. Paragraph must be grammatically correct, at least 150 words, and not have spelling or punctuation errors._

You need to make sure you are completely clear on what the instructor expects from you. If you misunderstand or misread the assignment, it will result not only in a bad grade but also in frustration. Taking the time to read the assignment carefully and ask questions will save you time and effort in the long run. Once you have cleared up any confusion by asking questions and you are certain you understand the assignment, you can pick a topic to write about.

Find a Good Topic

Any topic that you choose to write about should pass the following test.

Questions for finding a good topic

- Does this topic interest me?
- Can I find out more about it?

- Can I get involved with this topic? Is it relevant to my life in some way?
- Does it fit the assignment, focusing on a subject neither too broad nor too narrow to treat in the assigned length?

Choose one of the following broad topics or one of your own, and focus on one specific aspect of it that you think would make a good topic for a short essay.

My goals

Pet peeves

Personal responsibility

Taking risks

Relationships

Something I do well

Something I am interested in or enjoy doing

Family roles

Reality TV

Popular music

Significant places

PRACTICE 2   **Finding a good topic**

Ask the questions for finding a good topic (pp. 56–57) about the topic you have chosen. If you answer "no" to any of the questions, look for another topic, or modify the one you chose.

My topic: _Answers will vary._ _____

Keeping in mind the general topic you have chosen, read the rest of this chapter, and complete all of the practice activities. When you finish, you will have found a good topic to write about and explored ideas related to that topic.

Narrow Your Topic

To **narrow** a topic is to focus on the smaller parts of a general topic until you find a more limited topic or an angle that is interesting and specific. In real life, you narrow topics all the time: You talk with friends about a particular song rather than music, about a particular person rather than the human race, or about a class you are taking rather than about every class the college offers.

In college writing, you often need to do the same thing. A professor may give you a broad topic like "religion and culture," "cheating in our society," or "goals in life." These topics are too general to write about in a short essay, so you need to know how to narrow them.

ASK YOURSELF QUESTIONS

Shannon Grady was assigned the broad essay topic "religion and culture." What follows shows how she narrowed her topic. Shannon shares how she *thought* about the broad topic and the questions she asked to make it manageable.

First, I think about the words that are important. Here, that's <u>religion</u> and <u>culture</u>.

Then, I ask questions. (At first, the questions are all over the place, and I want to quit. But I tell myself I can't stop until I have something that might work, or else I'll be too frustrated to come back to it later.)

- <u>What religion—mine?</u> I don't go to church too often. But my grandmother's very religious. She came to this country from Ireland, and she always talks about her church back there. Plus, she goes to church here every single morning.

- <u>Whose culture—mine? This country's? Another country's? Now or in the past?</u> My grandmother loves to talk about her life in "the old country," and she has great stories.

- <u>What kind of culture—like art? Politics?</u> Well, Gran and all of her friends love storytelling, dancing, singing, and she's always playing Irish music. I never asked why everyone from Ireland seems to know how to sing, dance, play music, and tell great stories. But lots of the stories and songs are really sad—why?

- <u>Serious religion? Or things like Christmas music? Maybe both?</u> Talk with Gran. Ask her about the church in Ireland, and here.

Then, I review what I have so far. I've got two big topics to put together somehow:

- The Catholic church in Ireland (Gran's version)

- The Irish tradition of music, dance, storytelling, singing

The paper is supposed to be five pages long. How about:

- <u>My grandmother's religion?</u> No, this isn't really the topic.

- <u>The role of Catholicism in Ireland?</u> Too big.

- <u>Church and culture in small-town Ireland: One woman's story?</u> OK, try this as a start. I can talk to Gran about her town, her church, why the church was important, and how it relates to all the song, dance, music, storytelling. Maybe a separate paragraph for each?

Finally, I ask myself the questions for a good topic:

1. <u>Does the topic interest me?</u> Yes, I love my grandmother, and I can find out stuff I don't know about her!

2. <u>Can I find out more?</u> Yes.

3. <u>Can I get involved with this topic?</u> Yes. Is it relevant to my life in some way? Yes.

4. <u>Does it fit the assignment?</u> Yes, I think so—enough to say but narrowed topic.

MAP YOUR IDEAS

Use circles and lines to help visually break a general topic into more specific ones. Start in the center of a blank piece of paper, and write your topic. In the example below, the topic is "cheating." Circle your topic, and ask yourself some questions about it, such as "What do I know about it?" or "What's important about it?" Write your ideas around the topic, drawing lines from your topic to the ideas and then

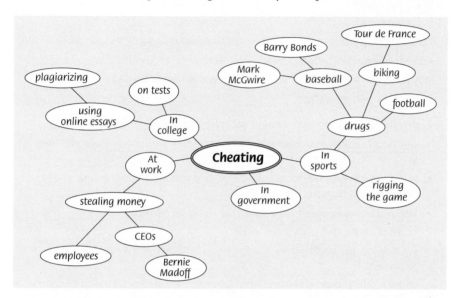

circling them. Keep adding ideas, connecting them with the lines and circles. This technique is called **mapping** or **clustering**. After mapping, look at each cluster of ideas, and consider using one of the narrower topics. In the example above, the student, Paul Desmots, started with the general topic of "cheating," but ended up writing about steroid use in sports and focused on recent examples in baseball.

LIST NARROWER TOPICS

A student, Roberta Fair, was assigned a short essay on the general topic "personal goals." First, she listed specific personal goals.

PERSONAL GOALS

Get a better job	Stop smoking
Get a college degree	No deadbeat guys
Learn to use my time better	Be nicer
Stay patient with my kids	Clean my house more often
Don't argue with my mother	Don't buy things I don't need

Then, she asked herself some questions to help her choose one of the narrower topics on her list.

- Which of the narrowed topics is the most important to me? They're all important, but some of them aren't as important to me as others, so I'll cross those out.

PERSONAL GOALS

Get a better job	Stop smoking
Get a college degree	~~No deadbeat guys~~
Learn to use my time better	~~Be nicer~~
Stay patient with my kids	~~Clean my house more often~~
~~Don't argue with my mother~~	Don't buy things I don't need

- Is it the right size for a short essay? Not really sure.
- Is it broad enough that I can make at least three or four points about it? I think so.
- Is it narrow enough that I can "dig deeply" and give good details in a short essay? I think all of these topics are.
- Which one is most important to you? They all are, in different ways.

  A better job would give me more money.

  A college degree would get me a better job, and I'd feel like I'd done something important.

  To get a college degree, I have to learn to use my time better.

  Maybe I'd be more patient with my kids if I had a better job and more money.

  Stop smoking. Right now I'm not ready.

  If I had a degree, a better job, and more money, I could buy things I want and not feel guilty.

Looking them all over again, though, I think the college degree would get me other things that are important—like a better job, more money, maybe more patience with my kids. I'm going to go with that.

Roberta then chose "Getting a college degree" as her narrowed topic.

TOPIC	NARROWED TOPIC
A personal goal	Getting a college degree

PRACTICE 3   **Narrowing a topic**

Use one of the three methods on pages 58–59 to narrow your topic. Then, write your narrowed topic below.

Narrowed topic: _Answers will vary._

Explore Your Topic

Explore a topic to get ideas you can use in your writing. **Prewriting techniques** are ways to come up with ideas at any point during the writing process—to find a topic, to get ideas for what you want to say about the topic, and to support your ideas.

Questions for exploring a topic

- What interests me about this topic?
- Why do I care about it?
- What do I know or want to know?
- What do I want to say?

The following sections detail prewriting techniques for exploring ideas and show how Roberta Fair used each one of them to get ideas about her topic, "Getting a college degree."

FREEWRITE

Freewriting is like having a conversation with yourself on paper. To freewrite, just start writing everything you can think of about your topic. Write nonstop for at least five minutes. Do not go back and cross anything out or worry about using correct grammar or spelling; just write.

> I don't know, I don't think about goals more than just handling every day—I don't have time. The kids, my job, laundry, food, school, it's a lot. So I just get by day by day but I know that won't get me or my kids anywhere. I really do wish I could get a better job that was more interesting and I wish I could make more money and get my kids better stuff and live in a better place and not be worried all the time about money and our apartment and all that. I really do need to get that degree cause I know we'd have a better chance then. I know I need to finish college.

LIST AND BRAINSTORM

List all the ideas about your topic that come to your mind. Write as fast as you can for five minutes without stopping.

Teaching tip If you are working in a computer classroom, ask students to turn off their monitors and freewrite by hand. Often, when freed from electronic spelling, grammar, and punctuation checks, they will produce more ideas.

Teaching tip To help generate ideas, have students switch papers or stations randomly and ask them to respond to the freewrite in front of them. What interests them about the topic? What do they like about the topic? What do they want to know more about? What three questions do they want to ask the writer?

> So hard to find time to study
>
> Good in the long run
>
> Lots of advantages
>
> Better job
>
> Better place to live
>
> More money
>
> More opportunities
>
> A big achievement—no one in my family's ever gotten a degree
>
> But they don't give me support either

ASK A REPORTER'S QUESTIONS

Ask yourself questions to start getting ideas. The following reporter's questions—Who? What? Where? When? Why? and How?—give you different angles on a narrowed topic, but you can also use other kinds of questions that come to you as you explore your narrowed topic.

> <u>Who?</u> Me, a single mother and student
>
> <u>What?</u> Getting a college degree
>
> <u>Where?</u> Stetson Community College
>
> <u>When?</u> Taking classes off and on now, want a degree in next couple of years
>
> <u>Why?</u> Because I want more out of life for my kids and me
>
> <u>How?</u> Working like a dog to finish school

DISCUSS

When you discuss ideas with someone else, you get more ideas and also feedback on them from the other person.

Team up with another person. If you both have writing assignments, first discuss one person's topic and then the other's. Ask questions about anything that seems unclear, and let the writer know what sounds interesting. Give thoughtful answers, and keep an open mind. It is a good idea to take notes when your partner comments on your ideas.

> <u>Roberta:</u> I guess my personal goal is getting a college degree.
>
> <u>Maria:</u> Why?
>
> <u>Roberta:</u> Well, I think it would help me.
>
> <u>Maria:</u> How?

Roberta: You know, I have a lousy job, no money, the kids, stuff like that.

Maria: Yeah, so how will a college degree help?

Roberta: I know I could get a better job that paid more, so I wouldn't have to work so much. I could spend more time with the kids, and we could live in a better place, you know.

Maria: So do it. What's the problem?

Roberta: Doing it. Time, money. But I know it's worth it, juggling everything for a while, till I get the degree.

CLUSTER AND MAP

You saw an example of clustering, also called mapping, on page 59. Here is Roberta's cluster.

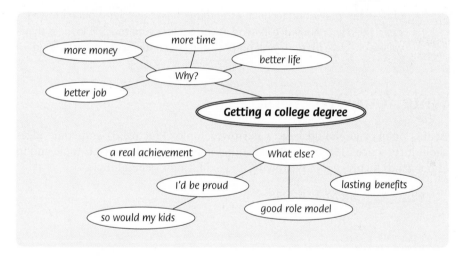

KEEP A JOURNAL

Another good way to explore ideas and topics for writing is to keep a journal. Set aside a few minutes a day, or decide on some other regular schedule to write in your journal. Your journal will be a great source of ideas when you need to find something to write about.

You can use a journal in many ways:

- To record and explore your personal thoughts and feelings
- To comment on things that happen either in the neighborhood, at work, at your college, in the news, and so on
- To examine situations you do not understand (as you write, you may figure them out)

By the time Roberta had used all of the prewriting techniques, she had decided that her narrowed topic (getting a college degree) was a good one and had also generated some ideas to discuss in her essay.

Roberta's Journal Entry

I've been taking courses at the college for a couple of years but not really knowing whether I'd ever finish or not. It's so hard, and I'm so tired all the time that I sometimes think it would be easier (and cheaper!) to stop or to go one semester and not another, but then it's so easy to get out of the habit. I need to decide whether getting a degree is worth all of the effort it will take, and I'm starting to think it is. I don't want to live like this forever. I want a better life.

PRACTICE 4   **Prewriting**

Choose *two* prewriting techniques, and use them to explore your narrowed topic. Keep your audience in mind as you explore your topic. Find ideas that will be effective for both your purpose and your audience's understanding.

Write Your Own Topic

At this point, you should have a narrowed topic (Practice 3) and some ideas about it (Practice 4). Use the checklist that follows to evaluate your topic and to understand the process of narrowing and exploring a general topic.

CHECKLIST

Finding a Good Topic

FOCUS
Read the assignment carefully and consider your audience and purpose.

ASK
- ☐ Is the topic too big for a short essay, if that is the assignment?
- ☐ If it is too big, what are some more limited parts of the topic?
- ☐ Once I have a narrowed topic, does it pass the "Questions for Exploring a Topic" on page 61.
- ☐ Do I or my audience have any assumptions or biases relating to my topic that I should be aware or? If so, what are they?
- ☐ What can I say about my topic? What ideas do I have about my topic?

WRITE
- ☐ Use a prewriting technique to explore ideas about your narrowed topic.

6

Developing a Thesis Statement

How to Develop a Good Thesis Statement

The **thesis statement** of an essay states the main idea you want to get across about your topic. It is your position on whatever you are writing about.

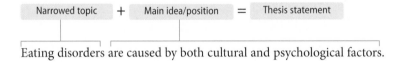

| Narrowed topic | + | Main idea/position | = | Thesis statement |

Eating disorders are caused by both cultural and psychological factors.

A strong thesis statement has several basic features.

Basics of a good thesis statement

- It takes your audience and purpose into account.
- It focuses on a single main idea or position on the topic.
- It is neither too broad nor too narrow.
- It is something that you can show, explain, or prove.
- It is written in confident, firm language.

Discussion Ask students for the titles of three movies they have seen, and write them on the board. Then, ask students to write down the main idea of each one. Compare notes to see whether everyone agrees. If not, briefly discuss their different interpretations.

Weak thesis statement   I think college is good, and there are lots of them.

The weak statement does not follow the basics of a good thesis statement: It focuses on two ideas, not one; it is very broad; the word *good* is not specific; and the words *I think* are not forceful or confident.

| Good thesis statement | A college degree brings many potential benefits such as better jobs, more career choices, and higher salaries. |

This statement has all the basics of a good thesis statement.

 Language note: In some cultures, people avoid making direct points. It is considered impolite to be too direct and self-assertive. In the United States, however, writers are expected to make clear, direct points. The audience wants to know early on what point the writer will make in the essay, the paragraph, or any other nonfiction text.

A good thesis statement is essential to most good essays. Early in your writing process, you may develop a *draft thesis* (or *working thesis*), a first-try version of the sentence that will state your main idea. You can revise it into a final thesis statement later in the writing process.

Consider Your Audience and Purpose

When you write your thesis statement you should always remember that you are writing to an audience. You need to consider the following as you construct a strong thesis statement:

- How old is your audience?
- How educated are they?
- How much do they already know about the topic?
- What do they want to know?
- Do they have a position on this topic?
- Are they married? With children?
- Do they have religious or political beliefs that may affect the way they view your paper?

Of course, with every paper you write, you will not consider all of these factors. You will choose the ones that are most appropriate to your own paper and keep them in mind as you construct your thesis statement.

After you have clearly identified who your audience is and what they will want to know about your topic, you need to make sure your purpose is clear in your paper. Because your general purpose in writing a paper is to communicate your idea as clearly as possible, the best way to clearly demonstrate your purpose is to write good, strong thesis statements. The explanations and practices in this section are organized according to the basics of a good thesis statement (p. 66). This section will help you develop effective thesis statements that will serve as firm foundations for the essays you write.

Teaching tip Have the class brainstorm and come up with other factors that writers need to consider about audience. Audience is treated in more detail in Chapter 7, but it is also important to consider early, in conjunction with thesis.

Focus on a Single Main Idea

Your thesis should focus on only one main idea. If you try to address more than one main idea in an essay, you will probably not be able to give adequate support for all the ideas. Also, you risk splitting your focus.

Thesis statement with two main ideas	In the next decade, <u>many high schools will have a drastic shortage of teachers</u>, and <u>high school teachers should have to take competency tests</u>.

The two ideas are underlined. The writer would need to explain why there will be a shortage of teachers and also why teachers should take competency tests. These are both meaty ideas, and any writer would have trouble supporting them equally in a single essay.

Revised	In the next decade, many schools will have a drastic shortage of high school teachers.
	or
	High school teachers should have to take competency tests.
Thesis statement with two main ideas	College students should be protected from taking on too much credit-card debt, and they should be allowed to stay on their parents' health insurance policies after graduation.
Revised	New laws and educational programs are needed to protect college students from taking on too much credit-card debt.
	or
	College students should be allowed to stay on their parents' health insurance policies after graduation.

Although a good thesis statement focuses on a single main idea, it may include more than one idea if these ideas directly relate to the main idea and are closely related.

A good thesis may or may not include other information that the essay will include. If you know the ideas or examples that you will make to support your thesis, you can include them. For example, see how the following revised thesis statements include some ideas (shown in *italics*) that support the writer's thesis.

Internships offer excellent learning opportunities—*seeing how people dress and act in offices, finding out the kinds of jobs the business has, and meeting people who are good future connections for you.*

The job market for students is tight, but there are things you can do to help get a job in your field, such as *asking for an informational interview, finding a mentor, or getting an internship.*

PRACTICE 1   Developing a thesis statement from
a narrowed topic

For each item, write a thesis statement from the narrowed topic. (Use a separate piece of paper for your answers if there is not enough room on the lines below.)

Example

General topic	Narrowed topic	Thesis
Foreign languages	Learning a foreign language	Learning a foreign language has many benefits.

General topic	Narrowed topic	Thesis
1. A memory	My first date	*Answers will vary.*
2. Music	My favorite kind of music	_____
3. Friendship	My best friend	_____
4. Owning a car	Costs of owning a car	_____
5. Reality TV	A show that you watch	_____

PRACTICE 2   Writing thesis statements that focus on a single
main idea

Rewrite the following thesis statements so that they focus on just one of the ideas mentioned. You can add information to make the statements more specific.

Example: Juggling college and other responsibilities can be challenging, and rising college costs are putting higher education out of reach for many.

Juggling college and other responsibilities can be challenging. _____

1. Planning for college financial aid should begin long before a student's first year of college, and prospective students should also consider how attending college will affect their family life.

   Answers will vary. _____

2. My first job taught me the importance of cooperation, and I also learned how to manage my time effectively.

   _____

3. For several reasons, I will never own my own business, but I do have what it takes to be a top athlete.

   _____

4. Organizations can reduce absenteeism by telling workers about several measures to prevent colds and flu, and they can increase morale by including employees on committees that explore workplace issues.

   _____

5. Given recent violent incidents, Riverside Mall needs to increase security, and the mall should also do a better job of plowing its parking lots in the winter.

   _____

Make Sure Your Thesis Is Neither Too Broad Nor Too Narrow

Your thesis should fit the size of the essay assignment. A thesis that is too broad is impossible to support fully in a short essay: There is just too much to cover well. A thesis that is too narrow gives you nothing on which to build a whole essay.

Too broad   Family is an essential part of life.

[Both *family* and *life* are broad concepts, and the thesis would be impossible to explain in a short essay.]

Revised   Time spent with my children is a welcome balance to time spent at work.

Too broad   The Industrial Revolution was important in this country.

[The Industrial Revolution is too broad to cover in an essay.]

| Revised | During the Industrial Revolution, women workers in the textile industry played an important role in Lowell, Massachusetts. |

A thesis that is too narrow leaves the writer with little to show, explain, or prove. It can also make the reader think, "So what?"

| Too narrow | My family members all have the same middle name. |

[Once the writer says what the middle name is, there is not much more to say, *unless* there is an interesting family story explaining why everyone has it.]

| Revised | An interesting event from long ago explains why my family members all have the same middle name. |

| Too narrow | I tweeted this morning. |

| Revised | Tweeting connects me to other people and their ideas. |

PRACTICE 3   **Writing thesis statements that are neither too broad nor too narrow**

Read the following thesis statements, and decide whether they are too broad, too narrow, or just right for a short essay. For statements that are too broad, write "B" in the space to the left; for statements that are too narrow, write "N"; and for statements that are just right, write "OK."

Example: __N__ **My dog will be ten years old next month.**

__B__ 1. Dogs tend to be loyal pets.

__B__ 2. I love food.

__OK__ 3. Being a vegetarian offers a wide range of healthy food choices.

__N__ 4. As a size 6, I find that when I want to wear fuchsia to work, that my options are limited because I have to find items that are "business casual."

__N__ 5. Another gourmet coffee shop opened last week, the third one on a single block.

Teamwork In small groups, have students identify the thesis statements in two or three of the readings at the back of the book, and then discuss how well those statements meet the criteria for good thesis statements.

PRACTICE 4   **Writing thesis statements that are specific**

Rewrite each of the following thesis statements by adding at least two specific details.

Example: Electronic devices in high schools can be a huge problem.

Cell phones that ring during a high school class disrupt students'

concentration and learning.

1. I have many useful skills.

   Answers will vary.

2. Technology makes studying easy.

   _____

3. I have always had trouble writing.

   _____

4. Allergies are increasing in children.

   _____

5. After I received my first paycheck, I had many feelings.

   _____

Make Sure You Can Show, Explain, or Prove Your Thesis

If a thesis is so obvious that it does not need support or if it states a known fact, you will not be able to say much about it.

Obvious	Most teenagers drive. Guns can kill people.
Revised	The high accident rates among new teen drivers could be reduced with better and more extended driver training. Accidental handgun deaths could be prevented through three sensible measures.
Fact	A growing number of American children are overweight. Each year, more companies outsource jobs to foreign workers.
Revised	We must, as a nation, act to reduce obesity in our children. As more companies export jobs to foreign countries, we will see numerous negative effects.

PRACTICE 5	**Writing thesis statements that you can show, explain, or prove**

Each of the following items is either obvious or a fact and therefore difficult to write about. Rewrite each sentence so that it would give you something to write in an essay.

Example: I have lived in this neighborhood for fourteen years. [Fact]

In the fourteen years I have lived in this town, I have learned a lot about small

towns.

1. Many teenagers experiment with drugs.

   Answers will vary.

2. Every year my college fees go up.

   _____

3. I make $8.00 an hour.

   _____

4. I have just finished my first college course.

   _____

5. Public transportation makes it easier to get to work.

   _____

Express Your Thesis Forcefully and Confidently

A strong thesis statement should be forceful and definite. Avoid writing a thesis statement that begins with "In this essay I will show . . ." or other filler. Do not say you will make a certain point. Just make it.

Note that the revised thesis statements in this chapter take a clear stand on issues and express a particular point of view. Starting with a topic that you care about can help. For more advice on choosing a topic, see Chapter 5.

Weak	In this essay, I will prove that high school dropouts have a difficult time in life.
Forceful	High school dropouts can expect to face surprising hardships in life.

Also, some words and phrases—such as *maybe* and *I think*—can indicate you lack confidence in your main idea. Avoid them. By saying that an idea is your opinion, you are telling the audience that you are unsure of this position and that they shouldn't trust you.

Weak	I think you have to be careful when buying a used car.
Forceful	Before you buy a used car, inform yourself about the basics so that you do not spend more than you need to.
Weak	Maybe it is time to evaluate our monthly spending.
Forceful	Our monthly spending needs close scrutiny.

PRACTICE 6 Writing forceful thesis statements

Rewrite the weak thesis statements that follow to make them more forceful.

Example: In my opinion, students who are involved with the community learn many important lessons.

Students who are involved with the community learn many important lessons.

1. I will explain some examples of history repeating itself.

   Answers will vary.

2. I am frustrated with where I had to park this morning at school.

3. Given that I have improved my job performance and shown a lot of initiative, I am pretty sure I will get a raise this year.

4. It would be a good idea to warn young people about the possible dangers of prescription drug abuse.

5. In this paper, I will describe three reasons why going to college has been a challenge for me.

PRACTICE 7 Revising thesis statements

In the spaces provided, revise each of the possible thesis statements that you wrote in Practice 1, improving them according to the basics of a good thesis statement (p. 66). Again, think of a statement that you would be interested in writing about. You may want to add more information to your thesis statements to make them more specific and forceful, but short, punchy thesis statements also can be powerful.

Possible thesis: When the sun is shining, people's moods improve.

Revised thesis: Bright sunshine dramatically improves people's moods.

1. *Answers will vary depending on the answers in Practice 1.*

2. _____

3. _____

4. _____

5. _____

Place Your Thesis Appropriately

A thesis statement does not have to come at the beginning or end of the first paragraph. Experienced writers may not get to the thesis for a few paragraphs, or they may imply their main idea rather than state it in a single sentence. In most college writing, however, you will need to have a clearly identifiable thesis statement, and it should be either the first or last sentence of your first paragraph. Your instructor may have a preference for putting the thesis statement as the first or last sentence in the first paragraph; if not, you can choose. In the following two paragraphs, one has the thesis statement first, and one has it last.

Thesis first

<u>Bright sunshine dramatically improves people's moods because of its effects on our brains.</u> Most people know this from experience because they tend to feel better during the long, sunny days of summer. In the shorter, darker days of winter, people usually feel more tired and less energetic. Until quite recently, people assumed that this was a psychological reaction, often tied, at least in the United States, with childhood memories of the long, happy, carefree days of summer when schools were not in session. But recently we have learned that feeling better in summer is not just in our heads.

Thesis last

Do your moods vary during the different seasons? For many of us, the short, dark days of winter are difficult: We feel tired, and we lack energy. Most of us want to sleep more and eat hearty, hot meals. In the bright, sunny days of summer, though, we come alive. Until quite recently, people assumed that this was a psychological reaction, often tied, at least in the United States, with childhood memories of the long, happy, carefree days of summer when schools were not in session. But recently we have learned that feeling better in summer is not just in our heads. <u>Bright sunshine dramatically improves people's moods because of its effects on our brains.</u>

What will both essays go on to describe? *How sunshine affects the brain*

Remember, the thesis statement you write first is a *draft thesis*: You can modify it as often as you like while you write your essay.

One Student's Process

Before selecting a writing assignment, read how student Takeesha Ellis developed a thesis statement from her narrowed topic. Before writing her thesis, Takeesha did some freewriting about it.

General Topic   Popular Culture

Narrowed Topic   Interest in Vampires

Freewriting: Our teacher said popular culture is the ideas that become popular at a specific time and that we should write about something that's popular now and I thought of vampires. There are all kinds of things about vampires now, like True Blood and Twilight and books and comics and movies. I don't know why but vampires are cool now. Because they live forever and are superhuman and have control over everything? Also, vampire guys are hot. I know Dracula was an old movie but I wonder why vampires are all of a sudden everywhere. Why now? What does it say about us? Because they're not like us, or are they? Is it about love, power, control, never having to die or get old?

Next, Takeesha decided on a point she might make about why we like vampires.

Point: Vampires are popular because they have things everyone wants but normal humans can't have.

She then wrote a draft thesis statement.

Draft thesis statement: We love vampires because they represent things we value and things we cannot have.

Finally, Takeesha revised her draft thesis statement to make it more specific.

Revised thesis statement: People are fascinated with vampires as creatures that have both human frailties, which we can all relate to, and superhuman powers, which we wish we had.

Write Your Own Thesis Statement

Write a thesis statement using the narrowed topic and ideas you developed in Chapter 5 or one of the following topics (which will need to be narrowed).

Friendship	Fashion or style	A good cause
Drug use	Video games	A waste of time
Popular music	Social media	A cultural icon
Exercise	Going "green"	Reality TV

Before writing, read the checklist that follows.

Teaching tip Even if you do not plan to read a student's entire first draft, it always helps to check the thesis statement. You can prevent problems by helping the student refine his or her main idea.

CHECKLIST

Writing a Thesis Statement

FOCUS

☐ Read your narrowed topic.

☐ Decide what you think is important about it. You may want to use a prewriting technique.

☐ Consider your audience and purpose.

ASK

☐ What is your position or your idea about your topic?

☐ Why is it important to you?

☐ Do you have assumptions or biases? Does your audience?

☐ What do you want to show, explain, or prove?

☐ Can you think of additional ideas to support it?

☐ Is your position a single idea?

☐ Is it a complete sentence?

WRITE

☐ Write a draft thesis statement, and make sure that it follows the basics of a good thesis statement (p. 66).

☐ Revise your draft statement according to the basics of a good thesis statement, and try to make it more specific and confident.

7

Supporting a Thesis

How to Support a Thesis

Support consists of the evidence, examples, or facts that show, explain, or prove your main idea, or thesis, so you need to keep that main idea in focus. **Primary support points** are the major support for your thesis. A short essay usually has between three and five primary points that support the thesis statement. Longer pieces of writing require more support. Each primary support point becomes the topic sentence of its own paragraph. **Supporting details** (or secondary support points) are specifics that explain your primary support points. Each paragraph presents details that support that topic sentence.

Without support, you *state* the main idea, but you do not *make* the main idea. Consider the following statements:

I did not break the bowl.

I do not deserve an F on this paper.

My neighborhood needs more markets.

These statements may be true, but without support they are not convincing. Perhaps you have received the comment "You need to support (or develop) your ideas" on your papers. This chapter will show you how to do so.

Writers sometimes confuse repetition with support. Restating the same idea several times using different words is not support; it is just repetition of an idea that does not help you support your thesis.

Repetition, not support	I do not deserve an F on this paper. It is not a failing paper. It should get a better grade.
Support	I do not deserve an F on this paper. It not only follows the assignment, but I was careful to apply the criteria for grading that was handed out. It has a thesis and support. Even though it has many grammar errors, the paper meets other criteria and should have received a better grade.

As you develop support for your thesis, make sure that each point has the following basic features. (See Chapter 6 for advice on developing thesis statements.)

Basics of good support

- It considers your audience and helps you achieve your purpose for writing.

- It relates directly and logically to your main idea, or thesis.

- It includes main support points as well as specific supporting details or examples.

Consider Your Audience and Purpose

Whenever you write, you need to be aware of your audience to determine what support will best support your ideas. If you assume that your audience understands something that they do not, your writing will have gaps or holes in it; while you may find the paper to be logical and clear, someone who does not share your background experiences, interest, and education may not be able to follow your logic.

Similarly, as you begin any writing project, you'll need to consider your purpose for writing. Do you want to make your audience "live" an experience through your eyes? If so, you'll have to provide plenty of descriptive detail, particularly if you know they probably haven't had a similar experience. Do you want your audience to agree with a proposal you're making about improving the campus cafeteria? If so, you'll need to provide evidence that it could use improving, along with specific, logical suggestions about what would improve it, and why.

Teaching tip
Emphasize that an opinion alone will not convince the audience. If students use an opinion, they should support it with factual evidence.

Prewrite to Find Support

Reread your thesis and imagine your audience asking, "What do you mean?" To answer this question and generate support for your thesis, try using one or more of the prewriting techniques discussed in Chapter 5.

> **PRACTICE 1**　　**Prewriting to find support**
>
> Choose one of the following sentences or one of your own, and write for five minutes using one prewriting technique. You will need a good supply of ideas from which to choose support points for your thesis. Try to find at least a dozen different ideas.
>
> **Suggested thesis statements**
>
> 1. Everyone in my family _Answers will vary._ _____.
>
> 2. Although people want to eat healthy _____.

Teamwork Practice 1 works well in pairs or small groups if you have students choose listing or discussing as their prewriting technique.

3. One way my city (or town) has improved is _____.

4. I have done some _____ things in my life, but the one I am most _____ of is _____.

5. Today, bullying is _____.

Drop Unrelated Ideas

After prewriting, remind yourself of your main idea. Then, review your prewriting carefully, and drop any ideas that are not directly related to your main idea. If new ideas occur to you, write them down.

> **PRACTICE 2**   **Dropping unrelated ideas**

Each thesis statement below is followed by a list of possible support points. Cross out the unrelated ideas in each list. Be ready to explain your choices.

1. **Thesis statement:** Written communication in the workplace must be worded precisely and formatted clearly.

    Possible support points

    use bulleted lists for important short points

    ~~once I wrote a ridiculous memo to my boss but never sent it~~

    try to keep communication to a single page; people are busy

    include the date

    ~~get it done by the end of the day~~

    read it over before sending

    ~~hate to put things in writing~~

    ~~takes too much time~~

    make a copy

    ~~getting forty e-mails in a day is too many~~

2. **Thesis statement:** Texting while driving should be against the law.

    Possible support points

    people have to look away from the road

    minds not on driving

younger drivers, who text most, lose control easily

texts come in all the time

statistics show how dangerous it is (get the numbers)

~~worse than talking on a cell phone~~

with cell phone, at least driver can watch the road at all times

~~people develop problems with their thumbs when they text too much~~

~~not fair to drivers who aren't texting~~

unsafe for all (find examples of accidents caused by texting)

3. **Thesis statement:** I know from experience that sometimes the customer is wrong.

   Possible support points

   work at supermarket

   customers often misread sale flyer

   they choose something like the item on sale but not it

   ~~get mad and sometimes get nasty~~

   ~~why do people bring screaming kids to the supermarket?~~

   ~~they don't have any right to be rude but they are~~

   ~~want to argue but I can't~~

   customers steal food like eating the grapes sold by the pound

   ~~sometimes they eat a whole box of cookies and bring up the empty box~~

   ~~then the kids are always grabbing at the candy and whining, sometimes they just rip the candy open or put it in their mouths~~

   customers misread the signs like ones that say "save $1.50" and think the item is on sale for $1.50

   ~~should get a different job~~

Select the Best Support Points

After dropping unrelated ideas, review the ones that remain, and select the ones that will be clearest and most convincing to your audience. As noted earlier, short essays usually have three to five primary support points. They will become the topic sentences for your support paragraphs.

Teaching tip
Encourage students to get in the habit of asking themselves the kinds of basic questions their audience will ask: "Such as?" "In what way?" "For example?" If a student's support points answer those questions, his or her audience should understand the main idea.

| PRACTICE 3 | **Selecting the best support points** |

For each item, circle the three points you would use to support the thesis statement. Be ready to explain your answers.

1. **Thesis statement:** A college degree should not be the only factor in hiring decisions.

   Possible support points

   job experience

   motivation and enthusiasm

   friends who work at the company

   appearance

   persistence in applying

   recommendations

   good transporation

   artistic talents

2. **Thesis statement:** Because people have a variety of learning styles, it helps to tailor your studying methods to your particular style.

   Possible support points

   learn by doing

   not interested in learning anything new

   learn by seeing

   do not bring their books to class

   disrupt the class

   learn by working with others

   get bored

   bad learners

   gifted students

Add Supporting Details

Once you have chosen your primary support points, you will need to add details to explain or demonstrate each of those points. These supporting details can be examples, facts, or evidence. As the following examples show, a supporting detail is always more specific than a primary support point.

Thesis statement	More research is needed on how to treat autism, a serious disorder affecting behavior, communication, and social interaction.
Primary support point	The disorder affects many people, their families, and communities.
Supporting details	Autism is now diagnosed in about 1 in every 68 children.
	This rate is much higher than it was thirty years ago (was 1 in 2,000).
	Parents and school staffs struggle to know how best to help autistic children.
Primary support point	Some people go online to buy risky treatments that are not science-based.
Supporting details	pressurized oxygen chambers
	drug and vitamin supplements
	special diets and nutrition consultations
	blood transfusions
Primary support point	More research has already started to have some good effects.
Supporting details	Funding has increased 15 percent a year between 2000 and 2010, with hundreds more scientists now studying autism.
	Many of the treatments advertised online have now been scientifically proven not to work.
	Children can now be diagnosed as young as one to two years old, when behavior therapy has a better success rate.

PRACTICE 4 Adding supporting details

In the space indicated, write the points you chose in Practice 3, item 1 (p. 82), as the best support. In the space to the right, add three details that would show, explain, or prove each primary support point.

Thesis statement: A college degree should not be the only factor in hiring decisions.

Teamwork Have students work in pairs to read their thesis statements and share possible supporting details. Together, partners can select the three best points. Suggest that they refer to the basics of good support (p. 79) when generating and selecting support points.

Primary support point	Supporting details
Answers will vary.	

Primary support point	Supporting details

Primary support point	Supporting details

Review Your Support

When you have developed support points for your main idea, along with supporting details, use your critical thinking and reading skills to evaluate it. Does the support make unwarranted assumptions? Does it reveal a bias in your point of view? It is important to review your support in this way because errors in reasoning make it difficult to express your main idea effectively.

Write Topic Sentences for Your Support Points

Your primary support points will form the topic sentences of the paragraphs that support your thesis statement. Each topic sentence should clearly relate to and show, explain, or prove your thesis.

Thesis statement	Playing a team sport taught me more than how to play the game.
Topic sentence (paragraph 1)	I learned the importance of hard practice.

Topic sentence (paragraph 2)	I also realized that, to succeed, I had to work with other people.
Topic sentence (paragraph 3)	Most important, I learned to be responsible to others.

Once you develop topic sentences to support your thesis, back up your topic sentences with supporting details.

> **PRACTICE 5**   **Writing topic sentences and supporting details**
>
> Using the support points you generated in Practice 3, write topic sentences that support the thesis statement. In the space under each topic sentence, list the details you selected. When you have completed this practice, you will have developed support for an essay.
>
> **Thesis statement: A college degree should not be the only factor in hiring decisions.**
>
> **Topic sentence (primary support point 1):** _Answers will vary._
>
> _____
>
> **Supporting details:** _____
>
> _____
>
> **Topic sentence (primary support point 2):** _____
>
> _____
>
> **Supporting details:** _____
>
> _____
>
> **Topic sentence (primary support point 3):** _____
>
> _____
>
> **Supporting details:** _____
>
> _____

One Student's Process

Before selecting a writing assignment, read how a student, Carson Williams, developed support for his thesis.

> **Thesis statement: Although my girlfriend and I are in love, we have some very different ideas about what a "good" relationship is.**

1. To generate ideas that might work as support, Carson used a prewriting technique: listing and brainstorming.

Listing and brainstorming

She always wants to talk

Asks me how I feel, what I think, what I'm thinking about

Gets mad if I don't answer or thinks I'm mad about something

~~Talks during movies and annoys me~~

~~Puts makeup on in the car~~

Always wants to be affectionate, holding hands, kissing

Wants me to tell her I love her all the time

Wants to hear she's pretty

Gets jealous if I'm looking at another girl even though I'm not interested

~~Always asks me if she looks fat and gets mad whatever I say~~

~~Even when we're out she talks on her cell forever~~

Wants to talk about our "relationship" but I don't have anything to say, it's fine

~~Talks about her girlfriends and their relationships~~

Not wild about cars

~~Loves cats and tiny dogs~~

If I just don't feel like talking, she imagines I'm in a bad mood or mad

Hates TV sports

Wants me to go shopping with her

Doesn't like me going out with the guys

2. Next, Carson read his list and crossed out some things that seemed unrelated to his main idea. (See the crossed-out items in the preceding list.)

3. He then reviewed the remaining ideas and noticed that they fell into three categories—differences about communication, differences about showing affection, and differences about how to spend time.

He grouped the ideas under these category labels and saw that the labels could serve as primary support points for his thesis. These support points could be turned into topic sentences of paragraphs backing his thesis, while the ideas under the labels could serve as supporting details for those topic sentences.

PRIMARY SUPPORT: *Differences in communication styles*

SUPPORTING DETAILS

She always wants to talk

Asks me how I feel, what I think, what I'm thinking about

Gets mad if I don't answer or thinks I'm mad about something

Wants to talk about our "relationship" but I don't have anything to say, it's fine

If I just don't feel like talking, she imagines I'm in a bad mood or mad

PRIMARY SUPPORT: *Differences about showing affection*

SUPPORTING DETAILS

Always wants to be affectionate, holding hands, kissing

Wants me to tell her I love her all the time

Wants to hear she's pretty

Gets jealous if I'm looking at another girl even though I'm not interested

PRIMARY SUPPORT: *Differences about how to spend time*

SUPPORTING DETAILS

Not wild about cars

Hates TV sports

Wants me to go shopping with her

Doesn't like me going out with the guys

4. Finally, Carson wrote topic sentences for his primary support points.

Topic sentences for primary support

One big difference is in our expectations about communication.

Another difference is in how we show affection.

Another difference is in our views of how we think a couple in a "good" relationship should spend time.

Write Your Own Support

Develop primary support points and supporting details for the thesis you wrote in Chapter 6 or for one of the following thesis statements.

> William Lowe Bryan said, "Education is one of the few things a person is willing to pay for and not get."
>
> Elderly people in this country are not shown enough respect.
>
> Few people know how to really listen.
>
> Some movies have made me cry from happiness.
>
> When I think of a book that really made me look at things in new ways and learn, I think of _____.

For examples of prewriting techniques, see pages 61–64.

Before writing, read the following checklist.

CHECKLIST

Supporting Your Thesis

FOCUS

- ☐ Read your thesis.
- ☐ Think about the people who will read your writing.
- ☐ Think about your purpose for writing.

ASK

- ☐ What support can you include that will show, explain, or prove what you mean?
- ☐ What does your audience need to know or understand to be convinced?
- ☐ What examples come to mind?
- ☐ What have you experienced yourself?
- ☐ What information can you find on the Internet, in a print source, or from people you meet and interview?
- ☐ What details could you use to strengthen the support?

WRITE

- ☐ Use a prewriting technique to find as many support points as you can.
- ☐ Drop ideas that are not directly related to your main thesis.
- ☐ Select the best primary support.
- ☐ Add supporting details.
- ☐ Review and evaluate your support.
- ☐ Write topic sentences for your primary support points.
- ☐ Make sure that all of your support points have the basics of good support (p. 79).

8

Planning and Drafting a Paper

How to Plan and Draft a Paper

A **plan** is a sketch or outline of a writing project. A **draft** is the first full version of your ideas in writing. Most effective writing needs to go through both stages, sometimes more than once. At this point, your goal is to arrange your ideas in a clear, logical order and to get them down on paper (or on the computer screen). Do the best job you can, but don't worry about making your work perfect the first time—that's what revision is for.

Basics of a good draft

- It has a thesis statement that presents the main idea.
- It has a logical organization.
- It has primary support points that are stated in topic sentences.
- It has supporting details that develop or explain each topic sentence.
- It follows standard essay structure (introduction, body paragraphs, conclusion) and uses complete sentences.
- The introduction captures the audience's interest and lets them know what the essay is about, and the conclusion reinforces the main idea and makes an observation.

Arrange Your Ideas

Once you have generated ideas, you need to arrange them in a logical **order**. Three common ways of ordering your ideas are **chronological order** (by the time sequence in which events happened), **spatial order** (by the physical arrangement of objects or features), and **order of importance** (by the significance of the ideas or reasons).

CHRONOLOGICAL ORDER

Use **chronological order** (time order) to arrange points according to when they happened. Time order works well when you are telling the story of an event or explaining how to do something. Usually, you go in sequence from what happened first to what happened last; in some cases, though, you can work back from what happened last to what happened first.

Example using chronological (time) order

The cause of the fire that destroyed the apartment building was human carelessness. The couple in apartment 2F had planned a romantic dinner. They lit candles all over the apartment and then ate a delicious meal. After dinner, they decided to go out to a club. Unfortunately, they forgot to blow out all of the candles, and one of them was too close to a window curtain, which caught fire. By the time another resident smelled smoke, the fire was uncontrollable. The building was destroyed. Fortunately, rescuers were able to save everyone who was in the building, but all of the tenants lost their homes and most of their possessions. Human carelessness caused much human misery.

How does the writer use chronological order to arrange information?

The writer orders events from first to last.

SPATIAL ORDER

Teamwork Have students break into pairs or small groups. Assign each pair or group one of the three sample paragraphs on pages 90–91 to rewrite using a different type of organization. After about 10 minutes, ask each group which order they tried and how the story changed with a new organization.

Use **spatial order** to arrange ideas so that your audience can see your topic as you do. Space order works well when you are writing about what someone or something looks like. You can move from top to bottom, bottom to top, near to far, far to near, left to right, right to left, back to front, or front to back.

Example using spatial (space) order

I stood watching in horror while all-powerful flames destroyed an entire building, including my apartment. The first few floors looked normal, except that firefighters were racing into the front entry. A couple of floors up, windows were breaking, and gray, foul-smelling smoke was billowing out. My eyes were drawn to the top two floors, where flames of orange and white leapt from the windows. A dog with brown and white spots barked furiously from the rooftop until it was rescued. Until you have actually witnessed a severe fire, you cannot imagine how powerful it is and how powerless you feel in its presence.

What type of spatial order does the writer use?

Bottom to top

ORDER OF IMPORTANCE

Use **order of importance** to arrange points according to their significance, interest, or surprise value. Save the most important point for last to end with a strong point.

Example using order of importance

Fires caused by human carelessness often have disastrous effects. In a recent incident, an apartment building was completely destroyed by a fire. The tenants lost all of their possessions: furniture, clothing, and irreplaceable treasured personal items. Worse than that, however, was that the owner and many of the tenants had no insurance to help them find new housing. Many had to depend completely on relatives and friends. The most disastrous effect of the fire, however, was that many tenants lost their beloved pets. Carelessness has no place around fire, which has the power to destroy.

What is this writer's most important point about the effects of fires?

Fires can cause loss of life.

As you arrange your ideas, consider what your purpose for writing is and what kind of organization would work best to make your main idea. Some examples follow in the chart.

Purpose	Organization
To describe an experience	Chronological
To explain how something works	
To explain how to do something	
To help your audience visualize whatever you are describing as you see it	Spatial
To create an impression using your senses—taste, touch, sight, smell, sound	
To re-create a scene	
To persuade or convince someone	Importance
To make a case for or against something	

Create an Outline

When you have decided how to order your ideas, make a written plan—an **outline**—starting with your thesis statement. Then, state each of your primary support points as a topic sentence for one of the body paragraphs of the essay. Add supporting details to develop or explain the topic sentence.

Some people find it useful to write full sentences as they plan so that their outline is a more complete guide for the essay. Others use phrases or single words. Either method works, as long as you stick to one or the other consistently.

The example that follows uses "standard" or "formal" outline format, in which numbers and letters distinguish between primary support points and secondary supporting details. Some instructors require this format. If you are making an outline for yourself, you might choose to write a less formal outline, simply indenting secondary supporting details under the primary support rather than using numbers and letters.

Thesis statement
   I. Topic sentence (primary support point 1)
      A. Supporting detail
      B. Supporting detail (and so on)
   II. Topic sentence (primary support point 2)
      A. Supporting detail
      B. Supporting detail (and so on)
   III. Topic sentence (primary support point 3)
      A. Supporting detail
      B. Supporting detail (and so on)
Concluding paragraph

For a diagram of the relationship between paragraphs and essays, see pages 34–35.

Teaching tip If students have difficulty outlining their essays, encourage them to try a visual approach, writing their outline as a cluster diagram or as a flowchart.

For more advice on primary support and supporting details, see Chapter 7.

PRACTICE 1   Outlining an essay

Outline the essay that follows. First, double-underline the thesis statement and the main idea in the concluding paragraph. Underline each topic sentence, and put a check mark next to each supporting detail.

We all know people who seem to fall in love over and over. They love being in love. But others have different patterns. Some people seem to fall in love once and stay there. Others avoid long-term commitment. Until now, we had no way to figure out why some people were steady lovers and others not. Some researchers now believe that the amount and type of certain hormones in a person's brain may determine a person's patterns of love.

Using mice as subjects, the researchers found that when two particular hormones (oxytocin and vasopressin) exist in the pleasure centers of the brain, they produce individuals with a pattern of long-lasting love. Male mice with these hormones in their pleasure centers were faithful to their partners. ✓ They stayed with their female mouse partners through pregnancy and the raising of offspring. ✓

In contrast, when those same hormones existed outside of the pleasure center, the male mice sought constant sources of new love. They did not have steady partners and did not stay around when a female mouse became pregnant. ✓ The mice with hormones in this location were the ones who ran from commitment. ✓

Unfortunately, the research did not deal with the most common love pattern: individuals involved in relationships that last for some time but not for life. In this pattern, people have serious relationships broken off when one person wants a commitment and the other does not. ✓ Perhaps this research will come next, as it is in these relationships where much of the pain of love exists. ✓

Though these behaviors may be built into the brain, scientists are working on ways to modify the effects. They hope to find a balance so that love patterns can be modified. One humorous researcher suggested that before we select our mates, we should ask them to have a brain scan to determine whether they are likely to stay or go.

The explanations and practices in this section will prepare you to write a good draft essay. See Chapter 7 for advice on support. For a diagram showing the parts of an essay, see page 35, and for a complete draft of an essay, see page 104.

Draft the Body of the Essay

Use your plan for your essay as you begin to write your draft. The plan should include your thesis statement, the primary support points for your thesis, and supporting details for your primary support points.

First, draft complete paragraphs that support your thesis. In general, essays have at least three body paragraphs, and they may have many more, depending on your assignment and purpose. Each should contain a topic sentence (usually the first sentence in the paragraph) that presents a primary support point as well as supporting details. At this point, draft only the body of your essay; you will write the introduction and conclusion later.

If you are having trouble with a word or sentence as you draft, make a note to come back to it and then keep going.

Teaching tip Suggest to students that a draft is similar to a dress rehearsal before a play or a scrimmage before a big game. In addition, require students to turn in their drafts with their final papers.

> **PRACTICE 2**   **Writing topic sentences**
>
> Writing topic sentences for primary support points is a good way to start drafting the body of an essay. Convert each of the following primary support points into a topic sentence that supports the thesis. You can make up details if you want.
>
> **Thesis statement: Being a good customer service representative in a retail store requires several important skills.**
>
>   I. Being pleasant and polite [Primary support point 1]
>
>   A. Smiling, saying hello [Supporting detail]
>
>   B. Looking at customer [Supporting detail]
>
> Topic sentence I: _Answers will vary._____
>
>   II. Listening carefully [Primary support point 2]
>
>   A. Making notes [Supporting detail]
>
>   B. Asking questions [Supporting detail]
>
> Topic sentence II: _____
>
>   III. Figuring out how to solve the problem [Primary support point 3]
>
>   A. Calling the right people [Supporting detail]
>
>   B. Filling out paperwork [Supporting detail]
>
> Topic sentence III: _____

Write an Introduction

The introduction to your essay should capture your audience's interest and present the main idea. Think of your introductory paragraph as a challenge. Ask yourself: How can I get my audience to want to continue reading?

Basics of a good introduction

- It should catch the audience's attention.

- It should present the essay's thesis statement (narrowed topic + main idea).

- It should give the audience an idea of what the essay will cover.

The thesis statement is often either the first or the last sentence in the introductory paragraph, though you may find essays in which it is elsewhere.

Here are examples of common kinds of introductions that spark the audience's interest.

ESL Remind nonnative speakers that it is a convention of academic English to present the main idea in the first paragraph, stated explicitly.

START WITH A SURPRISING FACT OR IDEA

Surprises capture people's attention. The more unexpected and surprising something is, the more likely people are to take notice of it and read on.

I was saved from sin when I was going on thirteen. But not really saved. It happened like this. There was a big revival at my Auntie Reed's church. Every night for weeks there had been much preaching, singing, praying, and shouting, and some very hardened sinners had been brought to Christ, and the membership of the church had grown by leaps and bounds. Then just before the revival ended, they held a special meeting for children, "to bring the young lambs into the fold." My aunt spoke of it for days ahead. That night I was escorted to the front row and placed on the mourners' bench with all the other young sinners, who had not yet been brought to Jesus.

—Langston Hughes, "Salvation" (See pp. 590–91 for the full essay.)

OPEN WITH A QUOTATION

A good short quotation can interest an audience. It must lead naturally into your main idea, however, and not just be stuck there. If you start with a quotation, make sure that you tell the audience who the speaker or writer is (unless it is a general quote, like the proverb in the following excerpt).

"Grow where you are planted" is an old proverb that is a metaphor for living. Although I had heard it before, it took me many years to understand and appreciate its meaning. If I had listened to that proverb earlier, I would have saved myself and others many painful experiences.

—Teresa Fiori, "Appreciate What You Have"

GIVE AN EXAMPLE OR TELL A STORY

Opening an essay with a brief story or illustration often draws the audience in.

Brian Head saw only one way out. On the final day of his life, during economics class, the fifteen-year-old stood up and pointed a semi-automatic handgun at himself. Before he pulled the trigger, he said his last words: "I can't take this anymore."

—Kathleen Vail, "Words That Wound" (See pp. 599–602 for the full essay.)

Teaching tip
Have students write introductions using two of the techniques. Have volunteers read them aloud and discuss how they catch attention.

OFFER A STRONG OPINION

The stronger the opinion, the more likely it is that people will pay attention.

> Sex sells. This truth is a boon for marketing gurus and the pornography industry but a rather unfortunate situation for women. Every issue of *Playboy*, every lewd poster, and even the Victoria's Secret catalog transform real women into ornaments, valued exclusively for their outward appearance. These publications are responsible for defining what is sexy and reinforce the belief that aesthetic appeal is a woman's highest virtue.

—Amy L. Beck, "Struggling for Perfection" (See pp. 665–67 for the full essay.)

ASK A QUESTION

A question needs an answer. If you start your introduction with a question, you engage your audience by inviting them to answer it.

> If you're a man, at some point a woman will ask you how she looks.
> "How do I look?" she'll ask.
> You must be careful how you answer this question. The best technique is to form an honest yet sensitive opinion, then collapse on the floor with some kind of fatal seizure. Trust me, this is the easiest way out. Because you will never come up with the right answer.

—Dave Barry, "The Ugly Truth about Beauty" (See pp. 658–60 for the full essay.)

Teamwork Practice 3 works well in pairs or small groups.

PRACTICE 3   **Identifying strong introductions**

Find a strong introduction in a newspaper, a magazine, a catalog, an advertisement—anything written. Explain, in writing, why you think it is a strong introduction. *Answers will vary.*

Teamwork Practice 4 works well in pairs or small groups. Students should be prepared to explain their choices to the rest of the class.

PRACTICE 4   **Selling your main idea**

As you know from watching and reading advertisements, a good writer can make just about anything sound interesting. For each of the following topics, write an introductory statement using the technique indicated. Make the statement punchy and intriguing enough to motivate your audience to stay with you as you explain or defend it.

1. Topic: Mandatory drug testing in the workplace

   Technique: Ask a question.

   Answers will vary.

2. Topic: Teenage suicide

   Technique: Present a surprising fact or idea (you can make one up for this exercise).

3. Topic: Free access to music on the Internet

   Technique: Give a strong opinion.

4. Topic: The quality of television shows

   Technique: Use a quotation (you can make up a good one for this exercise).

5. Topic: Blind dates

   Technique: Give an example or tell a brief story (you can just sum it up).

Write a Conclusion

Your conclusion should have energy and match the force of your thesis statement; it is your last chance to drive home your main idea. Fading out with a weak conclusion is like slowing down at the end of a race. In fact, you should give yourself a last push at the end because people usually remember best what they see, hear, or read last. A good conclusion creates a sense of completion: It not only brings the audience back to where they started but also shows them how far they have come.

Basics of a good conclusion
- It should refer to your main idea.
- It should briefly summarize the support you have developed.
- It should make a final observation.

A good way to end an essay is to refer back to something in the introduction.

- If you used a quotation, use another one—by the same person or by another person on the same topic—or refer back to the quotation in the introduction, and make an observation.
- If you stated a surprising fact or idea, go back to it and comment on it, using what you have written in the body of the essay.
- If you asked a question, ask it again, and answer it based on what you have said in your essay.
- If you started a story, finish it.
- Remind your audience of your original point, perhaps repeating key words that you used in your introduction.

Look again at three of the introductions you read earlier, each shown here with its conclusion.

Open with a quotation

Introduction A: "Grow where you are planted" is an old proverb that is a metaphor for living. Although I had heard it before, it took me many years to understand and appreciate its meaning. If I had listened to that proverb earlier, I would have saved myself and others many painful experiences.

Conclusion A: Finally, I have learned to grow where I am planted, to appreciate the good things in my life rather than look for the bad and be angry. I have learned to take advantage of the many opportunities I have for personal and professional growth, right here and now. And I have vowed to help others around me grow also. My life is much richer now that I follow that old wisdom, and I will pass its lesson on to my children.

—Teresa Fiori, "Appreciate What You Have"

Start with a strong opinion or position

Introduction B: Sex sells. This truth is a boon for marketing gurus and the pornography industry but a rather unfortunate situation for women. Every issue of *Playboy*, every lewd poster, and even the Victoria's Secret catalog transform real women into ornaments, valued exclusively for their outward appearance. These publications are responsible for defining what is sexy and reinforce the belief that aesthetic appeal is a woman's highest virtue. ▶

Conclusion B: Women are up against a long history of devaluation and oppression, and, unfortunately, the feminist movements have been only partially successful in purging those legacies. Sexually charged images of women in the media are not the only cause of this continuing problem, but they certainly play a central role.

—Amy L. Beck, "Struggling for Perfection"

Ask a question

Introduction C: If you're a man, at some point a woman will ask you how she looks.

"How do I look?" she'll ask.

You must be careful how you answer this question. The best technique is to form an honest yet sensitive opinion, then collapse on the floor with some kind of fatal seizure. Trust me, this is the easiest way out. You will never come up with the right answer.

Conclusion C: To go back to my main idea: If you're a man, and a woman asks you how she looks, you're in big trouble. Obviously, you can't say she looks bad. But you also can't say that she looks great, because she'll think you're lying, because she has spent countless hours, with the help of the multibillion-dollar beauty industry, obsessing about the differences between herself and Cindy Crawford. Also, she suspects that you're not qualified to judge anybody's appearance. This is because you have shaving cream in your hair.

—Dave Barry, "The Ugly Truth about Beauty"

> **PRACTICE 5**   **Analyzing conclusions**

After reading the paired introductions and conclusions above, indicate the techniques used in each conclusion to refer back to its introduction.

A. Technique used to link introduction and conclusion: _Reference back to a quotation_

B. Technique used to link introduction and conclusion: _Restatement of main idea_

C. Technique used to link introduction and conclusion: <u>Repetition of key words and restatement of main idea</u>

Teamwork Collect the examples students bring in, separate the introductions from the conclusions, and then scramble them. In a later class, have students work in small groups to match introductions and conclusions.

| PRACTICE 6 | Identifying good introductions and conclusions |

In a newspaper, magazine, or any other written material, find a piece of writing that has both a strong introduction and a strong conclusion. Answer the following questions about the introduction and conclusion.

1. What method of introduction is used? <u>Answers will vary.</u>

2. What does the conclusion do? Does it restate the main idea? Sum up the points made in the piece? Make an observation? _____

   _____

3. How are the introduction and the conclusion linked? _____

   _____

Teamwork Have students share their own drafts in small groups, exchanging comments and suggestions with group members. Students can use the checklist on page 105 as a prompt for discussing their drafts.

| PRACTICE 7 | Writing a conclusion |

Read the following introductory paragraphs, and write a possible conclusion for each one. Your conclusions can be brief, but they should each include the basics of a good conclusion (p. 97) and consist of several sentences.

1. **Introduction:** When it comes to long-term love relationships, I very much believe Anton Chekhov's statement, "Any idiot can face a crisis; it's the day-to-day living that wears you out." When faced with a crisis, couples often pull together. A crisis is a slap in the face that reminds you of who and what is important in your life. It is the routine necessities of living that can erode a relationship as couples argue over who does the laundry, who does the cleaning, or cooking, or bill paying. The constant skirmishes over day-to-day living can do more serious damage over the long term than a crisis.

   Conclusion: <u>Answers will vary.</u>

   _____

   _____

2. **Introduction:** Why do so many people feel that they must be available at all times and in all places? Until recently, the only way you could reach someone was by telephone or by mail. Now if you do not have a smartphone for texting, Facebook and Twitter accounts, and call waiting, people trying to reach you get annoyed. I resent the loss of privacy. I do not want to be available twenty-four hours a day.

Conclusion: _Answers will vary._

_____

_____

Title Your Essay

Even if your title is the *last* part of the essay you write, it is the *first* thing that the audience will read. Use your title to get your audience's attention and to tell them what your essay is about. Use concrete, specific words to name the topic of your essay.

Basics of a good essay title

- It makes the audience want to read the essay.
- It does not repeat the wording in your thesis statement.
- It may hint at the main idea but does not necessarily state it outright.

One way to find a good title is to consider the type of essay you are writing. If you are writing an argument (as you will in Chapter 18), state your position in your title. If you are writing a process analysis, in which you are telling your audience how to do something (as you will in Chapter 13), try using the term *steps* or *how to* in the title. This way, your audience will know immediately both what you are writing about and how you will present it. For example, "Five Steps to Financial Independence" may be a more inviting and more accurate title for a process analysis essay than "Financial Independence."

 Language note: A title is centered on the line above the first line of a paragraph or essay. The first letter of most words in a title should be capitalized (see p. 561 for more details).

> **PRACTICE 8**   **Writing a title**
>
> Read the following introductory paragraphs, and write a possible title for the essay each one begins. The first one is done as an example. Be prepared to explain why you worded each title as you did.
>
> **Example: The origin of this species of rant was a toothbrush—a new toothbrush that came with an instructional DVD. The user of this advanced piece of dental equipment had been brushing his teeth lo these many years without any educational aids at all. But now he was the proud owner of an IntelliCleanSystem equipped with packets of paste to be downloaded into the toothbrush's hard drive.**
>
> Possible title: _Making Life Better through Technology_
>
> 1. Many students plagiarize because they do not understand that information from Web sites must be acknowledged.

Possible title: *Answers will vary.*

2. Your sweetheart or your pet. Who would you choose to dump if one had to go? Most current pet owners said they would hold on to their spouse or significant other (84 percent), but a sizable 14 percent picked their pet, according to an *AP-Petside.com* poll.

—Leanne Italie

Possible title: *Answers will vary. Actual title is "AP-Petside Poll: Pet or Paramour? Many Say Pet." Source: Associated Press, 25 Jan. 2011.*

3. Is a girl named Gloria apt to be better-looking than one named Bertha? Are criminals more likely to be dark than blond? Can you tell a good deal about someone's personality from hearing his voice briefly over the phone? Can a person's nationality be pretty accurately guessed from her photograph? Does the fact that someone wears glasses imply that he is intelligent?

The answer to all these questions is obviously "no."

Yet, from all the evidence at hand, most of us believe these things.

Possible title: *Answers will vary.*

One Student's Process

Before writing your own draft, read Deshon Briggs's outline and draft.

Deshon's outline

Thesis statement (part of introductory paragraph): I learned that I can be the change in my life.

I. **Primary support 1 (paragraph 1):** One day, my English teacher wrote, "You are the change in your life" on the board.
    Supporting details:
    a. Said that we should explore this statement by writing about it for an assignment due in four weeks
    b. No idea what to do, figured I had plenty of time to think about it.

II. **Primary support 2 (paragraph 2):** I took my son to play basketball at a park near us and he gave me grief when I threw my Coke can off to the side.
    Supporting details:
    a. He got a bag from the car and picked up my can.
    b. Started picking up other cans and bottles, and I helped
    c. Guy I know came by with his kids, and they started collecting the stuff too

III. **Primary support 3 (paragraph 3):** We went to local freecycle.org and posted that we wanted a big trash can for bottles and cans
    a. Had a bunch of offers, and other guys said they'd help with clean-up
    b. Got the idea to use bottle and can deposit money for a new basketball net

IV. **Primary support 4 (paragraph 4):**
    a. Local paper called to do a story on the clean-up
    b. Got our pictures in the paper with story

Possible point for conclusion (part of concluding paragraph): Court is clean, we bought a bench, my son and I were the change in our lives.

Deshon's draft

Introductory paragraph

Thesis statement

One day, my teacher wrote "You are the change in your life" on the board. She said that statement related to our going to college and making our lives better. She gave us a writing assignment: to explore the statement that was due in four weeks. I did not really know what she was talking about but figured I had plenty of time to think about it. I learned that I really can be the change in my life.

Primary support 2

I took my son to play basketball at the park near us, and he gave me grief when I threw my Coke can off to the side. He got a bag from my car and picked up my can. He started picking up others, and I helped. A guy I know came by with his kids, and we all started picking up cans and bottles. There were a lot.

Primary support 3

I had the idea to go to the local freecycle.org and posted that we wanted a big trash can for bottles and cans for the park. I had a bunch of offers and other guys said they would help with the clean-up. We set up a schedule. My son and I got the idea of returning the bottles and cans for the deposit money that we could use to get a new basketball net. We did that.

Concluding paragraph

Point for conclusion

After a few weeks, the local paper called me and wanted to interview my son and me about the stuff we had done at the basketball court. We got our pictures in the paper, and we got some more people interested and some people made donations. Now we have enough money to get a bench. The court looks great, we met a lot of other people, and people gave us a lot of respect. It was great. And this is my paper for my English class, how my son and I were the change in our lives, starting with just picking up a Coke can.

Write Your Own Draft

Write an outline and a draft using the thesis and support you developed in Chapters 6 and 7, or use one of the following thesis statements.

With the advent of so many new technologies, teenagers no longer do much traditional dating.

Although cartoons are typically intended to entertain, they may also have important messages.

The most important skills a college student should have are

_____

My professor does not understand that _____

_____.

Living with roommates requires _____

_____.

Before writing, read the following checklist.

CHECKLIST

Writing a Draft Essay

FOCUS

☐ Review your support.

ASK

☐ Is your thesis clear?

☐ Are there topic sentences for each body paragraph?

☐ Do you have supporting details for each topic sentence?

☐ Is your support arranged in a logical order?

☐ What introductory technique will get your audience's attention and make your point stand out?

☐ How can you use the conclusion for one last chance to make your point?

☐ What is the strongest or most interesting part of the introduction? How might you refer back to it in your conclusion?

☐ Will your title make the audience want to read your essay?

WRITE

☐ Write a draft essay.

9

Revising a Draft

How to Revise a Draft

Revising is rewriting your draft to make your ideas clearer, stronger, and more convincing. When revising, you might add, cut, move, or change whole sentences or paragraphs.

Editing is correcting problems with grammar, style, usage, and punctuation. While editing, you usually add, cut, or change words and phrases instead of whole sentences or paragraphs. **Proofreading** is checking your paper one last time for any typographical errors (typos) or errors in formatting.

Revising (covered in this chapter) and editing (covered in Chapters 21–39) are two different ways to improve a paper. Most writers find it difficult to do both at once. It is easier to look first at the ideas in your essay and how effectively they're expressed (revising) and then to look for problems that need correcting (editing).

No one gets everything right in a draft—even professional writers need to revise. The following tips will help you with the revision process.

Tips for revising

- Take a break from your draft—set it aside for a few hours or a whole day.

- Read your draft aloud, and listen to what you have written.

- Imagine yourself as one of your readers.

- Get feedback from a friend, a classmate, or a colleague (see the next section of this chapter).

- Get help from a tutor at your college writing center or lab.

For more on audience and purpose, see Chapter 4.

You may need to read your draft several times before deciding what changes would improve it. Remember to consider your audience (your readers) and your purpose (your reason for writing it).

Understand Large-Scale and Small-Scale Revision

Teaching tip Stress to students that revision is not just copying a draft over neatly. It is rethinking, digging more deeply, and making it more powerful.

Large-scale or **global revision** means taking a step back to thoughtfully assess the project as a whole. Is the thesis as strong as it could be? Is there sufficient support? Have you addressed your audience and purpose effectively? Is the tone appropriate? Does the whole thing hang together well? Does all of it work together to support the thesis? If you need to make changes at this stage—and most of the time, you will—you are usually going to be adding or deleting entire paragraphs of your work.

Small-scale revision involves looking closely at the way you've expressed yourself and deciding whether it could be improved. When you perform small-scale revision, you may do any or all of the following:

- Improve your title to catch your audience's attention.
- Reword your thesis statement to make it clearer or more energetic.
- Rewrite your introduction to include a different attention-getter.
- Incorporate more transitional words or phrases.
- Revise the conclusion to help wrap up the ideas in the paper more concisely or memorably.

Returning to a paper you've already written and taking the time to work on any of these different aspects is not easy for a writer. We all would rather be perfect the first time, but a good writer knows that isn't possible. We need help from other readers. That's where peer review helps us as writers.

Revise Using Peer Review

Peer review is the exchange of feedback on a piece of writing from your fellow students, colleagues, or friends. Getting comments from a peer is a good way to begin revising your essay.

Other people can look at your work and see things that you might not—parts that are good as well as parts that need more explanation or evidence. The best reviewers are honest about what could be better but also sensitive to the writer's feelings. In addition, they are specific. Reviewers who say a paper is "great" without offering further comment do not help writers improve their work.

Basics of useful feedback

- It is given in a positive way.
- It is specific.
- It offers suggestions.
- It points out what is effective, as well as what needs work.

To get useful feedback, find a partner and exchange papers. Each partner should read the other's paper and jot down a few comments. The first time someone comments on what you have written, you may feel a little embarrassed, but you will feel better about the process once you see how your writing benefits from the comments.

Peer reviewers should consider the following as they read.

Questions for peer reviewers

1. What is the main idea?
2. After reading the introductory paragraph, do you have an idea of what the essay will cover, and why?
3. How could the introduction be more interesting?
4. Is there enough support for the main idea? Where might the writer add support?
5. Are there confusing places where you have to reread something to understand it? How might the writer make the points, the organization, or the flow of ideas clearer or smoother?
6. Does the writer have assumptions or biases that weaken the writing? What are they?
7. How could the conclusion be more forceful?
8. What do you most like about the essay? Where could it be better? What would you do if it were your essay?
9. What other comments or suggestions do you have?
10. How do you think the audience for the writing will respond to the thesis and its support?

Teamwork To model peer review, bring in a short paragraph or essay, and have students work with a partner to answer the eight questions for peer reviewers. Then, discuss the answers as a class. If possible, invite a writing center peer tutor to class to help facilitate discussion.

| PRACTICE 1 | **Reflecting on your experience with peer review** |

Think back to the last time you showed someone else something you wrote and asked for advice. As in the previous practice, pick something substantial—not necessarily an essay, but something longer than a text message. Then, answer the questions below.

1. What kind of advice did you get from the person to whom you showed your writing? Did that advice cause you to make any changes to it?
2. Take a moment to reflect on your experience. Would you change anything about the way you asked for advice? Would you have preferred to receive different kinds of advice? Would you ask again?

Revise for Unity

Unity in writing means that all the points are related to your main idea: They *unite* to support your main idea.

TOPIC SENTENCE: Online dating services have many benefits, but users should also be aware of the possible negatives as well.

SUPPORT POINT 1: One benefit of online dating services is that people do not have to cruise bars to meet people.

SUPPORT POINT 2: Contact via e-mail or text allows users to get to know each other a little before meeting.

SUPPORT POINT 3: The services also try to match compatible people by comparing profiles, so the likelihood of having something in common is greater than in a random encounter.

DETOUR

OFF MAIN IDEA: A good place to meet is a cheap restaurant. Most people like Italian food or burgers, so those types of places are safe.

SUPPORT POINT 4: Also, online dating services offer many choices of screened possible dates, more than anyone could meet in a bar in months.

SUPPORT POINTS 5, 6: On the negative side, online dating services can be expensive, and there are no guarantees of a good match. Also, although the companies do minor screening, nothing prevents a person from lying.

SUPPORT POINT 7: Arranging a date through a dating service can put more pressure on people than meeting in a natural way because people sometimes have unreasonably high expectations.

CONCLUDING SENTENCE: Online dating services can be successful, but people should be realistic about what to expect.

Sometimes writers drift away from their main idea, as the writer of the following paragraph did with the underlined sentences. The diagram on page 109 shows where readers might get confused.

Online dating services have many benefits, but users should be aware of the possible negatives as well. One benefit of online dating services is that people do not have to cruise bars to meet people. The Web sites offer subscribers potential matches, and the first contact is via e-mail. Contact via e-mail or text allows users to get to know each other a little before meeting. Sometimes a couple of exchanges can reveal that meeting is not necessary, so not only do users get to avoid cruising, they save time by eliminating bad matches. The services also try to match compatible people by comparing profiles, so the likelihood of having something in common is greater than in a random encounter. With all the online dating services available, people can choose ones that appeal to people with specific interests and preferences. <u>A good place to meet is a cheap restaurant. Most people like Italian food or burgers, so those types of places are safe.</u> Also, online dating services offer many choices of screened possible dates, more than anyone could meet in a bar in months. On the negative side, online dating services can be expensive, and there are no guarantees of a good match. Also, although the companies do minor screening, nothing prevents a person from lying. People often lie about their age, weight, and appearance. Arranging a date through a dating service can put more pressure on people than meeting in a natural way because people sometimes have unreasonably high expectations. Online dating services can be successful, but people should be realistic about what to expect.

PRACTICE 2 **Evaluating unity**

Read the following two paragraphs, and underline any detours from the main idea. In the lines provided at the end of paragraph 2, indicate which paragraph is more unified and explain why.

1. Identity theft is becoming common in this country, but people can take several precautions to protect themselves. One way is to buy an inexpensive paper shredder and shred documents that contain your Social Security number or personal financial information. <u>Shredded documents do not take up as much room in the trash, either.</u> Another precaution is to avoid mailing change-of-address postcards. Thieves can intercept these and use them to get mail sent to your old address. <u>Half the time people never keep these cards, so they just waste the postage.</u> It would be better to notify people of your address change by phone or e-mail. <u>When I moved I sent postcards that had a misprint, so they were not good anyway.</u> A third way is to avoid ever giving out your Social Security number. Even these precautions do not guarantee that your identity will not be stolen, but they will help prevent what is a time-consuming and expensive problem to set right.

2. Many new markets have appeared to meet the needs of pet owners who treat their pets as if they were precious children. The most thriving market is clothing, especially items that allow owners and their dogs to dress alike. This clothing includes cruisewear, formalwear, and jeweled loungewear. Another big market is made up of hotels all over the world that advertise themselves as pet-friendly. These hotels provide doggie or cat beds, on-site grooming, and pet care professionals. The rooms are uniquely decorated and provide special meals prepared and served to meet the needs of each "guest." Each guest also is treated to an individualized exercise program. These new markets do not cater to the conservative spender: They appeal to those pet owners who seem willing to spend any amount of money on luxuries for their pets.

More unified paragraph: _Paragraph 2_

Reasons that this paragraph is more unified than the other: _Answers will_ _vary, but students should note that all of the support in the second para-_ _graph clearly relates to the main idea._

PRACTICE 3   **Revising for unity**

Each of the following essays includes sentences that are off the main idea. Underline those sentences. The main idea in each essay is in boldface type.

1. Find four off-the-idea sentences.

   Oprah Winfrey is one of the most influential people of our times, but that does not mean that life is easy for her. As a child in rural Mississippi, she was dirt-poor and sexually abused. Somehow, she managed to climb out of that existence and become successful. But because she is now a superstar, every aspect of her life is under the media spotlight, and she is frequently criticized for everything from her weight to her attempts to help people spiritually.

   Oprah's roller-coaster weight profile is always news. Every supermarket tabloid, every week, seems to have some new information about Oprah and her weight. I can relate to how humiliating that must be. She looked like a balloon in an old picture I saw recently, even fatter than my Aunt Greta.

   Oprah is also criticized for her wealth, estimated to be $2.7 billion in 2010. She has a fabulous estate in Montecito, California, but does not spend all of her time there. Oprah is generous with her money, giving large amounts to charities and people in need. For example, she started a school

Teaching tip Choose a student to read these essays aloud to the class, and ask the rest of the class to stop the reader as soon as the essay detours from the main idea.

for girls in South Africa. Despite her good work, the media is always ready to portray her as too rich, even though many businesspeople are also very wealthy and do not give as much to worthy causes.

Oprah has even been criticized for her book club, although her recommendations prompted many people to become regular readers. When she recommended *The Corrections* by Jonathan Franzen, he said he did not want to be one of her choices because she sometimes recommended books he thought were not literary enough. <u>He is a real snob in my mind, and my friends think so, too.</u> When it was revealed that another author she recommended, James Frey, had made up some information in his memoir, some people said Oprah should have known. If the publisher did not know, how would Oprah?

Oprah Winfrey, despite her wealth and fame, does not have an easy life. Her critics feel free to cut her down at every turn. Instead, why not celebrate her personal and professional achievements? She deserves respect, not ridicule.

2. Find four off-the-idea sentences.

A recent survey of the places students prefer to study revealed some strange results. We would expect the usual answers, such as a library, bedroom, desk, and kitchen, and the survey respondents did in fact name such areas. But some people prefer less traditional places.

One unusual place cited was a church. The respondent said it was a great spot to study when services were not taking place because it was always quiet and not crowded. <u>Some churches are locked during the day because of vandalism. Other churches have had big problems with theft.</u>

Another unusual study area was the locker room during a football game. <u>A problem is that the person would miss the game.</u> Except for half-time, the large area was empty. The person who studied there claimed that there was a high energy level in the locker room that, combined with the quiet, helped him concentrate. <u>I wonder what the smell was like, though.</u>

The most surprising preference for a place to study was the bleachers by the pool of a gym. The light was good, said the student, she loved the smell of chlorine, and the sound of water was soothing.

The results may seem strange—a church, a locker room, and a pool—but they do share some characteristics: quiet, relative solitude, and no interruptions, other than half-time. Perhaps we should all think about new places that might help us study.

Revise for Support and Detail

Support is the evidence, examples, or facts that show, explain, or prove your main idea. **Primary support points** are the major ideas developed in the paragraphs that make up the body of your essay. **Supporting details** are the specifics that explain your primary support to your readers.

For more on primary support points and supporting details, see Chapter 7.

When you read your draft essay, ask yourself: Do you provide enough information for your readers to understand the main idea? Do you present enough evidence to convince your readers of that idea? Look for places where you could add more support and detail, and examine your writing for obvious biases (see p. 14).

Read the two paragraphs that follow, and note the support the writer added to the second one. Notice that she did not simply add to the paragraph; she also deleted some words and rearranged others to make the story clearer to readers. The additions are underlined; the deletions are crossed out.

This morning I learned that my local police respond quickly and thoroughly to 911 calls. I meant to dial 411 for directory assistance, but by mistake I dialed 911. I hung up after only one ring because I realized what I had done. A few seconds after I hung up, the phone rang, and it was the police dispatcher.She said that she had received a 911 call from my number and was checking. I explained what happened, and she said she had to send a cruiser over anyway.Within a minute, the cruiser pulled in, and I explained what happened. I apologized and felt stupid, but I thanked him. I am glad to know that if I ever need to call 911, the police will be there.

Revised to add support and detail

This morning I ~~learned that my local police~~ tested the 911 emergency system and found that it worked perfectly. Unfortunately, the test was a mistake. ~~learned that my local police respond quickly and thoroughly to 911 calls.~~ I meant to dial 411 for directory assistance, but without thinking ~~by mistake~~ I dialed 911. I frantically pushed the disconnect button ~~hung up~~ after only one ring because I realized my error. ~~what I had done.~~ As I reached for the phone to dial 411, ~~A few seconds after I hung up,~~ it rang like an alarm. ~~the phone rang, and it was the police dispatcher.~~ The police dispatcher crisply announced ~~She said~~ that she had received a 911 call from my number and was checking. I laughed weakly and explained what happened, hoping she would see the humor or at least the innocent human error. Instead, the crispness of her voice became brittle as ~~and~~ she said she had to send a cruiser over anyway. I went to meet my fate. Within a minute, the cruiser pulled in, and a police officer swaggered toward me. I explained what had happened, apologized, and thanked him humbly. I felt guilty of stupidity,

Teaching Tip
Try reading these or other examples out loud, removing any transitional words and phrases. Then discuss how the lack of transitions makes it difficult for readers to connect ideas in logical order. Also ask how the paragraph is organized—by time, space, or importance.

at the least. ~~and felt stupid, but I thanked him.~~ <u>We learn from our mistakes, and in this case</u> I am glad to know that if I ever need to call 911, the police will be there.

PRACTICE 4   **Evaluating support**

In the two paragraphs that follow, the main ideas are in bold. Underline the primary support points, and put a check mark by each supporting detail. Then, in the lines provided at the end of paragraph 2, indicate which paragraph provides better support and explain why.

1. **Women tend to learn the art of fly fishing more easily than men.** <u>For one thing, they have more patience, which is key to successful fishing.</u> ✓ It may take many hours of silent, solitary fishing to catch a single fish. Even long hours may net no fish, and men tend to be ✓ more eager for results. This eagerness can make them more ✓ careless. <u>Women also tend to be more sensitive to subtle movements.</u> This trait helps both in the casting motion and in the reeling in of a fish. <u>Women are more likely to take breaks than men,</u> who continue even when they are frustrated or tired. <u>Women may also spend money on the appropriate attire for fishing, gear that is waterproof and warm.</u> <u>Finally, women are more receptive to fishing advice than are men.</u> These feminine traits make a big difference in fly fishing.

2. **Because they are susceptible to certain safety problems, people over the age of seventy-five should be required by law to take a driving test every year.** Some people believe that such a law would represent age discrimination because many people are great drivers until they are in their nineties. But government statistics indicate that people over seventy-five have more accidents ✓ than younger drivers do. <u>One common failing of older drivers is impaired peripheral vision.</u> This vision problem makes it difficult ✓ for them to see cars on either side or at an intersection. <u>Another common problem is a longer response time.</u> Although older

drivers may know to stop, it takes them much longer to move their foot from the gas pedal to the brake than it does younger ✓ drivers. This lengthened response time is the most common cause ✓ of accidents among older drivers. <u>The most dangerous failing among older drivers is a loss of memory.</u> Consider this common scenario: The driver starts to back out of a parking space after ✓ checking to see that there is nothing behind him. He then notices ✓ that his sunglasses have fallen on the floor. He retrieves them and puts his foot back on the gas pedal without remembering that he needs to look again. Because he is still in reverse, the car moves ✓ quickly and hits the person or car now behind him. Although it may inconvenience older drivers to take annual driving tests, it will help prevent injuries and save lives.

Paragraph with better support: <u>Paragraph 2</u>

Reasons that this paragraph's support is better: <u>Answers will vary,</u> <u>but students might note that paragraph 2 provides supporting details for</u> <u>each primary support point, while paragraph 1 introduces certain points</u> <u>without backing them at all.</u>

PRACTICE 5 **Revising for support**

Read the following essay, and write in the space provided at least one additional support point or detail for each body paragraph and for the conclusion. Indicate where the added material should go in the paragraph by writing in a caret (^).

Anyone who has owned a dog knows that there is a special bond between dogs and humans. Even without speech, dogs seem to understand humans' words and emotions. Dogs have been beloved family pets for a very long time, but they are also being used effectively in new educational, workplace, and therapeutic settings.

Answers will vary.

Dog rescue organizations often bring dogs into schools to talk about the dogs' resilience and responsiveness to good care. For example, Greyhound Rescue, an organization that saves dogs from death after they are too old to race or when a track is being closed, is active in schools. Students meet the dogs and learn about caring for them and ways to help them. After visits, some students become volunteers.

Dogs work hard, too. They are sometimes brought into hotels to check for bedbugs, to airports for security checks, and to hospitals and nursing homes for patient therapy. There are also programs where chronically ill children are visited weekly by the same dog. The dogs seem to sense the children's pain or weakness, and their visits give the children something to look forward to. The dogs have the same effect on nursing home residents.

Dogs are also brought into prisons to be trained by prisoners. Sometimes inmates train these dogs as seeing-eye dogs for blind people. Other times prisoners ready abandoned puppies for adoption. Many violent prisoners have been successful trainers. The sad part is that they cannot keep the dogs they have trained.

It is said that dogs are man's best friend. They are trusting companions who love unconditionally. They are able to communicate and help where words sometimes do not.

Revise for Coherence

Coherence in writing means that all the support connects to form a whole that makes sense. In other words, even when the support is arranged in a logical order, it still needs "glue" to connect the various points.

A piece of writing that lacks coherence sounds choppy and is hard for readers to follow. Revising an essay for coherence helps readers see how one point leads to another. The best way to improve coherence is to add transitions.

Transitions are words, phrases, and sentences that connect ideas so that writing moves smoothly from one point to another. Transitions can connect sentences and ideas within a paragraph and also connect one paragraph to another. The box on page 117 lists some, but not all, of the most common transitions and their purpose.

The essay on page 118 shows how transitions link ideas within sentences and paragraphs and connect one paragraph to the next. It also shows another technique for achieving coherence: repeating key words and ideas related to the main idea. The transitions and key words in the essay are underlined.

Common Transitional Words and Phrases

Indicate space relation			
above	below	near	to the right
across	beside	next to	to the side
at the bottom	beyond	opposite	under
at the top	farther	over	where
behind	inside	to the left	

Indicate time order			
after	eventually	meanwhile	soon
as	finally	next	then
at last	first	now	when
before	last	second	while
during	later	since	

Indicate importance			
above all	in fact	more important	most important
best	in particular	most	worst
especially			

Signal examples			
for example	for instance	for one thing	one reason

Signal additions			
additionally	and	as well as	in addition
also	another	furthermore	moreover

Signal contrast			
although	in contrast	nevertheless	still
but	instead	on the other hand	yet
however			

Signal cause or consequence			
as a result	finally	so	therefore
because			

Teaching tip Have students bring in newspaper articles in which they have circled all the transitions. Then, have them try reading parts of the articles aloud without the transitions. Discuss the results.

I thought I would never make it to work today. I had an important meeting, and it seemed as if everything was conspiring against me. The conspiracy started before I even woke up.

I had set my alarm clock, but it did not go off, and therefore I did not wake up on time. When I did wake up, I was already late, not just by a few minutes but by an hour and a half. To save time, I brushed my teeth while I showered. Also, I figured out what I was going to wear. Finally, I hopped out of the shower ready to get dressed. But the conspiracy continued.

The next act of the conspiracy concerned my only clean shirt, which was missing two buttons right in front. After finding a sweater that would go over it, I ran to the bus stop.

When I got to the stop, I discovered that the buses were running late. When one finally came, it was one of the old, slow ones, and it made stops about every ten feet. In addition, the heat was blasting, and I was sweating but could not take off my sweater because my shirt was gaping open. Now I was sweating, and perspiration was running down my scalp and neck. At least, I thought, I will dry off by the time the bus gets to my work.

In fact, I did dry off a little, but the conspiracy did not end there. When I finally got to work, the elevator was out of service, so I had to walk up ten flights of stairs. I was drenched, late, and inappropriately dressed. By the time I got to my desk, I knew that the hardest part of the day was behind me.

Teamwork Practice 6 works well as a collaborative exercise. Have pairs of students try to find at least two transitional words to fill each blank and then discuss which word seems more appropriate and why.

| PRACTICE 6 | **Adding transitional words** |

Read the following paragraphs. In each blank, add a transition that would smoothly connect the ideas. In each case, there is more than one right answer. *Answers will vary. Suggested answers follow.*

Example: Many workers belong to labor unions that exist to protect worker rights. ____*However,*____ **until the 1930s, unions did not exist. In the 1930s, Congress passed laws that paved the way for unions.** ____*After that,*____ **workers had the right to organize, bargain, and strike.** ____*Today,*____ **unions remain a powerful force in American politics.**

1. The modern-day vending machine is based on an invention by a Greek scientist named Hero, who lived in the first century C.E. The machine that he invented required that the user insert a coin. ____*After*____ the coin fell, it hit a lever. ____*Then*____ out came the desired product—a cup of holy water.

2. ____*When*____ Jackie Robinson joined the Brooklyn Dodgers in 1947, he became the first African American to play major league baseball in

the twentieth century. ___*Because*___ he was the first, he was faced with what was called "breaking the color line" and received many death threats. ___*After*___ a few seasons of playing well, he spoke out against discrimination against African Americans. ___*During*___ his career, he played in six World Series and won the National League Most Valuable Player award in 1949.

3. Alcohol affects women more quickly than men. Their bodies inter-act with the alcohol in different ways. Women have more fat tis-sue, ___*and*___ men have more muscle tissue, which has more water than fat tissue. ___*When*___ men drink alcohol, it is diluted by the water in muscle. ___*But, However, In contrast,*___ when women drink, the alcohol is more concentrated. ___*Therefore, As a result,*___ women get drunk sooner.

PRACTICE 7   **Adding transitional sentences**

Read the following essay. Then, write a transitional sentence that would link each paragraph to the one following it. You may add your transitional sentence at the end of a paragraph, at the beginning of the next paragraph, or in both places.

   Many teenagers today do not date in the traditional sense—one boy and one girl going on dates or "going steady." Instead, they go out in groups rather than as couples. This new pattern gives many parents a sense that their sons and daughters are safe from premature sex and sexually transmitted diseases.

Answers will vary.
_____

_____

   Although teenagers do not pair off romantically, they are getting plenty of sex, just not with people they care about. They care about their friends and do not want to risk ruining friendships, so they "hook up" with strangers they meet while out at night or online. "Hooking up" means having sex with someone, and many teens hook up only with people they have no other contact with, preferably from different schools or towns.

_____

_____

Although teenagers often think that sex without emotional involvement will avoid heartbreak and breakups, many teens, both girls and boys, admit that it is difficult not to develop feelings for someone they are physically intimate with. If one person begins to feels an attachment while the other does not, a distancing occurs: That hurts. It is a breakup of a different sort.

_____

_____

Teenagers have always experimented with ways to do things differently than their parents did. Trying new ways to do things is an important stage in teenagers' development. Experimentation is normal and sometimes produces better ways of doing things. According to most teens, however, the "hook-up" is not the answer to heartbreak: It is just another road to it. Perhaps teenagers are destined to experience some pain as they try out what "love" means.

_____

_____

PRACTICE 8   **Adding transitions**

The following essay has no transitions. Read it carefully, and add transitions both within and between the paragraphs. There is no one correct answer. *Answers will vary. Possible answers shown.*

Skydiving is the most thrilling activity I can ever imagine. I was scared, euphoric, and proud during my one skydive. I would encourage anyone to have the experience of a lifetime.

_____First___ I was scared as I looked down out of the plane, ready to jump. The ground was barely visible. My instructor gave the ready sign, assuring me that he would be guiding me all the way. I closed my eyes, and we jumped out of the plane together. It felt as if we were dropping very fast. I opened my eyes and saw that, ___in fact,___ we were. I panicked a little, fearing that the parachute would not open or that my instructor would activate it too late, and we would be killed.

I was ___also___ euphoric. My instructor opened the chute, and we just glided silently through the air. It was like flying. It was peaceful and almost religious. I had never felt this way and knew that this was an important experience.

We landed, and I was proud of myself. It had taken a lot of courage to jump and to trust my life to another individual, my instructor. I had done it and done it well. I had benefited from the experience, mentally and spiritually. It was so thrilling and wonderful I probably will not do it again for fear that the second time would be an anticlimax. Do it!

One Student's Process

Before selecting a writing assignment, reread Deshon Briggs's draft in Chapter 8 (p. 104). Then, read his revised essay, which follows. His revisions are highlighted.

Deshon's revision

On the first day of my English class last spring, my teacher wrote "You are the change in your life" on the board. She said that ~~statement related to our going to college and making our lives better,~~ we had already taken a step toward change by coming to college to improve our lives. She said that we would be revisiting the theme of "people connecting to their communities" in our assignments and discussions and that we should be alert to ways that people are making a difference. She also gave us a writing assignment to explore ~~the statement that was due in four weeks~~ and find ways that we could make the statement true in our own lives. The paper would not be due for four weeks, but we should start taking action now. I did not really know what she was talking about but figured I had plenty of time to think about it. In those four weeks, though, I learned that I really can be the change in my life.

The weekend after we got the assignment, I took my son to play basketball at the park near us, and he gave me grief when I threw my Coke can off to the side. He said in his school they were learning about how litter is bad for the earth. He got a bag from my car and picked up my can. Then he started picking up others, and I helped. Once we started, I was surprised how many bottles and cans there were that I just had not noticed before. While we were working, a guy I know came by with his kids, and we all started picking up cans and bottles. ~~There were a lot.~~ We filled three big bags, just with bottles and cans. But then we kept going, filling another bag with paper and other litter. When we were done, we brought the bags home, threw away the trash, and took the cans and bottles to the supermarket to redeem the deposit money.

That night, I had the idea to go to the local freecycle.org and post that we wanted a big trash can bottles and cans for the park. By the next morning, I had a bunch of offers

Added detail

Details

Transition

Revised thesis

Transition

Detail

Transitions

Detail

Transition

Details

Transitions

Transitions

▶

Details

Transition

Details

Transition

Details

Revised
conclusion

seven offers for free trash cans and ~~other guys~~ four other guys with sons said they would help with clean-up. We set out the trash cans and labeled one for bottles and cans, one for other trash. Then we set up a schedule. The people responsible for pick-up would take the day's collection for deposit money and get rid of the trash. ~~My son and I got the idea of returning the bottles and cans for the deposit money that we could use to get a new basketball net. We did that~~ With the money we collected, we got a new basketball net and a bench. We felt proud of ourselves.

After a few weeks, the local paper called me and wanted to interview my son and me about ~~the stuff we had done at~~ our "campaign to improve" the basketball court. We got our pictures in the paper, and ~~we got some more people interested~~ some people who read about what we had done made donations. ~~Now we have enough money to get a bench.~~ Since then, we have made more improvements, and the court and park around it are clean. Someone had the idea of starting a community garden in the park, and now whole families come there. There are some picnic tables, and it is a wonderful and safe family recreation area. ~~The court looks great, we met a lot of other people, and people gave us a lot of respect. It was great.~~ My son and I have met many new people as we created our own little piece of paradise from what was just a junky basketball court in a park that no one used. And this is my paper for my English class: how my son and I ~~were~~ learned that we are the change in our lives. ~~starting~~ It all started with just picking up a Coke can.

Revise Your Own Essay

Revise the draft you developed in Chapter 8. Before revising, read the following checklist.

> **CHECKLIST**
>
> Revising Your Essay
>
> **FOCUS**
>
> ☐ After a break, reread your draft with a fresh perspective.
>
> **ASK**
>
> ☐ What is your main idea or position? Does your thesis statement clearly state your main idea?
>
> ☐ Does your essay have the following?
> – An introductory paragraph
> – Three or more body paragraphs
> – A topic sentence for each paragraph that supports the main idea
> – A forceful concluding paragraph that reminds readers of the main idea and makes an observation
>
> ☐ Does your essay have unity?
> – Do all of the support points relate directly to the main idea?
> – Do all of the supporting details in each body paragraph relate to the paragraph's topic sentence?
> – Have you avoided drifting away from the main idea?
>
> ☐ Do you have enough support?
> – Taken together, do the topic sentences of each paragraph give enough support or evidence for the main idea?
> – Do individual paragraphs support their topic sentences?
> – Would more detail strengthen your support?
>
> ☐ Is your essay coherent?
> – Have you used transitional words to link ideas?
> – Have you used transitional sentences to link paragraphs?
>
> **REVISE**
>
> ☐ Revise your draft, making any improvements you can. Be sure to look for bias or errors in reasoning.

Part 3

Different Types of Writing

"I write lab reports."

Aaron M.-D., student

PHOTO: ANDREW DILLON BUSTIN

10

Narration

Writing That Tells Stories

Understand What Narration Is

Narration is writing that tells a story of an event or experience. Whether they are serious or humorous, stories provide information and examples that can show, explain, or prove a point.

Four Basics of Good Narration

1 It conveys a **main idea** about an event or experience.

2 It includes all the major **events** of the story (primary support).

3 It uses descriptive **details** to bring the story to life for your audience (secondary support).

4 It presents the events in a clear **order,** usually chronological (time order).

In the following passage, each color corresponds to one of the Four Basics of Good Narration.

1 Thanksgiving is a time of repeating old traditions, such as gathering with family and friends and eating special foods like turkey, cranberry relish, and pumpkin pie. Every year, my family and I go to my older sister and brother-in-law's house, and we enjoy the whole traditional experience. But it was there that I also learned how unexpected new traditions can enter the mix and make a holiday even more meaningful.

2 My sister's son Jacob had spent a semester in Niger, a desert country in central Africa. There he made a good friend, Ibrahim, who later moved to

4 Transitional words and phrases clearly show the order of events.

the United States to study science and engineering. My sister and brother-in-law invited Ibrahim to Thanksgiving every year, so gradually we all came to know this warm and friendly person.

He would ask questions about Thanksgiving traditions, which were new and unfamiliar to him. We would ask questions about his country, which was unfamiliar to us. **3** In response he would often say, "Well, where I am from, whenever we gather, we drink a strong, sweet green tea called atai." It was as though, to him, this tea seemed strangely missing from the party.

2 One year he brought with him everything necessary to make the tea in the traditional way of his country: **3** two small metal pots with lids; tea leaves; sugar; special small glasses, like shot glasses; a tiny wire grill; and charcoal. He made the tea on my sister's back porch, though the weather was drizzly and cold. The process was complicated, and involved boiling the tea a long time, then pouring it from high up, to cool it. Patience is a necessary ingredient.

2 When the tea was finally ready, we all hesitatingly took sips from the little glasses, expecting to try it, set it aside, and think "that will be that." **3** But the tea was so pleasingly tasty—smoky and sweet—and so strikingly different that this custom quickly became an essential and beloved Thanksgiving tradition. Now **2** Ibrahim carefully makes this tea every year and serves it at the end of the big meal, and the holiday would not seem right otherwise.

1 I give thanks to Ibrahim for enlarging my world and proving that, when it comes to excellent customs, there is plenty of room at the table for one more.

Contexts for Narration

Telling stories is one important way in which we communicate with one another. Common types of narratives include stories of discovery, escape, journey, rescue, revenge, love, growth in self-knowledge, and transition to maturity. In other words, stories often involve people dealing with change. Through telling stories we figure out how to face trials and tragedies, large and small. We learn how to define or achieve success. We recall overcoming obstacles and breaking through cultural and personal limitations. And we wrestle with large forces and events beyond our control, often with the help of others.

Discussion As a class, generate other uses of narration in these areas.

Considering the **context** for your narration is just as important as writing the paper itself. The context for a narration consists of the **audience** and **purpose,** just as in any piece of effective writing. When you are thinking about the narrative you are writing, consider who the reader may be. Writing doesn't exist in a vacuum; there is always one or more readers and always some reason for them to read what you have written. The questions you need to ask about your audience can help you determine who your readers will be and why they may want to read your narrative. These questions can include, but are not limited to, the following:

- Who would want to read this story and why?
- What do they already know about this story? What do they not know?
- Have they had an experience like this before?
- Why are they reading this story?

Once you have clearly defined who your audience is, then you can consider your purpose for writing that story.

- Do I want my readers to learn something new?
- Is my purpose to entertain them?
- Am I trying to share advice about a situation my readers may encounter in the future, or am I helping them deal with an experience they may have encountered in the past?
- Do I want to take a serious or a humorous tone?

After reading the story, the audience should know why they were supposed to read it or what they were supposed to learn or gain. If you can't identify the purpose, don't expect the audience to be able to do so either.

You can use narration in many practical situations. Consider the following examples.

College	In a psychology course, you are asked to tell the story of one moment in your life that is connected to a significant memory in order to explore sense memories.
Work	A customer becomes angry with you and lodges a complaint with your boss. You recount in writing what happened.
Everyday life	A child asks you to tell a story before bedtime, so you make up a fairy tale.

Main Idea in Narration

Be clear on your **main idea**—what is important about the narration. Generally, college instructors will want your main idea to indicate what is important to you about a story. For clarity, state the main idea in the first paragraph and remind readers of it at the end of your narration.

Take another look at the passage under the Four Basics of Good Narration (p. 127). Note how the following sentence from that passage emphasizes the event's importance to the writer:

Discussion Bring in different types of stories (for example, a fairy tale, a synopsis of a popular television show, a summary of a popular book that the class may be familiar with) and determine who might be an appropriate audience for that particular narrative or story. What clues lead you to that conclusion?

I also learned how unexpected new traditions can . . . make a holiday even more meaningful.

In writing a narrative, make sure your topic sentence (for paragraphs) and thesis statement (for essays) communicate your general topic and the main idea you are making about the topic.

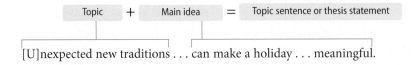

| Topic | + | Main idea | = | Topic sentence or thesis statement |

[U]nexpected new traditions . . . can make a holiday . . . meaningful.

Support in Narration

To **support** your main idea, you will present and explain the major events in the story and describe relevant details. As you write a narration, you will have decisions to make—what to include, what to leave out, and what perspective you will take on events. Your **point of view** determines how you will present the major events and details of the story and how you will support your main idea.

POINT OF VIEW

In a narration, the events you include and the way you describe them create a story that is based on your point of view. For example, two people who witness or participate in the same series of events may give different accounts because they perceive what happened differently.

The stories that Gloria and Mason tell in the following two paragraphs reflect their different points of view regarding the same experience.

Gloria's story
This morning, Mason and I set out for what was supposed to be a great day at the beach, but Mason's stubborn behavior ruined everything. First, he took the longest route, so we hit traffic that we would have avoided by going the short route. Then, we got lost. When I suggested that we stop and ask for directions, Mason refused. After another hour of driving, we passed an intersection that we'd crossed earlier. I again suggested that we stop and ask for directions, but Mason wasn't buying it. So we drove some more. Finally, we were about to run out of gas, so we pulled into a gas station. While Mason was filling the tank, I asked the attendant for directions. If we hadn't needed gas, we'd still be driving around looking for that beach.

Mason's story
This morning, Gloria and I set out for what was supposed to be a great day at the beach, but Gloria wanted to pick a fight. First, she insisted I was going the

wrong way, it was going to take us longer, and we'd hit more traffic. Then, she decided we were lost. I knew where we were going, but Gloria kept on nagging me to stop and ask for directions. When we were almost there, I decided to get gas, and she had to ask the attendant for directions. I don't know what was going on with her, but she was really on my case.

When you write a narration, describe events in a way that will tell the story you want to tell to your audience.

MAJOR EVENTS AND DETAILS

The **major events** of a story are your primary support in narration, and they will usually become the topic sentences for the body paragraphs in your essay. Ask yourself what the major events are and what makes them important. To help your readers experience the events as you did, give supporting details that bring the experience to life.

For example, one student stated the main idea of an event in the following thesis: *The theft of my wallet this morning showed me how easy it is for criminals to deceive unsuspecting victims.* The student then did some listing to come up with the major events and details about those events.

For more on support, see Chapter 7. For more on listing, see pp. 61–62.

MAJOR EVENTS	SUPPORTING DETAILS
(primary support)	(secondary support)
A woman bumped into me.	It was a light bump, but she dropped her folder of papers, and they scattered.
I bent down to help her collect the papers.	The wind was blowing, so I had to work fast.
A man stopped and asked if he could help.	I didn't get a good look at him because I was trying to get the papers, but he stood close to me and hung around for a minute just watching us. Then, he just left without saying anything.
The woman thanked me, and I said no problem.	She had her head down and walked off fast.
When I went to get coffee, I realized the wallet was gone.	I broke into a sweat at the café and had that horrible panicked feeling.
I realized that the man and woman were working together.	Looking back on the details, it was clear how carefully they had planned the theft.

DIALOGUE

For more on using quotation marks, see Chapter 37.

As you tell the story, you might want to include direct speech or **dialogue,** the words that you or other people said. If you report exactly what was said, use quotation marks.

> The woman said, "Oh, I'm so sorry! I'll never be able to get these papers before they blow away, and my boss will have a fit."

Using direct speech can bring a narration to life.

Organization in Narration

For more on chronological order, see page 90.

For more on transitions, see pages 116–17.

Because narration tells about something that has already happened, it often uses **chronological (time) order.** Start at the beginning of the story, and describe the events in the sequence in which they occurred.

Time transitions (words and phrases like *next* and *meanwhile*) are important in narration because they make the order of events clear to readers. Writers of narration use these common transitions not only within a paragraph—to move from one detail about the event to the next—but also between paragraphs to move from one major event to the next.

Common Time Transitions

after	eventually	meanwhile	soon
as	finally	next	still
at last	first	now	then
before	last	second	when
during	later	since	while

Read and Analyze Narration

For more examples of narration, see Chapter 40.

Before writing your narration essay, read the following examples of narration—one from the workplace, and one from college—and answer the questions that accompany them.

Profile of Success
Narration in the Real World

Monique Rizer

Journalist and Development Associate, National Military Family Association

Background   I was the oldest of six children, and before my mother married my stepfather, she was on welfare. She home-schooled me for five years until I begged her to let me go to a public high school. There I made friends with some people who expected to go to college, and I realized I wanted to go, too. I started at Green River Community College, but just then my parents' financial situation got really bad, and the eight of us had to move to a trailer. I stopped going to school until I met my future husband, who was going to a community college and encouraged me to go back. Several months later I became pregnant with my first son. I was determined to stay in college, so I completed one year at Highline Community College. That summer, I had my son, got married, and found loans to transfer to Pacific Lutheran University. While there, I received a Gates Millennium Scholarship, which made continuing college possible. Although I moved a few times, I graduated from college and went on to graduate school. After I finished graduate school, I had another son.

Writing at work   I have done many types of writing. I rewrote marketing material while working at an accounting firm, and when my husband was in Iraq, I wrote a newsletter for families of soldiers with advice on finding resources and keeping up morale and with news of what was going on with the soldiers in Iraq.

I had to find my own resources for military families, which was not easy. I had to write well, speak well, and be persistent. You have to communicate effectively to get what you need in life, and words give you the power to fight.

How Monique uses narration   Much of the writing I do involves telling people's stories so that readers can understand them and their unique problems.

For an example of Monique Rizer's narration writing, see page 587.

Workplace Narration

On April 19, 2013, actress Reese Witherspoon and her husband, James Toth, were arrested in Atlanta. The following is the narrative from a police report written by Officer J. Pyland of the Georgia Department of Public Safety.

Officer J. Pyland

Police Report

Guiding question Why are the descriptive details and the way they are arranged (chronological order) so important in writing this type of report?

Vocabulary The following words are *italicized* in the excerpt: *negotiated, initiated, HGN, PBT, implied.* If you do not know their meanings, look them up in a dictionary or online.

POLICE REPORT

Date: 4/19/13
_____

Reporting Officer: J. Pyland
_____

Detail of Event:

On April 19, 2013, at approximately 0040 hours, I was patrolling north on Peachtree Road. I observed a silver Ford Fusion fail to maintain its lane while it traveled in the left lane.

The Fusion traveled on the white dashed line that separated the left and center lanes with its passenger's side. I followed behind the Fusion in the left lane. As we *negotiated* a left curve, the Fusion traveled on top of the double yellow line that separated the northbound and southbound lanes with its driver's side tires. As we continued to travel northbound, the Fusion's left turn signal blinked on then off.

As we negotiated a sharp right curve the Fusion crossed into the center and straddled the solid white line that separated the left and center lanes. I *initiated* a traffic stop. The Fusion pulled to the right, into the driveway to the Walgreens.

The Fusion was partially in the northbound right lane of Peachtree Road. I approached the driver, Mr. James Joseph Toth, and told him that I needed to see his license. Mr. Toth handed me his license, and I explained the reason for the stop. As I explained the reason for the stop, I observed that Mr. Toth's eyelids were droopy. Mr. Toth's eyes were bloodshot and watery. I smelled the strong odor of an alcoholic beverage coming from Mr. Toth's breath.

I asked Mr. Toth how much he had to drink. Mr. Toth stated, "A drink." When asked where he had his drinks, Mr. Toth looked at the passenger, Mrs. Laura Jeanne Reese Witherspoon, and she began to answer. Mrs. Witherspoon stated that he had his drink at a restaurant. Mrs. Witherspoon stated that the drink was consumed two hours prior to the incident. I asked Mr. Toth if he would perform field sobriety. Mr. Toth gave verbal consent.

I had Mr. Toth back his car into the driveway of the Walgreens to get it out of the roadway. Mr. Toth was medically qualified for field sobriety. Mr. Toth performed all field sobriety asked of him. Just before Walk and Turn, Mr. Toth stated that he had a problem with his left leg. I asked Mr. Toth if it would prevent him from continuing, and he stated that it would not. Before we began field sobriety, Mrs. Witherspoon got out of the vehicle. I told Mrs. Witherspoon to stay in the vehicle, and she sat back in the vehicle.

I observed that Mr. Toth was chewing on something and asked him if it was gum. Mr. Toth stated that it was a mint. As I performed *HGN* on Mr. Toth, Mrs. Witherspoon got back out of the vehicle. I had to tell Mrs. Witherspoon several times to get back into the vehicle before she did so. I told Mrs. Witherspoon that I would arrest her the next time she got out of the vehicle. I went and explained to Mrs. Witherspoon the reason why I wanted her to stay in the vehicle. The reason was for my safety. Mrs. Witherspoon stated, "Yes sir."

During the rest of field sobriety, I observed that Mr. Toth had a hard time listening to and following my directions. Mr. Toth wanted to finish the rest of the tests on the sidewalk next to the Walgreens building.

After I had administered the *PBT*, Mrs. Witherspoon began to hang out the window and say that she did not believe that I was a real police officer. I told Mrs. Witherspoon to sit on her butt and be quiet. I placed Mr. Toth under arrest for DUI. When asked his age, Mr. Toth stated that he was 42 years old. Mrs. Witherspoon got out of the vehicle and walked up to me and Mr. Toth. I asked, "What had I already told you?" Mrs. Witherspoon asked what was going on.

I told Mrs. Witherspoon that Mr. Toth was under arrest. I told Mrs. Witherspoon to get back into the car. Mrs. Witherspoon stated that she was a "U.S. citizen" and that she was allowed to "stand on American ground." I put my hands on Mrs. Witherspoon's arms to arrest her. Mrs. Witherspoon was resistant, but I was able to put handcuffs on her without incident due to Mr. Toth calming her down.

Mrs. Witherspoon asked, "Do you know my name?" I answered, "No, I don't need to know your name." I then added, "Right now."

Mrs. Witherspoon stated, "You're about to find out who I am." I stated, "I am not worried about you, ma'am."

I stated, "I already told you how things work." I told Mrs. Witherspoon that she was obstructing my investigation of Mr. Toth. At approximately 0100 hours, I read Implied Consent Notice/Suspects Age 21 or Over from the orange card dated 06/08 and requested breath. Mr. Toth gave a verbal "Yea."

As I put Mrs. Witherspoon in the left side rear of my patrol car, she told me her name. Mrs. Witherspoon also stated, "You are going to be on national news." I advised Mrs. Witherspoon that was fine.

CPL Land # 570 met with me and transported Mrs. Witherspoon to Atlanta Pre-Trial Jail without incident. The vehicle was turned over to Futo's Wrecker Service. The backseat passenger was released to a taxicab. I transported Mr. Toth to the Atlanta Pre-Trial Jail. I set up the Intoxilyzer 5000 for the test. Mr. Toth gave two samples. Mr. Toth's lowest sample was 0.139 grams. Mr. Toth was turned over to the jail staff without incident.

1. Briefly summarize the police report. What is its purpose? Its intended audience? *Answers will vary.* _____

2. Which elements of the Four Basics of Good Narration (p. 127) does the police report have? Which does it lack? _____

   _____

3. How would you describe the language Officer Pyland uses in narrating the events of the arrest? _____

   _____

4. Do you think the police report fulfills its purpose? Explain. _____

   _____

A College Narration Essay

A student wrote the following essay for a college writing course. The assignment was "Write an essay describing an important decision in your life."

For the following essay, review the Four Basics of Good Narration (p. 127) and practice your critical reading process by doing the following.

> ## 2PR   The Critical Reading Process
>
> **P**review the text, including the guiding question.
>
> **R**ead the text, double-underlining the thesis statement, underlining the major support, and circling the transitions. Consider the quality of the support.
>
> **P**ause to question and interpret the text. Take notes and write down questions about what you are reading.
>
> **R**eview the text and your notes, and **respond** to it. Write answers to the Pause prompts.

Teaching tip The questions following the readings can be done either in writing or as class discussions.

Teamwork Have students work through the essay together to apply the 2PR Critical Reading Process and answer the questions after the essay.

Jordan Brown

A Return to Education

Guiding question How does Jordan feel about his return to college?

Vocabulary The following words are *italicized* in the essay: *anticipation, stamina*. If you do not know their meanings, look them up in a dictionary or online.

1   For me, college has been an experience marked by *anticipation*, fear, and pride. I sometimes find myself still surprised that I am really here. The journey to get here has been a long one, but if I can put my fears behind me, I believe I will be able to accomplish something that I can really be proud of.

2   Being able to go to college is something that I have been anticipating for many years. Since I left high school and the California Bay Area behind, I have been on the go in one way or another. After graduation, I felt that I wasn't ready for the commitments or responsibilities of college. Instead, I enlisted in the army. The army provided me with the maturity and self-discipline that I desperately needed in my life; however, being in the army also provided me with very little time or money to go to college, so I put it off until "a later date."

Pause Why did Brown join the army? Was it a good decision for him?

3   (After) the army, I sought a higher-paying job, (first) becoming a truck driver. This job provided me with money but no time. (Now) I work for the railroad, and with my apprenticeship behind me, I have some free time for the first time in my life.

4   What I have been anticipating for years is finally here. I (now) have the time and money for college, but do I have the ability? It has been eleven years since I last sat in a classroom. This made me question myself: Can I do this? Will I succeed? Will I fail? Am I even capable of learning in a classroom environment? Although I had these questions, I knew that the only way to face my fears was to attack them head-on. I reminded myself that the only thing I could do is try.

Pause How does Brown's first sentence here relate to the first paragraph? What questions does he have?

5   When I (first) walked into Front Range Community College, I was nervous. I couldn't help but notice how young everyone looked. I got to my study skills class, sat down, and looked around. I felt out of place. Most of the people in the class looked as if they had just graduated from high school. (When) we did our introductions, however, I learned that one of the women sitting across the room had graduated from high school eleven years ago. I started to feel a little younger.

Pause Why was Brown nervous?

6   (When) I got to my philosophy class, I watched the other students come in and noticed that not everyone looked like a kid. This class looked very much like an American melting pot, with students of many ages and cultures. (As) we went around the room introducing ourselves, I felt more confident about my decision to try college. Many students were even older than I was. A woman sitting near me, who looked about my mom's age, said she was in college because all of her kids were in college now. She told us that she wanted a college education and a better job. An older gentleman across the room said that he was a business executive from Germany. His job had become boring, and he was looking for something more challenging. (By the end) of the introductions, I was convinced that this "college thing" might just work.

Pause How do the other students help Brown feel better?

7   (Since) I have gone back to school, there has been a lot of pride surrounding me. My parents can't stop talking about me and how proud they are. My family and friends are excited for me and congratulate me on my decision. I am also proud of myself for making the tough decision to go back to school. I know that when I get my degree, I will have something to be truly proud of.

Pause How does Brown's first sentence here relate back to his thesis statement?

8   I (still) have fears and uncertainties. But I also have positive anticipation and hope. (Now,) I know that I am on the right course. I know
that as long as I have *stamina* and determination, nothing can stop
me from achieving my dream of getting my degree in mechanical
engineering.

Pause How does
Brown tie his conclusion
to his introduction?

1. **Respond.** How does Brown's experience relate to your own?
2. **Summarize.** Briefly summarize Brown's essay, including his **main
    idea,** his **purpose,** and the **major events** in his story. What is his point
    of view?
3. **Analyze.** Does Brown's **support** all relate to his main idea? Is it logically
    organized? Does he give you enough details? How do the topic sentences
    relate specifically to the thesis statement? Did the title give you an idea of
    what the essay would be about?
4. **Synthesize.** How does Brown's experience relate to other things you have
    thought about, read, or heard?
5. **Evaluate.** Does Brown achieve his purpose? Does his essay have the Four
    Basics of Good Narration (see p. 127)? What do *you* think of his essay, and
    why?

Write a Narration Essay

This section includes four assignments for writing a narration essay. Use
the following tools to help you as you complete one or more of these
assignments.

1. Review the Four Basics of Good Narration (p. 127).
2. Use **Narration at a Glance** as a basic organizer.
3. Use the Writing Guide: Narration (p. 142) as you write and revise.

| WRITING ASSIGNMENT 1 | **Writing a narration essay: suggested
topics** |

Write a narration essay on *one* of the following topics or on a topic of your
own choice.

College

*   Write about your first experiences of college, as Jordan
    Brown did.
*   Explain what led you to start college.

**Narration
at a glance**

Introduction with
thesis statement

Says what is
important about
the experience

↓

First major event

Details about
the event

↓

Second major
event

Details about
the event

↓

Third major
event

Details about
the event

↓

Conclusion

Reminds readers
of the main
idea and makes
an observation
based on it.

Work
- Explain what you learned from getting or doing your first job.
- Describe an incident that shows your boss as (supportive/unsupportive, fair/unfair, clueless/sharp, realistic/unrealistic, honest/dishonest).

Everyday life
- Recount a time when you took a risk.
- Recount the most embarrassing, rewarding, happy, or otherwise memorable moment in your life.

WRITING ASSIGNMENT 2   **Writing about an image**

Write a narration essay about what has happened (or is happening) in the image that follows. What is going on in the picture? What happened before or what is about to happen? What is the man thinking about? What else is going on in the room? Be as creative as you like, but be sure to apply what you know about reading a visual (see p. 22), and follow the Four Basics of Good Narration (p. 127).

© 2013 THANASIS ZOVOILIS/FLICKR SELECT/GETTY IMAGES

WRITING ASSIGNMENT 3   ## Writing to solve a problem

Problem Your school is mounting an antibullying campaign, and a committee consisting of the dean of student life, five faculty members, and five students has been formed to study the issue and make recommendations. You are part of that committee. As a first step, the committee has agreed that it needs to consider the various types of bullying that people experience and to involve as many students as possible. All committee members will write about bullying that they have experienced, participated in, or witnessed, describing the incidents in detail. The committee will select five of the essays to post online as examples, and posters displayed around campus will invite other students to submit their experiences.

Assignment Write an essay about bullying from your own experience. Consider the purpose and audience, and use what you have learned about good narration.

WRITING ASSIGNMENT 4   ## Writing about readings

The suggestions that follow ask you to read at least two different examples of narration and draw from them to write your own essay.

- Read Jordan Brown's essay "A Return to Education" (p. 137), Daniel Flanagan's essay "The Choice to Do It Over Again" (p. 180), and Monique Rizer's essay "When Students Are Parents" (p. 587). All are about education, especially the experience of returning to school after an absence. Drawing from these essays, write an essay about your experience of starting or returning to school.

- Read Langston Hughes's essay, "Salvation" (p. 590), and review Jordan Brown's and Monique Rizer's essays. These three narratives include the experience of wanting to fit in, but with different outcomes. Write an essay about a time you felt pressured to fit in, the ways you responded, and the outcome. Draw from the readings to relate your experience to that of the other writers.

Use the steps in the Writing Guide that follows to help you prewrite, draft, revise, and edit your narration. Check off each step as you complete it.

Teaching tip Break the class up into small groups and have students read their experiences aloud. Then, discuss the issue as a class.

Teamwork Have students, in pairs or small groups, share their plans for their narrative. Classmates can evaluate the order of the plan and suggest other supporting details.

For advice on summarizing, analyzing, synthesizing, and evaluating, see pages 39–49.

WRITING GUIDE: NARRATION

Steps in Narration	How to do the steps
Focus.	• Think about your audience and what is important about your story.
Explore your topic. See Chapter 5.	• Narrow your topic. • Prewrite, recalling what happened. Why is the story important?
Write a thesis statement. Topic + main idea = Thesis See Chapter 6.	• Say what is important about the story—how it affected you or others.
Support your thesis. See Chapter 7.	• Recall the major events. • Provide background information that your readers will need. • Describe the events with specific details.
Write a draft. See Chapter 8.	• Arrange the events chronologically. • Consider using one of the introductory techniques in Chapter 8, and include your thesis statement in your introduction. • Write topic sentences for each major event. • Write a paragraph for each event, giving details about each.
Revise your draft. See Chapter 9.	• Read to make sure that all events and details show, explain, or prove what is important about the story. • Add important events or details that occur to you. • Add time transitions. • Improve your introduction, thesis, and conclusion.
Edit your revised draft. See Parts 5 through 8.	• Correct errors in grammar, spelling, word use, and punctuation.
Evaluate your writing.	• Does it have the Four Basics of Good Narration (p. 127)? • Ask yourself: Is this the best I can do?

11

Illustration
Writing That Shows Examples

Understand What Illustration Is

Illustration is writing that uses examples to show, explain, or prove a point.

Four Basics of Good Illustration

1. It has a point.
2. It gives specific examples to show, explain, or prove the point.
3. It gives details to support the examples.
4. It uses enough examples to get the point across to the reader.

In the following paragraph, each number corresponds to one of the Four Basics of Good Illustration.

What is the strongest predictor of your health? **1** It may not be your income or age but rather your literacy. **2** People with low literacy skills have four times greater annual health costs than those with high skills. Why is literacy so important? **3** Most Americans read at an eighth- or ninth-grade level, and 20 percent read at just a fifth-grade level or below. However, most health-care materials are written above the tenth-grade level. **3** As many as half of all patients fail to take medications as directed, often because they don't understand the instructions. **2** Americans can improve their health literacy by asking their doctor or pharmacist **3** three questions: (1) "What is

4 Enough examples given to back the writer's main idea

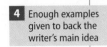

4 Enough examples given to back the writer's main idea

my main problem?" (2) "What do I need to do?" and (3) "Why is it important to do this?" If you're still confused, don't hesitate to ask your doctor, nurse, or pharmacist to go over the information again.

—"Literacy and Health," *Parade,* 18 January 2004

Contexts for Illustration

An illustration essay provides examples and details but doesn't necessarily tell a story. In writing an illustration, as with writing a narration, it's important to understand who your **audience** may be and what your **purpose** is. The following are some questions you may want to consider when identifying your audience:

- Who would want to read this illustration and why?
- How much information does the audience already have about the topic? What information will you need to give them as you write so they understand your paper?
- What kinds of examples or evidence are likely to be most effective?

Once you know who your reader will be, you need to consider your own **purpose** for writing your illustration. Broadly, your purpose is to show, explain, or prove your main idea through the use of clear and specific examples. However, since an illustration does have such a broad range of purposes, which one is specific to your own paper and the audience you have identified?

- Do you want them to learn something?
- Do you want them to better understand your main idea?
- Do you want them to be entertained?
- Do you want to prove something?
- Do you want to explain something?
- Do you have another purpose in mind?

As you can see, an illustration can cover a variety of assignments or types of papers. This is one of the main reasons why identifying the context, audience, and purpose is crucial to this particular type of writing.

Here are some ways you might use illustration.

College	In a criminal justice course, you discuss and give examples of the most common criminal violations.
Work	Your written self-evaluation for work includes specific and measurable examples of how well (or poorly) you performed.

Everyday life   You write to your mechanic to give examples that show how your car is not running properly.

Teaching tip
Photographer Susan Barnett studies how "people reveal a part of themselves" through their T-shirts. Ask students for other examples.

Main Idea in Illustration

Look at the opening sentences in the paragraph with the colored shading (p. 143):

> *What is the strongest predictor of your health?* It may not be your income or age but rather your literacy.

In this case, the topic—the strongest predictor of your health—is in the opening sentence, which is followed by a surprising **main idea:** that literacy might be a predictor of health. Because the idea is surprising, the reader will be interested in reading on to find out how it could be true. The writer demonstrates the main idea by giving examples.

Often, a thesis statement in illustration includes the topic and your main idea.

For more on thesis statements, see Chapter 6.

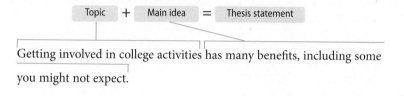

Topic + Main idea = Thesis statement

Getting involved in college activities has many benefits, including some you might not expect.

Support in Illustration

In illustration, the **examples** show or prove your stated main idea.

A student who had written the thesis *Homeschooling is beneficial to both the child and the parent* focused her prewriting on finding examples of benefits of homeschooling. Here are some examples from her brainstorming.

individualized to child	*parent and child have control*
parent and child together	*more flexibility*
at child's own pace	*considers child's learning style*
one-on-one	*education is part of regular life*

An illustration essay usually uses several examples as **support points.** The writer of the prewriting on homeschooling selected *individualized to child* as one support point and asked herself, "What do I mean? How? In what ways?" to find supporting details.

She also chose *parent and child have control* as another major example that would support the thesis. She then asked herself, "How do they have more control?" and listed potential supporting details.

> control over materials used (what books, what computer programs, what approach)
>
> control over time of instruction (what hours of the day, based on child's natural rhythms, vacations—not tied to a school's calendar)

Organization in Illustration

For more on order of importance, see pages 89–91.

Illustration often uses **order of importance** to organize several examples, saving the most vivid, convincing example for last.

Transitions are important in illustration because they signal to readers that you are moving from one example to another. Use transitions to move between sentences within a paragraph and also to move between paragraphs.

Common Transitions in Illustration

also	finally	for instance	in addition
another	for example	for one thing	one example . . .
			another example

Teamwork Have students work through the first essay together to apply the 2PR Critical Reading Process (p. 151) and answer the questions after the essay.

Read and Analyze Illustration

Before writing an illustration essay, read the following examples of illustration—from college and the workplace—and answer the questions that accompany them.

Profile of Success
Illustration in the Real World

Juan C. Gonzalez

Vice Chancellor for Student Affairs, University of California, San Diego

Background   I grew up in Amarillo, Texas, in a family of ten children. For most of my life, going to college never even occurred to me. I was a marginal student, on the slow track in school. I expected to either join the military or to work with the Rock Island Railroad, as my father did for thirty-seven years.

However, my circumstances changed when I was a sophomore in high school. That year, my father lost both of his legs in a railroad accident at work. As I sat with him through his long stay in the hospital, I realized that I wanted a different future. I knew then that I had to go to college, but I didn't know how I could accomplish that seemingly impossible goal.

Timing is often miraculous. Soon after making the decision to pursue higher education, I was approached by a TRiO/Upward Bound counselor who asked me to consider participating in the program. I jumped at the opportunity. The TRiO/Student Support Services program gave me the support, encouragement, and skills I needed for college work, and I will always be deeply grateful for their help.

Writing at work   Most of the writing I do at work is in creating lectures and presentations for a variety of different audiences, reviewing and revising statements of school policy, and writing and updating various reports on student life at the school. I work closely with graduate students, and much of our communication is oral—shared exchanges of ideas during class and meetings. However, in those meetings I take minutes of what occurs so that I have accurate records. I maintain active correspondence with students, with administrators in other areas of the college, and with faculty. I also spend a good amount of time writing e-mail messages to people at the university, in the community, and to colleagues around the country.

How Juan uses illustration   In reports to administration and in presentations to parents, trustees, and students, I have to give detailed examples of the work that our faculty and I achieve in our academic department.

Workplace Illustration

The following is from an address Dr. Gonzalez gave to a group of new students.

Teaching tip Have students take a look at the TRiO/Student Support Services page from the Illinois State University Web site that accompanies Angell Davis's Profile of Success in Chapter 15. What is the TRiO/Student Support Services program? Have the students explore your own school's Web site or promotional materials to see whether a similar program exists.

Guiding question What is the purpose of Student Affairs?

Vocabulary The following words are italicized in the excerpt: *embarking, striving, encapsulates, indicators, collaborative, integrated, aspire, complementing, facilitates, foster, engendering, status quo.* If you do not know their meanings, look them up in a dictionary or online.

As new students, you are *embarking* on an incredibly exciting and challenging time, a time of expanding knowledge, relationships, viewpoints, and achievements. In my role as vice president, I am constantly *striving* to match that energy level so that we can offer the highest level of service on this very diverse campus. I frequently marvel at college students who seem to have an unlimited amount of energy that allows them to attend classes, read and study, maintain a social life, run for political office, pursue a hobby, play an intramural sport, volunteer for a worthy cause, hold down a job. We in the Division of Student Affairs strongly encourage activities outside the classroom that enrich the academic experience, as we recognize that a university education is enhanced through involvement in our campus community.

Last November, a group of Student Affairs staff, students, and faculty began work on creating a strategic plan for the division. They have been laboring diligently on this document, and I am excited to share with you the fruit of that labor, our newly developed Student Affairs Strategic Plan, which has as its motto "Student Affairs: Where Life and Learning Intersect."

This phrase *encapsulates* the driving force behind the Division of Student Affairs. We exist, in essence, to help students succeed and grow, and we believe that growth and success must be measured in many ways. Academic success is one gauge of how well students are performing, but there are a variety of *indicators* other than grades. Those who take the most from their college experience are those who recognize that learning happens both inside and outside the classroom.

In fact, I recently had our units count the services they offer that are *collaborative* efforts with the academic side of the family, and a rough survey yielded 140 programs. This idea of *integrated* learning carries through most of what we do, whether it is a program to recruit the best students from around Texas like the Honors Colloquium, the increasingly popular "Academic Community Centers" for studying and advising on site in the residence halls, Summer Orientation, or the professor-led Freshman Reading Round-Up book discussions.

Our Vision Statement

Our vision statement lights the path we are following to where we *aspire* to be:

The Division of Student Affairs at The University of Texas at Austin seeks to become the premier organization of its kind. We envision a network of programs and services that excels in meeting students' out-of-classroom needs, *complementing* their academic experiences, and building community on a diverse campus. In doing so, we will contribute to developing citizens and leaders who will thrive in and enrich an increasingly complex world.

Our Mission

Our mission, or the explanation of what we do, is described this way:

The Division of Student Affairs *facilitates* students' discovery of self and the world in which they live. We enhance students' educational experiences through programs and services that support academic success. We provide for fundamental needs, including shelter, nourishment, and a sense of security. We create environments that *foster* physical, emotional, and psychological wellness, and advance healthy lifestyles. Student Affairs builds communities, both real and virtual, that encourage inclusiveness, invite communication, and add to the cultural richness of the institution. We focus on personal development, including career decision making, problem solving, and group dynamics, challenging students to work both independently and as part of a team.

The work group that wrote the strategic plan also composed a defining phrase to encapsulate Student Affairs: "Our passion is complete learning." These, I hope you will agree, are stirring words. We take our responsibility for providing an environment that is inclusive and promotes a healthy lifestyle seriously. We are committed to supporting you as you achieve your goals at this university.

Our Core Values

Sharing a fundamental belief in the value of Student Affairs and its ability to transform lives, we will pursue our vision by

- Focusing on the lifelong learning and personal growth of all members of the university community;
- *Engendering* a community that is inclusive, accessible, and secure;
- Conducting ourselves and our programs with the highest integrity;
- Enhancing our services by creating opportunities to collaborate and nurture partnerships;
- Challenging ourselves to move beyond the *status quo* and pursue higher levels of excellence with determination and enthusiasm;
- Strengthening a tradition of quality, compassion, and an unwavering belief in students and ourselves;
- Demonstrating the innovation and courage to adapt to changing conditions; and
- Realizing that both action and vision are necessary for a better future.

Our society benefits by having everyone educated, and education is a process that requires everyone to be engaged in the advancement of all peoples. The well-being of our state requires the next generation of leaders and scholars to understand our new world. This understanding means looking at the process of education as more than four years in college, the material in textbooks, or the contents of a classroom lecture but as a way to improve the world.

1. Who is the audience for Gonzalez's illustration? What is his purpose?

   The audience is students at the University of Texas at Austin; the purpose is to introduce them to Student Affairs, its strategic plan, and what it offers students.

2. Carefully reread the Four Basics of Good Illustration (p. 143) and decide whether you think Gonzalez's essay is a good example of illustration. Make notes to support your opinion. *Answers will vary.*

3. Use your own experience or do some research on the student services offered by your college. In a sentence or two, compare those services with those Gonzalez refers to in his illustration. *Answers will vary.*

4. In your own words, state what you think Gonzalez says about what a good education is. Does he give good examples? Do you agree with what he says? *Answers will vary.*

A College Illustration Essay

The following is an essay that Tam Nguyen wrote while she was a student at Bunker Hill Community College in Boston, Massachusetts, following a campus visit from the writer Tim O'Brien. Nguyen's essay was published in *Inside Higher Ed* as part of a piece titled "The Story of an Essay."

For more examples of illustration in writing, see Chapter 41.

For the following essay, review the Four Basics of Good Illustration (p. 143) and practice your critical reading process by doing the following.

2PR   The Critical Reading Process

Preview the text, including the guiding question.

Read the text, double-underlining the thesis statement, underlining the major support, and circling the transitions. Consider the quality of the support.

Pause to question and interpret the text. Take notes and write down questions about what you are reading.

Review the text and your notes, and **respond** to it. Write answers to the Pause prompts.

Tam Nguyen

Reflection

Guiding Question   Why does the writer feel such a deep connection to O'Brien?

Vocabulary   The following words are *italicized* in the essay: *concise, devoid, evoked, distorts, deconstruction, combatants, plaguing.* If you do not know their meanings, look them up in a dictionary or online.

1   The author Tim O'Brien came to Bunker Hill Community College for an event hosted by the Veterans Club. The event drew so many people that the A Lounge, where it took place, was overcrowded. People were standing wherever they could find a spot and those who wanted to attend spilled out into the hallway leading to the lounge. Despite the mass of people, the audience was silent. As I came into the room, I was drawn into an invisible circle that trapped me, and the force drawing the audience and me in was Tim O'Brien. He was casually dressed in jeans, a T-shirt, and his favorite baseball cap. He spoke slowly and quietly. Every word he uttered was clear, *concise*, factual, and *devoid* of excess emotion. Each word, however, trapped the audience in an emotion, and besides me, I saw a few others shedding tears from his presentation.

2   I joined the audience in the middle of the event, after finishing up at work. When I came, O'Brien was discussing "The Man I Killed," one of the most famous stories in his novel *The Things They Carried*. "The Man I Killed"

Combining modes
Notice that the author uses narration within her illustration essay.

Pause   What effect does O'Brien have on the audience?

describes O'Brien's reaction when he looked at the dead body of an enemy he just killed. O'Brien looked at the man's wounds and imagined different stories about him. He was a young boy with a typical life who wished every day that the Americans would leave, so he would not have to join the war. The story, at every moment it was discussed, *evoked* many personal feelings and memories from me.

3   It is commonly said that war *distorts* all the values of humanity. War allows only action, which is that a man kills another man, so he will not be killed himself. But to learn this *deconstruction* of humanity from a soldier who was put in a situation where it was either kill or be killed brings the cruelty of war to a new dimension. This extreme situation pushes a human into a dead end; it traps him or her in a corner where the only choice is either to give up on conscience or to die. Why does this type of situation dominate war, when people all across the world are taught not to kill? We understand that when a soldier kills another human, he has a good reason to do so: He is trying to protect himself and survive.

4   However, war causes *combatants* to lose sight of the value of humanity. The act of killing another human crosses a line which devalues the life of another human being. Once the line is crossed, what the soldiers see and feel becomes the hidden part of war that only a soldier, not an outsider, can tell. And this hidden part has been covered in the darkness of war trauma, which Vietnamese and American soldiers all experienced. At least, that is what I found out from my family members and friends.

Pause Why do you think Nguyen's family members avoid telling "specific" war stories?

5   My family has many members who were devoted to the war. They fought and killed to survive and contribute to a Vietnamese victory. They were honored and received many medals and awards which they should be proud of. Yet, besides their accomplishments, I have never heard a specific war story vividly describing a battle.

Pause What, exactly, does the writer want to know from her uncle?

6   For example, my uncle often used words like "we fought," "we won," and "we lost." He never told stories about what actually happened: whom he met, how he fought, or what he thought about the war. In fact, my uncle and the millions of participants, real people, are hidden behind characters. There is a key emotion that is always missing from history texts, novels, and movies, seemingly because no one really knows the truth or they just never tell. I wanted to get the answer from my uncle, but he usually stayed quiet and immersed himself in deep thought whenever I asked him about the battles he participated in. He would never tell me anything, and I could feel that the war created a secret circle around him which would haunt him for the rest of his life.

7   ⟨Another⟩ person that the war will bother for eternity is my friend Arthur. He is an American veteran of the Vietnam War who is devoted to obtaining an education and helping his fellow veterans. After leaving the war, he suffered for many years. In spite of the trauma *plaguing* Arthur, he fights the pain with optimism, which has gotten him through all his days.

Pause What qualities does Arthur illustrate?

8   ⟨One day,⟩ I asked him about his time in Vietnam. He smiled and joked about the "lousy" food he ate and the deep forests he had been through. But just like my uncle, he would not talk about the enemies he faced and how he fought. ⟨Again,⟩ the war remains hidden! How amazing it is that two individuals from two opposite cultures, who fought on opposing sides in a horrible war, share the same feelings.

9   ⟨Throughout⟩ the event, these experiences and connections were running through my head, and the stories were capturing me in the invisible circle. I wondered why, when Tim O'Brien was speaking about his own experiences, I couldn't get away from the similarities to my own experiences. The presentation came to an end, and I decided to stay afterward. I joined the line, which was meant for Tim O'Brien to sign his books, even though I didn't have one of his books and couldn't buy one, either. I just thought that I had to talk to him.

10   ⟨While⟩ I was waiting in line, memories again encircled me, and many thoughts came into my mind. I kept thinking about my grandfather who passed away. He was a general in the American War, and if all the soldiers I know keep the war hidden, my grandfather—who had more war stories than anyone in my family—also had more secrets as well. ⟨Then⟩ my mind wandered to my high school literature teacher who lost her whole family in the war and was disabled by a bomb in 1972. I ⟨also⟩ recalled a taxi driver whom I met last year, who was laughing when he told me that the Vietnam War cost him his two brothers. And right before I got to Tim O'Brien, I thought about my friend Arthur, who came back with a hidden part of his life which he barely shares with others. I wanted to tell Tim O'Brien all I knew and to express to him all my emotions. But once I came up to him all I could say was my name and that with all that I have heard, we, both Vietnamese and Americans, share the same feelings. The moment was unforgettable. We hugged each other, and just like the shared emotions, we both cried.

Pause What is significant about the fact that the author's grandfather was a general? How does it affect her perception?

11   I was drawn to Tim O'Brien by an invisible circle of war experiences and memories, probably because I somehow felt its existence by my own experiences and memories. He was the first one to open up and share such intensive stories of the war, and gave me the emotions that I have been searching for.

Pause What does Nguyen realize when she finally speaks to O'Brien?

I cried hard, as I felt connected to O'Brien and the soldiers on both sides. But above all, it was the greater understanding of my uncle, my grandfather, and Arthur that I appreciated the most. We know that nothing can be changed about the war. Time can never be turned back. There are wounds to be healed and others that won't disappear. However, we move on and find peace of mind by knowing that we at least share the same feelings with someone, somewhere.

Illustration at a glance

Introduction with thesis statement

Says what you want readers to know about the topic

First example

Details about the example

Second example

Details about the example

Third example (often the most powerful)

Details about the example

Conclusion

Reminds readers of the main idea and makes an observation based on it

---

1. **Respond.** Has there ever been a time when you experienced a personal connection with a writer, as Nguyen did?

2. **Summarize.** Briefly summarize Nguyen's essay including her **main idea, purpose,** and the major **examples** she gives. What is her point of view?

3. **Analyze.** Who do you think is the intended audience for Nguyen's essay? Why do you think she takes the time to stop and analyze the idea of war from so many different perspectives? How might the different perspectives affect Nguyen's audience?

4. **Synthesize.** Nguyen says, "It is commonly said that war distorts all the values of humanity. War allows only action, which is that a man kills another man, so he will not be killed himself. But to learn this deconstruction of humanity from a soldier who was put in a situation where it was either kill or be killed brings the cruelty of war to a new dimension." What does this statement mean? Have you ever had to rethink your views on a subject of great importance to you? What happens when we have to rethink something we believe in? How does it affect who we are and what we know?

5. **Evaluate.** Does Nguyen achieve her purpose? Does her essay have the Four Basics of Good Illustration (see p. 143)? What effect did her essay have on you, and why?

Write an Illustration Essay

This section includes four assignments for writing an illustration essay. Use the following tools to help you as you complete one or more of these assignments.

1. Review the Four Basics of Good Illustration (p. 143).

2. Use **Illustration at a Glance** as a basic organizer.

3. Use the Writing Guide: Illustration (p. 157) as you write and revise.

WRITING ASSIGNMENT 1	**Writing an illustration essay: suggested topics**

Write an illustration essay on one of the following topics or on a topic of your own choice.

College
- Write about what you expect to get out of college.
- Write about something you learned in another course, and give examples to explain it to a friend who has not taken the course.

Work
- Tell someone applying for a job like yours what his or her typical responsibilities might be.
- Demonstrate to an interviewer the following statement: "I am a detail-oriented employee."

Everyday life
- Write a letter to your landlord about how your apartment's maintenance needs to be done more regularly.
- Name the most influential person in your life, and give examples of his or her characteristics.

WRITING ASSIGNMENT 2	**Writing about an image**

© SETH JOEL/THE IMAGE BANK/GETTY IMAGES

The image shows a teacher applauding a student doing a presentation for the class. Teachers have to work with students who learn in different ways and have different backgrounds. Think about your own experiences in school, and write an illustration essay that identifies the qualities of a good teacher.

| WRITING ASSIGNMENT 3 | **Writing to solve a problem**

Problem A good friend of yours is being sexually harassed at work by a supervisor who is not her boss. Although she has let the supervisor know that the advances are not welcome, the offending behaviors have not stopped. Your friend is afraid that if she complains to her boss, she will be fired. She asks your advice about what to do.

Assignment Working on your own or with a small group, give your friend some advice about how she could handle the problem. Try to give her several good resources to think about or use; include resources that her company might offer.

Resources Review the chart on pages 708–709 for tips about problem solving. Also, check some Web sites for ideas about dealing with sexual harassment. You can start by typing *advice on sexual harassment* into a search engine. List any Web sites you use. Be sure to cite and document any sources you use in your papers. For advice, see Chapter 20.

| WRITING ASSIGNMENT 4 | **Writing about readings**

Choose one of the following options:

- Read Kathleen Vail's essay, "Words That Wound" (p. 599), and review Juan C. Gonzalez's piece on pages 148–50. Write a short essay explaining how schools can affect the quality of students' lives. Give examples of both positive and negative effects, drawing from Vail's essay and your own experience. You might want to write a thesis that makes use of Gonzalez's phrase "where life and learning intersect."

- Study the TRiO/Student Support Services Web page (pp. 211–12), written by Angell Davis and her colleagues, and read Monique Rizer's essay "When Students Are Parents" (p. 587). Write a letter to Davis that gives examples of programs that TRiO/Student Support Services could add to or improve in its lineup. How could the programs you propose serve the students Rizer is addressing? Include examples from your own experience, too.

Use the steps in the Writing Guide that follows to help you prewrite, draft, revise, and edit your illustration. Check off each step as you complete it.

WRITING GUIDE: ILLUSTRATION

Steps in Illustration	How to do the steps
Focus.	• Think about your topic and what your audience knows about it.
Explore your topic. See Chapter 5.	• Prewrite to give examples of your topic.
Write a thesis statement. Topic + main idea = Thesis See Chapter 6.	• Write a working thesis statement that includes your topic and main idea about it. You might also include some examples you will give in your support paragraphs.
Support your thesis. See Chapter 7.	• Choose at least three examples that demonstrate your main idea. • Consider what details about the examples your reader needs to know.
Write a draft. See Chapter 8.	• Arrange your examples in order of importance or time. • Write topic sentences for each major example. • Write a paragraph for each example, giving details about the examples.
Revise your draft. See Chapter 9.	• Make sure that your examples and details all relate to your main idea. • Add transitions. • Improve your introduction, thesis, and conclusion.
Edit your revised draft. See Parts 5 through 8.	• Correct errors in grammar, spelling, word use, and punctuation.
Evaluate your writing.	• Does it have the Four Basics of Good Illustration (p. 143)? • Ask yourself: Is this the best I can do?

12

Description

Writing That Creates Pictures in Words

Understand What Description Is

Description is writing that creates a clear and vivid impression of the topic. Description translates your experience of a person, place, or thing into words, often by appealing to the senses—sight, hearing, smell, taste, and touch.

Four Basics of Good Description

1	It creates a main impression—an overall effect, feeling, or image—about the topic.
2	It uses specific examples to support the main impression.
3	It supports those examples with details that appeal to the five senses.
4	It brings a person, place, or object to life for the reader.

In the following paragraph, each number corresponds to one of the Four Basics of Good Description.

1 Nojoqui Falls is a special place to me because its beauty provides a break from human worries. **2** At the start of the trail leading to the falls, the smell and sound of oak trees and pine trees make visitors feel they are up for the journey. **3** The sun hitting the trees makes the air fresh with a leafy aroma. Overhead, the wind blows through the leaves, making a soft noise. **2** Closer to the waterfall, the shade from the trees creates a shielding blanket. When the sun comes out, it fills the place with light, showing the vapor coming out of the trees and plants. To the left of the trail are rocks that are positioned perfectly for viewing the waterfall. **3** Water splashes as it hits

4 All the details bring the falls to life.

the rocks. **2** The waterfall itself is beautiful, like a transparent, sparkling window of diamonds. **3** The water is so clear that objects on the other side are visible. It is like a never-ending stream of water that splashes onto the rocks. **1** The total effect of these sights, sounds, and smells is a setting where daily cares can be set aside for a while.

4 All the details bring the falls to life.

—Liliana Ramirez, student

Contexts for Description

As with other kinds of writing, it is important to keep **audience** and **purpose** firmly in mind as you write description. The following are some questions you may want to consider:

- Who would want to read this description and why?
- What does your audience already know about the topic? What else do they need to know?
- What kinds of description are likely to be most effective for them?

Then, when you know who your audience will be, you need to consider your own purpose for writing your description. Broadly, your purpose is to describe your topic in such a way that it comes alive for your audience. The following questions may help you decide what else you want them to gain from your description:

- Do you want them to learn something?
- Do you want them to simply share your experience?
- Do you want them to be entertained?
- Do you have another purpose in mind?

Main Idea in Description

In descriptive writing, your **main idea** conveys the overall impression you want to give your readers.

Take another look at the paragraph starting on page 158. What if the topic sentence were written as follows:

I love Nojoqui Falls.

You would not know why the writer likes the place. But the actual topic sentence conveys a main impression of the falls and lets you know why this place is important to the writer:

Nojoqui Falls is a special place to me because its beauty provides a break from human worries.

This statement provides a preview of what is to come, helping the audience read and understand the description.

The thesis statement in description essays typically includes the topic and the main impression about it that the writer wants to convey.

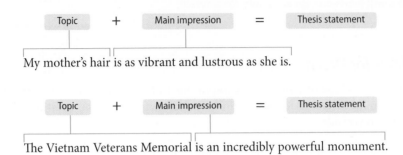

My mother's hair is as vibrant and lustrous as she is.

The Vietnam Veterans Memorial is an incredibly powerful monument.

Support in Description

Good description uses specific, concrete details to create the sights, sounds, smells, tastes, and textures that support and show your main impression.

Sight	Sound	Smell
Colors	Loud/soft	Sweet/sour
Shapes	Piercing/soothing	Sharp/mild
Sizes	Continuous/off-and-on	Good (like what?)
Patterns	Pleasant/unpleasant (how?)	Bad (rotten?)
Brightness	High/low	New (like what?)
Does it look like anything else?	Does it sound like anything else?	Does it smell like anything else?

Taste	Touch
Good (What does *good* taste like?)	Hard/soft
Bad (What does *bad* taste like?)	Liquid/solid
Bitter/sugary	Rough/smooth
Metallic	Dry/oily
Burning/spicy	Textures
Does it taste like anything else?	Does it feel like anything else?

As you think about the main impression you want to convey, ask yourself: What sensory details might bring this subject to life? Add additional details to convey each sensation more accurately or vividly.

For example, one student wrote this thesis statement:

When I wear my grandmother's old coat, she is standing beside me.

To support this main impression, the writer might include sensory details about the smell of the coat (*sweet like Grandma's perfume, with a faint odor of mothballs and home-baked bread*); the feel of the fabric (*nubby and rough, with some smooth spots where the fabric has worn thin*); and the candy in the pocket (*single pieces of butterscotch that rustle in their wrappings and a round cylinder that is a roll of wintergreen Life Savers*).

Organization in Description

Description may use any of the orders of organization, depending on the purpose of the description. If you are describing what someone or something looks like, you might use **spatial order,** the most common way to organize description. If you are describing something you want to sell, you might use **order of importance,** ending with the feature that would be most appealing to potential buyers.

Use transitions to help readers move smoothly from detail to detail.

Teaching tip Have students bring in descriptions of interesting places from books or newspapers. The Travel section of the *New York Times* (available at www.nytimes.com/pages/travel/index.html) often has such descriptions.

Teamwork Have students, working in small groups, choose an object from one group member's book bag or briefcase and agree on a main impression to use in describing that object.

Common Transitions in Description

Transitions to show spatial order	Transitions to show order of importance
above/underneath	even more
beyond	more
in front of/behind	the most
to the left/right	the most intense
	the strongest

Read and Analyze Description

Before writing your description essay, read the following examples—one from the workplace and one from college—and answer the questions that accompany them.

For more examples of description, see Chapter 42.

Profile of Success
Description in the Real World

Alex Espinoza
Writer and Associate Professor, California State University, Fresno

Background   I was born in Mexico, the youngest of eleven children. My father was an alcoholic who died when I was in high school. I didn't do well in school and was placed in the automotive program, where I barely passed my classes. At San Bernardino Community College, I discovered both writing and the Puente Project. In writing, I found my voice; in Puente, I found people who encouraged me academically. Although I had a low GPA, I had good recommendations and good grades in writing, so I was accepted at the University of California, Riverside, which has a great writing program. I then went on to get a master's degree in creative writing at the University of California, Irvine, which, although I didn't know it at the time, has one of the most selective creative writing programs in the country. My first novel,

Still Water Saints, was published in 2007, and I have a contract for a second one.

Writing at work   My job is writing and teaching writing, so I'm always writing. Here's some advice I always give my students: When you write, you are putting yourself on the page, and you can control how you are perceived. If you ignore the conventions of writing (like grammar, spelling, and punctuation), you will in turn be ignored by those whose attention you want.

How Alex uses description   In my own writing, I have to create vivid scenes for my readers. In my teaching, I help students form vivid images in their own writing.

For an example of Alex Espinoza's descriptive writing, see page 605.

Workplace Description

Done for a course in child development, this observational study emulates the kinds of professional observation carried out by teachers, social workers, and others who work with children.

Kimberly Lake

Sample Observation of a Developmentally Impaired Child

Guiding question What is the purpose of recording these specific details?

Vocabulary The following words are *italicized* in the essay: *Caucasian, siblings, co-parenting, phonetic, cognitive, deformities,* and *disposition.* If you do not know their meanings, look them up in a dictionary or online.

Introduction to Subject

Rena is a 4-year-old *Caucasian* female, with curly brown hair and green eyes. Rena is 31 inches tall and weighs 30 pounds.

Rena is experiencing delayed speech. I have known Rena's mother for 15 years and have frequent contact with her and the children.

Individual Functioning Level with the Physical Environment

Rena is not in preschool yet. She does interact normally with her siblings and friends. Rena deals well with her environment and gets along with others easily.

Rena lives with her mother, a 23-year-old female, and 2 female *siblings*, ages 1 and 6. They all live in an apartment on the northwest side of Fresno. The mother is a full-time student. Rena has a close relationship with her father, and the *co-parenting* is very effective between her two parents.

Rena enjoys playing outside. She loves animals and is very happy to interact with adults as well. Rena is very coordinated and enjoys dancing and climbing. She enjoys many physical activities and seems to avoid activities that include sitting, for example, watching television.

Social Skills: Ability to Function with People

Rena is very confident and outgoing. She has a healthy level of self-esteem and is able to engage in individualized tasks as well as group activities.

Rena is a very likable child. She gets along well with others and is extremely affectionate. She has a bright smile and is very patient when attempting to communicate.

Rena has many friends and is treated fairly by her siblings. Her oldest sister tends to Rena's needs during play and returns affection readily. Rena is very determined when she has a goal. Rena has to be reminded to share, and at times refuses to share.

After getting to know Rena, people like her and attend to her needs; they treat her with respect and patience when she is attempting communication.

Intelligence

Rena has delayed speech development. She understands simple directions and communication appropriate with her age group. She says 15 words and is far below expected performance. Rena has a difficult time with the *phonetic* sounds of words. In the last 3 months she has showed great improvement in her speech, adding about 5 words to her vocabulary. She is also learning sign language to help her communicate more easily.

Rena's father has a similar history of speech delay. He is able to speak a wide range of words, although not as clearly as would be expected.

Individualization

With proper speech therapy and the use of sign language I expect Rena to be able to learn to communicate at a normal level. She seems to understand when spoken to at an expected *cognitive* level for her age. I expect that she will be able to overcome her disability and function on a normal level as an adult with the help of sign language and phonetic practice. If Rena works hard and has the correct assistance, I believe she is capable of being successful in K–12 and on to college. I suggest that Rena should be examined for any physical *deformities* in her mouth that may be contributing to her difficulty in speech.

I have known Rena since birth and have seen her improve tremendously in the past few months. Because of her special need she has been catered to by her family and friends, and she tends to want her way at times and has not learned that she has boundaries and rules she needs to adhere to. As she matures, I am sure she will understand these. Rena is a beautiful girl with a wonderful and confident personality. She has a joyful *disposition*, and I believe she will have many friends when she attends school.

1. Briefly summarize this observation. Who is Lake observing and what specific qualities is she describing in this observation? *Answers will vary but should include the ideas that she is observing a 4-year-old named Rena. She is observing individual functioning with the environment, social skills, intelligence, and individualization.*

2. What is the purpose of this descriptive observation? *Answers will vary but should indicate that the writer is recording Rena's development.*

3. Does Lake use the five senses when she is writing her observation? If so, which ones does she use? Which ones doesn't she use? Should she use any senses that she leaves out? Why or why not? *Lake includes Rena's ability to speak, hear, and touch. Other answers will vary.*

4. Do you think Lake has written a complete and thorough observation that is descriptive enough to be helpful for someone who has never met Rena? If yes, why do you think so? If no, what do you think may be missing?

Answers will vary.

A College Description Essay

A student wrote the following essay for a college writing course. The assignment was "Write an essay describing an important event in your life."

For the following essay, review the Four Basics of Good Description (p. 158) and practice your critical reading process by doing the following.

2PR   The Critical Reading Process

Preview the text, including the guiding question.

Read the text, double-underlining the thesis statement, underlining the major support, and circling the transitions. Consider the quality of the support.

Pause to question and interpret the text. Take notes and write down questions about what you are reading.

Review the text and your notes, and **respond** to it. Write answers to the Pause prompts.

Kimberly Kirwan

Volunteering for a Fallen Soldier

Guiding question What is the main impression that Kirwan wants to share with her readers?

Vocabulary The following words are *italicized* in the essay: *squad, slated, adorned, dismounted, pronounced,* and *mourning.* If you do not know their meanings, look them up in a dictionary or online.

1   I am a member of the Tazewell Military Rites Team, a *squad* of approximately twenty members who attend veterans' funerals as volunteers. The

squad consists of six to eight flagbearers and six riflebearers. We stand in a strict order beside each other determined by the flags we hold, and we wear black shoes, black slacks, white shirts with black ties, and white gloves. On our left breasts, we wear a patch of the United States flag, and on our right arm, a patch that has "TMRT" on it. Some of the members wear additional patches that state what branch of the armed forces they served in. We volunteer out of a desire to honor the service of the soldiers and to show respect for their memory—something I believe more Americans should do.

Pause: What is the purpose of this description?

2   On Thursday afternoon at 11:15 a.m. I was due to meet my team at the VFW hall for the funeral of a fallen soldier. When we arrived at the VFW, we talked briefly about what the day would bring. As I looked around, I noticed that not everyone was there yet, so I quietly asked our commander, "What time is the funeral?" He replied, "We should be there around noon. The service starts at 12:30." I went to the table and asked the group if we should start loading the bus with the equipment. They agreed, so I unlocked the closet where the rifles and flags were kept and we began to empty it.

Combining modes Note that this descriptive essay is also a narrative with elements of a process analysis.

3   The ride to the site was very quiet. I looked around at my fellow volunteers as we rode. There were only two women on this particular day, myself and another. I was *slated* to hold the red flag for the United States Marine Corps, where I served, and she was set to carry the blue flag for the Army, where she served. The weather outside seemed to suit the events of the day: It was cold and misty, a typical day in late October. The dying leaves on the trees were dull orange and gold.

Pause: Are the events in this essay specific enough to make you feel like you are there with the writer?

4   When we arrived at the cemetery, the commander placed the six flag holders an arm's length apart, and then proceeded to do the same with the riflemen. As I looked around, I saw the family and friends of the deceased soldier arriving slowly one by one. Then, in the distance, I heard a low rumbling sound. Sometimes it's hard to know what you are hearing when you are way out in the fields, but when I turned around to look, I saw that the Patriot Riders were making their way to the entrance. Each rider had *adorned* his or her bike with American flags, which were now vibrant and waving happily as if in celebration. The Riders who arrived first lined their bikes up in a row, patiently waiting until all had arrived; then each person *dismounted* slowly and stood beside their flags—respectfully and with honor.

5   At 12:30, word spread that the service was about to start. The commander yelled, "Present arms!" We then carried our flags forward, and the minister began her service. After she *pronounced* her blessings, she turned to us; that was our riflemen's cue for the six-gun salute. The commander roared, "Ready, aim, fire!" The rifles went off with a crack so loud that it startled me, though I knew it was coming. The commander repeated his order two additional times, and when the report was finished, out in the distance, there came the sound of a serviceman playing the taps, a haunting melody played on a trumpet as a salute to the fallen soldier. <u>Standing there with my flag, listening to the music and watching the flags gently wave in the breeze, I felt shivers run up and down my spine. When I looked around, I saw relief on some faces that this soldier had served his time and was at peace now.</u> Others were clearly still *mourning*.

Pause: Which of the five senses does Kirwan use to describe the experience?

6   <u>This service moves me every time I take part; I get teary-eyed as I show my respect for the fallen soldiers' work and their service. Not many people understand what being a soldier is all about, but soldiers are doing and have done a lot for our country. I only wish more citizens would take the time to reflect on what they do.</u>

Pause: What sentence ties the conclusion to the thesis statement?

1. **Respond.** Respond to Kirwan's essay. What are your reactions to it? What did you learn about it or what do you feel after reading it?

2. **Summarize.** Briefly summarize Kirwan's essay. What were the main events or details?

3. **Analyze.** Remember that a description should have a main impression, use specific examples to support that impression, and use the five senses to bring that impression to life. What is the main impression Kirwan wants her readers to feel? Does she use specific examples and the five senses to help bring that image or impression to life for the readers? Were you able to visualize the event Kirwan described?

4. **Synthesize.** Do you have any experience with this topic? Is your experience similar or different? How does your own experience, or lack of experience, affect the way you read this essay?

5. **Evaluate.** Is Kirwan successful in her purpose? Does she convey her main impression and make you feel as though you are experiencing this event with her? Does the essay have the Four Basics of Good Description (see p. 158)? What do you think of the essay?

Description at a glance

```
┌─────────────────────┐
│ Introduction with   │
│ thesis statement    │
│                     │
│ Gives a main        │
│ impression          │
└─────────────────────┘
          ↓
┌─────────────────────┐
│ First major         │
│ sensory detail      │
│ Supporting details  │
└─────────────────────┘
          ↓
┌─────────────────────┐
│ Second major        │
│ sensory detail      │
│ Supporting details  │
└─────────────────────┘
          ↓
┌─────────────────────┐
│ Most important      │
│ sensory detail      │
│ Supporting details  │
└─────────────────────┘
          ↓
┌─────────────────────┐
│ Conclusion          │
│ Reminds readers     │
│ of the main         │
│ impression          │
│ Makes an            │
│ observation         │
└─────────────────────┘
```

Write a Description Essay

This section includes four assignments for writing a description essay. Use the following tools to help you as you complete one or more of these assignments.

1. Review the Four Basics of Good Description (p. 158).
2. Use **Description at a Glance** as a basic organizer.
3. Use the Writing Guide: Description (p. 171) as you write and revise.

WRITING ASSIGNMENT 1   **Writing a description essay: suggested topics**

Write a description essay on one of the following topics or on a topic of your own choice.

College
- Describe your favorite place on campus so that a reader understands why you like to be there.
- Describe an event or a setting that you learned about in one of your courses.

Work
- Describe a product your company makes or a service it provides.
- Describe a specific area at work that you see every day but have not really noticed. Look at it with new eyes.

Everyday life
- Describe a favorite photograph.
- Describe a favorite food without naming it. Include how it looks, smells, and tastes; also include what it means to you.

WRITING ASSIGNMENT 2   **Writing about an image**

Write a descriptive essay about the ivy-covered brick wall in the image on page 169. When thinking about the image, remember to use your five senses. What overall impression do the colors give you? How would it feel? Would it be rough or would it be smooth and worn down by the wind? What do you imagine the brick wall would taste like, if you were to actually taste it? Think carefully about the words you choose to describe the image and bring it to life for your readers. Help them think about it in a new way. Be sure to use plenty of details.

WRITING ASSIGNMENT 3   ## Writing to solve a problem

Problem A wealthy alumna has given your college money for a new student lounge. The college president has selected a group of students (including you) to advise him on the lounge and has asked that the group be as specific as possible in its recommendations.

Assignment Working on your own or, preferably, in a small group, write a description of an ideal student lounge to send to the president. Be sure to think about what various purposes the lounge should serve, where it should be located, what it should have in it, and what it should look like.

Resources Review the chart on pages 708–709 for advice about problem solving. Also, search the Web using the words *student lounges* and *design*. You might also go to the library and look for design or architecture books and magazines. List any Web sites or publications that you consult.

WRITING ASSIGNMENT 4   ## Writing about readings

The assignments that follow ask you to read one or more different descriptions and draw from them to write an essay.

- Read Rui Dai's essay "A Whiff of Memory" (p. 229) and Alex Espinoza's essay "Easy Like Sunday Morning" (p. 605). Both of these essays use food and smell as part of the description. Write your own description that focuses on a family meal, a particular food, or a smell that always reminds you of a particular event, memory, or person.

• Read Peter Van Buren's essay "The Day after a Day at the Embassy" (p. 611) and Brent Staples's "Just Walk On By" (p. 669). Even though these experiences took place in different parts of the world, both involved a sense of displacement or a feeling that something was surreal. Even though things appeared to be normal, for some reason the writer was able to step back and look at things in a different way for a short time due to a catalyst. In other words, there was an event that allowed the writer to step back and actually look at the place and surroundings in a different way. Write a descriptive essay about the power of a place, drawing from both of these essays and your own experiences.

• Read Tam Nguyen's essay "Reflection" (p. 151) and Kim Kirwan's essay "Volunteering for a Fallen Soldier" (p. 165). Both describe the experience of being a veteran in different ways. Write a descriptive essay about perspective. Nguyen learned that everyone she spoke to had a different way of thinking about war and being a soldier. Kirwan feels the same. Write a descriptive essay that highlights the fact that many people can feel differently about the same experience. Make sure to include your own experiences as well as ideas from these essays.

Use the steps in the Writing Guide that follows to help you prewrite, draft, revise, and edit your description. Check off each step as you complete it.

WRITING GUIDE: DESCRIPTION

Steps in Description	How to do the steps
Focus.	• Think about what you want to describe and who your readers are.
Explore your topic. See Chapter 5.	• Make sure your topic can be described in a short essay. • Prewrite to generate sensory images and details.
Write a thesis statement. Topic + Main impression = Thesis See Chapter 6.	• Decide your purpose for writing a description and what picture you want to create for your readers.
Support your thesis. See Chapter 7.	• Add images and details that will bring what you are describing to life for your audience. • Use your senses to create the images.
Write a draft. See Chapter 8.	• Arrange your main idea and the images that help create it in a logical order. • Write topic sentences for the supporting images and details that show them.
Revise your draft. See Chapter 9.	• Reread your essay, adding vivid details. • Add transitions to help show your reader your main impression of your topic. • Improve your introduction, thesis, and conclusion.
Edit your revised draft. See Parts 5 through 8.	• Correct errors in grammar, spelling, word use, and punctuation.
Evaluate your writing.	• Does it have the Four Basics of Good Description (p. 158)? • Ask yourself: Is this the best I can do?

13

Process Analysis
Writing That Explains How Things Happen

Understand What Process Analysis Is

Process analysis explains either how to do something (so your readers can do it) or how something works (so your readers can understand it). Both types of process analysis present the steps involved in the process.

Four Basics of Good Process Analysis

1 It helps readers either perform the steps or understand how something works.

2 It presents the essential steps in the process.

3 It explains the steps in detail.

4 It arranges the steps in a logical order (usually in chronological order).

In the following paragraph, each number corresponds to one of the Four Basics of Good Process Analysis.

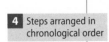
4 Steps arranged in chronological order

1 Two teenagers, Robbie and Brittany Bergquist, wanted to help American soldiers in combat zones call home, so in 2004 they founded the organization Cell Phones for Soldiers, which has proved to be extremely successful. 2 First, Robbie and Brittany pooled their own money, a total of $14. Realizing that would not go far, they then decided to hold fund-raising events. 3 Next, they enlisted friends and family to help them organize a

series of bake sales and car washes. As people learned about their efforts, more joined them, and they began to raise serious money to purchase phones. **2** Second, they started another fund-raising initiative: recycling old cell phones. **3** They collected old phones and brought them to a recycling company. **3** With this money, they purchased minutes on phone cards for the soldiers. **3** Then, they organized volunteers to wrap and send the cards to soldiers who had heard about their work and had contacted them. **2** To date, they have provided over 60 million minutes of phone time. Robbie and Brittany continue their efforts to include not only soldiers overseas but also returning veterans who are in the hospital.

4 Steps arranged in chronological order

Contexts for Process Analysis

Considering the context for a process analysis is important in determining your **audience** and **purpose.** You would use a process analysis when you want to help your readers understand the steps involved in a procedure. Think of it like a how-to guide. Your audience typically wants to read a process analysis either because they want to know the steps involved in how to do something or because they want to understand how something works. Therefore, when you are thinking about your audience, carefully consider the following:

- How old are they and what do they already know about the topic?
- What else do they want or need to know about the topic?
- Do they have experience with the topic, or is it new to them?

Once you have clearly identified your audience, you need to consider what they expect from you as a writer. In other words, what is your purpose?

- Do you want to explain how something works?
- Do you want to give step-by-step instructions?
- Do you want to provide in-depth information?

Once you know who your reader is and what information you want to give, you can begin to draft your paper.

Whenever you write directions or explain how something works, you are using process analysis. Here are some ways you might use process analysis.

College	In an information technology course, you write an essay explaining the process for implementing a new data management system.

Work	The office has a new security system, and you are asked to write a memo to employees explaining how to access their work areas during and after normal business hours.
Everyday life	You write directions telling your child how to operate the washing machine.

Main Idea in Process Analysis

Your **purpose** in process analysis is to explain a process so that the **audience** can either do it themselves or understand how it works. Your **main idea** in process analysis lets your audience know what you think about the topic—for example, whether a process is easy or complicated:

> Google Maps can get you from where you are to where you want to go in several easy steps.

A thesis statement for a process analysis usually identifies the process and the point you want to make about it. The thesis should also suggest what you want your audience to know or learn about the process.

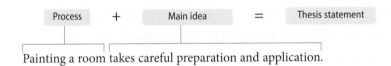

Painting a room takes careful preparation and application.

    In process analysis, include your thesis statement in your introduction so that the audience knows from the start what the process and the purpose are.

Support in Process Analysis

A clear process analysis presents all the essential steps in the process; these steps constitute the **major support.** Each step is explained by supporting details. For example, the writer of the thesis *Running a 5K may be very difficult, but anyone can start with a few simple steps* might use the following essential steps and details to explain the steps.

Essential Steps

    Step 1: Start by doing some light walking.

        Supporting Details

        Any exercise is good for you.

        Begin a routine that you can stick to.

Twenty minutes three times a week is a good start.

Your heart and muscles will start to get used to the exercise.

Step 2: After a week or two of walking, start to incorporate some light jogging.

Supporting Details

Warm up for 5 minutes with a brisk walk.

Try to jog for about 1 minute.

After jogging, walk for 2 minutes, and then jog again.

Continue to alternate for half an hour.

Step 3: Continue alternating your jogging and walking times until you build up to more jogging than walking.

Supporting Details

Eventually, you may start trying to jog certain distances rather than times.

Listen to your body and do what it can handle.

Make sure to always warm up and cool down.

Step 4: After approximately 9 weeks, you should be able to manage a 5k, or 3-mile, run.

Supporting Details

Runners will reach this goal at their own pace.

Remember that any brisk and regular exercise is good for your body.

Make sure to include all of the essential steps in the process, particularly if you want your audience to be able to do something using only your instructions. Read the following process analysis example. What essential step is missing?

Teamwork Have students, in pairs, discuss whether any other steps are missing.

Please do the laundry before I get home. The clothes are in the baskets next to the machine. One of the baskets has all dark clothes. Put these in the washing machine, with the heaviest, biggest items on the bottom. You can fill the machine to the top, but do not mash the clothes down. (If you put in too many clothes, the machine will stall.) After all of the clothes are in, set the level on Extra High. Then, turn the knob on the left to Warm Wash, Cool Rinse. Press the Start button. After about half an hour, the laundry should be done, and you can transfer it to the dryer.

Missing step: *These directions cover loading the machine and operating it, but they leave out adding the soap.*

Organization in Process Analysis

Because process analysis explains how to do something or how something works, it usually uses **chronological (time) order.** Start with the first step, and then explain each step in order.

Add transitional words and sentences to your essay to help readers follow the process.

Common Transitions in Process Analysis

after	eventually	meanwhile	soon
as	finally	next	then
at last	first	now	when
before	last	second	while
during	later	since	

Read and Analyze Process Analysis

Before writing a process analysis essay, read the following examples—one from the workplace and one from college—and answer the questions that accompany them.

Profile of Success
Process Analysis in the Real World

Melissa Erb

Counselor at a County Sheriff's Office

Background   I was a mediocre student in high school and did not have an interest in applying to colleges. However, my older sister went to community college, so I did, too. I didn't have an exact idea of where I wanted to go or what I wanted to do with my life, so community college was a good option for me. Shortly after starting, I surprised myself by finding the courses I was taking interesting, so I applied myself in each course. Early on, I took a few courses that discussed disparities in the world—topics such as hunger, racism, uneven wealth distribution, and injustice. I identified personally with some of these disparities because I was raised by a single mother. This triggered my interest in helping and empowering people whose circumstances made it difficult for them to help themselves.

After four years, I completed my associate's degree and then transferred to a four-year college, where I majored in psychology and minored in political science. With only a bachelor's degree, I had some trouble finding a satisfying job directly working with people, so I went on to get my master's degree in social work. I had two internships while getting my master's— one in child welfare, working in foster care, and the other in mental health, working in an intensive outpatient program as a therapist. I became a licensed social worker and currently work in my county's jail as a counselor. It's my job to prevent suicide and provide mental health services to inmates.

Writing at work   Among other responsibilities, I make regular progress notes containing observations of inmates' mental health status, comments about my counseling sessions with inmates, and recommendations for treatment.

How Melissa uses process analysis   My progress notes need to be clear, concise, and accurate so that personnel from other disciplines (attorneys, judges, counselors, and medical staff) can rely on them. This is particularly important because all writings about an inmate's mental health can be used in court, and, during a trial or appeal, counselors can be subpoenaed to answer questions about ambiguous information.

Workplace Process Analysis

The following is a progress report Melissa Erb wrote for one of her inmates, a thirty-four-year-old male with frequent suicidal tendencies. He was a victim of childhood abuse and has a history of traumatic brain injury. He has exhibited ongoing polysubstance abuse outside of jail and has been incarcerated for nine months.

Guiding question Why is it so important for Erb to record not only the order of the events during the meeting but also the specific details?

Vocabulary The following words are *italicized* in the excerpt: *euthymic, congruent, mania, deterrents, incarceration, referral, resilience*. If you do not know their meanings, look them up in a dictionary or online.

Progress Report

1. **IM:** inmate
2. **MHR:** mental health referral
3. **PO:** post officer

IM[1] was seen in building 1 due to MHR[2] from the PO[3] stating that the IM asked him "How do you know if you are *really* depressed?" The IM presented as calm, cooperative, friendly, and responsive to counselor with *euthymic* mood, *congruent* affect and speech. IM stated that he has been feeling very depressed lately but has been having moments of *mania* where he stays up all night and draws pictures and does not remember drawing them. IM reported still planning on committing suicide once he leaves jail when he is "free as a bird" in the woods but has no intention of doing it here. When asked why not here, IM reported that he would not do that to staff and that he wants to be free when he does it. IM

4. **TBI:** traumatic brain injury
5. **Hx:** history

has a TBI[4] Hx,[5] most recent in 2011. IM did not report any *deterrents* to suicide except current *incarceration*. Discussed IM's *resiliency* and to focus on positive. IM is currently taking 20 mg of Celexa for his depression, but current presentation does not match with IM's reports of depression (possible bipolar?). A chart review will be ordered to evaluate current meds and possible increase or change.

6. **SI:** suicide ideation
7. **CFU:** counselor follow-up

IM agreed to tell PO if thoughts of SI[6] increase or he thinks about doing it in jail. CFU[7] scheduled in 3 days to evaluate for current SI.

The Process of Writing a Progress Report

First, an officer submitted a mental health referral for the inmate, reporting that the inmate asked the officer, "How do you know when you are *really* depressed?" [Officers are trained to report serious concerns of mental health issues to the counselors. If it is not an emergency, then the officers ask the inmate to write an interoffice letter to the counselors.] The mental health *referral* further stated that the inmate appeared depressed and that he felt concerned for his safety (from self-harm).

Next, I saw the inmate a few hours after receiving the referral. The inmate and I discussed his depression. When I saw him two days prior he had just started some antidepressant medications and had been elated and happy. He now stated that they were not working for him and that he was having thoughts of committing suicide when he leaves jail. We discussed evidence of his past *resilience* and a safety plan: If thoughts recur, we will move inmate to safer environment. We also made a plan for working with the staff psychiatrist to reevaluate his medication. Inmate verbally agreed to tell an officer or counselor immediately if he has active thoughts of suicide.

I then returned to my office, printed the mental health referral, and signed it as completed. I wrote a progress note (see above) containing the information about our conversation and our plans for safety. I requested a psychiatric appointment for the inmate, asking for a review of his medications as soon as possible. Lastly, I sent an e-mail to my colleague who works on the weekend asking her to review my notes and visit him this weekend. I will follow up with the psychiatrist and inmate next week to discuss how the plan is working and will continue to document future interactions.

1. A process analysis typically is a step-by-step explanation of how to do something or an explanation to help someone understand something. What is the purpose of Erb's report? <u>*Answers will vary.*</u>

2. Note that a process analysis contains elements of other types of writing. What other modes does Erb use to write her report about the inmate? <u>*Answers will vary but should indicate some elements of narrative and descrip-*</u> <u>*tion in the report.*</u>

3. How would the report differ if its purpose were to teach counselors how to speak to inmates? <u>*It would give more details about the treatment.*</u>

4. Write a possible **thesis statement** for the report. <u>*Answers will vary.*</u>

5. Write a possible **concluding statement.** <u>*Answers will vary.*</u>

A College Process Analysis Essay

For the following essay, review the Four Basics of Good Process Analysis (p. 172) and practice your critical reading process by doing the following.

For more examples of process analysis, see Chapter 43.

Teamwork Have students work through the first essay together to apply the 2PR Critical Reading Process and answer the questions after the essay.

2PR The Critical Reading Process

Preview the text, including the guiding question.

Read the text, double-underlining the thesis statement, underlining the major support, and circling the transitions. Consider the quality of the support.

Pause to question and interpret the text. Take notes and write down questions about what you are reading.

Review the text and your notes, and **respond** to it. Write answers to the Pause prompts.

Daniel Flanagan

The Choice to Do It Over Again

Guiding question What did Flanagan do over?

Combining modes
Note that the essay is both a process analysis and a narration. It also presents causes and effects.

Vocabulary The following words are *italicized* in the essay: *degenerate, spiral, consequence, fragile, shortcomings.* If you do not know their meanings, look them up in a dictionary or online.

1   I do not know why I came to the decision to become a loser, but I know I made the choice at a young age. Sometime in the middle of fourth grade, I stopped trying. By the time I was in seventh grade, I was your typical *degenerate*: lazy, rebellious, disrespectful. I had lost all social graces. I was terminally hip and fatally cool.

2   Not long after that, I dropped out of school and continued my downward *spiral*. Hard physical labor was the *consequence* for the choices I made as an adolescent. At the age of twenty-one, I was hopelessly lost and using drugs as a way to deal with the fact that I was illiterate and stuck in a dead-end job carrying roof shingles up a ladder all day.

Pause What does the second sentence mean?

3   But now I believe in do-overs, in the chance to do it all again. And I believe that do-overs can be made at any point in your life, if you have the right motivation. Mine came from a surprising source.

Pause Why did Flanagan decide to change his life?

4   It was September 21, 2002, when my son Blake was born. It's funny that after a life of avoiding responsibility, now I was in charge of something so *fragile*. Over the years, as I grew into the title of Dad, I began to learn something about myself. In a way, Blake and I were both learning to walk, talk, work, and play for the first time. I began my do-over.

Pause Underline the steps in Flanagan's do-over.

5   It took me almost three years to learn how to read. I started with my son's books. Over and over, I practiced reading books to him until I remembered all the words in every one of them. I began to wonder if it was possible for me to go back to school. I knew I wanted to be a good

role model, so after a year and a half and a lot of hard work, <u>I passed my</u> <u>GED[1] test on my son's fourth birthday.</u> This may not sound like much, and I am not trying to get praise for doing something that should have been done in the first place, but all things considered it was one of the best days in my life. Today, <u>I am a full-time college student, studying to become a sociologist.</u>

6   Growing up, I always heard these great turn-around stories of triumph over *shortcomings*. But I never thought they applied to me. Now I believe it is a choice anyone can make: to do it all over again.

1. **Respond.** Think about Flanagan's experiences in relation to your own. What does your experience share with his? What is different?

2. **Summarize.** Briefly summarize Flanagan's essay, including the process he describes and the major steps.

3. **Analyze.** How does the title set up the essay? Why do you think Flanagan placed his thesis somewhere other than the first paragraph? How is his concluding sentence tied to his thesis statement?

4. **Synthesize.** What has Flanagan learned about choices? How does this relate to other stories and choices you have experienced or read about?

5. **Evaluate.** What is Flanagan's purpose for writing, and does he achieve it? Does he give enough information? Is the process he went through clear? Does his essay use the Four Basics of Good Process Analysis (p. 172)?

Write a Process Analysis Essay

This section includes four assignments for writing a process analysis essay. Use the following tools to help you as you complete one or more of these assignments.

1. Review the Four Basics of Good Process Analysis (p. 172).
2. Use **Process Analysis at a Glance** as a basic organizer.
3. Use the Writing Guide: Process Analysis (pp. 184–85) as you write and revise.

1. **GED:** General Education Development tests that substitute for high school graduation

Process analysis at a glance

Introduction with thesis statement
Includes the process you are describing

↓

First step in process
Details about the first step (how to do it or how it works)

↓

Second step in process
Details about the second step

↓

Third step in process
Details about the third step

↓

Conclusion
Reminds the audience of the process and makes an observation related to your main idea

WRITING ASSIGNMENT 1   ## Writing a process analysis essay: suggested topics

Write a process analysis essay on *one* of the following topics or on a topic of your own choice.

College
- How to apply for financial aid
- How to study for a test

Work
- How to do one of your major tasks at work
- How to get a job at your place of work

Everyday life
- How to wake up or how to get to sleep
- How to do something simple that most people don't think about (make a sandwich or cup of coffee, paint a wall, change batteries, etc.)

WRITING ASSIGNMENT 2   ## Writing about an image

Many accomplishments require practice and hard work. In this particular photo, you can see an example of Lego art. Although Legos are commonly known as a toy for children, many people enjoy working and playing with

these blocks—often going so far as to create complex and incredible pieces of art with them. Look at the photo carefully and think about Legos and the sculpture. Then, write an essay in which you help us understand this sculpture and what it means to the artist. How do you think he or she started? Do you think the sculpture began as a toy and turned into something more, or was it always intended to be art? How do you think the artist created something that looks like this?

WRITING ASSIGNMENT 3   ### Writing to solve a problem

Problem Your friend is in a terrible situation. Because of her great grades in high school, she was accepted at an excellent private university. To pay her tuition, she took out a lot of money in student loans and found a part-time job. Unfortunately, she could not manage work and class and had to drop out. At this point, her full loan payment came due. She wanted to transfer to a public university where the tuition was much lower; however, when she requested her transcript from the private university, she was told her records would not be sent until she had paid the charges on her loan. She wants to continue her studies but does not know how to manage this financially.

Assignment Working on your own or in a small group, research the options your friend has, and write some steps she could take to resolve her problem.

Resources There are many Web sites that offer advice on repayment of student loans. A good one to start with is FinAid (**www.finaid.org**). You can also type *student loan repayment* into a search engine. List any Web sites that you use.

Tip When you refer to an outside source, document it in the text and in a list at the end of your essay.

WRITING ASSIGNMENT 4   ### Writing about readings

Choose one of the following options:

- Read Jordan Brown's essay "A Return to Education" (p. 137), Daniel Flanagan's essay "The Choice to Do It Over Again" (p. 180), and Monique Rizer's essay "When Students Are Parents" (p. 587). Each essay deals with the author's decision to make life better. Drawing from at least two of the essays, write about each person's process, and include your own experience as well.

- Read Daniel Flanagan's essay "The Choice to Do It Over Again" (p. 180) and Malcolm X's essay "Learning to Read" (p. 617). In both of these essays, the author writes about deciding to improve his life through education. Drawing from the experiences of at least one of these authors, write an essay about your own educational process. Questions to think about include but are not limited to the following:

– What is your learning process? Flanagan and Malcolm X both took very different approaches to their own education. What approach have you chosen?

– Have you found that education has made a significant change in your life? How so?

Use the steps in the Writing Guide that follows to help you prewrite, draft, revise, and edit your process analysis essay. Check off each step as you complete it.

WRITING GUIDE: PROCESS ANALYSIS	
Steps in Process Analysis	**How to do the steps**
Focus.	• Think about a process and its essential steps.
Explore your topic. See Chapter 5.	• Make sure your process can be explained in a short essay. • Prewrite to decide on the steps and how you will explain them to your audience.
Write a thesis statement. Process + Main idea = Thesis See Chapter 6.	• Decide what you want your audience to know or learn about this process and write a thesis statement.
Support your thesis. See Chapter 7.	• List all of the essential steps and details to describe them for your audience. • Imagine you are not familiar with the process. Would you understand it from the support you have listed, or do you need more explanation?
Write a draft. See Chapter 8.	• Arrange the steps in a logical order (often chronological). • Write topic sentences for each essential step and paragraphs that describe them in detail.
Revise your draft. See Chapter 9.	• Ask another person to read and comment on your draft. • Read to make sure that all the steps are there and relate to the topic. • Add transitions (often chronological). • Improve your introduction, thesis, and conclusion.

WRITING GUIDE: PROCESS ANALYSIS

Steps in Process Analysis	How to do the steps
Edit your draft. See Parts 5 through 8.	• Correct errors in grammar, spelling, word use, and punctuation.
Evaluate your writing.	• Does it have the Four Basics of Good Process Analysis (p. 172)? • Ask yourself: Is this the best I can do?

14

Classification
Writing That Puts Things into Groups

Understand What Classification Is

Classification is writing that organizes people, ideas, or other things into categories. In classifying your chosen subjects, you are presenting and explaining them so that your audience understands what sets them apart.

Four Basics of Good Classification

1 It makes sense of a group of people, ideas, or other items by organizing them into useful categories.

2 It reflects a clear purpose and sense of audience in sorting the people or items.

3 It categorizes using a single, clear organizing principle.

4 It gives detailed examples or explanations of the things that fit into each category.

In the following paragraph, each number corresponds to one of the Four Basics of Good Classification.

Not all people learn in the same way, and **2** it is helpful to know what learning style you prefer. How do you naturally take in and absorb new information? The VARK learning styles inventory is a thirteen-item questionnaire that reveals which **3** learning style a person favors. **1** The first of its four learning styles is visual (V). **4** Visual learners absorb information best by looking at images or by drawing or diagramming a concept. For example, a visual learner may learn more by studying a flowchart of information rather than reading that same information in paragraph form. **1** The second learning style is auditory (A). **4** Auditory learners take in information most efficiently by hearing and listening. They remember information that they hear better than they remember information that they read. Even reading aloud is better than reading silently because hearing is key. Auditory learners benefit from discussion with others rather than working alone silently. **1** The third learning style is read/write (R). **4** Read/write learners learn best by reading written material. They also benefit from writing about what they have read. For example, many read/write learners study by reading and then writing a summary of what they have just read. Many people who are not naturally read/write learners have used that learning style in school because schools are oriented toward reading and writing. For example, a person whose score on the VARK is split evenly between auditory and read/write is probably an auditory learner who has learned to use a read/write learning style for school. **1** The final learning style is kinesthetic (K). **4** Kinesthetic learners learn by doing and by being active. For these learners, experiments in science may be easier to understand than reading a chapter in a book, listening to a lecture, or looking at an image. Kinesthetic learners often need to create activity in order to learn well: They may make flash cards, walk around as they study, or make a static activity interactive in some other way. All learners benefit from learning techniques such as highlighting and making notes, though different kinds of notes work for different learning styles. All learners are active learners: They learn best when they actively involve themselves in a task rather than passively observe it. **2** Taking a learning styles inventory is both fun and useful, particularly for students.

Contexts for Classification

Context, as you will recall, involves both your audience and your purpose. First, make sure you keep **audience** firmly in mind as you write classification:

- Who would want to read this classification and why?
- What background information do they already know?
- What other background information do they need to know?
- What do they want to learn about the topic?

You also need to consider your own **purpose** for writing your classification. Broadly, your purpose is to categorize your chosen items so that your audience sees their differences. To narrow your purpose, consider the following questions:

- Do you want your audience to learn something?
- Do you want them to think of a new way to classify or organize materials, thoughts, or objects?
- Do you want to share an experience or to entertain your readers?
- Do you have another purpose in mind?

The **organizing principle** of a classification essay is directly related to your purpose. For example, you might encourage a visit (your purpose) to an art museum (your topic) for a group of out-of-town visitors (your audience) using one of the following organizing principles: the most famous works of art; works from various geographical locations or periods; the kind of art, such as painting versus sculpture; or different areas or rooms in the museum.

You can use classification in many practical situations. Consider the following examples.

College	In a nursing course, you discuss three types of antibiotics used to treat infections.
Work	For a report on inventory at a software store, you list the types of software carried and report how many of each type you have in stock.
Everyday life	You look at the types of payment plans that are available for your car loan.

Main Idea in Classification

The **main idea** in classification uses a single **organizing principle** to sort items into useful categories that help achieve the **purpose** of the classification.

Imagine the following situation, in which a classification system is not logical or useful: You log on to your online movie service to find that the movies have been rearranged. The comedy, drama, and action categories are gone. Instead, the movies are arranged by length (for example, "longer than 2 hours," "between 1 and 2 hours"), and then alphabetically, by the lead actor's last name.

What would you think of this new arrangement?

1. Are the categories **useful**? (Do you choose movies to watch based on length? Based on who the lead actor is?)

2. Does it have a **single organizing principle**? (How are length and lead actor related?)

The following diagram shows how most online services classify movies.

Teaching tip Ask students to create another such chart for books, vehicles, music, or anything else they are interested in.

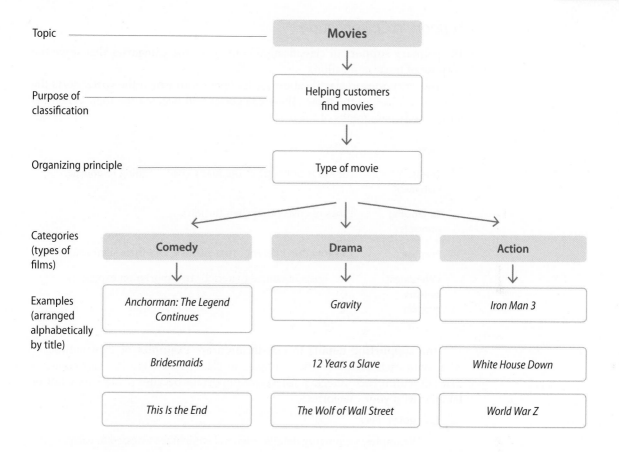

The following examples show how thesis statements for classification express the organizing principle and purpose.

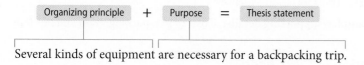

Several kinds of equipment are necessary for a backpacking trip.

In addition to the purpose and organizing principle, a thesis statement in a classification may also include the categories that will be explained.

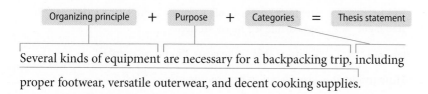

Several kinds of equipment are necessary for a backpacking trip, including proper footwear, versatile outerwear, and decent cooking supplies.

Support in Classification

The **primary support** in classification consists of the **categories** that serve the purpose of the classification.

The categories in classification are like piles into which the writer sorts the items that make up the topic. These categories will become the topic sentences for the body paragraphs of the essay.

Topic	College costs
Thesis statement	Tuition is only one of the many costs of going to college.
Organizing principle	Types of costs other than tuition
Purpose	To show the different kinds of costs and their significance
Categories/ primary support	Fees, costs of course materials, transportation expenses

The **supporting details** in classification are **examples** or explanations of what is in each category. The examples in classification are the various items that fall within each category. These are important because readers may not be familiar with your categories.

Category: Fees

> **Examples/supporting details:** General student fee assessed to each student, lab fees, computer fees

Category: Costs of course materials

> **Examples/supporting details:** Costs of books, lab manuals, software

Category: Transportation expenses

> **Examples/supporting details:** Costs of gas, parking, train and bus fare

Organization in Classification

A classification essay can be organized in different ways depending on its purpose. For example, read the thesis statements and purposes that follow.

Thesis statement	The high costs of college make completing a degree impossible for many students.
Purpose	To argue that some costs should be reduced

How might this classification be organized? *Order of importance*

Thesis statement	My daughter has every kind of mess imaginable in her room, making it clear that she needs a lesson in taking care of her space and her things.
Purpose	To prove the need for the lesson by describing the messes

How might this classification be organized? _Spatial order_

Thesis statement	During my teenage years, I adopted three distinct clothing styles.
Purpose	To show how a person's style changed

How might this classification be organized? _Chronological order_

As you write your essay, you might find the following transitions helpful as you lead from one category to the next or from one example to another.

Common Transitions in Classification

another   for example

another kind   for instance

first, second, third (and so on)

Read and Analyze Classification

Before writing a classification essay, read the following examples—one from the workplace and one from college—and answer the questions that accompany them.

Profile of Success
Classification in the Real World

Rebeka Mazzone

Director of Compliance, Internal Audit and Risk Management, Johnson & Wales University

Background   I was one of six daughters, raised by our mother. My parents were divorced when I was very young, so we lived with the help of welfare. We lived in an affordable housing complex, with many challenges and distractions. At the age of sixteen, I dropped out of high school and moved away on my own in search of a different life. I obtained a job in a fancy restaurant and got my GED while attending hairdressing school. After several years, a customer at the restaurant encouraged me to go to college, which I did not believe was possible without a great deal of money. I applied and was accepted to a local community college. I worked several part-time jobs while attending school full-time. After two years, I transferred to a small private college to pursue my bachelor's degree in accounting. I met a great faculty member, who became a mentor. He encouraged me to pursue my certified public accountant (CPA) license. In order to do this, I would need to work for a very conservative accounting firm. I knew the importance of looking the part. This entire process required me to transform my image during those next two years by learning to speak and write "proper" English, cutting and coloring my long platinum-blond hair, and dressing more conservatively. I was fortunate enough to get a great job with an international accounting firm, which gave me a great start to my career. While I now have a successful career and wonderful family, my journey of lifelong learning is far from over.

Writing at work   People think accountants are numbers people, and we are, but much of what I do is writing: documenting my findings in words for my clients, my colleagues, and my managers. So much depends on client communication. Only the accountant understands the numbers, and I have to explain those numbers clearly.

How Rebeka uses classification   I have to break complex financial strategies into categories that clients can understand so that I can help them make good financial choices.

Workplace Classification

The following curriculum vitae (or résumé) compiles Rebeka Mazzone's work experience, educational background, and other activities into one document for potential employers.

Rebeka Mazzone

Curriculum Vitae (CV)

Guiding question The term *curriculum vitae* (CV) stands for "the course of one's life." What is a CV usually used for?

Vocabulary The following words are *italicized* in the piece: *compliance, audit, implementing, enhance, execute, procedural, outsourcing, governance, paraprofessional, initiative*. If you do not know their meanings, look them up in a dictionary or online.

Rebeka J. Mazzone, CPA, CCEP

EXPERIENCE

Director—*Compliance***, Internal** *Audit***, and Risk Management**	June 2012–Present
Director of Internal Audit	April 2011–June 2012

Johnson & Wales University, Providence, RI

As the Chief Risk, Compliance, and Audit Executive, my responsibilities include developing, *implementing,* and overseeing university-wide risk management, compliance, policy, and internal audit functions to minimize risk, *enhance* compliance, and improve business operations. I perform risk assessments annually, and I develop and *execute* annual and long-range compliance and audit plans that address critical risks and areas of concern with internal controls, operational efficiencies, and/or compliance with regulations, policies, and procedures. I provide *procedural* counseling for implementation of audit recommendations, and I perform follow-up reviews of departments or campuses to monitor progress with implementation of corrective plans. I communicate with the audit committee of the board of trustees and other management.

Group Discussion Leader	October 2010–Present

American Institute of Certified Public Accountants (AICPA)

As a group discussion leader, I work with the AICPA to lead CPE course discussions for various state societies on topics related to not-for-profit accounting and management.

Director—Rhode Island Region	January 2008–April 2011
Senior Consultant	January 2003–January 2008

Accounting Management Solutions, Inc., Waltham, MA; New York, NY; and Providence, RI

As the Chief Financial Officer in the nonprofit division, my responsibilities included managing accounting *outsourcing* engagements, including all aspects of managing client's Finance Department, evaluating client's current accounting practices, and making recommendations based on that evaluation; selecting and implementing new accounting software; writing accounting policies and procedures manuals; conducting internal audits of all financial statement areas; preparing financial statements and schedules for audit and direct communication with auditors; budgeting and cash forecasting; monitoring and evaluating all aspects of finance; improving quality of financial statement presentation; training and supervising staff; making periodic progress reports to the Finance Committee; and managing client relationships. I was responsible for developing and teaching accounting and auditing updates to staff and several provider organizations and providing board *governance* training. I gained extensive experience in crisis management and analytical evaluations to immediately make decisions to minimize impact of crisis and plan for recovery. I was responsible for all aspects of business management, including writing proposals, hiring staff, supervising engagements, and overseeing billing and collections. I developed industry expertise in higher education, health care, real estate development, and property management.

Manager   January 1997–January 2003

KPMG, LLP, Washington, DC

As a Manager in the audit practice of a Big 4 Accounting Firm, my responsibilities included planning, managing, and performing audits. Daily tasks included managing and evaluating staff and other KPMG assisting offices; coordinating audit assistance of contracting audit firms and clients' internal auditors; training staff in areas of key competencies; researching technical accounting and reporting issues; reviewing financial and accounting policies to ensure compliance with applicable laws, regulations, and accounting principles; preparing and issuing financial reports, including entity consolidation; preparing and providing assistance to clients with journal entries and financial reports; conducting progress meetings and communicating performance improvement recommendations to client management; managing client expectations; and conducting performance and strategic analysis of clients' financial/strategic results; writing proposals; making Board presentations; conducting client training for contribution accounting and A-133 compliance; and billing for client services. I started as a *Paraprofessional* during my last semester of college and was promoted to Manager in less than three and a half years as a result of outstanding performance. I gained experience in all industries, including manufacturing, retail, health care, government, government contracting, higher education, membership organizations, research organizations, and other not-for-profits. I specialized in financial reporting and audits of higher education and not-for-profit institutions.

Associate   October 1995–January 1997

Butler & Butler, Certified Public Accountants, LLP, Rochester, New York

I started as an intern and was immediately promoted to permanent associate specializing in operational audits and management advisory services. I initiated several audits of various municipal offices focusing on management practices, employee procedures, and recommendations to strengthen internal controls. These *initiatives* resulted in recommended internal control changes and requests for additional services the following year.

Economic Crimes Assistant   August 1993–January 1994

Monroe County District Attorney, Economic Crimes Bureau, Rochester, New York

I developed cash flow charts and reconstructed bank transactions for trial and hearing evidence; researched laws and testimony to assist attorneys at trial; transcribed audiotapes for evidence and retrieved documents from various police agencies; and investigated defendant backgrounds and contacted victims and witnesses in preparation for hearings.

EDUCATION

B.S. Accounting, *Cum Laude,* St. John   May 1997
Fisher College, Rochester, New York

Computer Science Minor

- Dean's List 1995–1997

Technical/Interpersonal Skills

- Strong management, research, and analytical skills.
- Proficient on most accounting software, including Blackbaud Financial Edge, Peachtree, Microsoft GP (formerly Great Plains), and MIP. Proficient in all aspects of PCs using Microsoft Outlook, Word, PowerPoint, Access, and Excel software applications.
- Proficient in managing multiple priorities.
- Extensive knowledge of government grant compliance requirements, higher education, affordable housing development and management, and all aspects of not-for-profit accounting.
- Strong interpersonal skills.
- Ability to problem-solve from a collaborative perspective and exhibit open communication skills.

Volunteer Activities

- Member, CPE Advisory Committee, American Institute of CPAs (October 2012–Present)
- Board Member, Rhode Island Society of CPAs (May 2009–April 2012)
- Member and former Co-Chair, Rhode Island Society of CPAs Not-for-Profit Committee (January 2006–Present)
- Member, FASB Nonprofit Resource Group (June 2010–Present)
- Member, Finance Council and Co-Chair, Capital Campaign, St. Bernard's Church (April 2012–Present)

- Member, Audit Committee, Town of North Kingstown, Rhode Island (April 2010–August 2011)
- Past Board Member and Chair of the Asset Management Committee of the Pawtucket Citizens Development Corporation (April 2005–October 2006)
- President of Homeowners Association (June 2006–June 2009, July 2013–Present)
- Past Treasurer and member of the North Kingstown Newcomers Club (August 2004–August 2007)
- Various volunteer activities for the Greater Providence and West Bay Family YMCAs (August 2004–2012)

Membership/Certifications
- **Certified Public Accountant (CPA)**—New York State
- **Certified Compliance and Ethics Professional (CCEP)**
- **C3P Certified,** Tax Credit Certified through Spectrum
- **Sandler Sales Training,** Presidents Club
- **Member and Group Training Instructor**—American Institute of Certified Public Accountants (AICPA)
- **Member**—Rhode Island Society of Certified Public Accountants (RISCPA)
- **Member**—Eastern Association of College and University Business Officers (EACUBO)
- **Member**—National Association of College and University Business Officers (NACUBO)
- **Member**—Association of College and University Auditors (ACUA)
- **Member**—Northeast Higher Education Chief Audit Executives (NHECAE)

1. Briefly summarize Rebeka Mazzone's writing, including what she is classifying and what categories she uses. _Answers will vary. Mazzone is summarizing a list of her career experience. She classifies her background using categories such as education, experience, and volunteer activities._

2. What is her purpose? _To present her work experience to prospective employers._

3. Do you think the categories she uses are the only ones that matter? If not, what would you add? Would you delete any? _Answers will vary._

4. Do you think Mazzone achieves her purpose? Why or why not? _Answers will vary._

Of course, to develop a CV like Mazzone's takes years of experience and training. As a student, you are far more likely to have a résumé that does not look as extensive or involved as hers does. Many college students who are about to start their job search are encouraged to limit their résumé to one or two pages in order to present only the most important or significant information to potential employers. In those cases, you need to determine what information, or categories, will be most significant and most important to include and in what order. Consider the following college student's résumé as an example.

Street Address, City, State Zip Code • Phone Number • E-mail

Brittany Philpott

EXPERIENCE

| June 2009–June 2012 | Carol Stream Park District | Carol Stream, IL |

Head Gymnastics Instructor/Head Birthday Party Host

- Instructed gymnastics students of all levels (age range: six months to thirteen years)
- As a Head Coach, was responsible for instructing other coaches and providing insight into their coaching
- Hosted birthday parties with a specific theme for children of all ages sponsored by the park district. Responsible for setting up, developing, and carrying out activities, and conducting cleanup.

| May 2012–August 2012 | Safari Childcare | Streamwood, IL |

Teacher's Assistant

- Provided a learning environment for children from birth to age five
- Helped out in any classroom that needed assistance and taught children activities specific to that age group
- Developed lesson plans and kept a good communication with coworkers and parents

| October 2011–June 2012 | Wheaton Bible Church | West Chicago, IL |

Childcare Worker

- Cared for children during Sunday morning church services, specifically in the one-year-old room and the two-year-old room
- Cared for school-age children during weekday evenings when activities were going on for parents

| May 2013–May 2014 | University College Academic | Normal, IL |
| | Advisement for Illinois State University | |

Academic Peer Adviser

- Worked alongside a professional adviser and helped manage student case-load (making phone calls, sending e-mails to students, and holding advisement appointments with students)
- Helped manage the University College office (working the reception desk and phone bank)

Volunteer Experience (High School to College)

- Worked in the preschool in my high school (Freshman–Senior Year)
- Participated in Student Council, Class Council, Key Club (Volunteer Organization), Peer Leaders (introduced freshmen to the high school, gave tours, and mentored students), Volleyball Team, Show Choir, and Musicals (Freshman–Senior Year)
- Participated in College Mentors for Kids at Illinois State University, where we mentored children in grade school and encouraged college and the importance of school
- Participated in the Jumpstart Program at Illinois State University: worked with preschool children on literacy skills and phonemic awareness
- Served on the Student Board for Cornerstone Christian Fellowship at Illinois State University
- Volunteered at the Children's Museum in Normal, IL (2011–2012)
- Volunteered as a Tour Guide for Illinois State University (2012–2013)

EDUCATION

| August 2011–May 2015 | Illinois State University | Normal, IL |

Early Childhood Education

- Children's Studies Minor
- Reading Endorsement
- Special Education Letter of Approval

REFERENCES

Business References

- Arthur Morris, Director of Parks Department, Carol Stream District (331) 402-5267, a.morris@carolpark.com
- Joanna Davis, Supervisor, Safari Childcare (331) 625-8945, Joanna@safari.com

Personal References

- Brandon Chavez, Friend
  (331) 555-5631, b2014@yahoo.com
- Deborah Morales, Pastor, Wheaton Bible Church
  (331) 555-2252, debmorales@hotmail.com

1. Briefly summarize Brittany Philpott's writing, including what she
   is classifying and what categories she uses. _Answers will vary._

2. What is the purpose of this particular résumé? How can you tell? _Answers_
   will vary but should include something about teaching or working with
   children.

3. Do you think the categories Philpott uses are the only ones that matter? If
   not, what would you add? Would you delete any? _Answers will vary._

4. What makes this résumé different from Mazzone's CV? _Answers will vary._

A College Classification Essay

The following student essay was written for an English class. For this essay, review
the Four Basics of Good Classification (p. 186) and practice your critical reading
process by doing the following.

2PR The Critical Reading Process

Preview the text, including the guiding question.

Read the text, double-underlining the thesis statement, underlining the major
support, and circling the transitions. Consider the quality of the support.

Pause to question and interpret the text. Take notes and write down
questions about what you are reading.

Review the text and your notes, and **respond** to it. Write answers to the
Pause prompts.

For more examples of classification in writing, see Chapter 44.

Teamwork Have students work through the first essay together to apply the 2PR Critical Reading Process and answer the questions after the essay.

Teaching tip Read this essay aloud, give students a few minutes to respond to the questions in writing, and discuss the responses as a group.

Pause What are the key words here that tell you this may be a classification essay? How do you know what is going to be classified?

Pause What is the purpose for sorting these items? Is it a good purpose? Is it a clear purpose?

Pause What system of organization is he using? Are there clear details and examples for each category?

Josef Ameur

Video Game Genres

Guiding question What video game genres does Ameur describe?

Vocabulary The following words are *italicized* in the essay: *accessible, arcade, genres, asteroids, attributes, charisma, embark, epic, quests.* If you do not know their meanings, look them up in a dictionary or online.

1   Video games are an easily *accessible* way to cure the effects of boredom. Ever since the late 1970s, video games have been extremely popular. They started out as *arcade* units, costing 25 cents to $1 per play. Kids would spend hundreds of dollars playing these games. The accessibility of video games has evolved over time from pay-to-play arcade units to personal home TV consoles. The *genres* of games have also evolved over time: shooter, role-playing, and strategy are just a few.

2   Shooters are one of the oldest genres of games. This genre was born in arcade games such as *Asteroids* and *Galaga.* The early shooters were quite simple, and everything was on a two-dimensional plane. *Asteroids* consisted of a small spaceship avoiding *asteroids* by dodging and shooting at them. In *Galaga,* the players shot at enemy alien ships. Eventually, shooters evolved into third- and first-person shooters. In third-person, the player's view is from above, looking down at the character. In first-person, the player looks through the character's eyes. These shooters involve a character holding a gun shooting at enemies. Military, Sci-Fi, and Survival are a few subgenres.

3   Role-playing games (RPGs) started out on paper. *Dungeons & Dragons* was one of the more popular paper RPGs. Paper RPGs gave birth to computer-based ones. The benefit of computer-based RPGs is that with an Internet connection, they can be played with millions of other people. Players and their friends can create and control characters who live in a fantasy world. These characters are often class-based with classes such as thief, warrior, mage, and ranger. Players micromanage the *attributes* of their characters: *charisma*, strength, and magic, to name a few. Players *embark* on *epic quests*, slay beasts, find treasure, and fight in great battles.

4   Strategy games are similar to RPGs, but they are on a much larger scale. In strategy games, players often control a historic civilization. The

three main components of strategy games are economy, military, and politics. There are usually several types of resources that the players manage such as gold, stone, wood, and food. Players control the villagers, assigning them to gather resources. In the military aspect of this genre, players control the army and train different types of soldiers, taking into consideration the strengths and weaknesses of the different units. Politics determines allies and enemies and who wars with whom. In strategy games, there is no such thing as peace.

5   Many genres of games have been created to explore and play, but all video games offer the same core benefit: They offer a brief moment in time to escape the world around you. Video games not only cure boredom but also offer an experience that can rival that of books or films.

Pause Underline the sentence in which Ameur presents his categories.

Combining modes
Note that this classification essay also uses illustration.

Pause Note the detailed examples Ameur gives of each category.

1. **Respond.** Respond to Ameur's essay. What connections do you have to his topic? What, if anything, did you learn from it?
2. **Summarize.** Briefly summarize Ameur's essay, including what he is classifying and what categories he uses.
3. **Analyze.** Are the categories useful to Ameur's purpose of explaining video game genres? Are all of the details clearly related to each category? How does Ameur's conclusion remind readers of the purpose? What system of organization does he use?
4. **Synthesize.** What else do you know about the topic? Do you agree that the reason people play video games is to relieve boredom? What other ways are there to relieve boredom?
5. **Evaluate.** Does Ameur achieve his purpose? Do you agree that playing video games rivals the experience of reading a book or seeing a film? Does the essay have the Four Basics of Good Classification (see p. 186)? What do you think of the essay?

Write a Classification Essay

This section includes four assignments for writing a classification essay. Use the following tools to help you as you complete one or more of these assignments.

1. Review the Four Basics of Good Classification (p. 186).
2. Use **Classification at a Glance** as a basic organizer.
3. Use the Writing Guide: Classification (p. 204) as you write and revise.

Classification at a glance

Introduction with thesis statement
Organizing principle + purpose OR
Organizing principle + purpose + categories

↓

First category
Examples/explanations

↓

Second category
Examples/explanations

↓

Third category
Examples/explanations

↓

Conclusion
Refers back to the classification's purpose and makes an observation

| WRITING ASSIGNMENT 1 | ## Writing a classification essay: suggested topics |

Write a classification essay on one of the following topics or on a topic of your own choice.

| College | • Types of degree programs |
| | • Types of students |

| Work | • Types of working environments |
| | • Types of skills needed for a particular job |

| Everyday life | • Types of drivers |
| | • Types of parents |

| WRITING ASSIGNMENT 2 | ## Writing about images |

© RYAN MCVAY/PHOTODISC/ROYALTY-FREE/GETTY IMAGES

Take a close look at the image of different types of chairs. There are several ways the chairs can be classified: by colors, types, purposes, materials, and so on. Write a paper classifying them in an interesting way for the reader; make sure to use the Four Basics of a Good Classification (p. 186).

WRITING ASSIGNMENT 3   Writing to solve a problem

Problem When you were starting college, you received many credit card offers, and you signed up for three. Over time, you have run up a big debt, partly from the charges themselves and partly from the interest. Now you are seriously in debt and do not know how to get out of it.

Assignment Working on your own or in a small group, first classify your monthly expenses. Then, divide them into "necessary expenses" and "unnecessary expenses." Once you have done this, write an essay that classifies your expenses. Finally, cite some options you will pursue to pay down your debt.

Resources Check Web sites for advice about paying down debt without getting into even bigger trouble. You might start by typing the words *advice on how to pay off credit cards* into a search engine. List any Web sites that you use.

WRITING ASSIGNMENT 4   Writing about readings

In this chapter, Josef Ameur writes about an element of pop culture (video games). Read his essay (p. 200) and Caitlin Seida's "My Embarrassing Picture Went Viral" (p. 673). Then, drawing from the two essays and your own experience, write a classification essay describing the various dangers modern technology has the potential to create. For instance, are violent video games actually to blame for bullying or for increased violence in teens or in schools? Should students be more careful about sharing photos and other information through social media? Is our comfort level with technology creating dangerous situations that we aren't consciously thinking about?

Use the steps in the Writing Guide that follows to help you prewrite, draft, revise, and edit your classification essay. Check off each step as you complete it.

WRITING GUIDE: CLASSIFICATION

Steps in Classification	How to do the steps
Focus.	• Think about your topic and how you can sort it so that your audience will understand the categories.
Explore your topic. See Chapter 5.	• Prewrite to find possible categories to use and examples that will explain each category.
Write a thesis statement. Organizing principle + Purpose = Thesis Or Organizing principle + Purpose + Categories = Thesis See Chapter 6.	• Include your topic and either the method you are using to sort (the organizing principle) or the categories you will describe.
Support your thesis. See Chapter 7.	• Choose useful categories that will achieve your purpose. • Consider what your readers need to know to understand the categories.
Write a draft. See Chapter 8.	• Arrange the categories logically. • Write topic sentences for each category and paragraphs giving examples of each of the categories.
Revise your draft. See Chapter 9.	• Add any examples that will help your readers understand. • Add transitions. • Improve your introduction, thesis, and conclusion.
Edit your revised draft. See Parts 5 through 8.	• Correct errors in grammar, spelling, word use, and punctuation.
Evaluate your writing.	• Does it have the Four Basics of Good Classification (p. 186)? • Ask yourself: Is this the best I can do?

15

Definition

Writing That Tells What Something Means

Understand What Definition Is

Definition is writing that explains what a term or concept means.

Four Basics of Good Definition

1	It tells the audience what the term is and why it is being defined.
2	It presents a clear definition.
3	It uses examples to show what the writer means.
4	It gives details about the examples that the audience will understand.

In the following paragraph, each number corresponds to one of the Four Basics of Good Definition.

1 Internet addiction is **2** chronic, compulsive use of the Internet that interferes with the addicts' lives or their relationships with others. **3** For example, addicts may spend so much time online that they are unable to perform as expected at home, work, or school. **4** These addicts may spend hours surfing the Web, playing games, or e-mailing friends and family. **3** In more serious cases, the Internet addiction can cause financial problems, or worse. **4** For example, online shoppers who go to extremes can find

Teaching tip Have several dictionaries in your classroom. Advise students to have their own dictionary as well.

ESL Encourage ESL students to buy both an English dictionary and a bilingual dictionary.

themselves in debt and, as a result, damage their credit, not to mention personal relationships. **3** Still other Internet addictions involve potentially dangerous or illegal activities. **4** These activities can include meeting people online, gambling, viewing pornography, and engaging in cybersex. However, for Internet addicts, the problem usually isn't *how* they use the Internet; the problem is that they cannot stop using it, even if they want to.

Contexts for Definition

You will probably find that definition is one of the more common types of writing you will do as you progress through your college courses and even in your job. Definition writing is particularly important in college because it tends to show up on exams as well as writing assignments. In addition, many jobs require written definitions of some kind. As with any paper you write, it is important to first define the **audience** clearly. The following are some questions you may want to consider:

- Who could your audience be? Why might they be interested in this definition?
- What do they already know about this particular topic? What else do they need to know?
- What kinds of examples are likely to be most effective in explaining a definition to them?

Then, when you know who your audience will be, you need to consider the purpose for writing a definition. Broadly, your purpose is to define your topic in such a way that it is clear for your audience. But what do you want them to gain from your definition beyond this?

- Do you want them to learn something?
- Do you want them to better understand a concept they may already be familiar with?
- Do you have another purpose in mind?

Many situations require you to explain the meaning of a term, particularly how you are using it. Consider these examples.

College	On a U.S. history exam, you define the term *carpetbagger*.
Work	At a job interview, you are asked to choose one word that best defines you and explain what it means.
Everyday life	You explain the word *share* to your child when a friend comes over for a playdate.

Main Idea in Definition

In definition essays, your **main idea** typically defines your topic. The main idea is directly related to your **purpose,** which is to get your audience to understand the way that you are using a term or concept in your essay. Although writers do not always define a term or concept in a thesis statement, it helps the audience if they do.

A thesis statement in definition can follow a variety of different patterns, two of which include the term and its basic definition.

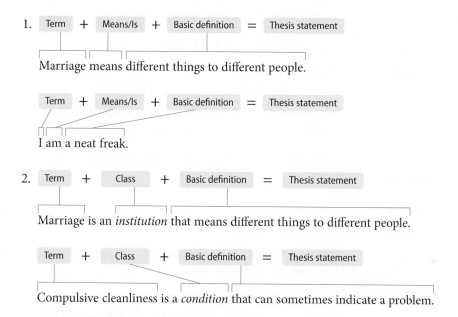

1.   Term + Means/Is + Basic definition = Thesis statement

   Marriage means different things to different people.

   Term + Means/Is + Basic definition = Thesis statement

   I am a neat freak.

2.   Term + Class + Basic definition = Thesis statement

   Marriage is an *institution* that means different things to different people.

   Term + Class + Basic definition = Thesis statement

   Compulsive cleanliness is a *condition* that can sometimes indicate a problem.

In essays based on the following thesis statements, your audience would expect the italicized terms and concepts to be defined through examples that show your meaning.

What does *marriage* mean today?

I am a *neat freak.*

Many people do not understand what *bullying* really means.

Support in Definition

If a friend says, "Summer in the city is awful," you may not know what it is that she finds awful. Is it the weather? The people? The transportation? Until your friend explains what she means, you may not know whether you would agree that summer in the city is awful.

Discussion Ask students to define *boring.* Then, ask them to give an example of something that they consider boring.

Support in definition provides specific examples of terms or concepts to help explain what they mean. Read the two thesis statements that follow and the lists of examples that could be used as support.

Thesis	Today, marriage means different things to different people.
Support	A union of one man and one woman
	A union of two people of either sex
	A union that is supported by state law
	A union that is supported by both civil and religious laws
Thesis	I am a neat freak.
Support	I clean compulsively.
	I am constantly buying new cleaning products.
	My cleaning habits have attracted the notice of friends and family.

In both of these examples, the writer would then go on to develop the examples with details.

Thesis	I am a neat freak.
Support	I clean compulsively.
	Details I clean in the morning and at night, and cannot let a spot on the counter go for a second.
Support	I am constantly buying new cleaning products.
	Details I buy new products every week, have a closet full of them, and believe every new sales pitch.
Support	My cleaning habits have attracted the notice of friends and family.
	Details My kids used to appreciate the clean house; now they complain that I am compulsive. Friends tease me, but I wonder if they think I go too far.

Organization in Definition

The examples in a definition essay are often organized by **importance,** or the impact you think the examples will have on your audience. Save the most important example for last.

As you write, add transitions to connect one example to the next.

Discussion Have students modify a dictionary definition for a variety of audiences.

> ### Common Transitions in Definition
>
> | another | for example |
> |---|---|
> | another kind | for instance |
> | first, second, third, and so on | |

Read and Analyze Definition

Before writing your definition essay, read the following examples—one from the workplace and one from college—and answer the questions that accompany them.

For more examples of definition, see Chapter 45.

Profile of Success
Definition in the Real World

Angell Davis

Academic Adviser and Technical Coordinator, TriO/Student Support Services Program at Illinois State University

Background   I was a high school dropout and was out of the education system for twelve years before beginning my college career at the age of twenty-eight. At the time, I was married and the mother of five children (one biological and four "bonus" children): my youngest was one, and my oldest was eleven. When I was pregnant with my daughter I daydreamed about all the things she could be when she grew up. I then realized that she would need a college degree for most of them. I knew I did not want to push her to do something that I was not willing to do myself, so I stayed home with her for a year and then started my college journey. I began at Heartland Community College (HCC) in August 2008 with a focus in psychology. I absolutely loved my experience at HCC. I felt like I belonged there regardless of my nontraditional status. I joined Project RISE, a student support program that helped me transition and be successful academically. The work was challenging, but my mind was set on succeeding. I transferred to Illinois State University with my associate's degree and completed my bachelor's degree two years later. My primary interest in psychology is on the family, but my specific passion is in preventing and repairing generational conflicts. This passion led me toward a master's degree in social work. While I was in my first year of graduate school, I was offered a full-time position working with special population students. Though I was working full-time, I was able to complete my program in three years. I am currently completing my first semester in the higher education administration doctoral program at Illinois State University.

I would say that I have always had to work extra hard in college. Having to focus on family, work, and my spiritual life while going to school made time scarce and sleep nonexistent. I was always a strong writer and critical thinker, however, which I believe are the two most important components to a successful college career.

How Angell uses definition at work
The writing I do for work is primarily assessment- and research-related. We are always looking for new ideas and methods to help our students reach their goal of graduation. We also do a lot of creation and promotion of events and have to find fun and innovative ways to interact with our students through newsletters and social media.

Workplace Definition

Angell Davis and her colleagues at the TRiO/Student Support Services program at Illinois State University need to communicate with students about how the program can help them. Their Web page, at **http://universitycollege.illinoisstate.edu/sss/,** is designed to define the program's goals and services clearly and succinctly.

Guiding question What is the definition of TRiO/Student Support Services?

Vocabulary The following words are *italicized* in the piece: *maximize, enhance, intrusive, pertinent.* If you do not know their meanings, look them up in a dictionary or online.

TRiO/Student Support Services

Student Support Services at Illinois State University is a student-oriented program that provides support services to individuals who are traditionally under-represented in post-secondary education.

The varieties of supportive services are designed to help program participants *maximize* their effectiveness as students and make successful progress toward graduation. From enrollment to graduation, Student Support Services staff members are dedicated to offering individualized assistance that will *enhance* the academic, personal, and professional potential of the students who participate in the program.

Program Eligibility

Students attending Illinois State University may be eligible for participation in the SSS program if they meet any of the following guidelines:

- First generation college student (neither parent graduated from a four-year college/university)
- Have a demonstrated financial need according to federal guidelines
- Have a documented disability

Services

Student Support Services (SSS) assists students by monitoring academic progress and providing information and assistance with educational and career concerns. Some of the specific, on-going services available to program participants are:

Academic Advising

Our advisors provide pre-registration advisement, drop/add counseling, referrals for tutoring and other areas, assistance in selecting a major, and assistance in developing realistic schedules and course loads.

Personal and Career Counseling

Advisors are available to help you understand and cope with the challenges students face in college. They help participants transition to college; assist in major and career selection; and provide assistance in identifying internship, employment, and study abroad opportunities that will enhance student experiences.

Academic Performance Monitoring

We monitor the academic progress of all participants, and provide *intrusive* advisement to help students successfully persist in their programs of study.

Investigation of Graduate/Professional School Opportunities

We assist in researching programs and institutions; helping students prepare for admission tests; and identifying opportunities to attend *pertinent* conferences and forums.

Participation in Student Leadership Conferences

Our office may sponsor student attendance to various State and Regional leadership conferences.

College Survival/Study Skills Workshops

Throughout the semester, workshops are offered to enhance the academic and personal growth of students in the program. These workshops may include financial aid, motivation, time management, study skills, law and graduate school preparation, and test-taking skills strategies.

Financial Aid Advisement

Our staff can assist in completing financial aid and scholarship applications; and determine and share resources.

Cultural and Educational Activities

Student Support Services assists students in exploring the world beyond classroom walls by arranging excursions to cultural and educational events or activities. Past experiences have included Mexican Fine Arts Museum, DeSable Museum of African-American History, *Les Miserables* at the Fox Theatre, Illinois State Theatre Productions, Medieval Times, and trips to St. Louis, New Orleans, Colorado Springs, and Washington D.C.

Referrals to Other University College Units and Campus Resources

We also assist in identifying additional campus resources that assist in our students' success.

---

1. Briefly summarize the information provided here on the TriO/Student Support Services Web page. What is the purpose of this program? *The program helps students who are underrepresented be more successful in college.*

2. What terms are being defined on this Web page? Is enough information provided to help the reader understand this program? *Answers will vary.*

3. Which of the Four Basics of Good Definition (p. 205) does this Web page have? _Answers will vary._

4. Do you think that this Web page fulfills its purpose and would be helpful to someone who needed the program's services? If not, what needs to be added to make the page more helpful? _Answers will vary._

A College Definition Essay

For the following essay, which was written for an English class, review the Four Basics of Good Definition (p. 205) and practice your critical reading process by doing the following.

2PR The Critical Reading Process

Preview the text, including the guiding question.

Read the text, double-underlining the thesis statement, underlining the major support, and circling the transitions. Consider the quality of the support.

Pause to question and interpret the text. Take notes and write down questions about what you are reading.

Review the text and your notes, and **respond** to it. Write answers to the Pause prompts.

Anna Puiia

What Is Hip?

Guiding question What examples does Puiia give to show her definition of *hip*?

Vocabulary The following words are *italicized* in the essay: *conspicuous, hodgepodge, conglomerate, dishevelment, aesthetic, amalgamated, apathy, nonchalance, ironic.* If you do not know their meanings, look them up in a dictionary or online.

Teamwork Have students work through the first essay together to apply the 2PR Critical Reading Process and answer the questions after the essay.

Pause Can you picture the type of person Puiia is describing?

1   You know who they are. You have seen their self-done haircuts, their skinny jeans, and their oversized sweaters and sunglasses. You have seen their bright colors, and mismatches, and secondhand-store hand-me-downs. You have seen that guy with the faux—or maybe real—knuckle tattoos that either make no sense or refer to something almost no one has heard of. You may spy them riding the bus wearing obnoxiously *conspicuous* headphones, which are blaring something that can only be described as indie rock. You may catch them pining over some skinny boy in oxfords and a kaffiyeh.[1] Hipsters are the kids everyone loves to hate.

1. **kaffiyeh:** a triangular-shaped Arab headdress

Pause Underline the details Puiia gives.

2   What is a hipster, anyway? Hipsterism, in general, is a to-each-his-own way of expressing oneself. Hipster fashion is a *hodgepodge* of past trends and styles—a recycled, updated *conglomerate* of former fashions. Hipsters combine elements of former subcultures to create their overall looks of *dishevelment*. Grunge's[2] flannel paired with skinny jeans and a book of Allen Ginsberg's[3] poetry or a copy of *On the Road*[4] in your backpack could characterize you as a hipster. A hipster may frame his or her face in lens-less or nonprescription Buddy Holly glasses[5] or stomp around in an old pair of Converse sneakers.[6] With hipsters, it's all about seeming (effortlessly) cool, or as if they did not think or care about their outfits when they got dressed (Robie).

2. **grunge:** a deliberately untidy style of dress

3. **Allen Ginsberg:** American poet and a leader of the 1950s Beat Generation

4. ***On the Road:*** a novel by Jack Kerouac, another leader of the Beat Generation

5. **Buddy Holly glasses:** thick-rimmed glasses worn by Buddy Holly, an American musician who was one of the first rock-and-roll artists

6. **Converse:** a brand of sneakers, particularly high-tops

Pause How does Puiia move the reader from one paragraph to the next?

3   But hipsterism goes beyond just fashion. The hipster subculture is very much defined by its musical tastes as well. The music of the hipster subculture is not defined by one genre. Most of the genres popularly associated with hipsters are combinations of other styles; they sometimes carry funny names, like shoegaze—a style of music characterized by the artists' use of effect pedals, which causes them to spend all of their live performances gazing at their feet (LaRose). Some hipsters prefer music of a moodier, folksier persuasion, while others prefer pure electronica and synthesizers. Some settle in between with bands that combine the simple, pretty melodies of folk with the intricate layering of electronica, creating an offbeat, experimental sound.

4   The hipster subculture is one of the most commonly criticized groups in American youth culture. A simple Google search of the word *hipster* provides one with links to pages and articles like "Hipster Subculture Ripe for Parody," or "Why the Hipster Must Die." Another link is to an article entitled "Hipster: The Dead End of Western Civilization." This

article discusses hipsterism as the "dead end of western civilization" (Haddow), because he claims that the hipsters are no longer producing anything new. He attacks the recycled *aesthetic* and *amalgamated* music styles of the hipsters and points to the use of past trends in new ways as a lack of creativity. This lack of creativity is reflected, he says, in today's youth culture "simply consuming cool, rather than creating it," (Haddow) as though hipsters are not making the things they buy and wear and listen to cool, but are instead being told these things are cool, and then consuming them. This criticism is founded in most of the things that hipsterism itself is based in: a sense of *apathy*, a projected *nonchalance* about fashion, the idea of recycling the past.

5   I do not see hipsters as a dead end. I see them as making progress for the fashion world. Hipsters are taking the trends of the past and making them cool in a new way—giving them new life. They are taking the untrends of the past and making them cool for the first time. They are wearing the flaws of their predecessors on their sleeves, or in the soles of their run-down boots, or in place of the lenses in their giant glasses. Their recycling is moving fashion along in a different way. So the individual items they are wearing are not new, but the hipsters have created a completely new look.

> **Pause** Do you agree with Haddow's opinion?

6   Now, as I get dressed in my skinny jeans and my oversized ugly sweater, sliding on some thrift-store loafers, I, a hipster, am wondering what the hippest response to being called a "dead end" would be. Maybe it was writing this paper, but I think I put in too much effort. It has to seem as if I did not care. Maybe it would be to laugh at it. Maybe I could name my band that someday, when I have a band. Or maybe I should just make a T-shirt with the saying "I Am the Dead End." That statement is simple, casual, and maybe even a little bit *ironic*. I like it.

Works Cited

Haddow, Douglas. "Hipster: The Dead End of Western Civilization." *Adbusters*. Adbusters.org, 29 July 2008. Web. 6 Apr. 2011. <https://www.adbusters.org/magazine/79/hipster.html>.

LaRose, Philip. "Know Your Subgenres: Shoegazing." *The KEXP Blog*. KEXP, 26 Apr. 2009. Web. 9 Apr. 2011. <http://blog.kexp.org/blog/2009/04/26/know-your-subgenres-shoegazing/>.

Robie, Elizabeth. "Culture: Hipster Fashion: The Ultimate in Urban Cool." *InsideVandy*. Vanderbilt University, 3 Jan. 2008. Web. 20 Apr. 2011. <http://www.insidevandy.com/drupal/node/6260>.

Definition at a glance

Introduction with thesis statement
Defines term or concept

↓

First example explaining the definition
Details about the first example

↓

Second example explaining the definition
Details about the second example

↓

Third example explaining the definition
Details about the third example

↓

Conclusion
Refers back to the defined term/concept and makes an observation about it based on what you have written

1. **Respond.** Puiia defines the term *hipster* in her essay. Do you agree with the definition she provides, or would you adjust it? Why might your definition be a bit different from hers? If it's the same, what about her definition makes the most sense to you?

2. **Summarize.** Briefly summarize Puiia's essay, including the term she is defining, her definition, and the examples she gives.

3. **Analyze.** In what paragraph does Puiia move toward her own definition of hipsterism, in contrast to Haddow's opinions? How does she mock his piece in the last paragraph?

4. **Synthesize.** Apart from Puiia's essay, what do you know about hipsters? Read Haddow's essay at **www.adbusters.org/magazine/79/hipster. html** and use both his essay and Puiia's to determine your own definition of *hip*.

5. **Evaluate.** Does Puiia give you a clear idea of how she understands the term *hipster*? What is her point of view? Do you think she is biased? If so, how? Does her essay have the Four Basics of Good Definition (p. 205)?

Write a Definition Essay

This section includes four assignments for writing a definition essay. Use the following tools to help you as you complete one or more of these assignments.

1. Review the Four Basics of Good Definition (p. 205).

2. Use **Definition at a Glance** as a basic organizer.

3. Use the Writing Guide: Definition (p. 219) as you write and revise.

WRITING ASSIGNMENT 1   **Writing a definition essay: suggested topics**

Write a definition essay on *one* of the following topics or on a topic of your own choice.

College	• A term or concept from another course you have taken
	• Honesty
Work	• Any term you use at work
	• A model employee
Everyday life	• Home
	• Road rage

WRITING ASSIGNMENT 2	**Writing about images**

Look at the chess pieces in the image. What words come to mind as you look at this photo? Is this image about colors? Shapes? Structure? Diversity? Acceptance? Or is it something else? Identify one word that best defines this picture, and then use clear examples to explain that definition to your reader.

WRITING ASSIGNMENT 3	**Writing to solve a problem**

Problem Your company is putting together a new employee handbook. To make the handbook both realistic and relevant, the company has decided that the contents will come directly from the employees. Your department has been assigned the section on communication.

Assignment Working on your own or with a small group, write a short piece defining *good communication skills,* giving detailed examples of how those skills should be applied in your company.

Resources You might:

- Set up an informational interview with a human resources worker to find out about your subject.

- Type *definition of good communication skills* into a search engine. Document any Web sites or references you use.

WRITING ASSIGNMENT 4   **Writing about readings**

The assignments that follow ask you to read one or more different definition essays and draw from them to write your own essay.

- Read Nancy Mairs's essay "On Being a Cripple" (p. 645) and Brent
  Staples's essay "Just Walk On By" (p. 669). Drawing from both essays,
  write a definition essay about labels. More specifically, what is a label
  that you have chosen for yourself or one that another has chosen for
  you? Define this label and use examples to explain your definition of it.

- Read Dave Barry's "The Ugly Truth about Beauty" (p. 658), Caitlin Seida's
  "My Embarrassing Picture Went Viral" (p. 673), and Amy L. Beck's "Struggling for Perfection" (p. 665). Drawing from these three selections to
  make your point, discuss the pressures that people feel to be young
  and beautiful.

Use the steps in the Writing Guide that follows to help you prewrite, draft,
revise, and edit your definition essay. Check off each step as you complete it.

WRITING GUIDE: DEFINITION

Steps in Definition	How to do the steps
Focus.	• Think about the term you are going to define and how to get your audience to understand the term as you do.
Explore your topic. See Chapter 5.	• Prewrite to get possible definitions and examples that will explain the definition.
Write a thesis statement. Topic + Definition = Thesis See Chapter 6.	• Include the term or concept you are defining and a basic definition of it.
Support your thesis. See Chapter 7.	• Choose examples of the definition and details about the examples that will show your audience how you see the term.
Write a draft. See Chapter 8.	• Arrange your examples. • Write topic sentences for each example and paragraphs that give details about them.
Revise your draft. See Chapter 9.	• Make sure the examples explain your definition. • Think about what other details your audience might need to understand your definition. • Add transitions. • Improve your introduction, thesis, and conclusion.
Edit your revised draft. See Parts 5 through 8.	• Correct errors in grammar, spelling, word use, and punctuation.
Evaluate your writing.	• Does it have the Four Basics of Good Definition (p. 205)? • Ask yourself: Is this the best I can do?

16

Comparison and Contrast

Writing That Shows Similarities and Differences

Understand What Comparison and Contrast Are

Comparison is writing that shows the similarities among subjects—people, ideas, situations, or items; **contrast** shows the differences. In conversation, we often use the word *compare* to mean either compare or contrast, but as you work through this chapter, the terms will be separated.

Four Basics of Good Comparison and Contrast

1 It serves a purpose by using subjects that have enough in common to be compared and contrasted in a useful way.

2 It presents several parallel points—either to help readers make a decision or to help them understand the subjects.

3 It uses examples to demonstrate the similarities or differences of the topics.

4 It uses either point-by-point or whole-to-whole organization (see p. 224).

In the following paragraph, which contrasts the subjects, each number corresponds to one of the Four Basics of Good Comparison and Contrast.

1 My current boyfriend **2** is a major improvement over **1** my ex-boyfriend **2** in terms of how he treats me. **3** One difference is that my current boyfriend opens the door when I get in the car as well as when I get out. In contrast, my ex-boyfriend never opened the door of the car or any other door. **3** My current boyfriend likes to tell me that he loves me. For example, we went to the beach, and he screamed that he loved me to the four winds so everyone could hear. My ex, on the other hand, always had a ready excuse for why he couldn't say that he loved me, ever. However, he wanted me to tell him I loved him all the time. **3** Another difference between the two is that my boyfriend spends money on me. When we go out

4 Uses point-by-point organization (see p. 224).

to a restaurant, he pays for the meal. My ex just never seemed to have money to pay for dinner or anything else. He would say he forgot to bring his wallet, and I would have to pay for the food. **3** To me, the most important difference between the two guys is that my current boyfriend is honest. He never lies to me about anything, and he makes me feel confident about our relationship. In contrast, I never could tell if my ex was lying or telling the truth because he often lied about his family and other things, and I never knew what to believe. **2** To sum it all up, my current boyfriend is a gentleman, and my ex was a pig.

4 Uses point-by-point organization (see p. 224).

—Liliana Ramirez, student

Contexts for Comparison and Contrast

Many situations will call for comparison and contrast writing. Perhaps you need to compare or contrast the features of a product you need to purchase, a particular class you want to take, or a job you want to pursue. Maybe you have been assigned a paper that asks you to identify the main similarities or differences between two objects, characters, symbols, or other works. Before you begin writing, you will need to determine the **audience** you will address. You may want to consider the following questions:

- Who would want to read your paper and why?
- What do they already know about the topics? What else do they want to know?
- How old are they? How much information will be appropriate for you to provide in your paper?
- What types of examples, details, features, or other information will be most useful to this particular audience?

Once you have identified who the audience is, you will then need to determine what the ultimate purpose of the paper will be.

- Do you want to help the audience make a decision between two products?
- Is your goal to help them see the pros and cons between two items or concepts?
- Do you want to help them understand something in greater detail so that they gain a fuller understanding of the subject?

No matter what purpose you decide on, remember that you should always choose two subjects that have enough in common that they can be compared and/or contrasted without great difficulty.

Many situations require you to use comparison and contrast.

College	In a business course, you compare and contrast practices in e-commerce and traditional commerce.
Work	You compare and contrast two health insurance options offered by your company in order to select the one that is best for you.
Everyday life	Before choosing a telephone plan, you compare and contrast the rates, services, and options each offers.

Main Idea in Comparison and Contrast

A comparison and contrast essay shows the audience how two or more subjects are alike or different. The **purpose** of a comparison and contrast essay may be to have the audience understand the subjects or to help them make a decision.

In comparison and contrast, your **main idea** expresses similarities or differences in your subjects. For example, in the paragraph on pages 220–21, Liliana Ramirez contrasts the different ways that her two boyfriends treated her. Her purpose is to help the audience understand why she prefers her current boyfriend over her ex.

Typically, thesis statements in comparison and contrast essays present the central subjects and indicate whether the writer will show similarities, differences, or both.

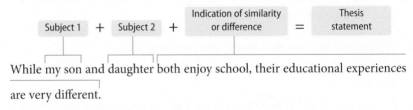

While my son and daughter both enjoy school, their educational experiences are very different.

[Purpose: to contrast educational experiences of her children]

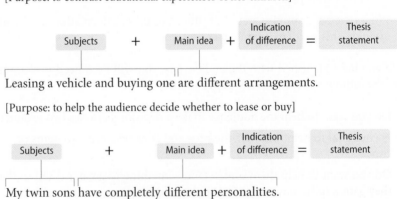

Leasing a vehicle and buying one are different arrangements.

[Purpose: to help the audience decide whether to lease or buy]

My twin sons have completely different personalities.

[Purpose: to help the audience understand the sons' personalities and how they differ]

To determine your thesis in a comparison and contrast essay, decide whether you want to show similarities, differences, or both. To make this decision, you need to think about what your purpose is—what you want the audience to under-stand—and what will be meaningful to that audience.

Support in Comparison and Contrast

The **support** in comparison and contrast demonstrates your main idea by show-ing how your subjects are the same or different. To find support, many people make a list with multiple columns—one for the points that will serve as the basis of the comparison or contrast and one for each of the subjects.

For example, one student, Sarah, wrote the following thesis statement, which indicates that her essay will focus on the differences between owning a laptop and owning a tablet computer.

> While both a laptop and a tablet computer offer similar programs and applications, there are definitely advantages and disadvantages to each.

To support this thesis, Sarah needs to find several points of contrast between a laptop and a tablet. She generates the following list.

DIFFERENCES BETWEEN LAPTOPS AND TABLETS

appearance

portability

price

Then, for each point of comparison, Sarah lists some details that explain the differences.

	LAPTOP	TABLET
APPEARANCE	smaller computer	more like a sheet of paper
	keyboard and screen	touchscreen/keyboard optional
PORTABILITY	larger	smaller
	needs bag	easily carried
	folds up	one screen only
PRICE	cheaper models available	pricey
	more programs	many apps/programs limited
	more options (mouse/keyboard/etc.)	options available at a price

Organization in Comparison and Contrast

Teaching tip Remind students that a whole-to-whole essay must include a strong transition to move from subject 1 to subject 2.

A comparison and contrast essay can be organized in two basic ways: A **point-by-point** organization first compares or contrasts one point between the two subjects and then moves to the next point of comparison or contrast. A **whole-to-whole** organization first presents all the points of comparison or contrast for one subject and then all the points for the second. To decide which organization to use, consider which of the two will best serve your purpose of explaining similarities or differences to your audience. Once you choose an organization, stick with it throughout the essay.

The two organization types look like this.

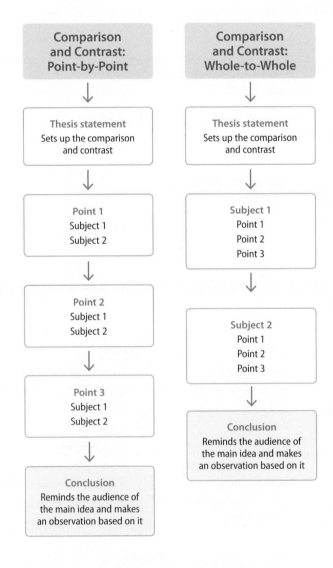

Comparison and Contrast: Point-by-Point	Comparison and Contrast: Whole-to-Whole
Thesis statement Sets up the comparison and contrast	**Thesis statement** Sets up the comparison and contrast
Point 1 Subject 1 Subject 2	**Subject 1** Point 1 Point 2 Point 3
Point 2 Subject 1 Subject 2	**Subject 2** Point 1 Point 2 Point 3
Point 3 Subject 1 Subject 2	**Conclusion** Reminds the audience of the main idea and makes an observation based on it
Conclusion Reminds the audience of the main idea and makes an observation based on it	

Using **transitions** in comparison and contrast essays is important to move readers from one subject to another and from one point of comparison to another.

Common Transitions in Comparison and Contrast

Comparison	Contrast
one similarity	one difference
another similarity	another difference
similarly	in contrast
like	now/then
both	unlike
	while

Read and Analyze Comparison and Contrast

Before writing a comparison and contrast essay, read the following examples— one from the workplace and one from college—and answer the questions that accompany them.

Profile of Success
Comparison and Contrast in the Real World

Garth Vaz

Physician, Community Health Centers of South Central Texas

Background   I was born in Jamaica, and at school, everyone thought I was lazy because I couldn't read. I knew I worked hard but didn't understand why I had such trouble reading. When it came time to go to high school, I dropped out and moved to Brooklyn, New York. Shortly thereafter, I was drafted and served as a medic in the military, where I got my GED. After completing my service, I went to Central Florida Community College and transferred to the University of Florida. I dropped out eventually and worked for a few years as an orderly.

I was accepted at the University of Florida Medical School but flunked out, at which point I finally discovered that my reading and writing problems were caused not by laziness but by dyslexia. I petitioned the school to return and passed my courses with the help of a note-taking service. But I failed the medical boards twice before I was allowed accommodation for dyslexia.

Today I am a doctor working at a community health clinic that, in addition to other medical services, provides care for migrant workers and their families. I also travel and speak extensively on learning behaviors, especially dyslexia and attention-deficit/hyperactivity disorder (ADHD).

Writing at work   For work, I write patient reports, speeches, and papers for publication. As a dyslexic, writing is still very difficult for me, though I have learned how to compensate for the difficulty. Because I still make lots of spelling errors, I have to read very carefully and reread anything I write to correct the mistakes.

Workplace Comparison and Contrast

The following is excerpted from an article that Dr. Vaz published on the subject of dyslexia.

Guiding question How are dyslexia and ADHD different?

Vocabulary The following words are *italicized* in the excerpt: *dyslexics, misconceptions, misdiagnoses, abound, deficient, remediation, diligent, squirm, fidget, excessively, blurts, norms, alienates, shun, ostracism, labored, intervention, contemporary.* If you do not know their meanings, look them up in a dictionary or online.

For decades, *dyslexics* have been one of the most misunderstood groups in our society. *Misconceptions* and *misdiagnoses abound,* as when dyslexics are mis-labeled stupid, retarded, or lazy and placed among the mentally *deficient.* Many dyslexics have been placed in special education programs along with the slow learners. Later, after appropriate *remediation,* these same students have gone on to become educators, lawyers, and doctors. It is therefore of great importance that we be aware of the sensitive nature of dealing with these prize products of our society, our dyslexic students. We must be *diligent* in our efforts to help them in their struggle for success.

Such misdiagnoses are due to the lack of understanding of dyslexia and conditions such as attention-deficit/hyperactivity disorder (ADHD), childhood depressive disorder (CDD), central auditory processing deficit (CAPD), and many others that share some similarities with common symptoms of dyslexia. I will now list, in brief, some of the differences in behaviors that characterize ADHD and dyslexia in children, particularly children in the elementary school classroom.

A young person with ADHD cannot easily sit still, certainly a problem in the classroom. He or she often leaves his assigned seat, running around and attempt-ing to climb on shelves, desks, and the like. When told firmly to remain in his seat, the child will try to obey but will *squirm* and *fidget* almost constantly, clearly in a state of agitation. He acts as if he is driven by a motor.

A child with ADHD often talks *excessively* and is unable to wait to be called on: Instead, he *blurts* out answers and responses. He seems to just butt into games and conversations, not observing social *norms* that require a give-and-take among group members. Such behavior often *alienates* other children and frustrates teachers and others who try to maintain control. Other children may *shun* the child with ADHD. This *ostracism,* in turn, results in further negative effects, such as low self-esteem and greater isolation.

In contrast, a young person with dyslexia can sit still but has trouble organiz-ing objects, belongings, and letters. She may mix up sounds, saying, for example, "plain" for "plan" or "seal" for "soul." She may have a stutter, furthering the frus-tration and embarrassment she already feels.

A dyslexic child typically reads poorly, confusing the order of letters, for example, in words such as "saw" and "was." Also, she may confuse words that have similar shapes or start and end with the same letters, as in "form" and "from" or the words cited in the last paragraph. While a dyslexic's reading is *labored,* his handwriting and spelling are usually worse. All of these symptoms of dyslexia, while quite different, often result in the same ostracism and loss of self-esteem. These problems then cause other behavior problems that are similar to those shown in children with ADHD and a number of other conditions. This explains why certain conditions are often confused. In addition, many children indeed have more than one condition. For example, over 40 percent of children with dyslexia have ADHD as well.

Unfortunately, because of budgeting restrictions, dyslexics are sometimes placed among the wrong group for remediation. In order for any *intervention* to succeed, it must be tailored specifically for the dyslexic. There are many improved techniques now being used successfully in reading remediation that are based on the Orton-Gillingham method. Many of these can be obtained on videocassettes and CDs. Arlene Sonday and the Scottish Rite Hospital have such programs on the market, and many other good ones can be located on the Internet (for example, **interdys.org/, dys.org/, kidshealth.org/,** and **ninds.nih.gov/disorders/dyslexia,** among many others).

There are many successful dyslexics in our society, some *contemporary* and others in the past. Albert Einstein, Benjamin Franklin, and General George Patton are a few who have made history. Athletes Bruce Jenner and Nolan Ryan and entertainers Whoopi Goldberg and Cher are among our contemporaries. Identifying with the successful dyslexic offers some hope to parents and children alike. The book *Succeeding with LD* is a collection of stories of successful dyslexics. The book was authored by Jill Lauren and published by Free Spirit Publishers. Each of these stories could make a book by itself but is short enough for the dyslexic to enjoy reading.

1. Briefly summarize Vaz's essay, including the terms being compared or contrasted and the major similarities or differences. *Answers will vary.*

2. What organization does Vaz use? *Whole to whole*

3. Why is dyslexia so often misunderstood, according to Vaz?
   Answers will vary.

4. Why is Vaz particularly interested in dyslexia? *He has it.*

For more examples of comparison and contrast, see Chapter 46.

A College Comparison and Contrast Essay

The essay on page 229 appeared in the Duke University newspaper, the *Chronicle,* in 2010. For the essay, review the Four Basics of Good Comparison and Contrast (p. 220) and practice your critical reading process by doing the following.

Teamwork Have students work through the first essay together to apply the 2PR Critical Reading Process and answer the questions after the essay.

2PR   The Critical Reading Process

Preview the text, including the guiding question.

Read the text, double-underlining the thesis statement, underlining the major support, and circling the transitions. Consider the quality of the support.

Pause to question and interpret the text. Take notes and write down questions about what you are reading.

Review the text and your notes, and **respond** to it. Write answers to the Pause prompts.

Rui Dai

A Whiff of Memory

Guiding question   What differences does Dai find between smells in the United States and in China?

Vocabulary   The following words are *italicized* in the piece: *etiquette, habituate, idiosyncratic, musk, endogenous, protocol,* and *olfaction.* If you do not know their meanings, look them up in a dictionary or online.

1   There are many things that distinguish China's street *etiquette* from the U.S. equivalent: For example, China forbids honking except in the most extreme cases. In the United States, there are no car horns to *habituate* to, nor are there so many people with so many voices. However, what is most distinctive about China is its smell.

2   Simply put, China smells different than America. It is a weird and completely overwhelming phenomenon that seems wholly inexplicable in scientific terms. How can one country smell different from another? China and the United States are both vast countries with obviously different, *idiosyncratic* odors in separate regions of each. The American Northeast smells of the sea, and the Midwest, dry cornfields. What is so distinctive

between the two that, without opening my eyes, I can tell which country is which? Let me explain. The smell of China carries a distinctive *musk* that is the combination of age and non-ammonia cleaning supplies. America, on the other hand, smells clean—literally, and not necessarily in a good way. Cleaning detergents are used almost ubiquitously in America, while relatively rare in China. In the States, the complex chemical combinations in cleaning agents destroy almost any *endogenous* smell of the environment, leaving only a hint of pine or lavender, or whatever oil extract the manufacturer had dropped into the mixture.

3   In every grocery store in America there is always an entire row of cleaning supplies, each with bottles of 409 or Scrubbing Bubbles lined neatly on steel shelves. In China, there are no comparable brands; there is classic soap and there is liquid soap: no ammonia in sight. Such a difference in cleaning *protocol* has a dramatic effect on the resulting odor of each country.

Pause According to Dai, why is smell distinctive?

4   The reason why the difference in odor between the two countries is so distinctive and apparent is because *olfaction* evokes strong emotional memories. Biologically, the olfactory system is one of the few senses in the human body that has a direct connection to the part of the brain that is in charge of emotional memories, the amygdala. The olfactory system's mitral cells and olfactory receptor neurons help send information about scents to the amygdala. This is the reason why the smell of cinnamon evokes more memories and emotions than just the sight of cinnamon. It also elicits memories of Christmas morning or the cinnamon rolls after a Thanksgiving dinner. In comparison, few other sensory faculties call to mind a similar distinctive memory. Hearing, for example, does not evoke as powerful memories as olfaction, or else every single time we heard something we would be reliving the past.

Combining modes Notice that in this contrast essay, the author also uses description.

5   To me, America smells like driving alone down a road really fast with the wind in your hair; it is freedom. China smells like getting breakfast with my grandmother at dawn in the street market just as it is beginning to bustle; it is nostalgia. As a Chinese American, it is always difficult to distinguish between which part of my heritage is which. I have always wondered what I would have been like if I stayed with my grandmother and had gotten breakfast with her every day at the street market. Would I still be as argumentative as I am today? Or would I be more pliable?

Pause What do the smells of America and China mean to Dai?

6   The distinction between my identity as both Chinese and American is even harder now that I am on a service project in China. I alternate sporadically as needed between my personalities as a Duke student and another Chinese pedestrian on the street. I converse normally with the rest of my service group as I would on Duke's campus, but the moment I turn to speak to a native or to translate something from English to Chinese, I become one of the more than 1.3 billion people who populate China.

7   Right now, the unique scent of China is correlated with a set of childhood memories. Once in a while, under the influence of a particular familiar waft of odor, memories of my childhood will rush me back in time. But memory is malleable. And soon, new memories will become associated with the scents of old, for better or for worse. I hope it will be for the better.

1. **Respond.** Dai writes about how smell and emotion are connected. Can you think of a smell and an emotion that are connected in your own life?

2. **Summarize.** Briefly describe Dai's comparison between China and America. What are the main reasons she believes that the smells are so different? Why is that so significant to her?

3. **Analyze.** From the beginning Dai acknowledges that China and America are different in numerous ways. Why do you think she decided to focus on only one? Why do you think that out of all the differences between the two cultures and countries she chose to focus on smell? What is the significance that smell has that other senses do not?

4. **Synthesize.** Toward the end of her essay, Dai talks about the fact that she is on a service project back in China after living in America and that she finds herself moving back and forth between the two cultures. She also says that memory is "malleable." What does she mean by that? Have you ever found yourself slipping back and forth between two families or two worlds and noticing that the differences you thought were so extreme were becoming less apparent after a while? Why do you think that happens?

5. **Evaluate.** What do you think is Dai's main purpose for writing this article? Does her essay follow the Four Basics of Good Comparison and Contrast (p. 220)?

Write a Comparison and Contrast Essay

This section includes three assignments for writing a comparison and contrast essay. Use the following tools to help you as you complete one or more of these assignments.

1. Review the Four Basics of Good Comparison and Contrast (p. 220).

2. Use the **Comparison and Contrast charts** on page 224 to help you with basic organization.

3. Use the Writing Guide: Comparison and Contrast (p. 234) as you write and revise.

WRITING ASSIGNMENT 1 **Writing a comparison and contrast essay: suggested topics**

Write a comparison and contrast essay on one of the following topics or on a topic of your own choice.

College	• Two courses you are taking or have taken
	• College and high school
Work	• Two jobs you have had
	• A job and a career
Everyday life	• Two places you have lived
	• Good customer service and bad customer service

WRITING ASSIGNMENT 2 **Writing about images**

1961 1962 1972 1978

1979 1992 2011

In 1961, the toymaker Mattel launched a new product—a Ken doll—advertised as the perfect boyfriend for the company's popular Barbie doll. In the fifty years since then, Ken's appearance has evolved in an effort to keep pace with the times and to appeal to each new generation of children and the parents who make the purchases.

Choose two or more of the images and compare and contrast the changing looks of Ken. In your essay, you might want to address how changes to Ken represent larger changes in society and culture. Also, answer this question: What do you think Ken might look like in ten or twenty years?

WRITING ASSIGNMENT 3   ### Writing about readings

Read "Learning to Read" by Malcolm X (p. 617) and "Mother Tongue" by Amy Tan (p. 633). Write a brief paper on one of the following:

- Although their tones are different, Malcolm X and Amy Tan both write about the importance of language in their lives. Explain that point, bringing in references from the two readings. In your concluding paragraph, indicate which of the readings makes the point most effectively to you and why.

- Think about the different languages you hear daily at work, at school, at home, or with your friends. Which of these are most influential in your life? How do you learn to navigate among them? How do we learn which are appropriate in which situations? Why do we need to learn to navigate among them? Use examples from the readings to support your position.

Use the steps in the Writing Guide that follows to help you prewrite, draft, revise, and edit your comparison and contrast essay. Check off each step as you complete it.

WRITING GUIDE: COMPARISON AND CONTRAST

Steps in Comparison and Contrast	How to do the steps
Focus.	• Think about what you want to compare and contrast and your purpose for writing.
Explore your topic. See Chapter 5.	• Make a side-by-side list of possible parallel points of comparison or contrast between your subjects.
Write a thesis statement. Subjects + Main idea = Thesis See Chapter 6.	• Include your subjects and some indication of whether you will be comparing or contrasting them.
Support your thesis. See Chapter 7.	• Choose the points of comparison or contrast that your audience will understand and that will serve your purpose.
Write a draft. See Chapter 8.	• Decide whether to use point-by-point or whole-to-whole organization and how to arrange your main ideas (by time, space, or importance). • Write topic sentences for your support paragraphs.
Revise your draft. See Chapter 9.	• Reread to add any examples that will help your audience understand. • Add transitions. • Improve your introduction, thesis, and conclusion.
Edit your revised draft. See Parts 5 through 8.	• Correct errors in grammar, spelling, word use, and punctuation.
Evaluate your writing.	• Does it have the Four Basics of Good Comparison and Contrast (p. 220)? • Ask yourself: Is this the best I can do?

17

Cause and Effect

Writing That Explains Reasons or Results

Understand What Cause and Effect Are

A **cause** is what makes an event or a situation happen. An **effect** is what happens as a result of one or more causes.

Four Basics of Good Cause and Effect

1	The main idea reflects the writer's purpose—to explain causes, effects, or both.
2	If the purpose is to explain causes, it presents real causes; likewise, if the purpose is to explain effects, it presents real effects.
3	It gives clear and detailed examples or explanations of the causes and effects.
4	It demonstrates how one point logically leads to the next point (how the cause produces the effect).

In the following paragraph, each number corresponds to one of the Four Basics of Good Cause and Effect.

1 Little doubt remains that global warming is a threat to our world, but not everyone understands why it is happening and what the effects are. Many experts believe that this warming trend is largely the result of **2** greenhouse gases, including **4** carbon dioxide emissions, mainly from cars, and pollutants from industrial processes. **2** Deforestation is another significant cause. If current warming trends continue, the United States is most at risk for **1** negative consequences, although the entire world will be affected. Scientists predict that **3** sea levels will rise dangerously and **4** flood coastal areas. There will also be **3** more droughts and changes in precipitation patterns, **4** such as more hurricanes and tornadoes. In addition and possibly most destructive is the **3** threat to plant and animal life and, consequently, to public health.

Contexts for Cause and Effect

A cause-and-effect paper may be particularly common in some of your science courses or in any kind of course that asks you to think critically about a situation. Whenever you begin to think about your **audience** for this kind of paper, stop and consider some of the following questions:

- Who will want to read this paper?
- How much does the audience know about this topic? What else do they want to know?
- Do they fully understand the cause that you will be writing about, or do they fully understand the effect? Will you need to provide more detail about one or the other so that they understand your position?
- Are you going to present a new cause or effect that the audience has never heard of before? If so, what examples or details will you need to include to help them fully understand the situation?

Once you have carefully considered and identified your audience, you need to think about what your particular **purpose** will be. Typically, a writer wants to explain the cause of something, the effect of something, or both. With that in mind, consider your assignment. Are you going to

- explain the cause of something?
- explain the effect of something?
- explain how a certain cause leads to a certain effect?

If this sounds a bit confusing, think of it this way: Writing about and analyzing causes and effects goes beyond asking "What happened?" to also ask "Why?" and "How?"

> **Situation:** On a hot summer day, you leave a rented DVD on the front seat of your car while you are at work. When you come out of work, you find that the DVD has melted.

The **cause** of the DVD's melting was *leaving it in a hot car all day*. The **effect** of leaving the DVD in a hot car all day was that *it melted*.

Many situations require you to determine causes or effects.

College   In an information technology course, you must discuss the effects of a virus on a local-area computer network.

Work   You analyze the likely effects of working five fewer hours per week.

Everyday life You try to figure out what is causing your phone to need a battery charge so often.

Main Idea in Cause and Effect

The **main idea** in a cause-and-effect essay should reflect your **purpose.** For example, if you are writing about why a certain event in history happened, your main idea would be to explain the causes. If you are writing about what happened as a result of that event, your main idea would be to explain the effects. Consider the following thesis from an essay on drunk driving:

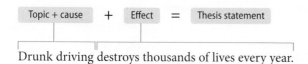

Drunk driving destroys thousands of lives every year.

The main idea of the essay is to discuss the effects of drunk driving—thousands of destroyed lives. The body of the essay will give examples.

Sometimes a thesis statement for a cause-and-effect essay will include both what caused the topic and what resulted from the topic. The following topic sentence shows this pattern:

Discussion Ask students to identify a local or campus-related change and list its apparent causes and effects.

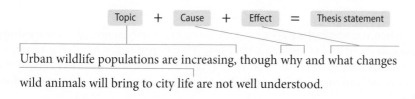

Urban wildlife populations are increasing, though why and what changes wild animals will bring to city life are not well understood.

Sometimes the writer does not directly indicate causes or effects in the thesis statement, as in the following example:

Until local police departments enforce restraining orders, victims of domestic violence will continue to be unprotected.

Although the writer does not indicate a specific cause or effect, the main idea of the essay is clear—to discuss how unenforced restraining orders have resulted in violence. The body of the essay will likely give examples of such situations.

As you begin to write cause-and-effect essays, you might find it helpful to include both the topic and an indicator of cause or effect in your thesis statement.

Support in Cause and Effect

In a cause-and-effect essay, **support** consists of explanations of causes and effects, and it demonstrates the main idea stated in your thesis. Take, for example, the following thesis statement:

> Irresponsible behavior caused my car accident.

The writer supported this thesis by presenting the causes with details that explain them.

Cause	Driving too fast		**Cause**	On my cell phone
Details	Rainy and slippery		**Details**	Not paying close attention
	Going too fast to control car			Hit a curve while laughing
	Could not stop			Did not react fast enough
Cause	Drinking			
Details	Not focused			
	Slowed reaction time			

When you are writing about causes, be careful that you do not say something caused an event or a situation just because it happened beforehand. For example, many of us have gotten sick after a meal and assumed that the food caused the sickness, only to find out that we had been coming down with the flu even before the meal.

When writing about effects, do not confuse something that happened after something else with an effect. In the previous example, just as the meal did not cause the illness, the illness was not the effect of the meal.

Organization in Cause and Effect

Cause-and-effect essays are organized in different ways depending on their purpose.

Main idea	Purpose	Organization
Global warming is a serious threat to life as we know it.	To explain the effects of global warming	Order of importance (saving the most serious effect for last)
Global warming will flood many coastal states.	To describe how the U.S. map eventually might look	Space order
Over the next century, the effects of global warming will be dramatic.	To describe the effects of global warming over the next century	Time order

As you write your essay, add transitions to show how each cause or effect relates to your main idea. Here are some common transitions that are used in cause-and-effect writing.

Common Transitions in Cause and Effect

one cause, reason, effect, result	as a result
also	because
another	thus
first, second, third, and so on	

Read and Analyze Cause and Effect

Before writing your own cause-and-effect essay, read the following examples— one from the workplace and one from college—and answer the questions that accompany them.

Profile of Success
Cause and Effect in the Real World

Jolanda Jones

Attorney, Houston City Councilor, and Consultant

Background   I grew up in a housing project in Houston, Texas, where I lost several relatives to street violence. I always did well in school, however, as a student and an athlete. I eventually graduated magna cum laude from the University of Houston, where I was a three-time NCAA heptathlon champion, and afterward enrolled in law school. In 1996, I qualified for the U.S. Olympic Team trials, and I won the high jump, beating Jackie Joyner-Kersee, who went on to win the gold medal. However, my brother was murdered at about this time, and for a variety of reasons, I did not do well in the rest of the trials. In 2000, I received the NAACP's Award for Legal Excellence for dedication to community service. I started my own consulting business, along with a law practice, and in 2007, I won a highly contested seat on the Houston City Council. Along the way, I was a contestant in season 10 of *Survivor.*

Writing at work   Legal briefs, proposals, letters, Web site content, speeches, presentations

How Jolanda uses cause and effect   As part of my community service and consulting, I speak to inner-city youth. When I address students, I emphasize the importance of understanding that for every action they take, there is a consequence they should consider. During my election campaign, I emphasized to voters how a vote for me would result in many changes in the city of Houston.

Workplace Cause and Effect

The following is a talk that Jolanda Jones gives to students.

Guiding question What does Jones want her audience to understand?

Vocabulary The following words are *italicized* in the essay: *consequences, abusive, coward, aspirations, humiliated,* and *capable.* If you do not know their meanings, look them up in a dictionary or online.

Some of the worst life situations I've seen were caused simply by people failing to consider the effects of their actions. Each of you in this room must learn for yourselves that every single decision you make has *consequences.* It is important that you think about the decisions you make before you make them because if you don't, then you will end up somewhere you didn't plan for.

My best decisions are the ones I make when I think my grandmother might find out about them. If I would be proud for her to know the decision I've made, then it's probably a good decision. If I have to sneak or would be ashamed for her to know my decision, then it is probably a bad decision. In any case, here are some examples of the thought process in good decision making. They show what happens when you don't consider consequences.

Some of you girls might be getting pressured by your boyfriends to have sex. What should you think about? Well, you're probably wondering what he'll say if you don't sleep with him. Will he break up with you or call you "prude"? Well, don't let him define you. What if you get pregnant? What if you get a sexually transmitted disease? What if you get AIDS? What if you break up after you have sex with him? Will he tell everyone how good you were in bed? Will everyone know your business?

Single parenthood is hard. I know from personal experience. I had graduated from college, was working as a minority recruiter and admissions counselor, and was training for the Olympics. I also planned to go to law school at Stanford. Then, I got pregnant without planning for it. Suddenly, I was expecting a child with a man who was both *abusive* and unsupportive. I was not married. I was disappointed in myself. I was ashamed of the shame I brought on my grandmother. I was a *coward.* I fled the United States and hid my pregnancy in Spain. I absolutely love my son, but I gave up my Olympic *aspirations* and Stanford Law School.

Some of you might be thinking about using drugs. Think long and hard. I have crackheads in my family whose lives have been destroyed. Some are homeless. Some are dying of AIDS. My aunt was murdered in a drug house. My brother was murdered buying marijuana. I have an alcoholic cousin who does not take care of her children, and she is on welfare. People who do drugs come to love drugs more than they love anyone or anything else. Then, the drugs control you. You lose control of your life.

What about crime—just little stuff, like shoplifting that little pair of earrings at the neighborhood Target? When I was sixteen, I'd worked to earn money to buy stuff I wanted. I wanted a pair of jeans. Instead, my mother took my check for herself. I still thought I was entitled to the jeans, so I went to Target and took a pair. I got caught. I was arrested, handcuffed, put in the back of a patrol car, and detained. I ducked my head down in the back of the patrol car. I just knew the whole world was looking at me. I was *humiliated.* I should have thought about the consequences. It wasn't right to steal from Target even if my mother took my check. You best believe I've thought about that ever since that date because I've never shoplifted again. I even told my son about it. I don't want him to make the same mistake that I did.

You have choices in life, and it's up to you to make the decisions that will most positively benefit your life. We are all *capable* of thinking through stuff and making the right decision. The question is: Are you going to do it, or are you going to just take the easy road through life? My grandmother said, "If you make a bad decision, learn from it and move on; that way it's not your fault. If, however, you make the same mistake twice, you're stupid and it is your fault." I don't know about you, but I'm not stupid.

I've made good and bad decisions in my life. Thankfully, I've made more good ones than bad. I hope to continue to make good decisions by considering consequences and learning from my mistakes. I hope that's your philosophy too.

Combining modes
Note the use of narration within the cause and effect.

1. Briefly summarize Jones's essay, including her main idea and purpose.

   Answers will vary.

2. Jones uses several cause-and-effect relationships throughout her essay to illustrate her purpose. Identify those relationships and how they support her purpose. *Answers will vary.*

3. Review the Four Basics of Good Cause and Effect (p. 235) and determine whether Jones's writing is a good cause-and-effect essay. Make specific notes to support your opinion. *Answers will vary.*

4. What is your reaction to Jones's essay? What would you ask her if you could? *Answers will vary.*

For more examples of cause and effect, see Chapter 47.

Teamwork Have students work through the first essay together to apply the 2PR Critical Reading Process and answer the questions after the essay.

For the following essay, review the Four Basics of Good Cause and Effect (p. 235) and practice your critical reading process by doing the following.

2PR   The Critical Reading Process

Preview the text, including the guiding question.

Read the text, double-underlining the thesis statement, underlining the major support, and circling the transitions. Consider the quality of the support.

Pause to question and interpret the text. Take notes and write down questions about what you are reading.

Review the text and your notes, and **respond** to it. Write answers to the Pause prompts.

A College Cause-and-Effect Essay

The following cause-and-effect essay was written for an introductory-level college writing course.

Laura Huber

Keep Moving: Why Exercise Benefits Parkinson's Disease Patients

Guiding question What reasons does Huber give in support of her position?

Vocabulary The following words are *italicized* in Huber's essay: *diagnosis, impacted, declined, gait, acquainted, clinical,* and *enlightened.* If you do not know their meanings, look them up in a dictionary or online.

1   Three years ago my father received a medical *diagnosis* that has greatly *impacted* his quality of life: he found out he has Parkinson's disease. Over the past few years, my family and I have watched my father, who is in his early seventies, physically and emotionally decline quite drastically. He has always been a very positive and happy man who was strong and physically active, but we witnessed him beginning to withdraw from social activity, and becoming physically weaker and unsteady in daily tasks. I noticed that my father's exercise routine *declined* as well; whereas my dad used to go to the gym multiple days a week, was an avid downhill skier, and rode his bike every chance he could, all of that activity was decreasing.

2   I started doing research after my father received his Parkinson's disease diagnosis to find out what could be done to halt or slow the progression of this disorder or at least minimize the side effects in order for him to still lead a productive and active life. Thankfully, I have succeeded in convincing him that he needed to continue exercising and even add to his existing routine. Persuading him took some effort, but it was worth it. Research has proved that exercise helps hold off the debilitating effects of Parkinson's disease when one is committed to an active routine.

3   Parkinson's disease (PD) is a debilitating disease that slowly decreases one's mobility and living independence. The Mayo Clinic's overview of the symptoms and side effects includes "muscle stiffness,

Pause What is the main argument or position of the essay?

tremors, bradykinesia (the slowdown of movement/gradual loss of spontaneous activity), changes in walking *gait* and posture, changes in speech and handwriting, and loss of balance with increased falls" ("Parkinson's Disease: Overview"). When my father was diagnosed, my goal was to keep him mobile as long as possible.

Pause By giving this information to the audience, what does Huber assume about them? Do they know a lot or a little about this disease? What do they want or need to know?

4   Many seniors do not have a regular exercise program. Anne Burnell, the founder and creator of Stronger Seniors, reports that statistically only 22 percent of those over 65 years of age report exercising regularly, and those who do spend no more than 17 minutes daily. Leading a sedentary lifestyle is typical for most seniors; however, my father is neither the typical senior nor the typical person with PD. Yet personally I am *acquainted* with several people diagnosed with PD who are statistically typical when it comes to their lack of exercising. Conferring with my father and with them, I have discovered they all seem to have misconceptions about exercise and their disorder. I have heard them excuse their lack of physical exercise due to three common issues: They don't see their need to exercise, they are too tired or despondent to exercise, and they are afraid of falling while exercising.

5   Seniors with PD may be even more reluctant to exercise due to their diagnosis. Therefore, an analysis of the reasons seniors with PD give for choosing a sedentary lifestyle is critical to helping them change their thinking about the benefits of exercise. First, those with PD do not understand the need for exercise. The Cleveland Clinic reports the point of exercising is to keep the disease from causing the body to decline at an accelerated rate ("Parkinson's Disease: An Overview"). Since currently there is no known cure for Parkinson's disease with medicine or alternative measures, patients need to do what they can to slow down the progression of the disease. Physical activity helps with maintaining and increasing bone and muscle mass which fight against the disabling factors of the disease and restore a sense of balance. These *clinical* findings are in strong support of proving there are substantial benefits to adding some type of physical activity to a daily routine.

Pause What reasons is Huber giving to support her position? Are they logical reasons? Are they well supported with good evidence?

6   The *New York Times* published an article titled "For Elderly, Fear of Falling Is a Risk in Itself," in which N. R. Kleinfield *enlightened* readers with firsthand accounts of the fears that older people have regarding falling and how the fear keeps them from exercising. The fear of falling equated to seniors being less mobile and less social, which are both

counterproductive in the long-term independence of seniors in general. Kleinfield surmised there is a direct connection between the ability to be unafraid of falling and the person's ability to have a positive outlook on life and to not give up being active.

7   In his book *Parkinson's Disease & the Art of Moving*, John Argue offers an affordable alternative to physical therapy sessions and gym memberships. Argue uses a blend of yoga and tai chi chuan, along with the principles of theater dance, for his specific type of exercise. Like other physical activity regimens, Argue's form of motion also increases strength and balance as well as mental sharpness and mood. He believes that the sooner people with PD implement a routine of physical activity, the better the patients' long-term quality of life can be.

Pause Is the purpose still clear at this point in the paper? Have all the points and claims stayed on topic and supported the main claim or position of the paper?

8   In closing, I hope those with Parkinson's disease will be convinced of their need to include a physical exercise routine to their lifestyle. Living with my parents has allowed me to have a firsthand observation of how my father has clearly profited from continuing to be very active in spite of his limitations. The benefits are abundant in improving and maintaining good physical and mental health. If patients choose to ignore the evidence, they will continue to lose ground in their mobility and their independence. Inevitably, the choice is theirs. I am glad that at least I have convinced my father to take control of his PD. One way I encourage my dad to continue his exercise routine is by saying to him, "Use it or lose it. Keep moving!"

Pause After reading, what is your overall impression of the essay? Are you persuaded by the evidence?

Works Cited

Argue, John. *Parkinson's Disease & the Art of Moving*. Oakland: New Harbinger, 2000. Print.

Burnell, Anne. "Statistics on Elderly Exercise." *Statistics on Elderly Exercise*. N.p., 10 Aug. 2011. Web. 25 June 2013.

Kleinfield, N. R. "For Elderly, Fear of Falling Is a Risk in Itself." *New York Times*. N.p., 5 Mar. 2003. Web. 25 June 2013.

"Parkinson's Disease: An Overview." *Cleveland Clinic*. N.p., 7 Oct. 2012. Web. 19 June 2013.

"Parkinson's Disease: Overview." *Mayo Clinic*. N.p., 11 May 2011. Web. 25 June 2013.

1. **Respond.** In a paragraph or two, record your response to Huber's essay. How does the information she presents connect to your experience or knowledge?

2. **Summarize.** Briefly summarize Huber's essay, including the topic, her position on it, and the main **support** she gives.

3. **Analyze.** How does Huber use **transitions** in her essay? How does she connect her concluding paragraph to her thesis statement? Is Huber biased or objective?

4. **Synthesize.** Huber attempts to connect the fears of senior citizens in general with those of senior citizens who have been diagnosed with Parkinson's disease. Do you think that the two can be compared or that more research is needed? If someone in your family was diagnosed with PD, would you want that person to be more active, or would you be afraid of injuries? Why do you feel that way?

5. **Evaluate.** Does Huber make a good argument? Do you agree with her? Does her essay have the Four Basics of Good Cause and Effect (p. 235)? Are there any logical fallacies?

Write a Cause-and-Effect Essay

ESL Invite ESL students to write about the causes or effects of a cultural or linguistic misunderstanding. Native English-speaking students might focus on causes or effects of a misunderstanding based on race, social class, gender, or age.

This section includes four assignments for writing a cause-and-effect essay. Use the following tools to help you as you complete one or more of these assignments.

1. Review the Four Basics of Good Cause and Effect (p. 235).

2. Use **Cause and Effect at a Glance** (p. 247) as a basic organizer.

3. Use the Writing Guide: Cause and Effect (p. 249) as you write and revise.

| WRITING ASSIGNMENT 1 | **Writing a cause-and-effect essay: suggested topics** |

Write a cause-and-effect essay on *one* of the following topics or on a topic of your own choice.

College
- The immediate effects of being in college or the desired long-term effects on your life of going to college
- Causes of a legitimate absence that resulted in your missing a test (directed to your professor)

Work
- Causes of low employee morale
- Effects of juggling work, school, and family

Everyday life
- Causes of an argument with a friend or a member of your family
- Effects of sleep deprivation (look for articles or Web sites)

WRITING ASSIGNMENT 2 **Writing about images**

DR. JUERG ALEAN/SCIENCE SOURCE

Closely examine these photos, which show the Trift glacier's evolution from 2002 to 2003. As you can see, there is a significant difference in the size of the glacier in each photo. After examining the photographs, write an essay that uses them as a jumping-off place for your own thoughts. The following are some questions you might wish to explore:

- What might have caused such a dramatic decrease in ice?

- What may be an effect on the land around these glaciers now that the ice has melted?

- How might melting ice affect animals or people in the surrounding areas?

- How might melting ice affect the weather or environment around the area?

You are also welcome to explore other questions of your own.

Cause and effect at a glance

Thesis statement
Indicates causes, effects, or both

↓

Cause 1 or effect 1
Detailed explanation or example of the first cause or effect

↓

Cause 2 or effect 2
Detailed explanation or example of the second cause or effect

↓

Cause 3 or effect 3
Detailed explanation or example of the third cause or effect

↓

Conclusion
Reminds the audience of your main idea and makes an observation about it based on what you have written

Writing to solve a problem

Problem Your child has been bullied at school, and you are deeply concerned about how it is affecting him or her. You have heard how desperate children can become in such circumstances, and you want to educate yourself on bullying in general and the situation in your child's school in particular. You have already contacted the principal, but so far nothing has been done.

Assignment Read Kathleen Vail's essay "Words That Wound" (p. 599) to consider the causes and effects of bullying. Then, go online and search for articles about bullying. Look particularly for common causes of bullying behavior and common effects on the victims. Write about these in a cause-and-effect essay.

Writing about readings

Standards of who and what are good or bad are reflected in television, magazines, music, and virtually every other type of media. Media images affect us all, whether or not we are aware of it, and several of the readings in this book deal with how people can be harmed by them. Choose one of the reading pairs that follow, and write an essay on the suggested topic:

1. Kathryn Arnett's "Media and Advertisement: The New Peer pressure?" (p. 264) and Amy L. Beck's "Struggling for Perfection" (p. 665).

   • Discuss the issue that Beck raises and how Arnett's piece on the media and body image supports Beck's point. Refer to both readings, and bring in your own experiences with media portrayals as well, including how you or people you know have been affected.

2. Dave Barry's "The Ugly Truth about Beauty" (p. 658) and Amy L. Beck's "Struggling for Perfection" (p. 665).

   • Discuss the authors' different approaches to a similar topic. Analyze the differences, and discuss which piece is more effective to you and why.

3. Amy L. Beck's "Struggling for Perfection" (p. 665) and Brent Staples's "Just Walk On By" (p. 669).

   • How have the two different groups the authors portray been negatively affected by portrayals in the media? Bring in references from each reading along with your experiences of how the media can cause people to have incorrect, and sometimes dangerous, perceptions of themselves and others.

Use the steps in the Writing Guide that follows to help you prewrite, draft, revise, and edit your cause-and-effect essay. Check off each step as you complete it.

WRITING GUIDE: CAUSE AND EFFECT	
Steps in Cause and Effect	**How to do the steps**
Focus.	• Think about an event or a situation that had concrete causes and/or effects.
Explore your topic. See Chapter 5.	• With your purpose in mind, prewrite to get ideas about causes and effects.
Write a thesis statement. Topic + Indication of cause or effect = Thesis See Chapter 6.	• Write a thesis statement that includes your topic and an indication of whether you will be showing causes, effects, or both.
Support your thesis. See Chapter 7.	• List the major causes and/or effects. • For each cause or effect, give details that will help your audience understand how they caused or affected an event.
Write a draft. See Chapter 8.	• Arrange the causes and/or effects in a logical order (often chronological or by importance). • Write topic sentences for each major cause and/or effect and paragraphs that describe them in detail.
Revise your draft. See Chapter 9.	• Ask another person to read and comment on your draft. • With your purpose and audience in mind, read to make sure that the causes and effects are real and you have explained them adequately. • Add transitions. **239** • Improve your introduction, thesis, and conclusion.
Edit your draft. See Parts 5 through 8.	• Correct errors in grammar, spelling, word use, and punctuation.
Evaluate your writing.	• Does it have the Four Basics of Good Cause and Effect (p. 235)? • Ask yourself: Is this the best I can do?

18

Argument
Writing That Persuades

Understand What Argument Is

Argument is writing that takes a position on an issue and offers reasons and supporting evidence to convince someone else to accept, or at least consider, that position. Argument is also used to persuade someone to take an action (or not to take an action).

Many situations require good argument skills.

Four Basics of Good Argument

1 It takes a strong, definite position on an issue or advises a particular action.

2 It gives credible supporting evidence to defend the position or recommended action.

3 It considers opposing views.

4 It avoids faulty reasoning.

In the following paragraph, each number corresponds to one of the Four Basics of Good Argument.

1 The drinking age should be lowered from twenty-one to eighteen. **2** The government gives eighteen-year-olds the right to vote. If they are adult enough to vote for the people and policies that run this country, they should be mature enough to have a drink. **2** The U.S. penal system also regards eighteen-year-olds as adults. If an eighteen-year-old commits a crime and goes to trial, he or she is tried and sentenced as an adult, not as a minor. That means that if the crime is murder, an eighteen-year-old

4 It avoids faulty reasoning.

could receive the death penalty. Eighteen-year-olds are not given special treatment. Most important is the fact that at eighteen, individuals can enlist in the armed forces and go to war. The government considers them old enough to die for their country but not old enough to have a drink? This makes no sense. **3** Opponents to lowering the drinking age justify their position by saying that if the age is lowered, teenagers will start drinking even earlier. However, there is no evidence to show that legal age is a major influence on teenage drinking. Other factors involved, such as peer pressure and the availability of fake IDs, have more impact on whether teenagers drink. While the government does need to address the issue of teenage drinking, forbidding eighteen-year-olds to drink while granting them other, more important rights and responsibilities at the same age is neither consistent nor reasonable.

4 It avoids faulty reasoning.

Contexts for Argument

Putting together a good argument is one of the most useful skills you can learn. Knowing how to argue well will equip you to defend effectively what you believe and to convince others to agree with you. With most papers, we tend to think of our audience first; however, with argument, in order to know who we are going to write to, we need to know what we are going to argue.

We present an argument for various **purposes:** to persuade someone to give us a job, to buy something we are selling, or to give us more time to finish a task. And we argue when something important is at stake, like keeping a job or protecting our rights. Here are some questions to consider when formulating your argument:

- What is your position on the topic?
- What are you trying to persuade your reader to think or believe?

When you are writing an argument, you will need a clearly defined **audience** so that you know how much information you will need to present. You cannot defend a position or persuade a reader if you do not take into account how much information that person already knows about the topic. Questions you may want to consider include, but are not limited to, the following:

- How old are your readers?
- How much do they know about your topic already?
- What do they want to know about your topic?
- How interested are they in the topic?

Discussion Ask students to identify some issues—whether local, national, or international—that have more than two sides.

- Do they currently have a position on the topic that you will need to consider as you write?
- Do they have any views that you will need to consider as you write? These views could be, for example, political, religious, ethical, or moral.

Discussion Ask students to give examples of situations in which they needed to defend a position.

College	An exit essay from a writing course contains the following instruction: "Develop a well-balanced argument on the subject of free speech on the Internet."
Work	You present reasons why you should get a promotion.
Everyday life	You convince a large company that it has made a mistake on your bill.

Main Idea in Argument

Your **main idea** in an argument is the position you take on the issue you are writing about. This main idea is the purpose of your paper, and it should be a clear and definite position. When you are free to choose an issue, choose something you care about. When you are assigned an issue, find one aspect that you feel strongly about and take a definite position. You should approach your argument feeling committed to and enthusiastic about your position. To help you get there, consider the following tips.

Tips for building energy and enthusiasm

- Imagine yourself arguing your position with someone who holds the opposite position.
- Imagine that your whole grade rests on persuading your teacher that your position is correct.
- Imagine how this issue could affect you or your family personally.
- Imagine that you are representing a large group of people who very much care about the issue and whose lives will be forever changed by it. It is up to you to win their case.

Take a few minutes to think about the issue, talk it over with a partner, or jot down ideas related to it. Once you have decided on your position and have built up some energy for it, write a thesis statement that includes the issue and your position on it.

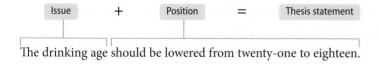

The drinking age should be lowered from twenty-one to eighteen.

Today's minimum wage is not enough to live on.

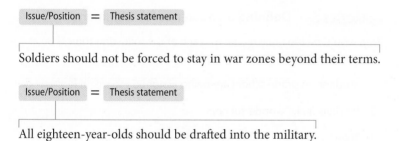

The important thing about a marriage is that two people love and respect each other, not what gender they are.

Sometimes the thesis combines the issue and the position, as in the following statements:

Issue/Position = Thesis statement

Soldiers should not be forced to stay in war zones beyond their terms.

Issue/Position = Thesis statement

All eighteen-year-olds should be drafted into the military.

Try to make the thesis statement for any argument as specific as possible to help guide your writing and your readers.

Vague   Our health-care system is disgraceful.

More specific   Two key reforms would make health care more affordable for all.

[The paper would detail the two reforms.]

Many thesis statements for arguments use words such as the following because they clearly express a position:

could (not)	ought (not)
must (not)	requires
must have	should (not)
needs	would

PRACTICE 1 **Writing a statement of your position**

Write your position on the following issues:

Free child care for college students

Answers will vary.
_____

Background checks for potential employees

_____

Restriction of social media

_____

Now, take one of the position statements that you just wrote, and put more energy into it.

_____

_____

PRACTICE 2 **Defining an audience for argument**

Who would be the ideal reader for each of the following topics? Be as specific as you can.

1. Students in grade school are being assigned too much homework.

2. Pit bulls make wonderful pets.

3. Teens and young adults tend to share too much information over Twitter.

4. A four-day workweek is not a good idea.

5. Reading to children every evening helps them learn.

PRACTICE 3 **Combining audience and purpose**

For the following topics, identify the audience that would be most interested in reading the argument. Then, write a strong, energetic position statement for that topic.

1. Adding alternative treatments into health-care packages.

2. Mandatory minimum sentencing for drug possession or use.

3. Career counseling opportunities at college.

Support in Argument

However strongly you may feel about an issue, if you do not provide solid **support** for your position, you will not convince anyone to see it your way. As you develop support for your position, think carefully about your readers and the kind of information that will be most convincing to them.

OFFERING REASONS AND EVIDENCE

The major support for your position consists of the **reasons** that you give for that position. These reasons must be backed up with **evidence**, such as facts, examples, and expert opinions. The success of your argument depends on the quality of the reasons and evidence that you present to support your position.

Facts are statements or observations that can be proved true. **Statistics**—numerical facts based on research—can be persuasive when used as evidence to back up your position. **Examples** are specific experiences or pieces of information that support your position. **Expert opinion** is the opinion of someone who is considered an expert in the area you are writing about. *Note:* The fact that a person's opinion appears on a Web site does not necessarily mean that he or she has any expertise. When in doubt about a source's authority, consult your instructor or a research librarian.

Position	It pays to stay in college.
Reason	College graduates earn more than high school graduates.
Evidence/fact	College graduates earn 55 percent more than high school graduates.
Reason	Students learn up-to-date skills that they will need to find a job.
Evidence/example	Understanding how to use technology in your field may make the difference between getting a job and coming in second.
Reason	Many jobs require college degrees.
Evidence/expert opinion	John Sterling, president of one of the largest employment recruiting agencies, said recently, "Ten years ago, a college degree was perceived as an advantage. Today, the college degree is the basic ticket of entry for the majority of jobs." (*Note:* When you use expert opinion, you need to identify the source.)

As you choose reasons and evidence to support your position, consider your readers. Are they likely to agree with you, to be uncommitted, or to be hostile?

For more on finding sources, using quotations, and citing sources, see Chapter 19.

Choose the support that is most likely to convince them, drawing on outside sources (such as the library or Internet) as needed.

ACKNOWLEDGING OPPOSING POSITIONS

Part of your support for your position involves the opposing position: Acknowledge it, and present some evidence against it. If, for example, you are arguing in favor of lowering the drinking age to eighteen, you should not ignore the position that it should be kept at age twenty-one. If you do not say anything about the other position, you are leaving your argument unprotected. To defend your own position, show some weakness in the opposing position.

The writer of the paragraph on pages 250–51 might consider the opposing position as follows:

Position   The drinking age should be lowered from twenty-one to eighteen.

Opposing position   The drinking age should not be lowered because people begin drinking before the legal age. If the age were lowered to eighteen, more sixteen-year-olds would drink.

Acknowledging the opposing position: First, laws should not be based on the extent to which they are likely to be abused or broken. They should be based on what's right. Even so, there is no evidence to show that legal age is a major influence on teenage drinking. Other factors involved, such as peer pressure and the availability of fake IDs, have more impact on whether teenagers drink.

As you gather support for your position, keep the opposing position in mind, and follow the tips given in the following box.

Tips for Supporting Your Position by Addressing the Opposing Position

- Visualize someone who holds the opposing position and what that person would say to defend it.

- In part of the body of your essay, acknowledge the opposing position. Do so politely; if you try to ridicule the opposing view, you will alienate people and immediately weaken your argument.

- Address the opposing position directly and show what's wrong, or misguided, about it. Again, do this politely.

- Return to the reasons and the evidence that support your position.

| PRACTICE 4 | **Acknowledging and addressing the opposing view** |

For each of the following positions, in the spaces indicated, state the opposing position and at least one point someone holding the opposing view might make against your position. *Answers will vary. Suggested answers follow.*

Teamwork Practice 4 works well in pairs.

Issue: The "Three Strikes and You're Out" rule in some high schools that requires students to be expelled after three serious offenses

Position: Against it

Opposing position: *In favor of the rule*

Point that someone holding the opposing position would make:
The rule serves as a deterrent.

Issue: Mandatory retirement at age sixty-seven

Position: In favor of it

Opposing position: *Opposed to mandatory retirement at age sixty-seven*

Point that someone holding the opposing position would make:
People live longer these days than they used to.

Issue: Stricter gun control laws

Position: Against it

Opposing position: *In favor of stricter gun control laws*

Point that someone holding the opposing position would make: *Stricter laws would decrease the number of accidental shootings.*

AVOIDING FAULTY REASONING

As you write and review the support for your position, be sure that your evidence is good and your reasoning is logical. Unfortunately, we are exposed to **faulty reasoning** all the time, especially in advertising. Certain kinds of errors in logic are so common that there is a name for them—**logical fallacies.** Be aware of the common fallacies so you can avoid them.

Logical Fallacies

Logical fallacy	Definition	Example	Faulty reasoning
Either/or extremes	Assuming that there are only two extreme choices with nothing in between.	*My country, love it or leave it.*	Should people really either applaud everything a government does or move to a different country?
Bad analogy	Comparing items or circumstances that are not alike enough to make a meaningful comparison.	*A human fetus should have the same rights as a human adult.*	While some specific rights may be shared by a fetus and an adult, saying they should have all the same rights does not make sense because they are different in many ways. Should a fetus be able to vote, for example?
Circular reasoning	Supporting a position by restating part of it.	*I deserve a raise because I deserve to make more money.*	While this may be true, it will not persuade your boss. You need to offer reasons why you are worth more than you are being paid.
"Everyone knows"	Appealing to people's general desire to be like the majority by supporting a statement with a claim that all or most other people believe something.	*Everyone knows that all politicians are liars.*	While some research studies might measure people's perceptions about how truthful politicians are, it is not likely that any

Continued

Logical fallacy	Definition	Example	Faulty reasoning
"Everyone knows" (continued)	A common occurrence of this is when a child says to a parent, "Everybody else's parents are letting them do *X*." This kind of faulty reasoning is also called the bandwagon effect.		study would reveal that all people believe that all politicians lie all the time.
Mistaken causes or effects	Assuming that one thing caused another simply because it occurred beforehand.	*The opening of the new liquor superwarehouse caused old Mr. Jones to close up his shop.*	Mr. Jones might have closed for a variety of reasons. Unless you have proof that Mr. Jones closed his shop because the superwarehouse opened, this statement alone is not evidence.
Overgeneralization	Making a broad statement that is not supported by enough evidence.	*Having grown up with three brothers, I know firsthand that boys are more violent than girls.*	A sample of one family is not enough to assume that all boys act in a particular way.
Oversimplification	Making something seem simple when it is not simple.	*If more parking spaces were available on campus, more students would come to class.*	Students miss class for many reasons, so saying parking is the problem is too simple.
Slippery slope	Saying that something will create a chain reaction, even though there is no evidence that this will happen.	*Using marijuana will lead to heroin addiction.*	There is no overall evidence that one leads all the way to another. To make such a claim, proof of each step of the chain reaction must be given.

Continued

Logical fallacy	Definition	Example	Faulty reasoning
"This, so that"	Pairing ideas or events that are not logically connected.	*I trust my doctor, so I ask him for advice about my finances.*	The fact that a medical adviser is trustworthy has no bearing on the doctor's financial reliability. This kind of faulty reasoning is also called a *non sequitur* (literally, "it does not follow").

Organization in Argument

Argument most often uses **order of importance** to organize reasons for the writer's position on the issue. Consider what you think your audience will find your most convincing reason. Arrange your reasons and evidence so that they build the strongest case for your position, and save the most convincing reason for last. Do not forget to acknowledge and address the opposing position somewhere in your argument.

As you write your argument, use transitions such as those in the following box to move your audience from one reason or point to the next.

Common Transitions in Argument

From one point to another	To add emphasis
also	above all
another fact to consider	best of all
another reason	especially
another thing	in fact
consider that	in particular
for example	more important
in addition	most important
in the first place	remember
	the last point to consider
	worst of all

Profile of Success
Argument in the Real World

Shawn Brown

Founder, Diamond Educators

Background   I had what is, unfortunately, a typical kind of life for many poor urban youth who are caught up in gangs, drugs, and violence. My brother was murdered in a crossfire, and I lived with my mother with no father around. I was an athlete and got away with not doing much in school. I had my first kid at age fifteen, and in that same year I almost shot a rival who had disrespected me. I didn't, mainly because I remembered my coach, who'd warned me not to leave my son fatherless. This coach, Ed Powell, had a saying I still repeat often: "He who fails to plan, plans to fail."

A few years ago, I got together a group of my friends, all college-educated African American men with families and steady jobs. We talked about how many young black men have no positive role models and decided that we wanted to help them the way we had been helped. From that meeting came Diamond Educators, a nonprofit organization that starts working with kids in third grade by teaching them how to behave, speak, and "play the game" in a way that will lead to success in life. Teens who are in the program give back by mentoring elementary school boys.

Writing at work   For Diamond Educators, I've written a mission statement, research projects, proposals for funding and support, and many other kinds of documents.

How Shawn uses argument   I use argument in both speech and writing to persuade the boys, members of the community, legal bodies, and potential donors. I have to think about who the person is, what he or she thinks, and how I can best make my case.

Read and Analyze Argument

Before writing your own argument essay, read the following examples—from college and the workplace—and answer the questions that accompany them. As you read, notice that argument uses many of the other kinds of writing you have studied to support a position. It may tell a story, give examples, describe something, explain how something works, break a large point into categories, define a term, compare two or more things, or show cause and effect.

Workplace Argument

Shawn Brown wrote this letter to support the parole request of a young man he had worked with.

Guiding question What is Brown's purpose, and what is his overall point?

Vocabulary The following words are *italicized* in the letter: *parole, mentor, multicultural, adverse, cope, invaluable, dedication, mentees, transform, jeopardize, essential,* and *incarcerated.* If you do not know their meanings, look them up in a dictionary or online.

To Whom It May Concern:

It is with enthusiasm that I am writing to support *parole* for Rodney Strong. In his work for Diamond Educators as a *mentor* to young men, he has made a positive contribution to the at-risk youth in the city of Boston.

Diamond Educators is a nonprofit mentoring program that serves at-risk young males who attend Boston public schools or who live in the inner-city neighborhoods of Boston. The mentors of the Diamond Educators program are *multicultural* male educators and professionals who grew up in the city of Boston and who dealt with *adverse* conditions that the majority of our young minority males face every day, conditions that often result in bad life choices. The adverse conditions I refer to are living in an environment where young men *cope* with peer pressure to join a gang and involve themselves with drugs, crime, and violence; single-parent homes; and a lack of positive male role models. Our mentors help young men chart a course through their difficult situations. These mentors are an *invaluable* resource for our young, urban, minority males.

As a mentor, Rodney demonstrated commitment and *dedication* to our program and to our students. Rodney worked long hours, but he found time to meet and counsel his *mentees*. He showed his mentees the importance of meeting commitments, taking responsibility, and having a positive purpose in life. He was a good example of how positive peer relationships can *transform* lives.

Rodney gave these young boys hope. He showed his mentees that by applying themselves and taking advantage of the resources available to them, they could achieve success in life. Many of the boys otherwise live without hope of any kind and choose paths that *jeopardize* their own well-being and that of others in the community. That hope is *essential* to becoming a productive member of the human community. Rodney is a leader with a strong will to achieve his own success and to help others find theirs.

The path to success for urban minority males is extremely difficult, and, as with many difficult courses, progress is not always direct and uninterrupted. Rodney stepped off course and made a poor decision when he committed a crime. However, he has demonstrated that he has learned from his mistake and is ready to return to his community as a positive force. He is ready to contribute to society, and to keep him *incarcerated* deprives us of a good man, a good leader, and a good role model for young men. His release will show his mentees that there is hope of a good, lawful life after jail.

Rodney is dedicated to being a good father and a good community influence. Unlike many who return to the community after incarceration, Rodney will not persist in a life of crime; he will return to his path of success and contribution. Keeping him from that serves no purpose.

I support Rodney Strong and will continue to support him after his return to the community. I urge you to consider his good work and to allow him to continue it.

Sincerely,
Shawn Brown, Cofounder
Diamond Educators

1. Briefly summarize Brown's essay, including the topic, his position on it, and the main reasons he gives. *Answers will vary.*

2. In what paragraph does Brown acknowledge and respond to an opposing view? 5

3. If you were an officer of the court, would Brown's letter alone persuade you to support parole for Rodney Strong? Why or why not? What else would you want or need to know? *Answers will vary.*

4. How might Brown's point of view differ from a member of the criminal justice system's? *Answers will vary.*

5. What, to you, is the strongest reason Brown presents? Why? _____
   Answers will vary.

For more examples of argument, see Chapter 48.

Discussion Ask students to identify a good argument or speech they have heard and explain what made it effective.

Teaching tip As an assignment, have students rewrite this argument, adding opposing positions, more support, and transitions.

A College Argument Essay

In learning how to construct a good argument, you use everything you have learned about good writing. Being able to make a good case for or against something you believe may be the most important skill you learn in college—and it can be applied to all other parts of your life.

For the following essay, review the Four Basics of Good Argument (p. 250) and practice your critical reading process.

The following essay was written in response to this assignment: "Identify a topic that is important in your field of study, and take a position on that topic."

2PR   The Critical Reading Process

Preview the text, including the guiding question.

Read the text, double-underlining the thesis statement, underlining the major support, and circling the transitions. Consider the quality of the support.

Pause to question and interpret the text. Take notes and write down questions about what you are reading.

Review the text and your notes, and **respond** to it. Write answers to the Pause prompts.

Kathryn Arnett

Media and Advertisement: The New Peer Pressure?

Guiding question   How might television and magazine ads be more influential to teens than their own friends?

Vocabulary   The following words are *italicized* in the essay: *chiseled, obligation, depicting, ultimately, impressionable, bouts, consumers,* and *clavicle*. If you do not know their meanings, look them up in a dictionary or online.

1   Growing up, I always felt different from my peers. Larger. I was taller and I was curvier than all the girls in my elementary school. As the years progressed, I flipped through magazines and compared myself to the tall, thin girls modeling the newest fashions. Why didn't I look like them? I started to look for ways to diet at age eleven, and what started as a controlled allowance of food at each meal morphed into constant guilt when I ate more than I had rationed. Now, you may be thinking, didn't she have enough food at home? I did. More than enough! So much so that my constant cycle of controlled eating, overeating, and feeling guilty lead to bulimia. I was a great student, and yet when I was twelve my school counselor was knocking at my door trying to reach my parents regarding my weight loss and lunchtime habits. I was desperate to look like what

I thought was normal. No one told me the models were airbrushed and dying to be skinny themselves.

2   Marketing and advertisement agencies focus on models such as a tall, thin woman or a muscular man with a *chiseled* jawbone when casting for photo shoots and television commercials. The problem with only portraying those types of men and women is that not everyone looks that way. When the majority of articles in magazines give readers tips on how to have the perfect abs or how to lose ten pounds in three days, it isn't hard to wonder why teenagers today are dressing more provocatively and worrying much more about what they look like than about the grades they are getting in school.

3   Parents have an *obligation* to their children to help safely guide them to become healthy adults. Because media and advertising are constantly being broadcast to our children, parents need to offer more information to help children form better opinions about the many messages they are being fed. One very strong message being advertised is that women who are tall and thin are attractive, just as men who are muscular and fit are attractive. If parents allow teenagers to view magazine advertisements and television commercials that depict this message, they are setting them up for a skewed view of what "beauty" is. This leaves teenagers feeling as if they do not fit in if they do not fall into this stereotype or image. And if they do not fit in, they are not beautiful.

4   Consider that nearly 50 percent of all teens and preteens categorize their exposure to television as "most of the time," so they are exposed to many advertisements every year. Of these advertisements seen, many are for diet pills, clothing, and hygiene products, products that show how to "fix" human flaws. Furthermore, there are television shows, movies, and commercials *depicting* scantily clad young women and buff young men in tight T-shirts. Many young people have no idea that the media are permitted to airbrush out imperfections from photos.

5   When a child grows up day to day becoming familiar with certain images, it doesn't take long before those images make an impact on each child and his or her future beliefs, whether about their body, their skin, or who they *ultimately* are as a person. Oftentimes, busy working-parent and single-parent homes end up with children watching more television because it is something inside the home that can safely entertain them. Haven't we all allowed our child to view a program so that we can have time to wash the dishes? But just how "safe" is this entertainment, especially for *impressionable* teens?

6   When a preteen or teenager is trying to find his or her style, thoughts, and self, having a healthy body image and healthy self-esteem are critical. Teens often have *bouts* of low self-esteem and feelings of loneliness as they progress from elementary school to high school. It is during this time of finding one's self that many teens are now requesting

Pause Why does Arnett feel she developed an eating disorder?

Pause Why does Arnett believe that television is having such a large influence on the lives of teens and younger adults today?

Pause What does Arnett mean when she talks about a "safe" environment?

Pause Do you agree with Arnett's opinion about plastic surgery?

cosmetic surgery as birthday gifts from their parents. It is hard to imagine that an adolescent with a crooked nose is requesting surgery for any other reason than to improve his or her body image.

7   Parents have the ability to take down the shroud of secrecy regarding magazine airbrushing techniques. Teenagers should know why this happens and how the media and advertising agencies try to trick *consumers*. When I think back to the photos and advertisements I viewed on my path to bulimia, I know that my body image could have been preserved with some guidance from my parents about the unrealistic picture painted by marketing and advertisement agencies trying to play on my naïveté. I was able to get help with my disorder, but only when I truly believed and understood the power and influence the media had on me. These pictures I viewed for so long were really touched up photos creating *clavicle* shadows and airbrushing away the cellulite in order to make me and other teens feel less normal. If parents can take away the power media has over us and our children, we can help guide our children toward a healthy self-image.

1. **Respond.** After reading Arnett's essay, do you agree with her position about the media and body image? Explain your answer.

2. **Summarize.** Briefly summarize Arnett's essay, noting what she believes is the cause and what she thinks is the effect.

3. **Analyze.** Arnett believes that many households rely on media such as television because there are so many single-parent and working-parent homes. Because of this, teens are now exposed to more unrealistic body images than ever before. Do you agree with this opinion or not? Could there be another reason why teens want to look or act a certain way? What might it be?

4. **Synthesize.** Arnett says that marketing and advertising agencies, along with parents, have an obligation to set realistic standards for everyone, especially teens. Is it really the job of those agencies to make sure that teens understand what a healthy body image and weight are? Or is it the job of parents and peers? Explain your answer.

5. **Evaluate.** Do you think Arnett proved her position? Explain. Did she use all of the Four Basics of Argument (p. 250)?

Civic Argument

As you can see, there are many ways to write an argument. One more example is called a **civic argument.** After a class discussion and assignment on the unfairness of federal financial aid regulations, student John Around Him, an Oglala Sioux from South Dakota, wrote the following letter to Senator John Kerry. Senator Kerry not only responded to the letter, promising to work to change the federal financial aid system, but he also visited Around Him's college class. Because of this contact, John Around Him was hired to work as a policy intern in Kerry's Massachusetts office.

Guiding question Why does the author think the financial aid system is not fair to many students?

Vocabulary The following words are *italicized* in the letter: *chaos, eligibility,* and *criteria.* If you do not know their meanings, look them up in a dictionary or online.

Dear Senator Kerry:

1   My name is John Around Him, and I am a student at Bunker Hill Community College in Boston, Massachusetts. I am Native American and a veteran of the war in Iraq. I know that you, as a veteran of the Vietnam War, can relate to putting your life on the line in an environment of gunfire, explosions, *chaos,* and confusion, wondering if the next second might be your last. For most young people, being in the middle of a dangerous war—being shot at and surrounded by death and violence—is not an appealing way to earn money for college. However, for students like me who do not qualify for federal financial aid, it may be the only way to go to college, and this is why I am writing to you. The federal financial aid system needs to be changed because it is not effective in helping students, especially low-income and minority students, pay for college.

2   I grew up on the Pine Ridge Reservation in South Dakota and graduated from Little Wound High School in 2001. I was an average student, with a grade-point average of just under 3.0. I always wanted to go to college, but I asked myself, "How would I pay for it?" I lived with a single-parent father and with two other families, and my father would often help others who needed it. My father was a language teacher, not highly paid, so for me family financial support for college was out of the question. I had to find another answer.

3   When I turned to the federal financial aid system, I found that there is money to help some students pay for college, but none for a student like me. According to the College Board's report, "Trends in College Pricing, 2006," the average tuition, room, and board costs for public universities is $12,796 (though many are much more, as is the case here in Massachusetts)—way out of line for my family's finances. Yet according to the financial aid formula, my father made too much money.

Note Partly as a result of this letter and his internship, Around Him received a full scholarship to Dartmouth College.

4   The formulas used to determine a student's financial need are not realistic: They do not represent the average student's situation. For example, according to the formula, to be considered independent (which largely determines *eligibility*) a student must meet one of the following *criteria:* He or she must be either twenty-four years of age or older, married, a veteran, or an orphan or ward of the court. Many students today, however, are financially independent as soon as they graduate from high school. In 2005, according to the National Center for Education Statistics, 64 percent of students at community colleges and 37 percent at public colleges and universities were financially independent. Fifty-eight percent of those students worked at least thirty-five hours per week, and 67 percent delayed entering college to earn money to help pay for it. Still, those under age twenty-four are not considered to be independent, and their

Pause How does Around Him appeal to his audience here?

Pause Note that Around Him uses narration in this paragraph.

family income is taken into consideration, even when the student receives no family support. As a result, many students have to try to meet one of the other eligibility requirements. For too many, the answer is joining the military, going to war.

5   I am not saying that students should not enlist in the military. Would I have signed on if I had received financial aid? I don't know. I support our troops and enjoyed my time in the service. The military's values and discipline and my experiences there have contributed to who I am today, and I am thankful for that. However, I don't believe that students should have to risk their lives to qualify for financial aid.

6   I am writing to you not only on my own behalf but for the well-being of my family and my country. The federal financial aid system ignores a majority of students in need of aid. Despite rising tuition costs, our financial aid options are slim, and more and more students are not able to achieve a college education, our path to success. This problem is like a cancer; unless treated, it will spread and will hurt our nation's future.

> Sincerely yours,
> John Around Him

Pause Summarize what Around Him says about the criteria for eligibility. What kind of evidence does he use in this paragraph?

Pause Why is this conclusion effective?

1. Briefly summarize John Around Him's argument, including his main idea and reasons. _Answers will vary._ _____

2. Where does Around Him acknowledge the opposing view? _____
   _____

3. Write three questions you would ask for a quiz on this essay (and be able to answer your own questions). _____

4. Is the argument a strong one? Why? _____

5. Which of the essays in this chapter is the best example of a good argument? Why? _____
   _____

Write an Argument Essay

This section includes four assignments for writing an argument essay. Use the following tools to help you as you complete one or more of these assignments.

1. Review the Four Basics of Good Argument (p. 250).
2. Use **Argument at a Glance** (p. 269) as a basic organizer.
3. Use the Writing Guide: Argument (p. 272) as you write and revise.

WRITING ASSIGNMENT 1   **Writing an argument essay: suggested topics**

Write an argument essay on one of the following topics or on a topic of your own choice. Select an issue that you care about so that you can argue powerfully.

College
- Defend the following statement: "A college degree means something."
- Write a letter to the student affairs office proposing a student service that does not currently exist.

Work
- Argue against a company policy you find unfair.
- Argue that employers should or should not monitor employee e-mail use.

Everyday life
- Argue against a rent increase.
- Write a letter to your congressional representative asking him or her to work to change a law or policy that you believe is unfair.

WRITING ASSIGNMENT 2   **Writing about images**

© MOODBOARD/BRAND X PICTURES/ROYALTY-FREE/GETTY IMAGES

Take a careful look at the image showing a young man holding a sign that says "Will Work for Food." Think about what the argument might be before going any further: What does or does not make sense to you on first glance? Now, consider a few statistics: In her article "Half of College Grads

---

Argument at a glance

Thesis statement
Includes the issue (topic) and your position on it

↓

Reason 1
Supporting examples, facts, and expert opinions

↓

Reason 2
Supporting examples, facts, and expert opinions

↓

Reason 3
Supporting examples, facts, and expert opinions

↓

Conclusion
Reminds readers of your position and makes a strong last attempt to convince them of that position

Are Working in Jobs That Don't Require a Degree," Susan Adams writes, "In 2011, 1.5 million, or 53.6%, of college grads under age 25 were out of work or underemployed, according to a 2012 Associated Press story that used an analysis of the U.S. government's 2011 Current Population Survey data by Northeastern University researchers, plus material from Drexel University economist Paul Harrington, and analysis from liberal Washington, D.C. think tank, the Economic Policy Institute."[1] With this information in mind, think about the above image. Going to college has become less of an option and more of a requirement for anyone who wants to find the kind of job that provides the stability, benefits, and salary needed to live independently and/or support a family.

Write an essay in which you respond to the image and discuss the argument you think the picture is making. Are there enough jobs for college graduates? Should everyone go to college, even if it means taking on loans or other debt? Are college graduates or young adults the new unemployed? How effective do you think this visual argument is? If you didn't have any background information on the unemployment rate or job rate in America, would the image alone be enough to create a strong argument?

1. **Susan Adams:** "Half of College Grads Are Working in Jobs That Don't Require a Degree," *Forbes*, May 28, 2013.

Teaching tip Have students work in groups to find out what the job outlook is for their intended major or for college graduates. Use this as an opportunity to explore sources and/or start thinking about using facts and statistics in an argument.

WRITING ASSIGNMENT 3   Writing to solve a problem

Problem An alumnus has given your college a large donation that is intended to improve the quality of student life. The president has set up a committee to determine several possible uses for the money, and you are one of the students on that committee.

Assignment Working either on your own or with a small group, first decide on three possible uses of the money that would improve the quality of student life. Then, choose one of them, and write a letter to the president arguing for this use of the donation. Be sure to include solid reasons for your choice.

Resources To help you decide which of the three possible uses you will argue for, you might type into a search engine keywords related to areas in need of improvement at your college (for example, *[your college] computer center*). List any Web sites that you use.

WRITING ASSIGNMENT 4   Writing about readings

The examples of argument in this chapter cover the issues of parole, media and body image, and unfair federal financial aid provisions. At the heart of each of these issues is a basic conflict between individual rights and institutional (or corporate) rules or laws. Keeping this in mind, choose *one* of the following assignments:

- Choose one of the readings in this chapter, and write your own pro or con argument on the same topic, using the evidence that the reading presents but also adding your own. Find at least one other source (either in print or online) on the subject, and refer to that source to support your position. Be sure to document your sources.

- Choose a different issue that pits individual rights against institutional policies. Here are some examples of such topics.

  - Should physician-assisted suicide be legal?

  - Should a college have the right to censor the contents of the college newspaper?

  - Should students be able to carry concealed weapons on a college campus if they have the proper permits?

  - Should the drinking age be lowered?

  - Should the government be able to require that you wear a seatbelt in your car?

  - Should the government be able to require that everyone have health insurance coverage?

  - Should students have to pass standardized tests to graduate from high school?

  - Should junk food be banned from all public schools, including both elementary and high schools?

  - Should college athletes be paid?

Write an essay responding to the question, and use at least one online or print source to support your position. Be sure to document the source.

- Choose another issue that is important to you. (If you cannot think of one, try looking through a newsmagazine or newspaper; go to an online news source such as *Slate, Salon,* or *Helium;* or visit a nonpartisan Web site such as *ProCon.org.*) Write an argument defending your position on the issue, using at least one source. Document any source that you use.

Use the steps in the Writing Guide that follows to help you prewrite, draft, revise, and edit your argument. Check off each step as you complete it.

Teaching tip Try introducing your students to thought-provoking questions such as these: Should all speech be protected, even hate speech? Should teachers or students be armed in the classroom?

WRITING GUIDE: ARGUMENT

Steps in Argument	How to do the steps
Focus.	• Think about your position on an issue and how you can persuade your readers of that position.
Explore your topic. See Chapter 5.	• Think about why you have taken the position you have. • Prewrite to find good support for your argument.
Write a thesis statement. Topic + Position = Thesis See Chapter 6.	• Write a thesis statement that includes your topic and your position. • Make sure it is a strong statement with a clear position.
Support your thesis. See Chapter 7.	• Provide facts, examples, and expert opinions to support your position. • Examine your reasons to make sure they are not faulty reasoning (see p. 257). • Consider the opposing view. • Give details to strengthen each of your main points.
Write a draft. See Chapter 8.	• Arrange your points by order of importance, leaving the one that will have the most impact until last. • Write topic sentences for each major point and paragraphs that demonstrate and prove them. • Write a conclusion that has energy and reminds your readers of your position and main support for it.
Revise your draft. See Chapter 9.	• With your audience in mind, read to make sure your supporting points are persuasive and complete. • Add transitions. • Improve your introduction, thesis, and conclusion.
Edit your draft. See Parts 5 through 8.	• Correct errors in grammar, spelling, word use, and punctuation.
Evaluate your writing.	• Does it have the Four Basics of Good Argument (p. 250)? • Ask yourself: Is this the best I can do?

Researched Writing

"I write presentations and speeches for work and school."

Katie F., student

PHOTO: JOEL BEAMAN

19

Doing Research
Preparing to Write a Research Essay

Most of your college classes will require you to write papers that draw not only on what you have observed, learned, and experienced but also on the knowledge of others, especially experts on the topic you are writing about. Using the knowledge of others to inform your work and to support the points you make is called using outside sources. Today, we have all kinds of information available to us, and finding information is usually easy. Your task, though, is not just to *find* information, but to find information that is reliable, objective, and relevant to your purpose. This chapter gives you the tools you will need to find and evaluate the vast information resources available to you before using it in your writing, or in any situation that requires you to make decisions or opinions based on information. You will use outside sources of information in such situations as the following.

College   You are assigned a paper on targeting consumer preferences in a marketing course.

Work   You want to find out what kinds of employment opportunities a new geographic area has. You also want to know what average salaries are for specific kinds of work.

Everyday life   You need information about a particular illness: its causes, symptoms, and treatments and questions you should ask a doctor.

Find Sources

Turn first to your college's library. Before even visiting the library, find its Web site by using a search engine and typing in your college's name and the word *library* (for example, "Santa Monica College library"). That will bring up the home page for the library. Look at the example of the Santa Monica College library's Web page, annotated to show the various entries there. Note that there is not only information on various sources (books, articles, and course materials) but also (in the left column) specific help on using the library and research topics.

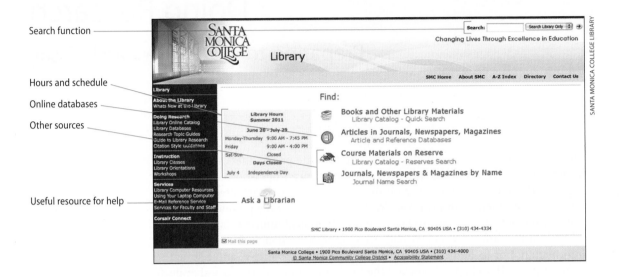

Next, visit the library in person. Most college libraries, like most public libraries, have hours that allow people with different schedules to use them.

Consult a Librarian

Librarians can help you find appropriate information in both print and electronic forms. If your library allows it, make an appointment with a librarian to discuss your project and information needs. You might arrange to go with other students for an orientation. Note in the lists of useful resources on the left side of the Santa Monica College Library page that instructors can schedule a library class. Your college library may also hold such classes. Before your appointment, orientation, or class, make a list of questions you would like to ask. Base your list either on what you have seen on your library's Web site or on some of the following questions.

Questions for the librarian

Teaching tip If the library offers group training on library resources, schedule such a session for your class.

- Can you show me how to use the library catalog? How do I use the information I find there?

- What are databases? How does database information differ from what I can find in the library catalog?

- Can I access the library catalog and article databases when I'm not on campus?

- Based on my topic, what other reference tools would you recommend that I use for my research?

- Once I identify a potentially useful source in the catalog or a database, how can I find the material?

- Can you recommend some keywords that I can use for my particular topic?

- Can you recommend an Internet search engine that will help me find information on my topic? Can you recommend some useful reference sites for my topic?

- How can I tell whether an online source is reliable?

- I have already found some online articles related to my topic. Can you suggest some other places to look? How can I find good print sources on my topic?

Use Library Resources

BOOKS

To find books on your topic, use the library catalog, which is likely to be online. Look at the Santa Monica College Library Web site on page 276, and see the "Library Catalog" link under the heading "Books and Other Library Materials." When you are beginning your research, using the library catalog's keyword search is often the best place to start. **Keywords** are individual words or phrases that are related to your topic. You type these keywords into the library catalog in the same way you'd type them into an online search engine. When you first look for sources, your keywords can be fairly general. For example, Michael McQuiston, a Temple College student whose essay on using native plants for landscaping appears on page 304, chose *green landscaping* as his keywords when searching his library's online card catalog for books. His keyword search returned the following entry:

Teaching tip Use your students' knowledge of electronic devices (smartphones, tablets, and so on) to help them find ways to research intelligently. Your library probably has an application (app) that students can download for free and use with ease.

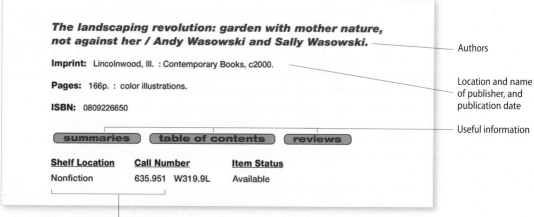

The landscaping revolution: garden with mother nature, not against her / Andy Wasowski and Sally Wasowski. ——— Authors

Imprint: Lincolnwood, Ill. : Contemporary Books, c2000. ——— Location and name of publisher, and publication date

Pages: 166p. : color illustrations.

ISBN: 0809226650

(summaries) (table of contents) (reviews) ——— Useful information

Shelf Location	Call Number	Item Status
Nonfiction	635.951 W319.9L	Available

Section of library where book is found, with specific identification number of book

In addition to giving the title, subtitle, and authors' names, this entry gives the publisher (the imprint) and length (166 pages), and notes that the book contains color illustrations. McQuiston could also have clicked on the buttons to see a summary of the book, its table of contents, and one or more reviews, all of which could help him decide whether this book is relevant to his research.

Along the bottom of the entry, McQuiston could see that the book was located in the nonfiction area of the library. The **call number** is a book's library identification number. With that information, McQuiston could go to the nonfiction section and, within that section, look for the book's number (635.951 W319.9L).

Since library holdings are organized by subject matter, the books on either side of the one you want may also be related to your research subject. If your library does not have a book you need, the librarian or you yourself can usually log on to the library's Web site and order it via interlibrary loan. If you have questions about what you find in the library catalog, consult the librarian.

Note For a complete online research guide, visit **macmillanhighered .com/researchroom**.

As you narrow your topic, you will likely also narrow your search by using more specific keywords. An example of how McQuiston did this is given in Chapter 20.

ONLINE DATABASES/PERIODICAL INDEXES

Most libraries, and college libraries in particular, subscribe to online **databases,** which are lists of **periodical** (journal, newspaper, and magazine) articles on different topics. Because the library pays a subscription fee for these databases, only library members may use them. By entering your student number on the college library Web site or your library card number on the public library's Web site, you can access all these helpful reference sources, which have already been checked for reliability. Some databases are general; some are specialized, with a focus on, for example, psychology or education. Some databases have the full texts of the periodicals online, which is handy.

Most college libraries subscribe to the most popular and comprehensive subscription databases: Academic Search Premier, LexisNexis Academic, ProQuest Research Library, and InfoTrac. These databases are excellent places to start looking for sources because they cover the widest range of periodicals. Michael McQuiston could search any of these databases, using his keywords, and immediately be referred to a variety of good sources on his topic.

Note Most resources referred to here can be accessed through a print reference guide as well as online. A librarian can direct you to the right area of the library and help you find good sources to start your research.

Because these databases include so many sources, a first search for McQuiston might show thousands of sites that included *green* and *landscaping*. An easy way to limit a keyword search is to enclose your topic in quotation marks ("green landscaping"). The search then shows only sources that include the two words together.

Some specialized subscription online databases might also be useful in your search. These include newspaper Web sites (such as the *New York Times* and the *Wall Street Journal*) and topical sites such as AccessScience, Business Source Premier, and Criminal Justice Index.

The Santa Monica College Library site (see p. 276) also provides links to journals, newspapers, and magazines. While library Web sites differ, they all have the goal of helping users navigate the library's resources.

ENCYCLOPEDIAS

Encyclopedias give brief, basic information on a wide range of subjects. Like databases, encyclopedias can be general or specialized. The *Encyclopædia Britannica*, a reliable general encyclopedia, is usually available in print in the reference section of the library and online (**www.britannica.com**). Specialized encyclopedias exist for almost any subject you can imagine; you can find them in the reference section or in the online catalog. Encyclopedias might be a good place to get an overview of your topic, but many instructors want students to use more specialized sources in their writing.

Note Do not rely on Wikipedia for accurate information.

Use Other Resources

Although your library is the best place to find good sources, other ways can work well, too. But you should always make sure these types of sources are reliable.

OPEN DATABASES

Many databases, both general and specialized, are free and open. Some particularly good ones are Infoplease (**www.infoplease.com**), the Internet Public Library (**www.ipl.org**), the Library of Congress Online (**catalog.loc.gov**), and Martindale's The Reference Desk (**www.martindalecenter.com**). To use these, follow the same search and keyword instructions covered earlier in this chapter.

Teaching tip Students have probably heard the "Do not use Wikipedia" rule before, but have they learned why? Put them in small groups and have them explore the accuracy of a particular entry that you know may be particularly vague or lacking information. An interesting assignment could be to have students edit or write an entry for Wikipedia and see what happens to it.

SEARCH ENGINES

Using a general search engine on the Web will likely bring you many sources on your topic, some reliable and some not. Some of the most popular search engines are

- Google (**www.google.com**)
- Bing (**www.bing.com**)
- Ask.com (**www.ask.com**)
- Yahoo! (**www.yahoo.com**)

To use a search engine, enter your keywords in the subject box. Michael McQuiston, the Temple College student, used Google and tried several variations on his search keywords, which netted the following results.

Keywords	Search returns
green landscaping	More than 19 million results
"green landscaping"	More than 500,000 results
"green landscaping in dry areas"	0 results
green landscaping in dry areas	More than 3 million results

These figures are a little surprising: Putting the keywords *green landscaping* in quotation marks narrowed the number of entries, but adding the words *in dry areas* within the quotation marks did not further narrow the search; instead, it provided no entries at all. Taking away the quotation marks from "green landscaping in dry areas" produced even more entries than "green landscaping." In this case, narrowing the search terms while using a general search engine resulted in the unwanted inclusion of many commercial sites, such as businesses that provided green landscaping services in dry areas. Finding good sites can require a long process of sifting through inappropriate sources for your research essay. Therefore, using library sources is often a better strategy than using general sources.

STATISTICAL SOURCES

Statistical data consist of facts and figures. When they are directly related to the thesis of your research essay and are from a reliable source, statistics can provide strong support. One good source of statistical data is the *Statistical Abstract of the United States,* which was published annually by the U.S. Census Bureau from 1878 until 2012 and is now published by ProQuest. It can help you find useful statistics related to social trends, social issues, population trends, economics, demographics, and other topics.

ONLINE RESEARCH SITES

Online research sites constitute another valuable source of information on how to do research. Bedford/St. Martin's, the publisher of this book, hosts the *Bedford Research Room* (**macmillanhighered.com/researchroom**), which includes guided tutorials on research processes; advice on finding, evaluating, and documenting sources; and tips on avoiding plagiarism. Other useful sites include Purdue University's Online Writing Lab (OWL) at **http://owl.english.purdue.edu.** This site offers a variety of materials and resources for writers, including research information.

Interview People

Personal interviews can be excellent sources of information. Before interviewing anyone, however, plan carefully. First, consider what kind of person to interview. Do you want information from an expert on the subject or from someone directly affected by the issue? How would the experience or comments of each person help support your points? The person should be knowledgeable about the subject and have firsthand experience. When you have decided whom to interview, schedule an appointment.

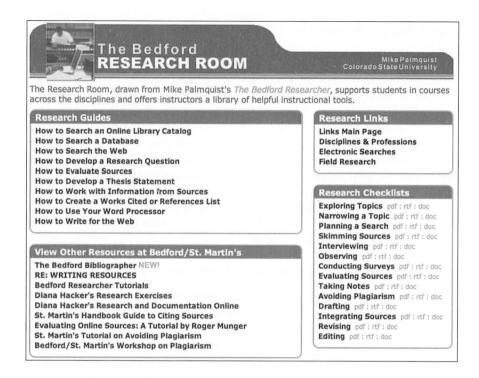

Next, to get ready for the interview, prepare a list of five to ten questions. Say, for example, you are writing about a proposed law to ban drivers from using cell phones. Choose open-ended questions (What is your position on regulating cell-phone use by drivers?) rather than questions that require only a simple yes-or-no response (Do you favor regulating cell-phone use by drivers?). Leave space for notes about the person's responses and for additional questions that may occur to you during the interview. Include in your notes the person's full name, his or her qualifications, and the date of the interview.

As you conduct the interview, listen carefully and write down any important ideas. If you plan to use any of the interviewee's exact words, put them in quotation marks in your notes. Confirm the wording with the interviewee to be sure you have it correctly in your notes. For more on using direct quotations, see Chapter 20 (p. 293) and Chapter 37.

Evaluate Sources

Evaluating sources means judging them to determine how reliable and appropriate they are for your topic, your assignment, your purpose, and your audience. To evaluate sources, use the critical thinking and reading skills you have learned and used in earlier chapters. Before using a source for your paper, apply the following questions to all sources, whether print or electronic.

Note If you plan to record an interview (whether using an audio or video recorder), get your subject's permission first. Recording what a person says without being granted permission is unethical and, in some states, against the law.

Teamwork Have students interview each other on their research topics. They can write a short summary of the interview using both direct quotations and paraphrases.

Questions for Evaluating All Sources

WHO IS THE AUTHOR?

Is the author actually an expert on the topic? Many celebrities, for example, are involved in worthwhile charitable causes that they learn a great deal about. But while Matt Damon, George Clooney, or Angelina Jolie may write a statement or an article about a cause, he or she may not be considered an expert.

Most sources provide some information about their authors. Books often have an "About the Author" section, usually at the end or on the book jacket. Periodicals may have biographical headnotes or notes about the author at the end of the article. If information about the author does not appear in the source itself, you can probably find out more about the author by conducting an online search. Read the information you find to make sure that the author has the authority and knowledge to make the source reliable.

IS THE SOURCE WELL-KNOWN AND RESPECTED?

Certain sources are generally agreed to be reliable, though not always unbiased. National magazines such as *Time, The New Yorker,* and *National Geographic* verify information before publishing it. Periodicals that you find on a subscription database are also usually reliable. Newspapers, too, usually verify information before using it. Tabloids (like the ones sold in the supermarket checkout lines) are not reliable, however; their purpose is to shock and entertain, not necessarily to tell the truth.

IS THE SOURCE UP-TO-DATE?

Look to see when a source was published. If your topic is in a rapidly changing field (for example, science or medicine), your source should be as recent as possible to include the most current knowledge. In contrast, if your topic concerns a person or a work that is considered classic (something that has been respected for a long time), the publication date is not as important. For example, Michael McQuiston's topic, green landscaping, is a relatively new practice, so he should be looking for works that have been published recently. In his reading, however, if he learns of a practice that changed the whole direction of landscaping, that would be considered classic work. Depending on his purpose, he might want to include a reference to that work, in addition to new findings. Whatever your topic is, judge each possible source for how current the information is.

IS THE SOURCE UNBIASED?

Every writer reflects some personal opinion on the subject he or she writes about. However, a good source balances those opinions with reasonable evidence. But facts and numbers can be used differently by people with different biases. For example, a researcher who believes in strict gun control may cite statistics about how many children are killed each year in gun accidents. A researcher who believes in the individual right to own guns may use statistics about how many people are killed in robberies or burglaries. Both writers can use accurate numbers to argue different positions.

Consider the author's background to determine whether he or she is likely to be biased in a way that interferes with reliability. In the gun issue, if an author is president of the Brady Campaign to Prevent Gun Violence, he has a bias toward gun control. If an author is president of the National Rifle Association, he has a bias toward gun ownership. If you think an author is strongly advocating one side of an issue without addressing the other side, move on to another source or include both sides in your essay.

Questions for Evaluating Web Sites

The Web is open to anyone with Internet access, which is one of the great things about it. Anyone can develop a Web site to promote anything he or she wants. That very openness means, though, that you have to be even more critical in evaluating information from a Web site than you would from a print source, especially if you are using a general search engine such as Google or Bing.

The first part of an address, or uniform resource locator (URL), is often the name of the person or organization sponsoring the site; the extension to the URL consists of the letters after the first period (that is, the dot). Different extensions convey information about the site's sponsor.

Extension	Indicates
.com	a commercial or personal site
.edu	an educational institution's site
.gov	a government agency's site
.net	a commercial or personal site
.org	a nonprofit group's site

As a general rule, educational (.edu) and government (.gov) sites are likely to be reliable. The commercial and personal sites (.com, .net) may be good sources, but they may also be promoting the opinions of a biased person or group of people. A nonprofit group's site (.org) also may present either good or biased information. When a search brings you to Web sites with .com, .net, or .org extensions, find out about the sponsors of the sites and examine the sites for evidence of strong bias.

In addition to the questions that you would ask to evaluate any source, add the following, which use your critical reading and thinking skills.

Questions to ask in evaluating a Web site

- What is the URL extension?
- Who sponsors the site?
- Is there an "About" link? What does it tell me when I click on it?
- What is the purpose of the site?
- What kind of information is on the site?
- Does the site material indicate a bias? What is it?
- How easy is it to navigate the site and access information? In other words, can I easily find the information I'm looking for, or am I constantly being forced to click on pop-up ads and other visual distractions?
- Based on the answers to the above, do I think information on the site is reliable and appropriate for my research essay?

PRACTICE

Look carefully at the two Web sites that Michael McQuiston found on his topic. In the space provided next to each number, explain what the corresponding numbered element tells you about the site.

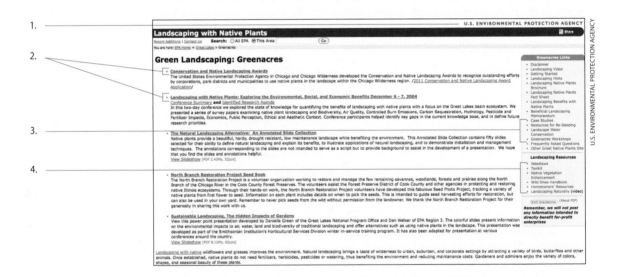

1.   *name of government agency (U.S. Environmental Protection Agency)*

2.   *links to information related to topic*

3.   *reports on native landscaping*

4. _links to information about landscaping resources_ _____

Other things I found out by going to the Web site: _Answers will vary._

_____

My evaluation of site: _Answers will vary._ _____

_____

1. _Banner heading indicates purpose of site._ _____

2. What do I learn from going to the "Home" and "About" pages?
   Answers will vary. _____

3. _Petition box provides visual, allows interactivity, and facilitates activism_

   among like-minded site visitors. _____

   My evaluation of site: _Answers will vary._ _____

   _____

   This chapter helps you find and locate good sources for a research essay. Chapter 20 shows you how to plan and write your research essay.

20

Writing the Research Essay

Using Outside Sources

This chapter will guide you through the process of writing a research essay. Throughout the chapter, we show how one student, Michael McQuiston, worked through key steps in the process. McQuiston's completed research essay appears on pages 304–308.

Make a Schedule

For more information on research papers, visit **macmillanhighered .com/researchroom**.

After you receive your assignment, make a schedule that divides your research assignment into small, manageable tasks. There is no way that you can do every step the day (or even a few days) before the assignment is due, so give yourself a reasonable amount of time.

You can use the following schedule as a model for making your own.

Choose a Topic

Teaching tip Walk students through the process of creating a schedule, starting with the date the essay is due and working backward. Suggest and discuss the amount of time they should allow for each key step.

Your instructor may assign a topic, or you might be expected to come up with one of your own. If you are free to choose your own topic, find a subject that you are personally interested in or curious about. If you need help, try asking yourself some of the following questions:

1. What is going on in my own life that I want to know more about?

2. What have I heard about lately that I would like to know more about?

3. What am I interested in doing in the future, either personally or professionally, that I could investigate?

4. What famous person—living or deceased—most interests me?

5. What do I daydream about? What frightens me? What do I see as a threat to me or my family? What inspires or encourages me?

6. Is there something I do in my spare time (sports, music, video games) that I would like to know more about?

Possible topics for a research essay

Assisted suicide	Music downloading
Banning texting (in class, while driving)	Obesity in the United States
	Outsourcing jobs to foreign countries
Dieting/eating disorders	Patients' rights
Environmental issues	Pets and mental health
Executive salaries	Presidential campaigns
The evolving family in America	Reality television programs
Gay/lesbian marriage/adoption	Rights of children of illegal immigrants
Global warming	
Gun control	Road rage
Identity theft	Sexual harassment
Local community service options	Standardized testing
Mandatory drug testing	Veterans' issues
Mandatory medical insurance	Violence in the media
Marijuana for medical purposes	Women in military combat

When you have chosen a general topic, you will need to narrow it using the same process you learned about in Chapter 5. Although a research essay may be longer than some of the other essays you have written, the topic still needs to be narrow enough to write about in the assigned length. It would be impossible, for example, to write a good five-page paper on "the family in America today." That general topic would have to be narrowed; one way to narrow it is shown in the following diagram (p. 288). The three topics in the second row are narrower than the main topic, and two of the three are further narrowed.

Next, the writer could try out one of the narrowed topics or further narrow those. Before moving ahead with a topic, check its appropriateness with your instructor if you have any doubt. You might also check library resources to see whether information is available on your planned topic. You do not need to actually look at the sources at this point, but you should assure yourself that a reasonable number of sources exist on your topic.

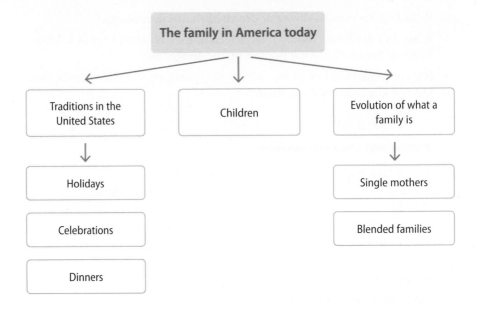

Before writing a working thesis statement, choose a **guiding research question** about your narrowed topic. For example, a writer using one of the narrowed topics related to today's American family, "celebrations," might start with a question like "What functions do common celebrations serve in the life of a family in America today?"

In this chapter, you will see how Michael McQuiston's paper on green landscaping developed.

Michael McQuiston's guiding research question

What are the benefits of green landscaping?

In Chapter 19, you learned how to find and evaluate sources for a research essay. After choosing and narrowing a topic and developing a guiding research question, you are ready to find sources of information related to that topic. As you read through a variety of sources, use your critical reading skills to help you understand and effectively use the information in your research essay. Remember the **2PR Critical Reading Process**.

> ## 2PR   The Critical Reading Process
>
> **P**review the text.
>
> **R**ead the text, looking for the main idea and support.
>
> **P**ause to question and interpret the text, taking notes as you read.
>
> **R**eview the text and your notes, and **respond** to it.

Avoid Plagiarism

Plagiarism is passing off someone else's ideas and information as your own. Turning in a paper written by someone else, whether it is from the Internet or written by a friend or family member who gives you permission, is deliberate plagiarism. Sometimes, however, students plagiarize by mistake because they have taken notes that do not distinguish a source's ideas from their own or that do not fully record source information, including publication data. As you find information for your research essay, do not rely on your memory to recall details about your sources; take good notes from the start. For more on how to avoid plagiarism, visit the Bedford Research Room (**macmillanhighered.com /researchroom**).

Note: This section's advice on recording, citing, and documenting sources reflects Modern Language Association (MLA) style, the preferred style for the humanities.

ESL In some cultures, copying someone else's work is a gesture of respect. Be clear with students about what constitutes plagiarism.

Teaching tip Ask students to bring in a draft bibliography after they have gathered and read their sources but before they finish writing the research paper. This will allow you to make sure they are compiling one.

Keep a Running Bibliography

A **bibliography** is a complete list, alphabetized by author, of the outside sources you consult. A **list of works cited** is a complete list, alphabetized by author, of the outside sources that you actually use in your essay. Most instructors require a list of works cited at the end of a research essay. Some may require a bibliography as well.

You can keep information for your bibliography and list of works cited on notecards or on your computer. Whatever method you use, be sure to record complete publication information for each source at the time you consult it; this will save you from having to look up this information again when you are preparing your list of works cited.

The following is a list of information to record for each source.

Teaching tip Have students practice citing and documenting sources throughout the semester. For example, if they write summaries of readings from this textbook, articles, or Web sites, ask them to use in-text citations and to include a list of works cited at the end of each summary.

Books	Articles	Web pages/other electronic sources
Author name(s)	Author name(s)	Author name(s)
Title and subtitle	Title of article	Title of Web page/online material
—	Title of magazine, journal, or newspaper	Title of site/larger work (e.g., online periodical)
City of publication and publisher	—	Name of sponsoring organization OR name of database
Year of publication	Date of publication	Date of publication or latest update
—	Page number(s)	Page, section, or paragraph numbers (if provided)
—	Volume number	Date you accessed the site
Medium (print)	Medium (print or Web)	Medium (Web/URL, CD)

Create Clear, Complete Records of Source Information

For each source that you take notes on, create an individual notecard or file on your computer. It should include the source's author(s) and title, the page number(s) where you found the specific information, and what method you are using to present it: summary or paraphrase (which are called **indirect quotations**) or **direct quotation** (which is word for word what the source says). A sample card or entry might look like this:

Last name(s) of author(s): List as in works-cited list.

Category of information: McQuiston is sorting information into categories, each a benefit of green landscaping.

Information: Fact or idea to include in his paper.

Information source

Method used to record information: Direct quotation, summary, or paraphrase.

> Welsh, Welch, Duble
> Water Conservation
> "In urban areas of Texas about 25 percent of the water supply is used for landscape and garden watering."
> "Landscape Water Conservation: Xeriscape." *Aggie Horticulture.* http://aggie-horticulture.tamu.edu/extension/xeriscape/xeriscope.html
> Direct Quotation

It is essential to note how you have recorded the information you might use in your paper. For example, if you transfer the exact wording of your note to your paper but have not recorded whether the note was a summary, a paraphrase, or an exact quotation, you risk plagiarizing the author. Even when you do not quote a source directly, you still must cite the source both in the text of your essay and in the works-cited list. The numbers after the indirect and direct quotations in the examples that follow indicate the page numbers where the words or ideas appear in the original work.

Use Indirect Quotation: Summary

As you learned in Chapter 4, a summary is your condensed version of a longer piece of writing, which should include the main point of what you are summarizing. It should also be written as much as possible in your own words, and not by using many of the same words or phrases from the longer source.

One way to include outside source material as evidence or support in your own writing is to summarize. Look back at Kathryn Arnett's essay "Media and Advertisement: The New Peer Pressure?" on page 264, and then read the two summaries that follow here. The first is unacceptable because it uses too many words and phrases from the original. The second is an acceptable summary.

Teaching tip Remind students that they must cite source information even when they summarize and paraphrase. Students often think they need to cite only when quoting directly.

Unacceptable summary

In her essay "Media and Advertisement: The New Peer Pressure?" (264), Kathryn Arnett argues that parents have an *obligation* to their children to help safely guide them to become healthy adults. She talks about the reasons why some young women may, in fact, be dying to be skinny after looking at advertisements in the media. Many teens today are growing up in homes where televisions are background noise and are always on. With exposure to these images most of the time, seeing these familiar images of muscular and fit men or tall and thin women, then they may be seeing a skewed view of what beauty really is. Although it is up to the parents and the children to be aware of what they view and what reality actually is, not all parents have time to monitor their children's television habits. Teenagers should know why this happens and how the media and advertisement agencies try to trick consumers.

Direct quotation should be in quotation marks.

Though this phrase is a common expression, here it is part of a pattern of using exact phrases from the original and so should be in quotation marks.

Pattern of using exact phrases of the original.

Exact wording of original; should be in quotation marks.

Acceptable summary

In her essay "Media and Advertisement: The New Peer Pressure?" (264) Kathryn Arnett argues that parents need to be more careful and consistent in the way they teach their children to respect and take care of their bodies. As more and more parents are working full-time and as more households keep the television on as background noise or use the television as a primary form of entertainment, children and teens are becoming more exposed than ever to media advertisements. These advertisements typically depict an ideal woman as tall and thin and an ideal man as muscular and fit; however, they don't show what it takes to achieve that look or that this appearance may be airbrushed or falsified. If parents can make their children aware of techniques such as airbrushing, perhaps teenagers can start to form their own opinions about what a perfect body is, and perhaps they will start to think about being healthy instead of perfect.

This summary does not use the language of the original, other than those words that refer to the topic. It also focuses on the main point of the piece rather than including all the specific support points. This summary gives the big picture of the essay in a condensed form.

Use Indirect Quotation: Paraphrase

Unlike a summary, a paraphrase is not just a condensed version of the original. To paraphrase properly, you need to think about the main idea and express it in your own words. You cannot paraphrase a whole essay or article; instead, you should concentrate on paraphrasing paragraphs or other short passages.

When you are taking notes from a source and find an idea that you might want to use, try this: Look away from the source, write the idea in your own words, and then look back at the original piece. If what you have written repeats a large number of words or phrases in the original, either try again or use a direct quotation.

Look back at Rui Dai's essay "A Whiff of Memory," comparing the smells of China and the United States (p. 229). Then read the following unacceptable and acceptable paraphrases, which focus on the fourth paragraph of that essay.

Unacceptable paraphrase

The shaded words and phrases are too close to the original. Though they are not direct quotes, the wording is close enough and the pattern of the phrases is the same as in the original.

According to the author (Dai, 229–31), the difference in smell between the two countries is so distinct and clear because olfaction evokes strong memories connected to strong emotions. Speaking biologically, the olfactory system is one of the few senses that has a direct connection to the section of the brain that is in charge of a person's emotional memories. This part of the brain is called the amygdala, and the mitral cells and olfactory receptor neurons help send information about scents.

Acceptable paraphrase

According to the author (Dai, 229–31) humans owe much of their strong emotional response to smells to their olfactory system. Without it, the distinct difference between the odor of a Chinese street and that of an American one would not be so apparent or evoke so many memories in a person. This system creates an emotional connection between a smell and a person's brain because the olfactory system directly connects to the amygdala, the section of the brain in charge of emotional memories. With the help of mitral cells and olfactory receptor neurons to send information to the brain about different scents, the amygdala can create an emotional response and memory for a person based on a smell.

The ideas in this paraphrase are the author's, but the wording is very different from the original.

Use Direct Quotation

A direct quotation uses information from an outside source word for word, enclosing it in quotation marks (" "). Use a direct quotation when the words from the source directly support your thesis. Avoid using long direct quotations in a short research essay, however, since most of what you write should be your own words. If you do use a direct quotation that is more than about forty words or four typed lines, indent the whole quotation, and do not use quotation marks.

Short direct quotation

According to Rui Dai, "Hearing … does not evoke as powerful memories as olfaction, or else every single time we heard something we would be reliving the past" (230).

Longer direct quotation

When beginning to explore the distinction between the smells of China and the United States, Rui Dai states:

> The American Northeast smells of the sea, and the Midwest, dry cornfields. What is so distinctive between the two that, without opening my eyes, I can tell which country is which? Let me explain. The smell of China carries a distinctive musk that is the combination of age and non-ammonia cleaning supplies. America, on the other hand, smells clean—literally, and not necessarily in a good way. Cleaning detergents are used almost ubiquitously in America, while relatively rare in China. In the States, the complex chemical combinations in cleaning agents destroy almost any endogenous smell of the environment, leaving only a hint of pine or lavender, or whatever oil extract the manufacturer had dropped into the mixture. (229–30)

For more on using quotation marks correctly, see Chapter 37.

Again, be certain to include how the information on your notecards is recorded (summary, paraphrase, or direct quotation) and the page number. You may think you will remember, but honestly, you will not. No one does. Keep in mind that preparing good paraphrases is more difficult than recording direct quotations. As you draft your essay, you can think about direct quotations and take the time to paraphrase them carefully.

Write a Thesis Statement

For more on writing a thesis statement, see Chapter 6.

After you have taken notes on the sources you gathered, you should be ready to write a thesis statement, which states the main idea of your research essay. You can start by turning your guiding research question into a statement that answers the question, as Michael McQuiston did for his essay on green landscaping. Note how he revised his thesis to make it more forceful and concrete.

> **Michael McQuiston's guiding research question** *What are the benefits of green landscaping?*
>
> **Draft thesis statement** *There are many clear benefits of green landscaping.*
>
> **Revised after taking notes from sources** *Landscaping with drought-tolerant native plants conserves water, reduces the use of toxic soil conditioners, and makes maintenance easier.*

As you write and revise your essay, your thesis statement may change, but having a good working one helps you focus your writing and see where you might need to do additional research.

Make an Outline

For more on outlining, see Chapter 8.

To organize your notes, you need to make an outline that shows how you will support your thesis. First, write down your thesis statement. Then, review your notes to decide what your three or four major support points will be. Write these under your thesis statement and number them. Under each of your major support points, write two or three supporting details, and number them.

As you read McQuiston's outline, note that although he started with four benefits of green landscaping (*water conservation, fertilizers/safety, effect on wildlife, maintenance*), as he read and took notes, he decided to put *effect on wildlife* into the *fertilizers/safety* category. Note also that he reviewed his organized notes and sources and tried to fit them into appropriate places in his essay. (The names in parentheses and **boldface** are the authors of his sources.)

Michael McQuiston's outline

I. **Thesis Statement (introductory paragraph):** Landscaping with drought-tolerant native plants conserves water, reduces the use of toxic soil conditioners, and makes maintenance easier.

II. **Water Use** ———————————————————————————— First support point
    a. A limited natural resource already strained
    b. Landscaping uses lots of water **(Welsh?)** ———— Supporting details
    c. Native plants **(Tufts?)**
        1. Use less water, drought-tolerant
        2. Many kinds
        3. Lower water bills/save money and water

III. **Fertilizers/Pest Control/Safety** ———————————— Second support point
    a. Poisonous, kids, pets **(Native Plant, Texas Wildscapes?)**
    b. Good bugs/wildlife ———————————————————— Supporting details
    c. Native plants use little or none

IV. **Maintenance** ——————————————————————————— Third support point
    a. Foreign plants, lots of water, lots of time and money
    b. Native plants, not much maintenance **(Lueck?)** —— Supporting details

V. **Conclusion**
    a. Review benefits
    b. Observation

Write Your Essay

Using your outline, write a draft of your research essay. (For more information on writing a draft, see Chapter 8.)

Your **introduction** should include your thesis statement and a preview of the support you will provide in the body of the essay. If you are taking a stand on an issue, the introduction should let your readers know what your position is. The **body** of the essay will present your major support points for your thesis backed by supporting details from your research. The **conclusion** will remind readers of your main idea and make a further observation based on the information you have presented.

As you write, incorporate your sources into your paper with **introductory phrases.** Most often, you will state the name of the source or author before adding the information you are using. Use a comma after the introductory phrases.

Introductory phrase identifying source

Introductory phrase   Source

As shown on the Web site of the Texas Parks and Wildlife Department,

Introductory phrase identifying author and source

In his article "Sustaining Mother Nature with Native Plants," Bill Ward states,

Common Introductory Phrases

according to [source]

as [source] claims   says

        explains   shows

        notes   states

        points out   writes

When you have finished writing your draft essay, take a break from it. Then, definitely allow yourself time to reread, revise, and edit it. At this point, you might read the draft essay and see that you need a bit more support from outside sources. Perhaps you can find more in the sources you have already been using, or you may want to find another source to support your thesis statement.

All the sources that you use must be cited correctly where you use them in your paper, as well as at the end of the paper, in the works-cited list. The sections that follow give you the correct format for documenting in-text citation and works cited. If you are using a type of source that you do not find in these sections, visit the Bedford Research Room (**macmillanhighered.com/research room**), where you will find the documentation format for every kind of source imaginable.

Cite and Document Your Sources

You need to include **in-text citations** of sources as you use them in the essay. You also need to document, or give credit to, your sources at the end of your research essay in a **list of works cited.**

Few people can remember the specifics of correct citation and documentation, so be sure to refer to this section or the reference text that your instructor prefers. Be sure to include all of the correct information, and pay attention to where punctuation marks such as commas, periods, and quotation marks should go.

There are several different systems of documentation. Most English professors prefer the Modern Language Association (MLA) system, which is used in this chapter. However, when you are writing a research paper in another course, you may be required to use another system. When in doubt, always ask your instructor.

For more information on documenting sources, visit **macmillanhighered.com/researchroom**.

Use In-Text Citations within Your Essay

Along with an introductory phrase that smoothly incorporates information from an outside source into your writing, your sources need to be cited where they are used and according to correct documentation format. In-text citations are short versions of the entries in the works-cited list.

The following section shows you what you need to include in an in-text citation for various kinds of sources. Use this format for any source material you are using: a summary, a paraphrase, or a direct quotation. In every case, insert the citation after the material you have used. If you use a direct quotation, the citation comes after the end quote and before the period ending the sentence.

Note: The formats given in this section are for print sources. When you cite a Web source, use page numbers if available. If the source is not paged, use the paragraph number instead. If there are no paragraphs, cite the author, title of the part of the Web site, or the Web site's sponsor.

The series of dots (called ellipses) in the following examples indicate that words have been left out.

Two examples are provided for each citation:

1. The author is named in an introductory phrase, with the page or paragraph number in parentheses.

2. The author is not named in the introductory phrase, and the author's name and page or paragraph number appear in parentheses.

One Author

As David Shipler states, "..." (16).

The number of people who work and fall below the poverty line has increased dramatically (Shipler 16).

Two or Three Authors   Use all authors' last names.

Quigley and Morrison found that ... (243).

Banks and credit card companies are charging many more fees ... (Quigley and Morrison 243).

Four or More Authors   Use the first author's last name and the words *et al.* (*et al.* means "and others").

According to Sen et al., ... (659).

The overuse of antibiotics can result in ... (Sen et al. 659).

Group, Corporation, or Government Agency Use the name of the group, corporation, or government agency. The source can be abbreviated in the parentheses, as shown in the second example.

> The Texas Parks and Wildlife Department offers guidelines for
> landscaping . . . (26).

> Texas has more native plants than any other . . . (Texas Parks and Wildlife
> Dept. 26).

Author Not Named Use the article title in quotations, shortened if it is a long title.

> In the article "Texas Wildscapes," . . . (7).

> Many areas of Texas are filled with drought-tolerant native . . . ("Texas
> Wildscapes" 7).

Encyclopedia or Other Reference Work Use the name of the entry you are using as a source.

> In its entry on xeriscaping, the *Landscape Encyclopedia* claims that . . .
> ("Xeriscaping").

> Xeriscaping is often used in . . . ("Xeriscaping").

Work in an Anthology Use the name of the author(s) of the piece you are using as a source.

> As Rich Chiappone believes, . . . (200).

> Fly fishing is as much a spiritual . . . (Chiappone 200).

Interview, E-mail, Speech Use the name of the person interviewed or the author of an e-mail.

> As University of Texas Vice President of Student Affairs Juan Gonzalez
> said in an interview, . . .

> Students have many resources available to . . . (Gonzalez).

Use a Works Cited List at the End of Your Essay

Note: In MLA style, works-cited entries that have a month and day as part of the publication date are formatted so that the day appears before the month; the month is abbreviated (Jan., Apr., Sept.); and there is no comma between the month and year:

Works cited date style: 14 Mar. 2011

BOOKS

One Author

For each set of entries, the first example shows the format; the second is an example of the format.

Author's Last Name, First Name. *Title of Book: Subtitle.* Publisher Location: Name of Publisher, Publication Date. Medium of Publication.

Shipler, David K. *The Working Poor: Invisible in America.* New York: Knopf, 2004. Print.

Two or Three Authors

Note that titles of books are in *italics*.

Author's Last Name, First Name, and Other Authors' First and Last Names. *Title of Book: Subtitle.* Publisher Location: Name of Publisher, Publication Date. Medium of Publication.

Picciotto, Richard, and Daniel Paisner. *Last Man Down: A New York City Fire Chief and the Collapse of the World Trade Center.* New York: Berkeley, 2002. Print.

Four or More Authors

Author's Last Name, First Name, et al. *Title of Book: Subtitle.* Publisher Location: Name of Publisher, Publication Date. Medium of Publication.

Roark, James L., et al. *The American Promise: A History of the United States.* 5th ed. Boston: Bedford/St. Martin's, 2012. Print.

Group, Corporation, or Government Agency

Name of Group, Corporation, or Agency. *Title of Book: Subtitle.* Publisher Location: Name of Publisher, Publication Date. Medium of Publication.

American Cancer Society. *American Cancer Society's Guide to Pain Control: Understanding and Managing Cancer Pain.* New York: American Cancer Society, 2004. Print.

Editor

Editor's Last Name, First Name, ed. *Title of Book: Subtitle.* Publisher Location: Name of Publisher, Publication Date. Medium of Publication.

Canellos, Peter S., ed. *The Last Lion: The Fall and Rise of Ted Kennedy.* New York: Simon & Schuster, 2009. Print.

Work in an Anthology

Selection Author's Last Name, First Name. "Title of Selection in the Anthology." *Anthology Title: Subtitle.* Ed. First and Last Name of Anthology Editor(s). Publisher Location: Name of Publisher, Publication Date. Pages of Selection. Medium of Publication.

Brown, Sterling A. "Riverbank Blues." *250 Poems: A Portable Anthology.* 3rd ed. Ed. Peter Schakel and Jack Ridl. Boston: Bedford/St. Martin's, 2014. 136-37. Print.

Encyclopedia

Note The citation here is for an online encyclopedia. Note that the entry includes the date the article was accessed (4 Apr. 2014).

Entry Author's Last Name, First Name. "Title of Entry." *Title of Encyclopedia.* Edition Number [1st, 2nd, 3rd] ed. Date of publication. Medium of Publication.

Araya, Yoseph. "Ecology of Water Relations in Plants." *Encyclopedia of Life Sciences.* Apr. 2007. Web. 4 Apr. 2014.

PERIODICALS

Magazine Article

Note that titles of periodicals are in *italics.*

Author's Last Name, First Name. "Title of Article." *Title of Magazine* Day Month Year of Publication: Page Numbers. Medium of Publication.

Kluger, Jeffrey. "One Weird Dinosaur." *Time* 11 Oct. 2010: 44-45. Print.

Newspaper Article

Author's Last Name, First Name. "Title of Article." *Title of Newspaper* Day Month Year of Publication: Page Number [if Print]. Medium of Publication.

Barringer, Felicity. "Indians Join Fight for an Oklahoma Lake's Flow." *New York Times* 12 Apr. 2011: A1+. Print.

Editorial in a Magazine or Newspaper, Author Known

Author's Last Name, First Name. "Title of Editorial." Editorial. *Title of Newspaper* Day Month Year of Publication: Page Number [if Print]. Medium of Publication.

Udall, Don. "When Someone Is Alive but Not Living." Editorial. *Newsweek* 14 June 1999: 12. Print.

Editorial in a Magazine or Newspaper, Author Unknown

"Title of Editorial." Editorial. *Title of Magazine or Newspaper* Day Month Year of Publication: Page Number [if Print]. Medium of Publication.

"Growing Smart." Editorial. *Miami Herald* 29 Apr. 2010. Web. 20 May 2014.

Article, Scholarly Journal with Numbered Volumes

Author's Last Name, First Name. "Title of Article." *Title of Journal* Volume Number.Issue Number (Year of Publication): Page Numbers [if Print]. Medium of Publication.

Fountain, Glinda H. "Inverting the Southern Belle: Romance Writers Redefine Gender Myths." *Journal of Popular Culture* 41.1 (2008): 37-55. Print.

Article, Scholarly Journal without Numbered Volumes

Author's Last Name, First Name. "Title of Article." *Title of Journal* Issue Number (Year of Publication): Page Numbers [if Print]. Medium of Publication.

Thiel, Peter. "The Optimistic Thought Experiment." *Policy Review* 147 (2008): 17-37. Print.

ELECTRONIC SOURCES

The format for citing electronic periodicals follows much of the same format as for print periodicals, so refer to the entries in the previous section for journals with numbered volumes.

Work from a Library Subscription Database (such as InfoTrac)

Author's Last Name, First Name. "Title of Article." *Title of Periodical* Volume number.Issue number (Year of Publication): Page Numbers. *Name of Database*. Web. Day Month Year of access.

McManus, John F. "Global Warming Skeptic Remains Adamant." *New American* 27.2 (2011): 9. *InfoTrac*. Web. 31 Mar. 2014.

Online Periodical

Author's Last Name, First Name. "Title of Article." *Title of Online Periodical*. Name of Periodical Publisher, Day Month Year of Article Publication. Web. Day Month Year of Access.

Manjoo, Farhad. "Is Something Rotten at Apple?" *Slate*. Slate Group, 25 Aug. 2008. Web. 14 Feb. 2014.

Short Work from a Web site If no author is given, omit this information. If no site sponsor is listed, use N.p. If no date of publication is available, use n.d.

Note that titles of Web sites are in italics.

Author's Last Name, First Name. "Title of Work." *Title of Web Site*. Name of Site Sponsor, Day Month Year of Publication. Web. Day Month Year of Access.

"In Her Own Words." *Lady Bird Johnson Wildflower Center*. Univ. of Texas at Austin, 2010. Web. 4 Apr. 2014.

OTHER SOURCES

For citation examples for other electronic sources, visit **macmillanhighered .com/researchroom**.

Personal Interview

Last Name, First Name of Person Interviewed. Personal interview. Day Month Year of Interview.

Okayo, Margaret. Personal interview. 16 Apr. 2014.

E-mail

Last Name, First Name of Author of E-mail Message. "Subject of E-mail." Name of Person Who Received E-mail. Day Month Year E-mail Received. E-mail.

Willey, Liz. "Happy Holidays from Paraguay." Message to Susan Anker. 4 Jan. 2014. E-mail.

Revise and Edit Your Essay

After a break, reread your draft with fresh eyes and an open mind. Then, ask yourself these questions.

- Does my introduction state my thesis?

- Does each of the body paragraphs contain a topic sentence that directly supports my thesis? Do the supporting details in each paragraph relate to and explain the topic sentence?

- Do I provide a conclusion that reminds readers of my main idea and makes a further observation?

- Have I included enough support for the thesis that readers are likely to see my topic the way I do? Is there anything else I could add to make my point?

- Do transitions help readers move from one idea to the next?

- Have I integrated source material smoothly into the essay? Do I need to smooth out anything that seems to be just dumped in?

- Have I reread the essay carefully, looking for errors in grammar, spelling, and punctuation?

- Have I cited and documented my sources?
- Are all of my citations and works-cited entries in the correct form (MLA or whatever style the instructor specifies)?
- Is this the best I can do?

For more on revising, see Chapter 9. When checking for grammar, spelling, and punctuation errors, consult Parts 5 through 8 of this book.

After reading the annotated student essay that follows, use the Writing Guide on pages 309–10 to write your research essay.

Sample Student Research Essay

The student essay that follows is annotated to show both typical features of research essays (such as references to sources) and elements of good writing (such as the thesis statement and topic sentences). The paper also shows formatting (such as margins, spacing between lines, and placement of the title). Your instructor may specify different or additional formatting in class or in your syllabus.

Student's name and page number at top of each page

McQuiston 1

Michael McQuiston

Professor Bicknell

Course — Composition 1

Date — 21 Apr. 2014

Title centered — To Be Green or Not to Be Green

Introductory phrase — When people make landscaping decisions, many do not realize that the choices they make affect not just the immediate appearance of their yard but also the present and future environment. Lady Bird Johnson, a champion of native landscaping, once said, "My special

Direct quotation — cause, the one that alerts my interest and quickens the pace of my life, is to preserve the wildflowers and native plants that define the regions of our land—to encourage and promote their use in

Introduction — appropriate areas" ("In Her Own"). Many people share her feelings and might want to know how landscaping can accomplish such preservation. When planning your landscaping, it is important to choose plants that will be not only aesthetically pleasing but low-maintenance and cost-effective as well. After owning a lawn care and landscape business in Texas for six years, I am a firm believer in green landscaping. Landscaping with drought-tolerant native plants

Thesis statement — conserves water, reduces the use of toxic soil conditioners, and requires little maintenance.

Body paragraphs — As the world's population grows, it strains our earth's limited supply of natural resources. One resource essential to both plants and animals is water. Many cities and towns already restrict watering during the hot summer months to certain days of the week or certain times of day. In an online article written for Texas A&M University, Welsh, Welch, and Duble state that "in urban areas of Texas about 25 percent of the water supply is used for landscape and garden watering." Some homeowners argue that water is necessary to ensure the survival of the plants in their yards.

However, part of the problem lies with the types of flowering plants, trees, and grass used in urban and suburban landscaping, many of them to achieve a certain "look." But these plants can require a great deal of water, as they often originate in areas with much higher rainfall per year or a more constant amount of rain throughout the year. In order to sustain plants native to a

McQuiston 2

climate zone that gets more rain, many homeowners not only see
their water bills double during the arid summer months, but also
contribute to the overall potential environmental water-shortage
problem.

Fortunately, there is a way to have a beautiful yard in Texas
without depleting our water supply: use plants that are drought-
tolerant or native to the area. The nonprofit organization Wild Ones
Natural Landscapers defines *native plants* as "those that were
growing naturally in the area before humans introduced plants
from a distant place" ("Landscaping"). Plants native to a certain
area can survive with the amount of water available through local
bodies of water and rainfall. Some native Texas plants that will still
look beautiful in the midsummer after two weeks of record-high
temperatures and drought include flowers such as the Bluebonnet,
Indian Blanket, Indian Paintbrush, Lantana, and many others, as
well as many shrubs and trees. Homeowners need only ask at
their local nursery or ask a landscape professional to find out what
plants, grass, and trees are native and drought-tolerant. Many
respected Web sites also provide similar advice. Green landscaping
significantly reduces people's water bills and at the same time
conserves water, a limited natural resource.

On a typical Saturday in suburbia, one might hear, "Don't let the
kids go in the yard today. I put down fertilizer." But, wait—aren't the
pets and other wildlife out there too? Although many homeowners
and landscape services recognize the harmful effects of fertilizer and
pesticides, they think having the "best-looking yard on the block" is
worth the risk. According to the California Department of Pesticide
Regulation's "Community Guide to Recognizing and Reporting
Pesticide Problems," pesticides are safest if used properly, but they
are still dangerous. Children and people with asthma or other chronic
diseases are much more likely to get sick from pesticides than healthy
adults, and "some individuals are also more sensitive to the odor or
other irritant effects of certain pesticides" (29).

Using native plants and grasses instead of turf grass in the
landscape eliminates the need for fertilizers and pesticides, making
the yard a safer place for both people and beneficial insects. Jane

First support point

In-text citation

Body paragraphs

Support point

In-text citation

McQuiston 3

Paraphrase

Scott, a gardener and naturalist, argues in her book *Field and Forest* that although the creation of a landscape of any kind causes some disturbance of land and soil, not all the harm landscaping and gardening does is necessary, and native plants would help reduce our environmental impact (4). Native plants do not need fertilizer to condition the soil because it is the soil they will naturally grow best in; there is no need to worry about the correct Ph balance or the perfect balance of nitrogen-potash-iron in the fertilizer. The need for pesticides is also diminished because plants that grow naturally in an area have developed defenses against harmful local insects.

Body paragraphs

Green landscaping also saves local wildlife, which can have a hard time finding food and water in the hot, dry summer months. Natural vegetation not only provides a safe haven for these creatures but also nourishes them. Planting native and drought-tolerant vegetation in the yard transforms it into an extension of these creatures' homes, and in exchange for food, water, and shelter, the creatures offer homeowners an exclusive peek into the wild world around them. The Texas Parks and Wildlife Department recognizes the importance of native plants in providing food for native species of animals, birds, and butterflies, even going so far as to offer a "habitat restoration and conservation plan for rural and urban areas" ("Texas Wildscapes"). Bill Ward's article "Sustaining Mother Nature with Native Plants" illustrates the necessity of native plants for insect life. Monarch butterfly larvae depend on the milkweed for their survival, but as can be gathered from its name, this Texas native is often eradicated because it is considered a weed. "Bugs in native plant gardens," Ward states, "are helping to sustain the ecosystem by supporting a diverse and balanced food web. The same cannot be said about yards landscaped with predominantly exotic plants."

In addition to the environmental effects of nonnative landscape plantings, the regular upkeep of a nonnative lawn can prove too much for busy homeowners. What began as the best-looking yard on the block can quickly deteriorate into the neighborhood eyesore without the necessary maintenance and regular application of extra water and pesticides. While all plants require some care, native

McQuiston 4

plants require far less than the transplanted ones, and Jane Scott argues that native plants are just as attractive as common exotics: "The more we know about the native plant communities that surround us, the more we will come to appreciate their inherent beauty and diversity and the more effectively we can accommodate them in the places where we live" (4). So, native plants offer peace of mind that the yard will look good season after season without constant daily care.

Body paragraphs

In this time of growing environmental awareness, planting nonnative, high-maintenance plants is irresponsible. Native plants do not strain the environment, and they provide food and shelter for various species of wildlife. The low-maintenance nature of native plants makes them friendly to the busy homeowner concerned about the environment. With less fertilizer and pesticide on the lawn, the yard will be a healthier place for families to spend their time and enjoy the outdoors. Green landscaping makes sense for everyone, for now and for the future. Be green.

Observation

Review of support

Works Cited

"Community Guide to Recognizing and Reporting Pesticide
Problems." *California Department of Pesticide Regulation*. State
of California, Apr. 2008. Web. 11 Apr. 2014.

"In Her Own Words." *Lady Bird Johnson Wildflower Center*. Univ. of
Texas at Austin, 2010. Web. 4 Apr. 2014.

"Landscaping with Native Plants." *Wild Ones*. Wild Ones Natural
Landscapers, May 2008. Web. 3 Apr. 2014.

Scott, Jane. *Field and Forest*. New York: Walker, 1992. Print.

"Texas Wildscapes: Gardening for Wildlife in Backyards,
Schoolyards, and Corporate Parks." *Texas Parks and Wildlife*.
Texas Parks & Wildlife Department, Feb. 2010. Web. 2 Apr.
2014.

Ward, Bill. "Sustaining Mother Nature with Native Plants." *Native
Plant Society of Texas*. Native Plant Soc. of Texas, 29 May 2010.
Web. 11 Apr. 2014.

Welsh, Douglas F., William C. Welch, and Richard L. Duble.
"Landscape Water Conservation: Xeriscape." *Aggie
Horticulture*. Texas A&M Univ. Dept. of Horticultural Science, 26
Oct. 2000. Web. 3 Apr. 2014.

Note that in works-cited entries, all lines after the first are indented.

Source without author

After you have taken notes, found outside sources, and written a draft thesis statement, use the writing guide that follows to help you write your research essay.

WRITING GUIDE: RESEARCH ESSAY	
Steps	**How to do the steps**
Make a schedule. See page 286.	• Include the due date and dates for doing research, finishing a draft, revising, documenting sources, and editing.
Choose a topic. See pages 286–89.	• Choose a topic that interests you. • Make sure the topic is narrow enough to cover in the assigned length of the paper.
Ask a guiding question. See page 288.	• Ask a question that will guide your research.
Find and evaluate sources. See Chapter 19.	• Use library resources. • Consider the reliability of each source.
Take notes to avoid plagiarism. See pages 289–94.	• Note the publication information. • Make an entry for each piece of information (p. 290).
Write a thesis statement. See Chapter 6.	• Based on what you have read, write a thesis statement that includes the main idea of your essay. • Turn your research question into a statement: **Research question:** What are the benefits of green landscaping? **Thesis statement:** There are many clear benefits of green landscaping. **Revised after taking notes from sources:** Landscaping with drought-tolerant native plants conserves water, reduces the use of toxic soil conditioners, and requires little maintenance.
Support your thesis. See Chapter 7.	• Review all notes to choose the best points. • Do further research if you do not have enough support to convince your readers of your main point. →

Steps in Research Essay	How to do the steps
Write a draft essay. See Chapter 8.	• Make an outline that organizes your support. • Write an introduction that includes your thesis statement. • Write topic sentences and paragraphs that give support and supporting details. • Work in your outside sources using introductory phrases (see pp. 295–96). • Write a conclusion that reminds your readers of your main idea and support and makes an observation. • Title your essay.
Revise your draft. See Chapter 9.	• Is the thesis clear? • Do I have enough support? • Do I end strongly? • Have I integrated outside sources smoothly in the essay (and cited them)? • Are all sources documented correctly?
Cite and document your sources.	• For in-text citations, see pages 296–98. For works-cited entries, see pages 298–302.
Edit your essay.	• Reread your essay, looking for errors in grammar, spelling, and punctuation.

Part 5

The Four Most Serious Errors

"I write cover letters to go with my resume."

Myra C., student

PHOTO: PATRICIA LEE

21

The Basic Sentence

An Overview

The Four Most Serious Errors

This book emphasizes the four grammar errors that people most often notice.

These four errors typically cause misunderstanding within your writing, and they definitely give readers a bad impression of you. Making any of these errors is like going for a job interview in pajamas. People *will* notice.

1. Fragments (see Chapter 22)

2. Run-ons (see Chapter 23)

3. Problems with subject-verb agreement (see Chapter 24)

4. Problems with verb form and tense (see Chapter 25)

These four errors all have to do with the basic elements of the sentence. This chapter covers those elements, and the next four chapters each cover one of the four most serious errors.

The Parts of Speech

There are seven basic parts of speech in English:

1. A **noun** names a person, place, or thing.

   Stephanie is a girl.

2. A **pronoun** replaces a noun in a sentence. A pronoun can be the subject of a sentence (*I, you, he, she, it, we, they*), or it can be the object of a sentence

e Log in to **macmillanhighered .com/realessays LearningCurve** > The Parts of Speech; **Additional Grammar Exercises** > The Parts of Speech

Discussion Ask students how much time they leave for editing their papers before turning them in. Remind them that even the most experienced writers leave time for editing and proofreading.

In the examples in this chapter, subjects are underlined once and verbs are underlined twice.

313

(*me, you, him, her, us, them*). A pronoun can also show possession (*mine, yours, his, her, its, our, their*).

She likes gymnastics.

3. A **verb** tells what the subject does, or it links a subject to another word that describes it.

   Stephanie *performs* competitively.   [The verb *performs* is what the subject Stephanie does.]

   It *is* difficult.   [The verb *is* links the subject *It* to a word that describes it: *difficult*.]

4. An **adjective** describes a noun or pronoun.

   Gymnastics is a *difficult* sport.   [The adjective *difficult* describes the noun *sport*.]

   It is *competitive*.   [The adjective *competitive* describes the pronoun *It*.]

5. An **adverb** describes an adjective, a verb, or another adverb. Many adverbs end in *-ly*.

   Gymnastics is *very* difficult.   [The adverb *very* describes the adjective *difficult*.]

   Injury occurs *quickly*.   [The adverb *quickly* describes the verb *occurs*.]

   Injury occurs *very* quickly.   [The adverb *very* describes the adverb *quickly*.]

6. A **preposition** introduces a phrase that modifies a noun, pronoun, or verb (*across, around, at, in, of, on, over*, and *to* are some prepositions).

   Coaches often train athletes *in* gyms.   [The preposition *in* begins the phrase *in gyms*, which modifies the verb *train*—where do the athletes train?]

7. A **conjunction** (*for, and, nor, but, or, yet, so*) connects words, phrases, or clauses.

   Language note: Any idea that ends with a period needs a subject and a verb to be a complete sentence. For a review of subjects and verbs, see pages 315–21.

   If you are not sure about the order in which words in a sentence usually appear, see Chapter 32.

> **PRACTICE 1**   **Using the parts of speech**

In the following sentences, fill in each blank with a word that is the part of speech called for in parentheses after the blank. *Note:* Some verbs may be in the past tense, and some verbs may use a helping verb such as *is* or *was*.
Answers will vary. Possible edits shown.

Example: The ____*soccer*____ **(*adjective*)** ____*coach*____ **(*noun*), a former drill**
 sergeant, ____*demanded*____ **(*verb*) that** ___*she*___ **(*pronoun*)**
 arrive ___*promptly*___ **(*adverb*)** ___*for*___ **(*preposition*) practice.**

1. The young ____*student*____ (*noun*), who was new ___*at*___ (*preposition*) the

   school, ____*wanted*____ (*verb*) to join the debating ____*and*____ (*conjunction*)

   fencing clubs.

2. ____*Her*____ (*pronoun*) dream ___*was*___ (*verb*) to play the ____*trumpet*____

   (*noun*) ___*in*___ (*preposition*) the ____*state*____ (*adjective*) band.

3. The ____*cars*____ (*noun*) that ____*continually*____ (*adverb*) went by ____*made*____

   (*verb*) it difficult for the hotel's ____*angry*____ (*adjective*) customers to sleep.

4. The ____*small*____ (*adjective*) ____*store*____ (*noun*), a recent addition ___*to*___

   (*preposition*) the neighborhood, ___*had*___ (*verb*) the freshest fruit ____*and*____

   (*conjunction*) vegetables that ___*he*___ (*pronoun*) had ever seen.

5. Shaking his head ____*decisively*____ (*adverb*), ___*he*___ (*pronoun*) looked up

   and ____*refused*____ (*verb*) to get out ___*of*___ (*preposition*) the car.

The Basic Sentence

A **sentence** is the basic unit of written communication. A complete sentence written in standard English must have three elements:

- A **subject**
- A **verb**
- A **complete thought**

To edit your writing, you need a clear understanding of what a sentence *is* and what a sentence *is not*. You can find out whether a group of words is a complete sentence by checking to see whether it has a subject, a verb, and a complete thought.

Teaching tip
Consider having students use different-colored highlighters to mark subjects and verbs.

 Log in to
**macmillanhighered
.com/realessays**
**Additional Grammar
Exercises** > The Basic
Sentence

Subjects

The **subject** is the person, place, or thing that the sentence is about. The subject of the sentence can be a noun (a word that names the person, place, or thing) or a pronoun (a word that replaces the noun, such as *I, you, she,* or *they*).

> 🌐 Language note: English sentences always have a subject.
>
> | **Incorrect** | Is hot outside. |
> |---|---|
> | **Correct** | It is hot outside. |

To find the subject, ask yourself: Who or what is the sentence about?

Person as subject	Vivian works for the police department.

[*Who* is the sentence about? *Vivian*]

Thing as subject	The tickets cost $65 apiece.

[*What* is the sentence about? The *tickets*]

> 🌐 Language note: In the preceding two sentences the word *the* appears before a noun (*the police department, the tickets*). *The, a,* and *an* are called *articles*. If you have trouble deciding whether to use an article or which article to use with which nouns, see page 500.

A **compound subject** consists of two or more subjects joined by *and, or,* or *nor.*

Two subjects	Nick and Chelsea have a new baby girl.
Several subjects	The jacket, pants, and sweater match perfectly.
Several subjects	Kim, Juan, or Melba will bring dessert.

The subject of a sentence is *never* in a prepositional phrase. A **prepositional phrase** is a word group that begins with a preposition; ends with a noun or pronoun; and modifies a noun, pronoun, or verb.

> 🌐 Language note: If you have trouble deciding which prepositions to use, see page 502.

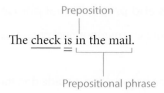

The subject of the sentence is *check*. The subject cannot be the word *mail,* which is in the prepositional phrase *in the mail.*

Although the word *friends* may seem to be the subject of the sentence, it is not. *One* is the subject. The word *friends* is not the subject because it is in the prepositional phrase *of my best friends.*

When you are looking for the subject of a sentence in your writing, it may help to cross out any prepositional phrases, as in the following sentences:

The rules ~~about smoking~~ are posted everywhere.

The sound ~~of lightning striking a tree~~ is like gunfire.

Many ~~of the students~~ work part-time.

Common Prepositions

about	beneath	like	to
above	beside	near	toward
across	between	next to	under
after	by	of	until
against	down	off	up
along	during	on	upon
among	except	out	with
around	for	outside	within
at	from	over	without
before	in	past	
behind	inside	since	
below	into	through	

> **PRACTICE 2**   **Identifying subjects and prepositional phrases**

In each of the following sentences, cross out any prepositional phrases, and underline the subject of the sentence.

Example: For several months, <u>Ronald</u> has been raising a guide dog for the blind.

1. Many other <u>people</u> around the country are raising guide dog puppies.

2. However, Ronald's <u>situation</u> is unusual because he is in prison.

3. <u>Ronald</u> is participating in a program called Puppies Behind Bars.

4. The <u>dog</u> he is raising, a black Labrador puppy named Cooper, lives with Ronald twenty-four hours a day.

5. Whenever Ronald's cell is locked, <u>Cooper</u> stays in the cell with him.

6. In the cell, <u>Ronald</u> plays with the dog, rolling on the floor with him and talking to him in a high voice.

7. <u>Ronald</u> teaches Cooper manners and obedience before the start of Cooper's formal guide dog training.

8. In return, <u>Ronald</u> gains a sense of responsibility.

9. When he finishes his formal training, <u>Cooper</u> will be matched with a blind person.

10. <u>Ronald</u> believes that he and Cooper are contributing an important service to society.

Verbs

Every sentence has a **main verb**, the word or words that tell what the subject does or that link the subject to another word that describes it. Verbs often follow the subject immediately, but that is not always the case: Other words may come between the subject and the verb.

There are three kinds of verbs—action verbs, linking verbs, and helping verbs.

> 🌐 **Language note:** Be careful with *-ing* and *to* forms of verbs (*reading, to read*).
>
> **Incorrect**   Terence <u><u>loves</u></u> to be reading.
>
> **Correct**   Terence <u><u>loves</u></u> reading. *or* Terence <u><u>loves</u></u> to read.
>
> If you make errors like this, see page 498.

ACTION VERBS

An **action verb** tells what action the subject performs.

To find the main action verb in a sentence, ask yourself: What action does the subject perform?

Action verbs

The baby cried all night.

The building collapsed around midnight.

After work, we often go to Tallie's.

My aunt and uncle train service dogs.

LINKING VERBS

A **linking verb** connects (links) the subject to a word or group of words that describes the subject. Linking verbs show no action. The most common linking verb is *be*, along with all its forms (*am, is, are, was, were*). Other linking verbs, such as *seem* and *become*, can usually be replaced by the corresponding form of *be*, and the sentence will still make sense.

To find linking verbs, ask yourself: What word joins the subject and the words that describe the subject?

Linking verbs

The dinner is delicious.

I felt great this morning.

This lasagna tastes just like my mother's.

The doctor looks extremely tired.

Common Linking Verbs

Forms of be	Forms of *become* and *seem*	Forms of sense verbs
am	become, becomes	appear, appears
are	became	appeared
is	seem, seems	feel, feels, felt
was	seemed	look, looks
were		looked
		smell, smells
		smelled
		taste, tastes, tasted

Some words can be either action verbs or linking verbs, depending on how they are used in a particular sentence.

Action verb	The <u>dog</u> <u>smelled</u> Jake's shoes.
Linking verb	The <u>dog</u> <u>smelled</u> terrible.

🌐 Language note: The verb *be* cannot be left out of sentences in English.

Incorrect	<u>Tonya</u> well now.
Correct	<u>Tonya</u> **is** well now.

HELPING VERBS

A **helping verb** joins with the main verb in the sentence to form the **complete verb**. The helping verb is often a form of the verb *be, have,* or *do.* A sentence may have more than one helping verb along with the main verb.

Helping verb + Main verb = Complete verb

Helping verbs + main verbs

<u>Sunil</u> <u>was talking</u> on his cell phone.

[The helping verb is *was,* and the main verb is *talking.* The complete verb is *was talking.*]

<u>Charisse</u> <u>is taking</u> three courses this semester.

<u>Tomas</u> <u>has missed</u> the last four meetings.

My <u>brother</u> <u>might have passed</u> the test.

Common Helping Verbs

Forms of *be*	Forms of *have*	Forms of *do*	Other
am	have	do	can
are	has	does	could
been	had	did	may
being			might
is			must
was			should
were			will
			would

Language note: The helping verb *be* cannot be left out when forming sentences in English.

Incorrect   Greg studying tonight.

Correct   Greg **is** studying tonight.

PRACTICE 3   ## Identifying the verb (action, linking, or helping + main)

In the following sentences, underline each subject and double-underline each verb. Then, identify each verb as an action verb, a linking verb, or a helping verb + a main verb.

Example: At first, Miguel did not want to attend his high school reunion.
helping verb + main verb

1. Miguel's family moved to Ohio from Escuintla, Guatemala, ten years

   ago. *action verb*

2. He was the new kid at his high school that fall. *linking verb*

3. Miguel was learning English at that time. *helping verb + main verb*

4. The football players teased small, quiet boys like him. *action verb*

5. After graduation, he was delighted to leave that part of his life

   behind. *linking verb*

6. Recently, the planning committee sent Miguel an invitation to his high

   school reunion. *action verb*

7. His original plan had been to throw the invitation straight into the

   trash. *helping verb + main verb*

8. Instead, he is going to the reunion to satisfy his curiosity about how his

   former classmates are doing. *helping verb + main verb*

9. His family is proud of Miguel's college degree and his new career as a

   graphic artist. *linking verb*

10. Perhaps some of the other students at the reunion will finally get to

    know the real Miguel. *helping verb + main verb*

Complete Thoughts

Discussion Have students discuss the differences between a complete thought in speaking and one in writing. Remind them that the context for speaking can be different from that for writing—and that in writing, a complete sentence always needs a subject and a verb.

A **complete thought** is an idea that is expressed in a sentence and that makes sense by itself, without other sentences. An incomplete thought leaves readers wondering what is going on.

Incomplete thought	as I was leaving [*What is going on?*]
Complete thought	The phone rang as I was leaving.
Incomplete thought	the people selling the car [*What is going on?*]
Complete thought	The people selling the car placed the ad.

e Log in to macmillanhighered .com/realessays **Additional Grammar Exercises** > Complete Thoughts

To identify a complete thought, ask yourself: Do I know what is going on, or do I have to ask a question to understand?

Incomplete thought	in the apartment next door

[Do I know what is going on, or do I have to ask a question to understand? *You would have to ask a question, so this is not a complete thought.*]

Complete thought	Carlos lives in the apartment next door.

PRACTICE 4   **Identifying complete thoughts**

Some of the following items contain complete thoughts, and others do not. In the space to the left of each item, write either "C" for *complete thought* or "I" for *incomplete thought*. If you write "I," add words to make a sentence.

Answers will vary. Possible edits shown.

Example: __I__ **The success of recent 3-D movies** *has surprised some people.*

__I__ 1. Although 3-D movies are more expensive, *, many viewers are happy to pay extra to see them.*

__I__ 2. People in the audience, *enjoy the feeling of being in the scene.*

__C__ 3. They are thrilled.

__I__ 4. ~~Complain~~ about wearing the special glasses. *Some people complain*

__C__ 5. The glasses can be uncomfortable.

<u>__I__</u> 6. However, if people have a choice between watching *Hunger Games* in 2-D or 3-D/
, they tend to choose 3-D.
∧

<u>__I__</u> 7. *Today's 3-D technology is much*
~~Much~~ better than it used to be.
∧

<u>__C__</u> 8. It is more expensive, too.

<u>__I__</u> 9. *It is hard to know whether*
~~If~~ 3-D is just a fad or not.
∧

<u>__C__</u> 10. Time will tell.

Six Basic Sentence Patterns

In English, there are six basic sentence patterns, some of which you have already worked with in this chapter. Although there are other patterns, they build on these six.

1. Subject-Verb (S-V)

This is the most basic pattern, as you have already seen.

       S   V
Airplanes pollute.

2. Subject–Linking Verb–Noun (S-LV-N)

   S LV   N
Fuel is a pollutant.

3. Subject–Linking Verb–Adjective (S-LV-ADJ)

   S   LV   ADJ
Travel seems cheap.

4. Subject-Verb-Adverb (S-V-ADV)

    S   V   ADV
Pollution costs dearly.

5. Subject–Verb–Direct Object (S-V-DO)

A *direct object* directly receives the action of the verb.

  S   V   DO
It degrades ozone.

6. Subject–Verb–Indirect Object–Direct Object

An *indirect object* does not directly receive the action of the verb.

S   V IO DO

Biofuels offer us hope.

> **PRACTICE 5**   **Identifying basic sentence patterns**
>
> In each of the following sentences, identify the basic sentence pattern by writing "S" above the subject, "V" above an action verb, "LV" above a linking verb, "N" above a noun (other than the subject), "ADJ" above an adjective, "ADV" above an adverb, "DO" above a direct object, and "IO" above an indirect object. Note: Not all of the sentences follow the six basic patterns described above.
>
>   S   V   IO   DO
> **Example:** **Dogs teach people manners.**
>
>   S   V
> 1. Dogs teach.
>
>   S   LV   ADJ   N
> 2. Dogs are natural coaches.
>
>   S   LV   ADJ
> 3. Dogs appear submissive.
>
>   S   V   IO   DO
> 4. They teach people lessons.
>
>   S   LV   ADV
> 5. They instruct unintentionally.
>
>   S   ADV   V
> 6. They clearly teach.
>
>   S   V   IO   ADJ   DO
> 7. Dogs give owners valuable lessons.
>
>   S   V   DO   ADV
> 8. Dogs greet owners excitedly.
>
>   S   V   ADV
> 9. Dogs respond promptly.
>
>   S   LV   ADV   ADJ
> 10. Dogs are extremely alert.

Editing Practice

> **EDITING REVIEW 1**

Underline each subject, double-underline each verb, and correct the six incomplete thoughts. *Answers will vary. Possible edits shown.*

    1 It is easier to help others than many people think. 2 For example,
a person can donate his or her
~~donating~~ hair. 3 Some people need donated hair in the form of wigs.
    ∧

    4 Who uses these wigs? 5 Mostly, children with cancer or other diseases that

need wigs

cause hair loss. 6 <u>Donating</u> <u>is</u> popular, especially with young girls.
^

7 More and more frequently, though, <u>men</u> and <u>boys</u> <u>are contributing</u> hair.

organization receives

8 For example, one nonprofit ~~organization.~~ ~~9 It receives~~ up to two thousand
^

locks of hair every week. 10 Unfortunately, <u>most</u> of the donated hair <u>is</u>

The

unusable for this charity's wigs. 11 ~~Because the~~ charity's <u>guidelines</u> <u>are</u> quite

The <u>organization</u> <u>must reject</u> ^

strict. 12 ~~Rejecting~~ hair that is gray, wet, moldy, too short, or too processed.
^

13 <u>It</u> <u>is</u> able to sell some rejected hair to help meet the group's costs.

the organization

14 But <u>continues</u> to encourage donations. 15 Obviously, <u>contributors</u> <u>feel</u>
^

they are getting more than they are giving.

EDITING REVIEW 2

Underline each subject, double-underline each verb, and correct the six
incomplete thoughts.

blue and

1 New <u>parents</u> commonly <u>dress</u> their baby boys in ~~blue.~~ ~~2 And~~ their
^

girls in pink. 3 Now, a recent <u>study</u> <u>suggests</u> that males actually do prefer

pink, or

blue and females prefer ~~pink.~~ ~~4 Or~~ at least a redder shade of blue. 5 The
^

, who

<u>study</u> <u>involved</u> 208 men and women ages twenty to twenty-six. ~~6 Who~~ were
^

asked to quickly select their preferred color/ ~~7 Choosing~~ from about one

thousand colored rectangles on a computer screen. 8 <u>Women</u> and <u>men</u>

according

both <u>like</u> blue/, 9 ~~According~~ to the study. 10 However, <u>women</u> clearly
^   ^

<u>express</u> a greater preference for the pinker end of the blue color spectrum.

11 The <u>researchers</u> <u>think</u> that females may have developed a preference for

which

more reddish colors/, ~~12 Which~~ resemble riper fruit and healthier faces.
^   ^

EDITING REVIEW 3

In each blank, fill in a word that is the appropriate part of speech.

1 Taking a peek __at__ (*preposition*) a fellow passenger's computer screen is OK to do, right? 2 This is a serious question at a time when airplane flights __are__ (*linking verb*) tightly packed __and__ (*conjunction*) laptop use is common. 3 What if the __person__ (*noun*) in the next seat is watching an offensive movie __without__ (*preposition*) headphones? 4 A recent survey __showed__ (*verb*) that 45 percent __of__ (*preposition*) business travelers admit to peeking at someone else's laptop in a public place. 5 In many cases, it is __nearly__ (*adverb*) impossible to avoid getting a glimpse of a nearby screen. 6 So, what is the __proper__ (*adjective*) etiquette for in-flight laptop use? 7 If __you__ (*pronoun*) are using your laptop, bring headphones. 8 Do not watch __movies__ (*noun*) that are in poor taste. 9 If a neighbor seems interested, invite __him or her__ (*pronoun*) to watch. 10 If you are sitting next to a laptop user, don't peek. 11 However, if the movie __he or she__ (*pronoun*) is watching looks interesting, it is OK to ask __politely__ (*adverb*) to watch. 12 If the sound is __too__ (*adverb*) high __or__ (*conjunction*) the content offensive, tell the laptop user. 13 If that does not work, __ask__ (*verb*) a flight attendant for assistance.

EDITING REVIEW 4

In each sentence of the following paragraph, identify the basic sentence pattern by writing "S" above the subject, "V" above an action verb, "LV" above a linking verb, "DO" above a direct object, and "IO" above an indirect object.

     S LV   S   LV
1 It is afternoon. 2 At this hour, many people become drowsy.
  S   V   DO   S   V   S   V
3 Most fight this "post-lunch dip." 4 Some people nap. 5 Others give
  IO   DO   S   V   DO
themselves a coffee transfusion. 6 Some try exercise. 7 The cleverest,
       V   DO   S   LV
however, use simple planning. 8 For these people, the "dip" is the time for
                        S   V   IO   DO
simple, noncreative tasks. 9 They give their brains a well-deserved break.
                            S   V   S   V
10 Later in the afternoon, their energy returns. 11 At this point, they resume
       DO   S   LV
more complex tasks. 12 Sometimes, the path of least resistance is best.

22

Fragments
Incomplete Sentences

Understand What Fragments Are

A **sentence** is a group of words that has a subject and a verb and expresses a complete thought, independent of other sentences. A **fragment** is a group of words that is missing a subject or a verb or that does not express a complete thought.

> **Fragment**   *At Memorial Arena.*
>
> [*At Memorial Arena* does not have a subject or a verb.]
>
> **Sentence**   <u>I</u> <u><u>am going</u></u> to a concert on Friday at Memorial Arena.

Language note: Remember that any idea that ends with a period needs a subject and a verb to be complete. For a review of subjects and verbs, see pages 316–21.

In the Real World, Why Is It Important to Correct Fragments?

A fragment is one of the grammatical errors that people notice most. Consider the following example.

Situation: A student responds to an ad for a work-study position at the college.

Teaching tip Ask students to take a few minutes to write out some fragment samples and then to look at them as a group. Does everyone in the group come to the same conclusions about what is a fragment and what is a complete sentence? Are there any samples that the group can't come to a conclusion about? If so, what makes those particular samples confusing? Identifying what your students already know about fragments will help give the entire class a starting point for this chapter.

In the examples in this chapter, <u>subjects</u> are underlined once and <u><u>verbs</u></u> are underlined twice.

Discussion Distribute and discuss "What Business People Think about Grammar and Usage" by Maxine Hairston, available on the Web at www.d.umn .edu/cla/faculty/troufs/ comp3160/Hairston. Business_People.html.

Dear Professor Espinoza:

I am interested in the position for an assistant that I saw. <u>On the work-study Web site.</u> I have attached a résumé for you to review. <u>That describes my experience.</u> I would very much like to work for you next semester. <u>Helping with your writing and research.</u> I type very fast.

Thank you for your consideration.

Sincerely,
Carson Watson

Teaching tip Ask students to share any tips they have for finding fragments in their own writing. How do they know the difference between a sentence and a fragment when they are editing their own papers?

Find and Correct Fragments

To find fragments in your own writing, look for the five kinds of fragments in this chapter. They represent common trouble spots.

When you find a fragment, you can usually correct it in one of two ways.

Ways to correct fragments

- Add what is missing (a subject, a verb, or both).
- Attach the fragment to the sentence before or after it.

> **PRACTICE 1** **Finding and correcting fragments**
>
> Underline the three fragments in Carson Watson's letter.

Fragments That Start with Prepositions

For a list of common prepositions, see page 317.

Whenever a preposition starts what you think is a sentence, check for a subject, a verb, and a complete thought. If any one of those is missing, you have a fragment.

e Log in to macmillanhighered .com/realessays LearningCurve > Fragments; **Additional Grammar Exercises** > Find and Correct Fragments > Correcting Fragments that Start with Prepositions

Fragment The <u>plane</u> <u>crashed</u> into the house. *With a deafening roar.*

[*With a deafening roar* is a prepositional phrase that starts with the preposition *with* and ends with the noun *roar*. The phrase has neither a subject nor a verb. It is a fragment.]

Fragment <u>You</u> should <u>take</u> the second left and head west. *Toward the highway.*

[*Toward the highway* is a prepositional phrase that starts with the preposition *toward* and ends with the noun *highway*. The phrase has neither a subject nor a verb. It is a fragment.]

Remember, the subject of a sentence is *never* in a prepositional phrase (see p. 316).

Correct a fragment that starts with a preposition by connecting the fragment to the sentence either before or after it. If you connect a fragment to the sentence after it, put a comma after the fragment to join it to the sentence.

Fragment	The plane crashed into the house. *From a height of eight hundred feet.*
Corrected	The plane crashed into the house, From a height of eight hundred feet.
Corrected	From a height of eight hundred feet, the plane crashed into the house.

Teaching tip Have students read a piece of their writing and underline any of the common prepositions listed on page 317. Then, have them highlight any fragments that start with a preposition. Ask students to give examples of fragments from their papers, and copy the fragments on the board. Have the whole class work together to create complete sentences from the fragments.

Fragments That Start with Dependent Words

A **dependent word** is the first word in a dependent clause, which does not express a complete thought even though it has a subject and a verb. Whenever you use a dependent word, think about what else you will need to form a complete thought.

Some dependent words are **subordinating conjunctions** (*after, because, before, since, until,* and so on).

Discussion Ask students what the word *dependent* means in the real world. Then, ask them how that definition will help them remember what a *dependent clause* is.

Fragment	I took the bus. *Because I missed my ride.*

[*Because* is a dependent word introducing the dependent clause *because I missed my ride.* The clause has a subject, *I,* and a verb, *missed,* but it does not express a complete thought.]

Corrected	I took the bus because I missed my ride.

[The dependent clause is attached to the sentence before it.]

Corrected	Because I missed my ride, I took the bus.

[The dependent clause is in front of the sentence. Note that when the dependent clause comes at the beginning of the sentence, it needs a comma after it.]

Some dependent words—*that, which, who, whose*—are **relative pronouns**; they relate one clause to another. When a word group starts with a relative pronoun it is not a complete sentence.

Fragment	*Whose brother is an astronaut.*

[In this case, *Whose* is a relative pronoun and the word group is a fragment. If, however, this word group were a question—Whose brother is an astronaut?—*Whose* would function as a regular pronoun, not a relative pronoun, and this would be a complete thought.]

Corrected	I visited my friend John, whose brother is an astronaut.

Common Dependent Words

after	if	what(ever)
although	since	when(ever)
as	so that	where
because	that	whether
before	though	which(ever)
even though	unless	while
how	until	who
		whose

🌐 **Language note:** For help with forming questions with pronouns, see Chapters 26 and 32.

PRACTICE 2 **Correcting fragments that start with prepositions or dependent words**

In the following items, circle any prepositions or dependent words starting a fragment. Then, correct the fragments by connecting them to the previous or next sentence.

Example: **Most dogs are content to have a daily walk. While some dogs need more.**
walk, while

1. Even after having a walk. These dogs become nervous and overly excited.

2. This, of course, greatly upsets the dogs' owners. Who have to deal with the messes that these agitated dogs leave around the home.

3. To address this growing need. A new type of service is springing up, especially in the larger cities of the country.

4. Because walking does not offer enough exercise for these high-spirited dogs. This new service provides someone to run with the dogs.

5. A runner will come to the owner's home and take the dog out for some vigorous exercise. At a price of around thirty to forty dollars.

6. Many of the runners are marathoners. With a large number also being actors, singers, writers, and students.

7. The runners have the chance to earn some much-needed cash/ ,W While
they get some great exercise for both the dogs and themselves.

8. Some dogs, such as English bulldogs, are not good candidates for
this service/ ,S Since they are not built for running.

9. But the larger dogs, especially young retrievers, Dalmatians, and
Weimaraners, are perfect for this/ ,I If they are strong and healthy.

10. Many dog owners who use this service say it has solved a huge problem for them/ ,W With their exhausted dogs eagerly packing away their
dinners and then lying down for the entire night.

PRACTICE 3   ### Correcting fragments that start with prepositions or dependent words

Read the following paragraph, and circle the ten fragments that start with prepositions or dependent words. Then, correct the fragments.

For decades, scholars have argued/ ,a About when and how chickens reached the Americas. One theory is that Portuguese and Spanish settlers brought them/ ,W When they arrived after 1500. Another suggests that the chickens were brought over by Polynesian visitors before Columbus's voyages. Most scholars once believed that the Portuguese and Spanish brought chickens to the Americas/ ,a Along with seeds, medicinal plants, and other necessities. Now researchers think they finally know what happened/ ,t Thanks to some revealing evidence found on the coast of Chile, where chicken bones were discovered/ ,a Along with some pottery that was dated between 1304 and 1424, or even earlier. Anthropologists performed a DNA analysis on the bones/ ,t That revealed that the chickens from Chile had a close genetic relationship to chickens from several Polynesian sites/ ,O On the islands of Tonga and American Samoa. When these findings were published/ ,S Some anthropologists said that the discovery supports the idea that Polynesians had by that time populated the Pacific and had even reached the Americas. Though the chicken bones matched Polynesian chickens/ ,t The pottery found with the bones was of the local Chilean style.

However, it is still unclear whether it was the local Chileans or the visiting Polynesians, Who ate the chickens back then.

Fragments That Start with -ing Verb Forms

An **-ing verb form** (also called a **gerund**) is the form of a verb that ends in -ing: *walking, writing, swimming*. Unless it has a helping verb (*was walking, was writing, was swimming*), it is not a complete verb in a sentence. Sometimes an -ing verb form functions as a noun and is used as a subject at the beginning of a complete sentence.

-ing verb form used as a subject

Swimming is a wonderful form of exercise.

[In this sentence, *swimming* is the subject and *is* is the verb.]

Running strains the knees.

[In this sentence, *running* is the subject and *strains* is the verb.]

-ing verb form used with a helping verb as a verb

I *am working* full-time this semester.

[In this sentence, *am* is the helping verb and *am working* is the complete verb.]

Tom *was running* when he saw the accident.

[In this sentence, *was* is the helping verb and *was running* is the complete verb.]

> **Language note:** English uses both -ing verb forms (*Kara loves singing*) and infinitives, a form in which *to* comes before the verb (*Kara loves to sing*). If these forms confuse you, pay special attention to this section and to the section that starts on page 334.

Whenever a word group begins with a word in -ing verb form, look carefully to see whether the word group contains a subject and a verb and whether it expresses a complete thought.

Fragment   Snoring so loudly I couldn't sleep.

[Is *Snoring* the subject? No. Is there a helping verb used with *snoring*? No. This word group is a fragment.]

Fragment   *Hoping for a faster route.* I took a back road to school.

[Is *Hoping* the subject? No. Is there a helping verb used with *hoping*? No. The first word group is a fragment.]

Correct a fragment that starts with an -ing verb form either by adding whatever sentence elements are missing (usually a subject and a helping verb) or by connecting the fragment to the sentence before or after it. Usually, you will need to put a comma before or after the fragment to join it to the complete sentence.

-ing **fragment**	The audience applauded for ten minutes. *Whistling and cheering wildly.*
Corrected	The audience applauded for ten minutes, W^Whistling and cheering wildly.
Corrected	They were whistling The audience applauded for ten minutes. Whistling and cheering wildly.
-ing **fragment**	*Working two jobs and going to school. I am tired all the time.*
Corrected	Working two jobs and going to school, I am tired all the time.
Corrected	I am working Working two jobs and going to school. I am tired all the time.

PRACTICE 4   **Correcting fragments that start with *-ing* verb forms**

In the following items, circle any *-ing* verb form that appears at the beginning of a word group. Then, correct any fragment either by adding the missing sentence elements or by connecting it to the sentence before or after it. *Answers may vary. Possible edits shown.*

Example: (Quilting) with a group of other women, m^My grandmother found a social life and a creative outlet.

1. My grandmother spent her entire life, (Living) on a farm in eastern Wyoming.

2. (Growing) up during World War II, S^she learned from her mother how to sew her own clothes.

3. She was a natural seamstress. My grandmother created (Creating) shirts and dresses more beautiful than anything available in a store.

4. (Joining) a quilting circle at the age of twenty, m^My grandmother learned how to make quilts.

5. The quilting circle made quilts for special occasions, u^(Using) scraps of cloth left over from other sewing projects.

6. *The quilters laid*
   ~~Laying~~ the scraps out in an interesting pattern. The women then chose a traditional design for the stitching that joined the top and bottom parts of the quilt.

7. Celebrating the birth of her first child, my father. ^,t^ The quilting circle gave my grandmother a baby quilt that is now a treasured heirloom.

8. She told me that the quilt was made of memories. *It incorporated* ~~Incorporating~~ fabric from her wedding dress, her maternity outfits, and all of the baby clothes she had stitched.

9. Looking at each bit of cloth in that quilt. ^,m^ My grandmother could still describe, years later, the garment she had made from it.

10. Trying to ensure that those memories would survive/, I asked her to write down everything she recalled about the quilt.

e Log in to macmillanhighered .com/realessays Additional Grammar Exercises > Correcting Fragments That Start with *to* and a Verb

Fragments That Start with *to* and a Verb

An **infinitive** is the word *to* plus a verb: *to hire, to eat, to study.* These phrases are all called *infinitive forms.* Although they contain verbs, infinitive forms function as nouns, adjectives, or adverbs.

If a word group begins with *to* and a verb, it must have another verb or it is not a complete sentence.

Fragment   I will go to the store later. *To buy a card.*

[The first word group is a sentence, with *I* as the subject and *will go* as the verb. In the second word group, there is no subject and there is no verb with the infinitive *to buy.*]

Fragment   Last week, a couple in New York fulfilled their wedding fantasy. *To get married on the top of the Empire State Building.*

[The first word group is a sentence, with *couple* as the subject and *fulfilled* as the verb. In the second word group, there is no subject and there is no verb with the infinitive *to get.*]

Correct a fragment that starts with *to* and a verb by connecting it to the sentence before or after it or by adding the missing sentence elements (a subject and a verb).

Fragment   Geri climbed on the roof. *To watch the fireworks.*

Corrected   Geri climbed on the roof/ ^t^ To watch the fireworks.

Corrected	Geri climbed on the roof. *She wanted to* ~~To~~ watch the fireworks.
Fragment	*To save on her monthly gas bills.* Tammy sold her SUV and got a hybrid car.
Corrected	To save on her monthly gas bills/, Tammy sold her SUV and got a hybrid car.
Corrected	*Tammy wanted to* ~~To~~ save on her monthly gas bills. *She* ~~Tammy~~ sold her SUV and got a hybrid car.

🌐 **Language note:** Do not confuse the infinitive (*to* before the verb) with *that.*

Incorrect	My brother wants *that* his girlfriend cook.
Correct	My brother wants his girlfriend *to cook.*

> **PRACTICE 5** **Finding and correcting fragments that start with *to* and a verb**

In the following items, circle any examples of *to* and a verb that begin a word group. Then, correct each fragment either by adding the missing sentence elements or by connecting it to the previous or the next sentence. *Answers may vary. Possible edits shown.*

Example: In the 1940s, Joe Gold decided/ To become a member of the Muscle Beach Weightlifting Club.

1. To lift weights/ Bodybuilders then met at Muscle Beach in Los Angeles.

2. When Joe Gold thought of opening a gym in 1965, he knew exactly where/ To locate it.

3. Muscle Beach had become known as Venice by then, but bodybuilders still went there/ To lift railroad ties and buckets filled with concrete.

4. Gold invented several new workout machines/ To give the bodybuilders more useful exercise.

5. To get the best possible workout/, Arnold Schwarzenegger regularly went to Gold's Gym in Venice.

6. Schwarzenegger won the title of Mr. Universe and later successfully ran in an election/ To become governor of California.

7. To have a realistic setting for the 1977 movie *Pumping Iron*/ The film-maker selected Gold's Gym.

8. *Pumping Iron*, featuring Schwarzenegger and other weight lifters, helped/ To make Gold's Gym famous.

9. In the early 1970s, however, Joe Gold made a decision/ To sell his origi-nal business along with the name *Gold's Gym* to another company.

10. Later, Gold went on/ To create World Gym, which now has more than three hundred locations around the world.

Fragments That Start with Examples or Explanations

As you edit your writing, pay special attention to groups of words that are exam-ples or explanations of information you presented in the previous sentences. These word groups may be fragments.

Fragment	Shoppers <u>find</u> many ways to save money on food bills. *For example, using double coupons.*

[The second word group has no subject and no verb. The word *using* is an *-ing* verb form that needs either to be the subject of a sentence or to have a helping verb with it.]

Fragment	<u>Parking</u> on this campus <u>is</u> a real nightmare. *Especially between 8:00 and 8:30 a.m.*

[The second word group has no subject and no verb.]

Finding fragments that start with examples or explanations can be difficult, because there is no single kind of word to look for. The following are a few start-ing words that may signal an example or explanation, but fragments that are examples or explanations do not always start with these words:

especially	for example	like	such as

When a group of words that you think is a sentence gives an example or explanation of information in the previous sentence, stop to see whether it has a subject and a verb and whether it expresses a complete thought. If it is missing any of these elements, it is a fragment.

Fragment	The <u>Web</u> <u>has</u> many job search sites. *Such as Monster.com.*

[Does the second word group have a subject? No. A verb? No. It is a fragment.]

Fragment	I wish I had something to eat from Chipotle right now. *A giant burrito, for example.*

[Does the second word group have a subject? No. A verb? No. It is a fragment.]

Fragment	I pushed seven different voicemail buttons before I spoke to a real person. *Not a helpful one, though.*

[Does the second word group have a subject? No. A verb? No. It is a fragment.]

To correct a fragment that starts with an example or an explanation, connect it either to the previous sentence or to the next one. Sometimes, you can add the missing sentence elements (a subject, a verb, or both) instead. When you connect the fragment to a sentence, you may need to reword or to change some punctuation. For example, fragments that are examples and fragments that are negatives are often set off by commas.

Fragment	The Web has many job search sites. *Such as Monster.com.*
Corrected	The Web has many job search sites_{, s}/ $uch as Monster.com. ^
Fragment	I pushed seven different buttons before I spoke to a real person. *Not a helpful one, though.*

Corrected	I pushed seven different buttons before I spoke to a real
	                , *though not a helpful one.*
	person./ ~~Not a helpful one, though.~~
	      ^

Corrected	I pushed seven different buttons before I spoke to a real
	              He was not
	person. ~~Not~~ a helpful one, though.
	     ^

PRACTICE 6 **Correcting fragments that are examples or explanations**

In the following items, circle any word groups that are examples or explanations. Then, correct each fragment either by connecting it to the previous sentence or by adding the missing sentence elements. *Answers may vary. Possible edits shown.*

Example: Some studies estimate that the number of teenage girls suffering dating abuse is very high. (Perhaps as many as one out of three girls,) *experiences some type of abuse from her boyfriend.*
                 ^

1. Many parents believe that they would know whether their daughters were being abused,/ (Either physically or emotionally.)
            ^

2. Most parents would certainly be concerned to see signs of violence on their children,/ (Such as bruises or scratches.)
         ^

3. A young man can be abusive without laying a finger on his girlfriend. ~~A guy who~~ (He might) monitors her actions and keeps her from spending time with other friends.

4. Abusive boyfriends often want to control their partners. ~~Make~~ (They may want to make) sure that their girlfriends dress a certain way, for example.

5. Around her parents, a teenage girl's boyfriend may act like a perfect gentleman. ~~Polite~~, (He may be polite,) attentive, and kind to the young woman.

6. When the couple is alone, however, he may be giving her verbal abuse, like telling her that she is fat, stupid, and ugly.

7. A young woman with an abusive boyfriend may develop psychological problems that will be difficult to treat, such as low self-esteem.

8. Parents should look for signs that their daughter needs help, like slipping grades, loss of interest in her friends, and unwillingness to confide in parents.

9. Friends who think that a young woman is involved in an abusive relationship should try to be supportive of her, not turn away even if she refuses to leave her boyfriend.

10. Young women need to know that help is available, from parents, guidance counselors, women's support services, and even the police, if necessary.

Editing Practice

As you edit the following paragraphs and your own writing, use the checklist that follows. You may also want to refer to the chart on page 342.

CHECKLIST

Editing for Fragments

FOCUS
Whenever you see one of the five trouble spots in your writing, stop to check for a possible fragment.

ASK
- ☐ Does the word group have a subject?
- ☐ Does it have a verb?
- ☐ Does it express a complete thought?

EDIT
- ☐ If your answer to any of these questions is "no," you have a fragment that you must correct.

Find and correct any fragments in the following paragraphs. *Answers may vary. Possible edits shown.*

Resources For cumulative Editing Review Tests, see pages 564–80.

> **EDITING REVIEW 1**   (5 fragments)
>
> 1 Genetically modified foods are being marketed/ 2 ^a^As the foods of the future. 3 For the past decade, gene technology has been advancing dramatically. 4 Inserting a gene from one species into the DNA of another species is easily possible. 5 A gene from a fish may be found/ 6 ^t^To make tomatoes more resistant to disease. 7 Of course, genetic modification may have unintended effects/, 8 ^a^As in the case of genetically modified corn/, 9 ^w^Which may harm monarch butterfly caterpillars. 10 Arguing that the long-term effects of genetic modification may not be known for years to come/, 11 ^s^Some scientists urge caution before marketing genetically modified foods.

Teamwork Divide the class into small groups and have each group present a corrected Editing Review. Compare the different ways in which the groups correct the fragments.

EDITING REVIEW 2   (4 fragments)

1 The term *organic* means different things/2 ^t^To different people.
3 Organic foods are supposed to be grown without pesticides/, 4 ^a^A method that reduces a farm's impact on the environment. 5 But is organic food a healthier choice for the person eating it? 6 Most people who buy organic food think so. 7 They pay premium prices for organic products because they think the food is good for their own well-being/, 8 ^n^Not just that of the environment. 9 Surprisingly, however, some foods labeled organic today are highly processed. 10 The label merely means that the ingredients meet a certain government standard/, 11 ^w^While guaranteeing nothing about the nutritional content or health benefits of the food.

EDITING REVIEW 3   (5 fragments)

1 For several years/, 2 ^t^The U.S. Department of Agriculture has permitted the irradiation of certain foods sold in American supermarkets.
3 Irradiating produce kills bacteria on the food/, 4 ^i^Increasing its shelf life.
5 Without irradiation, a strawberry may last only a day or two after being purchased. 6 An irradiated strawberry, in contrast, can last a week or more/
7 ^b^Because the bacteria that would cause it to spoil are killed by radiation.
8 While some consumers worry about buying irradiated food/, 9 ^o^Others dismiss these concerns as the effect of too many science-fiction movies.
10 In stores where irradiated fruits and vegetables are sold under banners announcing the radiation treatment/, 11 ^t^The owners report a booming market.

EDITING REVIEW 4   (4 fragments and 4 formal English errors)

1 Bacteria that resist antibiotics could be a real health threat in the next century. 2 ~~Doctrz~~ ^Doctors^ have begun ^to^2 explain ^to^2 their patients/3 ^t^That antibiotics are useful only for certain kinds of infections and that patients must finish

every course of antibiotics they start. 4 Antibiotic use in agriculture, however, has continued. 5 To increase. 6 The government does not even keep records. 7 Of antibiotic use in farm animals. 8 Mne cattle, pigs, and chickens get antibiotics for economic reasons, 9 Such as to keep them healthy and to make them grow faster. 10 Many scientists fear that antibiotic residue in the meat Americans eat may contribute to antibiotic resistance. 11 If so, agricultural antibiotics could eventually endanger human health.

PRACTICE 7   **Editing your own writing for fragments**

As a final practice, edit fragments in a piece of your own writing—a paper you are working on for this class, a paper you've already finished, a paper for another course, or a recent piece of writing from your work or everyday life. For help, use the checklist on page 339 and the chart on page 342.

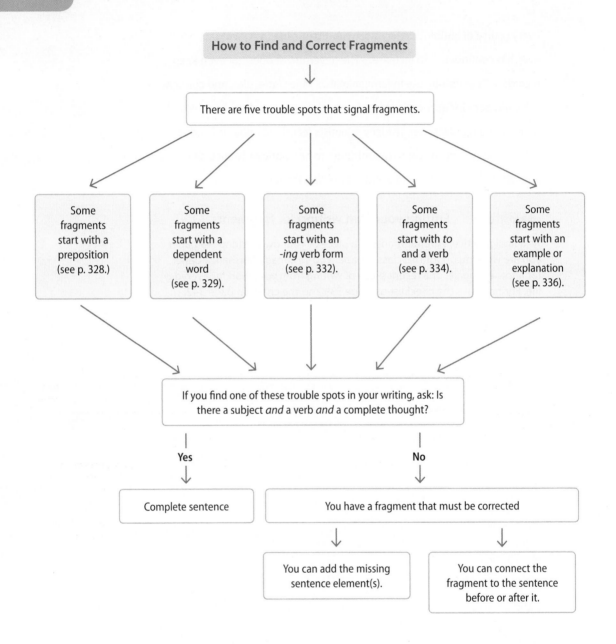

How to Find and Correct Fragments

There are five trouble spots that signal fragments.

Some fragments start with a preposition (see p. 328.)

Some fragments start with a dependent word (see p. 329).

Some fragments start with an *-ing* verb form (see p. 332).

Some fragments start with *to* and a verb (see p. 334).

Some fragments start with an example or explanation (see p. 336).

If you find one of these trouble spots in your writing, ask: Is there a subject *and* a verb *and* a complete thought?

Yes

No

Complete sentence

You have a fragment that must be corrected

You can add the missing sentence element(s).

You can connect the fragment to the sentence before or after it.

23

Run-Ons
Two Sentences Joined Incorrectly

Understand What Run-Ons Are

A sentence is also called an **independent clause**, a group of words with a subject and a verb that expresses a complete thought. Sometimes, two independent clauses can be joined correctly in one sentence.

In the examples throughout this section, the <u>subject</u> is underlined once, and the <u>verb</u> is underlined twice.

e Log in to **macmillanhighered.com/realessays** **LearningCurve** > Run-On Sentences; **Additional Grammar Exercises** > Find and Correct Run-Ons

Sentences with two independent clauses

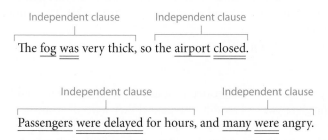

The <u>fog</u> <u><u>was</u></u> very thick, so the <u>airport</u> <u><u>closed</u></u>.

<u>Passengers</u> <u><u>were delayed</u></u> for hours, and <u>many</u> <u><u>were</u></u> angry.

A **run-on** is two sentences (each containing a subject and a verb and expressing a complete thought) that are joined incorrectly and written as one sentence. There are two kinds of run-ons: **fused sentences** and **comma splices**.

A **fused sentence** is two complete sentences joined without any punctuation.

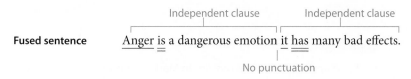

Fused sentence <u>Anger</u> <u><u>is</u></u> a dangerous emotion <u>it</u> <u><u>has</u></u> many bad effects.

343

A **comma splice** is two complete sentences joined by only a comma instead of a comma and one of these words: *and, but, for, nor, or, so, yet.*

Comma splice   Anger is a dangerous emotion, it has many bad effects.

|
Comma

Log in to
**macmillanhighered
.com/realessays
Additional Grammar
Exercises** > Identifying a
Run-On or Comma Splice

In the Real World, Why Is It Important to Correct Run-Ons?

Run-ons are errors that many people, including instructors and employers, will notice. In the following example, notice how the ideas are difficult to follow because of the run-ons.

Situation: Marion is new to her position as a licensed practical nurse at a large hospital. Each day, she updates patients' records and writes brief summaries of their progress for other nurses. The following is a report that Marion wrote in her first week on the job:

Trudari Kami is a premature infant she was born with a birth weight of 1.7 pounds her lungs were not fully developed, she was not able to breathe on her own. As of 2:15 a.m. on Thursday, April 6, she remains in stable condition her condition is still critical though she is being carefully monitored.

Find and Correct Run-Ons

To find run-ons, focus on each sentence in your writing one at a time. Until you get used to finding run-ons, this step will take time, but after a while you will not make the error as often.

Read the following paragraph. Does it include any run-ons? __*yes*__ If so, how many? __2__

The concert to benefit AIDS research included fabulous musicians and songs. One of the guitarists had six different guitars they were all acoustic. One had a shiny engraved silver shield on it, it flashed in the lights. The riffs the group played were fantastic. All of the songs were original, and many had to do with the loss of loved ones. At the end of some songs, the audience was hushed, too moved with emotion to begin the applause right away. When the concert was over, the listeners, many of them in tears, gave the performers a standing ovation.

> **PRACTICE 1**   **Finding run-ons**
>
> Find and underline the four run-ons in Marion's report.

When you find a run-on in your writing, you can correct it in one of four ways.

Ways to correct a run-on

- Add a period.
- Add a semicolon.
- Add a comma and a coordinating conjunction.
- Add a dependent word.

Add a Period

You can correct a run-on by adding a period to make two separate sentences.

Fused sentences (corrected)

I called about my bill. I got four useless recorded messages.

I finally hung up my question remained unanswered.

Comma splices (corrected)

My sister found a guy she likes in a chat room, she plans to meet him tomorrow.

I warned her that she should choose a public place. Applebee's at lunch would be good.

Add a Semicolon

A second way to correct a run-on is to join the two independent clauses into one sentence by adding a semicolon (;). Use a semicolon only when the two independent clauses express closely related ideas that make sense in a single combined sentence.

Teaching tip
Remind students that a semicolon balances two independent clauses. What is on either side of the semicolon must be able to stand alone as a complete sentence with a subject and a verb.

Fused sentences (corrected)

My father had a heart attack he is in the hospital.

My mother called 911 the ambulance was there in just under four minutes.

Comma splices (corrected)

The emergency room was like the one on the show *Grey's Anatomy,* the doctors and nurses were efficient.

He was in the emergency room for over three hours, there was no bed for him.

A semicolon is sometimes used before a transition from one independent clause to another, and the transition word is followed by a comma.

Transition between sentences

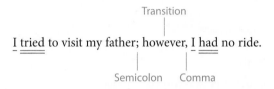

I tried to visit my father; however, I had no ride.

Semicolon   Comma

<hr />

PRACTICE 2   **Correcting a run-on by adding a period or a semicolon**

For each of the following run-ons, indicate in the space to the left whether it is a fused sentence (FS) or a comma splice (CS). Then, correct the run-on by adding a period or a semicolon. *Answers may vary. Possible edits shown.*

Example: ___CS___ **Social networking sites allow users to connect with one another, the sites also allow users to access each other's personal information.**

___CS___ 1. Online profiles often include photographs, group associations, and personal preferences, this information can sometimes be embarrassing.

___FS___ 2. Many sites, like Facebook, allow users to choose their own privacy settings. Users can limit how much information they want to share and who has access to their personal data.

___CS___ 3. Some people take steps to protect their privacy, they actively monitor their information and protect their online reputations.

CS   4. Most people assume that younger social networkers are freer with their personal information. **Y**/young people, however, are more likely than older people to limit what they share online.

FS   5. In a recent survey, 44 percent of Internet users ages eighteen to twenty-nine reported limiting the information available about themselves online**;** only 25 percent of users ages fifty to sixty-four reported doing so.

CS   6. Some people argue that older users are simply less knowledgeable about how to protect themselves. **Y**/younger users are more likely to know how to adjust settings and remove unwanted information.

FS   7. On the other hand, many observers note that security policies at sites like Facebook change frequently**;** even young people struggle to keep up with complicated and confusing privacy controls.

FS   8. The survey also reported that younger people are generally less trusting of social networking sites. **M**/more than a quarter of them said they "never" trust such sites.

CS   9. The truth is that younger users spend much more time on social networking sites than older users do**;**/twenty-somethings simply have more information online to protect and more reason to be concerned.

CS   10. Fortunately, few of the people surveyed reported problems with private information being released. **T**/taking precautions, as the younger users do, still seems wise.

Add a Comma and a Coordinating Conjunction

A third way to correct a run-on is to add a comma and a **coordinating conjunction**: a word that joins independent clauses to form one sentence. Some people remember the seven coordinating conjunctions (*and, but, for, nor, or, so, yet*) by using the memory device of *fanboys*, for **f**or, **a**nd, **n**or, **b**ut, **o**r, **y**et, **s**o.

To correct a fused sentence, add both a comma and a coordinating conjunction. A comma splice already has a comma, so just add a coordinating conjunction that makes sense in the sentence.

Tip Note that there is no comma *after* a coordinating conjunction.

e Log in to **macmillanhighered .com/realessays Additional Grammar Exercises** > Correcting a Run-On by Adding a Comma and a Conjunction

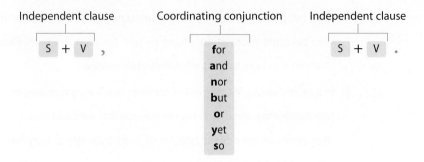

Independent clause — S + V ,   Coordinating conjunction — for and nor but or yet so   Independent clause — S + V .

Fused sentences (corrected)

We warned Tim to wear a seat belt ∧ he refused.   *, but*

He hit another car ∧ he went through the windshield.   *, and*

Comma splices (corrected)

He was unbelievably lucky, ∧ he got just scrapes and bruises.   *for*

He is driving again, ∧ he always buckles his seat belt before starting the car.   *but*

> 🌐 Language note: **Coordinating** conjunctions need to connect two independent clauses. They are not used to join a dependent and an independent clause.

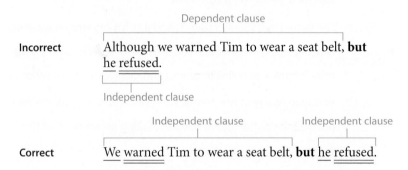

Dependent clause

Incorrect   Although we warned Tim to wear a seat belt, **but** he refused.

Independent clause

Independent clause   Independent clause

Correct   We warned Tim to wear a seat belt, **but** he refused.

| PRACTICE 3 | **Correcting a run-on by adding a comma and a coordinating conjunction** |

Correct each of the following run-ons. First, underline the subjects and double-underline the verbs to find the separate sentences. Then, add a comma (unless the run-on already includes one) and a coordinating conjunction. *Answers may vary. Possible edits shown.*

Example: Tasmania, an island off the coast of Australia, is the home of
but
many unusual kinds of wildlife, it also has been the site of several oil
spills.

1. Fairy penguins, a small breed of penguin, live in Tasmania these birds
, and
have often been the victims of oil spills.

2. The birds clean their feathers with their beaks they swallow the oil on
, and
their feathers.

3. Unfortunately, the penguins' attempts to clean off their feathers can be
, for
fatal crude oil is poisonous to penguins.

4. Wildlife conservationists in Tasmania expected future spills, they
so
created a plan to save the penguins.

5. One of the conservationists created a pattern for a sweater for the pen-
, and
guins volunteers from around the world knitted these unusual sweaters.

6. The sweaters cover everything but the penguins' heads and feet, they
so
cannot lick the oil-poisoned feathers.

7. Most of the sweaters were made by elderly nursing-home residents in
but
Tasmania, some were sent from as far away as Japan.

8. After future spills, a fairy penguin may wear a sweater it also might
, or
wear a tiny football jersey.

9. Some creative knitters made tuxedo-patterned sweaters a few of these
, and
penguin suits even have bow ties.

10. The penguins have a variety of protective outfits they do not like any
, but
of the garments.

Discussion The entire class can complete this practice together. Have students suggest appropriate conjunctions for each pair of independent clauses. Discuss how the choice of conjunction can change the meaning of a sentence.

Add a Dependent Word

The fourth way to correct a run-on is to make one of the complete sentences a dependent clause by adding a dependent word (a **subordinating conjunction** or a **relative pronoun**), such as *after, because, before, even though, if, though, unless,* or *when.* Choose the dependent word that best expresses the relationship between the two clauses.

Fused sentences (corrected)

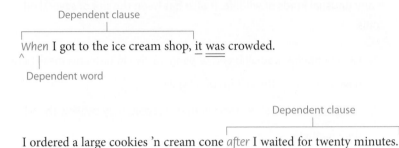

Dependent clause

When I got to the ice cream shop, <u>it</u> <u><u>was</u></u> crowded.

^ |

Dependent word

Dependent clause

<u>I</u> <u><u>ordered</u></u> a large cookies 'n cream cone *after* I waited for twenty minutes.

^ |

Dependent word

Comma splices (corrected)

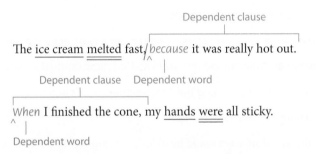

Dependent clause

The <u>ice cream</u> <u><u>melted</u></u> fast, *because* it was really hot out.

^ |

Dependent clause   Dependent word

When I finished the cone, my <u>hands</u> <u><u>were</u></u> all sticky.

^ |

Dependent word

When the dependent clause starts off the sentence, you need to add a comma after it, as in the first and fourth sentences in the preceding examples. When the dependent clause is after the independent clause, there is no comma, as in the second and third examples. (Refer to the list of common dependent words on page 330.)

> **PRACTICE 4**   **Correcting a run-on by making a dependent clause**
>
> Correct each of the following run-ons. First, underline the subjects and double-underline the verbs to find the separate sentences. Then, make one of the clauses dependent by adding a dependent word. When the dependent clause comes first in the sentence, add a comma after it if there is not one there already. *Answers may vary. Possible edits shown.*
>
> *which is*
> **Example:** <u>Everyone</u> <u><u>knows</u></u> where a compass points, ~~it points~~ toward the ^
> north.
>
> *Although this*
> 1. ~~This~~ <u>phenomenon</u> <u><u>is</u></u> something we take for granted, <u>it</u> <u><u>may be</u></u> ^
> changing.

2. A change in magnetism is possible *because* the earth's magnetic field is getting weaker.

3. Such a change happened before in the earth's history, *when* magnetic materials pointed south instead of north for long periods.

4. *Although a* A complete reversal could take thousands of years, some effects of the weaker magnetic field are already apparent.

5. The change in magnetism has affected some satellites, *which* ~~the satellites~~ have been damaged.

6. Animals may also be affected *because* some of them use the earth's magnetic field to sense where they are located.

7. *Because bees,* ~~Bees,~~ pigeons, salmon, turtles, whales, newts, and even bacteria need the magnetic field to navigate, they will adjust to the magnetic change.

8. However, it could take five thousand to seven thousand years *before* compasses would point south instead of north.

9. *Because the* ~~The~~ processes affecting magnetism may unfold much more slowly, the magnetic change may not occur for millions of years.

10. *While the* ~~The~~ dinosaurs roamed the earth for about thirty-five million years, the earth's magnetic field did not change during all this time.

A Word That Can Cause Run-Ons: Then

Many run-ons are caused by the word *then*. You can use *then* to join two sentences, but if you add it without the correct punctuation and/or joining word, the resulting sentence will be a run-on. Often, writers mistakenly use just a comma before *then*, but that makes a comma splice. To correct a run-on caused by the word *then*, you can use any of the four methods presented in this chapter.

Comma splice I grabbed the remote, then I ate my pizza.

Corrected I grabbed the remote*. Then* then I ate my pizza.

[period added]

Corrected I grabbed the remote*;* then I ate my pizza.

[semicolon added]

Corrected   I grabbed the remote, *then* I ate my pizza.

[coordinating conjunction *and* added]

Corrected   I grabbed the remote, *then* I ate my pizza.

[dependent word *before* added to make a dependent clause]

Editing Practice

Teaching tip Have
students review a rough
draft and highlight
problem sentences.
Then, have them
edit each sentence
systematically to
make sure it has one
subject and one verb
and expresses a single
complete thought.

As you edit the paragraphs in this practice and in your own writing, use the checklist that follows. You may also want to refer to the chart on page 356.

CHECKLIST

Editing for Run-Ons

FOCUS
Read each sentence aloud, and listen carefully as you read.

ASK
- ☐ Am I pausing in the middle of the sentence?
- ☐ If so, are there two subjects and two verbs?
- ☐ If so, are there two complete sentences in this sentence?
- ☐ If there are two sentences (independent clauses), are they separated by punctuation? If the answer is "no," the sentence is a **fused sentence**.
- ☐ If there is punctuation between the two independent clauses, is it a comma only, with no coordinating conjunction? If the answer is "yes," the sentence is a **comma splice**.

EDIT
- ☐ If the sentence is a run-on, correct it using one of the four methods for editing run-ons.

Resources For
cumulative Editing
Review Tests, see pages
564–80.

Find and correct any run-ons in the following paragraphs. Use whichever of the four methods of correcting run-ons that seems best to you. *Answers may vary. Possible edits shown.*

EDITING REVIEW 1   (6 run-ons)

1 Your memory can play tricks on you. 2 It is often easy to forget things
when
you want desperately to remember them. 3 You have probably had the
                                                            , which
experience of forgetting an acquaintance's name ~~the name~~ comes to your
                                                            ^
mind only when it is too late. 4 You have also probably been unable to
                                            because
find your keys once in a while/ you put them down somewhere without
                                        ^
thinking. 5 At other times, however, you may find it difficult to forget some
            even though
things, you wish you could never think of them again. 6 If you have an
            ^
annoying song in your mind, you may spend hours wishing desperately
to forget it. 7 Sometimes, you may find yourself forced to relive your most
                                                                            ;
embarrassing moment over and over again in your mind your memory will
                                                                ^
not let you leave that part of your past behind. 8 Some scholars believe that
                                                            . It
these annoying habits of memory evolved for a reason/ it is hard to imag-
                                                            ^
ine, though, any good reason for developing the ability to forget where you
left your keys.

EDITING REVIEW 2   (10 run-ons)

                                                            ;
1 Cooking for astronauts can be difficult most food crumbles too easily.
                                        ^   *. For*
2 Looking for crumbs in a space station is no fun ~~for~~ the same reason, salt
                                                        ^
and pepper for astronauts are always in liquid form. 3 Space cuisine has
                                                            ;
come a long way since the first astronauts went up in 1961 those *Gemini*
                                                                ^
astronauts primarily had gelatin-coated food cubes and aluminum tubes of
apple sauce. 4 They now get fresh fruit on occasion as well as such choices
as shrimp cocktail, mashed potatoes with bacon, green beans with garlic,
                                . They
and New Orleans jambalaya/ ~~they~~ have to be especially careful with some
                                ^
food choices, though. 5 For example, the Russians often bring tomatoes
                                                            ;
when it is their turn to supply the space station it is not wise to bite right
                                                        ^
into a fresh tomato because it can squirt out juice, which then has to be
tracked down. 6 Every dish is eventually consumed, even if it is not liked,
because
wasting food makes no sense when anything can happen in space. 7 NASA's
^

current challenge is preparing and packaging food for the planned expedi-

since

tions to Mars this food will have to have a five-year shelf life. 8 The food will
                                                    ∧   . *First*
be shot into space before the astronauts are / ~~first~~ the food will go up, which
                                                                                              ∧
will take six months. 9 Getting the astronauts to Mars will take another six
                                      . *Returning*
months / returning adds yet another six months, and delays have to be
                    ∧
anticipated due to possible weather or mechanical problems. 10 A lot of
                                                                                       , *for*
thought is going into minimizing bacterial growth in the food bacteria is
                                                                                    ∧
the last thing one wants on a space mission.

EDITING REVIEW 3   (12 run-ons)

1 The number of bike riders is growing, especially in American cities
, *because*
riding bikes to work and for exercise is now seen as a smart choice. 2 This
∧
makes it all the more important for drivers and bike riders to learn to share
                    . *Every*
the road / ~~every~~ year, approximately 46,000 bike riders are injured in crashes
               ∧
with motor vehicles. 3 The good news is that most of these accidents are
                                        but
preventable, it takes special care on the part of both drivers and riders.
                    ∧
4 Car drivers need to recognize that bicycles have a legal right to use most
                    , *although*
roads bikes must ride on the shoulder when the speed limit is over 50 miles
               ∧   ;
per hour. 5 When coming up on a cyclist, slow down / when passing, give
                                                                                ∧
the bike at least three feet of clearance. 6 Be especially careful with young
                                                                    because
cyclists, even those on the sidewalks, they can suddenly dart out in traffic
                                                                                  ∧
without looking. 7 When making a right turn, make sure there is no bicycle
                                                                                  ;
on the right / when waiting to turn left or at a stop sign, yield to a bicycle
                    ∧
that has the right of way. 8 Check carefully for bicycles before opening a car
                    . *Cyclists*
door ~~cyclists~~ have been killed by headlong crashes into suddenly opened
          ∧
car doors. 9 Bike riders need to follow the same traffic rules that apply to
                    . *Wait*
drivers ~~wait~~ for a green light before crossing intersections, and signal
          ∧
before all turns and stops. 10 Try to ride at least three feet from parked cars
                                                                                                          ;
do not weave in and out between parked cars. 11 Do not ride wearing   ∧
                                                                          and
headphones or while talking on a cell phone, always wear a properly fitted
                                                            ∧

bike helmet. 12 Increasing bike riding is a good sign for the environment

but

and for Americans' expanding waistlines, ^ for everyone's safety, both drivers

and riders must vigilantly follow the rules of road-sharing.

EDITING REVIEW 4   (10 run-ons and 7 formal English errors)

1 In times past, when a Ping-Pong player could not find someone to

. Those

play against, that meant there was no Ping-Pong, ~~those~~ times are now over.

2 More and more, people are installing in their basements and garages the

, which

perfect Ping-Pong partner ~~it~~ ^ is a robot that endlessly serves fast-moving Ping-

are ^ different   but

Pong balls. 3 There ~~R~~ several ~~dfrnt~~ Ping-Pong robots on the market, ^ they all do

basically the same thing. 4 They pitch balls one by one to the person on the

;

other side of the table ^ the fancier ones have nets that can catch return balls

can

and funnel them back to the automatic server. 5 The human player ~~cn~~ control

and

the speed, placement, and spin of the balls, ^ the more elaborate models allow

random serves or a programmed series of serves that can, for example, go

to   can be more

~~2~~ ^ alternate sides of the table. 6 Some players feel that the robots ~~cn b mo~~

because   ^

challenging to play against than a human opponent ^ it is hard to see where

the ball is coming from. 7 Human players partially give away their intentions

;

with their body position, the angle of the paddle, and the type of stroke ^ none

of these cues is visible with a robot server. 8 The ability of some robots to spin

, for

balls is also helpful, say some players ^ the machine can be set to replay the

exact same spinned serve repeatedly, allowing the person to better learn how

to counter it. 9 The Ping-Pong robots with retrieving nets can save the human

; however,

player time and effort ^ some humans appreciate the break to pick up balls.

which

10 The relentless machine can provide an exhausting workout, of course, ^ for

many robot owners, is the whole point.

PRACTICE 5   **Editing your own writing for run-ons**

As a final practice, edit run-ons in a piece of your own writing—a paper you
are working on for this class, a paper you've already finished, a paper for
another course, or a recent piece of writing from your work or everyday life.
Use the checklist on page 352 and the chart on page 356 to help you.

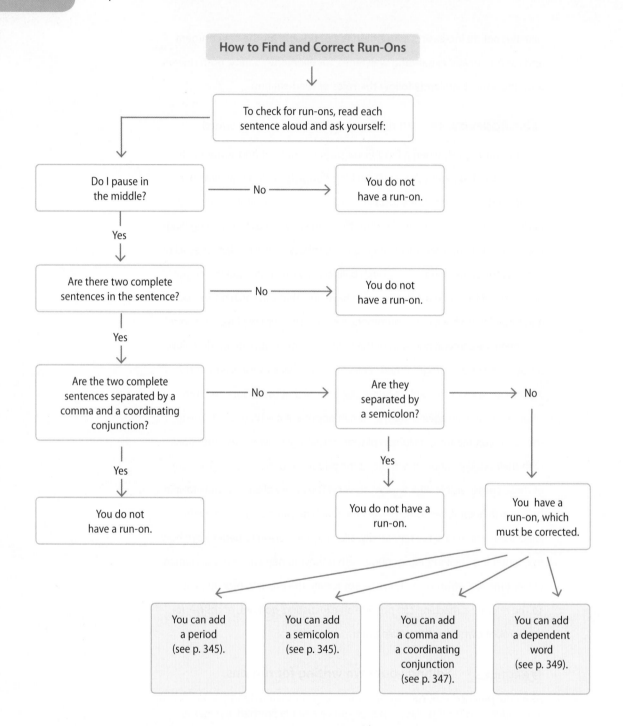

How to Find and Correct Run-Ons

To check for run-ons, read each sentence aloud and ask yourself:

Do I pause in the middle? — No → You do not have a run-on.

Yes ↓

Are there two complete sentences in the sentence? — No → You do not have a run-on.

Yes ↓

Are the two complete sentences separated by a comma and a coordinating conjunction? — No → Are they separated by a semicolon? — No →

Yes ↓

You do not have a run-on.

Yes ↓

You do not have a run-on.

You have a run-on, which must be corrected.

You can add a period (see p. 345).

You can add a semicolon (see p. 345).

You can add a comma and a coordinating conjunction (see p. 347).

You can add a dependent word (see p. 349).

24

Problems with Subject-Verb Agreement

When Subjects and Verbs Do Not Match

Understand What Subject-Verb Agreement Is

In any sentence, **the subject and the verb must match—or agree—in number**. If the subject is singular (one person, place, or thing), the verb must also be singular. If the subject is plural (more than one), the verb must also be plural.

e Log in to
macmillanhighered
.com/realessays
LearningCurve >
Subject-Verb Agreement

Singular   The <u>phone</u> <u><u>rings</u></u> constantly at work.

[The subject, *phone*, is singular—just one phone—so the verb must take the singular form: *rings*.]

Plural   The <u>phones</u> <u><u>ring</u></u> constantly at work.

[The subject, *phones*, is plural—more than one phone—so the verb must take the plural form: *ring*.]

In the examples throughout this chapter, the subject is underlined once, and the verb is underlined twice.

Regular verbs, verbs that follow standard English patterns, have two forms in the present tense: one that does not add an ending and one that ends in *-s*. First-person (*I, we*) subjects, second-person (*you*) subjects, and plural subjects (more than one person, place, or thing) have verbs with no *-s* ending. Third-person singular subjects (*he, she, it,* and singular nouns) always have a verb that ends in *-s*. The chart that follows shows the differences.

For more on regular verbs and how they differ from irregular verbs, see Chapter 25.

357

Regular Verbs, Present Tense

	Singular form	**Plural form**
First person	I walk.	We walk.
Second person	You walk.	You walk.
Third person	He/she/it walks.	They walk.
	Percy walks.	Percy and Don walk.
	The dog walks.	The dogs walk.

 Language note: Some nouns that do not end in *-s* are plural, so they need plural verbs. For example, *children* and *people* do not end in *-s*, but they mean more than one child or person, so they are plural.

Incorrect	The people owns their apartments.
Correct	The people own their apartments.

In the Real World, Why Is It Important to Correct Subject-Verb Agreement Problems?

Like fragments and run-ons, subject-verb agreement errors are significant problems that can make a bad impression on instructors, employers, and others.

Situation: McKayla Benjamin regularly shops at one particular clothing store in her local mall; however, she has recently been displeased with the quality of the merchandise. Even though the prices have remained the same, she thinks that the clothes are starting to fall apart or wear out more quickly than they used to. After approaching the manager of her local store and getting an unsatisfactory response, she decides to write a formal letter to the company to express her feelings with the current situation.

Dear X:

My name is McKayla Benjamin and I has been a loyal customer of your store for five years. I notice that your sales become less frequent. Your prices have got higher. Your clothes fell apart sooner. I like the way they look and I wanting to shop there, but I don't think you appreciating your customers. The manager at the local store choose not to help me. Please fix this issue as soon as possible so that I continue to shop at your store and enjoy your clothing.

Find and Correct Errors in Subject-Verb Agreement

To find problems with subject-verb agreement in your own writing, read carefully, and look for the five trouble spots covered in this chapter.

Teaching tip Remind students that correcting each of the four most serious grammar errors depends on being able to identify the subject and the verb in a sentence.

> **PRACTICE 1** **Finding subject-verb agreement problems**
>
> Find and underline the eight subject-verb agreement problems in the letter McKayla Benjamin wrote on page 358.

The Verb Is a Form of Be, Have, or Do

The verbs *be, have,* and *do* do not follow the regular patterns for forming singular and plural forms; they are **irregular verbs**.

These verbs cause problems for people who use only one form of the verb in casual conversation: *You be the richest* (incorrect). *You are the richest* (correct). In college and at work, use the correct form of the verbs *be, have,* and *do,* as shown in the charts on the next two pages.

e Log in to **macmillanhighered .com/realessays** **Additional Grammar Exercises** > Find and Correct Errors in Subject-Verb Agreement > Correcting Subject-Verb Agreement Problems with the Verbs *Be, Have,* and *Do*

    are
You ~~is~~ the craziest person I have ever known.

    has
Johnson ~~have~~ the best car in the lot.

    does
Valery ~~do~~ the bill paying on the first of every month.

Forms of the Verb *Be*

Present tense	Singular	Plural
First person	I am	we are
Second person	you are	you are
Third person	she/he/it is	they are
	the student/Joe is	the students are

Past tense		
First person	I was	we were
Second person	you were	you were
Third person	she/he/it was	they were
	the student/Joe was	the students were

Forms of the Verb *Have*, Present Tense

	Singular	Plural
First person	I have	we have
Second person	you have	you have
Third person	she/he/it has	they have
	the student/Joe has	the students have

Forms of the Verb *Do*, Present Tense

	Singular	Plural
First person	I do	we do
Second person	you do	you do
Third person	she/he/it does	they do
	the student/Joe does	the students do

Teaching tip
Complete the practices in this chapter as a group, and ask students to read the sentences aloud. What differences do they find in formal versus informal communication? How do they account for those differences?

PRACTICE 2 **Choosing the correct form of *be*, *have*, or *do***

In each sentence, underline the subject of the verb *be, have,* or *do,* and circle the correct form of the verb.

Example: The microwave oven (am /(is)/ are) a common fixture in most American homes.

1. Even so, many people (has /(have)) concerns about the safety of this standard appliance.

2. They (am / is /(are)) worried that standing close to an operating micro-wave oven can expose them to harmful radiation.

3. Some microwave ovens (does /(do)) in fact leak radiation, but the levels that might be released are quite small.

4. The <u>Center for Devices and Radiological Health</u>, a unit of the U.S. Food and Drug Administration, (has / have) responsibility for regulating microwave oven safety.

5. According to the center, the allowed <u>amount</u> of leakage from each microwave oven that reaches the market (am / is / are) far below the level of radiation that is harmful to humans.

6. <u>Manufacturers</u> of microwave ovens (does / do) even more than required by law to ensure the safety of their products.

7. All microwave <u>ovens</u> (has / have) a type of door latch that prevents the production of microwaves whenever the latch is released.

8. Also, the <u>doors</u> of microwave ovens (am / is / are) lined with a metal mesh that stops microwaves from escaping.

9. Furthermore, the radiation <u>level</u> from a microwave oven (am / is / are) extremely low at a distance of even a foot from the oven.

10. Therefore, the <u>radiation</u> from an operating microwave oven (do / does) not pose a threat to anyone.

PRACTICE 3 **Using the correct form of *be, have,* or *do***

In each sentence, underline the subject and fill in the correct form of the verb (*be, have,* or *do*) indicated in parentheses.

Example: **Our <u>professor</u> __has__ (*have*) forty papers to grade this weekend.**

1. Most <u>students</u> __are__ (*be*) used to the idea that computers sometimes grade tests.

2. <u>You</u> __have__ (*have*) probably taken standardized tests and filled in small ovals with a pencil.

3. A <u>computer</u> __does__ (*do*) not have to be sophisticated to read the results of such tests.

4. Surprisingly, one software <u>program</u> <u>_is_</u> (be) designed to grade student essays.

5. The <u>program</u> <u>_has_</u> (have) the ability to sort words in an essay and compare the essay to others in its database.

6. The <u>software</u> <u>_does_</u> (do) not check grammar or spelling.

7. <u>Teachers</u> <u>_are_</u> (be) still needed to supplement the computer grade, according to the software manufacturer.

8. If a computer grades your essay, <u>you</u> <u>_have_</u> (have) to write about one of five hundred specified topics.

9. A <u>computer</u> <u>_does_</u> (do) check the organization, clarity, and style of your writing.

10. Some <u>teachers</u> <u>_are_</u> (be) excited about their computerized assistant, but I <u>_do_</u> (do) not like the idea of a computer grading my essays.

Words Come between the Subject and the Verb

When the subject and the verb are not right next to each other, it can be difficult to make sure that they agree. Most often, what comes between the subject and the verb is either a prepositional phrase or a dependent clause.

PREPOSITIONAL PHRASE BETWEEN THE SUBJECT AND THE VERB

A **prepositional phrase** starts with a preposition and ends with a noun or pronoun: The line *for the movie* went *around the corner.*

Remember, the subject of a sentence is never in a prepositional phrase. When you are looking for the subject, you can cross out any prepositional phrases. This strategy should help you find the real subject and decide whether it agrees with the verb.

For a list of common prepositions, see page 317.

e Log in to macmillanhighered .com/realessays **Additional Grammar Exercises** > Correcting Subject-Verb Agreement Problems When the Subject and Verb are Separated by a Prepositional Phrase

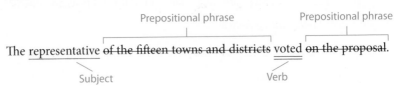

Prepositional phrase   Prepositional phrase

The representative ~~of the fifteen towns and districts~~ voted ~~on the proposal.~~

Subject   Verb

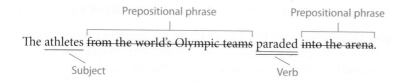

Prepositional phrase   Prepositional phrase

The athletes ~~from the world's Olympic teams~~ paraded ~~into the arena~~.

Subject   Verb

PRACTICE 4 **Making subjects and verbs agree when they are separated by a prepositional phrase**

In each of the following sentences, first cross out the prepositional phrase between the subject and the verb, and then circle the correct form of the verb. Remember, the subject of a sentence is never in a prepositional phrase.

EXAMPLE: Twenty-eight million people ~~in the United States~~ (am / is /(are))
deaf or hard of hearing.

1. Most parents ~~with hearing loss~~ (has /(have)) children who can hear.

2. Many ~~of these children~~ (learns /(learn)) sign language as a first language.

3. Communication ~~with words~~ ((comes)/ come) later.

4. Few people ~~in the hearing world~~ (understands /(understand)) the lives of deaf people completely.

5. Many deaf people ~~in this country~~ (feels /(feel)) closer to deaf people from other parts of the world than to hearing Americans.

6. The hearing children ~~of deaf parents~~ (comes /(come)) closer to understanding deaf culture than most hearing people.

7. A hearing child ~~in a deaf household~~ ((resembles)/ resemble) a child of immigrant parents in many ways.

8. Adapting ~~to two different cultures~~ ((makes)/ make) fitting in difficult for some young people.

9. Sometimes, ties ~~to the hearing world and the deaf world~~ (pulls /(pull)) in opposite directions.

10. Bridges ~~between cultures~~ (am / is /(are)) more easily built by people who understand both sides.

DEPENDENT CLAUSE BETWEEN THE SUBJECT AND THE VERB

A **dependent clause** has a subject and a verb, but it does not express a complete thought. When a dependent clause comes between the subject and the verb, it usually starts with the word *who, whose, whom, that,* or *which*.

The subject of a sentence is never in the dependent clause. When you are looking for the subject, you can cross out any dependent clauses.

Teaching tip Have students practice placing prepositional phrases or dependent clauses between a subject and a verb in sentences from their own writing. Point out that the addition does not affect the subject-verb agreement.

Dependent clause

The FBI agent ~~who conducted the investigation~~ interviewed Rosa Martin.

Subject   Verb

Dependent clause

The house ~~that slid off the cliff~~ was designed by a local architect.

Subject   Verb

| PRACTICE 5 | **Making subjects and verbs agree when they are separated by a dependent clause** |

e Log in to macmillanhighered .com/realessays **Additional Grammar Exercises** > Correcting Subject-Verb Agreement Problems When the Subject and Verb are Separated by a Dependent Clause

In each of the following sentences, cross out any dependent clauses. Then, correct any problems with subject-verb agreement. If a sentence has no problem, write "OK" next to it.

Example: A person ~~who lies in job applications~~ ^{is} are likely to get caught.

1. A résumé, ~~which is a job applicant's first contact with many prospective employers,~~ ^{contains} ~~contain~~ details about work experience and education.

2. Many people ~~who write résumés~~ are tempted to exaggerate. OK

3. Perhaps an applicant ~~who held a previous job for two months~~ ^{claims} ~~claim~~ to have spent a year there.

4. A job title ~~that sounds impressive~~ ^{looks} ~~look~~ good on a résumé, whether or not it is accurate.

5. Often, a person ~~who never received a college degree~~ wants to add one to a résumé anyway. OK

6. A person ~~who is considering untrue résumé additions~~ *needs* ~~need~~ to think
   ∧
   twice.

7. Employers ~~who like a résumé~~ *check* ~~checks~~ the information provided by the
   ∧
   applicant.

8. A résumé ~~that contains false information~~ goes in the reject pile. OK

9. Even if they somehow avoid having their résumés rejected, many people ~~who invent material on a résumé~~ *forget* ~~forgets~~ the inventions when they
   ∧
   face a prospective employer in an interview.

10. Even a company ~~that does not check all of the information on résumés~~
    pays attention when interviewees seem to forget some of their qualifi-
    cations. OK

The Sentence Has a Compound Subject

e Log in to
macmillanhighered
.com/realessays
**Additional Grammar
Exercises** > Correcting
Subject-Verb Agreement
Problems with
Compound Subjects

A **compound subject** consists of two (or more) subjects connected by *and, or,*
or *nor* (as in *neither/nor* expressions). If two subjects are joined by *and,* they
combine to become a plural subject, and the verb must take a plural form as
well.

    Subject *and*   Subject   Plural form of verb

The <u>director</u> *and* the <u>producer</u> <u>decide</u> how the film will be made.

If two subjects are connected by *or* or *nor,* they are considered separate, and the
verb should agree with the subject closest to it.

    Subject *or* Singular subject Singular form of verb

The <u>director</u> *or* the <u>producer</u> <u>decides</u> how the film will be made.

    Subject *nor* Singular subject   Singular form of verb

Neither the <u>director</u> *nor* the <u>producer</u> <u>wants</u> to give up control.

    Subject *or* Plural subject Plural form of verb

The <u>director</u> *or* his <u>assistants</u> <u>decide</u> how the film will be made.

Subject   *nor*   Plural subject   Plural form of verb

Neither the <u>director</u> *nor* his <u>assistants</u> <u>want</u> to give up control.

PRACTICE 6   **Choosing the correct verb in a sentence with a compound subject**

In each of the following sentences, underline the word (*and, or,* or *nor*) that joins the parts of the compound subject. Then, circle the correct form of the verb.

Example: A child <u>and</u> an adult (has /(have)) different nutritional needs.

1. Fruits <u>and</u> vegetables (does /(do)) not make up enough of most Americans' diets.

2. The U.S. government <u>and</u> other organizations concerned with health and nutrition (recommends /(recommend)) that people eat at least five servings of fruits and vegetables a day.

3. Whole-grain cereal <u>or</u> bread ((is)/ are) another important part of a healthy diet.

4. Neither vitamins <u>nor</u> fiber ((is)/ are) found in many popular snack foods.

5. Potato chips <u>and</u> candy (contains /(contain)) few useful nutrients.

6. Neither fat <u>nor</u> sugar ((helps)/ help) build a healthy body.

7. However, in small amounts, fat <u>and</u> sugar (contributes /(contribute)) beneficially by making food taste good.

8. Motivated dieters <u>and</u> certain health fanatics (eats /(eat)) nutritious food that tastes terrible.

9. Neither dieters <u>nor</u> health fanatics (is /(are)) likely to keep eating the unappetizing food for a lifetime.

10. Choosing nutritious food <u>and</u> preparing it well (allows /(allow)) a person to feel healthy and satisfied.

The Subject Is an Indefinite Pronoun

Indefinite pronouns, which refer to unspecified people or objects, are often singular, although there are exceptions.

When you find an indefinite pronoun in your writing, use the table that follows to help you determine the correct verb form, singular or plural. To determine what verb form to use when the pronoun may be singular or plural, you will need to check whether the word to which it refers is singular or plural.

e Log in to
**macmillanhighered
.com/realessays**
**Additional Grammar
Exercises** > Correcting
Subject-Verb Agreement
Problems When the
Subject Is an Indefinite
Pronoun

Everyone loves vacations.

[*Everyone* is always singular, so it takes the singular verb *loves*.]

Some of the wreckage was recovered after the crash.

[In this case, *some* is singular, referring to *wreckage,* so it takes the singular verb *was recovered*.]

Some of the workers were delayed by the storm.

[In this case, *some* is plural, referring to *workers,* so it takes the plural verb *were delayed*.]

Often, an indefinite pronoun is followed by a prepositional phrase or a dependent clause; remember that the subject of a sentence is never found in either of these. To choose the correct verb, you can cross out the prepositional phrase or dependent clause to focus on the indefinite pronoun.

Indefinite Pronouns

Always singular

anybody	everyone	nothing
anyone	everything	one (of)
anything	much	somebody
each (of)	neither (of)	someone
either (of)	nobody	something
everybody	no one	

May be singular or plural

all	none
any	some

All ~~of my first day on the job~~ <u>was</u> <u>devoted</u> to filling out forms.

<u>Some</u> ~~who are longtime residents~~ <u>recommend</u> a rent strike.

PRACTICE 7   **Choosing the correct verb when the subject is an indefinite pronoun**

In each of the following sentences, underline the indefinite pronoun that is the subject, and cross out any prepositional phrases or dependent clauses that come between the subject and the verb. Then, circle the correct verb.

Example: **One** ~~of the oldest types of exercise that people use to stay in~~ **shape ((is) / are) once again fashionable.**

1. <u>Many</u> ~~who choose this newly trendy type of exercise, which is walking,~~ (is / (are)) middle-aged or older.

2. <u>Someone</u> ~~with aching joints, past injuries, or an aging body~~ (want / (wants)) a relatively gentle form of exercise.

3. But <u>everybody</u>, ~~even people who are young and in great shape,~~ (need / (needs)) exercise that is safe, practical, and enjoyable.

4. <u>Those</u> ~~who walk for aerobic exercise~~ ((sustain) / sustains), on average, fewer fitness-related injuries than people who run.

5. <u>Nobody</u> ~~with good sense or serious concern for his or her health~~ (pursue / (pursues)) activities that might risk bodily damage.

6. Furthermore, <u>anyone</u> ~~who sets aside the time and makes the effort to walk regularly~~ (benefit / (benefits)) in several ways.

7. <u>Some</u> ~~of today's active walkers~~ ((do) / does) it to lose weight.

8. <u>Anybody</u> ~~with a waistline problem, which is a category that includes too many people these days,~~ (appreciate / (appreciates)) the opportunity to shed 300 calories by walking briskly for an hour.

9. <u>Others</u> ~~who have the time for an energetic yet leisurely walk~~ ((enjoy) / enjoys) looking at people, stores, and the outdoors as they exercise.

10. Depending on their specific situations and preferences, many people want a steady, low-impact type of exercise, like walking, and many others choose something more strenuous and demanding, such as running; either ~~type of exercise~~ (help /(helps)) them to have more active and healthy lives.

The Verb Comes before the Subject

In most sentences, the subject comes before the verb. Two kinds of sentences reverse that order—questions and sentences that begin with *here* or *there*. In these two types of sentences, you need to check carefully for errors in subject-verb agreement.

QUESTIONS

In questions, the verb or part of the verb comes before the subject. To find the subject and verb, you can turn the question around as if you were going to answer it.

Where is the nearest gas station? The nearest gas station is . . .

Are the keys in the car? The keys are in the car.

 Language note: Forming questions correctly is difficult for many people, especially those whose first language is not English. For charts that summarize how to correctly form questions, see Chapter 32.

SENTENCES THAT BEGIN WITH *HERE* OR *THERE*

When a sentence begins with *here* or *there*, the subject always follows the verb. Turn the sentence around to find the subject and verb.

Here are the hot dog rolls. The hot dog rolls are here.

There is a fly in my soup. A fly is in my soup.

 Language note: *There is* and *there are* are common in English. If you have trouble using these expressions, see page 489.

| PRACTICE 8 | **Correcting a sentence when the verb comes before the subject** |

Correct any problems with subject-verb agreement in the following sentences. If a sentence is already correct, write "OK" next to it.

are
Example: There is several openings for bilingual applicants.

are ^
1. Where is the corporation's main offices located?

are
2. There is branch offices in Paris, Singapore, and Tokyo.
^

^ *does*
3. How well do the average employee abroad speak English?

does^
4. What do the company manufacture?
^

is
5. How many languages are the manual written in?
^

6. Does the company employ college graduates as entry-level

translators? OK

are
7. There is some machines that can do translation.
^

8. Does learning a second language give an applicant an advantage? OK

9. There is never a disadvantage in knowing another language. OK

are
10. Here is the names of several qualified people.
^

Editing Practice

As you edit the following paragraphs and your own writing, use the checklist on page 371. You may also want to refer to the chart on page 374.

Find and correct any problems with subject-verb agreement that you find in the following paragraphs.

Resources For cumulative Editing Review Tests, see pages 564–80.

| EDITING REVIEW 1 | (7 errors) |

are
1 School systems around the country is embracing educational stan-
sounds ^
dards. 2 The idea of standards sound reasonable. 3 Does anyone want
^
to argue that students should not have to meet certain requirements to
has
graduate? 4 A national standard for all American students have many sup-
^
porters, too. 5 If the requirements for graduation in Oregon and Tennessee
are
is the same, everyone with a high school diploma gets a similar education.

6 There is a catch, of course. 7 Not everyone with a professional or personal interest in school quality is able to agree on these requirements. 8 Math-
are *are*
ematics and writing ~~is~~ important, but so ~~is~~ music and physical education.
are ^
9 How ~~is~~ parents, teachers, and administrators ever going to find standards
^
that everyone accepts?

EDITING REVIEW 2   (9 errors)

is
1 Agreeing on school standards ~~are~~ only part of the battle over educa-
are ^
tion. 2 How ~~is~~ students going to prove that they have met the standards
^   *is*
before graduation? 3 The answer, in many cases, ~~are~~ testing. 4 School tests
are ^
that are required by state law ~~is~~ becoming more and more common. 5
^
These tests are standardized, so all of the students taking an eighth-grade
are
test in a particular state ~~is~~ given the same test. 6 Both the individual student
^   *are*
and his or her school district ~~is~~ evaluated by the scores. 7 The parents of a
learn   ^
student ~~learns~~ not only what their child's score is but also how the school
^
compares with others around the state. 8 Then, children who need extra
are
help ~~is~~ supposed to receive it, and schools with very low scores year
^   *become*
after year ~~becomes~~ eligible for additional resources.

CHECKLIST

Editing for Subject-Verb Agreement

FOCUS

☐ Whenever you see one of the five trouble spots in your writing, stop to check that the subject and the verb agree.

ASK

☐ Where is the subject in this sentence? Where is the verb?

☐ Do the subject and verb agree in number? (Are they both singular or both plural?)

EDIT

☐ If you answer "no" to the agreement question, you need to correct the sentence.

EDITING REVIEW 3   (6 errors)

1 In reality, standardized tests for schools have many problems.
2 Most school districts that have a testing program ~~uses~~ *use* tests that can be
scored by a computer. 3 Computers cannot assess answers to essay questions, so computer-scored tests usually ~~offers~~ *offer* multiple-choice questions.
4 A multiple-choice test in science or mathematics ~~do~~ *does* not allow students to
demonstrate critical thinking. 5 How ~~does~~ *do* students show their writing ability on such a test? 6 There ~~is~~ *are* tricks to answering multiple-choice questions
that many students learn. 7 Frequently, a high score on such a test says
more about the student's test-taking ability than about his or her knowledge of a subject. 8 Nevertheless, the low cost and the quick results of a
computer-graded multiple-choice test ~~means~~ *mean* that this imperfect testing
system is used in many school systems.

EDITING REVIEW 4   (7 errors and 4 formal English errors)

1 Another problem with standardized tests ~~are~~ *is* that test material ~~cn~~ *can*
begin to change the curriculum. 2 Everyone who teaches ~~want~~ *wants* his or her
students ~~2~~ *to* get high scores on the tests. 3 For one thing, a teacher of under-
performing students ~~are~~ *is* likely to be criticized for not preparing them ~~btr.~~ *better*
4 One result of teachers' fears ~~are~~ *is* that they spend most of the class time
preparing students for the test. 5 In some cases, the phenomenon of
"teaching to the test" ~~become~~ *becomes* school policy. 6 A creative teacher or one
who has been teaching for years ~~are~~ *is* no longer trusted to engage students
with a subject. 7 ~~Skul~~ *School* officials, who also want high scores for their districts,
encourage teachers to focus on material that the test will cover.
8 Other material, which may be fascinating to students, ~~are~~ *is* ignored
because the test does not require it.

PRACTICE 9	**Editing your own writing for subject-verb agreement**

As a final practice, edit for subject-verb agreement in a piece of your own writing—a paper you are working on for this class, a paper you have already finished, a paper for another course, or a recent piece of writing from your work or everyday life. Use the checklist on page 371 and the chart on page 374 to help you.

Teamwork Have students exchange and read drafts of their writing, focusing on subject-verb agreement.

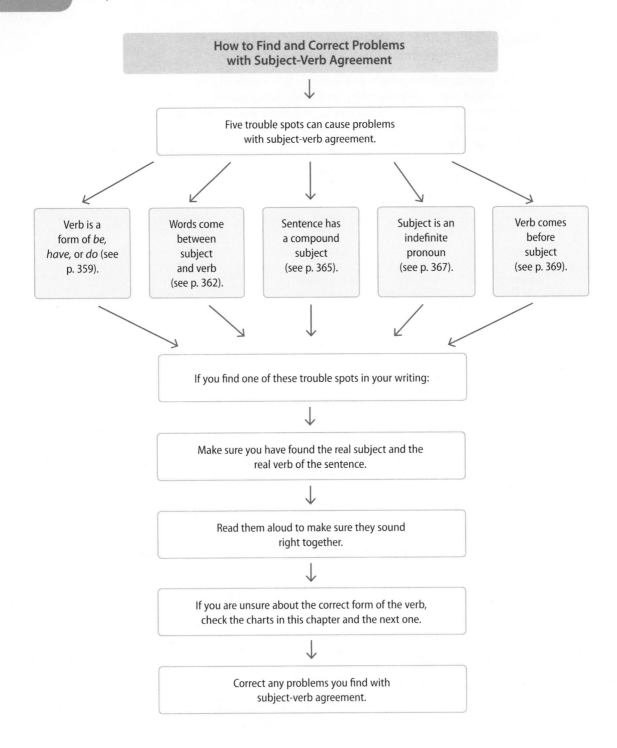

How to Find and Correct Problems with Subject-Verb Agreement

Five trouble spots can cause problems with subject-verb agreement.

Verb is a form of *be, have,* or *do* (see p. 359).

Words come between subject and verb (see p. 362).

Sentence has a compound subject (see p. 365).

Subject is an indefinite pronoun (see p. 367).

Verb comes before subject (see p. 369).

If you find one of these trouble spots in your writing:

Make sure you have found the real subject and the real verb of the sentence.

Read them aloud to make sure they sound right together.

If you are unsure about the correct form of the verb, check the charts in this chapter and the next one.

Correct any problems you find with subject-verb agreement.

25

Verb Problems
Avoiding Mistakes in Verb Tense

Understand What Verb Tense Is

Verb tense tells *when* the action of a sentence occurs—in the present, in the past, or in the future. Verbs change their form and use the helping verbs *have* or *be* to indicate different tenses.

To choose the correct form and tense, consider whether the subject is singular or plural *and* when the action occurs.

In the examples throughout this chapter, the subject is underlined once, and the verb is underlined twice.

Present tense	Teresa and I talk every day. [Plural subject]
Present tense	She also talks to her mother every morning. [Singular subject]
Past tense	Yesterday, they talked for two hours. [Plural subject]
Future tense	Tomorrow, they will talk again. [Plural subject]

🌐 **Language note:** Remember to add the endings on present-tense and past-tense verbs, even if they cannot be heard in speech.

Present tense	Krystal plays varsity basketball.
Present tense	She rides downtown on her bike.

Regular verbs follow a few standard patterns in the present and past tenses, and their past-tense and past-participle forms end in *-ed* or *-d*.

ⓔ Log in to **macmillanhighered .com/realessays LearningCurve** > Verb Tenses

For more on subject-verb agreement and singular versus plural verb forms, see Chapter 24.

375

Irregular verbs change spelling in the past-tense and past-participle forms. (For more on irregular verbs, see pp. 388–94.)

	Regular verb: *walk*		Irregular verb: *eat*	
Past tense	walked	[I walk**ed**.]	ate	[I ate.]
Past participle	walked	[I have/had walk**ed**.]	eaten	[I have/had eaten.]

In the Real World, Why Is It Important to Use Correct Verb Tense?

Errors in verb tense can create a negative impression of the writer, as the following example shows.

Situation: A student that Shawn has been working with shows him the script for an oral presentation he has to give in school the following week. Here is what the student wrote as an introduction.

> Last week I gone to the awards day for Diamond Educators and receive my first prize ever. I receive the prize because last semester I work with younger kids to help them do things right, like doing their homework and why it be important to go to school. Before I meet people at Diamond, I never understand why school matter. I believe that only fools cared about school, but now I know education can change my life. Trying to get a good education don't mean selling out: It mean making something of myself.

E Log in to
macmillanhighered
.com/realessays
**Additional Grammar
Exercises** > Using the
Correct Verb Form for
Regular Verbs in the
Present Tense

Use Correct Verbs

Verbs have several tenses to express past, present, and future time. This section will explain what those tenses are and how to use them correctly when you write.

Regular Verbs

To avoid mistakes with regular verbs, understand the basic patterns for forming the present, past, and future tenses.

PRESENT TENSE

The **simple present tense** is used for actions that are happening at the same time that you are writing about them and about actions that are ongoing. There are two forms for the simple present tense of regular verbs: **-s ending** or **no added ending**. Use the *-s* ending when the subject is *she, he,* or *it,* or the name of one person or thing. Do not add any ending for other subjects.

Regular Verbs in the Simple Present Tense

	Singular	**Plural**
First person	I laugh.	We laugh.
Second person	You laugh.	You laugh.
Third person	She/he/it laugh**s**.	They laugh.
	The baby laugh**s**.	The babies laugh.

PRACTICE 1   **Finding verb errors**

Find and underline the eleven errors in the student's writing on page 376.

PRACTICE 2   **Using the simple present tense of regular verbs**

In each of the following sentences, first underline the subject, and then circle the correct verb form.

Example: Most elevator riders (share / shares) a common complaint.

1. Too often, elevator doors (open / opens) at practically every floor even when there are just a few people in the car.

2. Now, guests at one big hotel (enjoy / enjoys) faster, more direct elevator rides, thanks to a new "smart elevator" system.

3. The system (work / works) well because it knows where people want to go before they get into their elevator car.

4. Whenever someone (want / wants) to take an elevator, he or she must first punch in the desired floor number at a keypad in the lobby.

5. A digital display then (indicate / indicates) the letter of the elevator car that will directly go to a floor close to the person's destination.

6. To ensure that guests do not get confused with the new system, employees of the hotel (help / helps) them use it correctly.

7. The hotel's managers (claim / claims) that the system reduces the average trip time by up to 30 percent.

8. However, some <u>guests</u> (express / expresses) irritation with the system.

9. <u>They</u> sometimes (wait / waits) a long time for an elevator, and then they cannot get into the first car that comes because it is not going near their floor.

10. Still, most <u>people</u> who use the system (consider / considers) it to be a welcome improvement in elevator technology.

Two other present-tense forms are the present progressive tense and the present perfect tense. The **present progressive tense** is used to describe actions that are in progress. It is formed as follows:

| Present-tense form of *be* (helping verb) | **+** | Main verb with *-ing* ending |

Present Progressive Tense

	Singular	Plural
First person	I am laugh**ing**.	We are laugh**ing**.
Second person	You are laugh**ing**.	You are laugh**ing**.
Third person	She/he/it is laugh**ing**.	They are laugh**ing**.
	The baby is laugh**ing**.	The babies are laugh**ing**.

Language note: Some languages, such as Russian, do not use the progressive tense. If your first language does not use the progressive tense, pay special attention to this section.

PRACTICE 3 **Using the present progressive tense**

In each of the following sentences, underline the helping verb (a form of *be*), and fill in the correct form of the verb in parentheses.

Example: My grandmother is <u>looking</u> (*look*) **into our family history.**

1. She is ___starting___ (*start*) with my grandfather's side of the family, the Mancinis.

2. To learn more about the Mancinis, she is ___contacting___ (*contact*) several of my grandfather's relatives to get birth documents and other information.

3. Also, she is ___gathering___ (*gather*) information about the Mancinis through genealogy sites on the Internet.

4. She is ___learning___ (*learn*) a lot about my grandfather's ancestors; for instance, they were peasants who fled Italy around 1910 because of difficult living conditions.

5. My sister and I are ___helping___ (*help*) our grandmother by looking at online records from Ellis Island.

6. Also, we are ___thinking___ (*think*) of taking a course in genealogical research at a local college.

7. Even our mother is ___pitching___ (*pitch*) in.

8. For example, she is ___calling___ (*call*) older Mancinis to get family stories.

9. She is constantly ___sharing___ (*share*) the stories with my sister and me; for instance, she learned that our great-grandfather helped to organize a coal-miner strike soon after coming to America.

10. "These stories are ___reminding___ (*remind*) me of some modern Mancinis," she said. "We like to stir things up."

The **present perfect tense** is used for an action that started in the past and is ongoing into the present or that was completed at some unspecified time in the past. It is formed by using a **past participle**, a verb form that uses the helping verb *have*. The past participle of the verb *play*, for example, is *has played* or *have played*. The **present perfect** is formed as follows:

Be and *have* are irregular verbs. For more details on irregular verbs, see pages 388–94.

| Present-tense form of *have* (helping verb) | + | Past participle |

Present Perfect Tense

	Singular	**Plural**
First person	I have laughed.	We have laughed.
Second person	You have laughed.	You have laughed.
Third person	She/he/it has laughed.	They have laughed.
	The baby has laughed.	The babies have laughed.

 Language note: Be careful not to leave out *have* when it is needed for the present perfect. Time-signal words like *since* or *for* may mean that the present perfect is needed.

Incorrect	Krystal *played* basketball since she was ten.
Correct	Krystal *has played* basketball since she was ten.

PRACTICE 4   **Using the present perfect tense**

In each of the following sentences, underline the helping verb (a form of *have*), and fill in the correct form of the verb in parentheses.

Example: My father has ___served___ (*serve*) in the army for twenty years.

1. My father's military career has ___forced___ (*force*) our family to move many times.

2. We have ___lived___ (*live*) in seven towns that I remember.

3. I have ___attended___ (*attend*) three different high schools.

4. None of the towns has ever really ___seemed___ (*seem*) like home.

5. I have never ___objected___ (*object*) to my family's traveling life.

6. None of us has ever ___expected___ (*expect*) to stay in one place for long.

7. My closest friends have all ___traveled___ (*travel*) a lot, too.

8. One of them has ___visited___ (*visit*) Egypt, Australia, Turkey, Pakistan, and seventeen other countries.

9. She has always ___liked___ (*like*) the idea of becoming a travel agent.

10. But she has ___decided___ (*decide*) to accept a position with a large international corporation that will allow her to travel.

PAST TENSE

The **simple past tense** is used for actions that have already happened. An **-ed ending** is needed for all regular verbs in the past tense.

Log in to **macmillanhighered.com/realessays** **Additional Grammar Exercises** > Using the Correct Verb Form for Regular Verbs in the Past Tense

Regular Verbs in the Simple Past Tense

	Simple present	Simple past
First person	I rush to work.	I rush**ed** to work.
Second person	You lock the door.	You lock**ed** the door.
Third person	Rufus seems strange.	Rufus seem**ed** strange.

PRACTICE 5   **Using the simple past tense**

In each of the following sentences, fill in the correct past-tense form of the verb in parentheses.

Example: **After the Revolutionary War** ___ended___ (*end*), **American politicians** ___turned___ (*turn*) **their anger against each other.**

(1) In general, politicians after the war ___decided___ (*decide*) to support either Alexander Hamilton, who favored a strong central government, or Thomas Jefferson, who advocated states' rights. (2) Rival politicians were ___concerned___ (*concern*) about the direction of the new democracy, so they ___attacked___ (*attack*) one another with great passion. (3) Few people ___cared___ (*care*) about facts or honesty in their attacks. (4) Some politicians eagerly ___challenged___ (*challenge*) President George Washington and ___called___ (*call*) him a would-be king. (5) Hamilton ___engaged___ (*engage*) in personal attacks that were especially nasty. (6) In return, Hamilton's enemies ___accused___ (*accuse*) him of planning to bring back the British monarchy.

Teaching tip Have students write a paragraph about something annoying they experienced in the past week. Ask each student to write one sentence from his or her paragraph on the board. As a class, edit for correct past-tense verb forms.

(7) In six different instances, Hamilton ___participated___ (*participate*) in fierce arguments that ___stopped___ (*stop*) just short of causing a duel. (8) He ___failed___ (*fail*) to avoid a duel in his long dispute with Vice President Aaron Burr. (9) For years, Hamilton ___charged___ (*charge*) Burr with being corrupt and dishonest. (10) When they ___dueled___ (*duel*) in 1804, each ___fired___ (*fire*) a shot from a pistol. (11) Burr was not hit, but Hamilton was seriously wounded, and he ___died___ (*die*) the next day.

Simple past tense   My car <u>stalled</u>.

[The car stalled at some point in the past but does not stall now, in the present.]

Be careful not to confuse the simple past tense with the present perfect tense (see p. 379).

Present perfect tense   My car <u>has stalled</u> constantly at work.

[The car began to stall in the past and may continue to do so into the present.]

PRACTICE 6   **Using the simple past tense and present perfect tense**

In each of the following sentences, circle the correct verb form.

Example: Within the last twenty years, racial profiling (became / has become) a significant source of disagreement between law enforcement agencies and some communities of color.

1. Numerous charges of racial profiling (increased / have increased) the tension between local police and members of various ethnic groups.

2. Law enforcement agencies (used / have used) criminal profiling for a long time.

3. With this practice, they (attempted / have attempted) to identify people who might be participating in criminal activity by their behavior and the conditions of a particular situation.

4. Once the individuals who fit the criminal profile (have been singled out / were singled out), the police questioned or searched them for drugs, guns, or other illegal material.

5. In 1998, an investigation of the New Jersey State Police (raised / has raised) the public's awareness of racial profiling, a troublesome aspect of criminal profiling.

6. The extensive publicity from this investigation (defined / has defined) *racial profiling* as the separating out of members of racial or ethnic groups for minor traffic or criminal offenses.

7. Investigators reviewing past law-enforcement activity concluded that the New Jersey State Police (violated / have violated) civil rights laws on numerous occasions.

8. Since this case was made public, other police departments (initiated / have initiated) investigations into their own possible racial profiling activities.

9. Similarly, communities (started / have started) to demand that the police be more accountable in their relationships with members of minority racial or ethnic groups.

10. The issue of racial profiling (endured / has endured) in the public mind and continues to be controversial.

Two other past-tense forms are the past progressive tense and the past perfect tense. The **past progressive tense** is used to describe actions that were ongoing in the past. It is formed as follows:

Past-tense form of *be* (helping verb)	+	Main verb with *-ing* ending

Past Progressive Tense

	Singular	**Plural**
First person	I was laughing.	We were laughing.
Second person	You were laughing.	You were laughing.
Third person	She/he/it was laughing.	They were laughing.
	The baby was laughing.	The babies were laughing.

PRACTICE 7   **Using the past progressive tense**

In each of the following sentences, first underline the helping verb (a form of *be*), and then fill in the correct form(s) of the verb in parentheses.

Example: **When Victoria graduated from college, she <u>was</u> _looking_ (look) for a good job.**

1. Because she was not sure exactly what kind of job she wanted, she <u>was</u> _hoping_ (hope) to find a city with a lot of opportunities.

2. However, because she had college loans to repay, she <u>was</u> _looking_ (look) to find a city that was not too expensive.

3. Discouraged by the recession, many of her friends <u>were</u> _struggling_ (struggle) to figure out where to go.

4. After doing some research, Victoria discovered that some cities <u>were</u> _experiencing_ (experience) growth in both population and employment.

5. Many of these cities <u>were</u> _drawing_ (draw) large numbers of young people in their twenties and early thirties as well.

6. Soon, Victoria <u>was</u> _focusing_ (focus) her attention on three cities.

7. According to a 2010 study, Austin, Texas; Washington, D.C.; and Raleigh, North Carolina, <u>were</u> _providing_ (provide) the best job markets for young adults.

8. Victoria <u>was</u> _having_ (have) trouble deciding among the three cities until she read about Austin's South-by-Southwest Festival.

9. A city that supported music, film, and technology <u>was</u> _going_ (go) to make her happy.

10. Before long, Victoria <u>was</u> _trying_ (try) to convince several of her friends to move to Austin with her.

The **past perfect tense** is used for an action that began and ended in the past before some other past action took place. It is formed as follows:

Past-tense form of *have* + Past participle

Be and *have* are irregular verbs. For more details on irregular verbs, see pages 388–94.

Past tense of *have*   Past participle

Past perfect My head had ached for a week before I called a
tense doctor.

[Both of the actions (*head ached* and *I called*) happened in the past, but the ache happened before the calling.]

Be careful not to confuse the simple past tense with the past perfect tense.

Simple past My daughter left.
tense

[One action (the daughter leaving) occurred in the past.]

Past perfect By the time Jill arrived, my daughter had left.
tense

[Two actions (Jill's arrival and the daughter leaving) occurred in the past, but the daughter left before Jill's arrival.]

PRACTICE 8   Using the past perfect tense

In each of the following sentences, circle the correct verb form. Note that some of the verbs are irregular. For a chart showing forms of these verbs, see pages 392–94.

**Example: By the time I reached home, rolling blackouts (darkened /
(had darkened)) the city.**

1. The temperature was unseasonably hot when I ((got) / had gotten) out
   of bed that morning.

2. By noon, the air conditioners at the office (were running / (had been)
   (running)) at high power for three hours.

3. My boss told me that she (heard / (had heard)) that energy use that day
   was skyrocketing.

4. I ((asked) / had asked) how we could conserve energy.

5. I mentioned that I (just learned / (had just learned)) that some household and office machines use power even when they are turned off.

For more practice on the past and perfect tenses, see Chapter 32.

6. My boss (read /(had read)) the same information, so we unplugged computers in the office that were not in use.

7. We also ((raised)/ had raised) the office temperature from sixty-eight degrees to seventy-two, and then we turned off some of the lights.

8. By late afternoon, we (did /(had done)) everything we could think of to save energy, but it was not enough.

9. We knew that the city (warned /(had warned)) residents that rolling blackouts were possible.

10. However, when the office ((suddenly darkened)/ had suddenly darkened), everyone was stunned.

FUTURE TENSE

The **simple future tense** is used for actions that will happen in the future. It is formed with the helping verb *will*.

Two other future tense forms to be familiar with are the future progressive tense and the future perfect tense. The **future progressive tense** is used to describe actions that will be ongoing in the future. It is formed as follows:

> *will* + *be* + Main verb with *-ing* ending

The **future perfect tense** is used to describe actions that will be completed in the future before another action in the future. It is formed as follows:

> *will have* + Past participle

Simple Future Tense

	Singular	**Plural**
First person	I will graduate in May.	We will graduate in May.
Second person	You will graduate in May.	You will graduate in May.
Third person	She/he/it will graduate in May.	They will graduate in May.
	My son will graduate in May.	My sons will graduate in May.

Future Progressive Tense

	Singular	**Plural**
First person	I will be working Friday.	We will be working Friday.
Second person	You will be working Friday.	You will be working Friday.
Third person	She/he/it will be working Friday.	They will be working Friday.
	The boss will be working Friday.	The bosses will be working Friday.

Future Perfect Tense

	Singular	**Plural**
First person	I will have finished by ten o'clock.	We will have finished by ten o'clock.
Second person	You will have finished by ten o'clock.	You will have finished by ten o'clock.
Third person	She/he/it will have finished by ten o'clock.	They will have finished by ten o'clock.
	The painter will have finished by ten o'clock.	The painters will have finished by ten o'clock.

PRACTICE 9   **Using the future perfect tense**

The future perfect tense is formed with helping verbs *will* and *have* plus a verb's past participle. Using the list of past participles on pages 392–94 (see the third column in the boxed chart), circle the correct form of the past participle in the following sentences.

Example: Rebekah will have ((woken) / woke) with the roosters and eaten a hearty breakfast.

1. A student in the year-long Learn to Farm program in Athol, Massachusetts, Rebekah will have (rose / (risen)) early to give the sheep some
   garlic oil, a natural deworming agent.

2. Rebekah's fellow student Lee will have (chosen / chose) which sheep from the herd to put in the holding pen for treatment.

3. Their instructor, Josh, will have (gave / given) them tips on how to get the animals to hold still and swallow the deworming medicine.

4. Josh's instructions will have (came / come) with a lot of encouragement.

5. For these experiences, Lee, Rebekah, and eleven other college students will have (paid / pay) $12,500 tuition to the Farm School, for lessons, room, and board.

6. Students who graduate from the program will have (driven / drove) diesel tractors and operated other large pieces of farm equipment.

7. They will have (ridden / rode) horses, planted beans, weeded fields of broccoli, and met many new friends.

8. In the coming years, the director of the Farm School, Patrick Connors, will have (grew / grown) more confident and seen enrollments increase.

9. Some graduates of the Learn to Farm program will have (taken / took) jobs on farms or gone on to study veterinary medicine.

10. Other graduates will have (seen / saw) how satisfying it is, in hard economic times, to be able to grow their own food.

Irregular Verbs

Unlike regular verbs, which have past-tense and past-participle forms that end in *-ed* or *-d,* **irregular verbs** change spelling in the past-tense and past-participle forms.

PRESENT-TENSE IRREGULAR VERBS

Only a few verbs are irregular in the present tense. The ones most commonly used are the verbs *be* and *have.*

The Verb *Be*, Present Tense

	Singular	Plural
First person	I am	we are
Second person	you are	you are
Third person	she/he/it is	they are
	the dog is	the dogs are
	Chris is	Chris and Dan are

e Log in to macmillanhighered .com/realessays **Additional Grammar Exercises** > Using the Correct Verb Form for *Be* and *Have* in the Present Tense

The Verb *Have*, Present Tense

	Singular	Plural
First person	I have	we have
Second person	you have	you have
Third person	she/he/it has	they have
	the dog has	the dogs have
	Chris has	Chris and Dan have

PRACTICE 10   **Using *be* and *have* in the present tense**

In each of the following sentences, fill in the correct form of the verb indicated in parentheses.

Example: **Disc golf ___is___ (be) played with Frisbees.**

1. I ___am___ (be) a fanatical disc golfer.

2. The game ___has___ (have) eighteen holes, like regular golf, but uses a Frisbee instead of a ball.

3. A disc golf course ___has___ (have) fairways and holes.

4. A tee ___is___ (be) at the beginning of each fairway.

5. Players ___are___ (be) eager to get the Frisbee from the tee into a metal basket in the fewest possible throws.

6. Some disc golfers ___have___ (*have*) special Frisbees for teeing off and putting.

7. My brother, who also plays disc golf, ___has___ (*have*) thirty different Frisbees for the game.

8. His wife ___is___ (*be*) surprisingly patient with his enthusiasm for the sport.

9. "You ___are___ (*be*) in the middle of a second adolescence," she tells him.

10. However, she, too, ___has___ (*have*) formidable Frisbee technique.

e Log in to
macmillanhighered
.com/realessays
Additional Grammar
Exercises > Using the
Correct Verb Form for
Irregular Verbs in the
Past Tense

PAST-TENSE IRREGULAR VERBS

As discussed earlier, the past-tense and past-participle forms of irregular verbs do not follow a standard pattern. For example, they do not use the *-ed* ending for past tense, although the past participle uses a helping verb, just as regular verbs do.

Present tense	Past tense	Past participle
Tony makes hats.	Tony made hats.	Tony has/had made hats.
You write well.	You wrote well.	You have/had written well.
I ride a bike.	I rode a bike.	I have/had ridden a bike.

The verb *be* is tricky because it has two different forms for the past tense—*was* and *were*.

The Verb *Be*, Past Tense

	Singular	Plural
First person	I was	we were
Second person	you were	you were
Third person	she/he/it was	they were
	the car was	the cars were
	Jolanda was	Jolanda and Ti were

PRACTICE 11   **Using past-tense forms of the verb *be***

In the paragraph that follows, fill in each blank with the correct past-tense form of the verb *be*.

Example: The many visitors to President Lincoln's White House __*were*__ generally polite.

(1) Lincoln __*was*__ respectful of his visitors as well, but they took up a great deal of his time. (2) Most of his visitors __*were*__ politicians, army generals, journalists, job seekers, and relatives of Mrs. Lincoln. (3) Nearly every visitor __*was*__ seeking something from the president, such as promotions, policy changes, or pardons. (4) Whenever a visitor came asking for nothing, Lincoln __*was*__ clearly relieved. (5) Mrs. Lincoln's relatives __*were*__ especially troublesome for the president. (6) Many of the Todds __*were*__ Confederate sympathizers or even Confederate combatants. (7) Usually, though, a Todd visiting Lincoln __*was*__ looking for a job. (8) Nearly everyone who had known Lincoln at some point in his life __*was*__ welcomed by the president. (9) His manner __*was*__ almost always so friendly and gracious that his visitors __*were*__ quickly put at ease. (10) Although in the Lincoln Memorial the statue has a serious face, whenever the president greeted a visitor, he __*was*__ usually smiling.

As you write and edit, consult the chart on pages 392–94 to make sure that you use the correct form of irregular verbs.

Irregular Verb Forms

Present tense	Past tense	Past participle (with helping verb)
be (am/are/is)	was/were	been
become	became	become
begin	began	begun
bite	bit	bitten
blow	blew	blown
break	broke	broken
bring	brought	brought
build	built	built
buy	bought	bought
catch	caught	caught
choose	chose	chosen
come	came	come
cost	cost	cost
dive	dived, dove	dived
do	did	done
draw	drew	drawn
drink	drank	drunk
drive	drove	driven
eat	ate	eaten
fall	fell	fallen
feed	fed	fed
feel	felt	felt
fight	fought	fought
find	found	found
fly	flew	flown
forget	forgot	forgotten
freeze	froze	frozen
get	got	gotten
give	gave	given
go	went	gone
grow	grew	grown
have/has	had	had
hear	heard	heard
hide	hid	hidden

Present tense	Past tense	Past participle (with helping verb)
hit	hit	hit
hold	held	held
hurt	hurt	hurt
keep	kept	kept
know	knew	known
lay	laid	laid
leave	left	left
let	let	let
lie	lay	lain
light	lit	lit
lose	lost	lost
make	made	made
mean	meant	meant
meet	met	met
pay	paid	paid
put	put	put
quit	quit	quit
read	read	read
ride	rode	ridden
ring	rang	rung
rise	rose	risen
run	ran	run
say	said	said
see	saw	seen
sell	sold	sold
send	sent	sent
set (to place)	set	set
shake	shook	shaken
show	showed	shown
shrink	shrank	shrunk
shut	shut	shut
sing	sang	sung
sink	sank	sunk
sit (to be seated)	sat	sat
sleep	slept	slept

Present tense	Past tense	Past participle (with helping verb)
speak	spoke	spoken
spend	spent	spent
stand	stood	stood
steal	stole	stolen
stick	stuck	stuck
sting	stung	stung
strike	struck	struck, stricken
swim	swam	swum
take	took	taken
teach	taught	taught
tear	tore	torn
tell	told	told
think	thought	thought
throw	threw	thrown
understand	understood	understood
wake	woke	woken
wear	wore	worn
win	won	won
write	wrote	written

PRACTICE 12   **Using past-tense irregular verbs**

In each of the following sentences, fill in the correct past-tense form of the irregular verb in parentheses. If you do not know the answer, find the word in the chart of irregular verb forms on pages 392–94.

Example: The *Titanic* ___set___ (*set*) out from Southampton, England, in 1912.

1. The White Star Line ___built___ (*build*) the *Titanic*, which was the biggest moving object in the world at that time.

2. The huge ship ___held___ (*hold*) over 2,200 passengers on its maiden voyage.

3. The newspapers ___wrote___ (*write*) that twenty lifeboats, which could hold 1,178 people altogether, hung from the upper deck of the *Titanic*.

4. The shipbuilders ___felt___ (*feel*) that the giant liner was the safest ship in the world and that more lifeboats were simply unnecessary.

5. On April 14, 1912, during its first trip across the Atlantic, the

   Titanic __struck__ (*strike*) an iceberg.

6. The sharp ice __tore__ (*tear*) a gaping hole in the bottom of the ship.

7. Icy ocean water __began__ (*begin*) to pour into the hold, dragging the

   Titanic down in the water.

8. Few passengers __understood__ (*understand*) the danger at first.

9. Half-empty lifeboats __left__ (*leave*) the sinking ship while other pas-

   sengers __stood__ (*stand*) on deck, refusing to depart.

10. Hundreds of people __froze__ (*freeze*) to death in the ocean before the

    nearest ship __came__ (*come*) to rescue the Titanic's 705 survivors.

PRACTICE 13 **Using past-tense irregular verbs**

In the following paragraph, replace any incorrect present-tense verb
forms with the correct past-tense form of the verb. If you do not know
the answer, look up the verbs in the chart of irregular verb forms on
pages 392–94.

Example: Dewayne faced a judge and jury of his fellow high school
                                             hit
students after he ~~hits~~ a boy in the classroom.
                 ^

                                    set
(1) Two years ago, my high school ~~sets~~ up a student court to give stu-
                                  ^
dents a voice in disciplining rule breakers. (2) Before the court opened its
                 taught
doors, adults ~~teach~~ students about decision making and about courtroom
             ^
                                                              became
procedures. (3) Some of us served as members of juries, and others ~~become~~
                                      sat   ^
advocates or even judges. (4) I ~~sit~~ on a jury twice when I was a junior.
                               ^
(5) Then, last spring, my friend Dewayne appeared before the student court
      lost   *struck*
after he ~~loses~~ his temper and ~~strikes~~ a fellow student. (6) I agreed to be his
        ^   *thought* ^   *told*
advocate because I ~~think~~ he truly regretted his behavior. (7) I ~~tell~~ the jury
                  ^   ^
                                                    sent
that he knew his violent reaction was a mistake. (8) The jury ~~sends~~ Dewayne
                                                             ^
for counseling to learn to manage his anger and made him write an apol-
                                                          shook
ogy to the other student. (9) After hearing the verdict, Dewayne ~~shakes~~
                                                                ^
hands with all the jurors and thanked them for their fairness. (10) The expe-
      made
rience ~~makes~~ me eager to learn more about America's system of justice.
      ^

For more practice on using past forms of irregular verbs, see Chapter 32.

PRACTICE 14   Using past-participle forms for irregular verbs

In each of the following sentences, underline the helping verb (a form of *have*) and fill in the correct past-participle form of the verb in parentheses. If you do not know the correct form, find the word in the chart on pages 392–94.

Example: Because many of the city's jobs had ___been___ (*be*) in the auto industry, Detroit's economy suffered when the car factories closed.

1. Over the last fifty years, the population of Detroit has ___shrunk___ (*shrink*) by 50 percent.

2. Many people have ___begun___ (*begin*) to argue that the city itself needs to shrink as well.

3. The mayor of Detroit has ___said___ (*say*) that the city needs to take drastic measures to save itself.

4. In the past, urban renewal has ___meant___ (*mean*) new buildings and fancy projects.

5. However, despite such efforts, Detroit has ___fallen___ (*fall*) further into decline.

6. Now, the mayor says the time has ___come___ (*come*) to close schools, cut services, and bulldoze neighborhoods.

7. A third of the city has ___become___ (*become*) vacant.

8. Even some who had ___held___ (*hold*) out hope that Detroit might regain its old size and strength agreed with the mayor when he presented his plan for right-sizing the city.

9. Others have ___grown___ (*grow*) angry and scared that their neighborhoods will be the ones destroyed.

10. However, given the failure of previous renewal strategies, right-sizing has ___won___ (*win*) many supporters.

Passive Voice

A sentence in the **passive voice** has a subject that performs no action. Instead, the subject is acted upon. To create the passive voice, combine a form of the verb *be* with a past participle.

$$\boxed{be \text{ (helping verb)}} \ + \ \boxed{\text{Past participle}} \ = \ \boxed{\text{Passive voice}}$$

             be (helping verb)   Past participle

Passive   My memo <u>was written</u> by an employee.

[The subject, *memo,* did not write itself. An employee wrote the memo, but the subject in the sentence, *memo,* performs no action.]

In sentences that use the **active voice**, the subject performs the action.

Active   An <u>employee</u> <u>wrote</u> the memo.

Use the passive voice when no one person performed the action, when you don't know who performed the action, or when you want to emphasize the receiver of the action. Use the active voice whenever possible, and use passive voice sparingly.

Passive   The <u>dog</u> <u>was hit</u> by a passing car.

[If the writer wants to focus on the dog as the receiver of the action, the passive voice is acceptable.]

Active   A passing <u>car</u> <u>hit</u> the dog.

Log in to
**macmillanhighered
.com/realessays**
**Additional Grammar
Exercises** > Identifying
Active and Passive Voice

🌐 **Language note:** Do not confuse the passive voice with the present-perfect tense or past-perfect tense. The passive uses a form of the verb *be* (*is, was, were*), and the subject performs no action. The present-perfect tense and the past-perfect tense have subjects that perform an action, and they use a form of the verb *have.*

Passive   The <u>boat</u> <u>was crushed</u> by huge waves.

[The subject *boat* performs no action. The verb uses *was,* a form of *be.*]

**Passive
incorrect**   The <u>boat</u> was <u>been</u> crushed by huge waves.

[The verb in the passive voice should not use *two* forms of *be* (*was, been*). Use *was.*]

Present perfect   Huge <u>waves</u> <u>have crushed</u> all the boats.

[The subject *waves* performs the action, *crushed,* using the present form of *have.*]

Past perfect   Huge <u>waves</u> <u>had crushed</u> all the boats.

[The subject *waves* performed the action, *crushed,* using the past form of *have.*]

PRACTICE 15   **Changing from passive voice to active voice**

Rewrite the following sentences in the active voice. *Answers may vary.*
Possible edits shown.

Officers can control the
Example: The *Queen Mary 2*, one of the world's largest cruise ships, ~~can be controlled~~ with a joystick.
                          ^

has
1. The *Queen Mary 2* ~~is equipped with~~ a grand lobby and an old-style
   ^
   three-story restaurant.

features
2. Its bridge, however, ~~is filled with~~ advanced consoles, screens, and
   ^
   joysticks.

The ship's computer systems can automatically correct the
3. ~~The~~ effects of the wind, waves, and ocean currents. ~~can be automati-~~
   ^
   ~~cally corrected by the ship's computer systems.~~

captain did not touch the
4. During the ship's first docking in New York, the joystick. ~~was not~~
   ^   ^
   ~~touched by the captain.~~

he would probably use
5. He said the joystick ~~would probably be used~~ more ~~by him~~ in the
   ^
   future.

Log in to macmillanhighered.com/realessays Additional Grammar Exercises > Correcting Problems with Consistency of Verb Tense

Consistency of Verb Tense

Consistency of verb tense means that all the actions in a sentence that happen (or happened) at the same time are in the same tense. If all of the actions happen in the present, use the present tense for all verbs in the sentence. If all of the actions happened in the past, use the past tense for all verbs in the sentence.

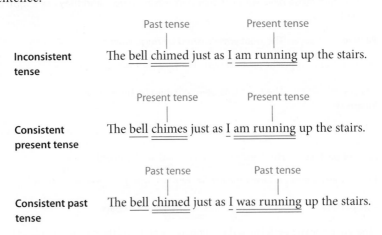

PRACTICE 16   **Using consistent tense**

In each of the following items, double-underline the verbs in the sentence, and correct any unnecessary shifts in verb tense by writing the correct form of any incorrect verb in the blank space provided.

Example: ___*use*___ **People either ride bicycles for leisurely journeys, or they used bikes for serious exercise.**

1. ___*need*___ Those who want a good workout needed different kinds of equipment than those interested in an easy ride.

2. ___*have*___ For example, serious cyclists who had bikes with wide padded seats face the chance of injuries.

3. ___*causes*___ A wide seat makes the rider shift from side to side, and it caused painful rubbing.

4. ___*should be*___ In addition, the seat should have been high enough so that the rider cannot put his or her feet on the ground.

5. ___*wear*___ Serious riders wore special shoes that snap onto the pedals to allow pulling up as well as pushing down.

6. ___*are*___ Serious money is also a factor because custom bicycles were expensive.

7. ___*chooses*___ Once an experienced cyclist chose the proper bicycle, he or she knows how to ride it properly.

8. ___*exercise*___ For instance, knowledgeable riders move around as they ride so that they exercised different muscle groups.

9. ___*keeps*___ The smart rider also kept his or her knees slightly bent, which eases the strain on the knees.

10. ___*wish*___ Of course, those who just wished to have a fun ride through the park ignore all of this advice.

Editing Practice

As you edit the following paragraphs and your own writing, use the following checklist and the Verb Tense Reference Charts that begin on page 404.

CHECKLIST

Editing for Verb Problems

FOCUS
Read all of your sentences carefully, looking for verb problems.

ASK
- ☐ Is my sentence about the present? About the past? About something that happened before something else?
- ☐ Is each verb a regular verb or an irregular verb?
- ☐ Have I used the tense that tells the reader when the action happened?
- ☐ Have I used the correct form of the verb?
- ☐ If the verbs in the sentence are not all in the same tense, is it because the actions actually happened at different times?

EDIT
- ☐ Edit to correct any problems with verb form or verb tense.

Find and correct any problems with verb form or tense in the following paragraphs.

Resources For cumulative Editing Review Tests, see pages 564–80.

EDITING REVIEW 1   (7 errors)

1 Since 1835, trapeze artists ~~consider~~ *have considered* the triple somersault the most dangerous maneuver. 2 That year, a performer tried to do a triple somersault on a trapeze for the first time and ~~dies~~ *died* in the attempt. 3 Only one person ~~has~~ managed to do the trick successfully in the next sixty-three years. 4 That man, a trapeze artist named Armor, did a triple somersault in 1860 and ~~is~~ *was* afraid to try it again. 5 According to circus legend, the second person to survive the triple, Ernie Clarke, once ~~done~~ *did* a quadruple somersault in private. 6 Ernie Lane, the third person to complete a triple

somersault, was later killed by the maneuver. 7 Circus historians now

believe

~~believed~~ that Alfredo Codona, a performer in the 1920s and 1930s, was the

^

gone

greatest master of the triple somersault. 8 He has ~~went~~ down in history as

^

the King of Trapeze.

EDITING REVIEW 2   (8 errors)

1 Many people go through life without ever knowing that there is a

record for peeling an apple or hopping on a pogo stick. 2 However, some

people are very aware of such records, and ordinary folks around the world

done

have ~~did~~ some peculiar things to qualify for the *Guinness Book of World*

^

Records. 3 For example, a New Zealand disc jockey, Nikora Curtis, recently

set

~~setted~~ a new record for the longest continuous radio broadcast. 4 In the

^

summer of 2010, he ~~has~~ stayed on the air for 176 hours with no sleep.

held

5 Another world record, for hopping up steps on a bicycle, is ~~hold~~ by Javier

^

Zapata of Colombia. 6 He climbed 943 steps without letting his feet touch

had

the ground, breaking a record that he himself ~~has~~ previously set. 7 Ashrita

^

is

Furman of New York also ~~be~~ a record breaker. 8 He balanced a milk bottle

^ *walked*

on his head and then ~~walks~~ almost eighty-one miles around a track. 9 These

^

strange endurance contests may not make Curtis, Zapata, and Furman

have

famous, but their names ~~had~~ entered the record book.

^

EDITING REVIEW 3   (9 errors)

1 The Olympic Games first let women compete in swimming events

began

in 1912, and with that, the swimsuit revolution ~~begun~~. 2 In 1913, the

^

first mass-produced women's swimsuit hit the market. 3 Before that year,

had

women ~~have~~ only been able to wade at the beach in bathing costumes

^

were

with long, baggy legs. 4 The 1913 suits, designed by Carl Jantzen, ~~was~~

^

ribbed one-piece outfits that allowed actual swimming. 5 An engineer,

came

Louis Réard, ~~comed~~ up with the next major development in swimwear in

^

1946 while working in the lingerie business. 6 He ~~has~~ called it the "bikini,"

after a Pacific island used for testing the atomic bomb. 7 In the 1950s, few

Americans ~~had~~ *were* dared to wear bikinis, which ~~was~~ considered scandalous.

8 Two-piece swimsuits ~~catch~~ *caught* on in the 1960s and 1970s. 9 The bikini ~~losted~~ *lost* ^

some popularity in the last decades of the twentieth century, but it has

made a triumphant return in the new millennium.

<hr>

EDITING REVIEW 4   (13 errors and 6 formal English errors)

1 Located in southern Utah, Best Friends Animal Sanctuary ~~are~~ *is* the larg-

est "no-kill" animal shelter in the United States. 2 For over twenty-five years,

the sanctuary ~~had~~ *has* provided a refuge *for* 4 unwanted, abused, and neglected

animals, and has promoted spay and neuter programs. 3 Dogs '*n* cats, as

well as birds, ~~piggies~~ *pigs*, horses, and rabbits, ~~were coming there~~ *come to the sanctuary* ^ from all over

the country. 4 The organization ~~took~~ *takes* in animals from other shelters ~~but~~ *and*

also ~~rescue~~ *rescues* animals from disaster areas and inhumane situations. 5 After

Hurricane Katrina, volunteers from Best Friends ~~find, rescue, care~~ *found, rescued, cared* for, and

transported many lost or abandoned ~~critters~~ *animals* ^. 6 In 2008, twenty-two of

football player Michael Vick's fighting dogs were taken in by the sanctuary.

7 Best Friends' goal is ~~being~~ to rehabilitate animals so that they ~~could~~ *can* find

new homes. 8 ~~Cuz~~ *Because* the animals often need to learn how to be around peo-

ple, the sanctuary ~~was encouraging~~ *encourages* visitors. 9 Visitors can even take a dog

or cat home overnight. 10 These home visits ~~had been~~ *are* fun for the ~~peeps~~ *people*,

help the animals get used to new environments, and sometimes lead to

adoption.

PRACTICE 17   ### Editing your own writing for correct verb tense and form

As a final practice, edit for verb problems in a piece of your own writing—
a paper you are working on for this class, a paper you have already finished, a paper for another course, or a recent piece of writing from your
work or everyday life. Use the Verb Tense Reference Charts starting on
page 403.

Verb Tense Reference Charts

English verbs, like verbs in most other languages, have different tenses to show when something happened: in the past, present, or future.

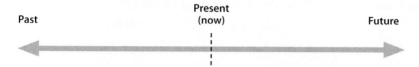

This section covers the most common tenses. The discussions of each tense start with a chart that tells you what time the tense is used for. The chart then shows how to use the tense in statements, negative sentences, and questions. You can use the verb charts both to learn tenses and to edit your own writing. Following the charts are lists of common errors to avoid.

THE SIMPLE TENSES

Tense	

Simple present

Timeline: situations that exist always (now, in the past, and in the future)

Present
Past   (now)   Future

I **like** pizza.

STATEMENTS

In the third-person singular, regular verbs end in -s or -es. (For irregular verb endings, see pages 392–94.)

I / you **like** pizza.   We **like** pizza.

She / he **likes** pizza.   They **like** pizza.

NEGATIVES

| Present of *do* | + | *not* | + | Base verb |

I / you **do not like** pizza.   We **do not like** pizza.

She / he **does not like** pizza.   They **do not like** pizza.

QUESTIONS

| Present of *do* | + | Subject | + | Base verb |

Do I / you **like** pizza?   **Do** we **like** pizza?

Does she / he **like** pizza?   **Do** they **like** pizza?

Simple past

Timeline: situations that began and ended at a specific time in the past

Present
Past   (now)   Future

I **worked** last night.

STATEMENTS

| Base verb | + | -d or -ed (regular verbs) |

I / you **worked** last night.   We **worked** last night.

She / he **worked** last night.   They **worked** last night.

NEGATIVES

| Past of *do (did)* | + | *not* | + | Base verb |

I / you **did not work** last night.   We **did not work** last night.

She / he **did not work** last night.   They **did not work** last night.

QUESTIONS

| Past of *do (did)* | + | Subject | + | Base verb |

Did I / you **work** last night?   **Did** we **work** last night?

Did she / he **work** last night?   **Did** they **work** last night?

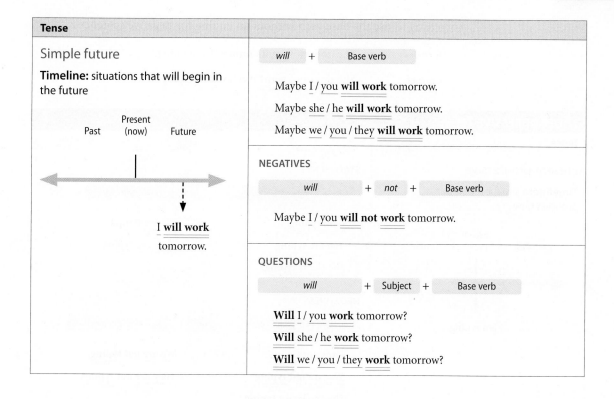

Tense	
Simple future **Timeline:** situations that will begin in the future *[timeline diagram: Past — Present (now) — Future, with "I will work tomorrow."]*	*will* + Base verb Maybe I / you **will work** tomorrow. Maybe she / he **will work** tomorrow. Maybe we / you / they **will work** tomorrow. **NEGATIVES** *will* + *not* + Base verb Maybe I / you **will not work** tomorrow. **QUESTIONS** *will* + Subject + Base verb **Will** I / you **work** tomorrow? **Will** she / he **work** tomorrow? **Will** we / you / they **work** tomorrow?

Forgetting to add *-s* or *-es* to verbs that go with third-person singular subjects (*she/he/it*):

Incorrect	She know the manager.
Correct	She knows the manager.

COMMON ERRORS FORMING SIMPLE PAST

Forgetting to add *-d* or *-ed* to regular verbs:

Incorrect	Gina work late last night.
Correct	Gina work**ed** late last night.

Forgetting to use the correct past form of irregular verbs (see the chart of irregular verb forms on pages 392–94):

Incorrect	Gerard speaked to her about the problem.
Correct	Gerard **spoke** to her about the problem.

Forgetting to use the base verb without an ending for negative sentences:

Incorrect	She does not wants money for helping.
Correct	She does not **want** money for helping.

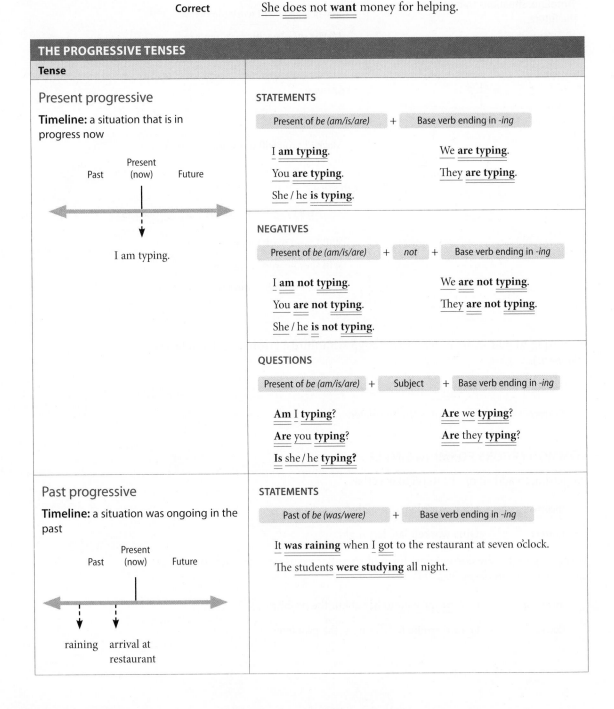

THE PROGRESSIVE TENSES

Tense

Present progressive

Timeline: a situation that is in progress now

Past   Present (now)   Future

I am typing.

STATEMENTS

Present of *be (am/is/are)* + Base verb ending in *-ing*

I **am typing**.   We **are typing**.
You **are typing**.   They **are typing**.
She / he **is typing**.

NEGATIVES

Present of *be (am/is/are)* + *not* + Base verb ending in *-ing*

I **am not typing**.   We **are not typing**.
You **are not typing**.   They **are not typing**.
She / he **is not typing**.

QUESTIONS

Present of *be (am/is/are)* + Subject + Base verb ending in *-ing*

Am I **typing?**   **Are** we **typing?**
Are you **typing?**   **Are** they **typing?**
Is she / he **typing?**

Past progressive

Timeline: a situation was ongoing in the past

Past   Present (now)   Future

raining   arrival at restaurant

STATEMENTS

Past of *be (was/were)* + Base verb ending in *-ing*

It **was raining** when I got to the restaurant at seven o'clock.
The students **were studying** all night.

Tense	
Past progressive (cont.)	**NEGATIVES**

Past of *be (was/were)* + *not* + Base verb ending in *-ing*

It **was not raining** when I got to the restaurant at seven o'clock.

The students **were not studying** all night.

QUESTIONS

Past of *be (was/were)* + Subject + Base verb ending in *-ing*

Was it **raining** when I got to the restaurant at seven o'clock?

Were the students **studying** all night?

Future progressive

Timeline: a situation that will be ongoing at some point in the future

Present
(now)
Past | Future

working Jan's
arrival

STATEMENTS

will be + Base verb ending in *-ing*

I / you **will be working** when Jan gets home.

She / he **will be working** when Jan gets home.

We **will be working** when Jan gets home.

They **will be working** when Jan gets home.

NEGATIVES

will + *not* + *be* + Base verb ending in *-ing*

I / you **will not be working** when Jan gets home.

She / he **will not be working** when Jan gets home.

We **will not be working** when Jan gets home.

They **will not be working** when Jan gets home.

QUESTIONS

will + Subject + *be* + Base verb ending in *-ing*

Will I / you **be working** when Jan gets home?

Will she / he **be working** when Jan gets home?

Will we **be working** when Jan gets home?

Will they **be working** when Jan gets home?

COMMON ERRORS FORMING THE PRESENT PROGRESSIVE

Forgetting to add -*ing* to the verb:

Incorrect	I am type now.
	She/he is not work now.
Correct	I am typ**ing** now.
	She/he is not work**ing** now.

Forgetting to include a form of *be* (*am/is/are*):

Incorrect	He typing now.
	They typing now.
Correct	He **is** typing now.
	They **are** typing now.

Forgetting to use a form of *be* (*am/is/are*) to start questions:

| Incorrect | They typing now? |
| Correct | **Are** they typing now? |

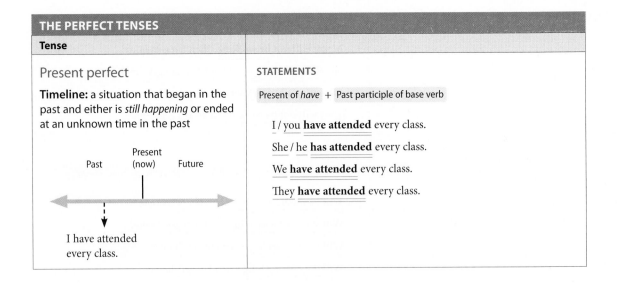

THE PERFECT TENSES

Tense	
Present perfect	**STATEMENTS**
Timeline: a situation that began in the past and either is *still happening* or ended at an unknown time in the past	Present of *have* + Past participle of base verb
	I / you **have attended** every class.
	She / he **has attended** every class.
	We **have attended** every class.
	They **have attended** every class.

Past — Present (now) — Future

I have attended every class.

Tense	
Present perfect (cont.)	**NEGATIVES**

NEGATIVES

Present of *have* + *not* + Past participle of base verb

I / you **have not attended** every class.

She / he **has not attended** every class.

We **have not attended** every class.

They **have not attended** every class.

QUESTIONS

Present of *have* + Subject + Past participle of base verb

Have I / you **attended** every class?

Has she / he **attended** every class?

Have we **attended** every class?

Have they **attended** every class?

Past perfect

Timeline: a situation that began and ended before some other past situation occurred

Past   Present
(now)   Future

(somebody)   Gil's
left   arrival

STATEMENTS

Past of *have (had)* + Past participle of base verb

I / you **had left** before Gil arrived.

She / he **had left** before Gil arrived.

We **had left** before Gil arrived.

They **had left** before Gil arrived.

Tense	
Past perfect (cont.)	**NEGATIVES** Past of *have (had)* + *not* + Past participle of base verb Usually used for *if* situations If you **had not left**, you would have seen him. If she / he **had not left**, she / he would have seen him. If we **had not left**, we would have seen him. If they **had not left**, they would have seen him.
	QUESTIONS Past of *have (had)* + Subject + Past participle of base verb **Had** I / you **left** before Gil arrived? **Had** she / he **left** before Gil arrived? **Had** we **left** before Gil arrived? **Had** they **left** before Gil arrived?
Future perfect **Timeline:** a situation that will be completed in the future before another future situation Past · Present (now) · Future graduation · moving	**STATEMENTS** *will have* + Past participle of base verb I / you **will have graduated** before you move. She / he **will have graduated** before you move. We **will have graduated** before you move. They **will have graduated** before you move.
	NEGATIVES *will not have* + Past participle of base verb I / you **will not have graduated** before you move. She / he **will not have graduated** before you move. We **will not have graduated** before you move. They **will not have graduated** before you move.

Tense	
Future perfect (cont.)	**QUESTIONS** *will* + Subject + *have* + Past participle of base verb **Will** I / you **have graduated** before you move? **Will** she / he **have graduated** before you move? **Will** we **have graduated** before you move? **Will** they **have graduated** before you move?

COMMON ERRORS FORMING THE PERFECT TENSE

Using *had* instead of *has* or *have* for the present perfect:

Incorrect	We **had** lived here since 2003.
Correct	We **have** lived here since 2003.

Forgetting to use past participles (with *-d* or *-ed* endings for regular verbs):

Incorrect	She has attend every class.
Correct	She has attend**ed** every class.

Using *been* between *have* or *has* and the past participle of a base verb:

Incorrect	I have **been** attended every class.
Correct	I have attended every class.

Incorrect	I will have **been** graduated before I move.
Correct	I will have graduated before I move.

→

MODAL AUXILIARIES/HELPING VERBS	
HELPING VERB (MODAL AUXILIARY)	
Modal auxiliaries join with a main (base) verb to make a complete verb.	**STATEMENTS** Subject + Helping verb + Base verb **PRESENT** Dumbo <u>can</u> <u>fly</u>. **PAST** Forms vary—see below. **NEGATIVES** Subject + Helping verb + *not* + Base verb **PRESENT** Dumbo <u>cannot</u> <u>fly</u>. **PAST** Forms vary—see below. **QUESTIONS** Helping verb + Subject + Base verb **PRESENT** <u>Can</u> Dumbo <u>fly</u>? **PAST** Forms vary—see below.
Can Means *ability*.	**STATEMENTS** **PRESENT** Beth <u>**can**</u> <u>work</u> fast. **PAST** Beth <u>**could**</u> <u>work</u> fast. **NEGATIVES** **PRESENT** Beth <u>**can**</u>not <u>work</u> fast. **PAST** Beth <u>**could**</u> not <u>work</u> fast. **QUESTIONS** **PRESENT** <u>**Can**</u> Beth <u>work</u> fast? **PAST** <u>**Could**</u> Beth <u>work</u> fast?

HELPING VERB (MODAL AUXILIARY)	
Could Means *possibility*. It can also be the past tense of *can*.	**STATEMENTS** **PRESENT** — Beth **could** work fast if she had more time. **PAST** — Beth **could** have worked fast if she had more time.
	NEGATIVES *Can* is used for present negatives. (See above.) **PRESENT** — Beth **could** not have worked fast.
	QUESTIONS **PRESENT** — **Could** Beth work fast? **PAST** — **Could** Beth have worked fast?
May Means *permission*. For past-tense forms, see *might*.	**STATEMENTS** **PRESENT** — You **may** borrow my car.
	NEGATIVE **PRESENT** — You **may** not borrow my car.
	QUESTIONS **PRESENT** — **May** I borrow your car?
Might Means *possibility*. It can also be the past tense of *may*.	**STATEMENTS** **PRESENT (with *be*):** Lou **might** be asleep. **PAST (with *have* + past participle of *be*):** Lou **might** have been asleep. **FUTURE:** Lou **might** sleep.
	NEGATIVES **PRESENT (with *be*):** Lou **might** not be asleep. **PAST (with *have* + past participle of *be*):** Lou **might** not have been asleep. **FUTURE:** Lou **might** not sleep.
	QUESTIONS *Might* in questions is notably formal and not often used. →

HELPING VERB (MODAL AUXILIARY)	

Must
 	
Means *necessary*.
	STATEMENTS
	
	   PRESENT: We **must** try.
	
	   PAST (with *have* + past participle of base verb):
	
	   We **must** have tried.

	NEGATIVES
	
	   PRESENT: We **must** not try.
	
	   PAST (with *have* + past participle of base verb):
	
	   We **must** not have tried.

	QUESTIONS
	
	   PRESENT: Must we try?
	
	   (Past-tense questions with *must* are unusual.)

Should
 	
Means *duty* or *expectation*.
	STATEMENTS
	
	   PRESENT: They **should** call.
	
	   PAST (with *have* + past participle of base verb):
	
	   They **should** have called.

	NEGATIVES
	
	   PRESENT: They **should** not call.
	
	   PAST (with *have* + past participle of base verb):
	
	   They **should** not have called.

	QUESTIONS
	
	   PRESENT: Should they call?
	
	   PAST (with *have* + past participle of base verb):
	
	   Should they have called?

HELPING VERB (MODAL AUXILIARY)	
Will Means *intend to* (future). For past-tense forms, see *might*.	**STATEMENTS** FUTURE: I **will** succeed.
	NEGATIVES FUTURE: I **will** not succeed.
	QUESTIONS FUTURE: **Will** I succeed?
Would Means *prefer* or is used to start a future request. It can also be the past tense of *will*.	**STATEMENTS** PRESENT: I **would** like to travel. PAST (with *have* + past participle of base verb): I **would** have traveled if I had the money.
	NEGATIVES PRESENT: I **would** not like to travel. PAST (with *have* + past participle of base verb): I **would** not have traveled if it had not been for you.
	QUESTIONS PRESENT: **Would** you like to travel? *Or* to start a request: **Would** you help me? PAST (with *have* + past participle of base verb): **Would** you have traveled with me if I had asked you?

COMMON ERRORS USING MODAL AUXILIARIES

Using more than one helping verb:

Incorrect	They **will can** help.
Correct	They **will** help. (future intention)
	They **can** help. (are able to)

For more on the modal auxiliaries, see Chapter 32.

Using *to* between the helping verb and the main (base) verb:

Incorrect	Emilio **might to** come with us.
Correct	Emilio **might** come with us.

Using *must* instead of *had to* in the past:

Incorrect	She **must** work yesterday.
Correct	She **had to** work yesterday.

Forgetting to change *can* to *could* in the past negative:

Incorrect	Last night, I **can**not sleep.
Correct	Last night, I **could** not sleep.

Forgetting to use *have* with *could/should/would* in the past tense:

Incorrect	Tara **should** called last night.
Correct	Tara **should have** called last night.

Using *will* instead of *would* to express a preference in the present tense:

Incorrect	I **will** like to travel.
Correct	I **would** like to travel.

Part 6

Other Grammar Concerns

"I write e-mails to my friends and family."

Jonatan T., student

PHOTO: PATRICIA LEE

26

Pronouns
Using Substitutes for Nouns

Understand What Pronouns Are

Pronouns replace nouns (or other pronouns) in a sentence so that you do not have to repeat the nouns.

> *her*
> Tessa let me borrow ~~Tessa's~~ jacket.
> *He* ^
> You have met Carl. ~~Carl~~ is my cousin.
> ^

The noun (or pronoun) that a pronoun replaces is called the **antecedent**. The word *antecedent* means "something that comes before." In most cases, a pronoun refers to a specific antecedent nearby. In the second example above, *Carl* is the antecedent and *He* is the pronoun that replaces *Carl*.

There are three basic types of pronouns—**subject** pronouns, **object** pronouns, and **possessive** pronouns. Note the pronouns in the following sentences.

> Object   Subject
> | |
> The linebacker tackled him, and he went down hard.

> Possessive
> |
> His shoulder was injured.

e Log in to
macmillanhighered
.com/realessays
LearningCurve >
Pronouns; **Additional
Grammar Exercises** >
Identifying Pronouns

ESL Students may have particular trouble with pronouns and would benefit from extra practice. Encourage these students to pay special attention to pronouns as they revise their own writing.

Pronoun Types

	Subject	Object	Possessive
First person (singular/plural)	I/we	me/us	my/our, mine, ours
Second person (singular/plural)	you/you	you/you	your, yours/your, yours
Third person (singular)	he, she, it	him, her, it	his, her, hers, its
Third person (plural)	they	them	their, theirs
	who/who	whom/whom	whose

 Language note: Notice that third-person pronouns have gender (*he/she, him/her, his/her/hers*). The pronoun must agree with the gender of the antecedent.

Incorrect	Tonya lives with *his* cousin.
Correct	Tonya lives with *her* cousin.

Also, notice that English has different forms for subject and object pronouns, as shown in the preceding chart.

For more help with pronouns, see Chapter 32.

Check for Pronoun Agreement

A pronoun must agree with (match) its antecedent in number: It must be singular (one) or plural (more than one). If it is singular, it must also match its antecedent in gender (*he*, *she*, or *it*).

Consistent   Sherry talked to *her* aunt.

[The pronoun *her* agrees with *Sherry* because both are singular and feminine.]

Consistent   The Romanos sold *their* restaurant.

[The pronoun *their* agrees with *Romanos* because both are plural.]

Watch out for singular nouns that are not specific. If a noun is singular, the pronoun must be singular as well.

Inconsistent   Any athlete can tell you about *their* commitment to practice.

[The noun *athlete* is singular, but the pronoun *their* is plural.]

Consistent   Any athlete can tell you about *his* or *her* commitment to practice.

[*Athlete* is singular, and so are the pronouns *his* and *her*.]

As an alternative to using the phrase *his or her,* make the subject plural if you can. (For more on this, see the note in the next section.)

> **Consistent** All athletes can tell you about *their* commitment to practice.

Two types of words often cause errors in pronoun agreement—indefinite pronouns and collective nouns.

INDEFINITE PRONOUNS

An **indefinite pronoun** does not refer to a specific person, place, or thing; it is general. Indefinite pronouns often take singular verbs. Whenever a pronoun refers to an indefinite person, place, or thing, check for agreement.

> ~~~~his~~~~
> Someone forgot ~~their~~ coat.
> ^
> ~~~~his or her~~~~
> Everybody practiced ~~their~~ lines.
> ^

Note: Although it is grammatically correct, using a masculine pronoun (*he, his,* or *him*) alone to refer to a singular indefinite pronoun such as *everyone* is now considered sexist. Here are two ways to avoid this problem:

1. Use *his or her.*

   Someone forgot his or her coat.

2. Change the sentence so that the pronoun refers to a plural noun or pronoun.

   The children forgot their coats.

Tip Focus on the "significant seven" indefinite pronouns: *any, each, either, neither,* and words ending in *-one, -thing,* or *-body.*

 Log in to **macmillanhighered .com/realessays Additional Grammar Exercises** > Using Indefinite Pronouns > Making Pronouns Agree with Indefinite Pronouns

Indefinite Pronouns

Always singular

anybody	everyone	nothing
anyone	everything	one (of)
anything	much	somebody
each (of)	neither (of)	someone
either (of)	nobody	something
everybody	no one	

May be singular or plural

all	none
any	some

COLLECTIVE NOUNS

Teaching tip Have students work in small groups to expand the list of collective nouns. Have all students write the added words next to the box.

A **collective noun** names a group that acts as a single unit.

Common Collective Nouns

audience	company	group
class	crowd	jury
college	family	society
committee	government	team

Log in to **macmillanhighered .com/realessays** **Additional Grammar Exercises** > Making Pronouns Agree with Collective Nouns

Collective nouns are usually singular, so when you use a pronoun to refer to a collective noun, it too must usually be singular.

The class had ~~their~~ final exam at 8:00 a.m. *(its)*

The group turned in ~~their~~ report. *(its)*

If the people in a group are acting as individuals, however, the noun is plural and should be used with a plural pronoun.

The audience took *their* seats.

The drenched crowd huddled under *their* umbrellas.

Make Pronoun Reference Clear

If the reader isn't sure what a pronoun refers to, the sentence may be confusing.

AVOID AMBIGUOUS OR VAGUE PRONOUN REFERENCES

In an **ambiguous pronoun reference**, the pronoun could refer to more than one noun.

Ambiguous   Michelle told Carla that she needed new shoes.

[Did Michelle tell Carla that Michelle herself needed new shoes? Or did Michelle tell Carla that Carla needed new shoes?]

Edited   Michelle needed new shoes. She told her friend Carla.

Ambiguous   I threw my present on the table, and it broke.

[Was it the present or the table that broke?]

Edited   My present broke when I threw it on the table.

In a **vague pronoun reference**, the pronoun does not refer clearly to any particular person or thing. To correct a vague pronoun reference, substitute a more specific noun for the pronoun.

Vague	After an accident at the intersection, they installed a traffic light.

[Who installed the traffic light?]

Edited	After an accident at the intersection, the highway department installed a traffic light.
Vague	When I heard it, I laughed.

[Heard what?]

Edited	When I heard the message, I laughed.

AVOID REPETITIOUS PRONOUN REFERENCES

In a **repetitious pronoun reference**, a pronoun directly follows a noun instead of replacing it. Remove the repetitious pronoun.

The police officer ~~he~~ told me I had not stopped at the sign.

The sign~~, it~~ was hidden by a tree.

> 🌐 **Language note:** In some languages, like Spanish, it is correct to repeat the noun with a pronoun. In formal English, however, a pronoun is used to replace a noun, not to repeat it.
>
> | **Incorrect** | My son he is a police officer. |
> |---|---|
> | **Correct** | My son is a police officer. |

ESL Read aloud some sentences from ESL students' writing, and ask them to raise their hands when they hear a repetitious reference. Then, ask students to edit the sentence for clarity.

Use the Right Type of Pronoun

As you can see on the chart on page 420, there are several types of pronouns—*subject* pronouns, *object* pronouns, and *possessive* pronouns—each of which has a different function.

SUBJECT PRONOUNS

Subject pronouns serve as the subject of a verb.

She took my parking space.

I honked my horn.

For more on subjects, see Chapter 21.

Language note: Some languages omit subject pronouns, but English sentences always have a stated or written subject.

Incorrect	Hates cleaning.
Correct	*He* hates cleaning.

OBJECT PRONOUNS

Object pronouns either receive the action of a verb (the object of the verb) or are part of a prepositional phrase (the object of the preposition).

Object of the verb	Carolyn asked *me* to drive.
	Carolyn gave *me* the keys.
Object of the preposition	Carolyn gave the keys to *me*.

POSSESSIVE PRONOUNS

Possessive pronouns show ownership. Note that you never need an apostrophe with a possessive pronoun.

Giselle is *my* best friend.

That jacket is *hers*.

Certain kinds of sentences can make choosing the right type of pronoun a little more difficult—ones that have compound subjects or objects; ones that make a comparison; and ones in which you have to choose between *who* or *whom*.

e Log in to macmillanhighered .com/realessays **Additional Grammar Exercises** > Using the Right Type of Pronoun with Compound Subjects and Objects

PRONOUNS USED WITH COMPOUND SUBJECTS AND OBJECTS

A **compound subject** has more than one subject joined by a conjunction such as *and* or *or*. A **compound object** has more than one object joined by a conjunction.

Compound subject	*Tim and I* work together.
Compound subject	Kayla baked the cookies for *Jim and me*.

To decide what type of pronoun to use in a compound construction, try leaving out the other part of the compound and the conjunction. Then, say the sentence aloud to yourself.

~~Jerome and~~ (me / $\boxed{\text{I}}$) like chili dogs.

[Think: *I* like chili dogs.]

The package was for ~~Karen and~~ (she / her).

[Think: The package was for *her*.]

When you are writing about yourself and others, always put the others first, choosing the correct type of pronoun.

Incorrect	*Me* and my friends went to the movies.
Correct	My friends and *I* went to the movies.

[The sentence puts others first and uses the subject pronoun *I*.]

Incorrect	Gene bought the tickets for *I* and my friends.
Correct	Gene bought the tickets for my friends and *me*.

[The sentence puts others first and uses the object pronoun *me*.]

If a pronoun is part of a compound object in a prepositional phrase, use an object pronoun.

Please keep that information just between you and *me*.

[The phrase *between you and me* is a prepositional phrase, so it uses the object pronoun *me*.]

Many people make the mistake of writing *between you and I*. The correct pronoun is the object pronoun *me*.

PRONOUNS USED IN COMPARISONS

Using the wrong type of pronoun in comparisons can give a sentence an unintended meaning. Editing sentences that contain comparisons can be tricky because comparisons often imply words that are not actually included in the sentence.

To find comparisons, look for the words *than* or *as*. To decide whether to use a subject or object pronoun in a comparison, try adding the implied words and saying the sentence aloud.

Bill likes Chinese food more than *I*.

[This sentence means Bill likes Chinese food more than I like it. The implied word after *I* is *do*.]

Bill likes Chinese food more than *me*.

[This sentence means Bill likes Chinese food more than he likes me. The implied words after *than* are *he likes*.]

Log in to **macmillanhighered .com/realessays** **Additional Grammar Exercises** > Using the Right Type of Pronoun in Comparisons

The professor knows more than (us /|we|).

[Think: The professor knows more than *we know.*]

Jen likes other professors more than (he /|him|).

[Think: Jen likes other professors more than *she likes him.*]

Log in to
**macmillanhighered
.com/realessays**
**Additional Grammar
Exercises** > Choosing
between *Who* and *Whom*

CHOOSING BETWEEN *WHO* AND *WHOM*

Who is always a subject; use it if the pronoun performs an action. *Whom* is always an object; use it if the pronoun does not perform any action.

Who = subject	Janis is the friend *who* introduced me to Billy.
Whom = object	Billy is the man *whom* I met last night.

In most cases, for sentences in which the pronoun is followed by a verb, use *who.* When the pronoun is followed by a noun or pronoun, use *whom.*

The person (|who|/ whom) spoke was boring.

[The pronoun is followed by the verb *spoke.* Use *who.*]

The person (who /|whom|) I met was boring.

[The pronoun is followed by another pronoun: *I.* Use *whom.*]

Whoever is a subject pronoun; *whomever* is an object pronoun.

Log in to
**macmillanhighered
.com/realessays**
**Additional Grammar
Exercises** > Making
Pronouns Consistent in
Person

Make Pronouns Consistent

Pronouns have to be consistent in **person**, which is the point of view a writer uses. Pronouns may be in first person (*I, we*); second person (*you*); or third person (*he, she, it,* or *they*). (See the chart on page 420.)

Inconsistent person	*I* wanted to use the copier, but the attendant said *you* had to have an access code.

[The sentence starts in the first person (*I*) but shifts to the second person (*you*).]

Consistent person	*I* wanted to use the copier, but the attendant said *I* had to have an access code.

[The sentence stays with the first person, *I.*]

Inconsistent person	After *a caller* presses 1, *you* get a recording.

[The sentence starts with the third person (*a caller*) but shifts to the second person (*you*).]

Consistent person   After *a caller* presses 1, *he or she* gets a recording.

Consistent person, plural   After *callers* press 1, *they* get a recording.

[In these last two examples, the sentence stays with the third person.]

Editing Practice

Edit the following paragraphs for pronoun errors, referring to the chart on page 430 as you need to. *Answers may vary. Possible edits shown.*

Resources For cumulative Editing Review Tests, see pages 564–80.

EDITING REVIEW 1   (13 errors)

1 The first year a woman driver ~~she~~ qualified for the Indianapolis 500 was 1977. 2 Janet Guthrie, ~~whom~~ *who* also competed in the Daytona 500 that year, became a role model for aspiring female drivers. 3 Though progress has been slow, auto racing has become more welcoming to women drivers, and audiences now see many more women competing in the big races. 4 These days, fans have several strong female drivers to follow, one of ~~who~~ *whom* is the famous Danica Patrick. 5 Patrick has made a name for ~~himself~~ *herself* by being a strong competitor. 6 In particular, she has shown male racers that women can be as ambitious and talented as ~~them~~ *they*. 7 Because of her talent and perhaps her willingness to promote herself, no other female car racer receives as much attention as ~~her~~ *she*. 8 However, other women drivers ~~they~~ have joined Patrick at the big Indianapolis races. 9 In 2010, ~~her~~ *she* and three other women qualified for and raced in the Indianapolis 500. 10 For driver Sarah Fisher, the 2010 race was her ninth time competing in the Indy 500. 11 Though none of them placed in the top five, each of the four women said ~~they were~~ *she was* there to win. 12 The car-racing audience now has ~~their~~ *its* eyes on NASCAR. 13 Few female racers have appeared in NASCAR races, and many say ~~they need~~ *NASCAR needs* to encourage more women to join ~~their~~ *its* ranks.

EDITING REVIEW 2   (12 errors)

1 If someone arrives home carrying a heavy bag of groceries, ~~they~~ *(he or she often has)* ~~often have~~ to struggle to get out the house keys to open the door. 2 To avoid such a struggle, a person in this situation can use a type of door lock that allows ~~he or she~~ *(him or her)* to enter with just the swipe of a finger. 3 The lock is a scanner that stores the fingerprints of those ~~whom~~ *(who)* are authorized to have access. 4 If the person's fingerprint matches a stored print, the lock ~~it~~ slides open. 5 The user does not need to do any wiring to install the lock, and ~~it needs~~ *(he or she needs)* only four AA batteries to operate it. 6 Using radio waves, the lock detects distances between ridges and valleys of a finger just below the skin's surface, so it doesn't even matter if ~~they have~~ *(the user has)* a minor cut or scratch. 7 While it may be possible for criminals to somehow get a photocopy of a homeowner's fingerprint, ~~him or her is~~ *(they are)* unlikely to get this opportunity. 8 Furthermore, the person ~~who~~ *(for whom)* the lock is intended ~~for~~ will never have this fingerprint information hacked because it is stored only by the lock itself and not in a central computer. 9 Homeowners with this device no longer need to remember their house keys because ~~his or her~~ *(their)* fingerprints are always with ~~him or her~~ *(them)*. 10 There is one thing homeowners do have to remember, though; ~~you~~ *(they)* have to make sure there are always fresh batteries in the lock.

EDITING REVIEW 3   (11 errors)

1 In 2006, NASA had trouble finding enough volunteers for experiments designed to test how well ~~you~~ *(they)* could counteract the effects of weightlessness. 2 The recruits were asked if ~~he or she~~ *(they)* would lie down in bed for three weeks. 3 ~~Each volunteer~~ *(The volunteers)* also had to have their feet about five inches higher than their heads. 4 The subjects ~~they~~ could not get up, ate while supported by one elbow, used bedpans, and showered lying down on a waterproof cart. 5 When people lie down for three weeks, ~~your~~ *(their)* muscles and bones can weaken, just as in real weightlessness. 6 To see if this weakening can be counteracted, ~~they~~ *(the researchers)* had some subjects spin around on a

centrifuge bed for thirty times a minute for one hour each day, which simu-

lated gravity. 7 To test the comparative effects of the centrifuge on men and

women, the researchers studied male-female pairs, but only one such pair

showed any difference. 8 (He was affected more than ~~her.~~) *she* 9 From the

start, the project was hampered by ~~their~~ inability to recruit more than *the researchers'* ^

ten subjects. 10 Most of the researchers, ~~whom~~ had hoped for thirty *who*

participants, were puzzled by the small number of volunteers. 11 But one

scientist, for ~~who~~ this was no surprise, noted that the centrifuge experience, *whom*

combined with three weeks of lying in bed, probably scared off a lot of

people. 12 She also wondered if many people could take so much time off

from ~~his or her job.~~ *their jobs*

EDITING REVIEW 4   (12 errors)

1 For those ~~whom~~ have some clothes they no longer want, there is *who*

now a new way to put those clothes to use. 2 A trend called clothes swap-

ping allows a person to donate ~~their~~ unwanted but still usable clothing in *his or her*

exchange for someone else's clothes. 3 People ~~they~~ are swapping clothes in

many American cities and even in other countries. 4 It started in the 1990s

when groups of women would get together and someone would bring

along ~~their~~ unwanted clothes to see if anyone else wanted them. 5 But now *her*

there are advertised clothes swaps, and ~~it draws~~ men as well as women. *they draw*

6 ~~At some swap events, they~~ require a donation of clothes in order to enter; *Some swap events*

at others, there might be an admission fee. 7 There is also the chance

of finding a smelly or dirty T-shirt ~~as you rummage~~ through a stack of *while rummaging*

clothing. 8 But most swaps have a rule that participants clean and press

~~his or her~~ donated clothing. 9 The attraction ~~it~~ is a combination of the thrill *their*

of bartering and the anticipation of coming across some free clothes that

fit one's size and personality. 10 Swaps do not have changing rooms, so

~~they~~ just put on an item over the clothes they are already wearing and *participants*

ask others ~~whom~~ are nearby how it looks. 11 Getting clothes at no cost *who*

is, of course, the main advantage, but participants are also aware that, if *the clothes*

~~they~~ look awful when tried on at home, they can simply be donated at the
  ^
next swap.

> **PRACTICE**   **Editing your own writing for pronoun use**

As a final practice, edit a piece of your own writing for pronoun use. It can be
a paper you are working on for this course, a paper you have already finished,
a paper for another course, or a recent piece of writing from your work or
everyday life. You may want to use the chart that follows as you edit.

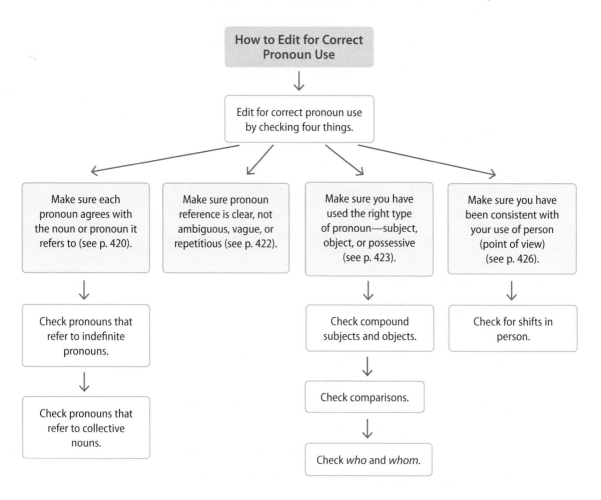

27

Adjectives and Adverbs

Describing Which One? *or* How?

Understand What Adjectives and Adverbs Are

Adjectives describe nouns (words that name people, places, or things) and pronouns (words that replace nouns). They add information about what kind, which one, or how many.

City traffic was *terrible* last night.

The highway was *congested* for *three* miles.

Two huge old trucks had collided.

> 🌐 **Language note:** In English, adjectives do not indicate whether the word they modify is singular or plural, unless the adjective is a number.
>
> **Incorrect** My two new classes are *hards*.
>
> [The adjective *two* is fine because it is a number, but the adjective *hard* should not end in -*s*.]
>
> **Correct** My two new classes are *hard*.

Adverbs describe verbs (words that tell what happens in a sentence), adjectives, or other adverbs. They add information about how, how much, when, where, why, or to what degree. Adverbs often end with -*ly*.

e Log in to **macmillanhighered.com/realessays LearningCurve** > Parts of Speech: Verbs, Adjectives, and Adverbs

Modifying verb	Dave drives *aggressively*.
Modifying adjective	The *extremely* old woman swims every day.
Modifying another adverb	Dave drives *very* aggressively.

Adjectives usually come *before* the words they modify, or they follow a linking verb and modify the subject of the sentence. Adverbs come either before or after the words they modify. You can also use more than one adjective or adverb to modify a word.

The happy, funny old man spoke quickly and humorously.

Language note: Sometimes, students confuse the *-ed* and *-ing* forms of adjectives. Common examples are *bored/boring, confused/confusing, excited/exciting,* and *interested/interesting.* Often, the *-ed* form describes a person's reaction, while the *-ing* form describes the thing being reacted to.

Incorrect	James is *interesting* in all sports. [James is not interesting; sports are.]
Correct	James is *interested* in all sports. [*Is interested* describes James's reaction to sports.]

Another common confusion is between when to use an adjective and when to use an adverb. Remember that adverbs modify verbs, adjectives, and other adverbs but not nouns. Adverbs often end in *-ly*.

Incorrect	James is a *carefully* driver.

[The word *carefully* should not be used to describe a noun, *driver*. The noun *driver* should be modified by an adjective, *careful*. The adverb *carefully* can be used to modify a verb, *drives*.]

Correct	James is a *careful* driver. *or* James drives *carefully*.

Choosing between Adjective and Adverb Forms

For coordinate adjectives, see Chapter 35.

Many adverbs are formed by adding *-ly* to the end of an adjective. To decide whether to use an adjective form or an adverb form, find the word you want to describe. If that word is a noun or a pronoun, use the adjective form. If it is a verb, an adjective, or another adverb, use the adverb form.

Adjective	Adverb
The *new* student introduced himself.	The couple is *newly* married.
That is an *honest* answer.	Please answer *honestly*.

e Log in to **macmillanhighered .com/realessays Additional Grammar Exercises** > Choosing between Adjective and Adverb Forms

Using Adjectives and Adverbs in Comparisons

To compare two persons, places, or things, use the **comparative** form of adjectives or adverbs.

Sheehan drives *faster* than I do.

Francis is *more talkative* than Destina is.

Comparative and Superlative Forms

Adjective or adverb	Comparative	Superlative
Adverbs and adjectives of one syllable		
tall	taller	tallest
fast	faster	fastest
Adjectives ending in y		
happy	happier	happiest
silly	sillier	silliest
Adverbs and adjectives of more than one syllable		
graceful	more graceful	most graceful
gracefully	more gracefully	most gracefully
intelligent	more intelligent	most intelligent
intelligently	more intelligently	most intelligently

e Log in to **macmillanhighered .com/realessays Additional Grammar Exercises** > Comparative and Superlative Forms

To compare three or more persons, places, or things, use the **superlative** form of adjectives or adverbs.

Sheehan drives the *fastest* of all our friends.

Francis is the *most talkative* of the three children.

Comparatives and superlatives can be formed either by adding an ending to an adjective or adverb or by adding the word *more* or *most*.

Description of adjective or adverb	Comparative	Superlative
Short (one syllable): tall	Add *-er*: taller	Add *-est*: tallest
Adjective ends in *-y*: silly	Change *-y* to *-i* and add *-er*: sillier	Change *-y* to *-i* and add *-est*: silliest
More than one syllable: intelligent	Add the word *more*: more intelligent	Add the word *most*: most intelligent

Use either an ending (*-er* or *-est*) or an extra word (*more* or *most*) to form a comparative or superlative—not both at once.

One of the ~~most~~ easiest ways to beat stress is to exercise regularly.

It is ~~more~~ harder to study late at night than during the day.

Using Good, Well, Bad, *and* Badly

e Log in to
**macmillanhighered
.com/realessays**
**Additional Grammar
Exercises** > Using *Good,
Well, Bad,* and *Badly*

Four common adjectives and adverbs have irregular forms—*good, well, bad,* and *badly*.

People often are confused about whether to use *good* or *well*. *Good* is an adjective, so use it to describe a noun or pronoun. *Well* functions as an adverb when the meaning is "in a good or proper manner."

Adjective	She is a *good* friend.
Adverb	He works *well* with his colleagues.

However, *well* functions as an adjective when describing someone's health:

I am not feeling *well* today.

Likewise, *bad* and *badly* are words that are often misused or used incorrectly in different situations. *Bad* is an adjective that means "inferior or defective," while *badly* is an adverb that means "unsatisfactory or inferior."

Adjective	I blame all of my illness this year on a *bad* diet.
Adverb	That particular bridge was *badly* constructed.
	He managed the baseball team *badly*.

The comparative and superlative forms of *good*, *well*, *bad*, and *badly* are highly irregular.

Forms of *Good*, *Well*, *Bad*, and *Badly*

	Comparative	Superlative
Adjective		
good	better	best
bad	worse	worst
Adverb		
well	better	best
badly	worse	worst

Teamwork Using an article from the newspaper, a Web site, or some other source, have students draw arrows from the adjectives and adverbs to the words they modify. This activity can be done in small groups or assigned as homework and reviewed in teams the next day.

Editing Practice

Edit the following paragraphs for adjective and adverb errors, referring to the chart on page 439 as you need to.

Resources For cumulative Editing Review Tests, see pages 564–80.

EDITING REVIEW 1   (9 errors)

1 For an average European in the Middle Ages, wearing stripes was not
simply
~~simple~~ a fashion mistake. 2 According to Michel Pastoureau, a scholar of the
                                        worst
medieval period, wearing stripes was one of the ~~worse~~ things a European

Christian could do in the thirteenth and fourteenth centuries. 3 Stripes

might be taken as a sign that the wearer was ~~more~~ sillier than other people;

jesters, for example, often wore them. 4 Prostitutes also wore striped

clothes, so stripes might be seen as an indication that the person was
more sinful   *most dangerous*
~~sinfuller~~ than others. 5 Wearing stripes was ~~dangerousest~~ for clergymen.

6 At least one clergyman in fourteenth-century France was executed
            foolish
because he had been ~~foolishly~~ enough to wear striped clothes. 7 Carmel-
                                    frequently
ite monks who wore striped cloaks were ~~frequent~~ attacked, and several
                                    simpler
popes insisted that the monks change to a ~~more simple~~ costume. 8 People

seriously
in medieval Europe certainly took their clothing ~~serious.~~ 9 The only reason
⌃

some people don't wear stripes today is that they are afraid of looking fat.

EDITING REVIEW 2   (14 errors)

embarrassing
1 Many people no longer find it ~~embarrassingly~~ to admit that they
⌃
better
have seen a psychotherapist. 2 Some patients argue that it is ~~gooder~~ to
⌃
seek mental help than to suffer silently. 3 Others seem to feel that needing
more interesting
a therapist is a sign that their lives are ~~interestinger~~ than other people's.
⌃
4 At any rate, the stigma that some people once attached to psychotherapy
quickly   *more visible*
is disappearing ~~quick.~~ 5 Therapists have lately become ~~visibler~~ in popular
⌃   ⌃
culture, and this visibility may result in even wider acceptance of psycho-

therapy. 6 For example, when a mobster on the cable television show *The*

Sopranos asked a therapist to treat his panic attacks, viewers saw that the
toughest
~~most tough~~ of men was still able to discuss his relationships and feelings
⌃
with a mental health specialist. 7 If Tony Soprano could do it, what ordinary
bad
person is going to feel ~~badly~~ about seeking help for ordinary problems?
⌃

8 However, people considering seeing a therapist are not the only ones

who loved to watch Tony Soprano trying to work through his problems.
biggest
9 Indeed, *The Sopranos,* which was one of the ~~bigger~~ hits ever on cable
⌃
television, included many psychologists in its audience. 10 One online
regularly
magazine ~~regular~~ published a therapist's analysis of each episode. 11 Other
⌃
therapists chatted online about whether or not the psychologist on the

television show was practicing psychology. 12 The audiences of psycho-
more accurately
logical professionals seem to agree that therapy was portrayed ~~accurater~~
⌃
on the show than in many popular films. 13 As they pointed out, at least

the therapist was not in love with her patient, unlike several psychiatrists
recent
in ~~recently~~ movies. 14 Although Mr. Soprano, like many actual therapy
⌃
patients, did things that were not good for his mental health, his therapist
better   *honestly*
thought that he was functioning ~~best~~ than before. 15 Whenever he ~~honest~~
⌃   ⌃

discussed his criminal day job with her, even the therapists tuning in might

have had trouble figuring out the ~~bestest~~ *best* possible response.
                                               ^

EDITING REVIEW 3   (12 errors)

1 Many people assume that today's college students are ~~traditionaler~~ *more traditional*
                                                                              ^

than they really are. 2 Seventy-five percent of today's college students

~~actual~~ *actually* do not go to college right after high school, live in the dorms, or
  ^

finish in four years. 3 For many people, waiting a few years before start-

ing college is not a ~~worst~~ *bad* choice. 4 Some also find that taking ~~more long~~ *longer*
                        ^   ^

than four years to finish is ~~more good~~ *better* than trying to rush through school.
                                ^

5 Almost half of today's students find that going to school part-time is

the ~~goodest~~ *best* plan. 6 One of the ~~interestingest~~ *most interesting* statistics shows that half
       ^   ^

of today's students support themselves and do not receive money from

family. 7 In fact, because school is ~~surprising~~ *surprisingly* expensive, 38 percent of col-
                                        ^

lege students work full-time. 8 Some students are able to balance work

and school ~~good~~ *well*, but many struggle. 9 One of the ~~more~~ sadder statistics
             ^

shows that less than half of students finish their schooling. 10 The truth is

that older students tend to have more ~~complicate~~ *complicated* lives with more distrac-
                                         ^

tions and responsibilities. 11 When colleges and universities offer flexible

schedules and requirements, students have a better chance of ~~successful~~ *successfully*
                                                                 ^

finishing school.

EDITING REVIEW 4   (14 errors)

1 In large and small parks across the country, a common sight is a pair

of chess players ~~quiet~~ *quietly* and ~~intent~~ *intently* studying the pieces on the board between
                   ^   ^

them. 2 But lately, chess in the park has been taken to a ~~newest~~ *new* level.
                                                             ^

3 "Street chess," as it is ~~typical~~ *typically* called, is no longer recreation; instead, it
                             ^

is ~~most~~ *more* like a business. 4 ~~Normal~~ *Normally*, it is the same people, mainly men, who
     ^   ^

are at their chess boards every day. 5 These players—some call them

hustlers—take on anybody who is willing to try to beat them, ~~usual~~ *usually* for a
wager of about $5. 6 Most of them are ~~real~~ *very* skilled and able to defeat just
about any opponent who challenges them. 7 Some play ~~bad~~ *badly* sometimes
and lose a game ~~deliberate~~ *deliberately* so that their regular customers will keep coming back. 8 But most hustlers play to win all the time, even if they hold

back sometimes to avoid embarrassing or discouraging their customers.
9 Players say that ~~general~~ *generally (or "in general")* the police do not bother them, but most hustlers
still find it ~~best~~ *better* to use street aliases than their real names. 10 One player
claims never to play for money, adding that he gives lessons for $45 an
hour. 11 Some players treat the pastime ~~casual~~ *casually*, playing only when they're in
the mood. 12 But for many hustlers, street chess is their life; they start during the day, every day, and continue ~~good~~ *well* into the next morning.

PRACTICE   ### Editing your own writing for correct use of adjectives and adverbs

As a final practice, edit a piece of your own writing for correct use of adjectives and adverbs. It can be a paper you are working on for this course, a
paper you have already finished, a paper for another course, or a recent
piece of writing from your work or everyday life. You may want to use the
chart on page 439 as you edit.

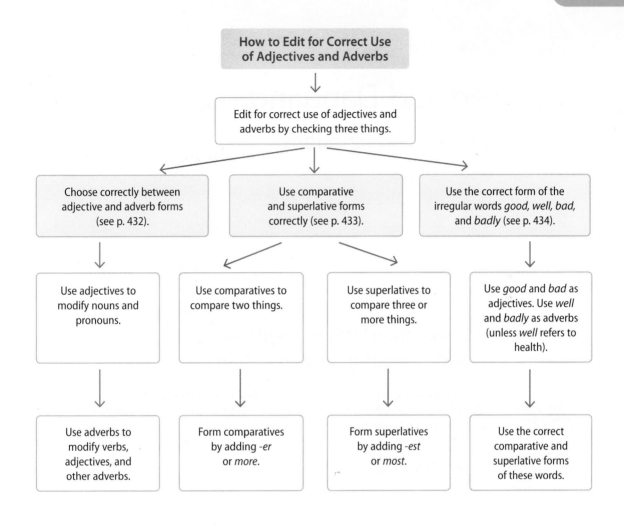

How to Edit for Correct Use of Adjectives and Adverbs

Edit for correct use of adjectives and adverbs by checking three things.

- Choose correctly between adjective and adverb forms (see p. 432).
- Use comparative and superlative forms correctly (see p. 433).
- Use the correct form of the irregular words *good, well, bad,* and *badly* (see p. 434).

Choose correctly between adjective and adverb forms (see p. 432).
- Use adjectives to modify nouns and pronouns.
  - Use adverbs to modify verbs, adjectives, and other adverbs.

Use comparative and superlative forms correctly (see p. 433).
- Use comparatives to compare two things.
  - Form comparatives by adding *-er* or *more*.
- Use superlatives to compare three or more things.
  - Form superlatives by adding *-est* or *most*.

Use the correct form of the irregular words *good, well, bad,* and *badly* (see p. 434).
- Use *good* and *bad* as adjectives. Use *well* and *badly* as adverbs (unless *well* refers to health).
  - Use the correct comparative and superlative forms of these words.

28

Misplaced and Dangling Modifiers
Avoiding Confusing Descriptions

Understand What Misplaced and Dangling Modifiers Are

📧 Log in to
macmillanhighered
.com/realessays
LearningCurve >
Misplaced and Dangling
Modifiers; **Additional**
Grammar Exercises >
Correcting Misplaced
Modifiers

Modifiers are words or word groups that describe other words in a sentence. Unless the modifier is near the words it modifies, the sentence can be misleading or unintentionally funny.

Misplaced Modifiers

A **misplaced modifier**, because it is not correctly placed in the sentence, describes the wrong word or words. To correct a misplaced modifier, move the modifier as close as possible to the word or words it modifies. The safest choice is often to put the modifier directly before the sentence element it modifies.

Misplaced Rudy saw my dog *driving his car on the highway.*

[Was my dog driving a car? No, Rudy was, so the modifier must come right before or right after his name.]

Correct *Driving his car on the highway,* Rudy saw my dog.

Misplaced Claudia could not see the stop sign *without sunglasses.*

[Did the sign need sunglasses? No, Claudia did.]

Correct *Without sunglasses,* Claudia could not see the stop sign.

Four sentence constructions in particular often lead to misplaced modifiers:

1. Modifiers such as *only, almost, hardly, nearly,* and *just*

I ~~only ordered~~ half a pound.
ordered only

Molly ~~almost~~ slept for ten hours.
almost

2. Modifiers that start with *-ing* verbs

Timothy bought the car. ~~using cash.~~
Using cash,

Elena took out the hot pizza. ~~wearing an oven mitt.~~
Wearing an oven mitt,

~~They~~ saw the Statue of Liberty. ~~looking out the window of the plane.~~
Looking out the window of the plane, they

[Note that when you move the phrase beginning with an *-ing* verb to the beginning of the sentence, you need to follow it with a comma.]

3. Modifiers that are prepositional phrases

Jim was carrying the bags ~~for his sister to the house.~~
to the house for his sister.

Julie found money ~~in her glove compartment for ice cream.~~
for ice cream in her glove compartment.

~~We~~ saw the rare bird. ~~with binoculars.~~
With binoculars, we

4. Modifiers that are clauses starting with *who, whose, that,* or *which*

I finally found the sock stuck to a T-shirt. ~~that was missing.~~
that was missing

Telemarketers are sure to be annoying. ~~who call people during dinner.~~
who call people during dinner

The computer died. ~~that I recently bought.~~
that I recently bought

For more on how to use relative pronouns—*who, which,* and *that*—see page 492.

Dangling Modifiers

A **dangling modifier** "dangles" because the word or words it is supposed to modify are not in the sentence. Dangling modifiers usually appear at the beginning of a sentence and may seem to modify the noun or pronoun that immediately follows—but they do not.

ℯ Log in to macmillanhighered .com/realessays **Additional Grammar Exercises** > Correcting Dangling Modifiers

Correct dangling modifiers either by adding the word being modified right after the opening modifier or by adding the word being modified to the opening modifier. Note that to correct a dangling modifier, you might have to reword the sentence.

| **Dangling** | *Talking on the telephone,* the dinner burned. |

[Was the dinner talking on the telephone? No.]

| **Correct** | *While Sharon was talking on the telephone,* the dinner burned. |
| | The dinner burned *while Sharon was talking on the telephone.* |

| **Dangling** | *While waiting in line,* the alarms went off. |

[Were the alarms waiting in line? No.]

| **Correct** | *While waiting in line,* I heard the alarms go off. |
| | *While I was waiting in line,* the alarms went off. |

Even if readers can guess what you are trying to say, misplaced and dangling modifiers are awkward. Be sure to look for and correct any misplaced and dangling modifiers in your writing.

Editing Practice

Edit the following paragraphs for misplaced and dangling modifiers, referring to the chart on page 444 as you need to. *Answers may vary. Possible edits shown.*

EDITING REVIEW 1

1 ~~When selling items online,~~ S shipping and handling costs can make or break a business. *that sells online* 2 By charging too much, ~~customers may~~ abandon *a site may force customers to* their order. *who feels that shipping and handling charges are too high* 3 A customer may never return to the site. ~~who feels that shipping and handling charges are too high.~~ 4 Most people have shipped packages, *at least occasionally,* so they know how much shipping costs. ~~at least occasionally.~~ 5 Going too far in the other direction, some online ~~customers get~~ free shipping and handling. *sites offer their customers* 6 If the sites lose money ~~that offer free shipping~~, they *that offer free shipping* may have to raise the prices on their products. 7 Most shipping companies charge by weight. 8 ~~Buying from the sites that use~~ these shippers, the *Using*

online sites must either charge a flat fee, which may be too much

or too little, or make the customer wait until the order is complete to

find out the shipping fee. 9 Neither option is perfect, so a business

that wants to keep expanding its online customer base
must choose the least unattractive solution. ~~that wants to keep expanding~~
^

~~its online customer base.~~

EDITING REVIEW 2

MEMO

To: All staff

From: Sara Hollister

Re: Dress code

employees were encouraged
1 After ~~encouraging employees~~ to wear casual clothing on Fridays, the
^

casual-dress code was soon in force all week long. 2 With some uncertainty

employees received
about what was appropriate casual wear, a memo ~~was circulated~~ last year
^
When all of the staff members began wearing
with guidelines for dress. 3 ~~Wearing~~ khakis and polo shirts, suits and ties
^

became rare in the halls of Wilson and Hollister. 4 Some younger staff

When Mr. Wilson arrived
members almost never wore anything but jeans. 5 ~~Arriving~~ in the office in
^ *him*

a Hawaiian shirt, some employees hardly recognized ~~Mr. Wilson~~ without his
^

trademark pinstriped suit. 6 Believing that informality improved productiv-

the company felt that
ity and morale, the casual dress code was well liked.
^

7 The company must recommend ~~for several reasons~~ changes in the
, for several reasons.
dress policy now/ 8 The human resources department feels that the relaxed
^

attitude toward dress may have contributed to the recent increases in

absenteeism and lateness at Wilson and Hollister. 9 Other problems

who have dropped in unexpectedly
have also surfaced. 10 Clients have sometimes expressed surprise. ~~who~~
^   ^

~~have dropped in unexpectedly.~~ 11 Hoping to keep their respect and

we have observed that
their business, the clients appear to feel more comfortable with
^

employees in suits. 12 Finally, fearing an increase in sexual harassment,
Wilson and Hollister will no longer permit
sleeveless shirts, shorts, miniskirts, and halter tops. ~~will no longer be~~
^   ^ *an almost*

~~permitted.~~ 13 Human resources ~~almost~~ recommends a complete change in
employees may continue
the casual-dress policy. 14 While ~~continuing~~ to wear casual clothing on
^

they must wear
Friday, business attire Monday through Thursday, is effective immediately.
^
I find
15 As an employee who prefers casual clothing, this news is rather sad, but
^

the decision is for the best. 16 Certain that you will understand the neces-
I appreciate
sity for these changes, your cooperation. ~~is appreciated.~~
^   ^

PRACTICE   **Editing your own writing for misplaced and dangling modifiers**

As a final practice, edit a piece of your own writing for misplaced and dangling modifiers. It can be a paper you are working on for this course, a paper you have already finished, a paper for another course, or a recent piece of writing from your work or everyday life. You may want to use the chart that follows as you edit.

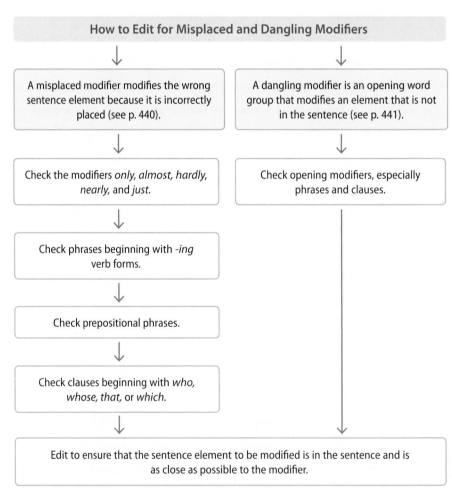

How to Edit for Misplaced and Dangling Modifiers

A misplaced modifier modifies the wrong sentence element because it is incorrectly placed (see p. 440).

A dangling modifier is an opening word group that modifies an element that is not in the sentence (see p. 441).

Check the modifiers *only, almost, hardly, nearly,* and *just.*

Check opening modifiers, especially phrases and clauses.

Check phrases beginning with *-ing* verb forms.

Check prepositional phrases.

Check clauses beginning with *who, whose, that,* or *which.*

Edit to ensure that the sentence element to be modified is in the sentence and is as close as possible to the modifier.

29

Coordination and Subordination

Joining Ideas

Understand Coordination and Subordination

Coordination is used to join two sentences with related ideas, using *for, and, nor, but, or, so,* or *yet*. The two sentences you join will still be independent clauses—otherwise known as complete sentences—joined with both a comma and a coordinating conjunction.

E Log in to
**macmillanhighered
.com/realessays
LearningCurve** >
Coordination and
Subordination

| **Two sentences** | The internship at the magazine is prestigious. Many interns have gone on to get good jobs. |

Independent clause

| **Joined through coordination** | The internship at the magazine is prestigious, *and* many interns have gone on to get good jobs. |

Independent clause

Subordination is also used to join two sentences with related ideas, using a dependent word such as *although, because, if,* or *that*. The resulting sentence will have one independent clause (a complete sentence) and one dependent clause (not a complete sentence).

| **Two sentences** | The internship was advertised last week. The magazine received many calls about it. |

445

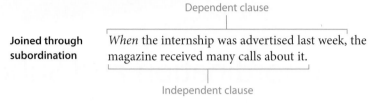

Joined through
subordination

Dependent clause

When the internship was advertised last week, the magazine received many calls about it.

Independent clause

[Adding the word *When* makes the first sentence dependent, or subordinate, to the second sentence.]

Both coordination and subordination are ways to join short, choppy sentences to get better rhythm and flow in your writing.

Practice Using Coordination and Subordination

Using Coordinating Conjunctions

Log in to
macmillanhighered
.com/realessays
**Additional Grammar
Exercises** > Using
Coordinating
Conjunctions

Conjunctions join words, phrases, or clauses. **Coordinating conjunctions** (*and, but, for, nor, or, so,* and *yet*) join independent clauses. You can remember them by keeping the word *fanboys* in mind: **f**or, **a**nd, **n**or, **b**ut, **o**r, **y**et, **s**o. Choose the conjunction that makes the most sense, and make sure to put a comma before it when joining two independent clauses.

	Coordinating conjunction	
Independent clause	, **for** , **and** , **nor** , **but** , **or** , **yet** , **so**	Independent clause

My friend is coming   , and   I'm excited to see her.

[The conjunction *and* simply joins two ideas.]

We were best friends   , but   I haven't seen her for years.

[The conjunction *but* indicates a contrast.]

I am a little nervous   , for   there may be rain.

[The conjunction *for* indicates a reason or cause.]

We haven't talked much   , nor   have we been in touch online.

[The conjunction *nor* indicates a negative.]

Maybe we will pick up our friendship   , or   we may be like strangers.

[The conjunction *or* indicates alternatives.]

We are meeting tonight   , so   we will know the answer soon.

[The conjunction *so* indicates a result.]

It is hard to keep in touch with old friends   , yet   they are very important.

[The conjunction *yet* indicates a contrast or a reason.]

Teaching tip
Emphasize that conjunctions are not interchangeable. Write two independent clauses on the board (*Lucy was hungry/She ate an apple*). Ask students which conjunctions would work and how the sentence would have to change to use others.

> **PRACTICE 1**   **Joining ideas with coordinating conjunctions**

In each of the following sentences, fill in the blank with an appropriate coordinating conjunction. There may be more than one correct answer for some sentences. *Answers will vary. Possible answers shown*

Example: Millions of people get motion sickness while traveling,
*and* **it can turn an enjoyable experience into a nightmare.**

1. Nearly 60 percent of children get carsick or airsick, _*and*_ many also get sick on amusement park rides.

2. Some amusement park operators are aware of this, _*for*_ a major theme park recently handed out "stomach distress" bags to customers.

3. Most people have experienced motion sickness at one time or another, _*yet*_ there are ways of easing or even avoiding its effects.

4. Motion sickness happens when a person's eyes and ears sense that she is moving one way, _*but*_ her brain detects movement in another way.

5. When in a car, you want to see the car's movement while you are feeling it, _*so*_ sit in the front seat and watch the road.

6. On a ship, you need to find a level point to focus on, _*so*_ you should keep your eyes on the horizon.

7. When you are flying, choose a window seat, _*and*_ look outside to watch and sense the plane's movement.

8. You can get a prescription for medication to prevent motion sickness, ___*but*___ you can also find some effective over-the-counter medications.

9. Taking ginger may be an even better way to prevent motion sickness, ___*for*___ you can simply buy ginger tea or raw ginger at a supermarket.

10. If you use a medication, be sure to take it one hour before you travel, ___*or*___ there may not be enough time for it to take effect.

PRACTICE 2   **Combining sentences with coordinating conjunctions**

Combine each pair of sentences into a single sentence by using a comma and a coordinating conjunction. In some cases, there may be more than one correct answer. *Possible edits shown.*

Example: For years, researchers have been trying to prove that media images have negative effects on women's body image, *yet some* ̶S̶o̶m̶e̶ **people are not convinced.**

1. Recently, two researchers decided to try to convince people once and for all, *so they* ̶T̶h̶e̶y̶ collected all the reliable research they could find.

2. They found seventy-seven trustworthy studies on the subject, *and they* ̶T̶h̶e̶y̶ analyzed the data.

3. The studies looked at different subjects and used a variety of methods, *but the* ̶T̶h̶e̶ findings were consistent.

4. Seeing super-thin models does make women feel dissatisfied with their own bodies, *and this* ̶T̶h̶i̶s̶ dissatisfaction is causing problems.

5. Women with poor body image are at risk for depression and low self-esteem, *for they* ̶T̶h̶e̶y̶ see themselves as flawed.

6. However, the super-thin body they see in advertisements is not realistic, *nor is that* ̶T̶h̶a̶t̶ body is̶ ̶n̶o̶t̶ always healthy.

7. Many women who strive for this "ideal" body will often engage in unhealthy dieting, *and some* ̶S̶o̶m̶e̶ may develop a more serious eating disorder.

8. Many women are aware that media images are unrealistic and manipu-

       , but that

       lative/ ~~That~~ awareness does not protect women from being influenced.

       ^

                         , for the

9. Education is not enough/ ~~The~~ images are simply too powerful.

                           ^

10. People need to acknowledge the problems these dangerous images

                    , and society

       are causing/ ~~Society~~ needs to develop solutions.

                  ^

Using Semicolons

A **semicolon** (;) is a punctuation mark that can join two sentences through coordination. When you use a semicolon, make sure that the ideas in the two sentences are closely related.

Equal idea	;	Equal idea
My computer crashed	;	I lost all of my files.
I had just finished my paper	;	I will have to redo it.

A semicolon alone does not tell readers much about the relationship between the two ideas. Use a **conjunctive adverb** after the semicolon to give more information about the relationship. Put a comma after the conjunctive adverb.

The following are some of the most common conjunctive adverbs, along with a few examples of how they are used.

Independent clause	; afterward, ; also, ; as a result, ; besides, ; consequently, ; frequently, ; however, ; in addition, ; in fact, ; instead, ; still, ; then, ; therefore,	Independent clause
My computer crashed	; as a result,	I lost all my files.
I should have made backup files	; however,	I had not done so.
The information is lost	; therefore,	I will have to try to rebuild the files.

Teaching tip
Remind students that a semicolon balances two independent clauses. What is on either side must be able to stand alone as a complete sentence.

PRACTICE 3   Joining ideas with semicolons

Join each pair of sentences by using a semicolon alone.

Example: In the wake of corporate scandals, many businesses are using new techniques to identify questionable job candidates*; graphology* ~~Graphology~~ is one such technique.

1. Graphology involves identifying personality features on the basis of a person's handwriting*; these* ~~These~~ features include honesty, responsibility, and loyalty.

2. Graphology is now used widely in Europe*; many* ~~Many~~ American graphologists, too, say their business has grown significantly in recent years.

3. An owner of a jewelry store turned to a graphology consultant following an increase in employee theft*; he* ~~He~~ says that handwriting analysis helped him identify the thieves.

4. On the other hand, many scientists and doctors believe that graphology is not reliable or scientific at all*; they* ~~They~~ state that there is no evidence that graphology can uncover a person's true character.

5. Nevertheless, even some job seekers are beginning to use graphology to help them find work*; one* ~~One~~ says he submitted his handwriting analysis report along with his résumé and got the job he wanted.

PRACTICE 4   Combining sentences with semicolons and connecting words (conjunctive adverbs)

Combine each pair of sentences by using a semicolon and a connecting word followed by a comma. Choose a conjunctive adverb that makes sense for the relationship between the two ideas. In some cases, there may be more than one correct answer. *Possible edits shown.*

Example: Most people do not own a gas mask*; however, after* ~~After~~ 9/11, some may have felt more comfortable having one available.

1. Two inventors believed that Americans would welcome the opportunity to have a gas mask/ ~~They~~ invented one that was part of a baseball
   ; as a result, they
   cap.

2. Professional gas masks are costly, heavy, and hard to use/ ~~Most~~ con-
   ; therefore, most
   sumers do not find them appealing.

3. The inventors' baseball-cap gas mask was small and lightweight/ ~~It~~
   ; in fact, it
   could fit in the corner of a drawer, in a coat pocket, or in a briefcase.

4. This mask was designed to fit children as well as adults/ ~~It~~ was meant
   ; in addition, it
   to sell for as little as twenty dollars.

5. The wearer slipped a thin sheet of transparent plastic attached to the
   hat over his or her head/ ~~He~~ or she could tie the plastic sheet at the
   ; then, he
   back of the neck.

6. Air from the outside was pulled in by a tiny fan/ ~~The~~ air was forced
   ; afterward, the
   through a filter of activated carbon in the hat's brim.

7. The inventors said that the plastic sheet allowed the wearer to see
   clearly/ ~~It~~ did not make the wearer feel too closed in.
   ; also, it

8. The mask was not intended for long-term use/ ~~It~~ was meant to be worn
   ; instead, it
   for about fifteen to thirty minutes.

9. The goal was to allow the wearer to get out of a contaminated area
   quickly/ ~~The~~ wearer could simply slip on the mask and then move into
   ; consequently, the
   fresh air.

10. The inventors looked for a company to make the new gas
    mask/ ~~They~~ did not find a manufacturer to bring the mask to the
    ; however, they
    market.

Using Subordinating Conjunctions

Conjunctions join words, phrases, or clauses. **Subordinating conjunctions** join two sentences, making the one after the dependent word a dependent clause.

e Log in to
macmillanhighered
.com/realessays
**Additional Grammar
Exercises** > Using
Subordinating
Conjunctions

Choose the conjunction that makes the most sense with the two sentences. Here are some of the most common subordinating conjunctions.

after	once
although	since
as	so that
as if	unless
because	until
before	when
even though	whenever
if	where
if only	while
now that	

Independent clause

Dependent clause

I decided to go to work   although   I had a terrible cold.

I hate to miss a day   unless   I absolutely cannot get there.

When the dependent clause ends a sentence (as in the preceding examples), it usually does not need to be preceded by a comma unless it is showing a contrast. When the dependent clause begins a sentence, use a comma to separate it from the rest of the sentence.

Subordinating conjunction	Subordinate idea	,	Main idea
Although	I had a terrible cold	,	I decided to go to work.
Unless	I absolutely cannot get there	,	I hate to miss a day.

Teaching tip Write two sentences where students can see them, and ask students how they would have to edit them to accommodate different subordinating conjunctions.

PRACTICE 5 **Joining ideas through subordination**

In the following sentences, fill in the blank with an appropriate subordinating conjunction. In some cases, there may be more than one correct answer. *Possible answers shown.*

Example: Smokey Bear spent most of his life in the National Zoo in Washington, D.C., __*where*__ he received so much mail that he had his own zip code.

1. Smokey Bear began reminding people "Only you can prevent forest fires" in 1944 __*because*__ government officials during World War II were concerned about preserving valuable resources like trees.

2. However, Smokey Bear existed only as a cartoon ___until___ a tragedy occurred six years later.

3. ___After___ a fire destroyed part of New Mexico's Lincoln National Forest in 1950, forest rangers found a badly burned bear cub clinging to a tree.

4. The "real" Smokey Bear became a celebrity ___when___ the public heard his story.

5. After his death twenty-six years later, Smokey Bear's body was returned to New Mexico ___so that___ he could be buried near his former home.

6. The character of Smokey Bear has been used continuously in U.S. fire safety campaigns ___since___ it first appeared more than seventy years ago.

7. Smokey has also appeared in public service announcements in Mexico, ___where___ he is known as Simon.

8. Recently, Smokey's famous line was changed to "Only you can prevent wildfires" ___because___ research indicated that most adults did not believe they could cause a wildfire.

9. However, humans can easily set fires ___if___ they discard cigarettes carelessly, burn trash on windy days, or even park a car with a catalytic converter in a dry field.

10. ___As___ the campaign heads into its eighth decade, Smokey is as recognizable to most Americans as Mickey Mouse and Santa Claus.

| PRACTICE 6 | **Combining sentences through subordination** |

Combine each pair of sentences into a single sentence by using an appropriate subordinating conjunction either at the beginning or between the two sentences. *Answers may vary. Possible edits shown.*

Example: Although
Michael had heard about lengthy delays for some air
      , he
travelers. He had never experienced one himself.

1. His turn came on a flight back to school in Austin, Texas, from
Minneapolis, Minnesota. *, where he* ^He was staying with his family during winter
break.

2. *Even though the* ^The flight took off on time and was going smoothly. *he* ^He had heard
some fellow passengers talking about a possible storm in the Austin
area.

3. He paid no attention to the rumors. *until the* ^The pilot announced to the passengers that the flight was landing in Wichita, Kansas, due to severe
weather in Austin.

4. The pilot added that they would be taking off again soon. *because he* ^He expected
the weather in Texas to clear.

5. *As* ^Michael sat in his seat and tried to sleep. *, he* ^He heard some people
ask the flight attendants to allow the passengers to wait in the air
terminal.

6. *After everyone* ^Everyone had waited on the plane for more than two hours. *the* ^The flight
crew finally told the passengers to go out to the air terminal.

7. Five hours later, Michael and his fellow passengers still did not
know when they would be able to resume their flight. *since there* ^There were
no announcements from anybody about what would happen
next.

8. *When an* ^An announcement finally came. *the* ^The passengers learned that the bad
weather in Texas would prevent the flight from continuing on to Austin
that day.

9. *If* ^Michael was already upset by the hours-long delay with no announcements. *he* ^He was even angrier at the thought of sleeping overnight in the
air terminal.

10. *While he* ^He was sitting uncomfortably in his terminal seat, feeling miserable. *, a* ^A
few other passengers asked him if he wanted to join them in renting a
car to complete the trip to Austin, which he did.

Teamwork Have
students in small groups
write five sentences
that use coordination
and/or subordination.
Then, ask them to copy
half of each sentence
(without conjunctions,
punctuation, or
beginning capital letters)
on a slip of paper. Have
the groups shuffle the
slips and give them to
another group. Each
group then puts the
pieces together and
reads the sentences
aloud.

Editing Practice

Join the underlined sentences by using either coordination or subordination, referring to the chart on page 457 as you need to. Be sure to punctuate correctly. *Answers may vary. Possible edits shown.*

Resources For cumulative Editing Review Tests, see pages 564–80.

EDITING REVIEW 1   (6 sets of sentences to be joined)

1 ~~A~~ *Whenever a* patient misunderstands a doctor's explanation and recommendations,/2 ~~There~~ *there* can be serious consequences. 3 If patients do not use medications properly or take preventive measures, their health risks increase. 4 These problems are common with people of all ages, races, and educational levels,/5 ~~They~~ *but they* are especially prevalent among the elderly. 6 The individual patient, of course, is affected in a personal and sometimes life-threatening way, but society in general also has to pay for the resulting increased medical costs. 7 ~~You~~ *If you* as a patient can follow a few simple guidelines,/8 ~~You~~ *you* can better understand what is wrong and what to do about it. 9 First, make absolutely sure that you understand the doctor's instructions. 10 The doctor will probably ask whether you have any questions,/11 ~~Think~~ *so think* over each step of the instructions and focus on anything that's confusing. 12 Repeat the instructions back to the doctor and ask, "Is that right?" 13 Another tip is to take notes on what the doctor recommends;/14 ~~Either~~ *either* write the notes yourself, or bring along someone else to jot them down. 15 It is easy to feel intimidated when you are partially unclothed in the examination room. 16 Ask to hear the necessary instructions in the doctor's office/17 ~~You~~ *when you* are fully clothed. 18 Finally, follow the doctor's instructions carefully, for recovery depends just as much on you as the patient as it does on the doctor.

EDITING REVIEW 2   (7 sets of sentences to be joined)

1 Al-Qurain is a community in the small Middle Eastern country of Kuwait. 2 Forty years ago, Kuwait City officials began to use an abandoned

quarry in al-Qurain as a garbage dump/ 3 ~~None~~ *because none* of them thought the area would ever be populated. 4 Twenty-five years ago, the government began to build subsidized housing in al-Qurain. 5 The dump was supposed to be closed/ 6 *but* Kuwaitis continued to use the al-Qurain landfill. 7 People soon lived all around the foul-smelling garbage pit. 8 Residents of the area were teased and insulted for living in the neighborhood/ 9 ~~Al-Qurain~~ *which* housed sixty thousand people.

10 For years, the dump sickened people around it/ 11 ~~Sometimes~~ *sometimes* the garbage caught fire and sent fumes into the homes nearby. 12 Finally, the Kuwaiti Environment Public Authority decided to try to help. 13 The agency gets little government funding/ 14 ~~It~~ *so it* needed to rely on donations for the cleanup effort. 15 Soon, a mountain of garbage had been removed/ 16 ~~The~~ *and the* leveled site was covered with pebbles from the desert. 17 Engineers found a way to siphon methane gas from the seventy-five-foot-deep garbage pit. 18 Kuwait is famous for oil production/ 19 ~~A~~ *yet a* methane-powered generator was proposed to provide electricity for al-Qurain residents. 20 The air in the neighborhood now ranks among the country's cleanest. 21 For many environmentalists and residents of this neighborhood, the cleanup of al-Qurain is almost a miracle.

PRACTICE 7   **Editing your own writing for coordination and subordination**

As a final practice, edit a piece of your own writing for coordination and subordination. It can be a paper you are working on for this course, a paper you have already finished, a paper for another course, or a recent piece of writing from your work or everyday life. You may want to use the chart on page 457 as you edit.

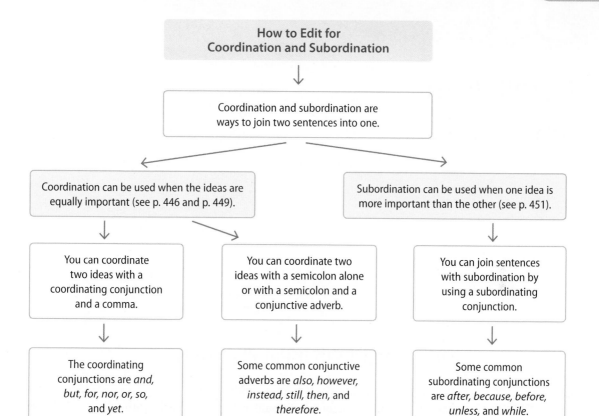

How to Edit for
Coordination and Subordination

Coordination and subordination are
ways to join two sentences into one.

Coordination can be used when the ideas are
equally important (see p. 446 and p. 449).

Subordination can be used when one idea is
more important than the other (see p. 451).

You can coordinate
two ideas with a
coordinating conjunction
and a comma.

You can coordinate two
ideas with a semicolon alone
or with a semicolon and a
conjunctive adverb.

You can join sentences
with subordination by
using a subordinating
conjunction.

The coordinating
conjunctions are *and,
but, for, nor, or, so,*
and *yet.*

Some common conjunctive
adverbs are *also, however,
instead, still, then,* and
therefore.

Some common
subordinating conjunctions
are *after, because, before,
unless,* and *while.*

30

Parallelism

Balancing Ideas

Understand What Parallelism Is

e Log in to
**macmillanhighered
.com/realessays**
LearningCurve >
Parallelism; **Additional
Grammar Exercises**
> Correcting Errors in
Parallelism

Parallelism in writing means that similar parts in a sentence are balanced by having the same structure. Put nouns with nouns, verbs with verbs, and phrases with phrases.

Not parallel	I like <u>math</u> more than <u>studying English</u>.

[*Math* is a noun, but *studying English* is a phrase.]

Parallel	I like <u>math</u> more than <u>English</u>.
Not parallel	In class, we <u>listened to the lecture</u>, <u>worked</u> in groups, and <u>were writing</u> an essay.

[Verbs must be in the same tense to be parallel.]

Parallel	In class, we <u>listened to the lecture</u>, <u>worked</u> in groups, and <u>wrote</u> an essay.
Not parallel	Last night we went <u>to a movie</u> and <u>dancing at a club</u>.

[*To a movie* and *dancing at a club* are both phrases, but they have different forms. *To a movie* should be paired with another prepositional phrase: *to a dance club*.]

Parallel	Last night we went <u>to a movie</u> and <u>to a dance club</u>.

ESL Tell students that parallel constructions often depend on using infinitives and idioms correctly. See Chapter 32 for details.

Practice Writing Parallel Sentences

Parallelism in Pairs and Lists

When two or more items in a series are joined by the word *and* or *or,* use a similar form for each item.

Teaching tip Review these examples with students, and ask them to explain why each of the nonparallel sentences needs correction.

Not parallel	The fund-raiser included a bake sale and also holding an auction.
Parallel	The fund-raiser included a bake sale and an auction.
Not parallel	Students got items for the auction from local businesses, from their families, and ran an advertisement in the newspaper.
Parallel	Students got items for the auction from local businesses, from their families, and from people who responded to a newspaper advertisement.

PRACTICE 1   **Making pairs and lists parallel**

In each sentence, underline the parts of the sentence that should be parallel. Then, edit the sentence to make it parallel.

Example: If you are a single parent, the morning routine can be difficult,
stressful
chaotic, and ~~you can feel stressed~~ without the proper organization.

Answers may vary. Possible edits shown.
and your children.
1. This is important because the beginning of the day affects both you/ ~~and your children are affected as well.~~

    keeping a cool head.
2. Get a good start by planning ahead, setting a few rules, and ~~also be sure to keep a cool head.~~

3. On the night before, make as many preparations for morning as possible, including preparing lunches, getting out clothes, and *organizing schoolbooks.*
    ~~it's important to organize schoolbooks.~~

    nutritious.
4. A quick cold breakfast can be easy, tasty, and ~~it can provide good nutrition.~~

5. Natural whole-grain cereal with fresh fruit, milk, or ~~adding some~~ plain yogurt, for example, is delicious and provides plenty of vitamins and minerals.

6. Allowing the kids to watch TV in the morning can either cause all sorts of problems or ~~you can let the TV~~ work to your advantage.
   [insert: *work to your advantage.*]

7. Set a rule that the kids must eat breakfast, wash up, ~~be sure of brushing their teeth~~, get dressed, and put their shoes on before they turn on the TV.
   [insert: *brush their teeth,*]

8. Prevent frantic, last-minute searches by establishing specific places for the items each of you needs for the day, such as car keys, backpacks, ~~making sure the kids have different pairs of shoes,~~ and coats.
   [insert: *shoes,*]

9. Save for the evening time-consuming tasks such as teaching a child to tie shoes or ~~if you~~ act as a referee in a dispute between siblings.
   [insert: *acting*]

10. Set aside some "me time," in which you stop rushing around, ~~taking a deep breath~~, and calmly prepare for your day.
    [insert: *take a deep breath,*]

Parallelism in Comparisons

In comparisons, the items being compared should have parallel structures. Comparisons often use the words *than* or *as*. When you edit for parallelism, make sure that the items on either side of the comparison word are parallel.

Not parallel	Driving downtown is as fast as the bus.
Parallel	Driving downtown is as fast as taking the bus.
Not parallel	Running is more tiring than walks.
Parallel	Running is more tiring than walking.
	Or
	A run is more tiring than a walk.

To make the parts of a sentence parallel, you may need to add or drop a word or two.

Teamwork Have students, in small groups, write three sentences that are not parallel. Ask groups to exchange and correct the sentences.

| **Not parallel** | A multiple-choice test is easier than answering an essay question. |

Parallel, word added	*Taking* a multiple-choice test is easier than <u>answering an essay question</u>.
Not parallel	The <u>cost</u> of a train ticket is less than <u>to pay the cost</u> of a plane ticket.
Parallel, words dropped	The <u>cost</u> of a train ticket is less than <u>the cost</u> of a plane ticket.

PRACTICE 2   Making comparisons parallel

In each sentence, underline the parts of the sentence that should be parallel. Then, edit the sentence to make it parallel. *Answers may vary. Possible edits shown.*

Example: <u>New appliances</u> are usually much more energy-efficient than <del>running</del> old ones.

1. For many people, <u>getting the household electric bill</u> is more worrisome
   paying
   than <del>to pay</del> the rent each month.
          ∧

2. The amount of the rent bill usually changes much less from month to
   the amount of the energy bill.
   month than <del>what an energy company charges</del>.
            ∧

3. <u>Saving money</u> appeals to many consumers more than <del>to use</del> less
   using
                                                              ∧
   <u>electricity</u>.

4. <u>Compact fluorescent lightbulbs</u> use less energy than <del>continuing to use</del>
   <u>regular incandescent bulbs</u>.

5. In most households, <u>running the refrigerator</u> uses more energy than
   using
   <del>the use of</del> all other appliances.
         ∧

6. Many people worry that <u>buying a new refrigerator</u> is more expensive
   simply keeping
   than <del>if they simply keep</del> the old one.
          ∧

7. However, <u>an energy-efficient new refrigerator</u> uses much less
           running
              ∧
   electricity than <u>running an inefficient older model</u>.

8. <u>Some new refrigerators</u> use only as much energy as <del>keeping</del> a 75-watt
   lightbulb <del>burning</del>.

9. Householders might spend less money <u>to buy an efficient new</u>
   <u>refrigerator</u> than <del>it would take</del> to run the old one for another five years.

10. Researching information about energy efficiency can save consumers

as much money as ~~when they remember~~ to turn off lights and air
   remembering

conditioners.

Parallelism with Certain Paired Words

When a sentence uses certain paired words called **correlative conjunctions**, the items joined by these paired words must be parallel. Correlative conjunctions link two equal elements and show the relationship between them.

both . . . and	neither . . . nor	rather . . . than
either . . . or	not only . . . but also	

Not parallel   Brianna dislikes *both* fruit *and* eating vegetables.

Parallel   Brianna dislikes *both* fruit *and* vegetables.

Not parallel   She would *rather* eat popcorn every night *than* to cook a meal.

Parallel   She would *rather* eat popcorn every night *than* cook a meal.

> **PRACTICE 3**   **Making sentences with paired words parallel**
>
> In each sentence, circle the paired words and underline the parts of the sentence that should be parallel. Then, edit the sentence to make it parallel. You may need to change the second part of the correlative conjunction. *Answers may vary. Possible edits shown.*
>
> **Example: A recent survey of young women reported that a majority of them would rather lose twenty pounds permanently than to live to be ninety.**

1. People in the United States are both pressed for time and ~~have gotten~~ used to convenient but fattening foods.

2. Many Americans are neither willing to exercise regularly nor ~~do they have~~ to do anything physical during a normal day.
   required

3. Being overweight can be unhealthy, but many Americans would rather look thinner than ~~to~~ stay the same size and get in better shape.

4. In fact, some Americans are not only out of shape but also ~~are~~
    dangerously obsessed with being thin.

5. The idea that thinner is better affects both overweight people and
    ~~it even influences~~ people of normal weight.

6. In their quest to lose weight, many Americans have tried either fad
    diets or ~~have taken~~ prescription drugs.

7. Dozens of healthy, average-sized Americans in the past ten years have
    died from either surgical procedures to remove fat or ~~they have died~~
    ~~from~~ dangerous diet drugs.

8. A thin person is neither guaranteed to be attractive nor ~~is he or she~~
    necessarily healthy.

9. Some people who are larger than average are not only healthy but also
    ~~can be~~ physically fit.

10. Americans who would rather pay for risky drugs and surgery than
    eat moderately and exercise
    ~~eating moderately and exercising~~ may have hazardous priorities.

PRACTICE 4   **Completing sentences with paired words**

The following items contain only the first part of a correlative conjunction.
Complete the correlative conjunction, and add more information to form a
whole sentence. Make sure that the structures on both sides of the correlative conjunction are parallel. *Answers may vary. Possible answers shown.*

Example: I am both enthusiastic about your company *and eager to work*
            for you .

1. I could bring to this job not only youthful enthusiasm *but also*
    leadership experience .

2. I am willing to work either in your Chicago office *or in your San*
    Francisco office .

3. My current job neither encourages creativity *nor allows flexibility* .

4. I would rather work in a difficult job *than work in an unchallenging one*

5. In college I learned a lot both from my classes *and from other students*

Editing Practice

Resources For cumulative Editing Review Tests, see pages 564–80.

Edit the following paragraphs for parallelism, referring to the chart on page 466 as you need to. *Answers may vary. Possible edits shown.*

> **EDITING REVIEW 1**   (8 errors)
>
> 1 Some employees who want to advance their careers would rather transfer within their company than ~~looking~~ _look_ for a new job elsewhere. 2 In-house job changes are possible, but employees should be sure that they both meet the criteria of the new job and ~~to~~ avoid making their present boss angry. 3 Because businesses invest money in each person they hire, many companies would rather hire from within ~~and not~~ _than_ bring an outsider into a position. 4 By hiring from within, a company neither needs to make an investment in a new employee ~~but may also prevent the current employee from leaving.~~ _nor loses a current employee._ 5 Transfers usually go more smoothly now than in the past; however, an in-house job move can still require diplomacy and ~~being honest.~~ _honesty._ 6 Experts caution employees who are considering an in-house transfer to tell their current manager the truth and ~~that they should~~ _to_ discuss their wish to transfer with the potential new manager. 7 Employees should neither threaten to quit if they do not get the new job nor ~~is it a good idea to~~ spread the word around the department that they are anxious to leave their present job. 8 Employees' goals for in-house transfers should be ~~career advancement~~ _advancing their careers_ and making sure that they create no bad feelings with the move.

> **EDITING REVIEW 2**   (15 errors)
>
> 1 Black motorists frequently arouse police suspicion either when driving in neighborhoods that are mainly white or when ~~they are~~ driving an expensive car. 2 A higher percentage of African Americans than ~~among people who are white~~ _whites_ are pulled over by the police. 3 Many African Americans feel insulted, endangered, and ~~react with anger~~ _angry_ when they are

stopped randomly. 4 African Americans are liable to be singled

out by police who suspect they are criminals not only while in a car but

while

~~African Americans~~ also report ~~being wrongly stopped~~ on foot.
^

5 Racial profiling is illegal yet a fairly common ~~.~~ ~~phenomenon.~~ 6 According
^   *of black women*

to a 2001 poll, ~~among black women the figure is~~ 25 percent, and 52 percent
^

of black men have been stopped by police. 7 Victims of racial profiling have

done nothing wrong, yet they are made to feel that others are either afraid
of them

or do not trust them. 8 Law-abiding African Americans should neither
^

expect such treatment nor ~~should they~~ put up with it from public officials

who are supposed to protect citizens. 9 Police departments around the

country must make their employees aware that automatically stopping,
questioning,

~~asking them questions,~~ and searching African Americans will not be
^   *Fair treatment of*

tolerated. 10 ~~Treating~~ all citizens ~~fairly~~ is more important than ~~that there is~~
^

a high arrest rate for the police.

| PRACTICE 5 | **Editing your own writing for parallelism** |

As a final practice, edit a piece of your own writing for parallelism. It can be a
paper you are working on for this course, a paper you have already finished,
a paper for another course, or a recent piece of writing from your work or
everyday life. You may want to use the chart on page 466 as you edit.

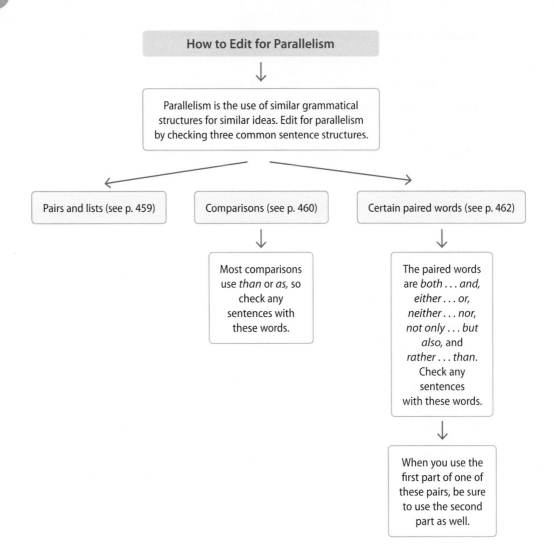

How to Edit for Parallelism

↓

Parallelism is the use of similar grammatical structures for similar ideas. Edit for parallelism by checking three common sentence structures.

Pairs and lists (see p. 459)   Comparisons (see p. 460)   Certain paired words (see p. 462)

↓   ↓

Most comparisons use *than* or *as,* so check any sentences with these words.

The paired words are *both . . . and, either . . . or, neither . . . nor, not only . . . but also,* and *rather . . . than.* Check any sentences with these words.

↓

When you use the first part of one of these pairs, be sure to use the second part as well.

31

Sentence Variety

Putting Rhythm in Your Writing

Understand What Sentence Variety Is

Having **sentence variety** in your writing means using assorted sentence patterns, lengths, and rhythms. Sometimes writers think that using short, simple sentences is always better than using long ones. That, however, is not true. Although avoiding wordiness is a worthy goal (see p. 510), writing that uses a lot of choppy sentences can be repetitious and hard to follow, as the following examples show.

With short, simple sentences

Age discrimination can exist even in unpaid jobs. In 2002, a magazine was accused of age discrimination. The magazine was the *Atlantic Monthly*. A woman was told she was too old to be an unpaid intern. The woman was forty-one. The position was for a senior in college. The woman was a senior. She had raised three children before going to college. She sued the magazine. The next day, another woman, age fifty-one, reported that the same thing had happened to her a year earlier. She had filed a discrimination suit. Her suit was brought to court by the Council on Age Discrimination. The magazine never showed up. The court never took any follow-up action against the magazine. Apparently, the matter was not of great importance to either the magazine or the justice system.

With sentence variety

Who said that a celebrity had to be a role model? Kids, teens, and young adults love to watch famous people. These famous people can often behave inappropriately, though. Remember when Britney Spears shaved her head? Lindsey Lohan was apparently taking drugs and driving under the influence. Miley Cyrus is dancing like a stripper. Who knows what Justin Bieber will do next? Most parents don't like it and think these people are bad role models. According to an article in *Inquisitor*, will.i.am, a member of the Black-Eyed Peas and

467

current *Voice* coach, disagrees. He believes that there are no rules for how these stars should act. Would you behave if cameras were in your face twenty-four hours a day, every day? Will.i.am believes that we want these stars to succeed and we want them to fail. We enjoy both situations because they are entertaining. For a pop star who is just becoming an adult, though, it is hard to have everyone see all your faults and successes all the time.

Too many short sentences make your writing sound like a list of ideas rather than a presentation of them. Sentence variety is what gives your writing good rhythm and flow.

Teamwork After completing the chapter, students can work in small groups to reexamine this paragraph. Have them identify which kinds of sentence variety the writer has used.

Practice Creating Sentence Variety

To create sentence variety, write sentences of different types and lengths. Because many writers tend to write short sentences that start with the subject, this chapter will focus on techniques for starting with something other than the subject and for writing a variety of longer sentences.

Remember that the goal of using sentence variety is to achieve a good rhythm. Do not simply change all your sentences from one pattern to another, or you still will not have variety.

For two additional techniques used to achieve sentence variety, coordination and subordination, see Chapter 29.

Start Some Sentences with Adverbs

Adverbs are words that describe verbs, adjectives, or other adverbs; they often end with *-ly*. As long as the meaning is clear, you can place an adverb at the beginning of a sentence or near the word it describes. An adverb at the beginning of a sentence is usually followed by a comma.

For more about adverbs, see Chapter 27.

Adverb at beginning	*Frequently,* stories about haunted houses surface at Halloween.
Adverb near a verb	Stories about haunted houses *frequently* surface at Halloween.
Adverb at beginning	*Often,* these tales reveal the life stories of former inhabitants.
Adverb near a verb	These tales *often* reveal the life stories of former inhabitants.

> **PRACTICE 1** **Starting sentences with an adverb**
>
> In each sentence, fill in the blank with an adverb that makes sense, adding a comma when necessary. There may be several good choices for each item. *Possible answers shown.*

Example: ____*Frequently,*____ **hurricanes hit barrier islands.**

1. ____*Suddenly,*____ a hurricane can destroy land and houses.

2. ____*Overnight,*____ most houses on an island are washed away.

3. ____*Quickly,*____ the ocean sweeps away the land under the houses.

4. ____*Afterward,*____ the island is a different shape.

5. ____*Later,*____ maps will have to be redrawn with the new configuration.

PRACTICE 2   **Writing sentences that start with an adverb**

Write three more sentences that start with an adverb, using commas as necessary. Choose from the following adverbs: *amazingly, frequently, gently, lovingly, luckily, often, quietly, sadly, stupidly.* Answers will vary.

Example: *Luckily, I remembered to save my file on a disk.*

1. _____

2. _____

3. _____

Join Ideas Using an -ing Verb Form

One way to combine sentences is to turn one of them into a phrase using an **-ing verb form** (such as *walking* or *racing*). The *-ing* verb form indicates that the two parts of the sentence are happening at the same time. The more important idea (the one you want to emphasize) should be in the main clause, not in the phrase you make by adding the *-ing* verb form. In the examples that follow, the idea the writer wanted to emphasize is underlined.

Two sentences	<u>Jonah did well in the high jump.</u> He came in second.
Joined with *-ing* **verb form**	<u>Jonah did well in the high jump</u>, coming in second.
	Doing well in the high jump, <u>Jonah came in second.</u>

To combine sentences this way, add *-ing* to the verb in one of the sentences and delete the subject. You now have a phrase that can be added to the beginning or the end of the other sentence, depending on what makes sense.

He also won the long jump. ~~He broke~~ *, breaking* the record.

Teaching tip Explain to students that in their own writing they will need to consider the context when deciding which sentence contains the more important idea.

ESL Remind students that an *-ing* verb form that modifies the subject cannot be the main verb in the sentence.

If you add the phrase to the end of a sentence, you will usually need to put a comma before it unless the phrase is essential to the meaning of the sentence, as in the following example.

using
The thief broke into the apartment/ ~~The thief used~~ a crowbar.

If you add a phrase starting with an *-ing* verb form to the beginning of a sentence, put a comma after it. Be sure that the word being modified follows immediately after the phrase. Otherwise, you will create a dangling modifier.

Two sentences	I dropped my bag. My groceries spilled.
Dangling modifier	Dropping my bag, my groceries spilled.
Edited	Dropping my bag, I spilled my groceries.

PRACTICE 3   **Joining ideas using an *-ing* verb form**

Combine each pair of sentences into a single sentence by using an *-ing* verb form. Add or delete words if necessary. *Answers will vary. Possible edits shown.*

Believing that
Example: Many fans of rap music ~~imagine it~~ is a recent development/
, many fans
~~They~~ are not aware that the roots of this music go back centuries.

Wandering
1. ~~Folk poets wandered~~ from village to village in West Africa hundreds
, folk poets
of years before the birth of the United States/ ~~They~~ rhythmically re-

cited stories and tales with the accompaniment of a drum and a few

instruments.

Using
2. ~~Rap music uses~~ rhymes and wordplay with a rhythmic delivery
, rap music's
to build on this heritage/ ~~Its~~ lyrics often deal with matters of race,

socioeconomic class, and gender.

Tracing   *, many fans*
3. ~~Many fans trace~~ the beginning of modern-day rap to the 1970s/ ~~They~~

still revere disc jockey Kool Herc, a Jamaican immigrant who lived in

the Bronx and who originated the new sound in America.

Reciting
4. ~~Kool Herc recited~~ lyrics to go along with the songs that he was playing
, Kool Herc
as a DJ/ ~~He~~ introduced this innovative music at private parties and then

later at well-known dance halls.

5. In the 1980s, rappers' lyrics focused on sharp sociopolitical content/
   , captivating
   ~~They captivated~~ listeners with increasingly creative wordplay.
   ∧
   Developing
6. ~~Rap songwriters developed~~ a rougher, more sinister edge in the 1990s/
   , rap songwriters
   ~~They~~ began narrating personal street experiences mixed with social
   ∧

   commentary.
   Branching   *, rap music today*
7. ~~Today, rap music has branched~~ out in several directions/ ~~It~~ has
   ∧   ∧

   southern, northern, midwestern, and even international forms

   alongside the more established styles.

8. Perhaps consciously and perhaps not, rappers extensively use forms
   , calling
   of wordplay that are also found in classical poetry/ ~~They call~~ on
   ∧

   such literary devices as double meanings, alliteration, similes, and

   metaphors.
   Emphasizing   *, nearly*
9. ~~Rap artists emphasize~~ the themes of wealth and class/ ~~Nearly~~ all
   ∧   ∧

   popular rappers in the United States are African American.
   Having   *, rap*
10. ~~Rap has~~ gained a solid foothold in American culture/ ~~It~~ is now widely
    ∧   ∧

    accepted as a form of mainstream American music.

PRACTICE 4   **Joining ideas using an *-ing* verb form**

Fill in the blank in each sentence with an appropriate *-ing* verb form. There
are many possible ways to complete each sentence. *Answers will vary.
Possible answers shown.*
Example: ___*Owning*___ the rights to the character Spider-Man, Marvel

Enterprises has been making big money lately.

1. ___*Switching*___ from losses of tens of millions of dollars a year, Mar-

   vel now turns a profit of more than $150 million a year, thanks to

   Spider-Man.

2. Marvel dominates the comic-book market, ___*producing*___ sixty comic

   books a month.

3. ___*Earning*___ 83 percent of its profits from licensing its characters for

   films and related merchandise, Marvel makes only 15 percent of its

   profits from comic-book sales.

4. Marvel keeps tight control of the characters it licenses to filmmakers,

_____allowing_____ no costume changes or added superpowers without

Marvel's approval.

5. _____Preventing_____ any film studio from having Spider-Man kill anyone, for

example, Marvel maintains the character as it believes he should be.

> **PRACTICE 5**   **Joining ideas using an *-ing* verb form**
>
> Write two sets of sentences, and join each set of sentences using an *-ing*
> verb form. *Answers will vary.*
>
> Example: **a.**   *Teresa signed on to eBay.com.* _____
>
> **b.**   *She used her password.* _____
>
> Combined: *Using her password, Teresa signed on to eBay.com.* _____
>
> *Teresa signed on to eBay.com using her password.* _____
>
> 1. a. _____
>
> b. _____
>
> Combined: _____
>
> 2. a. _____
>
> b. _____
>
> Combined: _____

Join Ideas Using an *-ed* Verb Form

For more on helping
verbs, see Chapters 21,
25, and 32.

Another way to combine sentences is to turn one of them into a phrase using an
-ed **verb form** (such as *waited* or *walked*). You can join sentences this way if one
of them has a form of *be* as a helping verb along with the *-ed* verb form.

Two sentences	Leonardo da Vinci was a man of many talents. He was noted most often for his painting.
Joined with *-ed* verb form	Noted most often for his painting, Leonardo da Vinci was a man of many talents.

To combine sentences this way, drop the subject and the helping verb from
a sentence that has an *-ed* verb form. You now have a modifying phrase that can
be added to the beginning or the end of the other sentence, depending on what

makes the most sense. Sometimes, you will need to change the word that the phrase modifies from a pronoun to a noun, as in the following example.

~~Leonardo was interested~~ *Interested* in many areas/ ~~He~~ *, Leonardo* investigated problems of geology, botany, mechanics, and hydraulics.

If you add a phrase that begins with an *-ed* verb form to the beginning of a sentence, put a comma after it. Be sure the word that the phrase modifies follows immediately, or you will create a misplaced or dangling modifier.

For more on finding and correcting misplaced and dangling modifiers, see Chapter 28.

Two sentences	The podium was where Marie paused. She was exhilarated by her achievement.
Misplaced modifier	Exhilarated by her achievement, the podium was where Marie paused.
Correct	Exhilarated by her achievement, Marie paused at the podium.

PRACTICE 6 **Joining ideas using an *-ed* verb form**

Combine each pair of sentences into a single sentence by using an *-ed* verb form. *Answers will vary. Possible edits shown.*

Example: **~~Alligators are hatched~~ *Hatched* from eggs when they are only a few inches long/ ~~Alligators~~ *, alligators* can reach a length of ten feet or more as adults.**

1. ~~An alligator was spotted in a pond in Central Park in New York City.~~ Many New Yorkers refused to believe in the existence of ~~the~~ *an* alligator/ *spotted in a pond in Central Park in New York City.*

2. ~~Alligators were released~~ *Released* by their owners for growing too large to be pets/ ~~These~~ *,* alligators were sometimes said to be living in New York City sewers.

3. ~~Rumors were believed~~ *Believed* by some gullible people/ ~~The~~ *, the* rumors about giant sewer alligators were untrue.

4. ~~The story of the alligator in Central Park was denied~~ *Denied* by city officials/ ~~The~~ *, the* story *of the alligator in Central Park* sounded like another wild rumor.

Reported
5. ~~Central Park alligator sightings were reported~~ by several New
   ^   *, the Central Park alligator*
   Yorkers/ ~~The~~ sightings were confirmed when a television news
                ^
   crew filmed a reptile in the pond.

Hired
6. ~~A professional alligator wrestler was hired~~ to catch the
   ^   *, a professional alligator wrestler*
   reptile/ He came to New York from Florida, accompanied by his wife.
            ^

Surrounded
7. ~~The pond in Central Park was surrounded~~ by news cameras and curious
   ^   *, the pond in Central Park*
   onlookers/ ~~It~~ was brightly lit just before 11:00 p.m. on the day the
                 ^
   alligator wrestler and his wife arrived.

Captured
8. ~~The creature was captured~~ in just a few minutes by the alligator
   ^   *, the*
   wrestler's wife/ ~~The~~ so-called alligator turned out to be a spectacled
                       ^
   caiman, a species native to Central and South America.

Surprised
9. ~~Some New Yorkers were surprised~~ to find that the caiman was only two
   ^   *, some New Yorkers*
   feet long/ ~~They~~ may have felt a bit foolish for expecting to see a giant
                  ^
   alligator in the park.

Removed   *, the caiman*
10. ~~The caiman was removed~~ from Central Park/ ~~It~~ soon found a home in a
    ^   ^
    warmer climate.

PRACTICE 7   **Joining ideas using an *-ed* verb form**

Fill in the blank in each sentence with an appropriate *-ed* verb form. There
are several possible ways to complete each sentence. *Answers will vary.*
Possible edits shown.

Example: ___*Enjoyed*___ **by many people around the world, online gambling**

is an increasingly popular recreational option.

1. ___*Used*___ regularly by Europeans, this venue for gambling is more dif-

   ficult for Americans to access.

2. ___*Prohibited*___ by some U.S. states, online gambling is a major worry of

   the government.

3. ___*Concerned*___ that Internet gambling can be used for hiding large

   exchanges of money, the U.S. Justice Department has asked major

Internet search engines to remove advertising for online gambling operations.

4. Also ___opposed___ to legalizing online gambling in the United States, some antigambling activists think the speed of the Internet makes it more likely for problem gamblers to give in to their addiction.

5. ___Considered___ a harmless pastime by some, easy-access online gambling can ruin even more lives than it already has.

PRACTICE 8   **Joining ideas using an -*ed* verb form**

Write two sets of sentences, and join them using an -*ed* verb form. *Answers will vary.*

Example: **a.** _Lee is training for the Boston Marathon._

b. _It is believed to have the most difficult hill to run._

Combined: _Lee is training for the Boston Marathon, believed to have_

the most difficult hill to run.

1. a. _Answers will vary._

b. _____

Combined: _____

_____

2. a. _____

b. _____

Combined: _____

_____

Join Ideas Using an Appositive

An **appositive** is a word or phrase that appears next to a noun and renames, defines, or clarifies it. Appositives, which are nouns or noun phrases, can be used to combine two sentences into one.

Two sentences	Elvis Presley continues to be popular many years after his death. He is "the King."
Joined with an appositive	Elvis Presley, "the King," continues to be popular many years after his death.

[The phrase *"the King"* renames the noun *Elvis Presley*.]

To combine two sentences by using an appositive, turn the sentence that renames, defines, or clarifies the noun into a phrase by dropping its subject and verb. The appositive should be placed before or after the noun to which it refers. Use a comma or commas to set off the appositive.

Millions of people make a special trip to visit Elvis's home ^*, Graceland,* each year. ~~It is called Graceland.~~

PRACTICE 9   Joining ideas using an appositive

Combine each pair of sentences into a single sentence by using an appositive. Be sure to use a comma or commas to set off the appositive.

Example: **William Shakespeare was famous and financially comfortable** ^*, one of the greatest writers in the English language,* **during his lifetime. ~~Shakespeare was one of the greatest writers in the English language.~~**

1. Shakespeare grew up in Stratford-upon-Avon, England. ^*, the son of a former town leader,* ~~He was the son of a former town leader.~~

2. Shakespeare attended the local grammar school until his father could ^*, a poor manager of money,* no longer afford it. ~~His father was a poor manager of money.~~

3. In 1582, Shakespeare, just eighteen, married twenty-six-year-old Anne Hathaway~~/~~, ~~She was~~ a farmer's daughter.

4. Three years later, he left for London~~/~~, ~~London was~~ the center of England's theater world.

5. Young Shakespeare, ~~was~~ once a simple country boy~~/~~, ~~He~~ soon became involved in acting, writing, and managing for one of London's theater companies.

6. By 1592, he was famous enough to be criticized in writing by one of the leading playwrights of the time~~/~~, ~~This playwright was~~ Robert Greene.

7. Greene's publisher soon printed a public apology for the criticism/, ~~This was~~ proof that Shakespeare had won the respect of some influential figures.

8. Shakespeare is said to have performed for Queen Elizabeth I/, ~~She was~~ a theater fan and supporter.

9. Eventually, Shakespeare returned to Stratford-upon-Avon and purchased a large home *, New Place,* where he lived until his death in 1616. ~~The house was called New Place.~~

10. Shakespeare remains highly popular today, and more than 250 movies have been made of his plays or about his life/, ~~His life is~~ a rich enough source of drama for any movie producer.

PRACTICE 10   **Joining ideas using an appositive**

Fill in the blank in each sentence with an appropriate appositive. There are many possible ways to complete each sentence. *Answers will vary. Possible answers shown.*

Example: My sister Clara, __*a busy mother of three*__ **, loves to watch soap operas.**

1. Clara's favorite show, __*Love and Desire*__ , comes on at three o'clock in the afternoon.

2. Clara, __*a hardworking seamstress*__ , rarely has the time to sit down in front of the television for the broadcast.

3. Instead, she programs her VCR, __*an aging but reliable machine*__ , and tapes the show for later.

4. Clara's husband, __*her childhood sweetheart*__ , used to tease her for watching the soaps.

5. But while he was recovering from the flu recently, he found her stack of tapes, __*a pile over two feet high*__ , and Clara insists that he watched every show of the previous season.

Join Ideas Using an Adjective Clause

An **adjective clause** is a group of words with a subject and a verb that describes a noun. Adjective clauses often begin with the word *who, which,* or *that* and can be used to combine two sentences into one.

Two sentences	Lorene owns an art and framing store. She is a good friend of mine.
Joined with an adjective clause	Lorene, who is a good friend of mine, owns an art and framing store.

Use *who* to refer to a person, *which* to refer to places or things (but not to people), and *that* for places or things.

To join sentences this way, use *who, which,* or *that* to replace the subject of a sentence that describes a noun that is in the other sentence. Once you have made this change, you have an adjective clause that you can move so that it follows the noun it describes. The sentence with the idea you want to emphasize should become the main clause. The less important idea should be in the adjective clause.

Two sentences	Rosalind is director of human services for the town of Marlborough. Marlborough is her hometown.

[The more important idea here is that Rosalind is director of human services. The less important idea is that the town is her hometown.]

Joined with an adjective clause	Rosalind is director of human services for the town of Marlborough, which is her hometown.

Note: If an adjective clause can be taken out of a sentence without completely changing the meaning of the sentence, put commas around the clause.

Lorene, who is a good friend of mine, owns an art and framing store.

[The phrase *who is a good friend of mine* adds information about Lorene, but it is not essential; the sentence *Lorene owns an art and framing store* means almost the same thing as the sentence in the example.]

If an adjective clause is essential to the meaning of a sentence, do not put commas around it.

The meat was recalled for possible salmonella poisoning. I ate it yesterday.

The meat that I ate yesterday was recalled for possible salmonella poisoning.

[The clause *that I ate yesterday* is an essential piece of information. The sentence *The meat was recalled for possible salmonella poisoning* changes significantly with the adjective clause *that I ate yesterday.*]

PRACTICE 11   Joining ideas using an adjective clause

Combine each pair of sentences into a single sentence by using an adjective clause beginning with *who, which,* or *that.*

Example: Some allergies cause sneezing, itching, and watery eyes/ They
Allergies that
^

can make people very uncomfortable.

1. Cats produce a protein/ It keeps their skin soft.
    that
    ^

2. This protein makes some people itch and sneeze/, The protein is the
    , which
    ^
    reason for most allergic reactions to cats.

3. Some cat lovers are allergic to cats/ They can control their allergies with
    who
    ^
    medication.

4. Allergic cat lovers may get another option from a new company/ The
    that
    company wants to create a genetically engineered cat.
    ^

5. Scientists have successfully cloned mice/ Some mice have been
    that
    ^
    genetically engineered for scientific study.

6. Researchers may soon have the technology to clone cats/ Cats could
    , which
    ^
    be genetically engineered to remove the allergen.

7. Many people have allergic reactions to cats. According to cat experts,
    who have allergic reactions to cats
    more than 10 percent of those people are allergic to something other
    ^
    than the skin-softening protein.

8. A single gene produces a cat's skin-softening protein. Scientists are not
    that produces a cat's skin-softening protein
    sure whether the gene is necessary for the cat's good health.
    ^

9. However, owning a genetically engineered cat would allow an allergic
    , which
    person to avoid taking allergy medications/ The medications can
    ^
    sometimes cause dangerous side effects.

10. Cloning and genetic engineering raise ethical questions/ These are
    that
    ^
    difficult to answer.

| PRACTICE 12 | **Joining ideas using an adjective clause** |

Fill in the blank in each of the following sentences with an appropriate adjective clause. Add commas, if necessary. There are many possible ways to complete each sentence. *Answers will vary. Possible answers shown.*

Example: Interactive television __*, which has started to become available to consumers,*__ **is a potential threat to viewers' privacy.**

1. Many Web sites __*that receive hundreds or thousands of hits each day*__ try to make a profit by selling information about visitors to the site.

2. Consumers __*who buy products online*__ must provide information to retail Web sites before being allowed to complete a purchase.

3. Consumer privacy __*, which is becoming rarer every day,*__ is suffering further with interactive television.

4. A viewer __*who tunes in to an interactive television program*__ may not realize that the broadcaster is collecting information about him or her.

5. The sale of personal information __*, which companies use to target potential customers,*__ can bring huge profits.

Editing Practice

Resources For cumulative Editing Review Tests, see pages 564–80.

Create sentence variety in the following paragraphs by joining at least two sentences in each of the paragraphs. Try to use several of the techniques discussed in this chapter. There are many possible ways to edit each paragraph. You may want to refer to the chart on page 484. *Answers will vary. Possible edits shown.*

| EDITING REVIEW 1 |

1 Rats might be nicer creatures than people think. *, which* 2 It's certainly hard to love and appreciate. *rats.* *, are* 3 They carry serious diseases like typhus, *Not only do they* salmonella poisoning, and bubonic plague. *, but rats also* 4 Rats have such huge appetites that it has been estimated that they destroy as much as one-third of humans' food supplies every year. 5 It has been estimated that rats have been responsible for ten million deaths over the past century

; however, rats
alone/ 6 ~~Rats~~ in the laboratory should probably be given credit for saving

as many lives as wild rats have taken.
              Used   *, rats*
    7 ~~Rats are used~~ widely in laboratory research/ 8 ~~Rats~~ have many
                          Being   *, when*
similarities to humans. 9 ~~Young rats are~~ ticklish/ 10 ~~When~~ a rat pup is gently

scratched at certain spots, such as the nape of the neck, it will squeal.
                          , which
11 The squeal can be heard only with an ultrasound scan/ 12 ~~The squeal~~ has

a similar soundgram pattern to that of a human giggle. 13 Rats can
                                              , craving
get addicted to the same drugs that humans do/ 14 ~~Rats crave~~ alcohol,
                                    Capable of overindulging,   rats
nicotine, amphetamine, and cocaine. 15 ~~Rats can also overindulge.~~ 16 ~~They~~

can continue consuming food or drugs until they die.

    17 Studies also show that rats, like humans, have personalities/
      being
18 ~~They can be~~ sad or cheerful depending on how they were raised and

their circumstances. 19 Rats that have been raised in stable, caring condi-
                          , while rats
tions tend to be optimists/ 20 ~~Rats~~ that have been reared in uneven and

unreliable conditions tend to be pessimists. 21 Both types of rats can learn
                                              , and they
to connect a certain sound with getting food/ 22 ~~They~~ can also associate

another sound with no food. 23 However, when they hear a new sound,
not associated with either food or no food,
the two types of rats react differently. 24 ~~The new sound is not associated~~

~~with either food or no food.~~ 25 The optimist will run to the food dispenser/
                                    , expecting nothing,
26 ~~It is~~ expecting to be fed. 27 The pessimist will go somewhere else. 28 ~~It is~~

~~expecting nothing.~~
              Demonstrating that rats   ,   researchers
    29 ~~Rats~~ can express kindness/ 30 ~~Researchers~~ put pairs of female rats

that had been littermates in a cage but separated them by wire mesh.
      Trained so that she
31 ~~Each rat~~ could pull a lever that would deliver food to her sister but not
              , each
to herself/ 32 ~~Each~~ rat experienced being a giver of food and a recipient of

a gift of food from her sister. 33 Then, one of the rats was replaced by an

unfamiliar and unrelated rat that had never learned about the food gift
              , revealing that those
process/ 34 ~~Those~~ rats that had recently received food gifts were 21 percent

more likely than rats that had not received food gifts to pull the lever to
                                              , believing
give food to their new, unknown partners. 35 The researchers ~~believe~~ that

these rats acted generously only because another rat had just been kind to
them/ 36 ~~Perhaps~~ *show us that perhaps* there is more to the rodents than previously thought.

EDITING REVIEW 2

1 Employees once wanted nothing more than to stay at their jobs as
long as possible/ 2 ~~They also viewed~~ *, viewing* career advancement as a high priority.
3 The optimal situation was to be valued on the job/ 4 ~~This~~ *, which* brought rewards
of satisfaction and money as well as the attainment of higher rungs on the
corporate ladder. 5 ~~Today's young employees are going~~ *Headed* in a different direc-
tion/ 6 ~~Young~~ *, young* workers these days have some expectations that few, if any,
jobs could satisfy.

7 A twenty-eight-year-old designer at an architecture firm had two
weeks of vacation every year/ 8 ~~This is~~ the standard vacation for most young
employees. 9 ~~Employees are commonly~~ *Commonly* encouraged to take only one of
these weeks off at a time/ 10 ~~Many~~ *, many employees* have trouble finding time to take any
vacation at all. 11 ~~The designer arranged~~ *Arranging* to take a job with another firm/
12 ~~He~~ *the designer* then resigned from his current firm. 13 ~~His~~ *After his* new firm agreed that he
could begin work in four weeks/ 14 ~~He then~~ *he* left on a leisurely motorcycle
trip beginning in the South, swinging over to the Rocky Mountains, and
returning across the Great Plains. 15 ~~He chose~~ *Choosing* an alternative to the entry-
level two-week vacation/ 16 ~~He~~ *he* quit, went on an adventure, and then
started a new job.
17 A thirty-three-year-old bankruptcy lawyer ~~was focused on a similar~~ *Focused on a similar quest, a*
~~quest.~~ 18 ~~She~~ quit her job; had an extended visit with her family; traveled
for four months throughout New Zealand, Australia, Southeast Asia,
and central Europe; and then found a new job at a different law firm.
19 In another telling example, ~~a software engineer, thirty-two,~~ *having* worked
hard with little vacation during the ten years he was with his company/
20 ~~He~~ *a software engineer, thirty-two,* quit to live his dream of visiting all fifty-eight national parks in the
United States. 21 ~~His~~ *Equipped with that* skills were in demand/ 22 ~~He~~ *he* did not worry about

finding another job. 23 He worried about feeling burned out by a job.

24 Finding a job is more difficult for applicants than it once was. 25 Find-

ing a new job was not the immediate concern for these people. 26 This is

perhaps a major difference between today's young employees and the

generation before them.

When a

27 A twenty-seven-year-old minister and his wife left their posts in

^ *,* *they*

Colorado Springs for new positions at a church in Philadelphia/ 28 ~~They~~

Saying ^ ^

took six weeks off between jobs. 29 ~~They say~~ the six weeks of unemploy-

, *they* ^

ment was healthy/ 30 ~~They~~ maintain that they are defined not by what

^ ^ *Emblematic*

they do but by who they are. 31 ~~They are emblematic~~ of their generation

, *they* ^

of workers/ 32 ~~They~~ took time off to renew relationships and pursue experi-

^ ^

ences that helped them reach a comfortable balance between work

and life.

PRACTICE 13 **Editing your own writing for sentence variety**

As a final practice, edit a piece of your own writing for sentence variety. It can be a paper you are working on for this course, a paper you have already finished, a paper for another course, or a recent piece of writing from your work or everyday life. You may want to use the chart on page 484 as you edit.

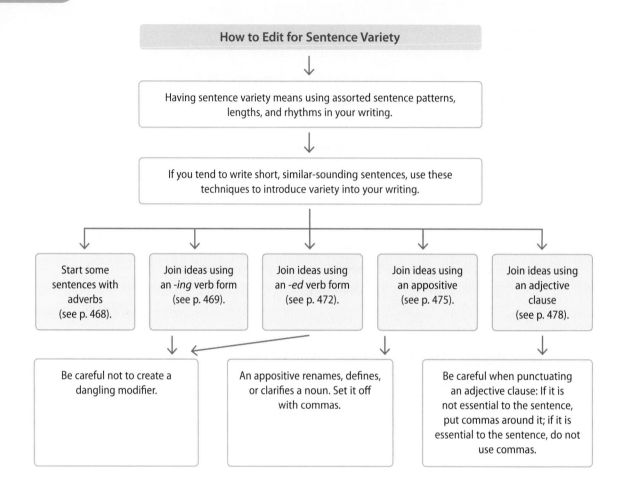

How to Edit for Sentence Variety

↓

Having sentence variety means using assorted sentence patterns, lengths, and rhythms in your writing.

↓

If you tend to write short, similar-sounding sentences, use these techniques to introduce variety into your writing.

| Start some sentences with adverbs (see p. 468). | Join ideas using an *-ing* verb form (see p. 469). | Join ideas using an *-ed* verb form (see p. 472). | Join ideas using an appositive (see p. 475). | Join ideas using an adjective clause (see p. 478). |

Be careful not to create a dangling modifier.

An appositive renames, defines, or clarifies a noun. Set it off with commas.

Be careful when punctuating an adjective clause: If it is not essential to the sentence, put commas around it; if it is essential to the sentence, do not use commas.

32

Formal English and ESL

Grammar Trouble Spots for Multilingual Students

Academic, or formal, English is the English you will be expected to use in college and in most work situations, especially in writing. If you are not used to speaking and writing formal English or if English is not your first language, this chapter will help you with the most common problems students have.

Note: In this chapter, the word *English* means formal English.

e Log in to
macmillanhighered
.com/realessays
LearningCurve >
Multilingual—Sentence
Structure

Basic Sentence Patterns

Statements

Every sentence in English must have at least one subject and one verb (**S-V**) that together express a complete idea. (Some languages, such as Spanish and Italian, do not always use a subject, because the subject is implied by the verb. In English, always include a subject.) The subject performs the action, and the verb names the action, as in the sentence that follows.

The pitcher throws.

Other English sentence patterns build on that structure. One of the most common patterns is subject-verb-object (**S-V-O**).

The pitcher throws the ball.

There are two kinds of **objects**:

A **direct object** receives the action of the verb.

The pitcher throws the ball.

[The ball directly receives the action of the verb *throws*.]

An **indirect object** does not receive the action of the verb. Instead, the action is performed *for* or *to* the person.

The pitcher throws me the ball.

For other common English sentence patterns, see Chapter 21.

[In this sentence, the word *me* does not receive the action of the verb *throws*. The action is performed *to* the person.]

Note that the **S-V-O** pattern differs from the sentence patterns in some other languages. In some languages (like Arabic) the pattern may be **S-O-V**; in other languages (like Spanish, Italian, and Russian) word order is not as strictly defined.

For more on prepositions, see pages 502–04. For more on the parts of sentences, see Chapter 21.

Another common sentence pattern is subject–verb–prepositional phrase. In standard English, the prepositional phrase typically follows the subject and verb.

```
S     V  Prepositional phrase
|     |          |
Lilah went to the movies.
```

Negatives

To form a negative statement, use one of the following words, often with a helping verb such as *can/could, does/did, has/have,* or *should/will/would.*

never	nobody	no one	nowhere
no	none	not	

Notice in the examples that the word *not* comes *after* the helping verb.

Sentence	The baby can talk.
Negative	The baby ~~no can~~ talk. *cannot*
Sentence	The store sells cigarettes.
Negative	The store ~~no~~ sell~~s~~ cigarettes. *does not*

Sentence	Jonah talks too much.
Negative	Jonah not talks̶ too much. *(does, ^)*

does inserted above "not talks", with caret ^ below.

Sentence	Johnetta will call.
Negative	Johnetta n̶o̶ will call. *(not, ^)*

not inserted above, caret ^ below.

Sentence	Caroline called.
Negative	Caroline n̶o̶ did call. *(not, ^)*

not inserted above, caret ^ below.

Sentence	Paul will come.
Negative	Paul n̶o̶ will come. *(not, ^)*

not inserted above, caret ^ below.

Common Helping Verbs

Forms of *be*	Forms of *have*	Forms of *do*	Other verbs
am	have	do	can
are	has	does	could
been	had	did	may
being			might
is			must
was			should
were			will
			would

The helping verb cannot be omitted in expressions using *not*.

Incorrect	The store *not sell* cigarettes.
Correct	The store *does not sell* cigarettes.

[*Does,* a form of the helping verb *do,* must come before *not.*]

Correct	The store *is not selling* cigarettes.

[*Is,* a form of *be,* must come before *not.*]

Double negatives are not standard in English.

Incorrect	Johnetta *will not call no one.*
Correct	Johnetta *will not call anyone.*
Correct	Johnetta *will call no one.*

For more on helping verbs and their forms, see Chapter 21.

Incorrect	Shane *does not have no* ride.
Correct	Shane *does not have a* ride.
Correct	Shane *has no* ride.

When forming a negative in the simple past tense, use the past tense of the helping verb *do*.

| *did* | + | *not* | + | Base verb without an *-ed* | = | Negative past tense |

| Sentence | I *talked* to Kayla last night. |

[The verb *talked* is in the past tense.]

| Negative | I *did not* talk to Kayla last night. |

For forming negatives in other tenses, see pages 404–15.

[Note that *talk* in this sentence does not have an *-ed* ending because the helping verb *did* conveys that past.]

| Sentence | Kerry *passed* the test. |
| Negative | Kerry *did not* pass the test. |

Questions

To turn a statement into a question, move the helping verb so that it comes before the subject. Add a question mark (**?**) to the end of the question.

| Statement | Danh *can work* late. |
| Question | *Can* Danh *work* late**?** |

If the only verb in the statement is a form of *be*, it should be moved before the subject.

| Statement | Phuong *is* smart. | Jamie *is* at work. |
| Question | *Is* Phuong smart**?** | *Is* Jamie at work**?** |

If there is no helping verb or form of *be* in the statement, add a form of *do* and put it before the subject. Be sure to end the question with a question mark (**?**).

| Statement | Norah sings in the choir. |
| Question | *Does* Norah sing in the choir**?** |

| Statement | Amy visited the elderly woman. |
| Question | *Did* Amy visit the elderly woman**?** |

Statement	The building burned.
Question	*Did* the building burn❓

Notice that the verb *visited* changed to *visit* and the verb *burned* to *burn* once the helping verb *did* was added.

For more on questions, see Chapters 24 and 25.

 Language note: *Do* is used with *I, you, we,* and *they. Does* is used with *he, she,* and *it.*

Examples   *Do* [I, you, we, they] practice every day?

Does [he, she, it] sound terrible?

There Is *and* There Are

English sentences often include *there is* or *there are* to indicate the existence of something.

There is a man at the door.   [You could also say, *A man is at the door.*]

There are many men in the class.   [You could also say, *Many men are in the class.*]

When a sentence includes the words *there is* or *there are*, the verb (*is, are*) comes before the noun it goes with. The verb must agree with the noun in number. For example, the sentence *There is a man at the door* uses the singular verb *is* to agree with the singular noun *man*, and the sentence *There are many men in the class* uses the plural verb *are* to agree with the plural noun *men*.

 Language note: The *there is/there are* structure does not exist in some other languages, so speakers of those languages sometimes leave out these words when writing in English.

Incorrect	My mother said much work to do.
	Much work to do.
Correct	My mother said *there is* much work to do.
	There is much work to do.

In questions, the word order in *there is* and *there are* is inverted.

Statements	*There is* plenty to eat.
	There are some things to do.
Questions	*Is there* plenty to eat?
	Are there some things to do?

Pronouns

For more on pronouns, see Chapter 26.

Pronouns replace nouns or other pronouns in a sentence so that you do not have to repeat them. There are three types of pronouns:

Subject pronouns serve as the subject of the verb (and every English sentence must have a subject).

         He
  Jonah is my cousin. ~~Jonah~~ lives next door to me.
         ^

Object pronouns receive the action of the verb or are part of a prepositional phrase.

  Jonah asked *me* for a ride.

  [The object pronoun *me* receives the action of the verb *asked.*]

  Jonah is my cousin. He lives next door *to me.*

  [*To me* is the prepositional phrase; *me* is the object pronoun.]

Possessive pronouns show ownership.

  Jonah is *my* cousin.

Use the following chart to check which type of pronoun to use.

Pronoun Types

Subject		Object		Possessive	
Singular	**Plural**	**Singular**	**Plural**	**Singular**	**Plural**
I	we	me	us	my/mine	our/ours
you	you	you	you	your/yours	your/yours
he/she/it	they	him/her/it	them	his/her/hers/its	theirs

Relative pronouns
who, which, that

The singular pronouns *he/she, him/her,* and *his/hers* show gender. *He, him,* and *his* are masculine pronouns; *she, her,* and *hers* are feminine.

Here are some examples of common pronoun errors, with corrections.

Confusing Subject and Object Pronouns

Use a subject pronoun for the word that *performs* the action of the verb, and use an object pronoun for the word that *receives* the action.

> *She*
> Dora is a good student. ~~Her~~ gets all A's.
> ^

[The pronoun performs the action *gets,* so it should be the subject pronoun *she.*]

> *her*
> Tomas gave the keys to ~~she~~.
> ^

[The pronoun receives the action of *gave,* so it should be the object pronoun *her.*]

Confusing Gender

Use masculine pronouns to replace masculine nouns and feminine pronouns to replace feminine nouns.

> *He*
> My brother passed the test. ~~She~~ got a B.
> ^

[The noun *brother* is masculine, so the pronoun must be masculine.]

> *him*
> The iPod belongs to Mr. Clark. Carla gave it to ~~her~~.
> ^

[*Mr. Clark* is masculine, so the pronoun must be masculine.]

Leaving Out a Pronoun

Some sentences use the pronoun *it* as the subject or object. Do not leave *it* out of the sentence.

> *It is*
> ~~Is~~ my birthday today.
> ^
> *It will*
> Annahita will travel by bus. ~~Will~~ arrive at 3:00 p.m.
> ^   *it*
> I tried calamari last night and liked very much.
> ^

Using a Pronoun to Repeat a Subject

Pronouns *replace* a noun, so do not use both a subject noun and a pronoun.

> The boss ~~he~~ is very mean.

[*Boss* is the subject noun, so the sentence does not also need a subject pronoun.]

The baseball ~~it~~ broke the window.

[*Baseball* is the subject, so no pronoun is needed.]

Using Relative Pronouns

The words *who, which,* and *that* are **relative pronouns**. Use relative pronouns in a phrase or clause that gives more information about the subject.

Use *who* to refer to a person or people.

The man *who* owns the building is strange.

Use *which* to refer to nonliving things.

The building, *which* was just painted, is for sale.

Use *that* to refer to either people or nonliving things. (Note that *who* is the preferred pronoun to refer to a person or people.)

The building *that* my uncle owns is for sale.

The present *that* you gave me is great.

Verbs

e Log in to
macmillanhighered
.com/realessays
LearningCurve >
Multilingual—Verbs

Verbs have different tenses to show when something happened: in the past, present, or future.

Learning how to use the various verb tenses is a challenge for everyone who is learning a new language. This section will give you examples that build on what you learned in Chapter 25.

Past   Present (now)   Future

This section covers some common errors in verb usage and also has full coverage of the progressive tenses. In addition, this section contains timelines, examples, and common errors for the simple, perfect, and progressive tenses. For full coverage of verbs and complete verb charts, see Chapter 25.

The Simple Tenses

SIMPLE PRESENT

Use the simple present to describe situations that exist now.

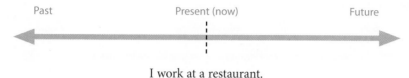

I work at a restaurant.

I/You/We/They <u>work</u> at a restaurant.

She/He <u>works</u> at a restaurant.

The third-person singular (*she/he*) of regular verbs ends in *-s* or *-es*. For irregular verb endings, see pages 392–94.

SIMPLE PAST

Use the simple past to describe situations that began and ended in the past.

You worked at a restaurant.

I/You/She/He/We/They <u>work**ed**</u> at a restaurant.

For regular verbs, the simple past is formed by adding either *-d* or *-ed* to the verb. For the past forms of irregular verbs, see the chart on pages 392–94.

SIMPLE FUTURE

Use the simple future to describe situations that will happen in the future. It is easier to form than the past tense. Use this formula for forming the future tense.

For charts, explanations, and practices on the simple tense, including how to use it to form negatives and questions, see Chapter 25.

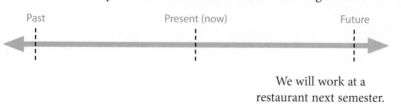

We will work at a restaurant next semester.

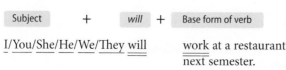

| Subject | + | *will* | + | Base form of verb |

I/You/She/He/We/They <u>will</u>   <u>work</u> at a restaurant next semester.

The Progressive Tenses

PRESENT PROGRESSIVE

Use the present progressive to describe situations that are happening now but began in the past.

working too many hours.

We are working too many hours.

For examples, explanations, and practices on the progressive tenses, along with a chart showing negatives and questions, see Chapter 25.

Use this formula to form the present progressive tense:

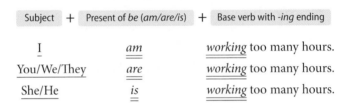

| Subject | + | Present of *be* (*am/are/is*) | + | Base verb with *-ing* ending |

I	*am*	*working* too many hours.
You/We/They	*are*	*working* too many hours.
She/He	*is*	*working* too many hours.

PAST PROGRESSIVE

Use the past progressive to describe situations that were going on in the past.

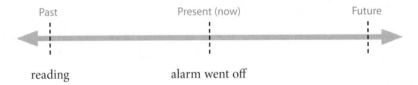

reading   alarm went off

I was reading when the alarm went off.

Use this formula to form the past progressive tense:

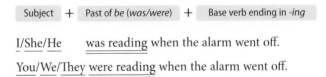

| Subject | + | Past of *be* (*was/were*) | + | Base verb ending in *-ing* |

I/She/He   was reading when the alarm went off.

You/We/They were reading when the alarm went off.

FUTURE PROGRESSIVE

Use the future progressive to describe situations that began and ended before some other situation happened.

I will be sleeping when Jin returns.

| Subject | + | *will be* | + | Base verb ending in *-ing* |

<u>I</u>/<u>You</u>/<u>She</u>/<u>He</u>/<u>We</u>/<u>They</u> <u>will be sleeping</u> when Jin returns.

The Perfect Tenses

PRESENT PERFECT

Use the present perfect to describe situations that started in the past and are still happening.

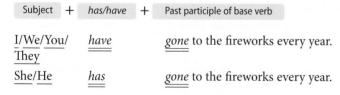

We have gone to the fireworks every year.

To form the present perfect tense, use this formula:

| Subject | + | *has/have* | + | Past participle of base verb |

| <u>I/We/You/</u>
<u>They</u> | <u>*have*</u> | <u>*gone*</u> to the fireworks every year. |
| <u>She/He</u> | <u>*has*</u> | <u>*gone*</u> to the fireworks every year. |

PAST PERFECT

Use the past perfect to describe situations that began and ended before some other situation happened.

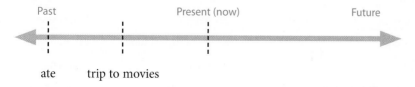

I had eaten before I went to the movies.

For charts, explanations, and practices on the perfect tense, including how to use it to form negatives and questions, see Chapter 25.

To form the past perfect tense, use this formula:

Subject + *had* + Past participle of base verb

I/You/She/   *had*   *eaten* before I/you/she/he/
He/We/They   we/they went to the movies.

FUTURE PERFECT

For more on the perfect tense, see Chapter 25. For a list of irregular verbs and their forms, see pages 392–94.

Use the future perfect to describe situations that begin and end before another situation begins.

I will have showered before Lee's arrival.

Use this formula to form the future perfect tense:

Subject + *will have* + Past participle of base verb

I/You/She/   *will have*   *showered* before Lee's arrival.
He/We/They

Modal Auxiliaries

Modal verbs are helping verbs that express the writer's attitude about an action. There aren't many of them to learn—see the following chart.

Modal auxiliary	Meaning	Example
can	ability	I can sing.
could	possibility	I could sing.
may	permission	You may sing.
might	possibility	I might sing.
must	obligation	I must sing.
should	advice or expectation	I should sing.
will	intention	I will sing.
would (often with the verb *like*)	desire, intention	I would sing.

For this section, you will need to refer to the charts on pages 412–15, which list statements, negatives, and questions for all of the modal auxiliaries.

SHOULD/MUST

As you see in the chart, *should* means that an action is expected or recommended. *Must* means that an action is required; it is an obligation.

Tomorrow, I *should* go to class.   [The writer has a choice about whether to go or not.]

Tomorrow, I *must* go to class.   [The writer has no choice about going to class: It is necessary.]

Read the two sentences that follow, and explain their meaning.

My grandmother *should* eat more.

My grandmother *must* eat more.

Two common student errors when using *should* or *must* are the following.

Using the Infinitive Instead of the Base Verb. The infinitive is *to* + a base verb. The base verb does not have *to* before it. When using *should* and *must*, use the base verb.

Incorrect	Children should *to obey* their parents.
Correct	Children should *obey* their parents.
Incorrect	They must *to work* late.
Correct	They must *work* late.

Using Two Modals. Using two modal auxiliaries together in a sentence is incorrect in English. Use only one.

Incorrect	I *must should* study harder.
Correct	I *must* study harder. *Or* I *should* study harder.

COULD/WOULD

Could means a possibility that an action will happen; *would* means an intention that an action happen. The meanings are similar, but the words are not interchangeable.

Gina *could* go to bed early.   [Gina has the ability to go to bed early; it is possible that she will.]

> Gina *would* like to go to bed early.   [Gina has the wish and intention to go to bed early, but she might not be able to.]

Read the two sentences that follow, and explain their meaning.

> Next semester, I *could* take two courses.

> Next semester, I *would* like to take two courses.

Two common student errors when using *could* or *would* are the following.

Using a Gerund Instead of an Infinitive or the Base Verb.   A gerund is a verb form that ends in *-ing* and functions as a noun in a sentence. When using the modal auxiliary *could,* follow it with the base verb. When using *would like,* follow it with the infinitive (*to* + base verb), not a gerund.

Incorrect	Today, I could *winning* the lottery.
Correct	Today, I could *win* the lottery.
Incorrect	I would like *graduating* in 2015.
Correct	I would like *to graduate* in 2015.

Omitting the Modal.   Just as you don't want to use two modal auxiliaries together in a sentence, you also don't want to forget a modal when it is required to show intention.

Incorrect	I *like* to take a vacation next month.
Correct	I *would like* to take a vacation next month.
Incorrect	Tomorrow, I *help* you.
Correct	Tomorrow, I *could help* you. Or Tomorrow, I *can help* you.

Gerunds and Infinitives

A **gerund** is a verb form that ends in *-ing* and acts as a noun. An **infinitive** is a base verb preceded by the word *to.* Gerunds and infinitives cannot be the main verbs in sentences; each sentence must have another word that is the main verb.

Gerund	I like *running.*

[*Like* is the main verb, and *running* is a gerund.]

Infinitive	I like *to run.*

[*Like* is the main verb, and *to run* is an infinitive.]

How do you decide whether to use a gerund or an infinitive? The decision often depends on the main verb in a sentence. Some verbs can be followed by either a gerund or an infinitive.

To improve your ability to write and speak standard English, read magazines and your local newspaper, and listen to television and radio news programs. Read magazines and newspaper articles aloud; it will help your pronunciation.

Verbs That Are Followed by Either a Gerund or an Infinitive

begin	forget	like	remember	stop
continue	hate	love	start	try

Sometimes, using an infinitive or gerund after one of the verbs listed in the preceding box results in the same meaning.

Gerund   I love *listening* to Ray Charles.

Infinitive   I love *to listen* to Ray Charles.

Other times, however, the meaning changes depending on whether you use an infinitive or a gerund.

Infinitive   Mario stopped to smoke a cigarette.

[This sentence means that Mario stopped what he was doing and smoked a cigarette.]

Gerund   Mario stopped smoking cigarettes.

[This sentence means that Mario no longer smokes cigarettes.]

Verbs That Are Followed by an Infinitive

agree	decide	need	refuse
ask	expect	offer	want
beg	fail	plan	
choose	hope	pretend	
claim	manage	promise	

Tony *expects to get* a raise.

Lana *plans to adopt* a child.

Verbs That Are Followed by a Gerund

admit	discuss	keep	risk
avoid	enjoy	miss	suggest
consider	finish	practice	
deny	imagine	quit	

Football players *avoid injuring* themselves.

Imagine sitting on a beach in Hawaii.

Do not use the base form of the verb when you need a gerund or an infinitive.

Incorrect   *Cook* is my favorite activity.

[*Cook* is the base form of the verb, not a noun; it can't function as the subject of the sentence.]

Correct gerund   *Cooking* is my favorite activity.

[*Cooking* is a gerund that can serve as the subject of the sentence.]

Incorrect   *Play* piano is fun.

Correct gerund   *Playing* piano is fun.

Incorrect   My goal is *graduate* from college.

Correct infinitive   My goal is *to graduate* from college.

[*To graduate* is an infinitive that can serve as the subject of the sentence.]

Incorrect   I need take vacation.

[There is already a verb, *need,* in the sentence, so there can't be another verb that shows the action of the subject, *I.*]

Correct infinitive   I need *to take* a vacation.

e Log in to
macmillanhighered
.com/realessays
LearningCurve >
Multilingual—Articles
and Types of Nouns

Articles

Articles announce a noun. English uses only three articles: *a, an,* and *the.* The same articles are used for both masculine and feminine nouns.

Language note: Articles (*a, an, the*) are not used in Russian or in many Asian languages. If you are not sure when to use an article or which one to use, pay close attention to this section.

Using Definite and Indefinite Articles

The is a **definite article** and is used before a specific person, place, or thing. *A* and *an* are **indefinite articles** and are used with a person, place, or thing whose specific identity is not known.

Definite article	*The* man knocked on *the* door.

[A specific man knocked on a specific door.]

Indefinite article	*A* man knocked on *a* door.

[Some man knocked on some door. We don't know what man or what door.]

Definite article	*The* hostess showed us to our seats.
Indefinite article	*A* hostess showed us to our seats.

When the word following the article begins with a vowel (*a, e, i, o, u*), use *an* instead of *a*.

An energetic hostess showed us to our seats.

Using Articles with Count and Noncount Nouns

To use the correct article, you need to know what count and noncount nouns are. **Count nouns** name things that can be counted. **Noncount nouns** name things that cannot be counted.

Count noun	I sold ten of my old *CDs* on eBay.
Noncount noun	I sold lots of *music* on eBay. [A *CD* can be counted; *music* cannot.]

Here are some examples of count and noncount nouns. This is just a brief list; all nouns in English are either count or noncount. To help determine whether a noun is count or noncount, try adding *s*. Most count nouns form a plural by adding *s;* noncount nouns do not have plural forms.

Count	Noncount		
apple/apples	advice	homework	rain
chair/chairs	beauty	honey	rice
dollar/dollars	equipment	information	salt
letter/letters	flour	jewelry	sand
smile/smiles	furniture	mail	spaghetti
tree/trees	grass	milk	sunlight
	grief	money	thunder
	happiness	postage	wealth
	health	poverty	

Prepositions

For more on prepositions, see Chapter 21. For a list of prepositions, see page 317.

A **preposition** is a word (such as *of, above, between, about*) that connects a noun, pronoun, or verb with other information about it. The correct preposition to use is often determined by idiom or common practice rather than by the preposition's actual meaning.

An **idiom** is any combination of words that is always used the same way, even though there is no logical or grammatical explanation for it. The best way to learn English idioms is to listen and read as much as possible and then to practice writing and speaking the correct forms.

e Log in to macmillanhighered .com/realessays LearningCurve > Multilingual— Prepositions

Prepositions after Adjectives

Certain prepositions often come after certain adjectives. Here are some common examples:

afraid of	full of	responsible for
ashamed of	happy about	scared of
aware of	interested in	sorry about/sorry for
confused by	nervous about	tired of
embarrassed about	proud of	worried about
excited about	reminded of	

Tanya is excited ~~of~~ *about* going to Mexico.

However, she is afraid ~~by~~ *of* taking time off.

Articles with Count and Noncount Nouns

Count nouns	Article used
Singular	
Specific →	*the*
	I want to read *the book* on taxes that you recommended.
	[The sentence refers to one particular book — the one that was recommended.]
	I can't stay in *the sun* very long.
	[There is only one sun.]
Not specific →	*a* or *an*
	I want to read *a book* on taxes.
	[It could be any book on taxes.]
Plural	
Specific →	*the*
	I enjoyed *the books* we read.
	[The sentence refers to a particular group of books — the ones we read.]
Not specific →	no article or *some*
	I usually enjoy *books*.
	[The sentence refers to books in general.]
	She found *some books*.
	[We do not know which books she found.]

Noncount nouns	Article used
Singular	
Specific →	*the*
	My son ate all *the food* we bought.
	[The sentence refers to particular food — the food we bought.]
Not specific →	no article or *some*
	There is *food* all over the kitchen.
	[The reader does not know what food the sentence refers to.]
	Give *some food* to the neighbors.
	[The sentence refers to an indefinite quantity of food.]

Prepositions after Verbs

Many verbs in English consist of a verb plus a preposition (or an adverb). The meaning of these combinations is not usually the literal meaning the verb and the preposition would each have on its own. Often, the meaning of the verb changes completely depending on which preposition is used with it.

You must *take out* the trash.   [*take out* = bring to a different location]

You must *take in* the exciting sights of New York City.   [*take in* = observe]

Here are a few common examples:

call in (telephone)	You can *call in* your order.
call off (cancel)	They *called off* the pool party.
call on (choose)	The teacher always *calls on* me.
drop in (visit)	*Drop in* when you are in the area.
drop off (leave behind)	Jerry will *drop off* the car.
drop out (quit)	Too many students *drop out* of school.
fight against (combat)	He tried to *fight against* the proposal.
fight for (defend)	We need to *fight for* our rights.
fill in (refill)	Please *fill in* the holes in the ground.
fill out (complete)	Please *fill out* this application form.
fill up (make something full)	Don't *fill up* with junk food.
find out (discover)	Did you *find out* what happened?
give up (forfeit)	Don't *give up* your place in line.
go over (review)	He wants to *go over* our speeches.
grow up (mature)	All children *grow up*.
hand in (submit)	You may *hand in* your homework now.
lock up (secure)	Don't forget to *lock up* before you go to bed.
look up (check)	I *looked up* the word in the dictionary.
pick out (choose)	Sandy *picked out* a puppy.
pick up (take or collect)	When do you *pick up* the keys?
put off (postpone)	I often *put off* doing dishes.
sign in (register, leaving name)	I have to *sign in* to work.
sign out (borrow, leaving name)	I want to *sign out* a book.
sign up (register for)	Cressia *signed up* for three classes.
think about (consider)	Patsy sometimes *thinks about* moving.
turn in (submit)	Please *turn in* your homework now.

"I write project summaries and answers to customers' questions."

Yamille R., student

PHOTO: PATRICIA LEE

33

Word Choice

Avoiding Language Pitfalls

Understand the Importance of Choosing Words Carefully

In conversation, much of your meaning is conveyed by your facial expression, your tone of voice, and your gestures. In writing, you have only the words on the page to make your point, so you must choose them carefully. If you use vague or inappropriate words, your readers may not understand you. Carefully chosen, precise words tell your readers exactly what you mean.

Two resources will help you find the best words for your meaning—a dictionary and a thesaurus. Both of these reference works are available in print and online forms.

e Log in to **macmillanhighered .com/realessays LearningCurve** > Word Choice and Appropriate Language

Dictionary

A dictionary provides all kinds of useful information about words—spelling, division of words into syllables, pronunciation, parts of speech, other forms of words, definitions, and examples of use.

ESL Students whose first language is not English can use a dictionary written especially for nonnative speakers (such as the *Longman Dictionary of American English*) in addition to a standard English dictionary.

The following is a part of a dictionary entry:

Spelling and end-of-line division   Pronunciation   Parts of speech

Other forms ————

Definition ————

Example ————

con • crete (kon´ krēt, kong´- krēt, kon krēt´, kong- kret´), *adj., n., v.* **-cret • ed, -cret • ing**, *adj.* **1.** constituting an actual thing or instance; real; perceptible; substantial: *concrete proof.* **2.** pertaining to or concerned with realities or actual instances rather than abstractions; particular as opposed to general: *concrete proposals.* **3.** referring to an actual substance or thing, as opposed to an abstract quality: The words *cat, water,* and *teacher* are concrete, whereas the words *truth, excellence,* and *adulthood* are abstract. . . .

—*Random House Webster's College Dictionary*

Thesaurus

To look up words in both the dictionary and the thesaurus, visit Merriam-Webster Online at www.m-w.com.

A thesaurus gives *synonyms* (words that have the same meaning) for the words you look up. Use a thesaurus when you cannot find the right word for what you mean or to avoid repeating the same word too often.

Concrete, *adj.* 1. Particular, specific, single, certain, special, unique, sole, peculiar, individual, separate, isolated, distinct, exact, precise, direct, strict, minute; definite, plain, evident, obvious; pointed, emphasized; restrictive, limiting, limited, well-defined, clear-cut, fixed, finite; determining, conclusive, decided.

—J. I. Rodale, *The Synonym Finder*

e Log in to macmillanhighered .com/realessays **Additional Grammar Exercises** > Using the Right Word

Practice Avoiding Four Common Word-Choice Problems

Four common problems with word choice can make it difficult for readers to understand your point. You can avoid them by using specific words that fit your meaning and make your writing clearer.

 Language note: Make sure to use the right kinds of words—nouns to name a person, place, or thing; adjectives to describe nouns; adverbs to describe adjectives or other adverbs.

N
Incorrect   Tyra seems *sadness*.

[*Sadness* is a noun. The kind of word needed to modify the noun *Tyra* is an adjective.]

ADJ
Correct   Tyra seems *sad*.

Vague and Abstract Words

Your words need to create a clear picture for your readers. **Vague and abstract words** are too general to make an impression. Here are some common vague and abstract words.

Teamwork Form groups, assign each group a column of words, and have them come up with more specific words to replace the words you've given them.

Vague and Abstract Words

a lot	dumb	OK (okay)	stuff
awesome	good	old	thing
awful	great	person	very
bad	happy	pretty	whatever
beautiful	house	sad	young
big	job	school	
car	nice	small	

When you see one of these words or another general word in your writing, try to replace it with a concrete or more specific word. A **concrete word** names something that can be seen, heard, felt, tasted, or smelled. A **specific word** names a particular individual or quality. Compare these two sentences:

Teaching tip Encourage students to look up in a dictionary words that they find in the thesaurus. Remind students that not all thesaurus words are interchangeable. Model specific examples of this problem for the class.

Vague and abstract   It was a beautiful day.

Concrete and specific   The sky was a bright, cloudless blue; the sun was shimmering; and the warm air was softened by a gentle breeze.

The first version is too general to be interesting. The second version creates a clear, strong image.

Some words are so vague that it is best to avoid them altogether.

Vague and abstract   It's like *whatever*.

[This sentence is neither concrete nor specific.]

Slang

Slang, the informal and casual language shared by a particular group, should be used only in informal and casual situations. Avoid it when you write, especially for college classes or at work. Use language that is appropriate for your audience and purpose.

Slang	Edited
I'm going to *chill* at home.	I'm going to relax at home.
I *dumped* Destina.	I ended my relationship with Destina.
I've been working *crazy* hard on my research project.	I've been working extremely hard on my research project.

If you are not sure whether a word is slang, check an online source, such as Slang Vocabulary (**www.slangvocabulary.com**) or the Slang and Idioms page at ManyThings.org (**www.manythings.org/e/slang.html**).

Wordy Language

Sometimes people think that using more words or using big words will make them sound smart and important. But using too many words in a piece of writing can obscure or weaken the point.

Wordy language includes phrases that contain too many words, unnecessarily modify a statement, or use slightly different words without adding any new ideas. It also includes overblown language—unnecessarily complicated words and phrases that are often used to make the writer or writing sound important.

Wordy	We have no openings *at this point in time.*
Edited	We have no openings now.

[The phrase *at this point in time* uses five words to express what could be said in one word—*now.*]

Wordy	*In the opinion of this writer,* tuition is too high.
Edited	Tuition is too high

[The qualifying phrase *In the opinion of this writer* is not necessary and weakens the statement.]

Wordy	In our advertising, we will *utilize* the *superlative photographic images* of ArtSense.
Edited	Our advertising will use ArtSense photographs.

[The words *utilize* and *superlative photographic images* are overblown.]

Common Wordy Expressions

Wordy	Edited
A great number of	Many
A large number of	Many
As a result of	Because
At that time	Then
At the conclusion of	At the end
At this point in time	Now
Due to the fact that	Because
In order to	To
In spite of the fact that	Although
In the event that	If
In this day and age	Now
In this paper I will show that	(Just make the point; don't announce it.)
It is my opinion that	I think (or just make the point)
The fact of the matter is that	(Just state the point.)

Clichés

Clichés are phrases used so often that people no longer pay attention to them. To get your point across and to get your readers' attention, replace clichés with fresh language that precisely expresses your meaning.

Clichés	Edited
Passing the state police exam is no *walk in the park*.	Passing the state police exam requires careful preparation.
I was *sweating bullets* until the grades were posted.	I was anxious until the grades were posted.

Common Clichés

as big as a house	last but not least
as hard as a rock	more trouble than it's worth
as light as a feather	no way on earth
best/worst of times	110 percent
better late than never	playing with fire
break the ice	spoiled brat
climb the corporate ladder	spoiled rotten
crystal clear	starting from scratch
drop in the bucket	sweating blood/bullets
easier said than done	24/7
hell on earth	work like a dog

Editing Practice

Edit the following paragraphs for vague and abstract language, slang, wordiness, or clichés, referring to the chart on page 516 as you need to. *Answers will vary. Possible edits shown.*

EDITING REVIEW 1   (24 possible edits)

1 Although people don't hear much about hobos in ~~this day and age~~ *these days*
of tightly sealed boxcars, there was a time not long ago when hobos were

a distinct segment of American culture. 2 Even then, however, few knew
the ~~handles~~ *names* of any hobos. 3 But to those who followed such social currents,

there was one hobo who ~~stood above the crowd~~ *stood out*—Steam Train Maury. 4 By
the time he ~~hung up his spurs~~ *retired* from his hobo wanderings, he was crowned

the king of the hobos five times; eventually, he achieved the status of

Grand Patriarch of the Hobos.
Born in
5 ~~Hailing from~~ Kansas in 1917 as Maurice W. Graham, Steam Train

Maury was the product of a troubled family. 6 He spent much of his youth
among parents and various relatives.
shifting ~~from here to there.~~ 7 In 1931, at the age of fourteen, he jumped on

a train and ~~at this point in time~~ he began his first time as a hobo.

hopping on trains and wandering

8 After ~~riding the rails and bouncing about~~ for several years, he became
      ^

a cement mason; operated his own school for masons in Toledo, Ohio;

and later served as a medical technician during World War II. 9 By 1971, he

had married

~~hooked up with a wife~~ and had two children, but he also developed hip
      ^

problems, was unable to work much, and became dissatisfied with his life.

thinking

10 Now fifty-four, he hopped on a freight train ~~with the vague intention~~
                                                              ^

~~and confused impression that~~ he'd just relive his hobo life for a few weeks

turned

and then return home. 11 Those two weeks ~~morphed~~ into ten years during
                                              ^

which Steam Train Maury became a hobo legend. 12 By 1981, Mr. Graham

eventful

had cowritten a book about his ~~sometimes exciting, sometimes boring,~~
                                    ^

~~and sometimes frightening~~ life as a hobo, helped to found the Hobo Foun-

dation, and took part in establishing the Hobo Museum in Britt, Iowa.

annual

13 At the National Hobo Convention held in Britt, ~~which was celebrated~~
          ^

~~every single year,~~ he was named the hobo king in 1973, 1975, 1976, 1978,

and 1981. 14 In 2004, he was crowned as the Grand Patriarch of the Hobos,

that title.

~~a title so prized that he was~~ the only person ever to have won ~~it.~~
                                                                      ^

15 Hobos have been hopping trains for free rides ever since the

helped to build

Civil War, when wandering field workers and laborers ~~took a~~
                                                          ^

~~significant and some say vital role in building~~ the American West.

Toward the end of the nineteenth century,

16 ~~Later,~~ some hobos, as a joke, named themselves "Tourist Union Local
      ^   *officials*

63." 17 In 1900, ~~the big shots~~ from Britt, Iowa, offered their town for Local
                      ^

63's hobo convention. 18 In the following decades, Britt became known as

the "hobo town," and by 1933, it was widely publicizing its four-day hobo

festivities.

convention and drawing tens of thousands to the ~~several widely varied~~
                                                      ^

~~events that were created just for the occasion.~~ 19 This was during the Great

Depression, when more than a million people were sneaking onto trains in

desperate

a ~~no-win~~ search for work.
      ^

an idealized

20 Mr. Graham always emphasized ~~a gussied-up~~ view of the hobo exis-
                                      ^

tence, the perspective that moved author John Steinbeck to call hobos "the

last free men." 21 ~~One of the typical and often-repeated examples~~ of Mr.
Typical

Graham's stories was that of a character called the Pennsylvania Kid, who

shaved with a piece of glass from a Coke bottle. 22 When asked if it was true
commented

that some hobos used deodorant, Mr. Graham ~~cracked~~ that it was a shame
died

but he didn't know what to do about it. 23 Steam Train Maury ~~croaked~~ of
Using

a stroke in 2006 at the age of eighty-nine. 24 ~~Making a fitting and~~

~~appropriate use of~~ the hobos' term for death, he had "taken the

westbound."

EDITING REVIEW 2   (22 possible edits)

something

1 Do humans have ~~a thing or two~~ to learn from honeybees? 2 A
experts

research study suggests that these hardworking insects may be ~~hotshots~~

at decision making. 3 This becomes evident when a hive of honeybees
becomes so large

~~keeps growing and growing so much~~ that it eventually outgrows its home.
flies away,

4 When that happens, the old queen ~~shoves off,~~ accompanied by a swarm
then

of about ten thousand bees. 5 Their challenge ~~at this critical and decisive~~

~~moment~~ is to find the best possible location for the new hive. 6 According
almost always

to the study, the bees~~, in the vast majority of cases in which this happens,~~

end up making good decisions.
manage   *somehow*

7 How do they ~~swing~~ that? 8 Do they ~~in one way or another~~ vote or
To find out,

have a method of coming to a consensus? 9 ~~As a means of discerning the~~

~~answer to this,~~ the researchers conducted several experiments as they
waited,

observed the honeybees making their decision. 10 While the swarm ~~took a~~

~~breather~~ huddling together on a tree branch, scout bees searched for suit-
returned,

able locations. 11 As the scout bees ~~wended their way back,~~ they did a

waggle dance to highlight what they had found. 12 Apparently, during this
changed their minds

process, some scouts ~~flip flopped~~ and ended up dancing to support other
all

scouts' finds. 13 The researchers concluded that the swarm doesn't wait for

~~each and every one of~~ the scouts to settle on one location. 14 Instead, the
enough

swarm senses when ~~a sufficient and satisfactory number of~~ scouts, perhaps

Resources For cumulative Editing Review Tests, see pages 564–80.

fifteen or twenty, have agreed on one site. 15 At that point, the entire

swarm gets ready to ~~make their move.~~ *go.* 16 For ~~an approximate period of~~ *about* an
^

hour, the bees warm up their flight muscles, and during this time, the

remaining scouts usually decide to support the chosen site. 17 In this way, a

solid consensus is achieved, and, in most cases, it is the ~~coolest~~ *best* possible
^

location for the new hive.

18 ~~As a result of these experiments, the~~ *The* researchers note that the bees'
^

process works because it makes sense. 19 ~~The inside story~~ *Information* is brought to the
^

group by independent individuals. 20 In the free marketplace of waggle

dancing, they openly ~~chew the fat over it~~ *confer* and eventually arrive at a mutual
^

decision. 21 ~~The fact of the matter is that it~~ *It* is almost always the right deci-
^   ^

sion. 22 Are humans capable of ~~pulling this off~~ *doing this?*?
^

PRACTICE   **Editing your own writing for word choice**

As a final practice, edit a piece of your own writing for word choice. It can
be a paper you are working on for this course, a paper you have already
finished, a paper for another course, or a recent piece of writing from your
work or everyday life. You may want to use the following chart as you edit.

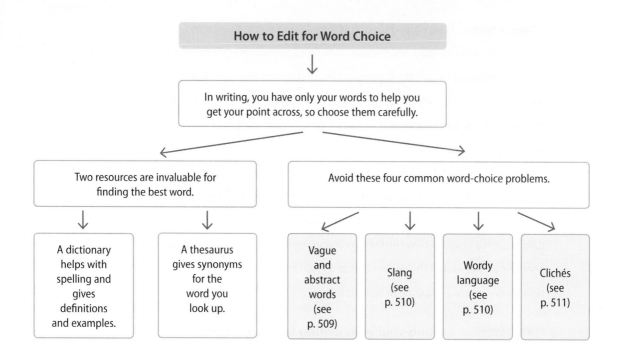

How to Edit for Word Choice

In writing, you have only your words to help you get your point across, so choose them carefully.

Two resources are invaluable for finding the best word.

A dictionary helps with spelling and gives definitions and examples.

A thesaurus gives synonyms for the word you look up.

Avoid these four common word-choice problems.

Vague and abstract words (see p. 509)

Slang (see p. 510)

Wordy language (see p. 510)

Clichés (see p. 511)

34

Commonly Confused Words

Avoiding Mistakes with Soundalikes

Understand Why Certain Words Are Commonly Confused

Certain words in English are confusing because they sound alike and may have similar meanings. In writing, words that sound alike may be spelled differently, and readers rely on the spelling to understand what you mean. Edit your writing carefully to make sure that you have used the correct words.

Practice Using Commonly Confused Words Correctly

Study the different meanings and spellings of these twenty-seven sets of commonly confused words. Complete the sentence after each set of words, filling in each blank with the correct word.

A / AN / AND

> **a:** used before a word that begins with a consonant sound
>
> **an:** used before a word that begins with a vowel sound
>
> **and:** used to join two words
>
> *A* friend *and* I got lost in *an* old maze.
>
> Most classrooms have __*a*__ worn-out chair __*and*__ __*an*__ old desk for the teacher.

Teaching tip Have students read the sentences in this section aloud so that they can focus on differences in pronunciation. Encourage them to exaggerate the pronunciation of words that do not sound exactly alike.

ACCEPT / EXCEPT

accept: to agree to receive or admit (verb)

except: but, other than (conjunction)

I *accept* all your requests *except* the one to borrow my car.

Do not ___*accept*___ anything from people at airports ___*except*___ from family members.

ADVICE / ADVISE

advice: opinion (noun)

advise: to give an opinion (verb)

Please *advise* me what to do; your *advice* is always helpful.

___*Advise*___ me of your plans, particularly if you don't follow my ___*advice*___ .

AFFECT / EFFECT

affect: to have an impact on, to change something (verb)

effect: a result (noun)

The sunny weather has had a positive *effect* on people's moods, but it will negatively *affect* the economy.

Since this year's drought will ___*affect*___ the cost of food, we'll be feeling its ___*effect*___ personally.

ARE / OUR

are: a form of the verb *be*

our: a pronoun showing ownership

Gardens *are* rare in *our* neighborhood.

___*Our*___ bulbs ___*are*___ arriving this week.

BY / BUY

by: next to or before

buy: to purchase (verb)

By the time I'm ready to leave the dollar store, I have found too much I want to *buy.*

I have decided to ___*buy*___ the model ___*by*___ the showroom entrance.

CONSCIENCE / CONSCIOUS

conscience: a personal sense of right and wrong (noun)

conscious: awake, aware (adjective)

Danny made a *conscious* decision to listen to his *conscience*.

The burglar was ___*conscious*___ that someone else was in the house and for a

moment felt a twinge of ___*conscience*___ .

Think about the second *n* in *conscience* to help you remember that *conscience* has to do with your *inner* thoughts.

FINE / FIND

fine: of high quality (adjective); feeling well (adverb); a penalty for breaking a law (noun)

find: to locate, discover (verb)

You will *find* a *fine* leather jacket in the coat department.

A ___*fine*___ partner is hard to ___*find*___ .

Some commonly confused words—such as *conscience* and *conscious*, *loose* and *lose*, and *of* and *have*—sound similar but not exactly alike. To avoid confusing these words, practice pronouncing them correctly.

ITS / IT'S

its: a pronoun showing ownership

it's: a contraction of the words *it is*

It's amazing to see a butterfly come out of *its* cocoon.

___*It's*___ good news for us that the bus changed ___*its*___ route.

If you are not sure whether to use *its* or *it's* in a sentence, try substituting *it is*. If the sentence does not make sense with *it is*, use *its*.

KNEW / NEW / KNOW / NO

knew: understood; recognized (past tense of the verb *know*)

new: unused, recent (adjective)

know: to understand, to have knowledge of (verb)

no: used to form a negative

I *knew* that Jason would need *new* shoes.

The ___*new*___ employee already ___*knew*___ some of the other employees.

There is *no* way to *know* what will happen.

Do you ___*know*___ that there is ___*no*___ school today because of the snow?

LOOSE / LOSE

loose: baggy, not fixed in place (adjective)

lose: to misplace, to forfeit possession of (verb)

If the muffler is *loose*, you might *lose* it.

You will ___lose___ that bracelet if it's too ___loose___.

MIND / MINE

mind: to object to (verb); the thinking or feeling part of one's brain (noun)

mine: belonging to me (pronoun); a source of ore and minerals (noun)

Keep in *mind* that the sweater is *mine*.

Your ___mind___ is a lot sharper than ___mine___.

Do not use of after would, should, could, and might. Use have after those words.

OF / HAVE

of: coming from; caused by; part of a group; made from (preposition)

have: to possess (verb; also used as a helping verb)

I would *have* helped if you had told me you were out *of* change.

Joe might ___have___ been part ___of___ the band.

PASSED / PAST

passed: went by or went ahead (past tense of the verb *pass*)

past: time that has gone by (noun); gone by, over, just beyond (preposition)

This *past* school year, I *passed* all of my exams.

If you go ___past___ the church, you have ___passed___ the right turn.

PEACE / PIECE

peace: no disagreement; calm (noun)

piece: a part of something larger (noun)

We will have no *peace* until we give the dog a *piece* of that bread.

Selling his ___piece___ of land will give Uncle Joe ___peace___ of mind.

PRINCIPAL / PRINCIPLE

principal: main or chief (adjective); head of a school or a leader of an organization (noun)

principle: a standard of beliefs or behaviors (noun)

The *principle* at stake is the *principal* issue of the court case.

The ___principal___ problem with many criminals is that they do not have good ___principles___.

QUIET / QUITE / QUIT

quiet: soft in sound; not noisy (adjective)

quite: completely, very (adverb)

quit: to stop (verb)

It is not *quite* time to *quit* yet.

The machine __quit__ running, and the office was __quiet__ .

RIGHT / WRITE

right: correct; in a direction opposite from left (adjective)

write: to put words on paper (verb)

Please be sure to *write* the *right* address.

__Write__ your name in the __right__ column.

SET / SIT

set: a collection of something (noun); to place an object somewhere (verb)

sit: to rest with one's rear end supported by a chair or other surface (verb)

Set your coat down before you *sit*.

Before you __sit__ down, __set__ your cup of coffee on the table.

SUPPOSE / SUPPOSED

suppose: to imagine or assume to be true (verb)

supposed: past tense of *suppose;* intended (verb)

You are *supposed* to call when you are going to be late, but I *suppose* that's too much to expect.

I was __supposed__ to take the ten o'clock train, but I __suppose__ the eleven o'clock is okay.

THAN / THEN

than: a word used to compare two or more things or persons (conjunction)

then: at a certain time (adverb)

I weigh a lot more *than* I used to back *then*.

If you want to lose weight, __then__ you will have to eat less __than__ you do now.

If you are not sure whether to use *their* or *they're*, substitute *they are*. If the sentence does not make sense, use *their*.

THEIR / THERE / THEY'RE

their: a pronoun showing ownership

there: a word indicating location or existence (adverb)

they're: a contraction of the words *they are* (pronoun plus verb)

Their windows are open, and *there* is a breeze, so *they're* not hot.

____They're____ going to be away, so my friend will be staying ____there____ and taking care of ____their____ cat.

THOUGH / THROUGH / THREW

though: however; nevertheless; in spite of (conjunction)

through: finished with (adjective); from one side to the other (preposition)

threw: hurled, tossed (past tense of the verb *throw*)

Jimmy *threw* the ball, and it went *through* the window, *though* he had not aimed it there.

____Though____ Amanda loved the shoes, she ____threw____ them out because she could not go ____through____ any more foot pain.

TO / TOO / TWO

to: a word indicating a direction or movement (preposition); part of the infinitive form of a verb

too: also; more than enough; very (adverb)

two: the number between one and three (adjective or noun)

They went *to* a restaurant and ordered *too* much food for *two* people.

The ____two____ friends started ____to____ dance, but it was ____too____ crowded to move.

USE / USED

use: to employ or put into service (verb)

used: past tense of the verb *use*. *Used to* can indicate a past fact or state, or it can mean "familiar with."

Paolo *used* to be a farmer, so he knows how to *use* all the equipment.

When you last ____used____ the oven, what did you ____use____ it for?

If you are not sure whether to use *whose* or *who's*, substitute *who is*. If the sentence does not make sense, use *whose*.

WHO'S / WHOSE

who's: a contraction of the words *who is* or *who has*

whose: a pronoun showing ownership

The person *whose* name is first on the list is the one *who's* going next.

___Who's___ the man ___whose___ shoes are on the table?

YOUR / YOU'RE

your: a pronoun showing ownership

you're: a contraction of the words *you are*

You're about to get paint all over *your* hands.

___Your___ teacher says ___you're___ always late to class.

If you are not sure whether to use *your* or *you're*, substitute *you are*. If the sentence does not make sense, use *your*.

Editing Practice

Edit the following paragraphs for commonly confused words.

Resources For cumulative Editing Review Tests, see pages 564–80.

> **EDITING REVIEW 1**   (18 errors)
>
> 1 Most people ~~no~~ *know* that Americans love to drive ~~there~~ *their* cars. 2 However, many people may not be ~~conscience~~ *conscious* of how much the government does to support our car culture. 3 For instance, the United States would never ~~of~~ *have* had so many good highways without federal and state assistance for road construction and maintenance. 4 New highways are usually paid for mainly ~~buy~~ *by* tax money. 5 It is rare for a new road ~~too~~ *to* be paid for with tolls, which would come exclusively from the people driving on it. 6 Americans also expect ~~they're~~ *their* roads to be well maintained, and they may ~~right~~ *write* to their representatives to complain about aging road surfaces. 7 The government even keeps gas prices lower here ~~then~~ *than* in most other nations.
>
> 8 Few people ~~mine~~ *mind* that the government assists drivers in these ways. 9 Some would argue that ~~its~~ *it's* a government's job to help pay for transportation. 10 However, other forms of transportation in this country are often ~~past~~ *passed* over when Congress hands out funds. 11 Amtrak, the U.S. railroad, may soon ~~loose~~ *lose* virtually all government funds, even though many government officials are skeptical of ~~it's~~ *its* ability to keep operating without government assistance. 12 ~~Accept~~ *Except* for a few places like New York and San Francisco, most U.S. cities do not have good mass transit systems. 13 Americans ~~who's~~ *whose*

travels have taken them to certain other countries praise the national train

systems and city transit systems they find there. 14 As traffic gets worse in

our nation's urban and suburban areas, some people ~~fine~~ _find_ it odd that the

United States does not invest more in transportation that would allow

people to leave ~~there~~ _their_ cars at home.

EDITING REVIEW 2   (14 errors)

1 Hoping to keep ~~are~~ _our_ nation's blood supply safe, the U.S. government

has placed restrictions on donating blood. 2 Anyone ~~whose~~ _who's_ spent more

than five years in Europe or more than three months in England since 1980

is not allowed to give blood. 3 Officials hope that asking about time in

Europe will help them ~~fine~~ _find_ people who might ~~of~~ _have_ been exposed to mad

cow disease. 4 Men are also asked whether they have had sexual relations

with other men in the ~~passed~~ _past_ ten years. 5 If they have, ~~their~~ _they're_ asked

not to give blood. 6 This is ~~suppose~~ _supposed_ to protect the blood supply from

the AIDS virus. 7 Of course, ~~they're~~ _there_ are some problems with these restric-

tions. 8 First, ~~know~~ _no_ one knows how much exposure to infected meat can

give a person mad cow disease, and ~~know~~ _no_ one is sure how long the disease

can hide in a human body. 9 Second, many gay men ~~our~~ _are_ not infected with

HIV, and many women, who are not asked about sexual activity, are

infected. 10 Restricting certain groups of people from giving blood may not

do anything to protect the blood supply, but it will certainly ~~effect~~ _affect_ the

amount of blood available. 11 Is it better to allow the blood supply to

become dangerously low ~~then~~ _than_ to allow people ~~who's~~ _whose_ blood might carry a

disease to donate blood?

PRACTICE   ### Editing your own writing for commonly confused words

As a final practice, edit a piece of your own writing for commonly confused
words. It can be a paper you are working on for this course, a paper you
have already finished, a paper for another course, or a recent piece of writing from your work or everyday life. Add any misused words you find to
your personal list of confusing words.

Part 8

Punctuation and Capitalization

"I write short
stories."

—Elijah M., student

PHOTO: PATRICIA LEE

35

Commas

Understand What Commas Do

Commas (,) are punctuation marks that help readers understand a sentence by introducing a pause at key points. Read aloud the following three sentences. How does the use of commas change the meaning?

No comma	After you call Jim I'll leave for the restaurant.
One comma	After you call Jim, I'll leave for the restaurant.
Two commas	After you call, Jim, I'll leave for the restaurant.

Commas signal particular meanings to your readers, so it is important that you understand when and how to use them.

Teaching tip Have a student read these sentences aloud, and ask the class to tell how they differ.

Practice Using Commas Correctly

Commas between Items in a Series

Use commas to separate three or more items in a series. This includes the last item in the series, which usually has the word *and* or *or* before it. The items can be either individual words or whole phrases.

e Log in to macmillanhighered .com/realessays LearningCurve > Commas

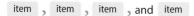

When you go to the store, please pick up *milk, bread, orange juice,* and *bananas.*

My math course last semester was *exciting, challenging,* and *engaging.*

Students may take the course as a *regular classroom course,* as an *online course,* or as a *distance learning course.*

Some periodicals and Web sites choose not to use a comma before the final item in a series. In college writing, however, it is always best to include it consistently throughout each piece of writing you do.

Commas between Coordinate Adjectives

Coordinate adjectives are two or more adjectives that independently modify the same noun and can be separated by the word *and*. Use a comma between coordinate adjectives.

> We had an entire month of *cold, damp, gray* weather.

> The *old, battered, rusty* car would not start.

Do *not* use a comma between the final adjective and the noun it modifies.

Incorrect	It was a *long, hard, complicated,* test.
Correct	It was a *long, hard, complicated* test.

Cumulative adjectives modify the same noun but form a unit and are not separated by commas. Cumulative adjectives cannot be joined by the word *and*.

> Our team wants to win the *big regional sales* trophy.

All of the words in italics are adjectives, but they build on one another. Moving left from *trophy,* each adjective becomes part of a larger unit.

1. *Sales* describes the trophy.
2. The next word to the left, *regional,* describes not just the trophy but the *sales* trophy.
3. The next word to the left, *big,* describes the *regional sales* trophy.

The team did not want to win just a *big* trophy or just a *regional* trophy or just a *sales* trophy. The team wanted the *big regional sales* trophy.

To summarize the rule: Use a comma to separate two or more coordinate adjectives. Do not use commas to separate cumulative adjectives.

PRACTICE 1   **Using commas in a series and with coordinate adjectives**

Add commas where they are needed in the following sentences. If the sentence is correct, write "C" next to it.

Example: The short, slim conductor stepped up to the elaborate, colorful podium.

1. We had prepared a wholesome, flavorful meal for the children, their parents, and their friends.

2. Lucas has painted three large pictures for the unfurnished, boring
living room.

3. The huge, confusing, and annoying airport desperately needed
renovating.

4. I have several urgent e-mail messages from Mr. Toland, Ms. Fry, and my
father.

5. Our scholarly English professor was once a professional baseball player. C

6. She loves to take long, slow walks in the rain.

7. My peer editor posts comments on my paper before I leave for my
session in the writing lab. C

8. Driving on this endless, dull, unsafe highway can be unpleasant.

9. The funny animated movie was based on a well-written graphic novel. C

10. We always buy rich, high-calorie candy bars when we go to the movies.

Commas in Compound Sentences

A **compound sentence** contains two independent clauses (sentences) joined by one of these words: *and, but, for, nor, or, so, yet.* Use a comma before the joining word to separate the two clauses.

e Log in to
macmillanhighered
.com/realessays
Additional Grammar
Exercises > Using
Commas in Compound
Sentences

| Sentence | **,** | *and / but / for / nor / or / so / yet* | sentence. |

Tom missed class yesterday, *and* he texted me to ask what he missed.

I would have been happy to help him, *but* I was absent too.

I told him I wasn't there, *so* he said he would e-mail the professor.

A comma is not needed if the word *and, but, for, nor, or, so,* or *yet* joins two sentence elements that are not independent clauses.

The words *and, but, for, nor, or, so,* and *yet* are called coordinating conjunctions. See Chapter 29 for more details.

 Language note: A comma by itself cannot separate two sentences: Doing so creates a run-on (see Chapter 23).

PRACTICE 2 **Using commas in compound sentences**

Edit the following compound sentences by adding commas where they are needed. If a sentence is already correct, put a "C" next to it.

Example: **The U.S. population is getting older, but the number of people**
trained to care for the elderly is declining.

1. Working in a nursing home is a difficult job, for elderly patients can sel-
   dom do much for themselves.

2. The labor is physically difficult, and it can also be mentally draining.

3. Few trained nurses and nurse's aides want nursing-home jobs, for the
   pay is also usually lower than that offered by hospitals.

4. Nursing-home workers have high turnover rates, and the facilities are
   constantly in need of new personnel.

5. More workers will be needed as the baby boomers become elderly, yet
   there is already a shortage of people willing to do the work.

6. A director sometimes must hire undertrained workers, or the nursing
   home will face a severe staff shortage.

7. Workers without education and training may have difficulty understanding a doctor's orders, so the patients' care may suffer. C

8. Home health aides and hospice workers are also in short supply, and
   the need for such workers is growing every day.

9. Solving these problems will be difficult, for long-term care for the elderly is already very expensive.

10. People caring for elderly patients must get better pay, or no one will be
    available to do the work in a few years.

e Log in to
macmillanhighered
.com/realessays
Additional Grammar
Exercises > Using
Commas after
Introductory Word
Groups

Commas after Introductory Word Groups

Use a comma after an introductory word or word group. An introductory word
group can be a word, a phrase, or a clause. The comma lets your readers know
when the main part of the sentence is starting.

Introductory word or word group	,	main part of sentence.

Introductory word	*Finally,* I finished the job.
Introductory phrase	*According to the paper,* the crime rate went down.
Introductory clause	*As you know,* the store is going out of business.

> **PRACTICE 3**   **Using commas after introductory word groups**

In each item, underline any introductory word or word group. Then, add commas after introductory word groups where they are needed.

Example: **Every year,** more than two hundred motorists die in collisions with animals.

1. <u>Along roadsides all across the country,</u> drivers see the bodies of animals hit by cars.

2. <u>Usually,</u> the victims are common species, such as deer and raccoons.

3. <u>Of course,</u> hitting a deer is not only disturbing but also potentially harmful or fatal to the occupants of a car.

4. <u>However,</u> the deer population has not suffered much of a decline from traffic accidents.

5. <u>On the other hand,</u> drivers in wilderness areas may accidentally kill endangered species.

6. <u>For instance,</u> experts believe that 65 percent of the population of Florida panthers has been killed on highways in the past twenty years.

7. <u>Maintaining the world's largest network of roads,</u> the U.S. Forest Service tries to balance the needs of humans and wildlife.

8. <u>To get access to wilderness areas,</u> humans, many of whom strongly favor protecting the environment, need roads.

9. <u>Unfortunately,</u> wilderness roads may isolate populations of animals that will not cross them and kill animals that make the attempt.

10. <u>Although expensive,</u> underpasses and overpasses have been successful in some areas at reducing human collisions with animals.

Commas around Appositives and Interrupters

An **appositive**—a phrase that renames, defines, or clarifies a noun—comes directly before or after the noun.

For more on appositives, see pages 475–77.

> Dick, *my neighbor,* has a new job.

> Apartment prices are high at Riverview, *the new complex.*

e Log in to
macmillanhighered
.com/realessays
Additional Grammar
Exercises > Using
Commas around
Appositives and
Interrupters

An **interrupter** is an aside or transition that interrupts the flow of a sentence but does not affect its meaning.

Campus parking fees, *you should know*, are going up by 30 percent.

A six-month sticker will now be $75, *if you can believe it.*

An interrupter that appears at the beginning of a sentence can be treated the same as an introductory word group.

As a matter of fact, the fees are the highest of any of the campuses in the city.

Putting commas around appositives and interrupters tells readers that these elements give extra information but are not essential to the meaning of a sentence. If an appositive or interrupter is in the middle of a sentence, set it off with a pair of commas, one before and one after. If an appositive or interrupter comes at the beginning or end of a sentence, separate it from the rest of the sentence with one comma.

Incidentally, your raise has been approved.

Your raise, *incidentally,* has been approved.

Your raise has been approved, *incidentally.*

Sometimes, an appositive is essential to the meaning of a sentence. When a sentence would not have the same meaning without the appositive, the appositive should not be set off with commas.

The actor *John Travolta* has never won an Academy Award.

[The sentence *The actor has never won an Academy Award* does not have the same meaning.]

The lawyer *Clarence Darrow* was one of history's greatest speakers.

[The sentence *The lawyer was one of history's greatest speakers* does not have the same meaning.]

PRACTICE 4   **Using commas to set off appositives and interrupters**

Underline any appositives or interrupters in the following sentences. Then use commas to set them off.

Example: **The reason for the delay, a mechanical problem with the airplane, was not mentioned.**

1. Road rage, as most people know, occurs when angry drivers overreact.

2. Another phenomenon, air rage, involves out-of-control and often in-toxicated passengers on an airplane.

3. One famous air rage incident, a confrontation between a drunken busi-nessman and a flight attendant, ended with the passenger tied to his seat for the rest of the flight.

4. Ground rage, like air rage, is a term used for incidents between airline passengers and airline employees.

5. Ground rage, as the name suggests, occurs in the terminal, not in the air.

6. Gate agents, the people who check tickets and allow passengers to board the plane, are frequent victims of ground rage.

7. Oversold seats, a common occurrence in air travel, can mean that some passengers are forced to miss a flight.

8. Passengers, many of whom are on tight schedules or have connecting flights to catch, find delayed flights infuriating as well.

9. Some delayed or bumped passengers take out their anger on the gate agent, a convenient target.

10. Although some airline employees may not be helpful or friendly, their attitudes do not excuse passengers who commit assault, a serious crime.

Commas around Adjective Clauses

An **adjective clause** is a group of words that often begins with *who, which,* or *that;* has a subject and verb; and describes the noun that comes before it in a sentence.

Whether or not an adjective clause must be set off from the rest of the sentence by commas depends on its meaning in the sentence. If an adjective clause can be taken out of a sentence without completely changing the meaning, put commas around the clause.

The mayor, *who was recently elected,* has no political experience.

SuperShop, *which is the largest supermarket in town,* was recently bought by Big Boy Markets.

I have an appointment with Dr. Kling, *who is the specialist.*

If an adjective clause is essential to the meaning of a sentence, do not put commas around it. You can tell whether a clause is essential by taking it out and seeing whether the meaning of the sentence changes significantly, as it would if you took the clauses out of the following examples:

The hair salon *that I liked* recently closed.

Salesclerks *who sell liquor to minors* are breaking the law.

Noun	,	adjective clause not essential to meaning	,	rest of sentence.

Noun	adjective clause essential to meaning	rest of sentence.

For more on adjective clauses, see page 478.

Use *who* to refer to a person; *which* to refer to places or things (but not to people); and *that* for people, places, or things. When referring to a person, *who* is preferable to *that*.

PRACTICE 5   Using commas to set off adjective clauses

Edit the following sentences by putting any needed commas around adjective clauses. Remember that if an adjective clause is essential to the meaning of the sentence, you should not use commas. If a sentence is already correct, put a "C" next to it.

Example: **Stephen King, who understands how to frighten his readers,
has depicted evil clowns in his work.**

1. The only thing that terrifies Maria is a person dressed as a clown. C

2. The fear of clowns, which is called *coulrophobia,* is fairly common.

3. Some young children who develop this fear are not prepared
    adequately before seeing a clown for the first time. C

4. Clowns, who usually wear heavy makeup and brightly colored wigs, do
    not look like ordinary people.

5. Clowns also make sudden movements that can frighten children. C

6. Most children who fear clowns will get over their phobia as they grow
    up. C

7. Those grown-ups, who may never love clowns, will still be able to
    tolerate having them around.

8. Many adults have seen movies that show clowns as evil killers. C

9. Few adults admit to having coulrophobia, which is most effectively
   treated when the sufferer confronts the fear.

10. Unlike some other phobias, which can trap people in their homes or
    make them unable to work, coulrophobia has little effect on most
    sufferers, who are not likely to meet clowns frequently in everyday life.

Other Uses for Commas

e Log in to
macmillanhighered
.com/realessays
Additional Grammar
Exercises > Other Uses
for Commas

COMMAS WITH QUOTATION MARKS

Quotation marks are used to show that you are using a direct quotation, repeating exactly what someone said or wrote. Generally, use commas to set off the words inside quotation marks from the rest of the sentence.

"Excuse me," said the old woman in back of me. "Did you know," she asked, "that you just cut in front of me?"

I exclaimed, "Oh, no. I'm so sorry!"

Notice that a comma never comes directly *after* a quotation mark.

For more on quotation
marks, see Chapter 37.

COMMAS IN ADDRESSES

Use commas to separate the elements of an address included in a sentence. However, do not use a comma before a zip code.

My address is 4498 Main Street, Bolton, Massachusetts 01740.

If a sentence continues after the address, put a comma after the address. Also, use a comma after individual elements used to name a geographical location such as a city and state.

The house was moved from Cripple Creek, Colorado, to the lot on Forest Street.

COMMAS IN DATES

Separate the day from the year with a comma. If you give only the month and year, do not separate them with a comma.

She wrote the letter on April 1, 2009.

The next session is in January 2011.

If a sentence continues after a date that includes the day, put a comma after the date.

He waited until April 15, 2010, to file his 2008 tax return.

COMMAS WITH DIRECT ADDRESS

Put commas before, after, or around the name or title of someone being addressed directly.

I want you to come look at this, Don.

Don, I want you to come look at this.

Unfortunately, Professor, I cannot finish the report by next week.

COMMAS WITH *YES* OR *NO*

Put a comma after the word *yes* or *no* in response to a question.

No, that isn't what I meant.

[To express a strong emotion, an exclamation mark is sometimes used instead of a comma: *No! That is not what I meant.* A word or phrase that expresses emotion and stands alone (like *No!*) is called an interjection.]

PRACTICE 6   Using commas

Edit the following sentences by adding commas where they are needed. If a sentence is already correct, put a "C" next to it.

Example: Strict telemarketing laws took effect on April 1, 2001.

1. My sister asked, "James, do you get a lot of telemarketing calls?"

2. "Yes, I do," I replied, "and they always come at dinnertime."

3. She told me that I could add my name to a list of those people not wanting calls from telemarketers. C

4. I wrote to the governor's office in Albany, New York, for information about the telemarketing registry.

5. My address, which is 21 Highland Road, Binghamton, New York 13901, has now been added to the state registry.

6. For a while, I still got occasional calls that began with an unfamiliar voice saying, "James, I have an exciting offer for you."

7. I simply replied, "No, I have news for you."

8. I pointed out that on August 11, 2010, I had added my name and address to a list of people who do not want to receive calls about exciting offers.

9. "As you probably know", I told my unwanted callers, "it is illegal for you
                ^   ^
   to contact me in this way."

10. The marketing calls had stopped completely by November 1. C

Editing Practice

Edit the following paragraphs by adding commas where they are needed.

Resources For cumulative Editing Review Tests, see pages 564–80.

> **EDITING REVIEW 1**   (17 commas)

1 Everyone who uses cleaning products at home has probably seen warning labels on those products, for most household cleaners contain harsh chemicals. 2 The warnings, which are required by law, are so common that many users probably ignore them. 3 However, all cleaning products should be used with care, and some of them can seriously injure children or anyone else who misuses them. 4 Drain cleaners, toilet bowl cleaners, and chlorine bleach can all cause serious damage to skin, eyes, and other sensitive tissue. 5 Glass cleaners can react with bleach to produce toxic fumes. 6 Alternative cleansers, nontoxic products that can be made from items in an average kitchen, are cheaper than brand-name cleaning products and usually work just as well. 7 For most cleaning jobs, a solution of vinegar and water or baking soda and water is effective. 8 A plunger can often fix a clogged drain as well as a drain cleaner can, and club soda cleans windows nicely. 9 As for air fresheners, one expert advises, "Open your windows." 10 Economy, efficiency, and safety are great reasons to choose homemade cleansers.

> **EDITING REVIEW 2**   (39 commas)

1 A few days ago, I received an e-mail that told a terrifying story. 2 At a large discount store in Austin, Texas, a four-year-old girl had disappeared, and her mother had asked for the store employees' help in finding the child. 3 Thinking quickly, the employees locked all of the doors, posted

an employee at every exit, and systematically searched the store. 4 The child, who was found in a bathroom, was safe, but half of her head had been shaved. 5 In addition, someone had changed her clothes, so it seemed obvious that an abductor had been trying to slip her out of the store unnoticed. 6 The e-mail message, which came from a distant acquaintance, ended by advising me, "Don't let your children out of your sight!"

7 Later that day, I was talking to my neighbor, and I happened to mention the message. 8 She too had seen it, and the story had shocked her. 9 Something about the story made me suspicious, however, so I decided to do some Internet research. 10 I found a site that discussed urban legends, Internet hoaxes, and chain letters. 11 On the site, I discovered an exact copy of the e-mail I had received. 12 I also learned that my neighbor and I were not the first people to fall for this hoax, for Ann Landers had even printed a version of it years earlier. 13 When she learned that she had been fooled, she printed a retraction, a column explaining that the story was fictional. 14 A reader wrote to her and said, "Reminding people to be cautious is one thing. Scaring them is another."

15 After doing the research, I felt better about the scary e-mail story, but I felt sad that we are so distrustful of one another. 16 Such stories can make us fear that potential abductors are everywhere. 17 Thirty years ago, most parents were not usually afraid to let children walk to school alone or play outside, but today's parents rarely let children out of their sight until the kids are in their teens. 18 The difference is not in the number of abductions of children, a very small number that has remained nearly constant over the decades. 19 No, the difference is that people now hear about these unusual and terrifying instances over and over. 20 Eventually, they reach the conclusion that these stories must be true, and they are convinced that such dreadful things must happen frequently. 21 The e-mail I had received was contributing, I decided, to this climate of irrational fear. 22 "Ann Landers's reader was right," I said to myself. 23 "We should teach our children caution,

but we can harm them and ourselves by making them believe that evil

strangers are lurking around every corner."

| PRACTICE 7 | **Editing your own writing for commas** |

As a final practice, edit a piece of your own writing for commas. It can be a paper you are working on for this course, a paper you have already finished, a paper for another course, or a recent piece of writing from your work or everyday life.

Teamwork Put students in small groups, and give each group one paragraph to edit. Then, have a member of each group read the edited paragraph aloud.

36

Apostrophes

⊟ Log in to
macmillanhighered
.com/realessays
LearningCurve >
Apostrophes; **Additional
Grammar Exercises** >
Using Apostrophes to
Show Ownership

Understand What Apostrophes Do

An **apostrophe** (') is a punctuation mark that either shows ownership (*Susan's book*) or indicates that a letter has been intentionally left out to form a contraction (*I'm, that's, they're*). Although an apostrophe looks like a comma (,), it is not used for the same purpose, and it is written higher on the line than a commas is.

apostrophe'   comma,

Practice Using Apostrophes Correctly

Apostrophes to Show Ownership

To understand this
chapter, you need to
know what nouns and
pronouns are. For a
review, see Chapters 21,
26, and 32.

- **Add 's to a singular noun to show ownership. Add the 's even if the noun already ends in *s*.**

  Darcy's car is being repaired.

  Joan fixed the mechanical problem with the bus's steering wheel.

- **If a noun is plural and ends in *s*, just add an apostrophe to show ownership. If it is plural but does not end in *s*, add 's.**

  Seven boys' coats were left at the school.

  The children's toys were all broken.

- **The placement of an apostrophe makes a difference in meaning.**

  My neighbor's twelve cats are howling. [One neighbor who has twelve cats]

My neighbors' twelve cats are howling. [Two or more neighbors who together have twelve cats]

- **Do not use an apostrophe to form the plural of a noun.**

Use the stair's or the elevator.

- **Do not use an apostrophe with a possessive pronoun. These pronouns already show ownership (possession).**

That basket is our's.

Possessive Pronouns

my	his	its	their
mine	her	our	theirs
your	hers	ours	whose
yours			

Its or *It's*

The single most common error with apostrophes and pronouns is confusing *its* (a possessive pronoun) with *it's* (a contraction meaning "it is"). Whenever you write *it's*, test to see whether it's correct by reading it aloud as *it is*.

PRACTICE 1   **Using apostrophes to show ownership**

Edit the following sentences by adding 's or an apostrophe alone to show ownership and by crossing out any incorrect use of an apostrophe or 's.

Example: ~~Fever's~~ *Fevers* are an important part of the human ~~bodys~~ *body's* system of defense against infection.

1. A ~~thermometers~~ *thermometer's* indicator mark at 98.6 degrees Fahrenheit is supposed to show a ~~persons~~ *person's* normal body temperature.

2. However, normal body temperature can range from 97.0 to 100.4 degrees, so most ~~doctors~~ *doctors'* view of a temperature lower than 100.5 is that ~~its~~ *it's* not a fever at all.

3. ~~Fever's~~ *Fevers* help the body combat ~~virus's~~ *viruses* and stimulate the immune
   system.

4. Unless a ~~persons~~ *person's* temperature is raised by an outside source, the
   ~~bodys~~ *body's* regulatory system will not usually let a fever go higher than
   106 degrees.

5. A ~~fevers~~ *fever's* appearance is not necessarily a reason to take fever-
   reducing ~~medication's~~ *medications*, which can lower a ~~bodys~~ *body's* temperature
   without doing anything to fight the infection.

6. Taking fever-reducing ~~drug's~~ *drugs* can actually make an illness take
   longer to run ~~it's~~ *its* course.

7. Many ~~doctors'~~ *doctors* do not recommend using any drugs to treat a fever if ~~its~~ *it's*
   lower than 102 degrees.

8. Parents should know that ~~childrens~~ *children's* fevers can go higher than ~~their's~~ *theirs*.

9. Some ~~parents~~ *parents'* fears of fever are so intense that they suffer from
   "fever phobia" and overreact to their ~~childrens'~~ *children's* symptoms.

10. Fever phobia can cause ~~parent's~~ *parents* to give their child extra medicine,
    but overdoses of ibuprofen and other fever reducers can impair the
    ~~livers'~~ *liver's* ability to work properly and can therefore complicate the ~~childs~~ *child's*
    sickness.

Apostrophes in Contractions

A **contraction** is formed by joining two words and leaving out one or more of the
letters. When writing a contraction, put an apostrophe where the letter or letters
have been left out, not between the two words.

   Note: In academic writing, contractions are rarely used.

I'll go when you come back. = *I will* go when you come back.

Be sure to put the apostrophe in the right place.

Don does'n't work here anymore.

Common Contractions

aren't = are not

can't = cannot

couldn't = could not

didn't = did not

doesn't = does not

don't = do not

he'd = he would, he had

he'll = he will

he's = he is, he has

I'd = I would, I had

I'll = I will

I'm = I am

I've = I have

isn't = is not

it's = it is, it has

let's = let us

she'd = she would, she had

she'll = she will

she's = she is, she has

there's = there is, there has

they'd = they would, they had

they'll = they will

they're = they are

they've = they have

who'd = who would, who had

who'll = who will

who's = who is, who has

won't = will not

wouldn't = would not

you'd = you would, you had

you'll = you will

you're = you are

you've = you have

Do not use contractions in papers or reports for college or work unless your instructor or boss specifically allows them.

 Language note: Contractions that include a *be* verb cannot be followed by the base verb or the helping verbs *can, does,* or *has.*

Incorrect   She's *work* late. Dan's *has* sick.

Correct   She's *working* late. Dan's sick.

PRACTICE 2   **Using apostrophes in contractions**

Read each sentence carefully, looking for any words that have missing letters. Edit these words by adding apostrophes where needed. Or, if apostrophes are misplaced, cross out and correct the error.

It's
Example: ~~Its~~ sadly true that some athletes will use performance-
⌃
enhancing drugs if they can get away with it.

they're
1. Those who do often say ~~theyre~~ using these drugs because their com-
⌃
petitors are probably using them, too.

2. Performance-enhancing drugs help some athletes win competitions,
   but for other athletes these drugs ~~arent~~ _aren't_ enough to ensure victory.

3. Most athletes taking steroids and other substances say they ~~would'nt~~ _wouldn't_
   use these drugs if they could be certain that their opponents ~~are'nt~~ _aren't_
   using them.

4. ~~Wholl~~ _Who'll_ be the one to put a stop to this drug use?

5. If sports organizations ~~do'nt~~ _don't_ eliminate drug use, we all know ~~whos~~ _who's_ the
   loser.

6. ~~Youre~~ _You're_ the loser, ~~Im~~ _I'm_ the loser, and all athletes are the losers.

7. When even one athlete gets away with using drugs, we ~~ca'nt~~ _can't_ trust that
   any athletic competition has been won fairly.

8. ~~Youve~~ _You've_ got to take a stand, ~~Ive~~ _I've_ got to take a stand, and anyone who believes in fairness has got to take a stand.

9. ~~Lets~~ _Let's_ eliminate performance-enhancing drugs now.

10. If we all ~~are'nt~~ _aren't_ ready to unite against drug use in sports, we might as
    well change the word _athlete_ to _actor_.

Apostrophes with Letters, Numbers, and Time

- **Use 's to make letters and numbers plural. The apostrophe prevents
  confusion or misreading.**

  Mississippi has four i's.

  In women's shoes, size 8's are more common than size 10's.

- **Use an apostrophe or 's in certain expressions in which time nouns are
  treated as if they possess something.**

  I get two weeks' vacation next year.

  Last year's prices were very good.

> **PRACTICE 3**   Using apostrophes with letters,
> numbers, and time

Edit the following sentences by adding apostrophes where needed and fix-
ing incorrectly used apostrophes.

Example: I just updated my blog by entering the last three *week's* worth

of entries.

[weeks']

1. Next ~~months~~ schedule is less busy, so I think I'll be able to keep my

    blog current then.

    [month's]

2. Arthur's blog offers an entire ~~winters~~ worth of detail on his social life.

    [winter's]

3. His blog is a little hard to read because he always leaves out certain let-

    ters, such as ~~as~~, ~~es~~, and ~~os~~.

    [a's   e's   o's]

4. Katie's blog also gets confusing when she puts all of her 4s and 8s in

    Roman numerals.

    [4's   8's]

5. When Manny's computer was stolen, he lost notes for his blog and two

    ~~year's~~ work on his novel.

    [years']

Editing Practice

Edit the following paragraphs by adding apostrophes where needed and crossing out incorrectly used apostrophes. In order to practice editing in professional and academic situations, some sentences will contain contractions that need to be corrected. If a sentence is already correct, put a "C" after it.

Resources For cumulative Editing Review Tests, see pages 564–80.

EDITING REVIEW 1   (15 errors)

1 Some of the first ~~discussion's~~ of global warming focused attention

[discussions]

on one of the gases that contributes to the greenhouse effect: methane.

2 Like other greenhouse gases, methane helps to keep the ~~earths'~~ heat

[earth's]

trapped in our atmosphere, and the temperature of the earth goes up as

a result. 3 Humans ~~are'nt~~ the only producers of methane; ~~its~~ also a by-

[aren't]   [it's]

product of ~~cow's~~ digestion of their food. 4 For a while, many ~~Americans~~

[cows']   [Americans']

knowledge of global warming ~~didnt~~ go much further than cow jokes. 5 As

[didn't]

~~scientists'~~ have become more convinced that global warming is real and

[scientists]

a potential threat to ~~human's~~, our knowledge of the causes of the green-

[humans]

house effect has expanded. 6 Cows ~~arent~~ completely off the hook, but

[aren't]

~~theyre~~ far less guilty of contributing to global warming than humans

[they're]

and cars are. 7 The amount of methane produced by ~~cows'~~ _cows_ adds up to about

3 percent of the total amount of greenhouse gases produced by people.
8 Getting a cow to change ~~it's~~ _its_ diet ~~wo'nt~~ _won't_ solve the ~~worlds~~ _world's_ warming

problem.

EDITING REVIEW 2   (13 errors)

1 In March 2001, the keyless entry systems of cars in Bremerton,

Washington, suddenly stopped working, and still no one knows why. C
2 The ~~cars~~ _cars'_ locks were supposed to respond when their ~~owner's~~ _owners_

pushed a button, and all at once they ~~wouldnt~~ _wouldn't_. 3 After a few ~~days~~ _days'_ wait, the

entry systems began functioning again. 4 Many ~~resident's~~ _residents_ of Bremerton, the

home of a Navy shipyard, were convinced that the ~~militarys~~ _military's_ technological

activity had affected the locks, but Navy ~~official's~~ _officials_ denied it. 5 Other people

wondered if radio transmissions might have jammed the frequency and

prevented the keyless ~~systems'~~ _systems_ from functioning. 6 Fortunately, people

whose cars had keyless entry systems ~~were'nt~~ _weren't_ locked out for those days.

7 These owners simply resorted to a backup system to open and lock

their ~~car's~~ _cars_—~~its~~ _it's_ called a "key." 8 To this day, the mystery ~~remain's~~ _remains_

unsolved and still happens occasionally in Bremerton and other ~~place's~~ _places_.

PRACTICE 4   **Editing your own writing for apostrophes**

As a final practice, edit a piece of your own writing for apostrophes. It can
be a paper you are working on for this course, a paper you have already
finished, a paper for another course, or a recent piece of writing from your
work or everyday life.

37

Quotation Marks " "

Understand What Quotation Marks Do

Quotation marks (" ") are punctuation marks with two common uses in college writing: They are used with direct quotations, and they are used to set off titles of short works. They always appear in pairs.

A **quotation** is the report of another person's words. There are two types of quotations: **direct quotations** (the exact repetition, word for word, of what someone said or wrote) and **indirect quotations** (a restatement of what someone said or wrote, not word for word). Quotation marks are used only for direct quotations.

To understand this chapter, you need to know what a sentence is. For a review, see Chapter 21.

Direct quotation	George said, "I'm getting a haircut."
Indirect quotation	George said that he was getting a haircut.

Practice Using Quotation Marks Correctly

Quotation Marks for Direct Quotations

When you write a direct quotation, you need to use quotation marks around the quoted words. These marks tell readers that the words used are exactly what was said or written.

Quoted words are usually combined with words that identify who is speaking. The identifying words can come after the quoted words, before them, or in the middle. Here are some guidelines for capitalization and punctuation.

e Log in to macmillanhighered .com/realessays **Additional Grammar Exercises** > Using Quotation Marks for Direct Quotations and Certain Titles

- Capitalize the first letter in a complete sentence that's being quoted, even if it comes after some identifying words.

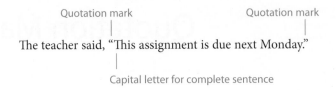

Quotation mark   Quotation mark

The teacher said, "This assignment is due next Monday."

Capital letter for complete sentence

- Do not capitalize the first letter in a quotation if it is not the first word in the complete sentence.

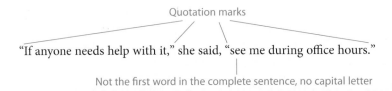

Quotation marks

"If anyone needs help with it," she said, "see me during office hours."

Not the first word in the complete sentence, no capital letter

- If it is a complete sentence and its source is clear, you can let a quotation stand on its own, without any identifying words.

Speaker (teacher) known

"My office hours are on the first page of your syllabus."

- Attach identifying words to a quotation with a comma; these identifying words cannot be a sentence on their own.

Identifying words attached with comma

A student asked, "May we e-mail questions?"

- Always put quotation marks *after* commas and periods. Put quotation marks after question marks and exclamation points if they are part of the quoted sentence.

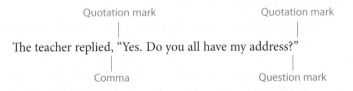

Quotation mark   Quotation mark

The teacher replied, "Yes. Do you all have my address?"

Comma   Question mark

- If a question mark or exclamation point is part of your own sentence, put it after the quotation mark.

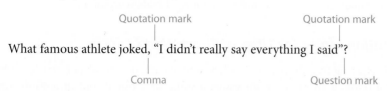

Quotation mark   Quotation mark

What famous athlete joked, "I didn't really say everything I said"?

Comma   Question mark

When you quote the exact words of an outside source in a paper, use quotation marks. You also need to cite, or give credit to, the source.

The government needs to ensure that when a company fails, employees' pensions are protected. An article in the *Boston Globe* reported, "When Polaroid collapsed, pension funds and employee stock programs were suddenly worthless. At the same time, however, the chief financial officer walked away with a package worth more than $2 million" (Richardson B3).

SETTING OFF A QUOTATION WITHIN ANOTHER QUOTATION

Sometimes you may directly quote someone who quotes what someone else said or wrote. Put **single quotation marks** (' ') around the quotation within a quotation so that readers understand who said what.

The student handbook reads, "Students must be given the opportunity to make up work missed for excused absences."

Terry told his instructor, "I'm sorry I missed the exam, but I would like to take a makeup exam. According to our student handbook, 'Students must be given the opportunity to make up work missed for excused absences,' and I have a good reason."

Terry's entire quotation

Here, Terry is quoting from the student handbook.

No Quotation Marks for Indirect Quotations

When you report what someone said or wrote but do not use the person's exact words, you are writing an indirect quotation. Do not use quotation marks for indirect quotations. Indirect quotations often begin with the word *that*.

Indirect quotation	Sophie said that the exam was postponed.
Direct quotation	Sophie said, "The exam was postponed."

Teaching tip As you read each of these guidelines, put a sentence on the board that should have quotation marks in it somewhere. Ask students where the quotation marks should go and which letters should be capitalized.

For more on commas with quotation marks, see page 535.

For information about how to use quotations in research papers, see Chapter 20.

For more on citing and documenting sources, see pages 296–302.

Teamwork Ask students to pair off, interview each other on a predetermined topic, and then write a one-paragraph report that includes at least one direct quotation and one indirect quotation. Photocopy several of these reports to use for a whole-class workshop on quotation marks.

| Indirect quotation | Carolyn told me that she had an accident. |
| Direct quotation | Carolyn told me, "I had an accident." |

Quotation Marks for Titles of Short Works

e Log in to
macmillanhighered
.com/realessays
**Additional Grammar
Exercises** > Punctuating
Direct and Indirect
Quotations
> Using Quotation Marks
for Titles

When referring to a short work such as a magazine or newspaper article, a chapter in a book, a short story, an essay, a song, or a poem, put quotation marks around the title of the work.

Newspaper article	"Mayor Warns of Budget Cuts"
Short story	"Everyday Use"
Essay	"Mother Tongue"

Usually, titles of longer works—such as novels, books, magazines, newspapers, movies, television programs, and CDs—are italicized. The titles of sacred books such as the Bible or the Koran are neither italicized nor surrounded by quotation marks. Typically, you will be writing papers on computers and will be able to use italics for longer titles; however, if you are writing a paper by hand or making corrections by hand, you should underline a title to indicate italics.

| Book | *The Chocolate War* |
| Newspaper | the *Washington Post* |

[Do not italicize or capitalize the word *the* before the name of a newspaper or magazine, even if it is part of the title. But do capitalize *The* when it is the first word in titles of books, movies, and other sources.]

If you are writing a paper with many outside sources, your instructor will probably refer you to a particular system of citing sources. Follow that system's guidelines when you use titles in your paper.

Note: When you write a paper, do not put quotation marks around the title.

Resources For
cumulative Editing
Review Tests, see pages
564–80.

Editing Practice

Edit the following paragraphs by adding quotation marks where needed and crossing out any incorrectly used quotation marks. Underline any book, magazine, or newspaper titles. Correct any errors in punctuation.

EDITING REVIEW 1   (17 errors)

1 "Here is one I've loved for years," said Evi as she held up a CD called "Kind of Blue" by the "jazz trumpeter" Miles Davis. 2 Charlie, who was also flipping through the jazz CDs, said that "he had gone through a Miles Davis phase but wasn't so interested in Miles's music now." 3 Shortly after they moved into the main section of the store, Charlie pulled out a book and opened it to an essay titled ~~Shooting an Elephant.~~ *"Shooting an Elephant."* 4 "Reading this had a big effect on me," he said, adding that "he eventually read most of what George Orwell had written." 5 They were browsing through the rows of books when Evi stopped and said, ~~this~~ *"This* is what led me to read all of Dylan Thomas's poetry." 6 Taking a book from the shelf, she opened it to a poem titled "Do Not Go Gentle into That Good Night," noting that "~~It~~ *it* was written for Thomas's dying father." 7 Pointing to a line in the poem, she said, ~~when~~ *"When* Thomas writes 'Rage, rage against the dying of the light,' he is talking to his father, to himself, and to me, bringing all of us into that special moment." 8 They continued on silently until Charlie exclaimed, ~~look~~ *"Look* at this—a book about the making of the Beatles' album Sgt. Pepper's Lonely Hearts Club Band!" 9 Evi reached for another copy of the book, saying that "her father had introduced her to the Beatles' music when she was ten and that it had been one of her favorite albums ever since." 10 Charlie picked up a copy of "Rolling Stone magazine" as they walked to the checkout counter, and he said, ~~a~~ *"A* trip to the bookstore turned out to be a lot more fun than I thought it would be."

EDITING REVIEW 2   (18 errors)

1 "Did you know that people our age could experience a life crisis"? my twenty-five-year-old friend Beth asked as we browsed at the newsstand. 2 She showed me an article called "The Trouble with Being 25" in a magazine she was looking at.

3 I told her that "she was crazy." 4 "You wait until midlife for your crisis, silly," I said. 5 I was imagining a middle-aged businessman suddenly buying an expensive sports car and driving around listening to Prince singing "Little Red Corvette."

6 Beth pointed out that she had plenty of anxiety about being twenty-five. 7 "It's as if people look at me and think I'm still basically a teenager, yet I have a grown-up job and grown-up responsibilities to go with it," she said.

8 I asked her "what kinds of responsibilities she was talking about."

9 "I have rent and bills to pay," she said, "and I'm trying to decide if I should take a couple of classes at night to get a better job." 10 She thought for a moment and then added, "And sooner or later I'll need to figure out whether I want to get married and have children." 11 She picked up a newspaper and idly turned the pages until she found a headline that read, "Confusion Reigns among Young Singles."

12 "Wow! You're right!" I blurted out. 13 "It's a good thing you read those stupid magazines," I said to Beth. 14 I was only partly kidding when I added that "she and I would never have realized that we were supposed to be having a crisis if we hadn't read about it."

15 "Let's do something to celebrate," said Beth. 16 That's why we spent the rest of the afternoon sitting around my kitchen table drinking coffee, listening to Beck singing "Loser," and reading out loud to each other from "How to Tell If You're Ready to Settle Down" in the new issue of Cosmopolitan.

> **PRACTICE**   **Editing your own writing for quotation marks**

As a final practice, edit a piece of your own writing for quotation marks. It can be a paper you are working on for this course, a paper you have already finished, a paper for another course, or a recent piece of writing from your work or everyday life.

38

Other Punctuation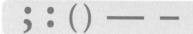

Understand What Punctuation Does

Punctuation helps readers understand your writing. If you use punctuation incorrectly, you send readers a confusing message—or, even worse, a wrong one. This chapter covers five marks of punctuation that people sometimes use incorrectly. Knowing what these marks do in a sentence can help you avoid such mistakes.

To understand this chapter, you need to know what sentences and independent clauses are. For a review, see Chapters 21 and 23.

Semicolon ;	Joins two independent clauses into one sentence
	Separates complete items in a list that already has commas within individual items
Colon :	Introduces a list
	Announces an explanation or example
Parentheses ( )	Set off extra information that is not essential to the sentence
Dash —	Sets off words for emphasis
	Indicates a pause
Hyphen -	Joins two or more words that together form a single description
	Shows a word break at the end of a line

Practice Using Punctuation Correctly

Semicolon ;

SEMICOLONS TO JOIN INDEPENDENT CLAUSES (SENTENCES)

Teaching tip Caution students not to use semicolons as a default solution when trying to increase sentence complexity; overuse and misuse are common.

Use a semicolon to join very closely related sentences and make them into one sentence.

> In an interview, hold your head up and don't slouch; it is important to look alert.

> Make good eye contact; looking down is not appropriate in an interview.

> 🌐 Language note: Do not use a comma instead of a semicolon to join two independent clauses; that would create a run-on (see Chapter 23).

SEMICOLONS WHEN ITEMS IN A SERIES CONTAIN COMMAS

For more on using semicolons to join sentences, see Chapter 29.

Use a semicolon to separate list items that themselves contain commas. Otherwise, it is difficult for readers to tell where one item ends and another begins.

> I have a cousin who lives in Devon, England; another cousin who lives in Derry, New Hampshire; and a third cousin who lives in Freeport, Maine.

Teaching tip After each of the explanations and examples in this chapter, ask students to write examples of their own.

Colon :

COLONS BEFORE LISTS

Use a colon to introduce a list after an independent clause.

> In the United States, three ice cream flavors are the most popular: vanilla, chocolate, and strawberry.

COLONS BEFORE EXPLANATIONS OR EXAMPLES

Use a colon after an independent clause to let readers know that you are about to provide an explanation or example of what you just wrote.

If the explanation or example is also an independent clause, some instructors and style guides may prefer that you capitalize the first letter after the colon; others may not.

> I use one criterion to choose a cereal: price.

> Sometimes, the choice of cereals is overwhelming: My supermarket carries at least five different types of raisin bran.

> OR:
> Sometimes, the choice of cereals is overwhelming: my supermarket carries at least five different types of raisin bran.

Note: A colon in a sentence must follow an independent clause. A common misuse is to place a colon after a phrase instead of an independent clause. Watch out especially for colons following the phrases *such as* or *for example*.

An independent clause contains a subject and a verb, and it expresses a complete thought. It can stand on its own as a sentence.

Incorrect	The resort offers many activities, such as: snorkeling, golf, and windsurfing.
Correct	The resort offers many activities: snorkeling, golf, and windsurfing.
Correct	The resort offers many activities, such as snorkeling, golf, and windsurfing.
Incorrect	Suzy has many talents. For example: writing, drawing, and painting.
Correct	Suzy has many talents: writing, drawing, and painting.

Teaching tip It may help students to think of the colon as a spotlight, especially in sentences where an example follows the colon (*The plan has one major problem: cost*).

COLONS IN BUSINESS CORRESPONDENCE

Use a colon after a greeting (called a *salutation*) in a business letter and after the standard heading lines at the beginning of a memorandum.

Dear Mr. Latimer:

To: Craig Kleinman

From: Susan Anker

Parentheses ( )

Use two parentheses to set off information that is not essential to the meaning of a sentence. Parentheses are always used in pairs and should be used sparingly.

My grandfather's most successful invention (his first) was the electric blanket.

My worst habit (and also the hardest to break) is interrupting.

Teaching tip Have students find examples of the overuse of parentheses from newspapers, magazines, or Web sites; edit these as a class.

Dash —

Use dashes as you use parentheses: to set off additional information, particularly information that you want to emphasize.

The essay question — worth 50 percent of the whole exam — will be open book.

Your answers should be well developed, and points—2 per error—will be deducted for major grammar mistakes.

A dash can also indicate a pause. It usually indicates a stronger pause than a comma does.

My son wants to buy a car—if he can find an affordable one.

Make a dash by typing two hyphens together. Some word processing programs also allow you to choose the dash from a menu of symbols or by using a keyboard shortcut. Do not leave any extra spaces around a dash.

Hyphen -

HYPHENS TO JOIN ADJECTIVES THAT FORM A SINGLE DESCRIPTION

Use a hyphen to join adjectives that together form a single description of a person, place, or thing.

The eighty-year-old smoker was considered a high-risk patient.

I followed the company's decision-making procedure.

HYPHENS WITH COMPOUND NUMBERS

Use a hyphen to spell out any number between twenty-one and ninety-nine.

HYPHENS WITH PREFIXES AND SUFFIXES

Use a hyphen with the following prefixes:

Ex-

Ex-athlete

Ex-student

Self-

Self-assured

Self-esteem

All-

All-encompassing

All-knowing

If you are unsure about whether or how to hyphenate a word or phrase, consult a dictionary or your instructor.

Use a hyphen with the following suffix:

-elect

> President-elect

HYPHENS IN OTHER SITUATIONS

Use a hyphen with numerical figures, and between a prefix and capital word:

> pre-2001

> anti-American

If you are not sure where to break a word, look it up in a dictionary. The word's main entry will show you where you can break the word: *dic • tio • nary*.

Editing Practice

Edit the following paragraphs by adding semicolons, colons, parentheses, dashes, and hyphens where needed. Keep in mind that more than one type of punctuation may be acceptable in some places. *Answers may vary. Possible edits shown.*

Resources For cumulative Editing Review Tests, see pages 564–80.

> **EDITING REVIEW**   (14 errors)
>
> 1 To avoid predators, many butterflies and moths randomly change directions as they fly about, but this is not their only strategy they also display striking colors like radiant and shiny reds, oranges, and blues and camouflage themselves in effective disguises. 2 For example, some butterflies have streaks composed of many dazzling colors across their wings to emphasize the speed of their flight sending a message that they're hard to catch. 3 Other butterflies use bold, attention-getting color patterns to signal that they are poisonous to eat Some are truly poisonous, and some are faking. 4 There are also species that attempt to look distasteful by imitating something that is not nutritious a bit of bird dropping, a dead leaf, or rotting vegetation. 5 One moth, *Oxytenis modestia,* is especially enterprising in its disguises In its first four caterpillar stages it looks like a bird dropping,

even including fake seeds⌃; the fifth stage imitates a green snake with a large

fake head and two fake eyes⌃; and the adult *Oxytenis* moth looks like a leaf

and, because it breeds twice a year, mimics the appropriate leaf for the

season. 6 *Oxytenis* moths that hatch in the dry season look like dry dead

leaves⌃; those hatching in the rainy season look dark and moldy. 7 Several

butterflies combine camouflage with eyecatching⌃- display⌃; for example,

Pieria helvetia has front wings that are bland and dull, but its hind wings

are bright red. 8 When it is resting, its wings are closed, and it can hardly be

seen, but when a predator threatens, it bursts into rapid, dramatic flight⌃— its

red patches make it conspicuously visible. 9 However, then it suddenly sets

down again, folds its wings in, and seemingly disappears⌃— a clever magic

act. 10 Birds and monkeys do their best to see past these disguises because,

according to one researcher⌃(one who will do anything for his research⌃,)

moths taste something like raw shrimp.

| PRACTICE | **Editing your own writing for other punctuation marks** |

Edit a piece of your own writing for semicolons, colons, parentheses, dashes, and hyphens. It can be a paper you are working on for this course, a paper you have already finished, a paper for another course, or a piece of writing from your work or everyday life. You may want to try more than one way to use these marks of punctuation in your writing.

39

Capitalization
Using Capital Letters

Understand Capitalization

There are three basic rules of capitalization: Capitalize the first letter of

- every new sentence.
- names of specific people, places, dates, and things.
- important words in titles.

If you can remember these three rules, you will avoid the most common errors in capitalization.

Teaching tip Remind students that their papers should not be written in all-capital letters.

Practice Capitalization

Capitalization of Sentences

Capitalize the first letter in each new sentence, including the first word in a direct quotation.

> Mary was surprised when she saw all the people.

> She asked, "What's going on here?"

e Log in to **macmillanhighered .com/realessays** **LearningCurve** > Capitalization; **Additional Grammar Exercises** > Capitalizing

Capitalization of Names of Specific People, Places, Dates, and Things

Capitalize the first letter in names of specific people, places, dates, and things. Do not capitalize general words such as *college* as opposed to the specific name: *Lincoln College*. Look at the examples for each group.

PEOPLE

Capitalize the first letter in names of specific people and in titles used with names of specific people.

Specific	Not specific
Carol Schopfer	my friend
Dr. D'Ambrosio	the physician
Professor Shute	your professor
Aunt Jane, Mother	my aunt, my mother

The name of a family member is capitalized when the family member is being addressed directly or when the family title is standing in for a first name.

Good to see you, Dad.   Mother is taking classes.

In other instances, do not capitalize.

It is my father's birthday.   My mother is taking classes.

PLACES

Capitalize the first letter in names of specific buildings, streets, cities, states, regions, and countries.

Specific	Not specific
Bolton Police Department	the police department
Washington Street	our street
Boston, Massachusetts	my hometown
Texas	this state
the West	the western part of the country
Italy	that country

Do not capitalize directions in a sentence: *Drive south for five blocks.*

DATES

Capitalize the first letter in the names of days, months, and holidays. Do not capitalize the names of the seasons (winter, spring, summer, fall).

Specific	Not specific
Monday	today
January 4	winter
Presidents' Day	my birthday

Language note: The first letter of all days, months, and proper names is capitalized.

Today is Tuesday, March 10.

ORGANIZATIONS, COMPANIES, AND GROUPS

Specific	Not specific
Santa Monica College	my college
Best Buy	the electronics store
Merrimack Players	the theater group

LANGUAGES, NATIONALITIES, AND RELIGIONS

Specific	Not specific
English, Greek, Spanish	my first language
Christianity, Buddhism	your religion

 Language note: The first letter of all languages and nationalities is capitalized.

Gina speaks Italian, but she is Chinese.

COURSES

Specific	Not specific
Nutrition 100	the basic nutrition course

COMMERCIAL PRODUCTS

Specific	Not specific
Diet Coke	a diet cola

The names of languages should be capitalized even if you are not referring to a specific course: *I am taking nutrition and Spanish.*

Capitalization of Titles

Capitalize the first word and all other important words in titles of books, movies, television programs, magazines, newspapers, articles, stories, songs, papers, poems, legislation, and so on. Words that do not need to be capitalized (unless they are the first word) include articles (*the, a, an*); coordinating conjunctions (*and, but, for, nor, or, so, yet*); and prepositions.

For more on punctuating titles, see page 550. For a list of common prepositions, see page 317.

American Idol is a popular television program.

Newsweek and *Time* often have similar cover stories.

"Once More to the Lake" is one of Chuck's favorite essays.

Editing Practice

Resources For cumulative Editing Review Tests, see pages 564–80.

Edit the following paragraphs by capitalizing as needed and removing any unnecessary capitalization.

> **EDITING REVIEW**   (88 errors)
>
> 1 In Robert Louis Stevenson's 1886 novella "the strange case of dr. jekyll and mr. hyde," a doctor uses himself as the subject of an experiment and the results are disastrous. 2 The novella was a great success, but stevenson didn't originate the idea of doctors experimenting on themselves.
>
> 3 one of the earliest known examples of self-experimentation goes back to the sixteenth century, when santorio santorio, of padua, italy, weighed himself every day for thirty years. 4 By weighing everything he ate and drank as well as his bodily discharges, Santorio discovered that the human body continually and imperceptibly loses large amounts of fluid. 5 today, that loss, called *insensible perspiration*, is routinely measured in hospital patients.
>
> 6 A key breakthrough to the modern age of cardiology was made in 1929 by a german, dr. werner forssmann, who as a surgical resident at a medical facility called the august victoria home, near berlin, conducted a daring self-experiment by inserting a thin tube into one of his veins and slid the tube into his own heart. 7 This idea was later developed by other researchers into the technique of cardiac catheterization. 8 Dr. forssmann, who used catheters on himself nine times, shared a nobel prize in 1956 for his pioneering experiments.
>
> 9 An important innovation in anesthesia occurred when a dentist in connecticut, Horace wells, watched a demonstration in which a volunteer inhaled nitrous oxide, cut his own leg, and felt no pain until the effects of the gas wore off. 10 dr. wells then had one of his own teeth extracted after he had inhaled the chemical, which people later

commonly called Laughing Gas. 11 He was amazed to have no Pain during
his extraction, declaring, "it is the greatest discovery ever made." 12 Others'
self-experimentation later aided the Development of ether, chloroform,
and additional Anesthetics.

13 In Medical circles, many people believe that major walter reed
experimented on himself in the early 1900s as the Leader of the group
in cuba that discovered that Mosquitoes transmit yellow fever. 14 In
fact, Dr. reed said he would allow mosquitoes to infect him to test the
Theory, but he returned to the united states before this was done.
15 Instead, other Members of his Team conducted the mosquito experiment on themselves, with one dying and another barely surviving. 16 after
these self-experimenters proved the crucial Connection between mosquitoes and yellow fever, dr. reed returned to Cuba, but he never did perform
the experiment on himself.

| PRACTICE | Editing your own writing for capitalization

Edit a piece of your own writing for capitalization. It can be a paper for this
course, a paper for another course, or a recent piece of writing from your
work or everyday life.

Editing Review Test 1

The Four Most Serious Errors (Chapters 21–25)

Directions: Each of the underlined word groups contains one or more errors. As you identify each error, write in the space the number of the word group containing the error. Then, edit the underlined word groups to correct the errors. If you need help, turn back to the chapters indicated above. *Answers may vary. Possible edits shown.*

Two fragments _3, 13_____

Two run-ons _1, 10_____

Two verb problems _5, 9_____

Four subject-verb
agreement errors _1, 7, 14, 15_____

              and

1 One opponent faces the other, during their personal battle nobody else in the universe

exists

~~exist.~~ 2 An attack prompts an immediate defense, often followed by a counterattack. ~~3 Starting~~

          , starting

~~the cycle again.~~ 4 In an age of precision-guided pilotless missiles and laser weapons, there would

                          has

seem to be no place for fencing. 5 Yet in recent years, fencing ~~had~~ been experiencing a surge

in popularity among women and men of all ages. 6 That is partly because, with training and

dedicated practice, even someone who is elderly or not adept at other sports can often learn to

hold his or her own quite well in a fencing encounter.

     7 Most beginning fencers are equipped with a training sword and protective equipment that

includes

~~include~~ a glove, a face mask, knee socks, knickers, and a special gray jacket. 8 The jacket is woven

                                is

with wire mesh for use with an electronic scoreboard. 9 At the tip of the sword ~~will be~~ a button

                        and

instead of a sharp point. 10 This is for safety, it is also useful for keeping track of valid hits.

11 When the button contacts a valid target on the jacket of an opponent, an electric signal

courses through the sword to a wire in the attacker's hand guard. 12 From the hand guard, the

wire runs to the back of the fencer's jacket and then up to an apparatus mounted on the ceiling

                    , causing

where the hit is registered. ~~13 Causing~~ a red light to go on. 14 In a typical match, the first fencer

                    wins.   *provides*

to score five valid hits on an opponent ~~win.~~ 15 All in all, fencing ~~provide~~ strenuous exercise,

competition, excitement, and a never-ending challenge.

Editing Review Test 2
The Four Most Serious Errors (Chapters 21–25)

Directions: Each of the underlined word groups contains one or more errors. As you identify each error, write in the space the number of the word group containing the error. Then, edit the underlined word groups to correct the errors. If you need help, turn back to the chapters indicated above. *Answers may vary. Possible edits shown.*

Two fragments _10, 17_____ Two verb problems _5, 11_____

Two run-ons _1, 3_____ Four subject-verb
agreement errors _7, 8, 13, 14_____ .

                                                          , but

1 Finding a venomous snake is not something most people go out of their way to do^that is exactly the goal of some scientists. 2 They are looking for precisely what everyone else wants to avoid: the snake's venom. 3 This is not a hunt for excitement or a dangerous thrill^*;*/it is a search for a medical breakthrough. 4 For over thirty years, scientists have been using snake venom to create new drugs. 5 One type of venom, for example, has ~~provide~~ ^*provided* a key ingredient for treating congestive heart failure.

    6 A snake creates venom in special glands in its upper jaw. 7 In latching onto prey, the snake squeezes these glands and ~~release~~ ^*releases* the venom. 8 Molecules from the venom then ~~attacks~~ *attack* the prey from the inside. 9 Some venom molecules cause muscle cells to relax^*, which*^. ~~10 Which~~ cuts off the victim's oxygen supply. 11 Other molecules ~~will have induced~~ ^*induce* the victim's immune system to attack its own organs. 12 Most venoms contain a combination of such molecules.

    13 In recent years, researchers have discovered how certain genes in venom ~~relaxes~~ ^*relax* the muscles in the prey's aorta, which pumps blood to the body's organs. 14 Relaxing these muscles ~~prevent~~ ^*prevents* the aorta from contracting, which lowers the blood pressure and allows time for deadly toxins to attack the victim's bloodstream. 15 Scientists are now trying to use these muscle-relaxing toxins to humans' advantage. 16 Controlled relaxation of the blood vessels around the heart helps blood flow more easily^*, reducing*~~. 17 Reducing~~ the effects of congestive heart failure.

Editing Review Test 3

3

The Four Most Serious Errors (Chapters 21–25)
Other Grammar Concerns (Chapters 26–32)

Directions: Each of the underlined word groups contains one or more errors. As you identify each error, write in the space the number of the word group containing the error. Then, edit the underlined word groups to correct the errors. If you need help, turn back to the chapters indicated above. *Answers may vary. Possible edits shown.*

Two fragments _9, 14_   One verb problem _2_

One run-on _4_   One pronoun error _6_

One adjective error _4_   One parallelism error _2_

Three subject-verb agreement errors _6, 7, 12_

1 Anyone who has ever gotten lost in a maze knows what a frightening experience it can be.
                                                            safe
2 But it is also challenging, exciting, and ~~there is no problem with safety~~ because few people ever
get
~~got~~ lost in mazes for long. 3 Mazes have become more popular than ever in recent years in the
  ^
United States and in many countries around the world.
                                                            , but   *largest*
    4 Mazes can be made of many different types of materials perhaps the ~~larger~~ number
                                                            ^   ^
of them are made of corn stalks. 5 Corn mazes have become big business in some farming
                                                    is
communities. 6 Building mazes ~~are~~ one way for farmers to market ~~his~~ farms as places for popular
                              ^   *their*
entertainment.
                                    is
    7 The point of this for some farmers ~~are~~ to adapt the small farm so that it can remain
                                          ^
competitive in today's economy. 8 Some farms are expanding on the maze idea by turning a
                                                parks, complete
section of land into small theme ~~parks. 9 Complete~~ with hay rides, petting zoos, and pig races.
                                  ^
10 Mazes are usually the major attraction, however, and many are quite elaborate. 11 There are
                                                            include
mazes shaped like butterflies, crowns, and sheriffs' badges. 12 Some mazes even ~~includes~~ such
                                                                                  ^
features as double-decker bridges.
                                                            , mazes
    13 Other mazes are designed to teach people about various farm crops and how they are
grown. 14 Whether entertaining, educational, or both. ~~15 Mazes~~ have become a significant way of
                                                      ^
raising people's awareness of and interest in farming.

Editing Review Test 4

The Four Most Serious Errors (Chapters 21–25)
Other Grammar Concerns (Chapters 26–32)

4

Directions: Each of the underlined word groups contains one or more errors. As you identify each error, write in the space the number of the word group containing the error. Then, edit the underlined word groups to correct the errors. If you need help, turn back to the chapters indicated above. *Answers may vary. Possible edits shown.*

Two fragments <u>2, 9</u>   One run-on <u>5</u>

One subject-verb agreement error <u>4</u>   Two pronoun errors <u>4, 6</u>

One misplaced/dangling modifier <u>4</u>   Two coordination/subordination errors <u>3, 12</u>

Two uses of inappropriately informal or
casual language <u>7, 16</u>

1 Many Internet users are not aware of the current debate over network neutrality. *, or what* ~~2 What~~ some call the argument over who owns the Internet. 3 People assume that open and equal access to Web content is a protected right*, but* ~~; some~~ companies are trying to change the way users access online information.

4 Companies like Comcast and AT&T, *that* ~~who~~ provide Internet service, *want* ~~wants~~ greater control over the data that travel through their lines and cables. 5 The companies argue that they built the roads *, so* they should be able to control who uses those roads. 6 By allowing some Web sites to pay more for faster transmission, *the Internet providers* ~~they~~ can earn more money. 7 The companies say they would like to use that money to develop new networks and ultimately provide *better* ~~killer~~ service.

8 Supporters of network neutrality argue that consumers should have equal access to all Web sites. *, not* ~~9 Not~~ just to those Web sites that pay more for faster delivery. 10 Internet service providers should not have the power to restrict, block, or slow down the delivery of any content. 11 Network neutrality advocates want to see the Internet remain free, open, and democratic. *however,* 12 The federal government supports network neutrality in theory; passing laws that protect network neutrality has been difficult. 13 Critics have found many flaws in the proposed legislation. 14 For example, without the power to filter content, unwanted material like spam

Editing Review Test 4, continued

cannot be prevented. 15 Nevertheless, many still hope that the government will find a way to

protect users' rights. 16 If service providers become self-appointed gatekeepers of the Web, many

be negatively affected.

fear that users are the ones who will ~~get the shaft~~.

                                        ∧

Editing Review Test 5

The Four Most Serious Errors (Chapters 21–25)
Other Grammar Concerns (Chapters 26–32)
Word Use (Chapters 33–34)

5

Directions: Each of the underlined word groups contains one or more errors. As you identify each error, write in the space the number of the word group containing the error. Then, edit the underlined word groups to correct the errors. If you need help, turn back to the chapters indicated above. *Answers may vary. Possible edits shown.*

One run-on <u>8</u>

One word choice error <u>10</u>

One adjective error <u>15</u>

One subject-verb agreement error <u>1</u>

Two commonly confused word errors <u>3, 12</u>

One verb problem <u>4</u>

Two pronoun errors <u>4, 14</u>

One misplaced/dangling modifier <u>6</u>

wants
1 Nobody <s>want</s> to go through life frightened that criminals might be lurking around every
                 ∧

corner. 2 But criminals do exist, and it makes sense to take precautions to avoid being victimized.
                                                    your
3 <u>There are prudent measures that you can work into <s>you're</s> everyday routines that can help</u>
                                                                      ∧

<u>prevent you from becoming a victim to some common scams.</u>

    4 <u>First, do not give out financial information, such as your bank account or Social Security</u>
                         whom   *do not*
<u>number, to anyone <s>who</s> you <s>did not</s> know and trust.</u> 5 It is surprisingly easy to create a fake
                         ∧   ∧

Social Security card and then a fake birth certificate to go with it. 6 <u>Using these fake documents,</u>
a criminal can ask   *to*
<u>the local motor vehicle department <s>will</s> issue a new driver's license with your name and the</u>
∧   ∧

<u>criminal's photo.</u>

    7 Second, beware of e-mail scams, one of which involves a so-called deposed Nigerian

leader who offers to pay you a substantial sum if you help him transfer his fortune out of

his country. 8 <u>Many of these scams use the same trick to get people to believe the sender is</u>
honest. The
<u><s>honest, the</s> criminal will send a postdated check for a share in the fortune in return for a check</u>
∧

<u>from the victim that is allegedly necessary to unfreeze the funds.</u> 9 Needless to say, the criminal's
                                                            use extreme caution.
checks always bounce. 10 <u>If you receive e-mail solicitations of any kind, <s>don't play with fire.</s></u> 11 Do
                                                                              ∧

thorough background checks on the sender before sending any money or information.

Editing Review Test 5, continued

12 Third, when ~~its~~ time to discard your old computer, remove the hard drive first to prevent
           it's
             ^

thieves from recovering any vital data. 13 On the positive side, you can relax a bit about your

household trash. 14 Most identity theft cases ~~they~~ do not start with scammers rummaging

through trash. 15 Instead, scammers use computer spyware or steal outgoing mail because they

find these methods ~~more easy~~.
                  easier.
                   ^

Editing Review Test 6

The Four Most Serious Errors (Chapters 21–25)
Other Grammar Concerns (Chapters 26–32)
Word Use (Chapters 33–34)

6

Directions: Each of the underlined word groups contains one or more errors. As you identify each error, write in the space the number of the word group containing the error. Then, edit the underlined word groups to correct the errors. If you need help, turn back to the chapters indicated above. *Answers may vary. Possible edits shown.*

Two run-ons 4, 11 _____

One subject-verb agreement error 14 _____

One parallelism error 7 _____

Two commonly confused words errors 2, 8 ____

One use of inappropriately informal or casual language 6 _____

One verb problem 2 _____

One pronoun error 11 _____

1 Eastern Egg Rock, a remote, treeless island off the coast of southern Maine, was for much of the twentieth century inhabited by a huge population of gulls. 2 By the mid-1980s, the gulls
had
~~have~~ been the dominant bird species ~~they're~~ *there* for about a hundred years. 3 But before that, the island was primarily the home of arctic terns and puffins. 4 By the late nineteenth century,
and
hunting had reduced the tern and puffin populations to nonviable levels, the gulls had taken over. 5 In 1973, the National Audubon Society decided to launch an experiment to try to bring puffins and terns back to Eastern Egg Rock. 6 Since then, Project Puffin has proved so successful
study it.
that biologists from all over the world now come to ~~check it out.~~
controlling
7 The Audubon team focused on restoring the nesting environment and ~~to control~~
to
predators. 8 The team moved puffin chicks from successful colonies in Newfoundland ~~too~~ carefully built burrows and fed them by hand. 9 Decoys and recorded calls helped attract puffins and terns to the nests. 10 Team members stayed on the island during every breeding season.
, so   *the gulls*
11 The large gulls do not like to nest around people this helped prevent ~~them~~ from returning. 12 There are now more than one hundred pairs of breeding puffins on Eastern Egg Rock. 13 In addition, there are sizable populations of terns, storm petrels, and black guillemots.

Editing Review Test 6, continued

14 Birdlife conservation efforts like Project Puffin ~~seems~~ *seem* to be having a significant effect worldwide. 15 A recent study found that, in the last century, thirty-one species of birds were saved from extinction due to conservation programs.

Editing Review Test 7

The Four Most Serious Errors (Chapters 21-25)
Other Grammar Concerns (Chapters 26–32)
Word Use (Chapters 33–34)
Punctuation and Capitalization (Chapters 35–39)

7

Directions: Each of the underlined word groups contains one or more errors. As you identify each error, write in the space the number of the word group containing the error. Then, edit the underlined word groups to correct the errors. If you need help, turn back to the chapters indicated above. *Answers may vary. Possible edits shown.*

One run-on 8 _____   One verb problem 7 _____

Two apostrophe errors 3, 11 _____   One pronoun problem 14 _____

One adverb error 11 _____   One quotation mark error 12 _____

One subject-verb agreement error 9 _____   One capitalization error 8 _____

One commonly confused word error 4 _____   One comma error 3 _____

One semicolon error 2 _____

   1 Many engineering students nationwide belong to a group called Engineers Without

Borders-USA (EWB-USA). 2 <u>EWB-USA is a nonprofit organization that allows engineering</u>

<u>students and professionals to volunteer in developing countries; using their knowledge to</u>

<u>help communities meet basic needs.</u> 3 <u>In particular, volunteer's work to improve shelter, water,</u>

<u>sanitation, and energy systems.</u>

   4 <u>One of the goals of EWB-USA is to train socially</u> *conscious* <u>~~conscience~~ engineers.</u> 5 By offering their

skills in places where those skills are most needed, students see how their education can help

people in very direct ways. 6 When designing projects, students work with local communities to

understand what the communities' needs are and to ensure that the local people can maintain

the projects once EWB volunteers have left. 7 <u>Throughout the process, professional engineers</u>
act
<u>~~acted~~ as mentors and technical consultants.</u>

Editing Review Test 7, continued

8 Currently, EWB-USA is working on projects in more than forty-five developing countries~~.~~
These
~~these~~ projects range from building bridges in El Salvador and Guatemala to digging wells
^ T
in ~~t~~anzania. 9 One group from Iowa State University ~~are~~ even helping local schools in Belize
^   *is*
build solar fruit dryers. 10 The dried fruit will provide the local children with healthy, inexpensive

snacks throughout the school year and will make use of the country's large supply of fresh fruit.
          EWB's   *simultaneously*
11 Most of ~~EWBs~~ projects have multiple benefits; for example, one project might ~~simultaneous~~
            ^   ^
reduce disease, decrease labor, allow children to spend more time in school, and improve living

conditions.

12 Bernard Amadei, who founded EWB-USA in 2002, explained billions of people all over the
                                                             "
                                                             ^
world are in need of basic services." 13 Given how popular EWB-USA has become, it appears that

many engineers and engineering students agree with Amadei. 14 The organization now has more
                                       its
than 12,000 members in ~~their~~ 250 chapters and is present on 180 campuses in the United States.
                        ^

Editing Review Test 8

The Four Most Serious Errors (Chapters 21–25)
Other Grammar Concerns (Chapters 26–32)
Word Use (Chapters 33–34)
Punctuation and Capitalization (Chapters 35–39)

8

Directions: Each of the underlined word groups contains one or more errors. As you identify each error, write in the space the number of the word group containing the error. Then, edit the underlined word groups to correct the errors. If you need help, turn back to the chapters indicated above. *Answers may vary. Possible edits shown.*

One run-on 6 _____

One pronoun error 1 _____

Two comma errors 2, 7 _____

One apostrophe error 8 _____

One use of inappropriately informal or casual language 11 _____

One capitalization error 3 _____

One commonly confused words error 6 _____

One semicolon error 10 _____

One verb problem 2 _____

Two adverb errors 10, 12 _____

One misplaced/dangling modifier 3 _____

Two hyphen errors 7, 9 _____

1 Some parents buy turtles for their children to keep as pets, but, apart from that, most
                                                      turtles
adults probably don't think about ~~them~~ at all. 2 Nevertheless, these slow, clumsy creatures
                                            ^   *would*   ^   *nearly*
possess two remarkable qualities that many people love to have. 3 Turtles are indestructible, and
                                         centuries.   ^   ^
they can ~~nearly~~ live for ~~Centuries.~~
                      ^

4 Most people attribute turtles' sturdiness to their tough shells, but turtles are tough in

other important ways as well. 5 A turtle can go without food or liquid for months at a time.
     Its
6 ~~It's~~ heart doesn't need to beat constantly, so a turtle can virtually turn it on (or off)
  ^   *wants. Turtles*
whenever it ~~wants, turtles~~ are built to survive through floods, heat waves, famines, ice ages,
              ^
and predators' attacks.

7 In March/2006, a 250-year-old turtle died in a zoo in Calcutta. 8 Scientists have recently
        turtle's   ^   ^
discovered that a ~~turtles~~ organs, unlike those of nearly every other animal studied, resist breaking
                    ^
                                                          one hundred years old
down or becoming less efficient over time. 9 A turtle that is over ~~one-hundred-years-old~~
                                                      ^

Editing Review Test 8, continued

can have a liver, lungs, and kidneys that are nearly identical to those of a turtle in
its teens.

  10 Although turtles resist disease and predators extremely ~~good,~~ _{well,} many turtle populations
are now facing dire threats they have never had to deal with before;threats from humans.
  11 Every year, ~~zillions of~~ _{many} turtles are killed by automobiles on new roads built across turtles'
migrational pathways. 12 People are also steadily encroaching on turtle habitats and, in some
areas, hunting them near to extinction in order to sell their valuable shells and meat. 13 The
resilient turtle might finally have met its match in humans.

Editing Review Test 9

The Four Most Serious Errors (Chapters 21–25)
Other Grammar Concerns (Chapters 26–32)
Word Use (Chapters 33–34)
Punctuation and Capitalization (Chapters 35–39)

9

Directions: Each of the underlined word groups contains one or more errors. As you identify each error, write in the space the number of the word group containing the error. Then, edit the underlined word groups to correct the errors. If you need help, turn back to the chapters indicated above. *Answers may vary. Possible edits shown.*

One fragment 15 _____   One dash error 10 _____

One run-on 2 _____   One semicolon error 9 _____

One pronoun error 2 _____   One parentheses error 6 _____

One parallelism error 12 _____   One use of inappropriately informal or casual

One apostrophe error 6 _____   language 4 _____

1 One of the most common afflictions people have is an allergy to pets. 2 Some ~~whom~~ *who* are

allergic simply refuse to have pets that can trigger a ~~reaction, these~~ *reaction. These* pets include cats, dogs, birds,

rabbits, gerbils, and hamsters. 3 Instead, allergic people may keep pets that do not ordinarily

cause an allergic reaction, such as fish, turtles, frogs, and lizards. 4 However, most pet-allergic

people who ~~are ga-ga about~~ *love* pets just go ahead and bring them into their homes anyway. 5 For

these pet-allergic pet lovers, there are some good ways to reduce the allergens in a home to

tolerable levels.

6 Allergens are spread from a ~~pets~~ *pet's* saliva, urine, skin secretions, and dander *(* the dead skin

particles that animals continually shed *)*. 7 These allergens disperse directly into the air. 8 The best

way to minimize pet allergies is to limit where the pet goes in the home. 9 Here is the single

most important rule *:* no pets in the bedroom. 10 Also, keep pets off of the furniture; instead *,*

get a dog or cat its own floor cushion, and choose a cushion with a washable cover. 11 Rabbits,

birds, gerbils, and hamsters need to be in their cages. 12 Another key is to thoroughly and

Editing Review Test 9, continued

frequently clean the pet, the areas where it spends most of its time, and ~~it's extremely important to clean~~ the bedrooms. 13 Install an air purifier in your bedroom and, if necessary, in other rooms where the pet is allowed. 14 Regularly clean the top blades of ceiling ~~fans.~~ *fans, which* ~~15 Which~~ are one of the main spreaders of allergens. 16 In many cases, with sufficient care and effort, pets and pet-allergic humans can coexist.

Editing Review Test 10

The Four Most Serious Errors (Chapters 21–25)
Other Grammar Concerns (Chapters 26–32)
Word Use (Chapters 33–34)
Punctuation and Capitalization (Chapters 35–39)

Directions: Each of the underlined word groups contains one or more errors. As you identify each error, write in the space the number of the word group containing the error. Then, edit the underlined word groups to correct the errors. If you need help, turn back to the chapters indicated above. *Answers may vary. Possible edits shown.*

One fragment _8_____   One comma error _5_____

One pronoun error _7_____   One semicolon error _13_____

One coordination/subordination error _2_____   One colon error _11_____

One subject-verb agreement error _2_____   One apostrophe error _13_____

One commonly confused words error _1_____

1 People are arriving at airports earlier ~~then~~ *than* they used to and spending more time there, and that has created an unexpected problem for travelers and airport managers. 2 ~~People~~ *As people* wait in security lines and for their flights*,* most of them ~~is~~ *are* using their cell phones and laptops. 3 This is not a problem in terms of cell phone and wireless Internet access because most airports can easily make these networks available. 4 The problem occurs when cell-phone and laptop users run out of battery power and need to plug into an electrical outlet. 5 In many airports*,* including some of the most heavily used ones, there are not enough outlets to go around.

6 Despite travelers' annoyance, many don't complain to airport personnel about not having enough outlets. 7 Most travelers mistakenly think that ~~he or she~~ *they* are not allowed to use the outlets*, assuming* 8 ~~Assuming~~ the outlets are only for airport management and cleaning staff. 9 Airport managers are definitely aware of the problem and have tried various ways of resolving it, including adding outlets in public seating areas and even in snack bars.

10 In the meantime, it's not unusual to see airport travelers carefully searching all the walls around them for a free outlet. 11 One experienced airport user offers other travelers this advice*:*

Editing Review Test 10, continued

Think like airport cleaning staff. 12 Look for the best place to plug in a vacuum cleaner. 13 Often,
                                                                                                      there's
he says, ~~theres~~ an outlet in a pillar,/ or behind some seats on a wall. 14 An especially kind traveler
                                  ^

brings along a power strip and invites others to share in the connection. 15 Until the airports

catch up on outlet availability, these makeshift solutions will have to do.

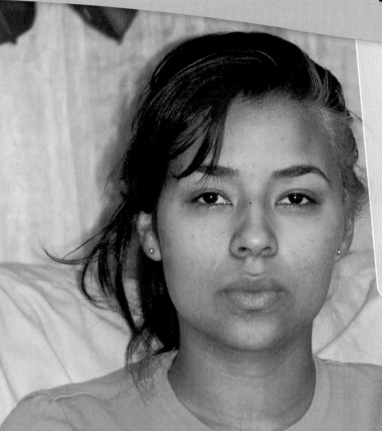

Part 9

Readings for Writers

"I write research papers and essay exams."

Chavella P., student

PHOTO: PATRICIA LEE

40

Narration

This part of the book (this chapter through Chapter 48) contains twenty-four essays that demonstrate the types of writing you learned in Part 3.

These essays are more than just good models of writing. They tell great stories, argue passionately about different issues, and present a wide range of perspectives and information. These essays can also provide you with ideas for your own writing. Most important, they offer you the opportunity to become a better reader and writer: By analyzing how others write, you can sharpen your own skills.

Each essay in this chapter uses narration to make its main idea. As you read these essays, consider how they achieve the four basics of good narration that are listed below and discussed in Chapter 10 of this book.

Four Basics of Good Narration

1	It reveals something of importance to your reader (your **main idea**).
2	It includes all the major events of the story (**primary support**).
3	It uses details to bring the story to life for your audience (**secondary support**).
4	It presents the events in a clear order, usually according to when they happened.

Bill Bryson

Coming Home

Bill Bryson is an American nonfiction writer whose many best-selling books include *A Walk in the Woods, A Short History of Nearly Everything,* and *At Home: A Short History of Private Life.* His most recent book, *One Summer: America 1927,* details how the summer of 1927 shaped the nation's future. He currently lives in the United Kingdom.

Guiding question Does Bryson really feel as though America is still his "home"?

Pause Before going further, stop to think about what Bryson may mean by, "you can't go home again."

Pause Based on the introduction, what do you think will happen to the narrator in the story?

Pause Underline the places where Bryson describes his feeling of being out of place.

1 I once joked in a book that there are three things you can't do in life. You can't beat the phone company, you can't make a waiter see you until he is ready to see you, and you can't go home again. Since the spring of 1995, I have been quietly, even gamely, reassessing point number three.

2 In May of that year, after nearly two decades in England, I moved back to the United States with my English wife and four children. We settled in Hanover, New Hampshire, for no other reason than that it seemed an awfully nice place. Founded in 1761, it is a friendly, well-ordered, prettily steepled community with a big central green, an old-fashioned Main Street, and a rich and gorgeous university, Dartmouth College, whose benignly dominant presence gives the town a backdrop of graceful buildings, an air of privileged endeavor, and the presence of five thousand students, not one of whom can be trusted to cross a road in safety. With this came other attractions—good schools, an excellent bookstore and library, a venerable movie theater (The Nugget, found in 1916), a good choice of restaurants, and a convivial bar called Murphy's. Helplessly beguiled, we bought a house near the center of town and moved in.

3 Coming back to your native land after an absence of many years is a surprisingly unsettling business, a little like waking from a long coma. Time, you discover, has wrought changes that leave you feeling mildly foolish and out of touch. You proffer hopelessly inadequate sums when making small purchases. You puzzle over ATM machines and automated gas pumps and pay phones, and are astounded to discover, by means of a stern grip on your elbow, that gas station road maps are no longer free.

4 In my case, the problem was intensified by the fact that I had left as a youth and was returning in middle age. All those things that you do as an adult—take out mortgages, have children, accumulate pension plans, take an interest in the state of your guttering—I had only ever done in England. Things like furnaces and storm windows were, in an American context, the preserve of my father. So finding myself suddenly in charge of an old New England house, with its mysterious pipes and thermostats, its temperamental garbage disposal and life-threatening automatic garage door, was both unnerving and rather exhilarating.

5 It is disconcerting to find yourself so simultaneously in your element and out of it. I can enumerate all manner of minutiae that mark me out as an American—which of the fifty states has a unicameral legislature, what a squeeze play is in baseball, who played Captain Kangaroo on TV. I even know about two-thirds of the words to "The Star-Spangled Banner," which is more than some people know who have sung it publicly.

6 But send me to the hardware store and even now I am totally lost. For months I had conversations with the clerk at our local True-Value that went something like this:

7 "Hi. I need some of that goopy stuff you fill nail holes in walls with. My wife's people call it Pollyfilla."

8 "Ah, you mean spackle."

9   "Very possibly. And I need some of those little plastic things that you use to hold screws in the wall when you put shelves up. I know them as rawl plugs."

10   "We call them anchors."

11   "I shall make a mental note of it."

12   Really, I could hardly have felt more foreign if I had stood there dressed in lederhosen.[1] All this was a shock to me. Although I was always very happy in Britain, I never stopped thinking of America as home, in the fundamental sense of the term. It was where I came from, what I really understood, the base against which all else was measured.

13   In a funny way nothing makes you feel more like a native of your own country than to live where nearly everyone is not. For twenty years, being an American was my defining quality. It was how I was identified, differentiated. I even got a job on the strength of it once, when in a moment of youthful audacity, I asserted to a managing editor of the *London Times* that I would be the only person on his staff who could reliably spell Cincinnati. (And it was so.)

14   Happily, there is a flipside to this. The many good things about America also took on a bewitching air of novelty. I was as dazzled as any newcomer by the famous ease and convenience of daily life, the giddying abundance of absolutely everything, the boundless friendliness of strangers, the wondrous unfillable vastness of an American basement, the delight of encountering waitresses and other service providers who actually seemed to enjoy their work, the curiously giddying notion that ice is not a luxury item and that rooms can have more than one electrical socket.

15   As well, there has been the constant, unexpected joy of reencountering all those things I grew up with but had largely forgotten: baseball on the radio, the deeply satisfying *whoing-bang* slam of a screen door in summer, insects that glow, sudden run-for-your-life thunderstorms, really big snowfalls, Thanksgiving and the Fourth of July, the smell of a skunk from just the distance that you have to sniff the air quizzically and say: "Is that a skunk?," Jell-O with stuff in it, the pleasingly comical sight of oneself in shorts. All that counts for a lot, in a strange way.

16   So, on balance, I was wrong. You can go home again. Just bring extra money for road maps and remember to ask for spackle.

> **Pause** Why do you think Bryson includes this exchange in the hardware store?
>
> 1. **lederhosen:** leather shorts, often worn with suspenders in an H-shape; traditional dress found in Bavaria.
>
> **Pause** Bryson claims that being an American was always his defining characteristic. What does he mean by this?
>
> **Pause** Underline the places where Bryson identifies positive aspects of his new life in America.

SUMMARIZE AND RESPOND

Summarize the main idea of "Coming Home." Then, go back and check off support for this main idea. Next, write a brief summary (three to five sentences) of the essay. Finally, jot down your initial responses to the reading. What do you think Bryson wanted to communicate to his readers? What do you learn about the narrator from his account of this experience?

CHECK YOUR COMPREHENSION

1. Which of the following would be the best alternative title for this essay?

   a.   "Problems with Moving"

   b.   "Going Home Again: The Difficulties and Joys of Returning to America"

   c.   "Memories of America"

   d.   "What Is Spackle?"

2. The main idea of this essay is that

   a.   the narrator enjoyed living in England.

   b.   there are too many differences between England and America.

   c.   the narrator enjoys the things he remembers about living in America, even if some of the adjustments have been difficult.

   d.   the narrator misses his life in England.

3. According to Bryson, coming back to the United States as an adult and dealing with the things his father used to do for him

   a.   was unnerving yet exhilarating.

   b.   was disturbing and uncomfortable.

   c.   was funny and humorous.

   d.   was scary and terrifying.

4. If you are unfamiliar with the following words, use a dictionary to check their meanings: reassessing (para. 1); steepled, benignly, beguiled (2); wrought, proffer (3); disconcerting, enumerate (5); foreign (12).

READ CRITICALLY

1. What does this experience lead the writer to believe?

2. What is your overall impression of the narrator?

3. Where in the essay does Bryson use transitions? How do they help the writer present the story in a clear order? Underline specific examples.

4. How do the supporting details Bryson uses make his narrative vivid and lively for readers? Point to a specific example.

5. How does the essay's conclusion refer to the essay's introduction? Do you find this choice effective? Why or why not?

WRITE AN ESSAY

Moving from one distinct culture to another shaped the way Bryson thought about his childhood memories. Things that were once familiar to him now seem strange because he has lived in a foreign country for so long. Although he said that this has made his life complicated, it also allowed him to reexperience certain things in a new way: the slam of a screen door, the Fourth of July, and Thanksgiving, to name a few. Think of a time in your life when you reexperienced something after a time away. If you haven't experienced returning to your home after moving away, your example could be revisiting a childhood playground after many years or going back to a school you graduated from. What was different about that experience? Did you feel any different about the place or the people? Did it still feel like home or the familiar place it used to be? If not, what made it seem strange? Share your thoughts and feelings about the experience.

Monique Rizer

When Students Are Parents

The following essay was published in the *Chronicle of Higher Education* in 2005. For more information about Monique Rizer, see her Profile of Success on page 133.

Guiding question　How has being a parent and student affected Rizer's decisions?

1　Crammed behind my desk, I fidgeted and shifted my eyes to observe the other students in the room. I tried not to look the way I felt—like I didn't belong there with them. I couldn't help noticing that all the other women were wearing shorts, sandals, flirty summer dresses: appropriate clothes for a warm September day. I tugged at the baggy clothes hiding my postpartum weight. I thought of my six-week-old son and hoped I'd make it home to nurse him at the scheduled time. The thought of him reminded me that however odd I felt, I was going to stay in college this time.

2　It was the summer of 1998. I was a twenty-year-old new mother and wife, and it was my first day of class, though not my first day of college. I'd begun my long journey through higher education three years before, but my plans to attend full time after high school graduation were put on hold when financial difficulties forced my family of eight to move. I then found a local community college and felt prepared to start again, but instead the registration papers sat abandoned in my car, where I practically lived since home was a 32-foot trailer filled with seven other people. In the summer of 1996, I packed my bags and left to live on my own; I enrolled again the next spring and had my son in July 1998. I knew I had to stay in school and go full time. I wanted more for my son and myself, even though I wasn't sure what exactly "more" was at the time.

Pause　Have you felt out of place in college or other places?

Pause　How do you think Rizer found the strength to go back to school after dropping out?

Discussion Many students face pressures when attending college, even those students who aren't parents. Explore some of the factors competing for their time, and analyze how being a college student is already a full-time job without the added obligations from outside of college.

Pause How was being a student parent both difficult and helpful?

Pause Do you have enough information to understand how Rizer got through college?

3   Focusing on my son helped me to persist in college during difficult times, and there were many. I did not have time to socialize with other students because when I was not in class, I had to rush to take care of the details of life as a mother. Grocery shopping, cooking, arranging for child care, taking my son to the doctor when he was sick, seemed to take every minute. I was exhausted every day, and finding the time and mental energy to study and do homework often seemed an overwhelming challenge. But I stuck with it, determined to finish, to do what my mother had not done. When she had me at nineteen, she quit college and never returned.

4   What helped me finish college, even after my marriage and the birth of my second son, was meeting other students who were also parents. I realized other people were in my situation, too, and probably felt just as stretched. As I met other mothers, we offered to baby-sit for each other or to get together with our children so that they could play, and we could study. All of us wanted more for our children than we had had, and that kept us going.

5   My commitment to finish college has paid off. Now, I have a bachelor's in journalism from Gonzaga University and a master's in information management from Syracuse University. During my years in school, my son kept me focused and ignited my ambition to be a better student. In my experience, there is no better motivation to finish college and to appreciate the full experience than a child whose future depends on your decisions. I had to continue to use my education to give him a better life and to set an example for him to follow.

6   I feel a tremendous sense of accomplishment: I've learned so many intangible lessons about myself; I've decided that I want to help other young parents achieve their educational goals; and I see a better future for my boys (I have two now). And I keep telling my mom that she doesn't have to live vicariously through me: She can return to college any time she wants. Being a student and a parent is challenging, but nothing is more rewarding than providing a bright future for your children.

SUMMARIZE AND RESPOND

Summarize the main idea of "When Students Are Parents." Then, go back to the text and check off support for this main idea. Next, write a brief summary (three to five sentences) of the essay. Finally, jot down your initial responses to the reading. What do you think Rizer wanted to communicate to her readers? What do you learn about the narrator from her account of this experience?

CHECK YOUR COMPREHENSION

1. An alternative title for this essay could be

   a.   "It's Important to Help Other Students with Children"

   b.   "Parents Can Be Successful in College"

   c.   "Professors Appreciate Successful Students"

   d.   "Parents Who Are Students Don't Fit In"

2. The main idea of the essay is that

   (a.) if they have the right resources, attitude, and support, parents can be just as successful as any other college students.

   b.   it's important to make sure that parents don't feel like outsiders on a college campus.

   c.   parents need the help of their friends in order to go to college.

   d.   children depend on the decisions of their parents.

3. Rizer believes that she was successful because

   a.   she was smart.

   b.   she was able to attend a good college.

   (c.) she was determined to do well for her son and her mother.

   d.   she enrolled in school full-time.

4. If you are unfamiliar with the following words, please use a dictionary to check their meanings: fidgeted, postpartum (para. 1); persist (3); intangible (6).

READ CRITICALLY

1. After completing college, what does Rizer believe about student parents?

2. What is your overall impression of the narrator?

3. Why does Rizer identify herself as an "outsider"? How does that affect her success as a student?

4. Why does Rizer specifically mention her mother and her sons in the essay? How do each of them inspire or shape her journey as a student?

5. How does the essay's conclusion refer to the essay's introduction? Do you find this choice effective? Why or why not?

WRITE AN ESSAY

Identify a time in your life that you felt like an outsider. This could be when you were younger and were left out of a game or when, more recently, you didn't understand something in a class. What made you feel like an outsider? Include the important details that help us understand your feelings. Why did you feel so different from others? How did you react to the situation?

Langston Hughes

Salvation

Langston Hughes (1902–1967) was born in Joplin, Missouri, and spent his high school years in Cleveland, Ohio. Later, he studied engineering at Columbia University, in New York City, but he eventually dropped out, soon becoming a central figure in the Harlem Renaissance, a period of creative innovation by writers, artists, and musicians in the African American section of New York. While he is primarily known as a poet, Hughes was also a prolific writer of stories, plays, and essays.

In this excerpt from his autobiography, *The Big Sea* (1940), Hughes recounts a childhood struggle to fulfill others' expectations while remaining true to his own ideas about being "saved."

Guiding question Was Hughes saved, or not?

Pause Based on the first paragraph, predict what this essay will be about.

1   I was saved from sin when I was going on thirteen. But not really saved. It happened like this. There was a big revival at my Auntie Reed's church. Every night for weeks there had been much preaching, singing, praying, and shouting, and some very hardened sinners had been brought to Christ, and the membership of the church had grown by leaps and bounds. Then just before the revival ended, they held a special meeting for children, "to bring the young lambs to the fold." My aunt spoke of it for days ahead. That night I was escorted to the front row and placed on the mourners' bench with all the other young sinners, who had not yet been brought to Jesus.

Teaching tip This essay is an excellent model of concrete language used to bring narration vividly to life. Have students consider Hughes's use of specific nouns, verbs, adjectives, and adverbs in several paragraphs.

2   My aunt told me that when you were saved you saw a light, and something happened to you inside! And Jesus came into your life! And God was with you from then on! She said you could see and hear and feel Jesus in your soul. I believed her. I had heard a great many old people say the same thing and it seemed to me they ought to know. So I sat there calmly in the hot, crowded church, waiting for Jesus to come to me.

3   The preacher preached a wonderful rhythmical sermon, all moans and shouts and lonely cries and dire pictures of hell, and then he sang a song about the ninety and nine safe in the fold, but one little lamb was left out in the cold. Then he said: "Won't you come? Won't you come to Jesus? Young lambs, won't you come?" And he held out his arms to all us young sinners there on the mourners' bench. And the little girls cried. And some of them jumped up and went to Jesus right away. But most of us just sat there.

4   A great many old people came and knelt around us and prayed, old women with jet-black faces and braided hair, old men with work-gnarled hands. And the church sang a song about the lower lights are burning, some poor sinners to be saved. And the whole building rocked with prayer and song.

5   Still I kept waiting to *see* Jesus.

Discussion Ask students about initiation practices in their own faiths. How do they respond to the practices within Hughes's Christian church?

6   Finally all the young people had gone to the altar and were saved, but one boy and me. He was a rounder's[1] son named Westley. Westley and I were surrounded

1. **rounder:** a man with a bad character

by sisters and deacons praying. It was very hot in the church, and getting late now. Finally Westley said to me in a whisper: "God damn! I'm tired o' sitting here. Let's get up and be saved." So he got up and was saved.

7   Then I was left all alone on the mourners' bench. My aunt came and knelt at my knees and cried, while prayers and songs swirled all around me in the little church. The whole congregation prayed for me alone, in a mighty wail of moans and voices. And I kept waiting serenely for Jesus, waiting, waiting—but he didn't come. I wanted to see him, but nothing happened to me. Nothing! I wanted something to happen to me, but nothing happened.

8   I heard the songs and the minister saying: "Why don't you come? My dear child, why don't you come to Jesus? Jesus is waiting for you. He wants you. Why don't you come? Sister Reed, what is this child's name?"

9   "Langston," my aunt sobbed.

10   "Langston, why don't you come? Why don't you come and be saved? Oh, Lamb of God! Why don't you come?"

11   Now it was really getting late. I began to be ashamed of myself, holding everything up so long. I began to wonder what God thought about Westley, who certainly hadn't seen Jesus either, but who was now sitting proudly on the platform, swinging his knickerbockered[2] legs and grinning down at me, surrounded by deacons and old women on their knees praying. God had not struck Westley dead for taking his name in vain or for lying in the temple. So I decided that maybe to save further trouble, I'd better lie, too, and say that Jesus had come, and get up and be saved.

12   So I got up.

13   Suddenly the whole room broke into a sea of shouting, as they saw me rise. Waves of rejoicing swept the place. Women leaped in the air. My aunt threw her arms around me. The minister took me by the hand and led me to the platform.

14   When things quieted down, in a hushed silence, punctuated by a few ecstatic "Amens," all the new young lambs were blessed in the name of God. Then joyous singing filled the room.

15   That night, for the last time in my life but one—for I was a big boy twelve years old—I cried. I cried, in bed alone, and couldn't stop. I buried my head under the quilts, but my aunt heard me. She woke up and told my uncle I was crying because the Holy Ghost had come into my life, and because I had seen Jesus. But I was really crying because I couldn't bear to tell her that I had lied, that I had deceived everybody in the church, and I hadn't seen Jesus, and that now I didn't believe there was a Jesus any more, since he didn't come to help me.

2. **knickerbockered:** wearing a pair of knee-length pants popular for boys in the early twentieth century

Pause What do you think Hughes might do next?

Pause Why did Hughes get up to be saved?

Pause Summarize Hughes's feelings.

SUMMARIZE AND RESPOND

Summarize the main idea of "Salvation." Then, go back and check off support for this main idea. Next, write a brief summary (three to five sentences) of the essay. Finally, jot down your initial response to the essay. What do you think Hughes wanted to communicate to readers by relating this story from his youth? What did you learn about Hughes as a young person?

CHECK YOUR COMPREHENSION

1. Which of the following would be the best alternative title for this essay?

   a. "Auntie Reed's Church"

   b. "The Power of Prayer"

   (c.) "Waiting for Jesus"

   d. "Westley and Me"

2. The main idea of this essay is that

   a. most religious people are hypocrites.

   b. a good preacher can stir a congregation to be saved.

   c. Hughes had a very religious upbringing that affected him throughout his lifetime.

   (d.) Hughes lost his faith because he didn't see Jesus when he pretended to be saved.

3. According to Hughes, his aunt

   (a.) deeply wanted him to be saved.

   b. raised him for most of his childhood.

   c. was herself saved when she was twelve years old.

   d. knew the real reason Hughes was crying after the revival meeting.

4. If you are unfamiliar with the following words, use a dictionary to check their meanings: escorted (para. 1); dire (3); gnarled (4); congregation, serenely (7); deacons (11); deceived (15).

READ CRITICALLY

1. How can you tell that Hughes truly wanted to be "brought to Christ" (para. 1)?

2. Why did Hughes finally join the other children who had been "saved"?

3. What does the fact that after the revival service Hughes cried "for the last time in [his] life but one" (para. 15) tell you about him?

4. What is the purpose of the exclamation points after the first three sentences of paragraph 2?

5. Note where Hughes uses direct quotation in the essay. What is the effect of these quotations?

WRITE AN ESSAY

Write an essay about a time in your youth when you desperately wanted to experience or achieve something but failed to do so, or missed your opportunity. In addition to narrating the events that occurred, share the thoughts and feelings you had at the time.

Narration: Linked Readings

Understanding Differences

Each of the following readings focuses on some idea of difference in the writer's life. It could be the difference between memories and experiences, what people mean versus what they say, or one culture versus another.

Tam Nguyen, "Reflection" (Chapter 11, p. 151)

Rui Dai, "A Whiff of Memory" (Chapter 16, p. 229)

Amy Tan, "Mother Tongue" (Chapter 44, p. 633)

Read the selections, and draw from at least one in addition to "Coming Home" to write an essay titled "Understanding Differences." You can refer to your own experience, but make sure to use material from the essays as well.

Overcoming Adversity and Trauma

Each of the following readings shows people overcoming adversity or trauma in different ways.

Daniel Flanagan, "The Choice to Do It Over Again" (Chapter 13, p. 180)

Nancy Mairs, "On Being a Cripple" (Chapter 45, p. 645)

Read the selections, and draw from at least one in addition to "When Students Are Parents" to write an essay titled "Overcoming Adversity." You can refer to your own experience, but make sure to use material from the essays as well.

The Pressure to Conform

Each of the following readings focuses on various aspects of the pressures people feel to conform.

Kathleen Vail, "Words That Wound" (Chapter 41, p. 599)

Brent Staples, "Just Walk On By: Black Men and Public Space" (Chapter 47, p. 670)

Read the selections, and draw from at least one in addition to "Salvation" to write an essay titled "The Pressure to Conform in Our Society." You can refer to your own experience, but make sure to use material from the essays as well.

41

Illustration

Each essay in this chapter uses illustration to get its main idea across. As you read these essays, consider how they achieve the four basics of good illustration that are listed below and discussed in Chapter 11 of this book.

Four Basics of Good Illustration

1. It has a good point.
2. It gives specific examples to show, explain, or prove the point.
3. It gives details to support the examples.
4. It uses enough examples to get the point across to the reader.

Liza Long

I Am Adam Lanza's Mother

Liza Long writes about her four children, their education, and mental health issues on her blog, *The Anarchist Soccer Mom*.

Guiding question What specific problems with the American health-care system does Long identify in her essay?

Pause Who was Adam Lanza and what happened in this situation?

1   Three days before 20-year-old Adam Lanza killed his mother, then opened fire on a classroom full of Connecticut kindergartners, my 13-year-old son

Michael (name changed) missed his bus because he was wearing the wrong color pants.

2   "I can wear these pants," he said, his tone increasingly belligerent, the black-hole pupils of his eyes swallowing the blue irises.

3   "They are navy blue," I told him. "Your school's dress code says black or khaki pants only."

4   "They told me I could wear these," he insisted. "You're a stupid bitch. I can wear whatever pants I want to. This is America. I have rights!"

5   "You can't wear whatever pants you want to," I said, my tone affable, reasonable. "And you definitely cannot call me a stupid bitch. You're grounded from electronics for the rest of the day. Now get in the car, and I will take you to school."

6   I live with a son who is mentally ill. I love my son. But he terrifies me.

Pause What do you think Long means when she says this?

7   A few weeks ago, Michael pulled a knife and threatened to kill me and then himself after I asked him to return his overdue library books. His 7- and 9-year-old siblings knew the safety plan—they ran to the car and locked the doors before I even asked them to. I managed to get the knife from Michael, then methodically collected all the sharp objects in the house into a single Tupperware container that now travels with me. Through it all, he continued to scream insults at me and threaten to kill or hurt me.

8   That conflict ended with three burly police officers and a paramedic wrestling my son onto a gurney for an expensive ambulance ride to the local emergency room. The mental hospital didn't have any beds that day, and Michael calmed down nicely in the ER, so they sent us home with a prescription for Zyprexa and a follow-up visit with a local pediatric psychiatrist.

9   We still don't know what's wrong with Michael. Autism spectrum, ADHD, oppositional defiant or intermittent explosive disorder have all been tossed around at various meetings with probation officers and social workers and counselors and teachers and school administrators. He's been on a slew of antipsychotic and mood-altering pharmaceuticals, a Russian novel of behavioral plans. Nothing seems to work.

Pause Underline the places where Long provides specific evidence of what might be problematic behavior in her son.

10   At the start of seventh grade, Michael was accepted to an accelerated program for highly gifted math and science students. His IQ is off the charts. When he's in a good mood, he will gladly bend your ear on subjects ranging from Greek mythology to the differences between Einsteinian and Newtonian physics to Doctor Who. He's in a good mood most of the time. But when he's not, watch out. And it's impossible to predict what will set him off.

11   Several weeks into his new junior high school, Michael began exhibiting increasingly odd and threatening behaviors at school. We decided to transfer him to the district's most restrictive behavioral program, a contained school environment where children who can't function in normal classrooms can access their right to free public babysitting from 7:30 to 1:50 Monday through Friday until they turn 18.

12   The morning of the pants incident, Michael continued to argue with me on the drive. He would occasionally apologize and seem remorseful. Right before we turned into his school parking lot, he said, "Look, Mom, I'm really sorry. Can I have video games back today?"

13   "No way," I told him. "You cannot act the way you acted this morning and think you can get your electronic privileges back that quickly."

Pause Predict: What will happen? What should Long do at this point? What might you do in this position?

14   His face turned cold, and his eyes were full of calculated rage. "Then I'm going to kill myself," he said. "I'm going to jump out of this car right now and kill myself."

15   That was it. After the knife incident, I told him that if he ever said those words again, I would take him straight to the mental hospital, no ifs, ands, or buts. I did not respond, except to pull the car into the opposite lane, turning left instead of right.

16   "Where are you taking me?" he said, suddenly worried. "Where are we going?"

17   "You know where we are going," I replied.

18   "No! You can't do that to me! You're sending me to hell! You're sending me straight to hell!"

19   I pulled up in front of the hospital, frantically waving for one of the clinicians who happened to be standing outside. "Call the police," I said. "Hurry."

Pause Why do you think Long says here "I won't be for much longer"?

20   Michael was in a full-blown fit by then, screaming and hitting. I hugged him close so he couldn't escape from the car. He bit me several times and repeatedly jabbed his elbows into my rib cage. I'm still stronger than he is, but I won't be for much longer.

21   The police came quickly and carried my son screaming and kicking into the bowels of the hospital. I started to shake, and tears filled my eyes as I filled out the paperwork—"Were there any difficulties with . . . at what age did your child . . . were there any problems with . . . has your child ever experienced . . . does your child have . . .?"

22   At least we have health insurance now. I recently accepted a position with a local college, giving up my freelance career because when you have a kid like this, you need benefits. You'll do anything for benefits. No individual insurance plan will cover this kind of thing.

Pause Number the steps that Long has taken to try to get help for her son. Have any of them been successful?

23   For days, my son insisted that I was lying—that I made the whole thing up so that I could get rid of him. The first day, when I called to check up on him, he said, "I hate you. And I'm going to get my revenge as soon as I get out of here."

24   By day three, he was my calm, sweet boy again, all apologies and promises to get better. I've heard those promises for years. I don't believe them anymore.

25   On the intake form, under the question, "What are your expectations for treatment?" I wrote, "I need help."

26   And I do. This problem is too big for me to handle on my own. Sometimes there are no good options. So you just pray for grace and trust that in hindsight, it will all make sense.

Pause Who are Dylan Klebold and Eric Harris? Who is James Holmes? Who is Jared Loughner? Who is Seung-Hui Cho? What do they have in common?

27   I am sharing this story because I am Adam Lanza's mother. I am Dylan Klebold's and Eric Harris's mother. I am James Holmes's mother. I am Jared

Loughner's mother. I am Seung-Hui Cho's mother. And these boys—and their mothers—need help. In the wake of another horrific national tragedy, it's easy to talk about guns. But it's time to talk about mental illness.

28   According to *Mother Jones*, since 1982, 61 mass murders involving firearms have occurred throughout the country. Of these, 43 of the killers were white males, and only one was a woman. *Mother Jones* focused on whether the killers obtained their guns legally (most did). But this highly visible sign of mental illness should lead us to consider how many people in the U.S. live in fear, like I do.

Pause Do these statistics and numbers show any patterns?

29   When I asked my son's social worker about my options, he said that the only thing I could do was to get Michael charged with a crime. "If he's back in the system, they'll create a paper trail," he said. "That's the only way you're ever going to get anything done. No one will pay attention to you unless you've got charges."

30   I don't believe my son belongs in jail. The chaotic environment exacerbates Michael's sensitivity to sensory stimuli and doesn't deal with the underlying pathology. But it seems like the United States is using prison as the solution of choice for mentally ill people. According to Human Rights Watch, the number of mentally ill inmates in U.S. prisons quadrupled from 2000 to 2006, and it continues to rise—in fact, the rate of inmate mental illness is five times greater (56 percent) than in the non-incarcerated population.

Pause Should mentally ill people be incarcerated? Is that the best place for treatment? If not, what is the best place? Who should pay for treatment in such a facility?

31   With state-run treatment centers and hospitals shuttered, prison is now the last resort for the mentally ill—Rikers Island, the LA County Jail, and Cook County Jail in Illinois housed the nation's largest treatment centers in 2011

32   No one wants to send a 13-year-old genius who loves Harry Potter and his snuggle animal collection to jail. But our society, with its stigma on mental illness and its broken health-care system, does not provide us with other options. Then another tortured soul shoots up a fast food restaurant. A mall. A kindergarten classroom. And we wring our hands and say, "Something must be done."

33   I agree that something must be done. It's time for a meaningful, nation-wide conversation about mental health. That's the only way our nation can ever truly heal.

34   God help me. God help Michael. God help us all.

SUMMARIZE AND RESPOND

Summarize the main idea of "I Am Adam Lanza's Mother." Then, go back and check off support for the main idea. Next, write a brief summary (three to five sentences) of the reading. Finally, jot down your initial response to the selection. How does the essay illustrate the broad topic of mental illness?

1. Which of the following would be the best alternative title for the essay?

    a. "He Didn't Understand"

    b. "She Can't Control Her Child"

    c. "Mental Illness Is Frightening"

    (d.) "Mental Illness Is Undertreated Too Often"

2. The main idea of this essay is that

    (a.) we don't have the right treatment for mental illness.

    b. mentally ill teens are too violent to be treated.

    c. statistics show that mentally ill teens are becoming more violent than ever.

    d. it's important to put mentally ill and violent teens in jail.

3. According to Long, *Mother Jones* found

    a. the mentally ill like to use drugs when they are violent.

    b. it's important to keep weapons away from teens.

    (c.) most of the killers in mass murder incidents involving firearms obtained their guns legally.

    d. some mentally ill teens function just fine on their own and don't need treatment at all.

4. If you are unfamiliar with the following words, use a dictionary to check their meanings: methodically (para. 7); burly (8); intermittent (9); exacerbates, pathology (30).

1. Identify three examples in the essay of Michael not behaving like a typical child. Why do these incidents scare the author?

2. What do you think Long intended to accomplish with this blog post? Who might her intended audience have been?

3. Long is told that the only way to help her son is to have him charged with a crime and put in prison. She, however, says that this is the least effective way to solve the nation's problem with violence and mental illness (para. 30). Do you agree or disagree with Long? Explain.

4. Long cites some statistics from *Mother Jones* about incidents of mass murder and about gun purchases. She then says that "this highly visible sign of mental illness should lead us to consider how many people in the U.S. live in fear, like I do" (para. 28). What does she mean by this?

5. Do you think Long provides enough examples and descriptions to illustrate her point? Explain your answer.

WRITE AN ESSAY

Long illustrates how untreated mental illness can tear a person's family apart. Write your own essay illustrating the effects of an illness—mental or physical. You can use examples from your own observations or experiences, or from current events.

Kathleen Vail

Words That Wound

Kathleen Vail was born in Pittsburgh, Pennsylvania, and received a bachelor's degree in journalism from California University of Pennsylvania. She has worked as an education reporter at daily newspapers in Pennsylvania, North Carolina, and Virginia, and in 1994 she became an assistant editor at the *American School Board Journal: The Source for School Leaders.* She has been managing editor there since 2006. Vail lives in Springfield, Virginia, with her husband and two sons. Originally published in the *American School Board Journal,* "Words That Wound" focuses on school bullying and its sometimes devastating consequences.

Guiding question What examples of bullying does Vail give?

1 Brian Head saw only one way out. On the final day of his life, during economics class, the fifteen-year-old stood up and pointed a semiautomatic handgun at himself. Before he pulled the trigger, he said his last words, "I can't take this anymore."

2 Brian's father, William Head, has no doubt why his child chose to take his life in front of a classroom full of students five years ago. Brian wanted everyone to know the source of his pain, the suffering he could no longer endure. The Woodstock, GA, teen, overweight with thick glasses, had been systematically abused by school bullies since elementary school. Death was the only relief he could imagine. "Children can't vote or organize, leave or run away," says Head. "They are trapped."

Pause Based on these two opening paragraphs, what do you predict that this essay will be about?

For many students, school is a torture chamber from which there is no escape. Every day, 160,000 children stay home from school because they are afraid of being bullied, according to the National Association of School Psychologists. In a study of junior high school students from small Midwestern towns, nearly 77 percent of the students reported they'd been victims of bullies at school—14 percent saying they'd experienced severe reactions to the abuse. "Bullying is a crime of violence," says June Arnette, associate director of the National School Safety Center. "It's an imbalance of power, sustained over a period of time."

4   Yet even in the face of this suffering, even after Brian Head's suicide five years ago, even after it was revealed this past spring that a culture of bullying might have played a part in the Columbine High School shootings,[1] bullying remains for the most part unacknowledged, underreported, and minimized by schools. Adults are unaware of the extent and nature of the problem, says Nancy Mullin-Rindler, associate director of the Project on Teasing and Bullying in the Elementary Grades at Wellesley College Center for Research for Women. "They underestimate the import. They feel it's a normal part of growing up, that it's character-building."

5   After his son's death, William Head became a crusader against bullying, founding an effort called Kids Hope to prevent others from suffering as Brian had. Unfortunately, bullying claimed another victim in the small town of Woodstock: thirteen-year-old Josh Belluardo. Last November, on the bus ride home from school, Josh's neighbor, fifteen-year-old Jonathan Miller, taunted him and threw wads of paper at him. He followed Josh off the school bus, hit the younger boy in the back of the head, and kicked him in the stomach. Josh spent the last two days of his life in a coma before dying of his injuries. Miller, it turns out, had been suspended nearly twenty times for offenses such as pushing and taunting other students and cursing at a teacher. He's now serving a life sentence for felony murder while his case is on appeal.

6   Bullying doesn't have to result in death to be harmful. Bullying and harassment are major distractions from learning, according to the National School Safety Center. Victims' grades suffer, and fear can lead to chronic absenteeism, truancy, or dropping out. Bullies also affect children who aren't victimized: Bystanders feel guilty and helpless for not standing up to the bully. They feel unsafe, unable to take action. They also can be drawn into bullying behavior by peer pressure. "Any time there is a climate of fear, the learning process will be compromised," says Arnette.

7   A full 70 percent of children believe teachers handle episodes of bullying "poorly," according to a study by John Hoover at the University of North Dakota at Grand Forks. It's no wonder kids are reluctant to tell adults about bullying incidents. "Children feel no one will take them seriously," says Robin Kowalski, professor of psychology at Western Carolina University, Cullowhee, NC, who's done research on teasing behavior.

8   Martha Rizzo, who lives in a suburb of Cincinnati, calls bullying the "dirty little secret" of her school district. Both her son and daughter were teased in school. Two boys in her son's sixth-grade class began taunting him because he

1. Columbine High School shootings: the April 1999 shootings at Columbine High School in Littleton, Colorado, in which two male students killed twelve students and a teacher, injured twenty-three others, and then killed themselves

Pause Underline the ways that bullying can be harmful, according to Vail.

wore sweatpants instead of jeans. They began to intimidate him during class. Once they knocked the pencil out of his hand during a spelling test when the teacher's back was turned. He failed the test. Rizzo made an appointment with the school counselor. The counselor told her he could do nothing about the behavior of the bullies and suggested she get counseling for her son instead. "Schools say they do something, but they don't, and it continues," says Rizzo. "We go in with the same problem over and over again."

9   Anna Billoit of Louisiana went to her son's middle school teachers when her son, who had asthma and was overweight, was being bullied by his classmates. Some of the teachers made the situation worse, she says. One male teacher suggested to her that the teasing would help her son mature. "His attitude was, 'Suck it up, take it like a man,'" says Billoit.

10   Much bullying goes on in so-called transition areas where there is little or no adult supervision: hallways, locker rooms, restrooms, cafeterias, playgrounds, buses, and bus stops. When abuse happens away from adult eyes, it's hard to prove that the abuse occurred. Often, though, bullies harass their victims in the open, in full view of teachers and other adults. Some teachers will ignore the behavior, silently condoning.[2] But even when adults try to deal with the problem, they sometimes make things worse for the victim by not handling the situation properly. Confronting bullies in front of their peers only enhances the bullies' prestige and power. And bullies often step up the abuse after being disciplined. "People know it happens, but there's no structured way to deal with it," says Mullin-Rindler. "There's lots of confusion about what to do and what is the best approach."

Pause Why can confronting bullies in front of their peers be counterproductive, according to Vail?

2. **condoning:** approving

11   Societal expectations play a part in adult reactions to childhood bullying. Many teachers and administrators buy into a widespread belief that bullying is a normal part of childhood and that children are better off working out such problems on their own. But this belief sends a dangerous message to children, says Head. Telling victims they must protect themselves from bullies shows children that adults can't and won't protect them. And, he points out, it's an attitude adults would never tolerate themselves. "If you go to work and get slapped on the back of the head, you wouldn't expect your supervisor to say, 'It's your problem—you need to learn to deal with it yourself,'" says Head. "It's a human rights issue."

12   Ignoring bullying is only part of the problem. Some teachers go further by blaming the victims for their abuse by letting their own dislike for the victimized child show. "There's a lot of secret admiration for the strong kids," says Eileen Faucette of Augusta, GA. Her daughter was teased so badly in the classroom that she was afraid to go to the blackboard or raise her hand to answer a question. The abuse happened in front of the teacher, who did nothing to stop it.

Pause What do you think of the point made here about teachers' "secret admiration for the strong kids"?

13   Head also encountered a blame-the-victim attitude toward his son. Brian would get into trouble for fighting at school, but when Head and his wife investigated what happened, they usually found that Brian had been attacked by other students. The school, Head said, wanted to punish Brian along with his attackers. "The school calls it fighting," Head says. "But it's actually assault and battery."

Pause Think about a time when you witnessed bullying behavior. How did you feel?

14   And changes are coming. This past April, five months after Josh Belluardo's death, the Georgia State Legislature passed an anti-bullying law. The law defines bullying as "any willful attempt or threat to inflict injury on another person when accompanied by an apparent present ability to do so" or "any intentional display of force such as would give the victim reason to fear or expect immediate bodily harm." Schools are required to send students to an alternative school if they commit a third act of bullying in a school year. The law also requires school systems to adopt anti-bullying policies and to post the policies in middle and high schools.

15   Head was consulted by the state representatives who sponsored the bill, but he believes the measure won't go far enough. He urges schools to treat bullying behavior as a violation of the state criminal law against assault, stalking, and threatening and to call police when the law is broken.

16   He knows it's too late for Brian, too late for Josh, too late for the teens who died in Littleton. But he continues to work, to educate and lobby on the devastating effects of bullying so that his son's death will not have been in vain.

17   "We should come clean and say what we've done in the past is wrong," says Head. "Now we will guarantee we'll protect the rights of students."

SUMMARIZE AND RESPOND

Summarize the main idea of "Words That Wound." Then, go back and check off support for this main idea. Next, write a brief summary (three to five sentences) of the reading. Finally, jot down your initial response to the selection. How do your own experiences with teasing and bullying in school affect your response?

CHECK YOUR COMPREHENSION

1. Which of the following would be the best alternative title for this essay?
    a.   "Bullying in Elementary School"
    b.   "The Tragic Story of a Bullied Teen"
    c.   "The Causes of Adolescent Suicide"
    d.   "Bullying: A Serious Problem"

2. The main idea of this essay is that
    a.   educators and policymakers need to realize that bullying has serious negative consequences and take steps to reduce its occurrence.
    b.   bullying should be made a criminal offense like assault, battery, stalking, and threatening.

   c.   adults who tolerate bullying among schoolchildren would never tolerate the same kind of behavior if it were inflicted in the workplace.

   d.   bullying is common in school settings because teachers, counselors, and administrators can do little about it.

3. According to Vail, teachers who ignore bullying

   a.   are afraid to intervene.

   (b.) send the signal that they see nothing wrong with it.

   c.   believe that parents have the responsibility for getting help for their children.

   d.   were probably bullies themselves.

4. If you are unfamiliar with the following words, use a dictionary to check their meanings: endure (para. 2); import (4); crusader, taunted, coma (5); distractions, chronic, truancy, compromised (6); intimidate (8); prestige (10); devastating (16).

READ CRITICALLY

1. Evaluate Vail's opening. How effective do you find it as a way of introducing her main idea?

2. Identify each of the examples that Vail presents. Do these examples convince you that the problem of bullying is serious and widespread? Why or why not?

3. Consider the statistics that Vail offers in paragraphs 3 and 7. What do they contribute to the essay? Which other kinds of statistics would you like to see?

4. In paragraph 12, Vail writes about "blaming the victims." What does she mean, and how does this idea contribute to the main point she is making?

5. In what ways does Vail tie her conclusion back to the opening part of her essay? What is the effect of this conclusion?

WRITE AN ESSAY

Write an essay developing your own ideas about what schools can do to reduce bullying among students. What policies might they adopt, and how could they enforce those policies? What could be done to stop the bullying that takes place in so-called transitional areas where students have no adult supervision? Use examples, either real or hypothetical, to help readers see that your plan would work.

Illustration: Linked Readings

The Pressure to Conform

Each of the following readings focuses on various aspects of the pressures people feel to conform.

Langston Hughes, "Salvation" (Chapter 40, p. 590)

Amy Tan, "Mother Tongue" (Chapter 44, p. 633)

Read the selections, and draw from at least one in addition to "Words That Wound" to write an essay titled "The Pressure to Conform in Our Society." You can refer to your own experience, but make sure to use material from the essays as well.

The Costs of War

Both of the following readings focus on the aftereffects and human costs of war and violence.

Liza Long, "I Am Adam Lanza's Mother" (Chapter 41, p. 594)

Peter Van Buren, "The Day after a Day at the Embassy" (Chapter 42, p. 611)

Read the selections, and draw from at least one to write an illustration essay titled "The Costs of Violence." You can refer to your own experience, but make sure to use material from the essays as well.

42

Description

Each essay in this chapter uses description to get its main idea across. As you read these essays, consider how they achieve the four basics of good description that are listed below and discussed in Chapter 12 of this book.

Four Basics of Good Description

1 It creates a main impression—an overall effect, feeling, or image—about the topic.

2 It uses specific examples to support the main impression.

3 It supports those examples with details that appeal to the five senses.

4 It brings a person, place, or object to life for the reader.

Alex Espinoza

Easy Like Sunday Morning

Alex Espinoza was born in Tijuana, Mexico, in 1971 and spent his childhood in La Puenté, a community near Los Angeles. He attended San Bernardino Community College and transferred to the University of California at Riverside, where he earned a bachelor of arts degree in creative writing. He went on to receive his master of fine arts degree from the University of California at Irvine, where he was editor of the university's literary magazine, *Faultline*. Espinoza published his first novel, *Still Water Saints,* in 2007. Espinoza is one of the Profiles of Success included in this book (see p. 162).

"Easy Like Sunday Morning" originally appeared on February 13, 2001, on *Salon*.

Guiding question   Which image or sensory detail in this essay do you find most memorable?

1   A photograph of my father sits above the television in our living room. My sister gave the picture to my mother as a Christmas present. It's not, however, the original photo.

2   The original black-and-white snapshot is stored in a photo album my mother keeps in her closet. In it, my father's stern face stares blankly at the camera, intense eyes crowned by thick bristly brows, square chin defining an angular face. My father had the picture taken when he was applying for a green card to come into the United States to work, leaving the rest of the family behind in Tijuana, Mexico.

3   My sister snuck the photo out of the album and took it to a copy center, where she had them blow it up, add color and remove the milky-colored crease from the corner.

Pause   Throughout the essay, Espinoza uses descriptive words to bring many different people, rooms, and scenes to life for the reader. Circle the descriptive words that use the five senses.

4   She had them color my father's shirt blue—an unnatural, manufactured blue, the kind of blue you see on birthday cakes. She placed it in a silver frame with a black velvet backing and little gold leaves on each corner. My mother put the photo on top of the television set, between a picture of Jesus Christ and a candle-holder shaped like a leaf.

5   It's early on a Sunday, a crisp, cold November morning, when the wind shakes the leaves loose, leaving bony branches that scrape against the windows of our house like long nails against a blackboard. These are the kinds of mornings I hated as a kid, because I always found it so hard to get out of bed. I realize that I still hate them now.

1. **menudo:** tripe stew seasoned with chiles; considered by some to be a hangover remedy; it is a very time-consuming dish to make and is often the center of a family meal.

6   My mother is making her *menudo*.[1] She stirs the simmering pot and complains about having to sweep the porch.

7   "I just swept this morning and those damn winds just carry more dead leaves back. *Como nada.*" She covers the pot, goes over to the counter and slowly dices an onion. She asks if I'll be having any menudo today. I tell her yes, but only a little, with no tripe and only a few pieces of hominy.

8   My mother frequently complains that I'm a finicky eater.

Pause   Espinoza chooses to use dialogue in his story. Why do you think he does this? What does it add to the story?

9   "Why can't you be more like your brothers when it comes to eating my food? Beto, Martin, they eat everything I make. When they lived at home and when they come over now. *Asi como nada,*" she says.

10   She places the finely chopped onions on one side of the little green bowl she always uses when she makes menudo, its edge warped from the time she accidentally placed it in the microwave. *"Ellos se comen todito. Pero tu? Nada!"*[2] she says.

2. **"Ellos se comen . . . Nada!":** "They eat absolutely everything. But you? Nothing."

11   She walks back over to the stove and stirs the soup, the water inside boiling the creamy white stomach lining whose smell and appearance have always made me sick.

12   "I just don't like it, Ma," I say as I flip the channels of the television.

13   I remember when I was younger, when we still lived in the house on Lang Avenue in La Puente near Los Angeles, when my father was still alive. Every Sunday morning my brothers would wake up, hung over from the previous evening's backyard parties. They would sit across from each other and piece together the highlights from their alcohol-saturated night—the mishaps, fights, hookups with girls (whose names always sounded like exotic ice-cream flavors)—and try to calculate the number of beers they had consumed.

14   They would sit in their thin boxer shorts, their eyes puffy from sleep, their hair mashed up against their heads, the creases from their sheets engraved into their arms, with their heads bent over their bowls in such a way that it looked as though they were praying.

15   I would sit there, watching and listening, with nothing to say. When they finished, they would wipe their mouths clean and go back to bed.

16   Then my father would come out of his room, sit in the chair closest to the glass window and eat his bowl, taking in the thick soup with a spoon whose handle was bigger than my arm, and rolling corn tortillas into thin tubes that he dipped into the bowl and ate one by one. He always ate slowly, staring out across the living room, while my mother argued with him about how late it was when he came stumbling home drunk the night before.

17   Again, I would sit there quietly, listening. I never understood why my father never talked back to my mother, and why he never turned to ask if I had eaten any menudo.

18   My mother tells me that both of my brothers are coming over today. She tells me that she hopes my brother Beto brings his tools to tighten the leaky sprinkler in the backyard that's flooding the grass. I laugh. It seems as though my mother always finds something to tighten, replace, patch up, hang up or tear down when she knows that one of my brothers is coming over.

19   My mother asks me what time my friend is coming over.

20   "This afternoon," I say.

21   Last week, my mother announced that she would be breaking out the pots and cutting up the tripe to make the menudo, because my brother Martin had said that it had been too long since he had had any of the stuff. I had almost forgotten that I had invited my boyfriend to join us for this Sunday morning ritual.

22   She asks me if my friend is white.

23   "Yes," I tell her.

24   What I don't tell her is that he is my boyfriend and that we have been dating for over three months now. I don't tell her that all those nights I said I'd be studying at the library, I was with him, drinking strong coffee in his living room with our shoes off, kissing on his green-and-white-striped couch with only the hum from his computer breaking the silence.

25   I don't tell her that the weekend I said I'd be in L.A. visiting my best friend Michael, I spent the night at his house and slept by his side with his chest pressed against my back and his long, thin fingers massaging my stomach.

26   I can't tell her that a few weeks ago, as we drove down the freeway with the windows rolled down and the radio blasting the latest Green Day album, he told me that he loved me. I can't tell her how good it made me feel.

27   She asks where I met my friend as she rubs her hands against her thin apron. The steam from the menudo fogs up the windows and seems to hang from the walls and slowly ooze down, clinging to everything, even my own skin, making the inside of the house feel moist and mysterious like the interior of a greenhouse or a sauna.

28   I tell her I met him at school. She asks if he is a student. I tell her that he finished school a few years ago. She asks if he has family. I tell her they live out of state.

Pause What is the purpose of this flashback? Why was it important for Espinoza to include this memory in his story?

Pause Espinoza is letting the reader in on a secret here—one that his family is not aware of. How does this confession add to the story? What do these details tell us about the writer and his relationship with his family?

29   I begin to get a sick feeling in my stomach. I begin to wonder if my boyfriend will have anything to talk to my brothers about and if my sisters-in-law will like him. I wonder if my family will see through my lie and discover that this man is my boyfriend, that this man is someone whom I love.

30   When the doorbell rings, my brother Beto's daughters are playing in the backyard, and my brother Martin's sons are sitting close to the television watching a puppet named Yankee Doodle Andy sing a song about the importance of friendship. I get up and open the door.

31   My boyfriend is standing on the porch with a bouquet of fresh flowers in one hand and a dozen Guerrero-brand flour tortillas in the other.

32   "You got the wrong brand," I say as I open the door to let him in.

33   He tells me he couldn't remember which ones I told him to get.

34   "La Rancher," I say. "Remember? The ones with the lady in the mariachi hat on the cover."

Pause How do you think the boyfriend feels after the author's greeting? How may that affect the way he acts?

35   He offers to go back. I tell him not to bother. I introduce him to my mother, who is coming out of the kitchen, wiping her forehead with the edge of her apron. She smiles and says *"Gracias"* when he gives her the flowers and tortillas.

36   He sits in the living room. My nephews stare at him for a few minutes. I see him smile and wave at both of them. They turn around and continue to watch *Yankee Doodle Andy*. I sit at the opposite end of our long, peach-colored sofa. I ask him if my directions were clear. He says they were. He can tell that I am nervous because I keep pulling on my earring. He smiles and tells me to relax.

37   My brothers and my sisters-in-law return from the market with bags of groceries. My brother Martin carries a 12-pack of beer in his hand. I introduce them to my friend. My brother Beto offers him a beer. He politely declines.

38   The menudo is ready and everyone sits at the dinner table to eat. My three nieces come in from the back and their mother tells them to say hello to my guest.

39   My mother serves my brothers and their wives big bowls of menudo. She turns and asks how much she should serve my boyfriend. I tell her to serve him a generous portion.

Pause Everything in the story up until this point has been in preparation for this meal, yet now there is silence. Why do you think the house is so silent?

40   She serves me a small bowl with only a few pieces of hominy and a flour tortilla on the side. Everything is quiet while we eat with our heads hovering over our bowls. Only the sound of our spoons gently tapping the sides of our porcelain bowls breaks the silence. And there is really no need for anyone to say or to ask anything at all.

41   Later I will go to my boyfriend's house. I will take him a bowl of menudo and three flour tortillas wrapped in aluminum foil. We will sit in front of the television, hold hands and talk about the future—a house tucked somewhere down a quiet, narrow street with a huge tree in front whose roots have broken through the concrete sidewalk, forcing it up like a camel's hump. We will talk about the photos gathering gray beards of dust that will crowd the top of our television set.

42   In the center will be the copy of my father's photo in the silver frame bought by my sister.

43   That night I will watch my boyfriend eat his menudo, leaving a red, swirly film at the bottom of the giant bowl. I will sit silently, listening to the easy, rhythmic sound of spoon hitting against bowl, knowing very well what is going into each careful tap. Knowing now, after all this time, what each one is trying to tell me in its own, simple way.

44   That night, I will listen.

45   I will hear the sound of my father's voice. I will hear my mother telling me to stop being such a picky eater and to learn to be more like my brothers. I will hear my boyfriend's love as he finishes his bowl, wipes his mouth, sighs and places his head gently on my stomach. It will be that easy. That simple.

46   I come home late at night, when the house is dark and thick with tranquillity, with my boyfriend's scent lingering faintly around my neck and fingernails.

47   I creep into my mother's room, remove the soft pink blanket from her face and gently kiss her pasty cheek.

48   Before I close the door, I hear her wake up and ask in a muffled voice what time it is. She asks where I have been.

49   I tell her I was with my friend.

50   She asks if he liked the menudo, if he ate it all.

51   I tell her he liked it. I tell her he ate it all.

52   "You are always alone," she says. "When are you going to bring a nice girl home? Doesn't your friend have a girlfriend? A wife?"

53   "No," I say softly, in the same voice I used as a kid whenever I knew I was in trouble. "He loves me, Ma. We love each other."

54   She pretends not to hear me. She clears her throat. She makes the sign of the cross and goes back to bed.

55   I stand there quietly with nothing left to say. I step out of the room and close the door behind me.

SUMMARIZE AND RESPOND

Summarize the main idea of "Easy Like Sunday Morning." Then, go back and check off support for this main idea. Next, write a brief summary (three to five sentences) of the reading. Finally, jot down your original response to the selection. What does Espinoza's experience with his family make him realize? How does it change him?

CHECK YOUR COMPREHENSION

1. Which of the following would be the best alternative title for this essay?

    a. "Introducing My Boyfriend to My Family"

    b. "Remembering My Father"

    c. "The Comfort of a Family Meal"

    d. "Combining Two Cultures"

2. The main idea of this essay is that

    a.   it's not the food that we remember, it's the experience of eating the food.

    (b.) our families and family rituals rarely change.

    c.   no matter what we do, we will always like certain things.

    d.   we always feel like children in our parents' homes.

3. The writer feels as though

    (a.) he can't tell his family who he really is.

    b.   his mother complains about him.

    c.   his mother keeps trying to make him like things he doesn't.

    d   he is more similar to his mother than he thought.

4. If you are unfamiliar with the following words, use a dictionary to check their meanings: tripe, hominy (para 7); finicky (8).

READ CRITICALLY

1. This essay is about an experience Espinoza had during a typical Sunday evening meal with his family, yet we learn more from his memories than from what is happening in the present. Why do you think Espinoza wrote the story in this way? What did he want us to think about by doing this?

2. Which paragraph do you think contains the most description and why? Where in the essay does the scene come to life for you? Where can you create a picture in your mind, hear what is going on, or smell what is cooking? What was it, in your opinion, that made that particular paragraph stronger than the others?

3. Espinoza starts the essay by describing the photograph of his father. Why is that the focus of the introduction? What is the father's role throughout the essay?

4. Espinoza says, "I will sit silently, listening to the easy, rhythmic sound of spoon hitting against bowl, knowing very well what is going into each careful tap. Knowing now, after all this time, what each one is trying to tell me in its own, simple way" (para. 43). What was it about this one particular meal that made it more special than any of the hundreds of meals like it before? What had changed or shifted?

WRITE AN ESSAY

Can you identify with or relate to Espinoza's experience? Write an essay about an event, experience, or encounter that inspired you or changed you in some way. What images and sensory details remain in your mind from the experience? How does the memory inspire you?

Peter Van Buren

The Day after a Day at the Embassy

Peter Van Buren worked for the U.S. State Department for twenty-four years and spent a year in Iraq before writing the book *We Meant Well: How I Helped Lose the Battle for the Hearts and Minds of the Iraqi People* (2011). His commentary has been featured on NPR and Al Jazeera, as well as in the *Nation* and the *Guardian*.

Guiding question What senses does the author appeal to in his essay?

1   We felt like hoboes, the four of us from the ePRT,[1] walking around the Embassy compound after the economics conference. Almost everything was a contrast to the world we lived in. Nothing was dusty, nothing covered with the fine tan silt that defined our Iraq. The air-conditioning was silent and even— smooth, cool air that we sought to draw into our pores and take back to our FOB.[2] The gleaming cafeteria always amazed us, from the sign apologizing for the Caesar salad station being temporarily closed to the surprisingly awkward, heavy feel of metal utensils (we used plastic, as if we were on a 365-day picnic) to the shock of a fruit-carving station stocked with fresh watermelon and papaya (we enjoyed those radioactive-orange-colored canned peaches in heavy syrup, more rumor than actual fruit). Unlike at the FOB, where the quality of the food made one thrifty about filling a plastic tray, we all loaded our china plates with fresh vegetables and crispy fries and ordered up Slurpees (choice of four flavors) and coffee drinks lush with real cream and sugar. It was all free, take as much as you wanted, here at Club Fed. The only surge in sight was in cholesterol.

2   At the Embassy, the men who held pointlessly long meetings with us sported bow ties and pressed linen pants, while the women wore earrings and perfume. No one was armed, civilians outnumbered uniformed military 20 to 1, there were water fountains in the hallways and marvelous real flush toilets that did not smell of the persons who used them before you. We rode an elevator for the only time in Iraq. We were like children raised by wolves, now among those who should have been our own kind yet weren't.

3   When you saw an American woman on the FOB, she was usually a soldier, dressed in military clothing designed to hide body shape better than any *hijab*[3]— one size fits no one, never a sense of, say, the lines of a summer dress hinting at the presence of her body. At the Embassy, you saw women in high heels, women in pants so impossibly tight that you died a little inside just to look; an employee imported from one of our embassies in South America wore black jeans and a yellow knit top with a black demi bra that stood out in bas relief. It might have looked crude in some universe, but here it was poetry, Old Testament–style temptation. Her body would leave an impression on history. Religions had been founded on less. The four of us looked like sad, desperate travelers from Mars as we stared.

1. **ePRT:** Embedded Provincial Reconstruction Team

2. **FOB:** Forward Operating Base

Pause What two scenes is Van Buren comparing in his introduction?

3. *hijab:* traditional covering for the hair and neck worn by Muslim women

Pause Van Buren describes the women he sees as "Old Testament– style temptation." What does he mean by that phrase? Why does he use a religious reference when describing women at the embassy?

4. **Sharia:** Islamic law based on the Koran

4   A key aspect of our Sharia[4] lifestyle on the FOB was the absence of alcohol, ostensibly banned by the military so as not to offend our Muslim hosts. But the Embassy knew no such restriction and the convenience store sold shampoo, magazines, cleaning supplies, and acres and acres of booze. You pushed through the swinging door to cases of cheap Budweiser, crates of Heineken, and every kind of liquor, liqueur, spirit, wine, and hooch known to man. Four varieties of flavored Grey Goose, Johnnie Walker in every color (including a $150 bottle of Blue), and types of vodka and gin I never knew existed. We stood there in air-conditioned comfort and browsed until the mere sight of it all made us inebriated, and only then did we carry our choices to the cash register, where we paid by credit card. A credit card, here at war! The wonder of it all wore off quickly given humans' astonishing ability to adjust, so we had to grab at each sensation and catalog it before it became part of our new evolving normal, as ordinary soon as the Embassy's Pizza Hut, the Starbucks clone Green Bean, the indoor swimming pool, the sign advertising swing dance lessons on Tuesdays, the Wi-Fi in the lounge, the lounge, the bar, the magazines published within the last two months, the hair salon that did highlights, the misters spraying cool water into the air to allow people to sit comfortably outside, the tennis courts, the driving range—all dizzying reminders that we Americans were strangers, useless to the needs of the place.

5   At the helipad, waiting for our ride home, we sat around for ninety minutes until it got dark enough to take off. Even with GPS, a lot of helicopter navigation is done by eye as the pilots try to avoid wires and land on small pads at remote installations. The pilots can fly easily in the daylight, and easily in the dark with night-vision gear, but it is tricky in the in-between times.

Pause Underline the descriptive words used in this paragraph to help the reader understand what it was like to wait for the helicopter in the darkness.

6   Darkness had new meaning here. Unlike in the States, where there were almost always some lights on, in the desert, when the moon was not out, you could not see your own feet beneath you. To better use their night goggles, the pilots blacked out the helicopter and switched off their outside lights. Flying this way was oddly therapeutic, as there was nothing to see, there were no reference points, just the enveloping sound of the helo and the comforting sensation of motion. We flew in a UH-1, the Vietnam-era helicopter everyone knows from the movies, which had a tendency to slide through the air in a series of long, lazy curves. Finally, we saw the lights that marked our home helo pad. The lights were not bright airport beams but small Chem-Light dots at the corners of the landing zone, almost invisible to the naked eye but nice and clear with night goggles.

7   We had to move by feel once on the ground. Vulnerable to mortar attack, the pilot was in a hurry to get airborne again. I got out of the helo and the crew chief, whose job it was to load and unload us, also jumped out to make sure I walked away properly. Because it was so dark, it was easy to get disoriented, and walking into the spinning tail rotor blades was death. The crew chief had night goggles and usually gave everyone a push from behind to get them moving in the right direction. Somebody eventually flashed a dim light to guide you. Not so easy, but you got used to it. This time the crew chief sent my colleagues off the LZ but held

me by the shoulder and shouted that I was to wait for a soldier with a lot of gear to get out and then help him carry the load.

8   Suddenly the helicopter engine engaged and the crew chief grabbed me by the jacket sleeve and jerked me backward onto the ground as the helo took off. The tail rotor spun over our heads and the bird disappeared with a roar into the black sky. There was no quiet like the hole left when a helo departed, the noise so powerful suddenly withdrawn. We were flat on the ground, with stuff spread all over by the downward blast of the rotors. Had the crew chief not flung me and himself down, we would have been killed. Dead without knowing it, just like that, dear Mrs. Van Buren, the Department of State regrets to inform you . . .

9   It was a rough way to break free from the Embassy cocoon, where their ignorant eagerness for things as they wanted them to be ran head-on into our thoughts about things as they were. We had not always gotten along, the four of us from the ePRT, arguing over the right thing to do, the best way to spend our money and get through our year. Still, though I was a bit in shock from the helo incident and scared after the fact, I was happy to be back with my teammates in the more familiar world of the FOB. Regrouped, we moved gracelessly to a small patio near our office outlined by a Conex shipping container on one side, a sloppy brick wall standing because it was too lazy to fall on a second, and the remnants of another building on the third. Usually when we came back with our secreted beer from the Embassy, we parceled the cans out in ones and twos, trying to make the stash last longer, like teens in our parents' basement. A can tonight, maybe two on Friday, and a couple of cases could pass the time for weeks. Tonight something unspoken made us greedy. We chugged cans, we popped the tops of the ever-warmer brew (room temperature was 104 degrees), and slurped the foam like Vikings on a New World bender. One of the benefits of not drinking often was that your body dried out, and so even a little alcohol thrown down that dry hole kicked your ass. A lot of alcohol drunk purposely under these conditions sent four adults into drunkenness marvelously rich and fine. It tasted of a high school June.

10   With a lot of dust in the air and only a toenail-clipping-shaped moon out, the darkness was complete as we sat drinking the last beers. A light would have embarrassed us. Seen in a photo, we could have been anywhere; there were no clues for an outsider to decode. We four felt closer to this place, and to one another, than we ever had.

Pause Van Buren compares his exit from the embassy to breaking free from a cocoon. Why does he choose that metaphor? How does it help the reader understand the experience?

SUMMARIZE AND RESPOND

Summarize the main idea of "The Day after a Day at the Embassy." Then, go back and check off descriptive details in the essay. Next, write a brief summary (three to five sentences) of the essay. Finally, jot down your initial response to the reading. What effect does the day at the embassy have on the author? Have you ever experienced anything similar?

CHECK YOUR COMPREHENSION

1. Which of the following would be the best alternative title for the essay?

   a.   "Finding My Way in the Dark"

   b.   "Comparing Two Worlds"

   c.   "Leaving My Comfort Zone"

   d.   "Not Knowing Whom to Trust"

2. The main idea of this essay is that

   a.   it was nice inside the embassy.

   b.   it was hard to move about in the dark without being able to see.

   c.   it was uncomfortable to try to live and work outside of the embassy.

   d.   it was hard to leave the embassy so quickly, knowing the difficulties that waited outside.

3. According to the author,

   a.   it was clear that everyone was treated the same in Iraq.

   b.   certain situations were different in Iraq.

   c.   different people were given different privileges in Iraq depending on their position.

   d.   everything had to be done in secret in Iraq.

4. If you are unfamiliar with the following words, use a dictionary to check their meanings: surge (para. 1); hijab (3); ostensibly, inebriated (4); mortar (7); secreted (9).

READ CRITICALLY

1. What is the author's purpose in this essay? How would you describe his tone?

2. Why do you think the author was so careful to describe everything he saw inside the embassy?

3. How is this essay both a description and a comparison and contrast essay?

4. Can you as a reader visualize what happened as the author tried to move through the darkness and get in the helicopter? What descriptive words and phrases, in particular, were unique to this story? How did the writer describe the night and the experience in a way that you hadn't heard or thought of before?

5. In your own words, describe how the author felt at the end of the essay when he was finally on the helicopter leaving the embassy. What is your evidence?

WRITE AN ESSAY

Van Buren's experience in the embassy made him more aware of how uncomfortable life was outside of the embassy. Write a description essay about a time when you have been in a place where you have felt uncomfortable. What was it about your experience that made you feel uncomfortable? Was it a problem because you didn't understand what was being discussed? Did you not understand the language? Were you at a party or gathering and didn't feel like you fit in? Make sure to include details that help your readers experience what you felt.

Description: Linked Readings

Feeling Foreign

Each of the following readings focuses on various aspects of feeling foreign and the ways people can have divided identities.

Rui Dai, "A Whiff of Memory" (Chapter 16, p. 229)

Bill Bryson, "Coming Home" (Chapter 40, p. 583)

Read the selections and draw from at least one in addition to "Easy Like Sunday Morning" to write an essay entitled "Feeling Foreign." You can use the word *foreign* in the sense of being from another country or in the sense of being in a new situation, such as starting at a new job or a new school.

Making Changes

Each of the following readings focuses on various ways people experienced change in their daily lives.

Langston Hughes, "Salvation" (Chapter 40, p. 590)

Malcolm X, "Learning to Read" (Chapter 43, p. 617)

Mary Elizabeth Williams, "Our Family's Week on a Food Stamp Budget" (Chapter 46, p. 654)

Read the selections and draw from at least one in addition to "The Day after a Day at the Embassy" to write an essay titled "Making Changes." Think about what happened when you made a change in your life, large or small. It could be a change in scenery, a change in your lifestyle, or a change in your education. Make sure you use at least one of the essays above, in addition to your own experience, to explain to your reader how this change affected your life.

Family Ties

Each of the following readings discusses family relationships and the ways they affect and shape people's lives.

Daniel Flanagan, "The Choice to Do It Over Again" (Chapter 13, p. 180)

Liza Long, "I Am Adam Lanza's Mother" (Chapter 41, p. 594)

Amy Tan, "Mother Tongue" (Chapter 44, p. 633)

Read the selections, and draw from at least one in addition to "Easy Like Sunday Morning" to write an essay entitled "How Family Ties Affect Our Lives." You may refer to your own experience, but make sure to use material from the essays as well.

43

Process Analysis

Each essay in this chapter uses process analysis to get its main idea across. As you read these essays, consider how they achieve the four basics of good process analysis that are listed below and discussed in Chapter 13 of this book.

Four Basics of Good Process Analysis

> **1** It helps readers either perform the steps themselves or understand how something works.
>
> **2** It presents the essential steps in the process.
>
> **3** It explains the steps in detail.
>
> **4** It arranges the steps in a logical order (usually in chronological order).

Malcolm X

Learning to Read

Born Malcolm Little on May 19, 1925, Malcolm X was one of the most articulate and powerful leaders of black America during the 1960s. A street hustler convicted of robbery in 1946, he spent seven years in prison, where he educated himself and became a disciple of Elijah Muhammad, founder of the Nation of Islam. In the days of the civil rights movement, Malcolm X emerged as the leading spokesman for black separatism, a philosophy that urged black Americans to cut political, social, and economic ties with the white community. After a pilgrimage to Mecca, the capital of the Muslim world, in 1964, he became an orthodox Muslim, adopted the Muslim name El Hajj Malik El-Shabazz, and distanced himself from the teachings of the black Muslims. He was assassinated in 1965. In the following excerpt from his autobiography (1965), coauthored with Alex Haley and published the year of his death, Malcolm X describes his self-education.

Guiding question What does Malcolm X mean by a "homemade education"?

1   It was because of my letters that I happened to stumble upon starting to acquire some kind of a homemade education.

2   I became increasingly frustrated at not being able to express what I wanted to convey in letters that I wrote, especially those to Mr. Elijah Muhammad. In the street, I had been the most articulate hustler out there. I had commanded attention when I said something. But now, trying to write simple English, I not only wasn't articulate, I wasn't even functional. How would I sound writing in slang, the way I would *say* it, something such as, "Look, daddy, let me pull your coat[1] about a cat, Elijah Muhammad—"

3   Many who today hear me somewhere in person, or on television, or those who read something I've said, will think I went to school far beyond the eighth grade. This impression is due entirely to my prison studies.

4   It had really begun back in the Charlestown Prison, when Bimbi first made me feel envy of his stock of knowledge. Bimbi had always taken charge of any conversations he was in, and I had tried to emulate him. But every book I picked up had few sentences which didn't contain anywhere from one to nearly all of the words that might as well have been in Chinese. When I just skipped those words, of course, I really ended up with little idea of what the book said. So I had come to the Norfolk Prison Colony still going through only book-reading motions. Pretty soon, I would have quit even these motions, unless I had received the motivation that I did.

5   I saw that the best thing I could do was get hold of a dictionary—to study, to learn some words. I was lucky enough to reason also that I should try to improve my penmanship. It was sad. I couldn't even write in a straight line. It was both ideas together that moved me to request a dictionary along with some tablets and pencils from the Norfolk Prison Colony school.

6   I spent two days just riffling uncertainly through the dictionary's pages. I'd never realized so many words existed! I didn't know *which* words I needed to learn. Finally, just to start some kind of action, I began copying.

7   In my slow, painstaking, ragged handwriting, I copied into my tablet everything printed on that first page, down to the punctuation marks.

8   I believe it took me a day. Then, aloud, I read back, to myself, everything I'd written on the tablet. Over and over, aloud, to myself, I read my own handwriting.

9   I woke up the next morning, thinking about those words—immensely proud to realize that not only had I written so much at one time, but I'd written words that I never knew were in the world. Moreover, with a little effort, I also could remember what many of these words meant. I reviewed the words whose meanings I didn't remember. Funny thing, from the dictionary first page right now,

Pause What does Malcolm X mean when he says that he wasn't "functional" when writing simple English?

1. **pull your coat:** to grab your attention

Pause Number the steps Malcolm X took to educate himself.

Discussion Ask students: Has there ever been a point in your life where you knew you needed to change something or fix something but you didn't know how to start? What was it? How did you begin?

Pause Why was this one moment so significant to the author? How did it encourage him to continue learning?

that "aardvark" springs to my mind. The dictionary had a picture of it, a long-tailed, long-eared, burrowing African mammal, which lives off termites caught by sticking out its tongue as an anteater does for ants.

10   I was so fascinated that I went on—I copied the dictionary's next page. And the same experience came when I studied that. With every succeeding page, I also learned of people and places and events from history. Actually the dictionary is like a miniature encyclopedia. Finally the dictionary's A section had filled a whole tablet—and I went on into the B's. That was the way I started copying what eventually became the entire dictionary. It went a lot faster after so much practice helped me to pick up handwriting speed. Between what I wrote in my tablet, and writing letters, during the rest of my time in prison I would guess I wrote a million words.

11   I suppose it was inevitable that as my word-base broadened, I could for the first time pick up a book and read and now begin to understand what the book was saying. Anyone who has read a great deal can imagine the new world that opened. Let me tell you something: from then until I left that prison, in every free moment I had, if I was not reading in the library, I was reading on my bunk. You couldn't have gotten me out of books with a wedge. Between Mr. Muhammad's teachings, my correspondence, my visitors—usually Ella and Reginald—and my reading of books, months passed without my even thinking about being imprisoned. In fact, up to then, I never had been so truly free in my life.

12   The Norfolk Prison Colony's library was in the school building. A variety of classes was taught there by instructors who came from such places as Harvard and Boston universities. The weekly debates between inmate teams were also held in the school building. You would be astonished to know how worked up convict debaters and audiences would get over subjects like "Should Babies Be Fed Milk?"

13   Available on the prison library's shelves were books on just about every general subject. Much of the big private collection that Parkhurst[2] had willed to the prison was still in crates and boxes in the back of the library—thousands of old books. Some of them looked ancient: covers faded; old-time parchment-looking binding. Parkhurst, I've mentioned, seemed to have been principally interested in history and religion. He had the money and the special interest to have a lot of books that you wouldn't have in general circulation. Any college library would have been lucky to get that collection.

14   As you can imagine, especially in a prison where there was heavy emphasis on rehabilitation, an inmate was smiled upon if he demonstrated an unusually intense interest in books. There was a sizable number of well-read inmates, especially the popular debaters. Some were said by many to be practically walking encyclopedias.

15   They were almost celebrities. No university would ask any student to devour literature as I did when this new world opened to me, of being able to read and *understand*.

Discussion Just like a student, Malcolm X had to start learning simpler material before working his way up to more advanced materials (books, language, debates, etc.). Ask students: What was a subject that was particularly difficult for you? When did you have a particular challenge that you had to tackle one step at a time? What was the process you followed?

2. **Parkhurst:** Charles H. Parkhurst (1842–1933) clergyman and social reformer. Parkhurst was particularly involved in education, politics, and criminal reform.

Pause Underline each achievement Malcolm X made in his learning.

16   I read more in my room than in the library itself. An inmate who was known to read a lot could check out more than the permitted maximum number of books. I preferred reading in the total isolation of my own room.

17   When I had progressed to really serious reading, every night at about ten p.m. I would be outraged with the "lights out." It always seemed to catch me right in the middle of something engrossing.

18   Fortunately, right outside my door was a corridor light that cast a glow into my room. The glow was enough to read by, once my eyes adjusted to it. So when "lights out" came, I would sit on the floor where I could continue reading in that glow.

19   At one-hour intervals the night guards paced past every room. Each time I heard the approaching footsteps, I jumped into bed and feigned sleep. And as soon as the guard passed, I got back out of bed onto the floor area of that light-glow, where I would read for another fifty-eight minutes—until the guard approached again. That went on until three or four every morning. Three or four hours of sleep a night was enough for me. Often in the years in the streets I had slept less than that.

Pause What does Malcolm X mean when he says that history has been "whitened"?

20   The teachings of Mr. Muhammad stressed how history had been "whitened"—when white men had written history books, the black man simply had been left out. . . . I never will forget how shocked I was when I began reading about slavery's total horror. It made such an impact upon me that it later became one of my favorite subjects when I became a minister of Mr. Muhammad's. The world's most monstrous crime, the sin and the blood on the white man's hands, are almost impossible to believe. . . . I read descriptions of atrocities, saw those illustrations of black slave women tied up and flogged with whips; of black mothers watching their babies being dragged off, never to be seen by their mothers again; of dogs after slaves, and of the fugitive slave catchers, evil white men with whips and clubs and chains and guns. . . .

21   Book after book showed me how the white man had brought upon the world's black, brown, red, and yellow peoples every variety of the sufferings of exploitation. I saw how since the sixteenth century, the so-called "Christian trader" white man began to ply the seas in his lust for Asian and African empires, and plunder, and power. I read, I saw, how the white man never has gone among the non-white peoples bearing the Cross in the true manner and spirit of Christ's teachings—meek, humble, and Christlike. . . .

22   I have often reflected upon the new vistas that reading opened to me. I knew right there in prison that reading had changed forever the course of my life. As I see it today, the ability to read awoke inside me some long dormant craving to be mentally alive. I certainly wasn't seeking any degree, the way a college confers a status symbol upon its students. My homemade education gave me, with every additional book that I read, a little bit more sensitivity to the deafness, dumbness, and blindness that was afflicting the black race in America. Not long ago, an English writer telephoned me from London, asking questions. One was, "What's your alma mater?" I told him, "Books." You will never catch me with a free fifteen minutes in which I'm not studying something I feel might be able to help the black man.

SUMMARIZE AND RESPOND

Summarize the main idea of "Learning to Read." Then, go back and check off the steps in the process. Next, write a brief summary (three to five sentences) of the essay. Finally, jot down your initial response to the reading. Is it a good process analysis essay? Why or why not?

CHECK YOUR COMPREHENSION

1. Which of the following would be the best alternative title for the essay?

    a.   "Living in Prison"

    b.   "Improving Your Handwriting"

    c.   "A Homemade Education"

    d.   "Using Your Prison Time Wisely"

2. The main idea of this essay is that

    a.   Malcolm X was interested in what was going on around him.

    b.   by taking the time to learn how to write and read on his own, Malcolm X changed his life.

    c.   it's possible to take steps to improve whatever situation you are in.

    d.   prison doesn't have to be a place that wastes your time.

3. What did his education give to the author?

    a.   More sensitivity to the plight of black people in America

    b.   A college degree

    c.   Ability to memorize books

    d.   Street smarts

4. If you are unfamiliar with the following words, use a dictionary to check their meanings: articulate (para. 2); emulate (4); inevitable (11); parchment (13); engrossing (17); feigned (19); atrocities (20).

READ CRITICALLY

1. What steps did Malcolm X take to learn how to read?

2. How did learning to read one word at a time help him become involved with more complex arguments and topics?

3. How does the essay demonstrate the Four Basics of Good Process Analysis?

4. How would you describe the author's tone in the essay?

Write about a time that you had difficulty learning a subject at school. What did you do to help yourself study for a test or master the subject? Detail the process you used so that readers could duplicate it on their own.

Felix Tarcomnicu

How the Hiring Process Has Changed over the Years

Since 2009, Felix Tarcomnicu has been a regular contributor to the blog he founded, *ResumeOK*, where he writes articles for job seekers. His work also appears on the Web sites the *Huffington Post* and *Entrepreneur*.

Guiding question How has the hiring process changed over the years?

Pause What do you think the main methods of hiring a candidate may be in today's workforce?

1   The process of hiring and recruiting manpower services has changed notably over the years and still continues to evolve as technology takes a giant leap forward. More and more companies are turning to a multi-faceted approach to recruit qualified applicants. To be able to stay at the top of the game, job seekers should be in the know of the various methods companies use to look for qualified applicants.

Free Job-Posting Websites

2   Apart from bringing entertainment and information to its users, the Internet has helped open the doors for many job hopefuls through employment posting websites such as Jobs DB and Jobstreet. With these sites, an applicant can simply look for job openings that match his skills and capacities, send out his résumé to prospective employers, and hope that he gets hired. Employment-posting websites have indeed changed the face of job hunting as we know it, as job seekers no longer need to scour the city for job openings, nor do they have to try their luck on the streets, hoping merchants have vacancies for them.

Pause Underline the ways the hiring process has changed from previous years.

3   These websites not only bring convenience to job seekers; they offer numerous advantages to employers as well. For one, they do not have to send out their HR personnel to job caravans in order to screen and interview applicants. They can now do so within the confines of their office, which means lowered operating expense for the company.

Social Networking Websites

4   Social networking websites are not just for getting in touch with long-lost family and friends anymore. In the recent years, these websites have become an excellent avenue for job seeking. Millions of people use social networking

websites such as Facebook, Twitter, and LinkedIn everyday. Their reach is beneficial for both parties, since the employer can let millions of people know about his job opening. At the same time, they give the job seeker the opportunity he would not have been presented with if he has not accessed these social networking websites.

LinkedIn

5   While Facebook and Twitter fare greatly in the world of job seeking, perhaps the best social networking site for those who wish to get hired is LinkedIn. This website features strong connections with thousands of companies from over 130 disciplines. With these members, LinkedIn registrants get the chance to view the numerous job openings from these respected companies. Like the traditional method of referring applicants, LinkedIn also fosters employee referrals, as the job posters can communicate easily with their former employees. Best of all, LinkedIn helps connect professionals from the same discipline, making the job search a lot easier and faster.

Facebook

6   Facebook is perhaps the most famous social media website in the world. Although it is commonly used for personal purposes, it is also very useful for those who are seeking employment. A Facebook profile enables a company to establish their brand presence and connect with many aspiring job seekers (fan base). At the same time, the company's employees who also use the social networking website can expand the reach more by sending out job invites to skilled people they know.

Pause How might understanding the hiring process from a company's viewpoint help a job seeker in his or her effort to gain employment?

Twitter

7   Tweets might be limited to 140 characters, but they are very useful for job seekers and employers as well. Since millions of users log on to Twitter every day, a company can use it to its advantage because it can be presented with a large pool of applicants. By posting tweets, your followers and employees can access the link of your job openings and file their applications online.

Craigslist

8   Craigslist is known to many as the online version of classified ads. Apart from posting about the items you wish to sell, Craigslist can also be instrumental to individuals who are looking to hire new employees. Just like employment-posting websites, Craigslist allows the employer to post his job opening and attract any interested applicants. Since it does not require résumés or job experience, this portal is oftentimes utilized by those looking for part-time employees, such as plumbers, painters, carpenters, to name a few.

Pause Consider your own use of social media. Would you want a potential employer to have access to your profile(s)? Why or why not?

Online Interviewing

9   Interviewing is an essential part of the recruitment process. Even if an applicant has a stellar résumé, an employer would like to talk to him personally.

Before, interviewing had to be done face to face. But with technological advancements such as VoIP, employers can now screen their applicants—even if they are located far away—with the use of programs such as Skype and Viber. As long as both individuals have a personal computer/smart device, internet connection and webcam (sometimes optional), they can go through the interview process right away. This method is very advantageous for both parties, too. The employer can conduct the interview at any set time, immediately if possible. On the other hand, the applicant does not have to spend money over fares or gas money just to be interviewed by the employer.

Online Outsourcing

10   Another trend that has taken the employment world by storm is outsourcing. More and more companies are basing their customer care centers in countries where English is the second language. Recognizing the money-saving benefits of this hiring trend, many employers, who are looking to complete small projects, are now practicing online outsourcing through websites such as oDesk or ELance. These websites provide employees with a talented pool of service providers from all around the world.

11   Just like "normal employment," contracts are put into place. Because projects are delivered through online messaging portals, the cost of hiring outsourced individuals is usually cheaper—and the quality of the projects is usually at par with that of traditionally hired professionals.

12   With the wide scale use of the internet and other online programs, the hiring process continues to change for the better. If you wish to keep up with these employment trends, then it is essential that you familiarize yourself with these processes—and how you can utilize them to your advantage.

SUMMARIZE AND RESPOND

Summarize the main idea of "How the Hiring Process Has Changed over the Years." Then, go back and check off support for this main idea. Next, write a brief summary (three to five sentences) of the essay. Finally, jot down your initial response to the essay. Do you think the Internet has made the hiring process easier or more difficult?

CHECK YOUR COMPREHENSION

1. Which of the following would be the best alternative title for this essay?

    a.   "How the Internet Is Changing Our Hiring Process"

    b.   "The Hiring Process Has Become Less Formal"

    c.   "Social Media Makes Finding a Job Easier"

    d.   "Finding a Job"

2. The main idea of this essay is that

    a. you need to make sure you use social media to help you find a job.

    (b.) you should use all the Internet tools available to you in order to assist you to find a job.

    c. finding a job today is different than it used to be thanks to advances in technology.

    d. you need to expect to conduct interviews online through Skype or Facebook when you are interviewing for a job.

3. According to the author,

    a. being technologically savvy can make up for gaps in a résumé.

    b. creating a strong technological profile is more important than any other skills.

    (c.) no matter how good your résumé is, you will still be required to interview.

    d. you should make all your social media networks public so employers can find you easily.

4. If you are unfamiliar with the following words, use a dictionary to check their meanings: multi-faceted (para. 1); registrants (5); stellar (9); VoIP, Skype, Viber (9); outsourcing (10).

READ CRITICALLY

1. Why does Tarcomnicu want to call attention to all of the distinct differences in the hiring process today versus the way it once was?

2. Tarcomnicu focuses heavily on technology in the essay. Can a person rely on technology alone to find a job today? Explain your answer using evidence from his essay.

3. Tarcomnicu presents a process analysis that doesn't look like a typical "first, second, third" essay. What are the steps in his process?

4. After reading his essay, do you think Tarcomnicu believes that technology is helping both businesses and job seekers or hurting them? Explain your answer.

WRITE AN ESSAY

According to Tarcomnicu, finding a job is different than it used to be, thanks to advances in technology. Write an essay that offers a process analysis of technology and employment. You could write about assisting others in finding a job, how to post a job opening to reach the greatest number of potential employees, or how to monitor or restrict the use of social media at work. You can consider other topics as well, but you need to write about a process.

Process Analysis: Linked Readings

Issues of Language

Each of the following readings focuses on the idea of unfamiliarity in some way.

> Bill Bryson, "Coming Home" (Chapter 40, p. 583)
>
> Amy Tan, "Mother Tongue" (Chapter 44, p. 633)

Read the selections, and draw from at least one in addition to "Learning to Read" to write an essay titled "Issues of Language." You can refer to your own experience, but make sure to use material from the essays as well.

The Pressure to Conform in Our Society

Each of the following readings discusses how it can be difficult to fit in with society's rules and regulations.

> Monique Rizer, "When Students Are Parents" (Chapter 40, p. 587)
>
> Liza Long, "I Am Adam Lanza's Mother" (Chapter 41, p. 594)
>
> Nancy Mairs, "On Being a Cripple" (Chapter 45, p. 645)
>
> Amy L. Beck, "Struggling for Perfection" (Chapter 47, p. 666)
>
> Brent Staples, "Just Walk On By: Black Men and Public Space" (Chapter 47, p. 670)

Read the selections, and draw from at least one in addition to "Learning to Read" to write an essay titled "The Pressure to Conform in Our Society." You can refer to your own experience, but make sure to use material from the essays as well.

44

Classification

Each essay in this chapter uses classification to get its main point across. As you read these essays, consider how they achieve the four basics of good classification that are listed below and discussed in Chapter 14 of this book.

Four Basics of Good Classification

1 It makes sense of a group of people or items by organizing them into useful categories.

2 It has a purpose for sorting the people or items.

3 It uses a single organizing principle.

4 It gives detailed examples or explanations of the things that fit into each category.

James Hamblin

How Much Caffeine before I End Up in the ER?

James Hamblin, MD, trained in residency in the Harvard, Northwestern, and UCLA medical systems, although he currently works in media. Now he enjoys doing stand-up and improvisational comedy. His work has appeared on National Public Radio and in *Salon*, the *Los Angeles Times*, and the *Atlantic*.

Guiding question In 2005, fewer than 2,000 trips to U.S. hospital emergency departments involved energy drinks. By 2011, that number was over 20,000. If energy drinks are safe, why are they sending us to the hospital?

Teaching tip Before you begin reading this essay, look around the room—chances are good that you'll see some students drinking coffee, energy drinks, or other caffeinated beverages. If not, then ask students whether they had such a drink earlier in the day. Have students look online or on the packaging to compare those ingredients to what they read in the Hamblin piece.

1   The Substance Abuse and Mental Health Services Administration (SAMHSA, a government behavioral health agency) issued a report on Friday that called energy drinks "a continuing public health concern." Yes, energy drinks like Red Bull, 5-Hour Energy, Monster, Full Throttle, CHARGE!, Neurogasm, Hardcore Energize Bullet, Facedrink, Eruption, Crakshot, Crave, Crunk, DynaPep, Rage Inferno, SLAP, and even good old Venom Death Adder.

Pause How dangerous do you believe energy drinks might be? What do you think the danger may be?

2   Everything is a public health concern, though, really. How publicly concerned should we be about energy drinks?

3   First off, the data from the SAMHSA report looks alarming. It tells us that the number of "energy drink-related" emergency department (ED) visits increased nearly tenfold between 2005 and 2011:

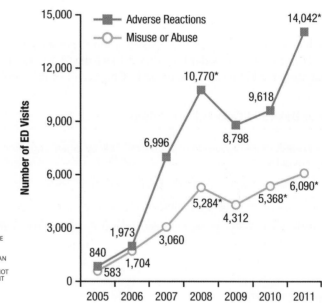

THIS GRAPH IS REPRODUCED COURTESY OF THE SUBSTANCE ABUSE AND MENTAL HEALTH SERVICES ADMINISTRATION (SAMHSA), U.S. DEPARTMENT OF HEALTH AND HUMAN SERVICES (HHS). INCLUSION OF THIS GRAPH IN THIS PUBLICATION DOES NOT CONSTITUTE OFFICIAL ENDORSEMENT BY SAMHSA OR HHS. SOURCE: 2011 SAMHSA DRUG ABUSE WARNING NETWORK (DAWN).

4   Energy drinks are not-uncommonly used along with alcohol and other drugs, so SAMHSA (say it aloud once, it's calming) makes the distinction that, of the 20,783 ED visits in 2011, 58 percent involved energy drinks alone; the remaining also involved other drugs.

5   The rise suggests an increasing propensity for abuse, though, given the rapidly increasing prevalence of energy drinks in the market since 2005 (now a $101 billion industry), probably a similar percentage of consumers are misusing them and/or having adverse reactions.

6   Those consumers are more commonly men, and most commonly 18–25-year-olds—though the over-40 demographic is growing the most rapidly, by degrees (up 379 percent between 2007 and 2011).

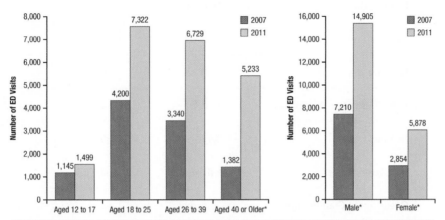

THIS GRAPH IS REPRODUCED COURTESY OF THE SUBSTANCE ABUSE AND MENTAL HEALTH SERVICES ADMINISTRATION (SAMHSA), U.S. DEPARTMENT OF HEALTH AND HUMAN SERVICES (HHS). INCLUSION OF THIS GRAPH IN THIS PUBLICATION DOES NOT CONSTITUTE OFFICIAL ENDORSEMENT BY SAMHSA OR HHS. SOURCE: 2011 SAMHSA DRUG ABUSE WARNING NETWORK (DAWN).

7   Why are these drinks sending people to the emergency room? The only ingredient(s) in common energy drinks that have been proven to have acute stimulant effects are caffeine and guarana (which SAMHSA defines as "a plant product containing concentrated caffeine"). The vitamins and amino acids that many drinks include shouldn't give you a noticeable burst of energy unless you were previously malnourished and vitamin-deficient. And they're not reasoned to play a role in intoxication effects.

8   So, essentially, energy drinks can be looked at as caffeine. And as the SAMHSA report puts it, "Large amounts of caffeine can cause adverse effects such as insomnia, nervousness, headache, fast heartbeat, and seizures that are severe enough to require emergency care."

9   How much is a "large amount" of caffeine? Like alcohol, it's relative to metabolism and tolerance. Most people can tolerate a lot. In caffeine-modified electroconvulsive therapy, for patients with depression, up to 2,000 mg has been given—intravenously. But that's in a controlled hospital environment where they are *trying* to give people seizures. And it does increase the likelihood they will have a seizure. For a frame of reference, SAMHSA notes, "The total amount of caffeine in a can or bottle of an energy drink varies from about 80 to more than 500 mg, compared with about 100 mg in a 5-ounce cup of coffee or 50 mg in a 12-ounce cola."

10   Those examples are a little misleading, though. The Center for Science in the Public Interest (CSPI) has a great list of how much caffeine specific foods/drinks contain. For energy drinks, "more than 500 mg" is far from the norm:

Pause Why are the numbers of those who have visited the emergency department because of energy drinks highest for young men (ages 18–25 and 26–39)? Also, why did the number jump so high between 2007 and 2011 for men over 40?

Pause Have you heard of guarana? Many times it's billed as a natural herb that may have positive effects. What other herbs or natural ingredients can you think of that are in your drinks or food? Look them up and see what they actually are. Are they good for you?

Discussion Ask students to divulge how much caffeine they drink in a day. Most are proud of the amount it takes to "keep them functional."

Energy Drinks	Serving Size	Caffeine (mg)
5-hour Energy	1.9 fl. oz.	208
Full Throttle	16 fl. oz.	200
Monster Energy	16 fl. oz.	160
Rockstar	16 fl. oz.	160
AMP Energy Boost Original	16 fl. oz.	142
Red Bull	8.4 fl. oz.	80
V8 V-Fusion+Energy	8 fl. oz.	80
Ocean Spray Cran-Energy	20 fl. oz.	55
Glacéau Vitaminwater Energy	20 fl. oz.	50

COURTESY OF CENTER FOR SCIENCE IN THE PUBLIC INTEREST

11   Cran-Energy is a thing, yes.

12   And the 50 mg that SAMHSA cites for a "cup of coffee" is pretty optimistic—at least in the way that many of us define coffee.

Coffees	Serving Size	Caffeine (mg)
Dunkin' Donuts Coffee with Turbo Shot	large, 20 fl. oz.	436
Starbucks Coffee	venti, 20 fl. oz.	415
Starbucks Coffee	grande, 16 fl. oz.	330
Panera Frozen Mocha	16.5 fl. oz.	267
Starbucks Coffee	tall, 12 fl. oz.	260
Starbucks Caffè Americano	grande, 16 fl. oz.	225
Panera Coffee	regular, 16.8 fl. oz.	189
Starbucks Espresso Frappuccino	venti, 24 fl. oz.	185

COURTESY OF CENTER FOR SCIENCE IN THE PUBLIC INTEREST

Coffees	Serving Size	Caffeine (mg)
Dunkin' Donuts Coffee	medium, 14 fl. oz.	178
Starbucks Caffè Mocha	grande, 16 fl. oz.	175
Starbucks Iced Coffee	grande, 16 fl. oz.	165
Maxwell House Ground Coffee—100% Colombian, Dark Roast, Master Blend, or Original Roast	2 Tbs., makes 12 fl. oz.	100-160
Dunkin' Donuts Cappuccino	large, 20 fl. oz.	151
Starbucks—Caffè Latte, Cappuccino, or Caramel Macchiato	grande, 16 fl. oz.	150
Starbucks Espresso	doppio, 2 fl. oz.	150

COURTESY OF CENTER FOR SCIENCE IN THE PUBLIC INTEREST

13   Still, despite the fact that a Starbucks venti coffee has three times as much listed caffeine as a can of Monster, some people swear they're more wired after drinking an energy drink. That may be because of the extra caffeine in guarana. Energy drinks can advertise that they have the same amount of caffeine as a cup of coffee; but when you include guarana, they have a much stronger stimulant effect. In Australia, listing quantified guarana content on beverages is mandatory.

14   The most interesting implication that the report mentions is from a study in which "bar patrons who consumed alcohol mixed with energy drinks were . . . four times more likely to intend to drive while intoxicated." Because, as SAMHSA puts it, "Individuals, especially young drinkers, may incorrectly believe that consumption of caffeine can 'undo' the effects of alcohol intake and make it safe to drive after drinking."

15   That sort of stimulant-empowered bullheaded behavior—rather than the ER admissions for caffeine-induced anxiety—is actually the most pressing public health concern.

16   So, caffeinate responsibly. "If I drink another Hardcore Energize Bullet, am I going to have to go to the hospital again?"

SUMMARIZE AND RESPOND

Summarize the main idea of "How Much Caffeine before I End Up in the ER?" Then, go back and check off support for this main idea. Next, write a brief summary (three to five sentences) of the essay. Finally, jot down your initial response to the reading. Have you ever considered the effects of caffeine? How much of an impact on health do you think it has?

CHECK YOUR COMPREHENSION

1. Which of the following would be the best alternative title for this essay?

    a. "Caffeine Is Found in Many Drinks"

    (b.) "Analyzing the Data on Caffeine"

    c. "Is Caffeine Really OK for You?"

    d. "Coffee: A Miracle Drug"

2. The main idea of this essay is that

    a. we underestimate the amount of caffeine we can handle.

    b. we don't understand what caffeine really does to our bodies.

    c. we don't understand what we're doing when we're mixing certain beverages together.

    (d.) we need to have a better understanding of the effects of caffeine on our body.

3. According to Hamblin, caffeine affects people differently because

    a. we all have a different tolerance.

    b. we aren't all able to read the labels and understand them.

    (c.) we all react differently to the amount of guarana in drinks.

    d. we are all seriously malnourished.

4. If you are unfamiliar with the following words, use a dictionary to check their meanings: propensity, adverse (para. 5); guarana (7); electroconvulsive (9); implication (14).

READ CRITICALLY

1. What are the different categories that Hamblin uses to determine how caffeine affects a person?

2. What transitions does the writer use? Underline them. How do they help structure the essay?

3. What specific examples does Hamblin use to support each of the categories about overuse of caffeine? How well do they support the main point?

4. After reviewing the entire article, do you agree with Hamblin? Can too much caffeine send you to the emergency room? In which of the circumstances that he describes is it most likely to happen? In which circumstances is it least likely to happen? Explain your answer.

5. Does this essay have the Four Basics of Good Classification? Explain your answer.

WRITE AN ESSAY

Hamblin uses data to make several arguments based on classifications. He classifies the number of emergency department visits based on abuse or misuse of caffeine as well as based on age and gender. In addition, he classifies energy drinks and coffee drinks by serving size and amount of caffeine. Using any of these classification systems, write an essay that draws on any one of the graphs or tables in the article. You can use your own experiences and observations, but you should also draw on the information from these classifications. For instance, perhaps you can categorize or classify the people you see in your classroom in a way that falls into line with what you see in this article. Your essay should show how caffeine affects people or how people use caffeine in a way that relates to this essay.

Amy Tan

Mother Tongue

Amy Tan was born in Oakland, California, in 1952, several years after her mother and father emigrated from China. She studied at San Jose City College and later San Jose State University, receiving a bachelor's degree with a double major in English and linguistics. In 1973, she earned a master's degree in linguistics from San Jose State. In 1989, Tan published her first novel, *The Joy Luck Club,* which was nominated for the National Book Award and the National Book Critics Circle Award. Tan's other books include *The Kitchen God's Wife* (1991), *The Hundred Secret Senses* (1995), *The Bonesetter's Daughter* (2001), and *Saving Fish from Drowning* (2005). Her short stories and essays have been published in the *Atlantic, Grand Street, Harper's,* the *New Yorker,* and other publications.

In the following essay, which was selected for *The Best American Essays 1991,* Tan discusses the different kinds of English she uses, from academic discourse to the simple language she speaks with her mother.

Guiding question In what ways did Tan's mother's "limited" ability to speak English affect Tan as she was growing up?

1   I am not a scholar of English or literature. I cannot give you much more than personal opinions on the English language and its variations in this country or others.

2   I am a writer. And by that definition, I am someone who has always loved language. I am fascinated by language in daily life. I spend a great deal of my time thinking about the power of language—the way it can evoke an emotion, a visual image, a complex idea, or a simple truth. Language is the tool of my trade. And I use them all—all the Englishes I grew up with.

3   Recently, I was made keenly aware of the different Englishes I do use. I was giving a talk to a large group of people, the same talk I had already given to half a dozen other groups. The nature of the talk was about my writing, my life, and my book, *The Joy Luck Club*. The talk was going along well enough, until I remembered one major difference that made the whole talk sound wrong. My mother was in the room. And it was perhaps the first time she had heard me give a lengthy speech, using the kind of English I have never used with her. I was saying things like "The intersection of memory upon imagination" and "There is an aspect of my fiction that relates to thus-and-thus"—a speech filled with carefully wrought grammatical phrases, burdened, it suddenly seemed to me, with nominalized forms, past perfect tenses, conditional phrases, all the forms of standard English that I had learned in school and through books, the forms of English I did not use at home with my mother.

Pause Summarize Tan's main idea in paragraph 4.

4   Just last week, I was walking down the street with my mother, and I again found myself conscious of the English I was using, the English I do use with her. We were talking about the price of new and used furniture and I heard myself saying this: "Not waste money that way." My husband was with us as well, and he didn't notice any switch in my English. And then I realized why. It's because over the twenty years we've been together I've often used that same kind of English with him, and sometimes he even uses it with me. It has become our language of intimacy, a different sort of English that relates to family talk, the language I grew up with.

5   So you'll have some idea of what this family talk I heard sounds like, I'll quote what my mother said during a recent conversation which I videotaped and then transcribed. During this conversation, my mother was talking about a political gangster in Shanghai[1] who had the same last name as her family's, Du, and how the gangster in his early years wanted to be adopted by her family, which was rich by comparison. Later, the gangster became more powerful, far richer than my mother's family, and one day showed up at my mother's wedding to pay his respects. Here's what she said in part:

1. **Shanghai:** a major city in eastern China

6   "Du Yusong having business like fruit stand. Like off the street kind. He is Du like Du Zong—but not Tsung-ming Island people. The local people call putong, the river east side, he belong to that side local people. That man want to ask Du Zong father take him in like become own family. Du Zong father wasn't look down on him, but didn't take seriously, until that man big like become a mafia. Now important person, very hard to inviting him. Chinese way, came only to show respect, don't stay for dinner. Respect for making big celebration, he shows up. Mean gives lots of respect. Chinese custom. Chinese social life that way. If too important won't have to stay too long. He come to my wedding. I didn't see, I heard it. I gone to boy's side, they have YMCA dinner. Chinese age I was nineteen."

2. **Forbes report:** a financial publication geared toward investors

3. **Shirley MacLaine:** actress whose works of autobiography often referred to her past lives

7   You should know that my mother's expressive command of English belies how much she actually understands. She reads the *Forbes* report,[2] listens to *Wall Street Week,* converses daily with her stockbroker, reads all of Shirley MacLaine's[3] books with ease—all kinds of things I can't begin to understand.

Yet some of my friends tell me they understand 50 percent of what my mother says. Some say they understand 80 to 90 percent. Some say they understand none of it, as if she were speaking pure Chinese. But to me, my mother's English is perfectly clear, perfectly natural. It's my mother tongue. Her language, as I hear it, is vivid, direct, full of observation and imagery. That was the language that helped shape the way I saw things, expressed things, made sense of the world.

8   Lately, I've been giving more thought to the kind of English my mother speaks. Like others, I have described it to people as "broken" or "fractured" English. But I wince when I say that. It has always bothered me that I can think of no other way to describe it other than "broken," as if it were damaged and needed to be fixed, as if it lacked a certain wholeness and soundness. I've heard other terms used, "limited English," for example. But they seem just as bad, as if everything is limited, including people's perceptions of the limited English speaker.

9   I know this for a fact, because when I was growing up, my mother's "limited" English limited *my* perception of her. I was ashamed of her English. I believed that her English reflected the quality of what she had to say. That is, because she expressed them imperfectly her thoughts were imperfect. And I had plenty of empirical[4] evidence to support me: the fact that people in department stores, at banks, and at restaurants did not take her seriously, did not give her good service, pretended not to understand her, or even acted as if they did not hear her.

> 4. **empirical:** based on direct experience or observation

10   My mother has long realized the limitations of her English as well. When I was fifteen, she used to have me call people on the phone to pretend I was she. In this guise, I was forced to ask for information or even to complain and yell at people who had been rude to her. One time it was a call to her stockbroker in New York. She had cashed out her small portfolio and it just so happened we were going to go to New York the next week, our very first trip outside California. I had to get on the phone and say in an adolescent voice that was not very convincing, "This is Mrs. Tan."

11   And my mother was standing in the back whispering loudly, "Why he don't send me check, already two weeks late. So mad he lie to me, losing me money."

12   And then I said in perfect English, "Yes, I'm getting rather concerned. You had agreed to send the check two weeks ago, but it hasn't arrived."

13   Then she began to talk more loudly. "What he want, I come to New York tell him front of his boss, you cheating me?" And I was trying to calm her down, make her be quiet, while telling the stockbroker, "I can't tolerate any more excuses. If I don't receive the check immediately, I am going to have to speak to your manager when I'm in New York next week." And sure enough, the following week there we were in front of this astonished stockbroker, and I was sitting there red-faced and quiet, and my mother, the real Mrs. Tan, was shouting at his boss in her impeccable broken English.

> **Pause** In paragraphs 9–14, what evidence does Tan use to support her claim that others believed that her mother's English showed a lack of intelligence?

Pause Have you or anyone you know not been taken seriously because of language, age, race, or some other trait?

Pause What has been your experience with the kinds of English tests that Tan writes about in paragraphs 16–17?

6. **semantic:** related to the meaning of words

14   We used a similar routine just five days ago, for a situation that was far less humorous. My mother had gone to the hospital for an appointment, to find out about a benign brain tumor a CAT scan[5] had revealed a month ago. She said she had spoken very good English, her best English, no mistakes. Still, she said, the hospital did not apologize when they said they had lost the CAT scan and she had come for nothing. She said they did not seem to have any sympathy when she told them she was anxious to know the exact diagnosis, since her husband and son had both died of brain tumors. She said they would not give her any more information until the next time and she would have to make another appointment for that. So she said she would not leave until the doctor called her daughter. She wouldn't budge. And when the doctor finally called her daughter, me, who spoke in perfect English—lo and behold—we had assurances the CAT scan would be found, promises that a conference call on Monday would be held, and apologies for any suffering my mother had gone through for a most regrettable mistake.

15   I think my mother's English almost had an effect on limiting my possibilities in life as well. Sociologists and linguists probably will tell you that a person's developing language skills are more influenced by peers. But I do think that the language spoken in the family, especially in immigrant families which are more insular, plays a large role in shaping the language of the child. And I believe that it affected my results on achievement tests, IQ tests, and the SAT. While my English skills were never judged as poor, compared to math, English could not be considered my strong suit. In grade school I did moderately well, getting perhaps B's, sometimes B-pluses, in English and scoring perhaps in the sixtieth or seventieth percentile on achievement tests. But those scores were not good enough to override the opinion that my true abilities lay in math and science, because in those areas I achieved A's and scored in the ninetieth percentile or higher.

16   This was understandable. Math is precise; there is only one correct answer. Whereas, for me at least, the answers on English tests were always a judgment call, a matter of opinion and personal experience. Those tests were constructed around items like fill-in-the-blank sentence completion, such as "Even though Tom was _____ , Mary thought he was _____ ." And the correct answer always seemed to be the most bland combinations of thoughts, for example, "Even though Tom was shy, Mary thought he was charming," with the grammatical structure "even though" limiting the correct answer to some sort of semantic[6] opposites, so you wouldn't get answers like, "Even though Tom was foolish, Mary thought he was ridiculous." Well, according to my mother, there were very few limitations as to what Tom could have been and what Mary might have thought of him. So I never did well on tests like that.

17   The same was true with word analogies, pairs of words in which you were supposed to find some sort of logical, semantic relationship—for example, "*Sunset* is to *nightfall* as _____ is to _____ ." And here you would be presented with a list of four possible pairs, one of which showed the same kind of relationship: *red* is to *stoplight*, *bus* is to *arrival*, *chills* is to *fever*, *yawn* is to *boring*. Well,

I could never think that way. I knew what the tests were asking, but I could not block out of my mind the images already created by the first pair, "*sunset* is to *nightfall*"—and I would see a burst of colors against a darkening sky, the moon rising, the lowering of a curtain of stars. And all the other pairs of words—red, bus, stoplight, boring—just threw up a mass of confusing images, making it impossible for me to sort out something as logical as saying: "A sunset precedes nightfall" is the same as "a chill precedes a fever." The only way I would have gotten that answer right would have been to imagine an associative situation, for example, my being disobedient and staying out past sunset, catching a chill at night, which turns into feverish pneumonia as punishment, which indeed did happen to me.

18   I have been thinking about all this lately, about my mother's English, about achievement tests. Because lately I've been asked, as a writer, why there are not more Asian Americans represented in American literature. Why are there few Asian Americans enrolled in creative writing programs? Why do so many Chinese students go into engineering? Well, these are broad sociological questions I can't begin to answer. But I have noticed in surveys—in fact, just last week—that Asian students, as a whole, always do significantly better on math achievement tests than in English. And this makes me think that there are other Asian American students whose English spoken in the home might also be described as "broken" or "limited." And perhaps they also have teachers who are steering them away from writing and into math and science, which is what happened to me.

19   Fortunately, I happen to be rebellious in nature and enjoy the challenge of disproving assumptions made about me. I became an English major my first year in college, after being enrolled as pre-med. I started writing nonfiction as a free-lancer the week after I was told by my former boss that writing was my worst skill and I should hone my talents toward account management.

20   But it wasn't until 1985 that I finally began to write fiction. And at first I wrote using what I thought to be wittily crafted sentences, sentences that would finally prove I had mastery over the English language. Here's an example from the first draft of a story that later made its way into *The Joy Luck Club*, but without this line: "That was my mental quandary[7] in its nascent[8] state." A terrible line, which I can barely pronounce.

21   Fortunately, for reasons I won't get into today, I later decided I should envision a reader for the stories I would write. And the reader I decided upon was my mother, because these were stories about mothers. So with this reader in mind—and in fact she did read my early drafts—I began to write stories using all the Englishes I grew up with: the English I spoke to my mother, which for lack of a better term might be described as "simple"; the English she used with me, which for lack of a better term might be described as "broken"; my translation of her Chinese, which could certainly be described as "watered down"; and what I imagined to be her translation of her Chinese if she could speak in perfect English, her internal language, and for that I sought to preserve the essence, but

Pause How do you think Tan might answer the questions she poses in paragraph 18?

Pause How do you respond when people make assumptions about you?

7. **quandary:** a state of uncertainty

8. **nascent:** developing; beginning to come into existence

neither an English nor a Chinese structure. I wanted to capture what language ability tests can never reveal: her intent, her passion, her imagery, the rhythms of her speech, and the nature of her thoughts.

22   Apart from what any critic had to say about my writing, I knew I had succeeded where it counted when my mother finished reading my book and gave me her verdict: "So easy to read."

SUMMARIZE AND RESPOND

Summarize the main idea of "Mother Tongue." Then, go back and check off support for this main idea. Next, write a brief summary (three to five sentences) of the essay. Finally, jot down your initial response to the reading. What do you think of Tan's relationship with her mother? Do you think that Tan's mother's "limited" English has affected their relationship for the better, for the worse, or in some more complex way? What impression do you have of Tan herself?

CHECK YOUR COMPREHENSION

1. Which of the following would be the best alternative title for this essay?
   - (a.) "The Englishes I Grew Up With"
   - b. "My Mother's Difficulties Communicating in English"
   - c. "How to Communicate with an Immigrant Parent"
   - d. "A Writer's Fascination with the English Language"

2. The main idea of this essay is that
   - a. children of immigrant parents have difficulties communicating in English because of their parents' "limited" command of the language.
   - b. there is no single, proper way to speak English because different people communicate in different ways.
   - c. teachers believe that Asian American students necessarily do better in math and science than they do in English and writing.
   - (d.) the kind of English one uses may change in different contexts.

3. Tan concludes that
   - a. to become a successful writer, she had to work harder than would someone who grew up in a home where English was the native language.
   - b. her mother found her book easy to read because her mother grew up speaking Chinese.
   - (c.) in finding her voice as a writer, she called on the memory of her mother and their communication with each other.

d. to prove her mastery of the English language, she had to write in a way that her mother would find impossible to understand.

4. If you are unfamiliar with the following words, use a dictionary to check their meanings: evoke (para. 2); keenly, wrought, burdened (3); intimacy (4); belies (7); fractured (8); guise (10); impeccable (13); benign (14); linguists, insular (15); associative (17); freelancer, hone (19); wittily (20).

READ CRITICALLY

1. Why, when speaking with her husband, does Tan sometimes switch to the kind of English her mother speaks? What does this tell you of her feelings about her mother's way of speaking?

2. Why does Tan dislike using labels such as "broken" or "limited" in referring to the English her mother speaks?

3. In what ways does Tan say that the language spoken within immigrant families can limit the possibilities of the children in such families? Do you agree with her?

4. What, exactly, does Tan classify in this essay? What are the specific classifications she writes about?

5. Tan divides her essay into three sections, indicated by the spaces between paragraphs 7 and 8 and paragraphs 17 and 18. What is the focus of each of these sections? Why do you suppose she chose to organize her essay in this way?

WRITE AN ESSAY

Write an essay classifying your use of language in different situations—at home with family members, with friends outside of home, at school, in your workplace, and elsewhere that your language may change because of the circumstances. For each situation, give examples of the kind of language you use that differs from the language you use in other situations.

Martin Luther King Jr.

The Ways of Meeting Oppression

Martin Luther King Jr. was a leading figure in the African American civil rights movement, a Baptist minister known for his activist work throughout the country before being assassinated in 1968. The youngest person to be given the Nobel Peace Prize (in 1964), he was posthumously awarded the Presidential Medal of Freedom in 1977 and the Congressional

Gold Medal in 2004. In "The Ways of Meeting Oppression," King discusses the failure of both acquiescence and physical violence as ways of responding to oppression and offers nonviolent resistance as the best means of fighting against racial injustice.

Guiding questions What is oppression? Where do you see oppression in the world today? How should people respond?

1. **acquiescence:** agreement by silence or lack of protest

2. **Moses:** a Hebrew prophet

3. **Shakespeare:** a renowned British playwright who wrote in the late 1500s and early 1600s

4. **fleshpots of Egypt:** biblical reference to cooking vessels and luxurious living (Exodus 16:3)

5. **yoke:** a harness that joins animals together as a team

Pause What makes some people give up in the face of oppression?

Pause What do you think King means by saying, "The oppressed must never allow the conscience of the oppressor to slumber"?

6. **an eye for an eye:** from the Hebrew Bible, meaning that the victim can seek amends that duplicate the original crime

1   Oppressed people deal with their oppression in three characteristic ways. One way is acquiescence:[1] The oppressed resign themselves to doom. They tacitly adjust themselves to oppression, and thereby become conditioned to it. In every movement toward freedom, some of the oppressed prefer to remain oppressed. Almost 2800 years ago, Moses[2] set out to lead the children of Israel from the slavery of Egypt to the freedom of the promised land. He soon discovered that slaves do not always welcome their deliverers. They become accustomed to being slaves. They would rather bear those ills they have, as Shakespeare[3] pointed out, than flee to others that they know not of. They prefer the "fleshpots of Egypt"[4] to the ordeals of emancipation.

2   There is such a thing as the freedom of exhaustion. Some people are so worn down by the yoke[5] of oppression that they give up. A few years ago, in the slum areas of Atlanta, a Negro guitarist used to sing almost daily: "Been down so long that down don't bother me." This is the type of negative freedom and resignation that often engulfs the life of the oppressed.

3   But this is not the way out. To accept passively an unjust system is to cooperate with that system; thereby the oppressed become as evil as the oppressor. Noncooperation with evil is as much a moral obligation as is cooperation with good. The oppressed must never allow the conscience of the oppressor to slumber. Religion reminds every man that he is his brother's keeper. So acquiescence—while often the easier way—is not the moral way. It is the way of the coward. The Negro cannot win the respect of his oppressor by acquiescing; he merely increases the oppressor's arrogance and contempt. Acquiescence is interpreted as proof of the Negro's inferiority. The Negro cannot win the respect of the white people of the South or the peoples of the world if he is willing to sell the future of his children for his personal and immediate comfort and safety.

4   A second way that oppressed people sometimes deal with oppression is to resort to physical violence and corroding hatred. Violence often brings about momentary results. Nations have frequently won their independence in battle. But in spite of temporary victories, violence never brings a permanent peace. It solves no social problem; it merely creates new and more complicated ones.

5   Violence as a way of achieving racial justice is both impractical and immoral. It is impractical because it is a descending spiral ending in destruction for all. The old law of an eye for an eye[6] leaves everybody blind. It is immoral because it seeks to humiliate the opponent rather than win his understanding; it seeks to annihilate rather than to convert. Violence is immoral because it thrives on hatred rather than love. It destroys community and makes brotherhood impossible. It leaves society in monologue rather than dialogue. Violence ends by defeating

itself. It creates bitterness in the survivors and brutality in the destroyers. A voice echoes through time saying to every potential Peter, "Put up your sword."[7] History is cluttered with the wreckage of nations that failed to follow this command.

6   If the American Negro and other victims of oppression succumb to the temptation of using violence in the struggle for freedom, future generations will be the recipients of a desolate night of bitterness, and our chief legacy to them will be an endless reign of meaningless chaos. Violence is not the way.

7   The third way open to oppressed people in their quest for freedom is the way of nonviolent resistance. Like the synthesis[8] in Hegelian[9] philosophy, the principle of nonviolent resistance seeks to reconcile the truths of two opposites—acquiescence and violence—while avoiding the extremes and immoralities of both. The nonviolent resister agrees with the person who acquiesces that one should not be physically aggressive toward his opponent; but he balances the equation by agreeing with the person of violence that evil must be resisted. He avoids the nonresistance of the former and the violent resistance of the latter. With nonviolent resistance, no individual or group need submit to any wrong, nor need anyone resort to violence in order to right a wrong.

8   It seems to me that this is the method that must guide the actions of the Negro in the present crisis in race relations. Through nonviolent resistance, the Negro will be able to rise to the noble height of opposing the unjust system while loving the perpetrators of the system. The Negro must work passionately and unrelentingly for full stature as a citizen, but he must not use inferior methods to gain it. He must never come to terms with falsehood, malice, hate, or destruction.

9   Nonviolent resistance makes it possible for the Negro to remain in the South and struggle for his rights. The Negro's problem will not be solved by running away. He cannot listen to the glib[10] suggestion of those who would urge him to migrate en masse to other sections of the country. By grasping his great opportunity in the South, he can make a lasting contribution to the moral strength of the nation and set a sublime[11] example of courage for generations yet unborn.

10   By nonviolent resistance, the Negro can also enlist all men of good will in his struggle for equality. The problem is not a purely racial one, with Negroes set against whites. In the end, it is not a struggle between people at all, but a tension between justice and injustice. Nonviolent resistance is not aimed against oppressors but against oppression. Under its banner, conscience, not racial groups, are enlisted.

7. **"Put up your sword":** order from Christ to Peter to put away his sword when Peter was trying to defend Christ from arrest (John 18:11)

8. **synthesis:** in philosophy, the combination of two contradictory ideas or propositions to attain a higher truth

9. **Georg Wilhelm Friedrich Hegel (1770-1831):** German philosopher

Pause How is nonviolence a "synthesis"?

10. **glib:** easy, insincere, or superficial

11. **sublime:** impressive; awe-inspiring

SUMMARIZE AND RESPOND

Summarize the main idea of "The Ways of Meeting Oppression." Then, go back and check off support for this main idea. Next, write a brief summary (three to five sentences) of the selection. Finally, jot down your initial response to the reading. Do you agree with King about nonviolence? Do you think there are circumstances and injustices that justify a violent response?

1. Which of the following would be the best alternative title for this essay?

    a. "Civil Rights Is a Racial Struggle"

    b. "Accepting Injustice Is Evil"

    c. "What the Bible Says about Oppression"

    (d.) "Nonviolent Resistance: The Moral and Practical Choice"

2. The main idea of this essay is that

    a. the struggle to achieve racial equality requires African Americans to take responsibility for their own actions.

    b. violence is justified when motivated by love, but immoral when motivated by hatred.

    (c.) nonviolent resistance is the best response to injustice, as it reconciles the truths of acquiescence and violence while avoiding their immorality.

    d. black people facing oppression in America should move to regions of the country that are more tolerant of racial diversity.

3. King argues that nonviolent resistance

    (a.) allows people to oppose an unjust system while still loving the perpetrators of that system.

    b. is dangerous and requires remarkable physical courage.

    c. may force white Americans to respond with violence, which would damage the cause of civil rights.

    d. is moral and idealistic, but ineffective at addressing real social problems.

4. If you are unfamiliar with the following words, check the dictionary for their meanings: tacitly, emancipation (para. 1); resignation, engulfs (2); conscience, inferiority (3); corroding (4); annihilate, monologue, dialogue (5); succumb, desolate, legacy (6); reconcile (7); perpetrators (8).

READ CRITICALLY

1. What is King's purpose in this essay? What effect do you think he wants his writing to have on his audience?

2. What different examples does King use to support his classifications? How effective are they? Explain.

3. Where in the essay does the writer use transitional words or phrases? Point to specific examples.

4. Why does King choose to present the different ways to meet oppression in this order? Would the essay be as effective if he had begun with nonviolent resistance? Why or why not?

5. According to King, the civil rights struggle is "not purely a racial one, with Negroes set against whites," but rather a "tension between justice and injustice." "Nonviolent resistance is not aimed against oppressors but against oppression" (para. 10). What do you think he means by these statements?

WRITE AN ESSAY

King's essay is "The Ways of Meeting Oppression." Write a classification essay entitled the "The Ways of Dealing with _____ ," filling in the blank with a particular problem or challenge—for example, bullying, stress, educational setbacks, family conflict, difficult bosses, or college pressures. Use specific examples, and make sure that the different ways of addressing the problem can be placed into at least three categories.

Classification: Linked Readings

Overcoming Adversity and Trauma

Each of the following readings shows people overcoming challenges, adversity, or trauma in different ways.

Monique Rizer, "When Students Are Parents" (Chapter 40, p. 587)

Malcolm X, "Learning to Read" (Chapter 43, p. 617)

Amy Tan, "Mother Tongue" (Chapter 44, p. 633)

Read the selections, and draw from at least one in addition to "The Ways of Meeting Oppression" to write an essay titled "Overcoming Adversity." You can refer to your own experience, but make sure to use material from the essays as well.

Stereotypes

Each of the following readings focuses on or uses stereotypes.

Nancy Mairs, "On Being a Cripple" (Chapter 45, p. 645)

Dave Barry, "The Ugly Truth about Beauty" (Chapter 46, p. 658)

Brent Staples, "Just Walk on By: Black Men and Public Space" (Chapter 47, p. 670)

Read the selections, and draw from at least one to write an essay titled "Stereotypes: Are They Wrong?" You can refer to your own experience, but make sure to use material from the essays as well.

Reading and Writing with Graphics

The following readings use different types of classifications, and two of them contain graphic images. Using graphics in writing can often help you make a complicated concept simple and easier for the reader to grasp. All of the following topics require the reader to understand a process or ask the reader to think about the different pieces of a larger topic.

Felix Tarcomnicu, "How the Hiring Process Has Changed over the Years" (Chapter 43, p. 622)

James Hamblin, "How Much Caffeine before I End Up in the ER?" (Chapter 44, p. 627)

Katy Hall and Chris Spurlock, "Paid Parental Leave: U.S. vs. the World" (Chapter 46, p. 661)

Read the selections, and draw from at least one to create an essay that uses some kind of graphic structure. Note that the word *graphics* doesn't necessarily mean pictures. Graphics can be as simple as subheadings, such as the ones in "How the Hiring Process Has Changed over the Years," or they can be integrated into the text to illustrate a concept, as in "How Much Caffeine Before I End Up in the ER?" In the case of "Paid Parental Leave," the entire essay is a graphic.

45

Definition

Each essay in this chapter uses definition to get its main idea across. As you read these essays, consider how they achieve the Four Basics of Good Definition that are listed below and discussed in Chapter 15 of this book.

Four Basics of Good Definition

1 It tells readers what term is being defined.

2 It gives a clear definition.

3 It uses examples to show what the writer means.

4 It gives details about the examples that readers will understand.

Nancy Mairs

On Being a Cripple

In her essays, memoirs, and poetry, Nancy Mairs often writes about multiple sclerosis and her experience, since 1993, of life in a wheelchair. Mairs attended Wheaton College and earned an M.F.A. and Ph.D. from the University of Arizona. Her essay collections include *Waist High in the World: A Life among the Nondisabled* (1996) and *A Troubled Guest* (2002).

This essay, from the collection *Plaintext* (1986), addresses the words we use to talk about people with disabilities. Mairs makes a case for honesty in language and explains what she means when she calls herself a cripple.

Guiding question How would you describe Mairs's attitude toward her disability?

To escape is nothing. Not to escape is nothing. —LOUISE BOGAN

Pause Why might this incident in the women's room have prompted Mairs to write her essay?

1 The other day I was thinking of writing an essay on being a cripple. I was thinking hard in one of the stalls of the women's room in my office building, as I was shoving my shirt into my jeans and tugging up my zipper. Preoccupied, I flushed, picked up my book bag, took my cane down from the hook, and unlatched the door. So many movements unbalanced me, and as I pulled the door open I fell over backward, landing fully clothed on the toilet seat with my legs splayed in front of me: the old beetle-on-its-back routine. Saturday afternoon, the building deserted, I was free to laugh aloud as I wriggled back to my feet, my voice bouncing off the yellowish tiles from all directions. Had anyone been there with me, I'd have been still and faint and hot with chagrin. I decided that it was high time to write the essay.

1. semantics: in general, the study of words; here, the choice of particular words

2 First, the matter of semantics.[1] I am a cripple. I choose this word to name me. I choose from among several possibilities, the most common of which are "handicapped" and "disabled." I made the choice a number of years ago, without thinking, unaware of my motives for doing so. Even now, I'm not sure what those motives are, but I recognize that they are complex and not entirely flattering. People—crippled or not—wince at the word "cripple," as they do not at "handicapped" or "disabled." Perhaps I want them to wince. I want them to see me as a tough customer, one to whom the fates/gods/viruses have not been kind, but who can face the brutal truth of her existence squarely. As a cripple, I swagger.

Pause Why does Mairs dislike the terms *disabled, handicapped,* and *differently abled*?

3 But, to be fair to myself, a certain amount of honesty underlies my choice. "Cripple" seems to me a clean word, straightforward and precise. It has an honorable history, having made its first appearance in the Lindisfarne Gospel in the tenth century. As a lover of words, I like the accuracy with which it describes my condition: I have lost the full use of my limbs. "Disabled," by contrast, suggests any incapacity, physical or mental. And I certainly don't like "handicapped," which implies that I have deliberately been put at a disadvantage, by whom I can't imagine (my God is not a Handicapper General), in order to equalize chances in the great race of life. These words seem to me to be moving away from my condition, to be widening the gap between word and reality. Most remote is the recently coined euphemism[2] "differently abled," which partakes of the same semantic hopefulness that transformed countries from "undeveloped" to "underdeveloped," then to "less developed," and finally to "developing" nations. People have continued to starve in those countries during the shift. Some realities do not obey the dictates of language.

2. euphemism: a word that puts a pleasant cover over an unpleasant condition

4 Mine is one of them. Whatever you call me, I remain crippled. But I don't care what you call me, so long as it isn't "differently abled," which strikes me as pure verbal garbage designed, by its ability to describe anyone, to describe no one. I subscribe to George Orwell's thesis that "the slovenliness[3] of our language makes it easier for us to have foolish thoughts." And I refuse to participate in the degeneration of the language to the extent that I deny that I have lost anything in the course of this calamitous disease; I refuse to pretend that the only differences between you and me are the various ordinary ones that distinguish any one

3. slovenliness: sloppiness

person from another. But call me "disabled" or "handicapped" if you like. I have long since grown accustomed to them; and if they are vague, at least they hint at the truth. Moreover, I use them myself. Society is no readier to accept crippledness than to accept death, war, sex, sweat, or wrinkles. I would never refer to another person as a cripple. It is the word I use to name only myself.

5   I haven't always been crippled, a fact for which I am soundly grateful. To be whole of limb is, I know from experience, infinitely more pleasant and useful than to be crippled; and if that knowledge leaves one open to bitterness at my loss, the physical soundness I once enjoyed (though I did not enjoy it half enough) is well worth the occasional stab of regret. Though never any good at sports, I was a normally active child and young adult. I climbed trees, played hopscotch, jumped rope, skated, swam, rode my bicycle, sailed. I despised team sports, spending some of the wretchedest afternoons of my life, sweaty and humiliated, behind a field-hockey stick and under a basketball hoop. I tramped alone for miles along the bridle paths that webbed the woods behind the house I grew up in. I swayed through countless dim hours in the arms of one man or another under the scattered shot of light from mirrored balls, and gyrated through countless more as Tab Hunter and Johnny Mathis gave way to the Rolling Stones, Creedence Clearwater Revival, Cream. I walked down the aisle. I pushed baby carriages, changed tires in the rain, marched for peace.

6   When I was twenty-eight I started to trip and drop things. What at first seemed my natural clumsiness soon became too pronounced to shrug off. I consulted a neurologist, who told me that I had a brain tumor. A battery of tests, increasingly disagreeable, revealed no tumor. About a year and a half later I developed a blurred spot in one eye. I had, at last, the episodes "disseminated[4] in space and time" requisite for a diagnosis: multiple sclerosis. I have never been sorry for the doctor's initial misdiagnosis, however. For almost a week, until the negative results of the tests were in, I thought that I was going to die right away. Every day for the past nearly ten years, then, has been a kind of gift. I accept all gifts.

7   Multiple sclerosis is a chronic[5] degenerative[6] disease of the central nervous system, in which the myelin that sheathes the nerves is somehow eaten away and scar tissue forms in its place, interrupting the nerves' signals. During its course, which is unpredictable and uncontrollable, one may lose vision, hearing, speech, the ability to walk, control of bladder and/or bowels, strength in any or all extremities,[7] sensitivity to touch, vibration, and/or pain, potency, coordination of movements—the list of possibilities is lengthy and, yes, horrifying. One may also lose one's sense of humor. That's the easiest to lose and the hardest to survive without. . . .

8   Like many women I know, I have always had an uneasy relationship with my body. I was not a popular child, largely, I think now, because I was peculiar: intelligent, intense, moody, shy, given to unexpected actions and inexplicable notions and emotions. But as I entered adolescence, I believed myself unpopular because I was homely: my breasts too flat, my mouth too wide, my hips too narrow, my clothing never quite right in fit or style. I was not, in fact, particularly ugly, old

4. **disseminated:** spread over

5. **chronic:** marked by a long duration; always present

6. **degenerative:** having a worsening effect; causing deterioration

7. **extremities:** limbs of the body

photographs inform me, though I was well off the ideal; but I carried this sense of self-alienation with me into adulthood, where it regenerated in response to the depredations of MS. Even with my brace I walk with a limp so pronounced that, seeing myself on the videotape of a television program on the disabled, I couldn't believe that anything but an inchworm could make progress humping along like that. My shoulders droop and my pelvis thrusts forward as I try to balance myself upright, throwing my frame into a bony S. As a result of contractures, one shoulder is higher than the other and I carry one arm bent in front of me, the fingers curled into a claw. My left arm and leg have wasted into pipestems, and I try always to keep them covered. When I think about how my body must look to others, especially to men, to whom I have been trained to display myself, I feel ludicrous, even loathsome.

9   At my age, however, I don't spend much time thinking about my appearance. The burning egocentricity of adolescence, which assures one that all the world is looking all the time, has passed, thank God, and I'm generally too caught up in what I'm doing to step back, as I used to, and watch myself as though upon a stage. I'm also too old to believe in the accuracy of self-image. I know that I'm not a hideous crone, that in fact, when I'm rested, well dressed, and well made up, I look fine. The self-loathing I feel is neither physically nor intellectually substantial. What I hate is not me but a disease.

10   I am not a disease.

Pause Why might Mairs have chosen to write this one-sentence paragraph (para. 10)?

11   And a disease is not—at least not singlehandedly—going to determine who I am, though at first it seemed to be going to. Adjusting to a chronic incurable illness, I have moved through a process similar to that outlined by Elisabeth Kübler-Ross in *On Death and Dying*. The major difference—and it is far more significant than most people recognize—is that I can't be sure of the outcome, as the terminally ill cancer patient can. Research studies indicate that, with proper medical care, I may achieve a "normal" life span. And in our society, with its vision of death as the ultimate evil, worse even than decrepitude, the response to such news is, "Oh well, at least you're not going to *die*." Are there worse things than dying? I think that there may be.

12   I think of two women I know, both with MS, both enough older than I to have served me as models. One took to her bed several years ago and has been there ever since. Although she can sit in a high-backed wheelchair, because she is incontinent she refuses to go out at all, even though incontinence pants, which are readily available at any pharmacy, could protect her from embarrassment. Instead, she stays at home and insists that her husband, a small quiet man, a retired civil servant, stay there with her except for a quick weekly foray[8] to the supermarket. The other woman, whose illness was diagnosed when she was eighteen, a nursing student engaged to a young doctor, finished her training, married her doctor, accompanied him to Germany when he was in the service, bore three sons and a daughter, now grown and gone. When she can, she travels with her husband; she plays bridge, embroiders, swims regularly; she works, like me, as a symptomatic-patient instructor of medical students in neurology. Guess which woman I hope to be.

8. **foray:** a trip, an outing

SUMMARIZE AND RESPOND

Summarize the main idea of "On Being a Cripple." Then, go back and check off support for this main idea. Next, write a brief summary (three to five sentences) of the reading. Finally, jot down your initial response to the selection. What impression of Mairs do you come away with? What did you learn from her description of her disease? If you could write a note to Mairs, what would you say to her?

CHECK YOUR COMPREHENSION

1. Which of the following would be the best alternative title for this essay?
   a. "The Painfulness of a Disease"
   b. "Surviving with Multiple Sclerosis"
   c. "Learning to Laugh at My Disability"
   d. "Coping with Others' Attitudes toward Disability"

2. The main idea of this essay is that
   a. multiple sclerosis is an incurable disease of the central nervous system that can affect movement, vision, hearing, and speech.
   b. many labels are used to describe disabled people, but most such people prefer the term *crippled*.
   c. one needs a strong sense of humor and a circle of supportive friends to live with a disability.
   d. being disabled presents many difficulties and obstacles, but one can learn to cope with these challenges.

3. Mairs makes the point that
   a. she is grateful to have the memory of being able-bodied as a young woman.
   b. the greatest drawback to her disability is that it makes her feel unattractive.
   c. she feels doctors are not doing enough to discover a cure for multiple sclerosis.
   d. she believes everyone should use the word *crippled* rather than *disabled* or *handicapped*.

4. If you are unfamiliar with the following words, use a dictionary to check their meanings: splayed, chagrin (para. 1); wince, swagger (2); incapacity, partakes, dictates (3); degeneration, calamitous (4); gyrated (5); neurologist (6); inexplicable, regenerated, depredations, contractures, ludicrous, loathsome (8); crone (9); decrepitude (11); incontinent (12).

READ CRITICALLY

1. How effective do you find Mairs's opening paragraph as an introduction to the essay as a whole?

2. Why do you think Mairs devotes paragraphs 2–4 to discussing her use of the word *cripple* to describe herself? How do you respond to this section of the essay? Mairs also objects to terms like *differently abled,* which do not tell the full truth about a condition. Can you think of other such words? Why do you think such words come into the language?

3. How would you evaluate "On Being a Cripple" as a definition essay? What have you learned from the essay that you did not know before?

4. Mairs writes at the end of paragraph 11, "Are there worse things than dying? I think that there may be." What does she mean? How do this question and answer lead into the subject of paragraph 12?

5. What do you think of Mairs's closing sentence? What image of Mairs does it leave you with?

WRITE AN ESSAY

Write an essay defining an important aspect of yourself. This definition might relate to a challenge you face in life, or it might focus on another facet of your identity—your family heritage, your membership in a particular group, a personality or physical trait that you believe sets you apart from others. Think about titling your essay "On Being ___" and, as Mairs does, relating experiences that help communicate your definition to readers.

Russel Honoré

Work Is a Blessing

Lieutenant General Honoré commanded the Joint Task Force Katrina in 2005, leading the Department of Defense in response to Hurricanes Katrina and Rita in Alabama, Mississippi, and Louisiana. He was responsible for directing the operations of over 22,000 service members, 2,000 aircraft, and 20 ships. In February 2008, he retired from the U.S. Army after thirty-seven years of active service and now focuses on disaster preparedness, response, and recovery activities.

Guiding question   Why is work a "blessing"?

Pause What do you think the reading will be about?

1   I grew up in Lakeland, La., one of 12 children. We all lived on my parents' subsistence farm. We grew cotton, sugar cane, corn, hogs, chickens and had a large garden, but it didn't bring in much cash. So when I was 12, I got a part-time

job on a dairy farm down the road, helping to milk cows. We milked 65 cows at 5 in the morning and again at 2 in afternoon, seven days a week.

2   In the kitchen one Saturday before daylight, I remember complaining to my father and grandfather about having to go milk those cows. My father said, "Ya know, boy, to work is a blessing."

3   I looked at those two men who'd worked harder than I ever had—my father eking out a living on that farm and my grandfather farming and working as a carpenter during the Depression. I had a feeling I had been told something really important, but it took many years before it sank in.

4   Going to college was a rare privilege for a kid from Lakeland. My father told me if I picked something to study that I liked doing, I'd always look forward to my work. But he also added, "Even having a job you hate is better than not having a job at all." I wanted to be a farmer, but I joined the ROTC[1] program to help pay for college. And what started out as an obligation to the Army became a way of life that I stayed committed to for 37 years, three months and three days.

5   In the late 1980s, during a visit to Bangladesh, I saw a woman with a baby on her back, breaking bricks with a hammer. I asked a Bangladesh military escort why they weren't using a machine, which would have been a lot easier. He told me a machine would put that lady out of work. Breaking those bricks meant she'd earn enough money to feed herself and her baby that day. And as bad as that woman's job was, it was enough to keep a small family alive. It reminded me of my father's words: To work is a blessing.

6   Serving in the U.S. Army overseas, I saw a lot of people like that woman in Bangladesh. And I have come to believe that people without jobs are not free. They are victims of crime, the ideology of terrorism, poor health, depression and social unrest. These victims become the illegal immigrants, the slaves of human trafficking, the drug dealers, the street gang members. I've seen it over and over again on the U.S. border, in Somalia, the Congo, Afghanistan and in New Orleans. People who have jobs can have a home, send their kids to school, develop a sense of pride, contribute to the good of the community, and even help others. When we can work, we're free. We're blessed.

7   I don't think I'll ever quit working. I'm retired from the Army, but I'm still working to help people be prepared for disaster. And I may get to do a little farming someday, too. I'm not going to stop. I believe in my father's words. I believe in the blessing of work.

1. **ROTC:** Reserve Officers' Training Corps

Pause The key to writing a good definition is to make sure the reader has enough evidence to understand your definition. Underline any sentence that defines the statement "Work is a blessing."

Pause The author says: "When we can work, we're free. We're blessed." What does he mean by that?

SUMMARIZE AND RESPOND

Summarize the main idea of "Work Is a Blessing." Then, go back and check off support for this main idea. Next, write a brief summary (three to five sentences) of the reading. Finally, jot down your initial response to the selection. Before reading this essay, did you consider the idea of working a blessing? Do you share Honoré's belief? How do you think the economic recession that began in 2008 changed the idea of work in America?

CHECK YOUR COMPREHENSION

1. Which of the following would be the best alternative title for this essay?

    a.   "Choose a Job You Love"

    b.   "Listen to Your Father"

    c.   "Choices Make You Free"

    d.   "Life Isn't Always Fair"

2. The main idea of this essay is that

    a.   if you can choose to work, you can make other choices in your life.

    b.   work isn't always miserable.

    c.   some people aren't lucky.

    d.   you should always go to college.

3. Honoré believes that work is a blessing because

    a.   it's part of life.

    b.   it's what you pass on to your children.

    c.   it's your choice to work.

    d.   it's what you do to survive.

4. If you are unfamiliar with the following words, use a dictionary to check their meanings: subsistence (para. 1); eking (3).

READ CRITICALLY

1. What would you describe as Honoré's purpose in this essay? Who might his intended audience be?

2. Why do you think Honoré brings up the story of the young woman in Bangladesh? What is the purpose of that story?

3. What do you think Honoré means when he says, "And I have come to believe that people without jobs are not free. They are victims of crime, the ideology of terrorism, poor health, depression and social unrest. These victims become the illegal immigrants, the slaves of human trafficking, the drug dealers, the street gang members" (para. 6)?

4. What is Honoré's actual definition of *work*?

5. Does Honoré's essay demonstrate the Four Basics of Good Definition? Why or why not?

WRITE AN ESSAY

Write an essay in which you focus on the kinds of jobs you have had in your life. Or, if you have not been employed before, think about jobs that your family and friends may have held. Then, think about why you are in school and what careers and classes you are interested in. Do you agree that Americans have the choice to pursue any career they wish? What evidence can you provide to support your answer?

Definition: Linked Readings

Stereotypes

Each of the following readings focuses on or uses stereotypes.

> Liza Long, "I Am Adam Lanza's Mother" (Chapter 41, p. 594)
>
> Amy Tan, "Mother Tongue" (Chapter 44, p. 633)
>
> Dave Barry, "The Ugly Truth about Beauty" (Chapter 46, p. 658)
>
> Amy L. Beck, "Struggling for Perfection" (Chapter 47, p. 666)
>
> Brent Staples, "Just Walk On By: Black Men and Public Space" (Chapter 47, p. 670)

Read the selections, and draw from at least one in addition to "On Being a Cripple" to write an essay titled "Stereotypes: Are They Wrong?" You can refer to your own experience, but make sure to use material from the essays as well.

Media Images and Realities

The following readings focus on the possible effects of media images on reality.

> Dave Barry, "The Ugly Truth about Beauty" (Chapter 46, p. 658)
>
> Amy L. Beck, "Struggling for Perfection" (Chapter 47, p. 666)
>
> Caitlin Seida, "My Embarrassing Picture Went Viral" (Chapter 47, p. 674)
>
> Wency Leung, "Does Social Media Make Us Closer—or Make Us Loners?" (Chapter 48, p. 686)

Read the selections, and draw from at least one in addition to "On Being a Cripple" to write an essay titled "Media Images and Reality" that examines how media images reflect or do not reflect real life. You can refer to your own experience, but make sure to use material from the essays as well.

46

Comparison and Contrast

Each essay in this chapter uses comparison and contrast to get its main idea across. As you read these essays, consider how they achieve the Four Basics of Good Comparison and Contrast that are listed below and discussed in Chapter 16 of this book.

Four Basics of Good Comparison and Contrast

1. It uses subjects that have enough in common to be usefully compared and contrasted.
2. It serves a purpose—either to help readers make a decision or to help them understand the subjects.
3. It presents several important, parallel points of comparison and/or contrast.
4. It is organized either point by point or whole to whole (see p. 224).

Mary Elizabeth Williams

Our Family's Week on a Food Stamp Budget

Mary Elizabeth Williams has written articles for the *New York Times* and the *Nation* and published a book titled *Gimme Shelter: My Three Years of Searching for the American Dream* (2009). This article, originally published in *Salon,* where she is a staff writer, sees her family living for a week on the budget given to families eligible for government assistance for food.

Guiding question What is the SNAP challenge?

1   I love to eat. You won't catch me on any diets or purifying cleanses or experiments in going gluten- or lactose-free. I plan meals in my dreams, and put baking ingredients on my Amazon wish list. My idea of going voluntarily hungry is waiting until the previews are over to open the candy. And I'm lucky as hell, because unlike one in every six Americans who don't have a choice in the matter, I don't have to go hungry.

2   After I wrote about Cory Booker's[1] decision last month to take the SNAP Challenge—to take "a view of what life can be like for millions of low-income Americans"—I couldn't get the idea of it out of my head. The challenge is simple in concept but demanding in its execution: see what it's like to live for one week on a food budget equivalent to your state's Supplemental Nutrition Assistance Program's (SNAP) benefits. Participants can use their existing spices and condiments, but no other foodstuffs, nor they can accept food "from friends, family, or at work." Because I live in New York, I'd have a slightly more generous allowance than New Jersey's Booker got—a total of $36.86 for a week of eating. And because my two daughters are awesome, they said they wanted to do it too as I soon as I mentioned it to them. So for the past week, we've been eating on a little over five bucks a person per day.

3   We didn't start this because we think our small action is going to change the cruelly paltry food allowances that our states hand out, or make any significant impact in the lives of the 50.1 million Americans living in food-insecure households. The only minute tangible effect of this week is that we're using the savings from our grocery bill to make a gift to the phenomenal City Meals on Wheels. Instead, what we hope for is a lesson in empathy; a reminder that hunger and food insecurity are real issues for our friends and neighbors. On our side of Broadway, the median household income is a modest $51,000. On the other side, it's half that.

4   And we did it for another reason too. We did it because we wanted to be part of a bigger conversation about how we are feeding ourselves in the country, right now, at every income level. We did it because families aren't eating together enough—or when they are, they're eating in front of the TV. We did it because a quarter of Americans eat fast food every day and half of them drink soda every day too. Even when we eat at home, nearly half our meals come from "fast food, delivery, or takeout from restaurants or grocery delis." We did it because while millions go hungry, we throw away almost half of our food. Perhaps not uncoincidentally, 60 percent of Americans are now overweight or obese. And a lot of the health problems we are facing could be eased if we got our butts in the kitchen and started cooking.

5   Somewhere along the way, cooking went from being something that normal Americans just did, on a daily basis, to something we instead watch as a gladiator sport on television. And while it's true that we no longer live in a world where nonna is stirring a pot all afternoon and the wifey is waiting when we come through the door with a drink, this isn't the fault of feminism. It's a fault of indifference. It's a fault of forgetting how important food is. We spend far less of our income on food now than our parents or grandparents did, because it's easy to get food that's cheap and convenient and can be gobbled down in a car.

Pause What do you think the article will compare and contrast?

1. **Cory Booker:** former mayor of Newark, New Jersey, and current U.S. senator

Pause What do you think will happen? What will the outcome of the challenge be?

Pause Underline the main criticisms of American eating habits outlined in the article.

Pause Take a moment to identify what is being compared. Number the reasons that Williams provides as evidence for her comparison.

6   Not long ago, I was at a party, making conversation with a hospital dietician. I told her I was planning on doing the SNAP Challenge and she told me that she'd done it herself a few months prior. "Do you cook?" she asked. "If you can cook, you'll be fine." Then she told me that most of her colleagues—fellow dieticians—don't even cook. We're losing a basic skill, one that we badly need to nourish ourselves, and one we need to teach our children. Cooking is emancipating. And my kids and I wanted to bust the notions that cooking takes a lot of money, or stupid fancy equipment. (Unless you think a Crock Pot is a fancy thing, it does not.)

7   My daughters and I spread the shopping and stocking up for the challenge over several days. We bought oranges and potatoes, vegetables and milk and a chicken and some flour. We bought things that are delicious, and you don't need to be a genius to prepare. And when the first day—Sunday—arrived, it came with a flourish and a big stack of pancakes. Over the past few days, I've made soups and sautéed sausages. I've baked bread and made yogurt and jam. I've sent the kids into the kitchen to make chili. These things aren't hard to do. They take a little thought and work, but why shouldn't nourishing yourself take a little thought and work? And what concerns me is that I suspect my daughters and I are eating a more healthy, balanced and pleasurable diet on a food stamp budget that a lot of families with a whole lot more to spend.

Pause How do these meals differ from the "average American meals" Williams discussed earlier?

8   It hasn't all been fun and easy. My daughters both have pined for regular old cereal instead of oatmeal or yogurt again. I went out for coffee with my mate and my coffee was a glass of water. I've had to put more effort into each meal, especially as the week has gone on and I've watched our supplies dwindle. But I've done it knowing that for us, this ends on Sunday. And I don't ever want to forget that feeling I had yesterday of wanting to buy an avocado, and being just two cents short. I want my daughters to learn to cook, but more than that I want them to learn to be compassionate, competent young women. I want them to be able to someday feed their own families, and I want them to feed themselves. Extraordinary things are possible when you can do that. Worlds of possibility open up when you know how to eat, because you know how to cook. When you don't need to rip open a box for sustenance. And it's a challenge that's worth taking, every day.

SUMMARIZE AND RESPOND

Summarize the main idea of "Our Family's Week on a Food Stamp Budget." Then, go back and check off support for this main idea. Next, write a brief summary (three to five sentences) of the reading. Finally, jot down your initial response to the selection. Do you agree that families may be better off doing more cooking for themselves? What was your reaction to Williams's experiment?

CHECK YOUR COMPREHENSION

1. Which of the following would be the best alternative title for this essay?
    (a.) "Take the Time to Eat Right"
    b.   "Eating Well Is Expensive"

    c.   "The SNAP Challenge Is Difficult"

    d.   "Americans Don't Have Time to Cook"

2. The main idea of this essay is that

    a.   families can't afford to eat in a way that is healthy and balanced.

    b.   there isn't enough time in the day or money to cook balanced and healthy meals.

    c.   we could cook healthy and balanced meals, but they are too expensive.

    (d.) we don't take the time to cook the meals that would be good for us, although we could probably afford it.

3. According to the essay,

    a.   cooking is an everyday chore.

    (b.) cooking has become a gladiator sport on TV.

    c.   cooking is too hard.

    d.   cooking takes too much time.

4. If you are unfamiliar with the following words, use a dictionary to check their meanings: condiments (para. 2); minute, tangible, empathy (3); emancipating (6).

READ CRITICALLY

1. Where in the essay does the author use point-by-point organization?

2. What tone does Williams create in this essay? How can you tell? What is her general position on this topic?

3. The author says, "Somewhere along the way, cooking went from being something that normal Americans just did, on a daily basis, to something we instead watch as a gladiator sport on television" (para. 5). What does she mean by this? How did cooking change in this way?

4. After reading this article, do you think Williams believes it is possible to continue living on the SNAP budget? Explain your answer.

5. What were the good parts of the SNAP challenge that Williams wanted her readers to understand? What does she think Americans have forgotten about eating?

WRITE AN ESSAY

Write an essay comparing and contrasting a favorite meal that you have had in two different places. Ideally, it would be a meal you have tried to make yourself, or that someone you know has cooked for you, and one that you have purchased in a restaurant or fast-food franchise. What makes the two meals different based on the way they smell? How do they taste different? Do the meals themselves evoke different emotions and/or memories for you?

Dave Barry

The Ugly Truth about Beauty

According to the *New York Times*, humorist Dave Barry is "the funniest man in America." Born in 1947 in Armonk, New York, Barry earned a B.A. from Haverford College. He then worked for several years as a newspaper reporter and a lecturer on business writing before discovering his talent as a humor columnist. The columns he wrote for the *Miami Herald* from 1983 to 2004 have been collected in numerous books. Barry's hilarious observations on American life won him the Pulitzer Prize for Commentary in 1988. His most recent books are *Insane City* (2013) and *You Can Date Boys When You're Forty* (2014).

In "The Ugly Truth about Beauty," first published in the *Miami Herald* in 1998, Barry compares and contrasts men's and women's beauty routines. The essay humorously highlights differences in the ways that men and women view themselves.

Guiding question Why do men and women think of their looks differently?

1   If you're a man, at some point a woman will ask you how she looks.

2   "How do I look?" she'll ask.

3   You must be careful how you answer this question. The best technique is to form an honest yet sensitive opinion, then collapse on the floor with some kind of fatal seizure. Trust me, this is the easiest way out. Because you will never come up with the right answer.

4   The problem is that women generally do not think of their looks in the same way that men do. Most men form an opinion of how they look in seventh grade, and they stick to it for the rest of their lives. Some men form the opinion that they are irresistible stud muffins, and they do not change this opinion even when their faces sag and their noses bloat to the size of eggplants and their eyebrows grow together to form what appears to be a giant forehead-dwelling tropical caterpillar.

5   Most men, I believe, think of themselves as average-looking. Men will think this even if their faces cause heart failure in cattle at a range of three hundred yards. Being average does not bother them; average is fine, for men. This is why men never ask anybody how they look. Their primary form of beauty care is to shave themselves, which is essentially the same form of beauty care that they give to their lawns. If, at the end of his four-minute daily beauty regimen,[1] a man has managed to wipe most of the shaving cream out of his hair and is not bleeding too badly, he feels that he has done all he can, so he stops thinking about his appearance and devotes his mind to more critical issues, such as the Super Bowl.

Pause Based on the first sentence of paragraph 4, how do you think Barry will go on to develop this essay?

1. **regimen:** routine

6   Women do not look at themselves this way. If I had to express, in three words, what I believe most women think about their appearance, those words would be: "not good enough." No matter how attractive a woman may appear to be to others, when she looks at herself in the mirror, she thinks: woof. She thinks that at any moment a municipal animal-control officer is going to throw a net over her and haul her off to the shelter.

7   Why do women have such low self-esteem? There are many complex psychological and societal reasons, by which I mean Barbie. Girls grow up playing with a doll proportioned such that, if it were a human, it would be seven feet tall and weigh eighty-one pounds, of which fifty-three pounds would be bosoms. This is a difficult appearance standard to live up to, especially when you contrast it with the standard set for little boys by their dolls . . . excuse me, by their action figures. Most of the action figures that my son played with when he was little were hideous-looking. For example, he was very fond of an action figure (part of the He-Man series) called "Buzz-Off," who was part human, part flying insect. Buzz-Off was not a looker. But he was extremely self-confident. You could not imagine Buzz-Off saying to the other action figures: "Do you think these wings make my hips look big?"

Pause What two subjects does Barry contrast in paragraph 7?

8   But women grow up thinking they need to look like Barbie, which for most women is impossible, although there is a multibillion-dollar beauty industry devoted to convincing women that they must try. I once saw an *Oprah* show wherein supermodel Cindy Crawford dispensed makeup tips to the studio audience. Cindy had all these middle-aged women applying beauty products to their faces; she stressed how important it was to apply them in a certain way, using the tips of their fingers. All the women dutifully did this, even though it was obvious to any sane observer that, no matter how carefully they applied these products, they would never look remotely like Cindy Crawford, who is some kind of genetic mutation.

Pause What is Barry's main idea in paragraph 8?

9   I'm not saying that men are superior. I'm just saying that you're not going to get a group of middle-aged men to sit in a room and apply cosmetics to themselves under the instruction of Brad Pitt, in hopes of looking more like him. Men would realize that this task was pointless and demeaning.[2] They would find some way to bolster their self-esteem that did not require looking like Brad Pitt. They would say to Brad: "Oh YEAH? Well what do you know about LAWN CARE, pretty boy?"

2. **demeaning:** degrading, lowering one's character

10   Of course many women will argue that the reason they become obsessed with trying to look like Cindy Crawford is that men, being as shallow as a drop of spit, WANT women to look that way. To which I have two responses:

11   1. Hey, just because WE'RE idiots, that does not mean YOU have to be; and

12   2. Men don't even notice 97 percent of the beauty efforts you make anyway. Take fingernails. The average woman spends 5,000 hours per year worrying about her fingernails; I have never once, in more than forty years of listening to men talk about women, heard a man say, "She has a nice set of fingernails!" Many men would not notice if a woman had upward of four hands.

13 Anyway, to get back to my original point: If you're a man, and a woman asks you how she looks, you're in big trouble. Obviously, you can't say she looks bad. But you also can't say that she looks great, because she'll think you're lying, because she has spent countless hours, with the help of the multibillion-dollar beauty industry, obsessing about the differences between herself and Cindy Crawford. Also, she suspects that you're not qualified to judge anybody's appearance. This is because you have shaving cream in your hair.

SUMMARIZE AND RESPOND

Summarize the main idea of "The Ugly Truth about Beauty." Then, go back and check off support for this main idea. Next, write a brief summary (three to five sentences) of the essay. Finally, jot down your initial response to the essay. Do you agree with Barry's assessment of why there are differences in the ways men and women view themselves? What examples from your experience do or do not support his points?

CHECK YOUR COMPREHENSION

1. Which of the following would be the best alternative title for this essay?
    a. "Barbie versus He-Man"
    b. "Men and Women: What They See in the Mirror"
    c. "It's Kinder to Lie"
    d. "The Beauty Industry's Dark Secret"

2. The main idea of this essay is that
    a. men don't know how to respond when women ask about their appearance.
    b. men don't care how much effort women put into their looks.
    c. because of society and the media, men and women view their physical appearances differently.
    d. childhood toys influence the way men and women think about their looks.

3. According to Barry,
    a. most men are concerned with how women view their appearance.
    b. women want men to be honest about their looks.
    c. most women are dissatisfied with their appearance.
    d. a woman's perception of her appearance is influenced by her moods and her female friends.

4. If you are unfamiliar with the following words, use a dictionary to check their meanings: societal, proportioned (para. 7); mutation (8); bolster (9).

READ CRITICALLY

1. Who is Barry's intended audience, and what do you think is his purpose in writing this essay?

2. In paragraphs 7 and 8, Barry discusses children's toys. Why did he choose these particular toys, and how do they help him explain his points of contrast?

3. What is Barry's attitude toward Cindy Crawford and Brad Pitt? Explain how he uses these examples to support his main idea.

4. Explain the significance of the title. What do you think Barry would say is the ugly truth about beauty?

5. Why do you think the beauty industry is so successful? Support your answer with examples from this essay.

WRITE AN ESSAY

Look through your family photographs, or use the Internet or magazines to view men's and women's fashions over the last fifty years. Think about how styles have changed, and write an essay that compares and contrasts fashion trends from two different decades. Use concrete examples to show differences and similarities in the two time periods' styles.

Katy Hall and Chris Spurlock

Paid Parental Leave: U.S. vs. the World

Katy Hall is the managing features editor of the *Huffington Post*. Chris Spurlock graduated from the Missouri School of Journalism and typically uses visuals in his articles because he firmly believes that a strong and well-designed visual is crucial to understanding a complicated story. A native of St. Louis, he held jobs at the *Columbia Missourian* and KTVI-TV/KPLR-TV before his current job as an infographic design editor for the *Huffington Post*.

Guiding question Why do countries other than the United States have paid parental leave?

1   When Australia passed a parental leave law in 2010, it left the U.S. as the only industrialized nation not to mandate paid leave for mothers of newborns. Most of the rest of the world has paid maternity leave policies, too; Lesotho, Swaziland and Papua New Guinea are the only other countries that do not. Many countries give new fathers paid time off as well or allow parents to share paid leave.

Pause Why might the United States not have a paid parental leave policy?

2   New parents in the U.S. are guaranteed their jobs for 12 weeks after the arrival of a new baby, thanks to the Family Medical Leave Act of 1993, but they do not have to be paid during that time and exemptions apply for small companies. Only about 16 percent of employers offer fully paid maternity leave and many families take on significant debt or turn to public assistance around the birth of a child. As America's falling fertility rate raises economic concerns, working families may long to procreate in Sweden, where parents are given 480 paid days per child, to be shared between them and used any time before the kid turns eight.

Paid Parental Leave: U.S. vs. The World

The U.S. joins Lesotho, Swaziland, and Papua New Guinea as the only countries that do not mandate paid maternity leave. Most countries ensure at least three months of paid leave for new mothers, and many give fathers benefits too.

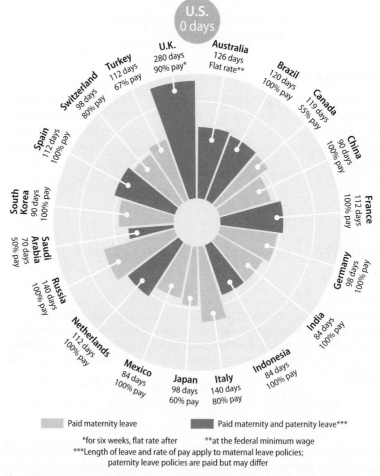

U.S. 0 days

U.K. 280 days 90% pay*

Australia 126 days Flat rate**

Turkey 112 days 67% pay

Switzerland 98 days 80% pay

Brazil 120 days 100% pay

Canada 119 days 55% pay

Spain 112 days 100% pay

China 90 days 100% pay

South Korea 90 days 100% pay

France 112 days 100% pay

Saudi Arabia 70 days 50% pay

Germany 98 days 100% pay

Russia 140 days 100% pay

India 84 days 100% pay

Netherlands 112 days 100% pay

Indonesia 84 days 100% pay

Mexico 84 days 100% pay

Japan 98 days 60% pay

Italy 140 days 80% pay

Paid maternity leave   Paid maternity and paternity leave***

*for six weeks, flat rate after   **at the federal minimum wage
***Length of leave and rate of pay apply to maternal leave policies; paternity leave policies are paid but may differ

3   Will the U.S. catch up with the rest of the world during President Obama's second term? Advocates are working to get a national law passed while some states are expanding family leave policies, the *Atlantic* reports. . . . In the meantime, certain companies understand that keeping new parents happy makes more sense than replacing them, which generally costs somewhere between 50 and 200 percent of a worker's salary. When Google lengthened its maternity leave from three months to five and made it fully paid, new-mom attrition fell by half.

SUMMARIZE AND RESPOND

Summarize the main idea of "Paid Parental Leave: U.S. vs. the World." Then, go back and check off support for the main idea. Next, write a brief summary (three to five sentences) of the reading. Finally, jot down your initial response to the selection. How does the United States compare with the rest of the world in terms of paid parental leave? Is this disparity surprising to you? Why or why not?

CHECK YOUR COMPREHENSION

1. Which of the following is the best alternative title for this essay?
    a.   "Caring for Your Newborn and Getting Paid"
    b.   "It's Good to Be American"
    c.   "It's Better to Be British"
    d.   "Taking Care of Parents around the World"

2. The main idea of this essay is that
    a.   other industrialized nations provide too much time for parents after the birth of a baby.
    b.   other industrialized nations do not need their employees to return to work as soon as they are needed in the United States.
    c.   other industrialized nations ensure parents have enough paid time off to take care of themselves and their baby before returning to work.
    d.   other industrialized nations expect parents to take care of themselves after the birth of a baby.

3. According to the essay, in the United States,
    a.   Family Medical Leave Act laws mean that new moms can spend 12 weeks at home with their newborns at full pay.
    b.   Family Medical Leave Act laws mean that new moms can spend 12 weeks at home with their newborns at half pay.

    c. Family Medical Leave Act laws mean that new moms can spend 12 weeks at home with their newborns at quarter pay.

    (d.) Family Medical Leave Act laws mean that new moms can spend 12 weeks at home with their newborns and keep their jobs.

4. If you are unfamiliar with the following words, use a dictionary to check their meanings: procreate (para. 2); advocates, attrition (3).

READ CRITICALLY

1. What is Hall and Spurlock's purpose in writing this column?

2. The graphic illustrates parental leave in the United States compared with that in the rest of the world. How does the United States compare? Why?

3. Why might Hall and Spurlock have chosen to use a graphic in this column? What did they think the graphic could achieve that writing could not? Were they more successful in achieving their purpose by using the graphic? Why or why not?

4. What role do you think the government should play in moderating or mandating parental leave? Why do you think this?

5. The final paragraph presents evidence that companies in the United States are finding it more effective to provide employees with parental leave packages than to hire new employees. Why is this? Do you agree with this statement? Explain your answer.

WRITE AN ESSAY

Write an essay comparing and contrasting the experience of a parent who is able to take the several weeks or months of paid leave after the birth of a child with that of a parent who has to immediately return to work for financial reasons. In what ways will that experience be different for each family? In what ways are they similar? Make sure you establish a basis for comparison (e.g., similarities and differences in bonding with the infant, establishing routines, and getting enough sleep).

Comparison and Contrast: Linked Readings

Conceptions of Gender

The following readings focus on various aspects of the effects of gender on people's behavior and lives.

Amy L. Beck, "Struggling for Perfection" (Chapter 47, p. 666)

Brent Staples, "Just Walk On By: Black Men and Public Space" (Chapter 47, p. 670)

Read the selections, and draw from at least one in addition to "The Ugly Truth about Beauty" to write an essay titled "How Gender Affects Behavior." You can refer to your own experience, but make sure to use material from the essays as well.

Being a Parent

The following readings focus on various struggles and hardships encountered by parents.

Monique Rizer, "When Students Are Parents" (Chapter 40, p. 587)

Liza Long, "I Am Adam Lanza's Mother" (Chapter 41, p. 594)

Read the selections and write an essay entitled "The Difficulties of Being a Parent." Draw from at least one selection in addition to "Paid Parental Leave: The U.S. vs. the World." You can refer to your own experience, but make sure to use material from the essays as well.

47

Cause and Effect

Each essay in this chapter uses cause and effect to get its main idea across. As you read these essays, consider how they achieve the Four Basics of Good Cause and Effect that are listed below and discussed in Chapter 17 of this book.

Four Basics of Good Cause and Effect

1. The main point reflects the writer's purpose—to explain causes, effects, or both.
2. If the purpose is to explain causes, it presents real causes.
3. If the purpose is to explain effects, it presents real effects.
4. It gives clear and detailed examples or explanations of the causes and/or effects.

Amy L. Beck

Struggling for Perfection

Amy L. Beck was born in 1979 in Greenwich, Connecticut. After graduating from Harvard University in 2000, Beck joined Teach for America, a program that places recent college graduates in inner-city or rural schools, and she taught first graders in Long Beach, California, for two years. She has also worked in France as a researcher for the travel guide *Let's Go* and as an intern with the French Public Health Administration. Beck is currently a pediatrician at the University of California, San Francisco Medical Center.

In "Struggling for Perfection," which she wrote for the *Harvard Crimson* in 1998, Beck explores eating disorders and domestic abuse. How are these two problems linked? According to Beck, they are both partly caused by media images.

Guiding question What is the cause-and-effect relationship that Beck writes about?

1   Sex sells. This truth is a boon[1] for marketing gurus and the pornography industry but a rather unfortunate situation for women. Every issue of *Playboy*, every lewd poster, and even the Victoria's Secret catalog transform real women into ornaments, valued exclusively for their outward appearance. These publications are responsible for defining what is sexy and reinforce the belief that aesthetic[2] appeal is a woman's highest virtue.

2   Some argue that the proliferation[3] of pornography and other sexually explicit images of women is both harmless for society and inevitable. Just this point was made in a recent *Crimson* column titled "In Defense of Hooters and the St. Pauli Girl." In the tone of an expert, the author boldly claims that the objectification[4] of women in the media does not affect the way men treat the real women in their lives, nor does it give those with pathological[5] tendencies "the decisive nudge into misogyny."[6] Furthermore, the author says, those women who feel pressure to conform to beauty standards set by the media are suffering from a classic psychosis in which they "confuse fiction with reality."

3   My first reaction was to ask how anyone could possibly believe that the pervasiveness[7] of pornography and sexually explicit depictions of women could fail to have any sort of effect on society. Having spent twelve weeks working in a psychiatric hospital last summer, I am writing from a starkly different perspective.

4   During my first eight weeks at the hospital, I worked on an eating disorder unit in constant contact with anorexics and bulimics. Many patients on the unit were so emaciated[8] that I could never accustom myself to their appearance; every time I saw them I experienced the same shock. Most had been in and out of countless other hospitals and treatment programs, improving slightly each time but always sliding back into eating-disordered behavior when released.

5   These people were truly at rock bottom, considered by many to be incurable. Their eating disorders had consumed them entirely, leaving no trace of the vibrant, intelligent people that once inhabited their now skeletal bodies. Certainly, these people also had family problems, alcoholic parents, histories of abuse and clinical depression, to name a few, all of which contribute to feelings of worthlessness and extremely low self-esteem—cited by experts as a major cause of eating disorders. What I find significant, however, is not the root of their problems but that these women (there were a few men, but never more than five percent of the patient population) turned to their bodies as a means of expression and self-healing. Profoundly influenced by the depiction of women by the fashion industry, they had been convinced that the only way to attain love, respect, and personal fulfillment was through a relentless pursuit of physical perfection. Most were perfectly aware that they would never look like a supermodel, but it was inconceivable not to try to do so. They found that they were good at dieting and that they were praised and rewarded for their success. And by the time things had gone too far, they had lost all sense of perspective.

6   Convinced by the media and popular culture to believe that, as women, they should look a certain way and that only if they looked that way would they be loved and respected, they turned to dieting as a means of personal fulfillment and self-definition. While cases as extreme as those I saw at the hospital are rare,

1. **boon:** a welcome benefit

2. **aesthetic:** having to do with beauty

3. **proliferation:** rapid growth

4. **objectification:** the treatment of a person as an object

5. **pathological:** abnormal, diseased

6. **misogyny:** hatred of women

7. **pervasiveness:** the extension or spread of one thing throughout something else

8. **emaciated:** extremely thin

Pause After reading her second paragraph, what do you predict that Beck will do in her essay?

Pause Underline the sentence that best expresses the main idea of paragraph 5.

9. debilitating: weakening

many women experience milder but still debilitating[9] forms of eating disorders. They may never get sick enough to require hospitalization, but they nonetheless devote excessive mental and physical energy to diet and exercise, often jeopardizing their health in the process.

7   For my last four weeks at the hospital I transferred from eating disorders to a general psychology unit. The diagnoses varied, but the number of patients with histories of abuse was astounding. After listening to and reading countless case histories, I began to recognize the patterns. In many cases, domestic battering was chronic, occurring weekly or daily whenever the victim broke some sort of household rule, such as serving dinner late or dressing "too sexy." The majority of the sexual abuse victims had been raped by people close to them: relatives, ex-boyfriends, or family friends. In one particularly striking case, a patient's boyfriend made her have sex with five of his friends on a frequent basis.

Pause Summarize the main idea of paragraph 7.

8   The men who committed these heinous crimes were rarely pathological rapists or batterers. Few would even be deemed mentally ill or classically misogynistic. Rather, they are men who view the real women in their lives in the same manner that they would view a *Playboy* model, a waitress at Hooters, or a prostitute—as objects that exist solely for their pleasure and convenience. These men are not genetically predisposed[10] to disrespect and abuse women. Their attitudes towards women were societally conditioned.

10. predisposed: inclined to something in advance

9   Some would argue that pornography did not contribute to these men's behavior towards women. I disagree. Rape and battery are not new problems, and objectification of women by the media reinforces historically entrenched beliefs that a woman's main reason for existence is procreation and the sexual pleasure of her mate. Pornographic magazines and lewd posters reduce women to a commodity[11] that can be purchased and owned, divorcing the physical manifestation[12] from the person within. The power of popular culture to affect how we eat, how we dress, and how we behave is enormous. Conceptions of gender are in no way immune to this phenomenon.

11. commodity: a thing of use, value, or advantage

12. manifestation: a visible presence, an outward show

10   Certainly some of us are more affected by the media than others. Not all teenage girls develop anorexia, nor do all men who read *Playboy* abuse their wives. Nonetheless, the prevalence of both eating disorders and various forms of domestic and sexual abuse indicate major societal trends. The American Anorexia/Bulimia Association reports that 5 percent of women will develop a full-fledged eating disorder, while 15 percent have "substantially disordered eating." The Family Violence Prevention Program documents that 4 million American women were battered last year. And, yes, I am absolutely convinced that the objectification of women by the media is an integral part of both of these problems, presenting women with unrealistic role models while encouraging men to think of women solely in terms of their sexuality.

Pause How are you and others you know affected by media images?

11   Women are up against a long history of devaluation and oppression, and, unfortunately, the feminist movements have been only partially successful in purging[13] those legacies. Sexually charged images of women in the media are not the only cause of this continuing problem, but they certainly play a central role.

13. purging: removing something unwanted

SUMMARIZE AND RESPOND

Summarize the main idea of "Struggling for Perfection." Then, go back and check off support for this main idea. Next, write a brief summary (three to five sentences) of the essay. Finally, jot down your initial response to the essay. Do you agree or disagree with Beck's points? What else do you think causes eating disorders and domestic abuse?

CHECK YOUR COMPREHENSION

1. Which of the following would be the best alternative title for this essay?

   a. "The Alarming Growth of Eating Disorders"

   b. "The Causes and Effects of Eating Disorders"

   c. "The Media's Influence on Eating Disorders and Domestic Abuse"

   d. "Pressure to Conform"

2. The main idea of this essay is that

   a. media images of women are not the only cause of eating disorders.

   b. publications such as *Playboy* and the Victoria's Secret catalog transform women into sexual objects.

   c. low self-esteem is a major cause of eating disorders.

   d. media images of women contribute to eating disorders and violence against females.

3. According to the author,

   a. women who try to look like supermodels are unable to tell the difference between fiction and reality.

   b. many of the women she met while working in the hospital had backgrounds that included abuse, family problems, and depression.

   c. patients with eating disorders are often incurable.

   d. feminist movements have been very successful in their attempts to lessen the prevalence of eating disorders and abuse against women.

4. If you are unfamiliar with the following words, use a dictionary to check their meanings: gurus, lewd (para. 1); inevitable, psychosis (2); anorexics, bulimics (4); depiction (5); chronic (7); heinous, genetically (8); entrenched, procreation (9); integral (10); devaluation, legacies (11).

1. Why do you think Beck begins her essay by discussing the column "In Defense of Hooters and the St. Pauli Girl" (para. 2)?

2. Media images of women lead to what two major problems, according to Beck? How are these problems linked?

3. Describe Beck's attitude toward men who commit domestic abuse. What examples from the essay support your response?

4. Does Beck provide clear links between media images of women and the effects of those images? Discuss some of the supporting details she uses to show these links.

5. Beck presents some statistics about eating disorders and domestic abuse. How does she use these statistics to make a further observation about her main point?

Beck acknowledges the fact that sexually charged media images of women are not the only cause of eating disorders and abuse. Write an essay about a different possible cause of one of these problems. You could also choose to write about a similar problem (what causes some men to take steroids, for example). If you addressed other causes of eating disorders and abuse for the Summarize and Respond section above, feel free to use those ideas.

Brent Staples

Just Walk On By: Black Men and Public Space

Brent Staples was born in 1951 in Chester, Pennsylvania. After graduating from Widener University, he earned a Ph.D. in psychology from the University of Chicago. He is a member of the editorial board of the *New York Times,* writing commentary on politics and culture. He has published a memoir, *Parallel Time: Growing Up in Black and White* (1994).

In "Just Walk On By: Black Men and Public Space," Staples observes how people, particularly women, react to him when he goes out for a walk. This essay was first published in *Ms.* magazine.

Guiding question How does Staples affect people, and why?

1   My first victim was a woman—white, well dressed, probably in her early twenties. I came upon her late one evening on a deserted street in Hyde Park, a relatively affluent neighborhood in an otherwise mean, impoverished section of

Chicago. As I swung onto the avenue behind her, there seemed to be a discreet, uninflammatory[1] distance between us. Not so. She cast back a worried glance. To her, the youngish black man—a broad six feet two inches with a beard and billowing hair, both hands shoved into the pockets of a bulky military jacket—seemed menacingly close. After a few more quick glimpses, she picked up her pace and was soon running in earnest. Within seconds she disappeared into a cross street.

2   That was more than a decade ago. I was twenty-two years old, a graduate student newly arrived at the University of Chicago. It was in the echo of that terrified woman's footfalls that I first began to know the unwieldy inheritance I'd come into—the ability to alter public space in ugly ways. It was clear that she thought herself the quarry[2] of a mugger, a rapist, or worse. Suffering a bout of insomnia, however, I was stalking sleep, not defenseless wayfarers. As a softy who is scarcely able to take a knife to a raw chicken—let alone hold one to a person's throat—I was surprised, embarrassed, and dismayed all at once. Her flight made me feel like an accomplice in tyranny.[3] It also made it clear that I was indistinguishable from the muggers who occasionally seeped into the area from the surrounding ghetto. That first encounter, and those that followed, signified that a vast, unnerving[4] gulf lay between nighttime pedestrians—particularly women—and me. And I soon gathered that being perceived as dangerous is a hazard in itself. I only needed to turn a corner into a dicey situation, or crowd some frightened, armed person in a foyer somewhere, or make an errant[5] move after being pulled over by a policeman. Where fear and weapons meet—and they often do in urban America—there is always the possibility of death.

3   In that first year, my first away from my hometown, I was to become thoroughly familiar with the language of fear. At dark, shadowy intersections, I could cross in front of a car stopped at a traffic light and elicit the *thunk, thunk, thunk, thunk* of the driver—black, white, male, or female—hammering down the door locks. On less traveled streets after dark, I grew accustomed to but never comfortable with people crossing to the other side of the street rather than pass me. Then there were the standard unpleasantries with policemen, doormen, bouncers, cabdrivers, and others whose business it is to screen out troublesome individuals *before* there is any nastiness.

4   I moved to New York nearly two years ago and I have remained an avid night walker. In central Manhattan, the near-constant crowd cover minimizes tense one-on-one street encounters. Elsewhere—in SoHo, for example, where sidewalks are narrow and tightly spaced buildings shut out the sky—things can get very taut indeed.

5   After dark, on the warrenlike[6] streets of Brooklyn where I live, I often see women who fear the worst from me. They seem to have set their faces on neutral, and with their purse straps strung across their chests bandolier-style, they forge ahead as though bracing themselves against being tackled. I understand, of course, that the danger they perceive is not a hallucination. Women are particularly vulnerable to street violence, and young black males are drastically overrepresented among the perpetrators of that violence. Yet these truths are no solace

---

1. **uninflammatory:** unlikely to cause fear

Pause After reading the title and the first paragraph, what do you predict Staples will write about in the rest of the essay?

2. **quarry:** one that is chased, as in a hunt

3. **tyranny:** the abuse of power

4. **unnerving:** upsetting

5. **errant:** stray, unintended

Pause In paragraph 3, what does Staples mean by "standard unpleasantries"?

6. **warrenlike:** narrow and having many blind spots

against the kind of alienation that comes of being ever the suspect, a fearsome entity with whom pedestrians avoid making eye contact.

Pause Summarize the point that Staples makes about himself in paragraphs 6 and 7.

6   It is not altogether clear to me how I reached the ripe old age of twenty-two without being conscious of the lethality nighttime pedestrians attributed to me. Perhaps it was because in Chester, Pennsylvania, the small, angry industrial town where I came of age in the 1960s, I was scarcely noticeable against a backdrop of gang warfare, street knifings, and murders. I grew up one of the good boys, had perhaps a half-dozen fistfights. In retrospect, my shyness of combat has clear sources.

7   As a boy, I saw countless tough guys locked away; I have since buried several, too. They were babies, really—a teenage cousin, a brother of twenty-two, a childhood friend in his mid-twenties—all gone down in episodes of bravado played out in the streets. I came to doubt the virtues of intimidation early on. I chose, perhaps unconsciously, to remain a shadow—timid, but a survivor.

8   The fearsomeness mistakenly attributed to me in public places often has a perilous flavor. The most frightening of these confusions occurred in the late 1970s and early 1980s, when I worked as a journalist in Chicago. One day, rushing into the office of a magazine I was writing for with a deadline story in hand, I was mistaken for a burglar. The office manager called security and, with an ad hoc[7] posse, pursued me through the labyrinthine halls, nearly to my editor's door. I had no way of proving who I was. I could only move briskly toward the company of someone who knew me.

7. **ad hoc:** made up of whatever is available (Latin, for this purpose)

9   Another time I was on assignment for a local paper and killing time before an interview. I entered a jewelry store on the city's affluent Near North Side. The proprietor excused herself and returned with an enormous red Doberman pinscher straining at the end of a leash. She stood, the dog extended toward me, silent to my questions, her eyes bulging nearly out of her head. I took a cursory look around, nodded, and bade her good night.

10   Relatively speaking, however, I never fared as badly as another black male journalist. He went to nearby Waukegan, Illinois, a couple of summers ago to work on a story about a murderer who was born there. Mistaking the reporter for the killer, police officers hauled him from his car at gunpoint and but for his press credentials would probably have tried to book him. Such episodes are not uncommon. Black men trade tales like this all the time.

Pause In paragraph 11, underline each of the precautions Staples says he takes to appear less threatening.

11   Over the years, I learned to smother the rage I felt at so often being taken for a criminal. Not to do so would surely have led to madness. I now take precautions to make myself less threatening. I move about with care, particularly late in the evening. I give a wide berth to nervous people on subway platforms during the wee hours, particularly when I have exchanged business clothes for jeans. If I happen to be entering a building behind some people who appear skittish,[8] I may walk by, letting them clear the lobby before I return, so as not to seem to be following them. I have been calm and extremely congenial[9] on those rare occasions when I've been pulled over by the police.

8. **skittish:** nervous, jumpy

9. **congenial:** pleasant, agreeable

10. **constitutionals:** walks taken for one's health

12   And on late-evening constitutionals[10] I employ what has proved to be an excellent tension-reducing measure: I whistle melodies from Beethoven and Vivaldi and the more popular classical composers. Even steely New Yorkers

hunching toward nighttime destinations seem to relax, and occasionally they even join in the tune. Virtually everybody seems to sense that a mugger wouldn't be warbling bright, sunny selections from Vivaldi's *Four Seasons*. It is my equivalent of the cowbell that hikers wear when they know they are in bear country.

Pause How do you respond to the image, in paragraph 12, of Staples whistling classical music as he walks at night?

SUMMARIZE AND RESPOND

Summarize the main idea of "Just Walk On By: Black Men and Public Space." Then, go back and check off support for this main idea. Next, write a brief summary (three to five sentences) of the reading. Finally, jot down your initial response to the selection. Did you find any of what Staples relates surprising, or do his observations match your own experience? Did reading about Staples's experiences change your attitudes in any way? What impression do you have of the writer himself?

CHECK YOUR COMPREHENSION

1. Which of the following would be the best alternative title for this essay?
   a. "Walking the Streets after Dark"
   b. "The Burdens of Racial Identity"
   c. "Being Mistaken for a Criminal Because of One's Skin"
   d. "How to Avoid Muggers and Other Street Criminals"

2. The main idea of this essay is that
   a. the author had to learn how to make himself appear less threatening to others.
   b. the author recognizes that strangers may be unjustifiably afraid of him because he is a black man.
   c. the author believes that people should try to see black men as individuals and not stereotype them as muggers.
   d. the author knew criminals as he was growing up but wants readers to understand that he himself is not one.

3. An important point that Staples makes in this essay is that
   a. the police and other authorities often stop black men for questioning for no good reason.
   b. he felt angry because of strangers' behavior toward him but found ways to suppress his anger.
   c. people in large cities like Chicago and New York are more likely than others to fear black men.
   d. he was once almost arrested because he was mistaken for a murderer he was writing a story about.

4. If you are unfamiliar with the following words, use a dictionary to check their meanings: menacingly (para. 1); unwieldy, insomnia, wayfarers, dismayed, indistinguishable, dicey (2); hallucination, perpetrators, solace, alienation, entity (5); lethality, retrospect (6); bravado (7); perilous, posse, labyrinthine (8); affluent, cursory (9); credentials (10); warbling (12).

READ CRITICALLY

1. What, specifically, is the cause-and-effect relationship that Staples is describing in the essay? How well do you think he shows this relationship? What is the effect of the situation on Staples himself?

2. Why do you suppose Staples opens his essay by referring to "my first victim"? What is the effect of this language?

3. Who would you say Staples imagined as his audience for this essay? What vision of himself does he seem to want his readers to come away with?

4. Why do you think Staples refers to the experience of another black man in paragraph 10, when all of his other examples are drawn from his own experience?

5. What is your response to Staples's final two paragraphs? To his final sentence? How would you evaluate this conclusion?

WRITE AN ESSAY

Write an essay, based on your own experiences, about the causes and effects of stereotypes and mistaken perceptions. You might focus on mistaken perceptions others have had of you or on mistaken perceptions you have had of others—or on both kinds of mistaken perceptions. You might also focus on instances of mistaken perceptions and stereotyping that you have witnessed. Be sure to establish clear cause-and-effect relationships.

Caitlin Seida

My Embarrassing Picture Went Viral

Caitlin Seida has been writing professionally since 2006. Her work has appeared on *Livestrong,* the *Daily Puppy,* and *Case to Case,* among other online publications.

This article appeared on *Salon* in October 2013. In it, Seida chronicles her experiences when an unflattering photo of her was spread around the Internet, inspiring her to take action and confront her anonymous adversaries.

Guiding question How carefully do you think about what you post on a social site?

COURTESY © CAITLIN SEIDA

1   I logged onto my Facebook one morning to find a message from a girlfriend. "You're Internet famous!" it read. She sent a link to a very public page whose sole purpose was posting images that mock people's appearances. There I was in full glory—a picture of me dressed as my hero Lara Croft: Tomb Raider for Halloween—but written over the image were the words "Fridge Raider."

2   Funny enough, I wasn't even angry at first. I was actually kind of amused. Who doesn't laugh at unfortunate shots of poorly dressed strangers? I've certainly done it before; the Internet runs on this kind of anonymous scorn. There are entire websites dedicated to the poor fashion choices of random people. And just like me, most of those people are fat.

3   I don't generally view my body size as positive or negative—it simply is. I eat right (most of the time) and I exercise (an inordinate amount), but it does little, thanks to a struggle with polycystic ovarian syndrome and a failing thyroid gland. I'm strong, I'm flexible and my doctor assures me my health is good, but the fact remains: I'm larger than someone my height should be.

4   None of this played into my decision to dress up as Lara Croft, one of the most kick-ass female video game characters ever. Croft is feminine but dangerous, well-educated but athletic, and she's also easily recognizable, which makes a Halloween costume fairly easy. That picture was taken late in the evening—I was red-faced from the heat, my makeup was sweating off and I was lacking proper boob support (a problem the pixelated Croft has never confronted). But I was having fun, and seeing the image again on that website, I still thought it showed.

5   So I laughed it all off at first—but then, I read the comments.

6   "What a waste of space," read one. Another: "Heifers like her should be put down." Yet another said I should just kill myself "and spare everyone's eyes." Hundreds of hateful messages, most of them saying that I was a worthless human being and shaming me for having the audacity to go in public dressed as a sexy video game character. How dare I dress up and have a good time!

Teaching tip While this article is equal parts social media and body acceptance issues, it is a good time to have a discussion about how social media posts will persist online. Many students, especially younger ones, do not consider the future consequences of posting potentially embarrassing content. (For instance, some employers may ask for access to their social media.) It's also beneficial to discuss the fact that nothing is ever fully deleted from the Internet. Students with personal experience in this area may be able to share a new view or perspective to help others understand more clearly.

Pause What do you think the essay will be about? Identify what the "cause" may be and what the "effect" may be, based on the introduction.

Pause Underline the places where Seida explains what caused her situation.

7   We all know the awful humiliation of a person laughing at you. But that feeling increases tenfold when it seems like *everyone* is laughing at you. Scrolling through the comments, the world imploded—and took my heart with it.

8   I called my friend Terri Jean, a photographer. She reminded me that I was beautiful, and told me I would get through this. And then, like any kick-ass heroines, we came up with a plan.

9   The first thing I needed to do was figure out where the picture came from. That wasn't hard—it came from me. I'd posted the image on Facebook, but like so many before me, I'd failed to pay attention to my privacy settings when I uploaded it. Instead of restricting access to my friend network, I'd inadvertently given access to the whole world.

10   But Facebook made it easy to find people who had commented on the images. By now, the picture had metastasized through reposts on Twitter, Tumblr, Reddit, 9Gag, FailBlog. But looking through the Facebook "like" function, I could track down the most offensive commenters.

11   Most of them were women. Shocked? I wasn't. Anyone who's survived high school can tell you how women slice each other up to make ourselves feel better. I sent several of those women a message.

12   "You're being an asshole," the note said. "Why don't you just do the right thing and delete the post and stop sharing it?"

13   The most common response was not remorse or defensiveness but surprise. They were startled that I could hear what they'd been saying. Their Facebook pages were set to private, after all. Most didn't realize that when you post to a public page through your Facebook account, it doesn't matter that your own content is restricted: The whole world can read your words anyway.

14   And of course, they hadn't really thought of me as a person. Why should they? These images are throwaways, little bursts of amusement to get through a long workday. You look, you chuckle, you get some ridicule off your chest and move on to the next source of distraction. No one thought about the possibility that I might read those words. Far less, that I would talk back.

15   Next, I began the monumental task of sending out copyright violation notices to the websites hosting the image—I would have to issue hundreds of them. My work as a paralegal had given me some training in this regard, but it was tedious, like pulling weeds out of the planet's largest garden. I had to seek out each instance of the image and sift around until I could find contact information.

16   I got a fair number of them taken down, but once something like this spreads, it's out there forever. Friends still send me emails asking if I know about this, and I can hear the anxious balancing act in their voices, trying to be a good friend and alert me to this danger while still trying to shield me from the hurtful attacks. I still go through the less tasteful side of the Internet monthly and issue take-down notices for new instances, but it'll never be completely gone, which is part of why I decided to post the image in this story. On my own terms. To own it again, without shame this time.

Pause Think of a time when you have posted something online and received an unexpected response. Why did it happen?

Pause Why did Seida and her friends feel it was necessary to find out who had made comments on her photo?

Pause Why do you think people were surprised to hear from Seida about the comments they had left on her photo?

Pause Seida says that the people she contacted hadn't thought of her as a real person. What does she mean by that?

Pause Seida notes that even though she has issued hundreds of copyright violation notices, the image will never be completely gone. Can you completely delete something from the Internet? Does anyone think about that question before they post something to a social media site?

17 But along the way, in my journey to control something that was ultimately uncontrollable, I encountered something that cut right through the haze of shock and depression: People were actually defending me.

18 Perfect strangers pointed out that there was nothing wrong with a woman of large size dressing up to have a good time. Some commenters even accurately guessed that I had polycystic ovarian syndrome. The disease is characterized by an accumulation of fat in the stomach, making it look, as one insensitive doctor told me, "like you've got a basketball shoved under your shirt." For every three negative and hateful comments, there was at least one positive one.

19 In the months since, my attitude toward these throwaway images of mockery on the Internet has changed. I no longer find them funny. Each one of those people is a real human being, a real person whose world imploded the day they found themselves to be a punch line on a giant stage. I speak up whenever a friend gets a cheap laugh from one of these sites. I ask one simple question: "Why do you think this is funny?" Very few have a good answer. Mostly they just say, "I don't know." Reminding people of our shared humanity hasn't exactly made me popular, but it feels like the right thing to do. I know what it's like to be the person in that horrible photograph. I can't inflict such pain on someone else.

20 I've also learned to keep a tighter rein on my privacy settings online. I don't always succeed at keeping my content private, but I'm certainly more guarded now.

21 And while my self-confidence took a large blow from the experience, I'm getting over it. My photographer friend Terri did a photo shoot with me after it all went down. She's a retro pinup photographer, and I've been posing for her for a while now, but that particular shoot felt great. Just to be seen a little bit more as I wanted to be.

22 But I refuse to disappear. I still go jogging in public. I don't hide my flabby arms or chubby ankles for fear of offending someone else's delicate sensibilities. I dress in a way that makes me happy with myself. And this Halloween, I'm thinking of reprising my role as Lara Croft just to give all the haters the middle finger.

23 And no, I won't be putting the pictures online this time.

Pause Seida uses terms here like "throwaway images" and "punch line on a giant stage." What is she talking about when she uses these phrases? Do most people stop to think about where viral pictures come from or who is in them?

Pause Put brackets around the places where Seida identifies the effects of her post.

SUMMARIZE AND RESPOND

Summarize the main idea of "My Embarrassing Picture Went Viral." Then, go back and check off support for this main idea. Next, write a brief summary (three to five sentences) of the reading. Finally, jot down your initial response to the selection. Did you find any of what Seida relates surprising, or have you had similar experiences online? Did reading about Seida's experiences change your attitudes in any way? How do you feel about sharing photos online?

CHECK YOUR COMPREHENSION

1. Which of the following would be the best alternative title for this essay?
   a. "My Photo as Lara Croft"
   b. "Learn to Accept Your Body"
   c. "Nothing Is Safe on the Internet"
   d. "I'm a Real Person" *(circled)*

2. The main idea of this essay is that
   a. the nameless people in pictures online are real people. *(circled)*
   b. make sure you copyright all of the images and material you post online.
   c. don't let your friends post anything online unless you approve it.
   d. don't let people get away with bad behavior.

3. An important point that Seida makes in this essay is that
   a. no one looks good late at night after a party, so we shouldn't judge.
   b. make sure you know the whole story before you make comments about someone.
   c. the Internet has made it very easy for us to remain hidden while we laugh at people we don't know. *(circled)*
   d. it's not OK to post pictures of someone without their knowledge or to share them with others.

4. If you are unfamiliar with the following words, use a dictionary to check their meanings: inordinate (para. 3); pixelated (4); heifers (6); tenfold, imploded (7); inadvertently (9); metastasized (10).

READ CRITICALLY

1. What, specifically, is the cause-and-effect relationship that Seida is describing in the essay? What steps did Seida take to attempt to fix what happened after her photo went viral?

2. Midway through the essay, Seida says, "Instead of restricting access to my friend network, I'd inadvertently given access to the whole world" (para. 9). How did this affect her experience with social media? Why might she have made this mistake?

3. Who would you say Seida imagined as the audience for this essay? What vision of herself does she seem to want her readers to come away with?

4. Seida could have just ignored the entire situation. Instead, she chose not only to track down and chastise the people who commented negatively on her picture but also to send copyright violations to Web sites that allowed it to be posted. Why do you think she made these choices? What did she gain by going through the trouble?

5. What is your response to Seida's final two paragraphs? To her final sentence? How would you evaluate this conclusion?

WRITE AN ESSAY

Write an essay, based on your own experiences, about the causes and effects of stereotypes and mistaken perceptions. You might focus on mistaken perceptions others have had of you or on mistaken perceptions you have had of others—or on both kinds of mistaken perceptions. You might also focus on instances of mistaken perceptions and stereotyping that you have witnessed. Be sure to establish clear cause-and-effect relationships.

Cause and Effect: Linked Readings

Conceptions of Gender

Each of the following readings focuses on various aspects of the effects of gender on people's behaviors and lives.

Dave Barry, "The Ugly Truth about Beauty" (Chapter 46, p. 658)

Caitlin Seida, "My Embarrassing Picture Went Viral" (Chapter 47, p. 674)

Read the selections, and draw from at least one in addition to "Struggling for Perfection" to write an essay titled "How Gender Affects Behavior." You can refer to your own experience, but make sure to use material from the essays as well.

Stereotypes

Each of the following readings focuses on or uses stereotypes.

Amy Tan, "Mother Tongue" (Chapter 44, p. 633)

Nancy Mairs, "On Being a Cripple" (Chapter 45, p. 645)

Dave Barry, "The Ugly Truth about Beauty" (Chapter 46, p. 658)

Read the selections, and draw from at least one in addition to "Just Walk On By: Black Men and Public Space" to write an essay titled "Stereotypes: Are They Wrong?" You can refer to your own experience, but make sure to use material from the essays as well.

48

Argument Casebook

Social Media

Four Basics of Good Argument

1 It takes a strong, definite position on an issue or advises a particular action.

2 It gives good supporting evidence to defend the position or recommended action.

3 It considers opposing views.

4 It avoids faulty reasoning.

This chapter includes four essays on the topic of social media. The first of these essays, written by Sherry Turkle, a Massachusetts Institute of Technology (MIT) professor who has done extensive research on both media and technology, focuses on the concept of reality in a world in which technology can create things that seem realistic. Turkle asks several questions: What is real? Is the definition of reality changing as technology becomes more advanced? Why does reality matter? These questions are central to any discussion of social media because, as the other articles argue, the concepts of friendship, loneliness, and society are all starting to form in alternate realities. Next is Wency Leung's essay "Does Social Media Bring Us Closer—or Make Us Loners?" Leung notes that social media are only as useful as the person using them allows them to be.

As you will see when you read these essays, the question of whether or not social media actually allow us to connect and become less lonely is a complex one. The essays provide both positive and negative views about social media and are written by reporters, journalists, and commentators—all of whom are familiar with different types of media and communication: print, video, audio, and social. They try to view the use of social media as a new way of sharing information and of connecting communities. Not only do social media make our communication with others more complex, but, as Kate Harding points out in her essay, "Social Networking Is Not Killing Friendship," the definition of the word *friend* is constantly shifting as technology makes it easier to share information and give more access to our personal lives. A friend is no longer just a person we see and interact with on a regular basis. Finally, everyone who uses social media creates one or more online identities, which may or may not be "real," as Stephen Marche discusses in his essay, "Is Facebook Making Us Lonely?"

While you may already have one or more opinions on the topic of social media, read the essays and carefully consider the opinions of their authors. Examine their points of view, and think about technology and social media from other perspectives. You may have grown up with social media all around you. How might you feel if all of this technology were new to you? If you did not grow up with social media, how might you perceive or think about these issues if you had?

Social Media

Sherry Turkle

Introduction from *Alone Together*

Sherry Turkle received a joint doctorate in sociology and personality psychology from Harvard University and is a licensed clinical psychologist; currently, she is the director of the MIT Initiative on Technology and Self. She is an expert on mobile technology, social networking, and sociable robotics. Her work has been featured in the *New York Times, Wired,* and *Scientific American,* and she has appeared as a media commentator on social and psychological effects of technology for CBS, NBC, ABC, CNN, the BBC, and NPR, among other media outlets. Her most recent book, *Alone Together: Why We Expect More from Technology and Less from Each Other*, was published in January 2011.

Guiding question   What does it mean to be "real"?

1   Technology proposes itself as the architect of our intimacies. These days, it suggests substitutions that put the real on the run. The advertising for Second Life, a virtual world where you get to build an avatar, a house, a family, and a social life, basically says, "Finally, a place to love your body, love your friends, and love your life." On Second Life, a lot of people, as represented by their avatars, are richer than they are in first life and a lot younger, thinner, and better dressed. And we are smitten with the idea of sociable robots, which most people first meet in the guise of artificial pets. Zhu Zhu pet hamsters, the "it" toy of the 2009–2010 holiday season, are presented as "better" than any real pet could be. We are told they are lovable and responsive, don't require cleanup, and will never die.

2   Technology is seductive when what it offers meets our human vulnerabilities. And as it turns out, we are very vulnerable indeed. We are lonely but fearful of intimacy. Digital connections and the sociable robot may offer the illusion of companionship without the demands of friendship. Our networked life allows us to hide from each other, even as we are tethered to each other. We'd rather text than talk. A simple story makes this last point, told in her own words by a harried mother in her late forties:

Pause Underline the sentence that you think is the main idea of the previous paragraph.

I needed to find a new nanny. When I interview nannies, I like to go to where they live, so that I can see them in their environment, not just in mine. So, I made an appointment to interview Ronnie, who had applied for the job. I show up at her apartment and her housemate answers the door. She is a young woman, around twenty-one, texting on her BlackBerry. Her thumbs are bandaged. I look at them, pained at the tiny thumb splints, and I try to be sympathetic. "That must hurt." But she just shrugs. She explains that she is still able to text. I tell her I am here to speak with Ronnie; this is her job interview. Could she please knock on Ronnie's bedroom door? The girl with the bandaged thumbs looks surprised. "Oh no," she says, "I would never do that. That would be intrusive. I'll text her." And so she sent a text message to Ronnie, no more than fifteen feet away.

3   This book [*Alone Together*], which completes a trilogy on computers and people, asks how we got to this place and whether we are content to be here.

4   In *The Second Self,* I traced the subjective side of personal computers—not what computers do for us but what they do to us, to our ways of thinking about ourselves, our relationships, our sense of being human. From the start, people used interactive and reactive computers to reflect on the self and think about the difference between machines and people. Were intelligent machines alive? If not, why not? In my studies I found that children were most likely to see this new category of object, the computational object, as "sort of" alive—a story that has continued to evolve. In *Life on the Screen,* my focus shifted from how people see computers to how they forge new identities in online spaces. In *Alone Together,* I show how technology has taken both of these stories to a new level.

Pause Predict what this new term may mean. What does it mean to be "alone together"?

5   Computers no longer wait for humans to project meaning onto them. Now, sociable robots meet our gaze, speak to us, and learn to recognize us. They ask us to take care of them; in response, we imagine that they might care for us in return. Indeed, among the most talked about robotic designs are in the area of care and companionship. In summer 2010, there are enthusiastic reports in the *New York Times* and the *Wall Street Journal* on robotic teachers, companions, and therapists. And Microsoft demonstrates a virtual human, Milo, that recognizes the people it interacts with and whose personality is sculpted by them. Tellingly, in the video that introduces Milo to the public, a young man begins by playing games with Milo in a virtual garden; by the end of the demonstration, things have heated up—he confides in Milo after being told off by his parents.

6   We are challenged to ask what such things augur. Some people are looking for robots to clean rugs and help with the laundry. Others hope for a mechanical bride. As sociable robots propose themselves as substitutes for people, new networked devices offer us machine-mediated relationships with each other, another kind of substitution. We romance the robot and become inseparable from our smartphones. As this happens, we remake ourselves and our relationships with each other through our new intimacy with machines. People talk about Web access on their BlackBerries as "the place for hope" in life, the place

where loneliness can be defeated. A woman in her late sixties describes her new iPhone: "It's like having a little Times Square in my pocketbook. All lights. All the people I could meet." People are lonely. The network is seductive. But if we are always on, we may deny ourselves the rewards of solitude.

The Robotic Moment

7   In late November 2005, I took my daughter Rebecca, then fourteen, to the Darwin exhibition at the American Museum of Natural History in New York. From the moment you step into the museum and come face-to-face with a full-size dinosaur, you become part of a celebration of life on Earth, what Darwin called "endless forms most beautiful." Millions upon millions of now lifeless specimens represent nature's invention in every corner of the globe. There could be no better venue for documenting Darwin's life and thought and his theory of evolution by natural selection, the central truth that underpins contemporary biology. The exhibition aimed to please and, a bit defensively in these days of attacks on the theory of evolution, wanted to convince.

8   At the exhibit's entrance were two giant tortoises from the Galápagos Islands, the best-known inhabitants of the archipelago where Darwin did his most famous investigations. The museum had been advertising these tortoises as wonders, curiosities, and marvels. Here, among the plastic models at the museum, was the life that Darwin saw more than a century and a half ago. One tortoise was hidden from view; the other rested in its cage, utterly still. Rebecca inspected the visible tortoise thoughtfully for a while and then said matter-of-factly, "They could have used a robot." I was taken aback and asked what she meant. She said she thought it was a shame to bring the turtle all this way from its island home in the Pacific, when it was just going to sit there in the museum, motionless, doing nothing. Rebecca was both concerned for the imprisoned turtle and unmoved by its authenticity.

9   It was Thanksgiving weekend. The line was long, the crowd frozen in place. I began to talk with some of the other parents and children. My question—"Do you care that the turtle is alive?"—was a welcome diversion from the boredom of the wait. A ten-year-old girl told me that she would prefer a robot turtle because aliveness comes with aesthetic inconvenience: "Its water looks dirty. Gross." More usually, votes for the robots echoed my daughter's sentiment that in this setting, aliveness didn't seem worth the trouble. A twelve-year-old girl was adamant: "For what the turtles do, you didn't have to have the live ones." Her father looked at her, mystified: "But the point is that they are real. That's the whole point."

10   The Darwin exhibition put authenticity front and center: on display were the actual magnifying glass that Darwin used in his travels, the very notebook in which he wrote the famous sentences that first described his theory of evolution. Yet, in the children's reactions to the inert but alive Galápagos tortoise, the idea of the original had no place. What I heard in the museum reminded me of Rebecca's reaction as a seven-year-old during a boat ride in the postcard-blue Mediterranean. Already an expert in the world of simulated fish tanks, she saw something in the water, pointed to it excitedly, and said, "Look, Mommy, a jellyfish! It looks

Pause Turkle makes several points in the previous paragraph that support her argument that we are "alone together." Underline those points.

Pause What do you think of Rebecca's position? Is it a good argument?

Pause Why do you think the parents and the children felt differently about this topic?

so realistic!" When I told this story to a vice president at the Disney Corporation, he said he was not surprised. When Animal Kingdom opened in Orlando, populated by "real"—that is, biological—animals, its first visitors complained that they were not as "realistic" as the animatronic creatures in other parts of Disneyworld. The robotic crocodiles slapped their tails and rolled their eyes—in sum, they displayed archetypal "crocodile" behavior. The biological crocodiles, like the Galápagos tortoises, pretty much kept to themselves.

11   I believe that in our culture of simulation, the notion of authenticity is for us what sex was for the Victorians—threat and obsession, taboo and fascination. I have lived with this idea for many years; yet, at the museum, I found the children's position strangely unsettling. For them, in this context, aliveness seemed to have no intrinsic value. Rather, it is useful only if needed for a specific purpose. Darwin's endless forms so beautiful were no longer sufficient unto themselves. I asked the children a further question: "If you put a robot instead of a living turtle in the exhibit, do you think people should be told that the turtle is not alive?" Not really, said many children. Data on aliveness can be shared on a "need-to-know basis"—for a purpose. But what are the purposes of living things?

SUMMARIZE AND RESPOND

Summarize the main idea of the introduction from *Alone Together*. Then, go back and check off support for this main idea. Next, write a brief summary (three to five sentences) of the selection. Finally, jot down your initial response to the reading. Do you think that Turkle's assertion that computers are taking away authenticity is true? What makes you think as you do?

CHECK YOUR COMPREHENSION

1. Which of the following would be the best alternative title for this essay?
   a. "Building Better Robots"
   b. "Understanding How to Interact with Computers"
   c. "Technology Takes Over"
   d. "Does It Need to Be Real?"

2. The main idea of this essay is that
   a. nothing will ever take the place of a human.
   b. it's important to remain in control of technology at all times.
   c. reality is a matter of opinion.
   d. technology has become too powerful.

3. According to Turkle, she was disturbed by her daughter's reaction to the tortoise because

   a.   the purpose was to visit the museum and see the live animal.

   (b.)   her daughter wasn't experiencing the exhibit in the same way that Turkle was.

   c.   she really wanted the tortoise to move around more.

   d.   she was upset that her daughter didn't understand the exhibit.

4. If you are unfamiliar with the following words, use a dictionary to check their meanings: tethered, harried (para. 2); mediated (6); venue, underpins (7); aesthetic, sentiment, adamant (9).

READ CRITICALLY

1. Evaluate the first seven paragraphs of Turkle's essay. What do they contribute to the rest? How do they set up the situation in the museum?

2. How well do you think the harried mother's account of her potential nanny's roommate demonstrates Turkle's argument that we are "alone together"?

3. What is the main argument that Turkle is trying to make? In which paragraph do you see that argument fully articulated?

4. Why does Turkle tell the reader about the experience with her daughter in the museum? What argument is she trying to make about technology and reality? What evidence does she use to support her point?

5. What is your overall evaluation of Turkle's argument? How effectively do you think she presents her case? How do you explain your evaluation?

WRITE AN ESSAY

Write an essay about a belief that you have come to hold through personal experience but that many other people might disagree with or find controversial. Like Turkle, show readers what happened to make you think as you do, and take a clear stand on the issue.

Wency Leung

Does Social Media Bring Us Closer— or Make Us Loners?

Wency Leung is a reporter on staff at the *Toronto Globe and Mail*. Her article asks readers to consider their relationship with social media and technology: Do they really bring us closer together with our friends and relations, or do they put up more barriers and create a more isolating experience for everyone involved?

Guiding question Are the people you talk to online your true friends?

Teaching tip Before reading the essay, ask students how many of them are active on social media sites, and discuss what types of sites they use and their level of activity. It can be surprising how quickly new social media sites are appearing and evolving. Ask students how much time on a social media site may be too much. In addition, ask students to define *social media*. Some will only identify sites like Facebook, Snapchat, Twitter, or Instagram, while others consider any technology that allows multiple people to interact—such as online video games or role-playing games.

1   It started as a marketing gimmick. In 2000, Mitch Maddox, also known as DotComGuy, holed himself up in a Dallas townhouse for a year, relying on visitors and his Internet connection to interact with the outside world. At the time, it was a novelty to be plugged in 24 hours a day, visiting chat rooms, making purchases online and having every moment captured on streaming video for the rest of the world to see.

2   For Maddox, being continuously wired was a stunt, devised to promote electronic *commerce*. Now, it is a way of life. Although we may not physically shut ourselves in as DotComGuy did, we often live in our own bubbles, simultaneously reaching out and closing ourselves off to others through the use of technology. At business meetings, we pay partial attention while responding to e-mails. When we are with our friends, we will stop to send text messages and Twitter updates. While we are connected, we are rarely fully engaged with those immediately around us.

Pause Underline the argument or main idea of the article.

3   "It's almost like I experienced what a lot of people maybe are experiencing now, only I experienced it 12 years ago," Maddox says in a phone interview from his home in Dallas, explaining that his year of wired living forced him to be constantly "on" for all his Internet followers.

4   Our obsession with smart devices and social media seems alarming. As U.S. psychologist Sherry Turkle, author of *Alone Together: Why We Expect More from Technology and Less from Each Other,* wrote in the *New York Times* last year, "we have sacrificed conversation for mere connection." With 2011 census data showing more Canadians living alone than in couple households with children for the first time, it would be easy to assume that people are becoming more alienated than ever. But technology's impact on our social lives may not be as detrimental, or as powerful, as we might think.

Pause Underline the counterargument in this paragraph.

5   In a 2011 study, Cornell University researcher Matthew Brashears examined national U.S. survey results that indicated a considerable decline in the number of people Americans consider close friends. Data from the General Social Survey, which offers a glimpse into the social environments of the average American, showed that respondents in 2004 had confided in roughly two friends on matters they considered important to them during the previous six months. This, Brashears noted, was down from an average of three friends in 1985.

6   More strikingly, the proportion of Americans who were socially isolated—those who discussed important matters with no one—had surged to 23 per cent from 8 per cent over the same period.

7   Brashears points out, however, that the social survey results should be taken with a grain of salt. First, the proportion of people who report having no discussions of important matters fluctuates wildly from year to year, and a sizable fraction of them may simply feel they have no important matters to discuss.

8   Another interpretation, he says, is that people's social networks are not necessarily shrinking; rather, they may be changing how they define their friends. "What I suspect is happening is that we're seeing a reallocation of all your associates into different categories," he said in an interview. "So fewer people are being considered as discussion partners, but maybe more of them are people you would spend time with."

9   In fact, recent research suggests that social media and modern communications technologies have either no effect, or a slightly positive effect, on people's face-to-face relationships and social circles, Brashears says. "So if you use Facebook and you use all this stuff, you may have slightly more friends than you might have otherwise."

10   Technology's bad rap can be partly attributed to how quickly it has become a fixture in our lives, Brashears suggests. Consider that Facebook came into general use only in 2006, the same year Twitter's early prototype was created. And although early research indicated that people who were highly plugged into the Internet had smaller social circles, those studies were conducted in the 1990s when the Internet was the domain of a relatively small group of early adopters.

11   But plugging in does not appear to help us make friends either. In a study released last year, University of Waterloo postdoctoral researcher Amanda Forest found that individuals who have low self-esteem were more likely to consider Facebook a safe place to express themselves and engage with others, without the awkwardness of face-to-face interaction. Yet they also were more likely to be downers online, posting updates that exhibited sadness, anger, fear and anxiety instead of more positive emotions. Forest found that coders who were asked to assess their Facebook messages found people with low self-esteem less likeable than those with high self-esteem on the basis of their status updates.

12   "The same people who are more negative in person seem to be the ones who are more negative on Facebook," Forest says, suggesting that the way we act online is more or less an extension of how we act in person. Even though we try to portray ourselves a certain way on social-media sites, we do this to some extent in real life as well, she says.

13   Back in Dallas, Maddox says his early immersion in electronic communications has caused him to moderate his use of mobile devices and social media. After leaving the office each evening, the software company employee and self-proclaimed technology junkie avoids checking e-mail on his iPhone. And even though he appreciates social-media sites, he does not check them every day. He says he logs onto Facebook only once every four months.

14   "I think it's great," he says, "but I had my year of that and it was just so much that I just kind of set those boundaries for myself."

Pause Leung uses statistical data to make a point here. Take a moment to figure out what all of these numbers mean. Circle each of the statistics that she uses, and then paraphrase (restate in your own words) what those statistics mean.

Pause Put brackets around Leung's points that support her main argument.

Pause The study found that people who acted in a certain way in real life acted similarly online. Why might this be?

SUMMARIZE AND RESPOND

Summarize the main idea of "Does Social Media Bring Us Closer—or Make Us Loners?" Then, go back and check off support for this main idea. Next, write a brief summary (three to five sentences) of the essay. Finally, jot down your initial response to the reading. Do you find that social media improves your social life, or makes you feel more isolated?

CHECK YOUR COMPREHENSION

1. Which of the following would be the best alternative title for this essay?
   a. "Making Friends Online Is Hard"
   b. "It's Easier to Make Friends Online"
   c. "It's Easier to Be Yourself Online"
   d. "Social Media Mimics Real Life"

2. The main idea of this essay is that
   a. people who had a negative attitude and small circle of friends in person seemed to have the same experience online.
   b. people created more successful versions of themselves online than in person.
   c. people were more popular online and were spending too much time online than in person when social media was developed.
   d. it was too easy for people to become socially isolated once social media became a popular option for them, so they decided to stop interacting with others in person.

3. Leung makes the point in the essay that
   a. as technology becomes more sophisticated, most people are becoming completely absorbed in social media and not interacting at all with life around them.
   b. as technology becomes more sophisticated, we are connected, but we are not fully engaged with life around us.
   c. as technology becomes more sophisticated, people are less absorbed in social media and pay attention to life around them more.
   d. as technology becomes more sophisticated, people are becoming better able to make intelligent choices about when to pay attention to technology and when to tune in to real life.

4. If you are unfamiliar with the following words, use a dictionary to check their meanings: commerce (para. 2); census, alienated, detrimental (4); fluctuates (7); reallocation (8); prototype (10).

READ CRITICALLY

1. What is the point of the example that Leung writes about in paragraph 1? Why do you suppose that she decided to begin the essay with it?

2. What is the purpose of the statistics in paragraphs 4, 5, and 6? Does the information that Leung offers here surprise you in any way? What does it all mean?

3. In paragraphs 7 and 8, Leung attempts to offer two different interpretations of her earlier data. How well are they supported? Explain your answer.

4. What is the purpose of paragraphs 11 and 12? What point is Leung trying to make here? Is it effective? Explain your answer.

5. How would you define Leung's intended audience? What evidence leads you to make that decision?

WRITE AN ESSAY

Write an essay in which you argue your views regarding this subject: Are people more or less isolated due to social media? Before you begin your essay, you should carefully define the terms *isolated* and *social media,* and you should make sure the reader understands which specific types of social media you are referring to. Use specific examples and evidence to support your position on this issue.

Kate Harding

Social Networking Is Not Killing Friendship

Kate Harding is the author of *Asking for It: The Alarming Rise of Rape Culture, and What We Can Do about It* (2014), coauthor of *Lessons from the Fatosphere: Quit Dieting and Declare a Truce with Your Body* (2009), and a contributor to *The Book of Jezebel* (2013). Her work has appeared in many media outlets and print anthologies.

"Social Networking Is Not Killing Friendship" first appeared on *Salon* in December 2009. Harding defends the benefits of social networking, arguing that it is not responsible for the death of the traditional concept of friendship.

Guiding question How does Harding define *friendship* in her article?

1   William Deresiewicz has written a long, lovely essay on friendship for *The Chronicle Review,* ranging from "Achilles and Patroclus, David and Jonathan,

Virgil's Nisus and Euryalus" all the way through present-day palhood. It's a fascinating read. Unfortunately, its conclusion—that social networking means the death of genuine friendship—is pretty specious for a piece that's otherwise so well-considered. "The Facebook phenomenon, so sudden and forceful a distortion of social space, needs little elaboration," writes Deresiewicz. "Having been relegated to our screens, are our friendships now anything more than a form of distraction? When they've shrunk to the size of a wall post, do they retain any content? If we have 768 'friends,' in what sense do we have any?" Whoa, whoa, whoa! Back up, my figurative friend. If you're going to automatically equate Facebook "friendship" and genuine companionship, then actually, the Facebook phenomenon *does* need some more elaboration.

2   At this writing, I have 658 Facebook friends. Without doing a proper audit of that list, I'd estimate that maybe 100 of them are people I've actually met, around 30 are people I would still call "friends" in any other context, and perhaps a dozen are good friends—people I talk to on the phone, over e-mail and (geography permitting) in person, on a regular basis. Then there's my husband, all three of my siblings, a niece and two nephews—people I wouldn't introduce as my "friends" in real life any more than the old classmate who unfriended me for being adamantly pro-choice. But somehow, this circumstance in which I have 658 "friends" while having only 30ish actual friends causes me no cognitive dissonance, much less despair for the future of human interaction.

3   I can handle an argument that social networking is sapping the word "friend" of its meaning. But then, as Deresiewicz himself acknowledges, that word has changed meaning many times throughout history. "Far from being ordinary and universal, friendship, for the ancients, was rare, precious, and hard-won." Then along came Christianity, which "discouraged intense personal bonds, for the heart should be turned to God. . . . In medieval society, friendship entailed specific expectations and obligations, often formalized in oaths." The Renaissance brought back friendship based in "truth and virtue, again, above all," which basically lasted through the 19th century, and changes in commercial relationships cemented it: "Capitalism, said Hume and Smith, by making economic relations impersonal, allowed for private relationships based on nothing other than affection and affinity." Later, "as industrialization uprooted people from extended families and traditional communities and packed them into urban centers, friendship emerged to salve the anonymity and rootlessness of modern life." So, eventually, did the trend toward delaying marriage and away from close-knit, multigenerational family units: "We have yet to find a satisfactory name for that period of life, now typically a decade but often a great deal longer, between the end of adolescence and the making of definitive life choices. But the one thing we know is that friendship is absolutely central to it." And that brings us pretty much up to the present day—so, why is friendship at risk again?

4   Because we no longer expect friends to be our soulmates, apparently.

5   That glib neologism "bff," which plays at a lifelong avowal, bespeaks an ironic awareness of the mobility of our connections: Best friends forever may not be on speaking terms by this time next month. We save our fiercest energies for sex.

Pause What do you predict the main argument of the article will be?

Pause Number all the different definitions of *friend* in this paragraph. Which is the one that seems most appropriate to you? Why?

Indeed, between the rise of Freudianism and the contemporaneous emergence of homosexuality to social visibility, we've taught ourselves to shun expressions of intense affection between "friends," male friends in particular, though even Oprah was forced to defend her relationship with her closest friend, and have rewritten historical friendships, like Achilles' with Patroclus, as sexual. For all the talk of "bromance" lately (or "man dates"), the term is yet another device to manage the sexual anxiety kicked up by straight-male friendships whether in the friends themselves or in the people around them and the typical bromance plot instructs the callow bonds of youth to give way to mature heterosexual relationships. At best, intense friendships are something we're expected to grow out of.

6   Instead, we have groups of friends we're not all that close to individually, which means that having hundreds of Facebook friends you've never even met is only the logical next step in the slow death of Platonic companionship.

7   For all Deresiewicz's writing talent and experience, he's getting a lot of words mixed up here. First, he confuses "Facebook friend" and "friend." Newsflash: People only end up with hundreds or thousands of "friends" on social networking sites because *nobody really thinks they mean the same thing.* The folks who are on my list because they read my writing on *Salon* are never going to call me to give them a ride home from the bar, or visit them at the hospital, or invite me over for a holiday dinner—if for no other reason than they don't have my phone number, seeing as how we are not actually friends, and no one is the least bit confused about this.

8   But more troublingly, I think Deresiewicz is using the word "we"—meaning all internet-savvy westerners—when the words he's really looking for are "some men." He's absolutely right about the shallowness of "bromance" as it's typically presented in pop culture, the way emotional reservation is held up as a masculine virtue, and the sexual anxiety that means a guy can't express affection toward a pal unless he follows it up with "no homo." But those things don't damage the whole concept of friendship as we know it—they damage *some men's* ability to form close, non-sexual relationships. And I would hardly be the first feminist to say that sucks. In fact, much has been written about how rigid gender roles force boys and men to squelch their feelings and keep their emotional distance from anyone they don't plan on marrying (and even then, they're expected to publicly roll their eyes at any expectation of intimacy that doesn't lead directly to a blow job). Meanwhile, much has also been written about the strength and value of female friendship bonds, especially as family ties became less binding over time.

9   In a recent essay on motherhood—which explores, among other things, the changing nature of modern family and friendships for women of the "creative class"—Sandra Tsing Loh describes her sister as "a fearsomely strong figure, who, if I were left for dead in a pile of leaves at the bottom of a 15-foot hole, would be the first to run to the edge and fashion a rope of her own hair to haul me out," and then suggests, "As a philosophical midlife exercise, you should make your own list of rescuers—that list may surprise or depress you." For me,

Pause What new terms did Harding define in this paragraph? Would you consider any of these to be the best definition of *friendship*? Why or why not?

it did neither. After my husband, I thought of half a dozen female friends who would get on the first plane to wherever that hole was and MacGyver up whatever device was needed to get me out of it. And I'd do the same for them, of course.

10   As it happens, we're all Facebook "friends," but that has exactly nothing to do with it. Years of love, loyalty, hard conversations, emotional vulnerability and just showing up are what make us, if not each other's classical soulmates, then at least each other's hypothetical rescuers. Social networking doesn't prevent anyone from maintaining that type of meaningful real-world relationship alongside hundreds of superficial connections—but the myth that real men don't have feelings or need emotional support like some kind of *girls* sure can prevent them from developing anything deeper than a fleeting bromance.

11   I'd say more about that, but now I have to go get on a plane to visit my BFF. I guess it's possible that in this crazy modern world, I'll have a new one of those in a month, but since this one's been around for about 20 years, I don't hesitate to use the term unironically. I do wish everyone could have that kind of friendship—but I really don't think it's Facebook that's stopping them.

Pause What argument is Harding making in the paragraph here? What makes a bromance different from any other kind of friendship?

SUMMARIZE AND RESPOND

Summarize the main idea of "Social Networking Is Not Killing Friendship." Then, go back and check off support for this main idea. Next, write a brief summary (three to five sentences) of the essay. Finally, jot down your initial response to the essay. What impression of Harding does the essay create for you? How do you react to her basic argument?

CHECK YOUR COMPREHENSION

1. Which of the following is the best alternative title for this essay?
   a. "Define 'Friend' for Me"
   b. "It's OK to Have a Lot of Friends"
   c. "You Can't Trust Everyone"
   d. "Your Definition of *Friend* Might Be Different from Mine"

2. The main idea of this essay is that
   a. you can't consider everyone you friend on Facebook to be a true friend.
   b. you have to be careful about getting close to people and trusting them.
   c. unfortunately, some men can't have close relationships with others without being labeled in a negative way.
   d. friendship is earned through time.

3. Harding doesn't like the way Deresiewicz talks about Facebook friends because

    a.　she thinks that any friend can be a true friend.

    b.　she believes that he can't understand friendship due to the way society treats friendship between two men.

    (c.)　she believes he oversimplifies his argument.

    d.　she has hundreds of friends and she likes them all, even if she hasn't met them.

4. If you are unfamiliar with the following words, use a dictionary to check their meanings: specious, relegated, figurative (para. 1); audit, cognitive dissonance (2); affinity (3); glib, neologism, bespeaks, ironic, contemporaneous, shun, callow (5); Platonic (6).

READ CRITICALLY

1. What is Harding's purpose of questioning Deresiewicz in paragraph 1? What does she disagree with? What argument does she set up with this quote?

2. Harding goes on, in paragraph 2, to tell us how many Facebook friends she has. Why do you think she does this? What is she trying to illustrate by doing this? Is she successful? Why or why not?

3. In paragraphs 5 and 8, Harding brings up different types of friendship. What is the purpose of defining these different kinds of friendship? Why does she want the audience to be aware of different kinds of friendship? Why is she so careful to clearly define each type?

4. In paragraph 8, Harding talks specifically about the trouble with the idea of bromance. What is a bromance, and why does she think that such a notion makes Deresiewicz criticize all Facebook friends?

5. Evaluate Harding's concluding paragraph. Who do you think is the intended audience? Do you think that it will have its intended effect on the audience? Why or why not?

WRITE AN ESSAY

Write an essay that argues for or against something that has changed because of technology. For instance, we can now speak through cell phones anywhere, instead of through landline phones restricted to specific locations. We can now take online courses at colleges far from home. We can see photos and videos instantly. We can even date online. Write an argument that claims some aspect of our lives is either better or worse thanks to technology. Make sure to clearly define what technology you are talking about, who and what it affects, and how it is used.

Stephen Marche

Is Facebook Making Us Lonely?

Canadian writer Stephen Marche is the author of the short-story collection *Shining at the Bottom of the Sea* (2007) and the novel *Raymond and Hannah* (2005). In 2011, his monthly column for *Esquire* magazine, "A Thousand Words about Our Culture," was a finalist for the American Society of Magazine Editors' National Magazine Award for Commentary. In addition, Marche writes opinion pieces for the *New York Times,* the *Wall Street Journal, Salon,* and Toronto's *Globe and Mail,* among others. His essay "Is Facebook Making us Lonely?" was published in the *Atlantic* in May 2012.

Guiding question What kinds of evidence and outside authorities does Marche cite to support his argument?

1   Yvette Vickers, a former *Playboy* playmate and B-movie star, best known for her role in *Attack of the 50 Foot Woman,* would have been 83 last August, but nobody knows exactly how old she was when she died. According to the Los Angeles coroner's report, she lay dead for the better part of a year before a neighbor and fellow actress, a woman named Susan Savage, noticed cobwebs and yellowing letters in her mailbox, reached through a broken window to unlock the door, and pushed her way through the piles of junk mail and mounds of clothing that barricaded the house. Upstairs, she found Vickers's body, mummified, near a heater that was still running. Her computer was on too, its glow permeating the empty space.

2   The *Los Angeles Times* posted a story headlined "Mummified Body of Former Playboy Playmate Yvette Vickers Found in Her Benedict Canyon Home," which quickly went viral. Within two weeks, by Technorati's count, Vickers's lonesome death was already the subject of 16,057 Facebook posts and 881 tweets. She had long been a horror-movie icon, a symbol of Hollywood's capacity to exploit our most basic fears in the silliest ways; now she was an icon of a new and different kind of horror: our growing fear of loneliness. Certainly she received much more attention in death than she did in the final years of her life. With no children, no religious group, and no immediate social circle of any kind, she had begun, as an elderly woman, to look elsewhere for companionship. Savage later told *Los Angeles* magazine that she had searched Vickers's phone bills for clues about the life that led to such an end. In the months before her grotesque death, Vickers had made calls not to friends or family but to distant fans who had found her through fan conventions and Internet sites.

3   Vickers's web of connections had grown broader but shallower, as has happened for many of us. We are living in an isolation that would have been unimaginable to our ancestors, and yet we have never been more accessible. Over the past three decades, technology has delivered to us a world in which we need not be out of contact for a fraction of a moment. In 2010, at a cost of $300 million, 800 miles of fiber-optic cable was laid between the Chicago Mercantile Exchange and the New York Stock Exchange to shave three milliseconds off trading times. Yet within this world of instant and absolute communication, unbounded by limits of time or space, we suffer from unprecedented alienation. We have never been more detached from one another, or lonelier. In a world consumed by ever more novel modes of socializing, we have less and less actual society. We live in an accelerating contradiction: the more connected we become, the lonelier we are. We were promised a global village; instead we inhabit the drab cul-de-sacs and endless freeways of a vast suburb of information.

4   At the forefront of all this unexpectedly lonely interactivity is Facebook, with 845 million users and $3.7 billion in revenue last year. The company hopes to raise $5 billion in an initial public offering later this spring, which will make it by far the largest Internet IPO in history. Some recent estimates put the company's potential value at $100 billion, which would make it larger than the global coffee industry—one addiction preparing to surpass the other. Facebook's scale and reach are hard to comprehend: last summer, Facebook became, by some counts, the first Web site to receive 1 trillion page views in a month. In the last three months of 2011, users generated an average of 2.7 billion "likes" and comments every day. On whatever scale you care to judge Facebook—as a company, as a culture, as a country—it is vast beyond imagination.

5   Despite its immense popularity, or more likely because of it, Facebook has, from the beginning, been under something of a cloud of suspicion. The depiction of Mark Zuckerberg, in *The Social Network,* as a bastard with symptoms of Asperger's syndrome, was nonsense. But it felt true. It felt true to Facebook, if not to Zuckerberg. The film's most indelible scene, the one that may well have earned it an Oscar, was the final, silent shot of an anomic Zuckerberg sending out a friend request to his ex-girlfriend, then waiting and clicking and waiting and clicking—a moment of superconnected loneliness preserved in amber. We have all been in that scene: transfixed by the glare of a screen, hungering for response.

6   When you sign up for Google+ and set up your Friends circle, the program specifies that you should include only "your real friends, the ones you feel comfortable sharing private details with." That one little phrase, *Your real friends*— so quaint, so charmingly mothering—perfectly encapsulates the anxieties that social media have produced: the fears that Facebook is interfering with our real friendships, distancing us from each other, making us lonelier; and that social networking might be spreading the very isolation it seemed designed to conquer.

7   Facebook arrived in the middle of a dramatic increase in the quantity and intensity of human loneliness, a rise that initially made the site's promise of greater connection seem deeply attractive. Americans are more solitary than ever before. In 1950, less than 10 percent of American households contained

Pause Why might Marche start with this anecdote? What is he trying to illustrate to the reader in his introduction?

Pause Underline the main argument of Marche's essay.

Pause Marche compares Facebook to a coffee addiction: In what way are the two similar? Why might he make this comparison?

only one person. By 2010, nearly 27 percent of households had just one person. Solitary living does not guarantee a life of unhappiness, of course. In his recent book about the trend toward living alone, Eric Klinenberg, a sociologist at NYU, writes: "Reams of published research show that it's the quality, not the quantity of social interaction, that best predicts loneliness." True. But before we begin the fantasies of happily eccentric singledom, of divorcées dropping by their knitting circles after work for glasses of Drew Barrymore pinot grigio, or recent college graduates with perfectly articulated, Steampunk-themed, 300-square-foot apartments organizing croquet matches with their book clubs, we should recognize that it is not just isolation that is rising sharply. It's loneliness, too. And loneliness makes us miserable.

Pause Is there a connection between being solitary and being lonely?

8   We know intuitively that loneliness and being alone are not the same thing. Solitude can be lovely. Crowded parties can be agony. We also know, thanks to a growing body of research on the topic, that loneliness is not a matter of external conditions; it is a psychological state. A 2005 analysis of data from a longitudinal study of Dutch twins showed that the tendency toward loneliness has roughly the same genetic component as other psychological problems such as neuroticism or anxiety.

9   Still, loneliness is slippery, a difficult state to define or diagnose. The best tool yet developed for measuring the condition is the UCLA Loneliness Scale, a series of 20 questions that all begin with this formulation: "How often do you feel . . . ?" As in: "How often do you feel that you are 'in tune' with the people around you?" And: "How often do you feel that you lack companionship?" Measuring the condition in these terms, various studies have shown loneliness rising drastically over a very short period of recent history. A 2010 AARP survey found that 35 percent of adults older than 45 were chronically lonely, as opposed to 20 percent of a similar group only a decade earlier. According to a major study by a leading scholar of the subject, roughly 20 percent of Americans—about 60 million people—are unhappy with their lives because of loneliness. Across the Western world, physicians and nurses have begun to speak openly of an epidemic of loneliness.

Pause Take a minute to study the data Marche presents in his argument. What does it all mean?

10   The new studies on loneliness are beginning to yield some surprising preliminary findings about its mechanisms. Almost every factor that one might assume affects loneliness does so only some of the time, and only under certain circumstances. People who are married are less lonely than single people, one journal article suggests, but only if their spouses are confidants. If one's spouse is not a confidant, marriage may not decrease loneliness. A belief in God might help, or it might not, as a 1990 German study comparing levels of religious feeling and levels of loneliness discovered. Active believers who saw God as abstract and helpful rather than as a wrathful, immediate presence were less lonely. "The mere belief in God," the researchers concluded, "was relatively independent of loneliness."

11   But it is clear that social interaction matters. Loneliness and being alone are not the same thing, but both are on the rise. We meet fewer people. We gather less. And when we gather, our bonds are less meaningful and less easy. The decrease in confidants—that is, in quality social connections—has been dramatic

over the past 25 years. In one survey, the mean size of networks of personal confidants decreased from 2.94 people in 1985 to 2.08 in 2004. Similarly, in 1985, only 10 percent of Americans said they had no one with whom to discuss important matters, and 15 percent said they had only one such good friend. By 2004, 25 percent had nobody to talk to, and 20 percent had only one confidant.

12   In the face of this social disintegration, we have essentially hired an army of replacement confidants, an entire class of professional carers. As Ronald Dworkin pointed out in a 2010 paper for the Hoover Institution, in the late '40s, the United States was home to 2,500 clinical psychologists, 30,000 social workers, and fewer than 500 marriage and family therapists. As of 2010, the country had 77,000 clinical psychologists, 192,000 clinical social workers, 400,000 nonclinical social workers, 50,000 marriage and family therapists, 105,000 mental-health counselors, 220,000 substance-abuse counselors, 17,000 nurse psychotherapists, and 30,000 life coaches. The majority of patients in therapy do not warrant a psychiatric diagnosis. This raft of psychic servants is helping us through what used to be called regular problems. We have outsourced the work of everyday caring.

13   We need professional carers more and more, because the threat of societal breakdown, once principally a matter of nostalgic lament, has morphed into an issue of public health. Being lonely is extremely bad for your health. If you're lonely, you're more likely to be put in a geriatric home at an earlier age than a similar person who isn't lonely. You're less likely to exercise. You're more likely to be obese. You're less likely to survive a serious operation and more likely to have hormonal imbalances. You are at greater risk of inflammation. Your memory may be worse. You are more likely to be depressed, to sleep badly, and to suffer dementia and general cognitive decline. Loneliness may not have killed Yvette Vickers, but it has been linked to a greater probability of having the kind of heart condition that did kill her.

> **Pause** Marche relies heavily on statistical evidence to prove his point. Underline the statistics and numerical data in his essay. Is it convincing? Why or why not?

14   And yet, despite its deleterious effect on health, loneliness is one of the first things ordinary Americans spend their money achieving. With money, you flee the cramped city to a house in the suburbs or, if you can afford it, a McMansion in the exurbs, inevitably spending more time in your car. Loneliness is at the American core, a by-product of a long-standing national appetite for independence: The Pilgrims who left Europe willingly abandoned the bonds and strictures of a society that could not accept their right to be different. They did not seek out loneliness, but they accepted it as the price of their autonomy. The cowboys who set off to explore a seemingly endless frontier likewise traded away personal ties in favor of pride and self-respect. The ultimate American icon is the astronaut: Who is more heroic, or more alone? The price of self-determination and self-reliance has often been loneliness. But Americans have always been willing to pay that price.

15   Today, the one common feature in American secular culture is its celebration of the self that breaks away from the constrictions of the family and the state, and, in its greatest expressions, from all limits entirely. The great American poem is Whitman's "Song of Myself." The great American essay is Emerson's "Self-Reliance." The great American novel is Melville's *Moby-Dick,* the tale of

> **Pause** If loneliness is a bad thing, why do people seek it out?

a man on a quest so lonely that it is incomprehensible to those around him. American culture, high and low, is about self-expression and personal authenticity. Franklin Delano Roosevelt called individualism "the great watchword of American life."

16   Self-invention is only half of the American story, however. The drive for isolation has always been in tension with the impulse to cluster in communities that cling and suffocate. The Pilgrims, while fomenting spiritual rebellion, also enforced ferocious cohesion. The Salem witch trials, in hindsight, read like attempts to impose solidarity—as do the McCarthy hearings.[1] The history of the United States is like the famous parable of the porcupines in the cold, from Schopenhauer's[2] *Studies in Pessimism*—the ones who huddle together for warmth and shuffle away in pain, always separating and congregating.

17   We are now in the middle of a long period of shuffling away. In his 2000 book *Bowling Alone,* Robert D. Putnam attributed the dramatic post-war decline of social capital—the strength and value of interpersonal networks—to numerous interconnected trends in American life: suburban sprawl, television's dominance over culture, the self-absorption of the Baby Boomers, the disintegration of the traditional family. The trends he observed continued through the prosperity of the aughts, and have only become more pronounced with time: the rate of union membership declined in 2011, again; screen time rose; the Masons and the Elks continued their slide into irrelevance. We are lonely because we want to be lonely. We have made ourselves lonely.

18   The question of the future is this: Is Facebook part of the separating or part of the congregating; is it a huddling-together for warmth or a shuffling-away in pain?

19   Well before Facebook, digital technology was enabling our tendency for isolation, to an unprecedented degree. Back in the 1990s, scholars started calling the contradiction between an increased opportunity to connect and a lack of human contact the "Internet paradox." A prominent 1998 article on the phenomenon by a team of researchers at Carnegie Mellon showed that increased Internet usage was already coinciding with increased loneliness. Critics of the study pointed out that the two groups that participated in the study—high-school journalism students who were heading to university and socially active members of community-development boards—were statistically likely to become lonelier over time. Which brings us to a more fundamental question: Does the Internet make people lonely, or are lonely people more attracted to the Internet?

20   The question has intensified in the Facebook era. A recent study out of Australia (where close to half the population is active on Facebook), titled "Who Uses Facebook?," found a complex and sometimes confounding relationship between loneliness and social networking. Facebook users had slightly lower levels of "social loneliness"—the sense of not feeling bonded with friends—but "significantly higher levels of family loneliness"—the sense of not feeling bonded with family. It may be that Facebook encourages more contact with people outside of our household, at the expense of our family relationships—or it may be that people who have unhappy family relationships in the first place seek companionship through other means, including Facebook. The researchers also found that

1. **McCarthy hearings:** televised 1954 Congressional hearings led by Senator Joseph R. McCarthy intended to investigate and identify Communists living and working in the United States during the Cold War

2. **Arthur Schopenhauer (1788–1860):** philosopher who contended that the universe is not a rational place and we should strive to make the world a more benevolent and beautiful place

Pause What do you think the author means when he talks about the idea of "social capital"?

Pause Think about the question the author asks here. Does the Internet make people lonely or are lonely people more attracted to the Internet? What are your reasons?

lonely people are inclined to spend more time on Facebook: "One of the most noteworthy findings," they wrote, "was the tendency for neurotic and lonely individuals to spend greater amounts of time on Facebook per day than non-lonely individuals." And they found that neurotics are more likely to prefer to use the wall, while extroverts tend to use chat features in addition to the wall.

21   Moira Burke, until recently a graduate student at the Human-Computer Institute at Carnegie Mellon, used to run a longitudinal study of 1,200 Facebook users. That study, which is ongoing, is one of the first to step outside the realm of self-selected college students and examine the effects of Facebook on a broader population, over time. She concludes that the effect of Facebook depends on what you bring to it. Just as your mother said: you get out only what you put in. If you use Facebook to communicate directly with other individuals—by using the "like" button, commenting on friends' posts, and so on— it can increase your social capital. Personalized messages, or what Burke calls "composed communication," are more satisfying than "one-click communication"—the lazy click of a like. "People who received composed communication became less lonely, while people who received one-click communication experienced no change in loneliness," Burke tells me. So, you should inform your friend in writing how charming her son looks with Harry Potter cake smeared all over his face, and how interesting her sepia-toned photograph of that tree-framed bit of skyline is, and how cool it is that she's at whatever concert she happens to be at. That's what we all want to hear. Even better than sending a private Facebook message is the semi-public conversation, the kind of back-and-forth in which you half ignore the other people who may be listening in. "People whose friends write to them semi-publicly on Facebook experience decreases in loneliness," Burke says.

22   On the other hand, non-personalized use of Facebook—scanning your friends' status updates and updating the world on your own activities via your wall, or what Burke calls "passive consumption" and "broadcasting"—correlates to feelings of disconnectedness. It's a lonely business, wandering the labyrinths of our friends' and pseudo-friends' projected identities, trying to figure out what part of ourselves we ought to project, who will listen, and what they will hear. According to Burke, passive consumption of Facebook also correlates to a marginal increase in depression. "If two women each talk to their friends the same amount of time, but one of them spends more time reading about friends on Facebook as well, the one reading tends to grow slightly more depressed," Burke says. Her conclusion suggests that my sometimes unhappy reactions to Facebook may be more universal than I had realized. When I scroll through page after page of my friends' descriptions of how accidentally eloquent their kids are, and how their husbands are endearingly bumbling, and how they're all about to eat a home-cooked meal prepared with fresh local organic produce bought at the farmers' market and then go for a jog and maybe check in at the office because they're so busy getting ready to hop on a plane for a week of luxury dogsledding in Lapland, I do grow slightly more miserable. A lot of other people doing the same thing feel a little bit worse, too.

Pause How might the term *social loneliness* differ from just the word *loneliness*?

23   Still, Burke's research does not support the assertion that Facebook creates loneliness. The people who experience loneliness on Facebook are lonely away from Facebook, too, she points out; on Facebook, as everywhere else, correlation is not causation. The popular kids are popular, and the lonely skulkers skulk alone. Perhaps it says something about me that I think Facebook is primarily a platform for lonely skulking. I mention to Burke the widely reported study, conducted by a Stanford graduate student, that showed how believing that others have strong social networks can lead to feelings of depression. What does Facebook communicate, if not the impression of social bounty? Everybody else looks so happy on Facebook, with so many friends, that our own social networks feel emptier than ever in comparison. Doesn't that *make* people feel lonely? "If people are reading about lives that are much better than theirs, two things can happen," Burke tells me. "They can feel worse about themselves, or they can feel motivated."

24   Burke will start working at Facebook as a data scientist this year.

25   John Cacioppo, the director of the Center for Cognitive and Social Neuroscience at the University of Chicago, is the world's leading expert on loneliness. In his landmark book, *Loneliness,* released in 2008, he revealed just how profoundly the epidemic of loneliness is affecting the basic functions of human physiology. He found higher levels of epinephrine, the stress hormone, in the morning urine of lonely people. Loneliness burrows deep: "When we drew blood from our older adults and analyzed their white cells," he writes, "we found that loneliness somehow penetrated the deepest recesses of the cell to alter the way genes were being expressed." Loneliness affects not only the brain, then, but the basic process of DNA transcription. When you are lonely, your whole body is lonely.

26   To Cacioppo, Internet communication allows only ersatz intimacy. "Forming connections with pets or online friends or even God is a noble attempt by an obligatorily gregarious creature to satisfy a compelling need," he writes. "But surrogates can never make up completely for the absence of the real thing." The "real thing" being actual people, in the flesh. When I speak to Cacioppo, he is refreshingly clear on what he sees as Facebook's effect on society. Yes, he allows, some research has suggested that the greater the number of Facebook friends a person has, the less lonely she is. But he argues that the impression this creates can be misleading. "For the most part," he says, "people are bringing their old friends, and feelings of loneliness or connectedness, to Facebook." The idea that a Web site could deliver a more friendly, interconnected world is bogus. The depth of one's social network outside Facebook is what determines the depth of one's social network within Facebook, not the other way around. Using social media doesn't create new social networks; it just transfers established networks from one platform to another. For the most part, Facebook doesn't destroy friendships—but it doesn't create them, either.

27   In one experiment, Cacioppo looked for a connection between the loneliness of subjects and the relative frequency of their interactions via Facebook, chat rooms, online games, dating sites, and face-to-face contact. The results were unequivocal. "The greater the proportion of face-to-face interactions, the less

Pause Burke's research finds that "correlation is not causation." What does that mean?

lonely you are," he says. "The greater the proportion of online interactions, the lonelier you are." Surely, I suggest to Cacioppo, this means that Facebook and the like inevitably make people lonelier. He disagrees. Facebook is merely a tool, he says, and like any tool, its effectiveness will depend on its user. "If you use Facebook to increase face-to-face contact," he says, "it increases social capital." So if social media let you organize a game of football among your friends, that's healthy. If you turn to social media instead of playing football, however, that's unhealthy.

28 "Facebook can be terrific, if we use it properly," Cacioppo continues. "It's like a car. You can drive it to pick up your friends. Or you can drive alone." But hasn't the car increased loneliness? If cars created the suburbs, surely they also created isolation. "That's because of how we use cars," Cacioppo replies. "How we use these technologies can lead to more integration, rather than more isolation."

29 The problem, then, is that we invite loneliness, even though it makes us miserable. The history of our use of technology is a history of isolation desired and achieved. When the Great Atlantic and Pacific Tea Company opened its A&P stores, giving Americans self-service access to groceries, customers stopped having relationships with their grocers. When the telephone arrived, people stopped knocking on their neighbors' doors. Social media bring this process to a much wider set of relationships. Researchers at the HP Social Computing Lab who studied the nature of people's connections on Twitter came to a depressing, if not surprising, conclusion: "Most of the links declared within Twitter were meaningless from an interaction point of view." I have to wonder: What other point of view is meaningful?

30 Loneliness is certainly not something that Facebook or Twitter or any of the lesser forms of social media is doing to us. We are doing it to ourselves. Casting technology as some vague, impersonal spirit of history forcing our actions is a weak excuse. We make decisions about how we use our machines, not the other way around. Every time I shop at my local grocery store, I am faced with a choice. I can buy my groceries from a human being or from a machine. I always, without exception, choose the machine. It's faster and more efficient, I tell myself, but the truth is that I prefer not having to wait with the other customers who are lined up alongside the conveyor belt: the hipster mom who disapproves of my high-carbon-footprint pineapple; the lady who tenses to the point of tears while she waits to see if the gods of the credit-card machine will accept or decline; the old man whose clumsy feebleness requires a patience that I don't possess. Much better to bypass the whole circus and just ring up the groceries myself.

31 Our omnipresent new technologies lure us toward increasingly superficial connections at exactly the same moment that they make avoiding the mess of human interaction easy. The beauty of Facebook, the source of its power, is that it enables us to be social while sparing us the embarrassing reality of society—the accidental revelations we make at parties, the awkward pauses, the farting and the spilled drinks and the general gaucherie of face-to-face contact. Instead, we have the lovely smoothness of a seemingly social machine. Everything's so simple: status updates, pictures, your wall.

Pause Which paragraphs are specifically meant to support Marche's position on the issue?

Pause What point is Cacioppo trying to make in comparing Facebook to cars?

32   But the price of this smooth sociability is a constant compulsion to assert one's own happiness, one's own fulfillment. Not only must we contend with the social bounty of others; we must foster the appearance of our own social bounty. Being happy all the time, pretending to be happy, actually attempting to be happy—it's exhausting. Last year a team of researchers led by Iris Mauss at the University of Denver published a study looking into "the paradoxical effects of valuing happiness." Most goals in life show a direct correlation between valuation and achievement. Studies have found, for example, that students who value good grades tend to have higher grades than those who don't value them. Happiness is an exception. The study came to a disturbing conclusion:

> Valuing happiness is not necessarily linked to greater happiness. In fact, under certain conditions, the opposite is true. Under conditions of low (but not high) life stress, the more people valued happiness, the lower were their hedonic balance, psychological well-being, and life satisfaction, and the higher their depression symptoms.

The more you try to be happy, the less happy you are. Sophocles made roughly the same point.

33   Facebook, of course, puts the pursuit of happiness front and center in our digital life. Its capacity to redefine our very concepts of identity and personal fulfillment is much more worrisome than the data-mining and privacy practices that have aroused anxieties about the company. Two of the most compelling critics of Facebook—neither of them a Luddite—concentrate on exactly this point. Jaron Lanier, the author of *You Are Not a Gadget,* was one of the inventors of virtual-reality technology. His view of where social media are taking us reads like dystopian science fiction: "I fear that we are beginning to design ourselves to suit digital models of us, and I worry about a leaching of empathy and humanity in that process." Lanier argues that Facebook imprisons us in the business of self-presenting, and this, to his mind, is the site's crucial and fatally unacceptable downside.

34   Sherry Turkle, a professor of computer culture at MIT who in 1995 published the digital-positive analysis *Life on the Screen,* is much more skeptical about the effects of online society in her 2011 book, *Alone Together:* "These days, insecure in our relationships and anxious about intimacy, we look to technology for ways to be in relationships and protect ourselves from them at the same time." The problem with digital intimacy is that it is ultimately incomplete: "The ties we form through the Internet are not, in the end, the ties that bind. But they are the ties that preoccupy," she writes. "We don't want to intrude on each other, so instead we constantly intrude on each other, but not in 'real time.'"

Pause If we don't want to intrude on each other, why are we constantly intruding on each other?

35   Lanier and Turkle are right, at least in their diagnoses. Self-presentation on Facebook is continuous, intensely mediated, and possessed of a phony nonchalance that eliminates even the potential for spontaneity. ("Look how casually I threw up these three photos from the party at which I took 300 photos!") Curating the exhibition of the self has become a 24/7 occupation. Perhaps not surprisingly, then, the Australian study "Who Uses Facebook?" found a significant

correlation between Facebook use and narcissism: "Facebook users have higher levels of total narcissism, exhibitionism, and leadership than Facebook nonusers," the study's authors wrote. "In fact, it could be argued that Facebook specifically gratifies the narcissistic individual's need to engage in self-promoting and superficial behavior."

36   Rising narcissism isn't so much a trend as the trend behind all other trends. In preparation for the 2013 edition of its diagnostic manual, the psychiatric profession is currently struggling to update its definition of narcissistic personality disorder. Still, generally speaking, practitioners agree that narcissism manifests in patterns of fantastic grandiosity, craving for attention, and lack of empathy. In a 2008 survey, 35,000 American respondents were asked if they had ever had certain symptoms of narcissistic personality disorder. Among people older than 65, 3 percent reported symptoms. Among people in their 20s, the proportion was nearly 10 percent. Across all age groups, one in 16 Americans has experienced some symptoms of NPD. And loneliness and narcissism are intimately connected: a longitudinal study of Swedish women demonstrated a strong link between levels of narcissism in youth and levels of loneliness in old age. The connection is fundamental. Narcissism is the flip side of loneliness, and either condition is a fighting retreat from the messy reality of other people.

Pause Where in the article is Marche using counterarguments? Identify those paragraphs.

37   A considerable part of Facebook's appeal stems from its miraculous fusion of distance with intimacy, or the illusion of distance with the illusion of intimacy. Our online communities become engines of self-image, and self-image becomes the engine of community. The real danger with Facebook is not that it allows us to isolate ourselves, but that by mixing our appetite for isolation with our vanity, it threatens to alter the very nature of solitude. The new isolation is not of the kind that Americans once idealized, the lonesomeness of the proudly nonconformist, independent-minded, solitary stoic, or that of the astronaut who blasts into new worlds. Facebook's isolation is a grind. What's truly staggering about Facebook usage is not its volume—750 million photographs uploaded over a single weekend—but the constancy of the performance it demands. More than half its users—and one of every 13 people on Earth is a Facebook user—log on every day. Among 18-to-34-year-olds, nearly half check Facebook minutes after waking up, and 28 percent do so before getting out of bed. The relentlessness is what is so new, so potentially transformative. Facebook never takes a break. We never take a break. Human beings have always created elaborate acts of self-presentation. But not all the time, not every morning, before we even pour a cup of coffee. Yvette Vickers's computer was on when she died.

38   Nostalgia for the good old days of disconnection would not just be pointless, it would be hypocritical and ungrateful. But the very magic of the new machines, the efficiency and elegance with which they serve us, obscures what isn't being served: everything that matters. What Facebook has revealed about human nature—and this is not a minor revelation—is that a connection is not the same thing as a bond, and that instant and total connection is no salvation, no ticket to a happier, better world or a more liberated version of humanity. Solitude used to be good for self-reflection and self-reinvention. But now we are left thinking

about who we are all the time, without ever really thinking about who we are. Facebook denies us a pleasure whose profundity we had underestimated: the chance to forget about ourselves for a while, the chance to disconnect.

SUMMARIZE AND RESPOND

Summarize the main idea of "Is Facebook Making Us Lonely?" Then, go back and check off support for this main idea. Next, write a brief summary (three to five sentences) of the selection. Finally, jot down your initial response to the reading. What do you think of the arguments that Marche makes here? Does anything in the essay tempt you to rethink your position on social media? What might you say to Marche about his stand on this issue?

CHECK YOUR COMPREHENSION

1. Which of the following would be the best alternative title for this essay?
    a. "Virtual Loneliness"
    b. "Does Technology Create False Friendship?"
    c. "Facebook Is a Tool, Not a Friend"
    d. "You Can't Be Happy All the Time"

2. The main idea of this essay is that
    a. even though we are now more connected to each other than at any other point in history, people are finding themselves more isolated due to their constant need to portray themselves as happy and fulfilled.
    b. social media creates loneliness and feelings of isolation because it keeps people from interacting on a personal level.
    c. the Internet and social media are destroying real relationships and meaningful bonds between people; therefore, people are feeling more isolated and alone than ever before.
    d. rather than living a meaningful and productive life, most people are content to allow machines to do their work and living for them and are choosing to isolate themselves.

3. Marche makes the point that
    a. Facebook users had slightly lower levels of "social loneliness"—the sense of not feeling bonded with friends—but "significantly higher levels of family loneliness"—the sense of not feeling bonded with family.

b. Facebook did not encourage people to have contact with others outside of their household, so these people became increasingly isolated.

c. Lonely people were less inclined to spend time on Facebook because they were neurotic.

d. Extroverts needed Facebook because they suffered from "social loneliness."

4. If you are unfamiliar with the following words, use a dictionary to check their meanings: unprecedented, cul-de-sacs (para. 3); initial public offering (4); Asperger's syndrome, indelible, anomic (5); quaint, encapsulates (6); reams, eccentric (7); intuitively, longitudinal, neuroticism (8); confidant (10); geriatric (13); deleterious, strictures, autonomy (14); secular, constrictions (15); cohesion (16); aughts (17); correlates (22); ersatz, gregarious, surrogate (26); unequivocal (27); omnipresent, gaucherie (31); Luddite, dystopian (33); nonchalance, narcissism (35).

READ CRITICALLY

1. In paragraph 9, the author claims that "loneliness is slippery." What does he mean by this? Do you agree or disagree? Explain your answer.

2. In paragraphs 21 and 22, the author briefly discusses a study done by Moira Burke about how different people use Facebook: personalized versus nonpersonalized use. What is the result of that study? Based on that study, do you think that Facebook makes a person lonely? Explain your answer.

3. In paragraph 34, the author quotes Sherry Turkle, who says, "The ties we form through the Internet are not, in the end, the ties that bind. But they are the ties that preoccupy. We don't want to intrude on each other, so instead we constantly intrude on each other, but not in 'real time.'" What does this mean? How could we be lonely but still intruding on each other? How can we intrude on each other, but not in "real time"?

4. Marche begins and ends his argument with an anecdote about Yvette Vickers. What is his purpose for doing so? Is the anecdote effective? Explain your answer.

5. Reread the introduction of Marche's argument and the conclusion. What was the main argument of the essay? Do you agree or disagree with it? Explain your answer.

For information on citing sources, see Chapter 20.

WRITE AN ESSAY

Write an essay in which you take a position on the question asked in Marche's essay: "Does the Internet make people lonely, or are lonely people more attracted to the Internet?" Assume that your audience is made up of readers who are approximately your age and at your level of education. They have the same experience with technology and understand social media to the same level that you do; however, they hold a different position on this issue than you do

WRITE AN ESSAY ABOUT SOCIAL MEDIA

Read the four essays about social media. Each of the authors has a different perspective on the subject. When you are thinking about the subject of social media, consider all the different aspects the authors touch on: What is reality? Does social media bring us closer together or make us lonelier? Are we depending too much on our virtual lives to bring us happiness? These are just a few of the many topics that the authors mention in their essays and that you could take a position on and research further. Drawing from at least two of the four essays, write your own argument about the subject. You may use your own experiences in your argument as well as outside sources. When you use material from the essays here or from another source, be sure to cite the source.

Your introduction should include a statement of your position on the issue. In the body of your essay, develop reasons for your opinion, using the essays and other sources. In your conclusion, summarize your reasons, and restate your opinion based on the evidence you have presented.

Write an Essay: What Do You Think?

Using material from at least three of the four essays in this chapter, write an essay either for or against social networking. In order to write a successful essay, you will want to narrow your topic and think about a specific aspect of the topic. Think about a particular question you could answer and take a position on, for example: Does social networking make us lonely?

In your introduction, state your position on the issue. In the body of your essay, acknowledge the opposite side of the issue—either pro (Harding) or con (Marche, Leung, and Turkle). Use the appropriate selections to support your position, along with any relevant experiences you have had and outside sources you use. Cite all sources. In your conclusion, restate your position, review the reasons you have given, and make a last pitch for your side of the argument. As you write your argument, think about your own experiences with social networking.

Appendix

Problem Solving in Writing

Some writing assignments, both in English and in other subjects, will require you to use problem-solving skills. Such assignments will ask you to read and analyze a problem to develop possible solutions, often by synthesizing information from various sources.

Problem-solving skills are necessary not only in college but also—and even more so—in the work world. Often, managers assign a team to pose possible solutions to a problem that the organization faces. Also, problem-solving skills will help you in your everyday life when you run into a situation you want to change.

Each of the chapters in Part 3 includes problem-based writing assignments ("Writing to Solve a Problem"). These assignments offer you the opportunity to solve real-world problems by working alone or as part of a team. Use the following section to complete those assignments or to address any problem you may face in college, at work, or in your everyday life.

Problem Solving

Problem solving is the process of identifying a problem and figuring out a reasonable solution.

Problems range from minor inconveniences like finding a rip in the last clean shirt you have when you're running late to more serious problems such as being laid off from your job. While such problems disrupt our lives, they also give us opportunities to tackle difficult situations with confidence.

Too often, people are paralyzed by problems because they don't have strategies for attacking them. However, backing away from a problem rarely helps solve it. When you know how to approach a challenging situation, you are better able to take charge of your life.

Problem solving consists of five basic steps, which can be used effectively by both individuals and groups.

The Problem-Solving Process

Understand the problem.

You should be able to say or write the problem in a brief statement or question.

> **EXAMPLE:** Your ten-year-old car needs a new transmission, which will cost at least $1500. Do you keep the car or buy a new one?

Identify people or information that can help you solve the problem (resources).

> **EXAMPLES**

- Your mechanic
- Friends who have had similar car problems
- Car advice from print or Web sources

List the possible solutions.

> **EXAMPLES**

- Pay for the transmission repair.
- Buy a new car.

Evaluate the possible solutions.

1. Identify the steps each solution would require.
2. List possible obstacles for each solution (like money or time constraints).
3. List the advantages and disadvantages of the solutions.

> **EXAMPLES (considering only advantages and disadvantages):**

- Pay for the transmission repair.

  Advantage: This would be cheaper than buying a new car.

  Disadvantage: The car may not last much longer, even with the new transmission.

- Buy a new car.

  Advantage: You would have a reliable car.

  Disadvantage: This option would be much more expensive.

Choose the most reasonable solution.

Choose the solution that is realistic—the simpler the better. Be able to give reasons for your choice.

> *Solution:* Pay for the transmission repair.

> *Reasons:* You do not have money for a new car, and you do not want to assume more debt. Opinions from two mechanics indicate that your car should run for three to five more years with the new transmission. At that point, you will be in a better position to buy a new car.

Acknowledgments

Dave Barry. "The Ugly Truth about Beauty." Originally published in the *Miami Herald*, February 1, 1998. Reprinted by permission of the author.

Jennifer Brett. "Officer J. Pyland Police Report." From "Reese Witherspoon Arrested in Atlanta: Read the Report." From *Access Atlanta*, April 21, 2013.

Bill Bryson. "Coming Home." Excerpt from *I'm a Stranger Here Myself: Notes on Returning to America after Twenty Years Away,* copyright © 1999 by Bill Bryson. Used by permission of Broadway Books, an imprint of the Crown Publishing Group, a division of Random House LLC and Doubleday Canada, a division of Random House of Canada Limited, a Penguin Random House Company. All rights reserved.

Rui Dai. "A Whiff of Memory." From *The Chronicle*, May 20, 2010.

Islam Elshami. "Why Join the Club." From *The Torch*, Bergen Community College, February 2010.

Alex Espinoza. "Easy Like Sunday Morning." From *Salon*, February 13, 2001. This article first appeared in Salon.com, at http://www.Salon.com. An online version remains in the *Salon* archives. Reprinted with permission.

Daniel Flanagan. "The Choice to Do It Over Again." From *This I Believe: On Fatherhood*, ed. Dan Gediman. Copyright © 2011 Jossey-Bass.

Katy Hall and Chris Spurlock. "Paid Parental Leave." From the *Huffington Post*, February 4, 2013.

James Hamblin. "How Much Caffeine before I End Up in the ER?" From *The Atlantic*, January 15, 2013.

Kate Harding. "Social Networking Is Not Killing Friendship." From *Salon*, December 9, 2009. This article first appeared in Salon.com, at http://www.Salon.com. An online version remains in the *Salon* archives. Reprinted with permission.

Don H. and Sandra E. Hockenbury. "Daily Hassles, That's Not What I Ordered!" From *Discovering Psychology*, Sixth Ed., p. 501, by Don H. and Sandra E. Hockenbury. Copyright © 2014 by Worth Publishers. Used with permission by the publisher.

Russel Honoré. "Work Is a Blessing." From *This I Believe: On Fatherhood*, edited by Dan Gediman with John Gregory and Mary Jo Gediman. Copyright © 2011 Jossey-Bass.

Langston Hughes. "Salvation." From *The Big Sea*. Copyright © 1940 by Langston Hughes. Copyright renewed 1968 by Arna Bontemps and George Bass. Reprinted by permission of Hill and Wang, a division of Farrar, Straus and Giroux, LLC.

Martin Luther King Jr. "Ways of Meeting Oppression." From *Stride Toward Freedom: The Montgomery Story*. Copyright © 1958 by Dr. Martin Luther King Jr. Copyright © 1986 by Coretta Scott King. Reprinted by arrangement with The Heirs to the Estate of Martin Luther King Jr., c/o Writers House as agent for the proprietor, New York, NY.

Kimberly Lake. "Sample Observations of a Developmentally Impaired Child." Reprinted by permission of the author.

Wency Leung. "Does Social Media Bring Us Closer—or Make Us Loners? *The Globe and Mail*, January 14, 2013.

Liza Long. "I Am Adam Lanza's Mother." *The Blue Review*, December 14, 2012. Reprinted by permission of the author.

Nancy Mairs. From *Plaintext*. Copyright © 1986 The Arizona Board of Regents. Reprinted by permission of the University of Arizona Press.

Stephen Marche. "Is Facebook Making Us Lonely?" From *The Atlantic*, April 2, 2012.

Monique Rizer. "When Students Are Parents" as appeared in *The Chronicle of Higher Education*, December 16, 2005. Reprinted by permission of the author.

Cailtlin Seida. "My Embarrassing Picture Went Viral." From *Salon*, October 2, 2013. This article first appeared in Salon.com, at http://www.Salon.com. An online version remains in the *Salon* archives. Reprinted with permission.

Brent Staples. "Just Walk On By: Black Men and Public Space." Reprinted by permission of the author.

Amy Tan. "Mother Tongue." Copyright © 1989. First appeared in *The Threepenny Review*. Reprinted by permission of the author and the Sandra Dijkstra Literary Agency.

Deborah Tannen. "It Begins at the Beginning." Excerpt from pp. 43–44 from *You Just Don't Understand* by Deborah Tannen. Copyright © 1990 by Deborah Tannen. Reprinted with permission of HarperCollins Publishers and International Creative Management, Inc.

Felix Tarcomnicu. "How the Hiring Process Has Changed over the Years." Originally published at the *Huffington Post*, May 31, 2013, from ResumeOK.com. Reprinted by permission of the author.

Sherry Turkle. "Introduction" from *Alone Together*. Copyright © 2012 Sherry Turkle (Author). Reprinted by permission of Basic Books, a member of the Perseus Books Group.

Kathleen Vail. "Words That Wound." Originally published in *American School Board Journal*, September 1999. Copyright © 1999 National School Boards Association. Reprinted by permission of the *American School Board Journal*. All rights reserved.

Peter Van Buren. "The Day after a Day at the Embassy." From the book *We Meant Well: How I Helped Lose the Battle for the Hearts and Minds of the Iraqi People* by Peter Van Buren. Copyright © 2011 by Peter Van Buren. Used by permission of Henry Holt and Company, LLC. All rights reserved.

Mary Elizabeth Williams. "Our Family's Week on a Food Stamp Budget." From *Salon*, February 1, 2013. This article first appeared in Salon.com, at http://www.Salon.com. An online version remains in the *Salon* archives. Reprinted with permission.

Malcolm X. "Learning to Read" from *The Autobiography of Malcolm X* by Malcolm X as told to Alex Haley. Copyright © 1964 by Alex Haley and Malcolm X. Copyright © 1965 by Alex Haley and Betty Shabazz. Used by permission of Random House, an imprint and division of Random House, LLC, and John Hawkins Associates. All rights reserved.

Index

A

a; *see also* Articles
    versus *an*/*and*, 517
    basics of, 500–02, 503
Abstract words, avoiding, 509
Academic English. *See* English, formal
accept/*except*, 518
Action verbs, 319, 320
Active reading, 16–23
Active voice, 397–98
Adams, Susan, 270
Additions, transitions that signal, 117
Addresses, commas in, 535
Adjective clauses
    commas around, 533–35
    definition of, 478, 533
    joining ideas with, 478–80
Adjectives, 431–39
    definition of, 314, 431
    editing, 435–39
    joining with hyphens, 556
    prepositions after, 502
    in six basic sentence patterns, 323
    understanding, 431–32
    using in comparisons, 433–34
Adverbs, 431–39
    choosing between forms of, 432–33
    definition of, 314, 431, 468
    editing, 435–39
    in six basic sentence patterns, 323
    starting sentences with, 468–69
    understanding, 431–32
    using in comparisons, 433–34
Advertisements, reading critically, 22–25
advice/*advise*, 518
affect/*effect*, 518
almost, misplaced modifiers and, 441
am. See be, and forms of
Ambiguous pronoun reference, 422
Ameur, Josef, "Video Game Genres," 200–201
an; *see also* Articles
    versus *a*/*and*, 517
    basics of, 500–502, 503
Analogies, bad, 258
Analysis
    definition of, 39, 43
    for responding to text, 43–45

and; *see also* Coordinating conjunctions
    versus *a*/*an*, 517
    comma before, in series of items, 527–28
    compound subjects and, 316, 365
    for coordination, 445, 446–51
    in parallelism, 459
    subject-verb agreement and, 365
Antecedent, 419, 420–22
Anthologies
    in-text citation for, 298
    works-cited documentation for, 299–300
Apostrophes
    basics of, 540–46
    possessive pronouns and, 424
Appositives
    commas around, 531–33
    joining ideas with, 475–77
"Appreciate What You Have" (Fiori), 95, 98
are/*our*, 518
Argument, 250–72
    definition of, 250
    four basics of, 250, 680
    reading and analyzing, 261–68
    readings for, 680–706
    understanding, 250–60
    writing, 268–72
Arnett, Kathryn, "Media and Advertisement: The New Peer
        Pressure?," 264–66
Around Him, John, 266–68
Arranging ideas, 89–91
Articles (*a, an, the*)
    basics of, 500–02, 503
    capitalization of, 561
    definition of, 500
    need for, 316
as, comparisons and, 425–26, 460
Assignments, decoding, 55–56
Assumptions, critical thinking and, 14
At a glance
    argument, 269
    cause and effect, 247
    classification, 201
    definition, 216
    description, 168
    illustration, 154
    narration, 139
    process analysis, 181

Useful Editing and Proofreading Marks

The marks and abbreviations below are those typically used by instructors when marking papers (add any alternate marks used by your instructor in the left-hand column), but you can also mark your own work or that of your peers with these helpful symbols.

Alternate symbol	Standard symbol	How to revise or edit (numbers in boldface are chapters where you can find help)
	adj	Use correct adjective form **Ch. 27**
	adv	Use correct adverb form **Ch. 27**
	agr	Correct subject-verb agreement or pronoun agreement **Chs. 24 and 26**
	awk	Awkward expression: edit for clarity **Ch. 9**
	cap or triple underline [example]	Use capital letter correctly **Ch. 39**
	case	Use correct pronoun case **Ch. 26**
	cliché	Replace overused phrase with fresh words **Ch. 33**
	coh	Revise paragraph or essay for coherence **Ch. 9**
	coord	Use coordination correctly **Ch. 29**
	cs	Comma splice: join the sentences correctly **Ch. 23**
	dev	Develop your paragraph or essay more completely **Chs. 3 and 6**
	dm	Revise to avoid a dangling modifier **Ch. 28**
	frag	Attach the fragment to a sentence or make it a sentence **Ch. 22**
	fs	Fused sentence: join the two sentences correctly **Ch. 23**
	ital	Use italics **Ch. 37**
	lc or diagonal slash [Example]	Use lowercase **Ch. 39**
	mm	Revise to avoid a misplaced modifier **Ch. 28**
	pl	Use the correct plural form of the verb **Ch. 25**
	ref	Make pronoun reference clear **Ch. 26**
	ro	Run-on sentence: join the two sentences correctly **Ch. 23**
	sp	Correct the spelling error **Ch. 34**
	sub	Use subordination correctly **Ch. 29**
	sup	Support your point with details, examples, or facts **Ch. 7**
	tense	Correct the problem with verb tense **Ch. 25**
	trans	Add a transition **Ch. 9**
	w	Delete unnecessary words **Ch. 33**
	wc	Reconsider your word choice **Chs. 33 and 34**
	?	Make your meaning clearer **Ch. 9**
	$\overset{\wedge}{,}$	Use comma correctly **Ch. 35**
	; : ( ) - —	Use semicolon / colon / parentheses / hyphen / dash correctly **Ch. 38**
	" " ˅ ˅	Use quotation marks correctly **Ch. 37**
	∧	Insert something
	℘ [exa mple]	Delete something
	⌣ [(words)(example)]	Change the order of letters or words
	¶	Start a new paragraph
	# [example words]	Add a space
	⌒ [ex ample]	Close up a space